ALCOHOL, BOAT CHASES, AND SHOOTOUTS!

HOW THE U.S. COAST GUARD AND CUSTOMS FOUGHT RUM SMUGGLERS AND PIRATES

The Trilogy:
1920s & '30s

by
JAMES MORRISON

Royal Exchange Publications
Charleston, SC

©2017 James Morrison. All rights reserved. This work may not be copied for sale or distribution without the express written permission of the author.

ISBN: 978-0-9800516-1-2

Library of Congress Control Number: 2017932360

Royal Exchange Publications, Charleston, South Carolina

About the Author

Photo by Linda Morrison

James Morrison grew up in Staten Island, NY and Lakewood, NJ. He lived in Charleston, SC for about 13 years. There, he was a tour guide at the Old Exchange Building and attended graduate school at the Citadel. His military career has spanned nearly two decades. He served for four years in the Marine Corps and was stationed at Camp Lejeune, NC. He spent six months aboard the USS Nassau on a Mediterranean deployment. After getting out of the Marines, he served in the Army National Guard where he attended military police school. He also volunteered for the Coast Guard Auxiliary for two years. After joining the Army Reserve, he was mobilized for active duty as a Drill Sergeant at Fort Jackson, SC. He is still in the Army Reserve as part of the Judge Advocate General Corps.

James has a bachelor's degree in military history from American Military University, a master's degree in history from the Citadel, and a law degree from Concord Law School. He currently lives in Richmond, VA.

DEDICATED TO

My greatest history teacher,
my father,
JOHN MORRISON

LINDA MORRISON

PATRICIA MORRISON

THERESA KORNSICHER

SUMMER ASHLEY MORRISON

MY BROTHER DAVE

MY SISTER CAROLYN

THE OLD EXCHANGE BUILDING

JOHN YOUNG

LINDA VEITCH

COURTNEY McINDOE

THE McINDOE FAMILY

In Memory of Grandma

Theresa Kornsicher 1928-2013

CONTENTS

Part I: 1919-1924

1. An Exciting Story..1
2. A Storm On the Horizon..9
3. Atlantic City's Mystery Ship..................................30
4. The Prohibition "Navy" Is Born.............................51
5. A Drunken Shooting Spree...................................67
6. Corruption..81
7. Pirates Attack Rum Ships.....................................93
8. Mystery Of the Sunken Rum Ship.......................111
9. A Letter From A Smuggler..................................116
10. The Government Attacks Rum Row....................130
11. The President's Unpleasant Trip.........................145
12. Rum Smuggler Tells All......................................152
13. The Real McCoy...159
14. Merry Christmas!...164
15. Nineteen Twenty-Four..174
16. "Stop Shooting, This is a Police Boat!"...............207
17. Secretary Mellon In the Hot Seat........................216
18. Pirates Attack A French Steamship.....................222
19. Aliens, Narcotics, and a Bulletproof Boat............237
20. A New Fleet..244
21. Into the Lion's Den..250
22. Reporter Visits Rum Row....................................261

Part II: 1925-1929

23. Crazy Sea Stories...271
24. Uncle Sam Chokes the Rum Fleet......................281
25. Misconduct...299
26. Nineteen Twenty-Six..304
27. The West Coast..316
28. The Dwyer Conspiracy.......................................329
29. The Plot Thickens...345

30. The Mysterious Envelope..................................354
31. Defeat and Denial...364
32. A Man Walked Into an Inn...............................371
33. Canada Opens the Floodgates.........................376
34. Bravery in Action...381
35. A Bad Year for Customs...................................390
36. Buffalo...394
37. *I'm Alone*..400
38. Florida...409
39. Detroit...418
40. Raiding a Fortress...435
41. The December Shootings.................................444
42. Ten Years of Prohibition..................................466

Part III: The 1930s

43. Tiny French Islands..481
44. The Radio Rum Ring..486
45. The *Josephine K*..495
46. The Tide Turns..504
47. Repeal..511
48. Hangover..521

Sources..532
Endnotes..535
Index..567

ILLUSTRATIONS

"Woman's Holy War" Against Alcohol.................3
NYC Children in the Summer of 1920..................5
New York Waterfront 1920..................7
Admiral Reynolds..................18
Customs Officials Search a Suspect for Liquor............24
Detroit Circa 1920..................28
CG 262 in San Francisco on Prohibition Duty..................52
Coast Guard Cutter *Bothwell*..................53
Coast Guard Cutter *Seneca*..................61
Agents Pouring Liquor into a Sewer..................69
Armored Rum-Runner Runs Aground..................87
Captain Byron L. Reed..................94
Officials and Reporters Look for Rum-Runners..........118
The *Katherine*..................120
The Rum Schooner *M.M. Gardner*..................122
Former Navy Eagle Boat..................125
Comic Depicting Teapot Dome Scandal..................127
Part of the "Prohibition Navy" in Port..................133
Rum Smuggler's Truck Sinks Through Ice..................136
Gun Aboard the *Seneca*..................139
Aboard the *Seneca*..................160
"The Weapons To Make The Ocean Dry"..................165
Candid Photo Of Admiral Reynolds..................180
Coast Guardsmen Man a 5-Inch Gun..................183
Rum-Runner *Linwood* on Fire..................184
Former Navy Destroyer in Dry Dock..................193
An Armored Rum-Runner..................241
"Three Cracking Good Destroyers"..................246
The *Seneca* Versus the K-13091..................266
Cartoon Depicting Prohibition's Transfer to DOJ.......269
Buffalo, NY in 1925..................395
Detroit in the 1920s..................421
Liquor Seizure on the Detroit River..................423
Lower Manhattan Waterfront..................501
Political Cartoon Depicting FDR..................514

About the Book

A lot can happen in ten years. When I began writing this trilogy, my niece, Summer, was just learning to walk. By the time I finished, she was in middle school. Over that decade, I had relocated a few times to three different states and made a few career changes. The proverbial roof caved in and the bottom dropped out several times. Friends had come and gone. Most of those who were cheering me on when I started this writing marathon were not at the finish line. But such is life. The most important part is not giving up on your dreams and finishing what you set out to do, no matter the obstacles.

I came across the topic for this book when I was in grad school at the Citadel. I was taking a course on maritime history and came across an old, dusty, out-of-print book titled *Rum War at Sea* by Malcolm Willoughby. The book was printed in 1964 by the Government Printing Office and was already over 50 years old by the time I read it. What I had read blew my mind, because in all my years of studying history I had never heard of the Rum War. I knew about Prohibition and the gangsters of the 1920s, but nothing about what happened at sea. The idea that there was a shooting war between the Coast Guard and rum-runners was amazing. And this wasn't just a small boat here and there with some contraband liquor, but massive fleets of cargo ships, loaded with liquor, and aided by speedboats and airplanes. Adding to my amazement was the fact that almost no one living knew anything about the Rum War, including most history buffs. I had struck historical gold!

Although Willoughby's book is very good, it is still a publication from the US Treasury Department. Government agencies tend to pat themselves on the back whenever they publish anything. My goal was to include both the flattering and unflattering stories in order to present the whole picture—to take the reader down the rabbit hole, with all its twists and turns.

Then came the task of piecing the story together. Since the events in question happened over 80 years earlier, interviews with witnesses were pretty much out of the question. I had to rely on documents. When I first started my research, old newspapers were still in the process of being digitized, so I spent endless hours scrolling through microfilm in the College of Charleston library. I also paid a visit to the Coast Guard historian's office in Washington, DC, and the National

Archives. I enjoyed digging for the information. It was a lot like a treasure hunt.

Once I gathered the "evidence," then came the process of writing something informative, yet entertaining at the same time—not an easy task. In graduate school, I learned to write papers for professors. I was forced to read many dry, unbelievably boring books and articles from scholarly journals. Since I wanted regular people to read my book, I threw a lot of what I learned in grad school (about writing style) out the window, and used something strictly forbidden in academia called a "narrative." A "narrative" tells a story. It has a beginning, a middle, and an end. It has characters that you can follow and keeps you turning the pages to see what happens next. Academics are trained to chop up the living body of a true story to present the dead body parts in an analytical format. This is a tragedy, because it sucks the life right out of history and does no justice to those who actually played important roles in our history.

After two years and many sleepless nights, Part I went into print. Originally, Parts II and III were supposed to be separate books, but I decided to combine the entire trilogy into one book instead. There's a saying that "we make plans and God laughs." Never was this truer than with this book. It was supposed to be finished years earlier, but life got in the way.

I hope that you become as absorbed in these stories as I did while writing about them. The sea is an exciting, timeless place, which never fails to capture the imagination. It takes us away from the humdrum of our daily lives. In this book are a lot of exciting stories that have not seen the light of day in about eight decades. I'm really happy to finally share them with you. Enjoy!

Semper Paratus,
James Morrison

Part I: 1919-1924

Courtesy US Coast Guard Headquarters

1
AN EXCITING STORY

"The reign of tears is over. The slums will soon only be a memory. We will turn our prisons into factories and our jails into storehouses and corn-cribs. Men will walk upright now, women will smile, and children will laugh. Hell will be forever for rent."
— Reverend Billy Sunday on the first day of Prohibition.

You are about to read an exciting story that the American public has not heard or read about in several decades. About half of the stories in this book have not been in print since the 1920s. This is a story that involves smuggling, high speed boat chases, pirates, corruption, and scandals.

Those who are familiar with the topic of Prohibition are aware of homemade beer and wine, bathtub gin, moonshine, and other types of homemade alcohol. However, a large percentage of the alcohol Americans drank during those years was imported. The Coast Guard and Customs had the extremely difficult task of preventing liquor from landing on America's shores and coming across the long, open land borders with Canada and Mexico.

Prohibition's goal was to prevent the manufacture, sale, and transportation of liquor to stop alcoholism and social drinking. Prohibition was attempted in Aztec society, ancient China, feudal Japan, Norway, Sweden, Russia, Canada, and India. However, only a few Muslim countries managed to effectively ban alcohol.

The Prohibition movement in the United States can be traced back to the religious revivalism of the 1820s and 1830s, which stimulated movements toward perfectionism, including temperance (abstaining from alcohol) and the abolition of slavery. Massachusetts passed a law in 1838, which was repealed two years later, prohibiting the sales of spirits in less than 15-gallon quantities. Maine passed the first state Prohibition law in 1846 and many other states soon passed similar laws before the Civil War.

The Anti-Saloon League, founded in 1893, led the state Prohibition drives from 1906 to 1913. During World War I, the US

Government passed a temporary Wartime Prohibition Act to save grain for use as food instead of an ingredient for alcohol. By January 1920, Prohibition was already in effect in 33 states covering 63 percent of the population.

A Surplus War

It became the duty of the US Coast Guard and Customs to curtail liquor smuggling at sea. As Prohibition dragged on, the war on smuggling escalated. This "war" was made possible by a surplus of both alcohol and military equipment. Much of the liquor smuggled in the US during the first few years of Prohibition was actually surplus from American distilleries. The surplus liquor and beer sat in bonded warehouses, where one only needed a permit to withdraw it. In many cases, distilleries and breweries sent their alcohol overseas only to have it smuggled back into the US at inflated prices.

The fighting between the Coast Guard and rum smugglers escalated quickly, largely because of America's war surplus. World War I ended before most American factories finished cranking out their war goods; so the government auctioned off the excess items to anyone who could afford it. The smugglers were usually a step ahead of the Coast Guard with their newly-purchased gear. Smugglers were soon using airplanes, machine guns, submarines, torpedoes, armored craft, and speedboats powered by 400-horsepower Liberty engines. Most of this equipment came from government surplus auctions.

The Coast Guard also relied on surplus gear. The early Prohibition fleet was made up of submarine-chasers, made of wood, and Eagle boats. Both types of vessels were World War I surplus Navy vessels. Later on, the Coast Guard acquired more than twenty surplus destroyers to fight the rum fleet.

Life In The Early 1920s

To get a real sense of the Prohibition days, one should consider what life was like for the average American. Hollywood films from then and now have given a very glamorous image to those times. Films and documentaries (sadly) depict the '20s as a relatively carefree time of economic prosperity when men and women wore flashy clothing and spent their free time drinking, doing dances like "the Charleston," and listening to jazz. According to this same Hollywood image, the average person lived in a beautifully-furnished, spacious home with heat and electricity, a phone, radio, record player, and a refrigerator. The image also includes at least one big, shiny car for every household and even a household servant.

Library of Congress

An 1874 illustration depicting "Woman's Holy War" against alcohol. Note the leg of a fleeing man at the lower right. Published in New York by Currier and Ives.

Unfortunately, that was not the case for most Americans. In the early 1920s, the nation went through a very bad recession. Millions of war veterans returned home to find that many factories and shipyards that produced military goods had shut down. Unemployment was widespread and workers went on strike in massive numbers to protest harsh working conditions and poor pay. There were no social safety nets such as unemployment checks, worker's compensation, Social Security, Medicaid, or food stamps. These economic conditions tempted the average worker to take part in bootlegging or rum-running. Smuggling liquor paid several times the salary of the average job for fewer hours of work, and, in many cases, the working conditions were better. Smuggling liquor by boat was usually far more bearable than working at a steel mill, coal mine, textile mill, or assembly line.

In addition to a bad economy, the government began Communist witch hunts in reaction to the Communist revolution in Russia. Politicians put striking workers and Communists in the same category, often drawing no distinction. On January 2, 1920, government agents in 33 cities rounded up thousands of suspected Communists and detained them without charges for long periods. In the face of widespread protest against the "Palmer Raids," Attorney General Palmer argued that his program was the only practical means to prevent a Bolshevik conspiracy to overthrow the US Government.

In addition to a recession and political turmoil, daily life for the average American was harsh by today's standards. In 1920, only 47 percent of city homes and 1.6 percent of farm homes had electricity. Americans prioritized installing electrical outlets over other modern conveniences, such as running water. Much of the American population in the early '20s did not have central heating, bathtubs, running water, or indoor toilets.

Rural people, especially women, knew what they were missing when they read magazine advertisements and mail-order catalogs. For example, without an electric pump, women had to haul water into the house from a nearby well or stream and then heat it for cleaning, bathing, or laundry. For those Americans fortunate enough to have electricity, there were new electrical gadgets on the market. Electric irons, fans, and vacuum cleaners were new and popular items. Those who did not have electricity had to heat an iron on the stove to have wrinkle-free clothes. Electric mixers, blenders, coffee makers, and washing machines were also new on the market and were, in 1920, only affordable to the wealthy. Washing machines at that time were very simple devices with a motor that agitated water, detergent, and soiled items. After the cycle was complete, a person would have to remove the drenched clothing from the machine, insert each piece through a motorized wringer, and then hang the clothing up to dry. Washing machines would not be equipped with a spin cycle until the late 1930s. In 1920, electric refrigerators were also very rare, even among the wealthy. Most families continued to rely on underground storage or iceboxes.[1]

Library of Congress
In this 1920 photo taken in New York City, children are licking a block of ice to stay cool in the summer. Electric refrigerators were extremely expensive in the early 1920s, so most people still used an "ice box."

Telephones were still a luxury in the early 1920s. Although the telephone had existed for a few decades by that point, only 35 percent of households had one. To provide an example, when Calvin Coolidge was Vice President, his hometown in Massachusetts only had one telephone, located in the general store. When the store closed in the evenings and on Sunday, the town's residents had no phone access.[2]

Radios were also a new item. The first commercial radio broadcast was in November of 1920. At the time, most radio receivers were homemade crystal sets that could be put together for about $2 and used with a $4 set of earphones. At the end of 1921, there were only ten radio stations in the US. A year later, there were 350 radio stations.

Films were also very popular in the early 1920s, but they had no sound. Theaters presented movies with the music of a live piano player, organist, or sometimes a live orchestra. During the period discussed in this book, Charlie Chaplain was a new silent movie star. The first feature-length "talking picture," *The Jazz Singer* starring Al Jolson, did not debut until 1927.[3]

The automobile brought swift changes to America during this period. In 1920, only one household in three owned an automobile. However, America had an extensive, reliable system of railroads that crossed the country and reached most small towns. Most cities and towns were designed for pedestrians, so car ownership was not a necessity.

During those years, most American roads were dirt roads and no paved highway existed to connect the East and West Coast. In a practical sense, this meant that during times of heavy rain, the roads could turn into muddy quagmires. On the other hand, if there were a drought, vehicles and horses kicked up large amounts of dust (including dried manure). The switch from horses to automobiles did not happen overnight. In the city and in the country, many people were still using horses and mules, each of which made about 15-25 pounds of manure a day. One can only imagine the stench of a city like New York or Chicago in those days.

Henry Ford revolutionized the assembly line system and his workers cranked out an affordable and durable car "for the masses" called the Model T. To sell his cars, Ford introduced consumer credit on a massive scale, making it possible for Americans to live beyond their means. In the 1920s, easy credit helped expand the American economy greatly, which worked out well until the credit bubble burst in 1929.

In order to accommodate the increased number of cars and trucks on the road, Congress approved a measure to subsidize highway construction. However, even by the 1929, only one fifth of America's roads were paved.[4]

One of the key things to know about the 1920s is that it was still a very Victorian decade. Most popular histories depict the 1920s as a time when everyone abandoned Victorian values almost overnight. Many documentaries simplify the entire decade by showing footage of men and women doing nothing but drinking and dancing, interspersed with footage of gangsters shooting tommy-guns. While it is true that a large number of America's youth adopted the new social freedoms that came with the "Jazz Age," a great portion of Americans did not. Bear in mind that the Victorian Age lasted up until World War I. People who reached adulthood before the 1920s had a tendency to hold onto Victorian values long after that era was over. One only has to briefly look through a newspaper from the '20s to realize that many Americans still viewed the world in 19th century terms. Many of the "hot" issues of the 1920s were actually carried over from the previous century. Prohibition, women's suffrage, racism, communism, immigration, workers' rights, anti-war sentiments, and isolationism were all old issues. They all just happened to converge and reach a boiling point around 1920.

Library of Congress
America did not modernize overnight. For example, this photo was taken in New York in 1920. Horses were still a common sight, even though the automobile had existed for two decades. The same applied to ships; in the early '20s, sailing ships were still almost as common as steamships.

In 1920, the Coast Guard and Customs were still equipped for the age of steam and sail. Men who grew old during the Victorian era led both of those organizations during the Prohibition years. A century later, we have come to take for granted the size, training, and equipment of both agencies. The sudden, overwhelming burden brought on by Prohibition enforcement caused growing pains in federal law enforcement. It was the job of both the Coast Guard and Customs to simultaneously work through these growing pains and carry out the mission of stopping an endless flood of smuggled liquor.

Some Things Never Change

While it is interesting to note how much has changed technologically and culturally since the 1920s, it is more important to note the things that have not changed. There are certain characteristics of our political system that have changed very little in the past century. Finger-pointing, mudslinging, and partisanship were as strong in the 1920s as they are today. The men of the Coast Guard and Customs were always caught in the crossfire. When the national Prohibition law took effect, both the Coast Guard and Customs were under-equipped, under-manned, poorly funded, yet expected to stop a tidal-wave of liquor from flooding the US.

The Prohibition law was extremely unpopular. It is interesting to note that the National Prohibition Act received two thirds of the vote in Congress and was ratified by 36 state legislatures. Although it soon became apparent that the law was extremely unpopular, even among police officers and politicians, Congress did not repeal the law until 13 years after it went into effect. Not only did Congress take a long time to repeal the law, it continually escalated the war on alcohol, spending hundreds of millions of dollars (billions in today's dollars) to enforce a policy that most Americans were against. Prohibition provides a classic example of a great gap between popular opinion and the workings of our political machinery. As far as Congress was concerned, the issue was not *how many* people supported Prohibition, but *who* supported it.

2

A STORM ON THE HORIZON

In 1919, President Wilson strongly promoted the idea that the US should join the League of Nations as part of his vision for world peace and the spread of democracy. Most of Congress did not buy the idea. So in early September, President Wilson went on a national speaking tour to rally popular support. The goals of his tour were ambitious. He was to travel by rail from coast to coast and North to South by rail, giving as many speeches as possible within a month. It was a stressful tour; Wilson happened to go on his tour while the nation was undergoing a massive labor crisis. His speeches were all about foreign problems while Americans were thinking about matters closer to home.

Wilson arrived in Seattle with his entourage and met with the Secretary of the Navy for a formal review of the Pacific Fleet in Puget Sound. During the motorcade on the way to the review, the street crowds cheered at a deafening volume. When his car reached Union Street, the employees of a store fired a homemade confetti gun, concealing the President and First lady in a shower of paper confetti. School children waved their flags and shrieked while drivers blared their car horns.

The President was standing and waving his silk high-hat when the noise and cheering came to a very abrupt and sobering end. Men in blue denim work clothes stood along the road on both sides with their arms folded, staring straight ahead, not at the President. They stood motionless and without making a sound. In their hats, the workers wore little signs reading RELEASE POLITICAL PRISONERS. These men were members of the International Workers of the World and were there to demonstrate their anger at the imprisonment of labor leaders on sedition charges. The President's smile quickly vanished and his face took on a flabbergasted look. He stood through the terrible silence for a few minutes. Instead of waving his hat, his arms hung limp at his sides. After two blocks he sank into his car seat beside his wife Edith. He put his tall hat back on his head, a little to one side. His face turned white as he sat in a crumpled-up posture. The denim-clad, statue-like men lined the street for six blocks. His car then began to pass cheering spectators again, but he did not stand. He just waved his hand and smiled weakly.[1]

Wilson and his entourage then went to the harbor and boarded an overcrowded launch that lurched violently, colliding with another boat before reaching the *Oregon*. They sailed several miles through the bay as warships fired twenty-one gun salutes, while their bands played the National Anthem.

A few days later, Wilson made a stop at Pueblo, Colorado, where he intended to give a speech at the Memorial Auditorium in front of thousands of spectators. He went up before the cheering crowd and began to speak. His voice was not strong, but he did well enough until he stumbled over a sentence. "Germany must never be allowed…" He stopped and was silent. "A lesson must be taught to Germany…" He stopped again. "The world will not allow Germany…" Reporter Joseph Jefferson O'Neill looked up from his notes and noticed the terror on the First Lady's face. Wilson had never stumbled like this in any of his presidential speeches. One of his bodyguards believed the President was about to collapse and prepared to catch him. But Wilson pulled himself together and, with a very weak voice, continued his speech on the League of Nations. He invoked the memories of fallen American soldiers to support his cause, bringing tears to the eyes of the audience, and then he stopped. Wilson, who always hid his emotions from the public, began crying in front of an audience of thousands. The President barely managed to say the last paragraph of his speech and left.[2]

That night, the President and his staff were on a train to Wichita, Kansas. Edith Wilson was in the compartment next to her husband's. Her maid was brushing her hair and giving her a massage. The two spoke in low tones so as not to awaken the President. But around 11:30, he knocked on her door. "Can you come to me Edith, I'm terribly sick." He was sitting on the edge of his bed, his head resting on the back of a chair. Mrs. Wilson sent for Dr. Grayson, who took a few minutes to arrive. Upon his arrival, there was nothing he could do to ease Wilson's pain. They brought in some pillows to make him more comfortable, but the President writhed in agony from the splitting pain in his head. After a few hours, he fell asleep sitting up.[3]

As the train approached Wichita, Wilson awoke, stood up and announced that he must shave before giving his next speech. He emerged from the bathroom clean-shaven and dressed, but Dr. Grayson advised him that to continue his speaking tour would be extremely hazardous to his health. However, Wilson was persistent and refused to give up. As he argued with Dr. Grayson, saliva dribbled down from the left side of his mouth, and the left half of his face was fallen and unmoving. Wilson's words came out mumbled and slurred. Joseph Tumulty, the President's friend, secretary, and closest political advisor, helped Dr. Grayson convince Wilson that appearing in public in such a state would do more harm than good both for himself and the nation. Wilson sat with Tumulty holding his hands. The President tried to move closer, but his left arm and leg remained motionless. He then insisted that he only needed a day of rest and would then be ready to continue, but his wife quickly crushed that idea. The rest of the speaking tour was cancelled, and the train headed straight back to Washington.[4]

By October 2, the President and his staff were all back at the White House. Wilson woke up and went to the bathroom. As he sat on a stool, he suffered a stroke. He tumbled to the floor, hitting his head on bathtub's protruding pipes. Mrs. Wilson heard his groans and found him unconscious. She dragged him to the bed and ran from the room to use a special phone to call the Usher's Room. She used that particular phone because she feared the operators might leak information to the public. "Please get Dr. Grayson, the President is very sick," she said. When the Chief Usher and Dr. Grayson arrived, Wilson lay stretched out on the large Lincoln bed. He looked as if he were dead. His face had a long cut above the temple, where blood was still evident; he also had another long cut down the length of his nose.[5]

After about two weeks, the President's staff decided he could be lifted out of bed for a few minutes and placed in a chair by the window. Meanwhile, Congress awaited his signature on the Volstead Act. The Volstead Act and the 18th Amendment[*] are actually two separate documents which banned the transportation and sale of alcohol. (For excerpts of the Volstead Act, see Appendix A.) Congress approved the 18th Amendment as early as 1917 and later overrode Wilson's veto. Wilson believed that education, not prohibition was the way to deal with the problem of alcoholism and that prohibition would be a major

---

[*] 18th Amendment of the US Constitution

Section 1. After one year from the ratification of this article the manufacture, sale, or transportation of intoxicating liquors within, the importation thereof into, or the exportation thereof from the United States and all territory subject to the jurisdiction thereof for beverage purposes is hereby prohibited.
Section 2. The Congress and the several States shall have concurrent power to enforce this article by appropriate legislation.
Section 3. This article shall be inoperative unless it shall have been ratified as an amendment to the Constitution by the legislatures of the several States, as provided in the Constitution, within seven years from the date of the submission hereof to the States by the Congress.

violation of American liberties. Three-fourths of the states had to ratify the 18th Amendment before it could become law. By January 16, 1919, thirty-six states did just that. However, the American people had a grace period of one year before the new law took effect.

In October 1919, Congress voted in favor of the Volstead Act, which outlined the details of Prohibition not included in the 18th Amendment. The Volstead Act was a complicated document full of loopholes. For example, one could still buy and consume a certain amount of alcohol for medical purposes.

Congress sent the approved bill to the White House. The First Lady placed the bill in front of the President. She put a pen in his hand, which trembled as he signed his name to veto the Volstead Act. The effort completely exhausted him. As soon as the Senators familiar with the President's handwriting saw his signature, they immediately began speculating about who had forged it. Most Senators thought it was Tumulty's work; others blamed the First Lady. The Senators even got a handwriting expert to study the signature with a microscope. Soon, several Senators offered strategies to oust the President. Senator Albert Fall of New Mexico vociferously declared that the elected President was not in office. He pounded his fist on the table and shouted, "We have a petticoat Government! Mrs. Wilson is President!" Congress overrode the President's veto and the Volstead Act soon became law.[6]

It was November and the nation was at a crucial point. The actions of the President were vital and time was critical. Prohibition laws, which would take a monumental effort to enforce, were to take effect in less than two months. While Wilson lay in bed crippled and disoriented, the Senators battled with each other over whether or not to join the League of Nations, which was included in the Treaty of Versailles. The American public, in general, was weary of war and entanglement in foreign affairs. Wilson's Covenant, which he added to the Treaty, was the part that most Republican Senators found unacceptable. Articles X and XI of the Covenant would commit all members of the League to protect the independence of any other member threatened by external aggression. This concept seemed little different than the alliance system that a few years earlier turned a relatively small conflict in the Balkans into a World War. However, when Edith Wilson brought compromise suggestions to her husband from Congress, he refused.

Since the President's health had begun to crumble on September 13, he had not met personally with any of his Cabinet members or members of Congress. November was no different. The day before the

Senate was to vote on the Treaty, the Cabinet caught its first glimpse of Wilson in two months. The men met in the White House Cabinet Room at the request of Secretary Lansing to discuss the Treaty. As they sat in the room debating what to do next, they looked out the window to see Wilson being pushed out onto the South Portico in a wheelchair. He sat there motionless, huddled under blankets and wearing a cap. His wife and doctor stood by him as he gazed at the sheep, which were kept there to keep the lawn short.

This was the President's first time outdoors since he had fallen in the bathroom. His wheel-chair was not an ordinary one. Wilson was unable to sit up in an ordinary wheel-chair. His body would slide down to one side, eventually hitting the floor if no one helped him. The chair his Cabinet members saw was modified so his legs stuck straight out to the front, offering more support. After about fifteen minutes, the President was wheeled back inside and put into his bed. The next day, the Senate took a vote on the Treaty and rejected it.[7]

December came and went. Wilson remained hidden from view and unreachable. Most of his letters piled up unanswered and dozens of bills were becoming law without his signature. This was possible due to a provision in the Constitution giving the President ten days to either approve or veto a bill before it became law without his signature. When the President actually did "respond", the letter would be sent back to its author with Edith Wilson's scribbled handwriting. Her sloppy pencil writing wrapped around the margins and across the top and bottom of the returned letters, usually beginning with "The President says" or "The President wants." Eventually, the First Lady began receiving Cabinet members in her sitting room, which was next to the President's room. She would tell the visiting Secretary what the President wanted done about a given situation. Sometimes, when one of the Cabinet members asked for more details, she went into her husband's room, closing the door behind her. Then, she emerged to tell the visiting Secretary what she claimed the President had said. During this time, none of the Cabinet members saw either the President or a single word in his own handwriting. The only evidence the US Government had of Wilson's existence was his 15 minutes outside during the November Cabinet meeting.[8]

A Phenomenal Amount of Drinking

As of January 15, 1920, there were 60,000,000 gallons of whisky in bonded warehouses.[9] Prohibition was to go into effect on January 17, 1920. As the fateful day approached, Americans who did drink made a mad dash for alcohol. Many Americans bought as much as they possibly could and filled rented storage spaces and safe deposit boxes with bottles of liquor. But on January 15, 1920, a New York judge decreed that all liquor stocks outside the home broke the law and were liable to seizure. Across the nation, there was a huge panic as millions of Americans rushed back to their storage units, safe-deposit boxes, and other stash sites outside the home. Americans hired trucks and even used baby carriages, wheel barrels, and anything else that rolled to transport liquor back to their homes.[10]

Out of fear that the Government would seize their liquor and beer, distillers and brewers rushed to export their alcohol for safekeeping outside of the United States. During January of 1920, US Customs cleared 3,384,766 gallons of spirits as exports to foreign countries. It was enough liquor to make 290,000,000 drinks. During January of the previous year, the exports totaled only 14,006 gallons. Most of the exported liquor would eventually wind up returning to the US in rum ships and as legitimate cargo for "medicinal purposes."[11]

A phenomenal amount of drinking took place across the nation on the night of January 16th. One popular theme for parties was a mock wake for alcohol. But, overall the mood was subdued. When the next day came, it was time for the "drys" to celebrate. In Norfolk, Virginia, Billy Sunday, a famous evangelist, staged a mock funeral for John Barleycorn, a fictitious figure representing alcohol. Sunday had a troupe of mimes, impersonating drunks and devils, accompany a 20-foot-long coffin to its final resting place. "The reign of tears is over," he told a huge crowd. "The slums will soon only be a memory. We will turn our prisons into factories and our jails into storehouses and corn-cribs. Men will walk upright now, women will smile, and children will laugh. Hell will be forever for rent."

In Chicago, on that same day, an event occurred that would be precursor of things to come. Six armed, masked men stole $100,000 worth of whiskey that was marked for "medicinal use".[12]

Attorney General Palmer gave a speech at a Prohibition jubilee in which he declared that 99.5% of Americans were for the enforcement of the law. He added:

"There is no longer any liquor question in America—that is settled. The question now is whether the law will be obeyed. The Americans are a law-abiding people and will support the prosecuting officers who enforce the law. The prohibition law looks just like any other law to the Department of Justice. And those who violate the prohibition law will be vigorously prosecuted while the department is under my control. The safety of the public depends more than any other thing on the respectful obedience of the people to the law of the land."[13]

Federal Law Enforcement

Prohibition was a federal law. In the early 1920s, the concept of federal law enforcement was a relatively new idea. When Prohibition first went into effect, the Bureau of Investigation (re-named the Federal Bureau of Investigation in 1935) was only twelve years old. In those days, the Bureau did not provide formal training, so previous law enforcement experience was preferred in candidates, but not necessary. The 300 agents of the Bureau investigated violations of laws involving national banking, bankruptcy, naturalization, anti-trust, peonage (compulsory service), and land fraud.

In the one-year gap between the ratification of the 18th Amendment and its adoption, Congress set up some of the new law enforcement machinery. Congress chose to give the Treasury Department responsibility for enforcing Prohibition laws through the Volstead Act. To most Americans, the Treasury Department might seem an unusual choice for this duty. Many people tend to think of printing money or picture a large federal bank in Washington, DC when they hear of the Treasury. However, there is much more to the department. The Treasury Department was created in 1789, right after the State Department, which means that the Secretary of the Treasury is the second-ranking member of the President's Cabinet. The Secret Service, which protects the President, his family, and former Presidents, is a part of the Treasury Department. The Secretary of the Treasury advises the President and shapes any policy that has to do with money, which is basically every US policy. The Treasury had several smaller bureaus under it that were vital to alcohol control even before the 18th Amendment was passed. To block rum smuggling by sea, the Treasury Department had the Coast Guard.† To block smuggling across the

---

† In 1915, the Treasury Department combined the Revenue Cutter Service with the

Canadian and Mexican border, there was the Customs Service. Customs also patrolled America's waterways and ports.

To stop bootlegging within the US, there was the Bureau of Internal Revenue. Under that bureau, Congress formed a new Prohibition Bureau of 1,500 agents plus several hundred clerical and administrative workers. These new agents were excluded from the Civil Service and exempt from its rules. In every state, these appointments were political. All an aspiring Prohibition agent had to do was endorse a local politician to secure his position. No other qualifications or character references were needed. Some of the new agents had criminal records. The job paid a salary of $2,300 a year, barely enough to live on. In the first few months of Prohibition, the agents were mostly Democratic appointees. When President Harding took over, almost all of them were dismissed and replaced by Republicans. The agents had a high turnover rate. In any given year, there were 10,000 applicants for 2,000 jobs, and the average length of service was only a few months. Many agents would eventually be fired for corrupt practices, although most charges were never proven.[14]

Choosing the right Secretary of the Treasury would be vital in waging the war against alcohol. As President Wilson lay crippled and isolated from the Legislative and Judicial branches of government, not to mention his own staff, he was supposed to appoint a new Treasury Secretary. The current Secretary would be leaving his post shortly, along with the Secretary of the Interior and the Assistant Secretary of Agriculture plus several members of the Civil Service Commission, Federal Trade Commission, Interstate Commerce Commission, Shipping Board, Tariff Committee, War Finance Corporation, Waterways Commission (seven vacancies), and the Rent Commission. He also needed to appoint new diplomats to nine different countries.[15]

The War on Rum Begins

The "war on rum" immediately began to cost as much as a real war. The Coast Guard was soon dubbed the "dry navy". Not even a month after Prohibition took effect, the Chief of the Customs Division through Secretary Glass requested an appropriation of $2,000,000 from Congress for an army of Customs officials to enforce the new laws at the ports and along the borders. This was in addition to the $1,000,000

Lifesaving Service to form the modern Coast Guard. The Coast Guard dates back to 1790, but originally went by the names Revenue Marine and Revenue Cutter Service.

Congress had already approved to guard 800 warehouses full of liquor. After only three weeks of Prohibition, the government estimated it would have to spend $8,000,000 just to keep the warehouses guarded. Keep in mind that in 1920, a brand new car cost approximately nine hundred dollars.[16]

One might have the idea that immediately after Prohibition went into effect, Coast Guardsmen and Customs agents jumped into their vessels and began a frantic pursuit of rum smugglers. However, this was far from the case. At the National Archives in Washington, DC, most of the original logbooks from that period are available for examination. If one looks through the logbooks of the Coast Guard Cutters *Manhattan, Seneca, Gresham,* and the *Hahn* for the years 1920 and 1921, rum smugglers are mentioned very rarely. The *Manhattan*, for example, has only nine logbook entries relating to smugglers for all of 1921. It is important to remember that these particular cutters were stationed in New York City, the busiest rum smuggling port in the nation. These vessels spent much of their time in port during those two years. When the cutters did go out, they went on short patrols. The cutters generally did not patrol at night, when rum smugglers were at their busiest. The crews of these vessels also had most Sundays off. However, from 1922 onward, the number of logbook entries reporting rum seizures increased steadily. By 1924, rum seizures were an almost daily occurrence for the crews aboard these cutters.[17]

Admiral Reynolds

The Commandant of the Coast Guard from September 1919 to January 1924 was William Edward Reynolds—a historical figure who has faded into obscurity. During his tenure as Commandant, Reynolds scarcely made any statements to the press. The press, in turn, rarely mentioned him. There are no published books on his life.

In the 1920s, Admiral Reynolds was the symbol of a bygone era. He was born in 1860, one year before the Civil War began. He was appointed a cadet in the Revenue Cutter Service in 1878 and commissioned a third lieutenant (a rank that no longer exists) in 1880. In 1881, Reynolds was a member of the small sled party sent out from the Revenue Cutter *Corwin* to search along the northern coast of Siberia for tidings of the Arctic exploring steamer *Jeannette*. On August 12, 1881, he was at the head of the party which landed on Wrangel Island and took possession of the island in the name of the United States. During the Spanish-American War he was in command of the Revenue Cutter

McClane and served in the fleet of Rear Admiral Sampson. During the World War, Reynolds was Chief of Staff of the Twelfth Naval District, headquartered in San Francisco.[18]

Reynolds was promoted to Captain by 1903 and Captain Commandant with the rank of Commodore in 1919. He became the first officer in the Coast Guard to hold the rank of Rear Admiral, which Congress provided for in the Act of January 12, 1923. When Admiral Reynolds retired on January 11, 1924, he had served for 45 years.

Courtesy US Coast Guard Headquarters

Admiral Reynolds

A "Petticoat Government"

Over tea, Edith Wilson asked Secretary of Agriculture Houston to take the Treasury Secretary position. His old position was to be filled by Edward Merideth. She also personally asked Judge John Barton Payne to leave the Shipping Board for the Department of the Interior. Neither Houston, Meredith, nor Payne were interviewed by the President before getting their new jobs.[19]

At night, while the President slept, the First Lady sat up late working on official papers. On one occasion, pointing at a pile of newspapers, she said to a maid, "I don't know how much more criticism I can take." Things were so bad that Edith Benham, her secretary, had a complete nervous breakdown and had to resign.[20]

After seven months without direct contact with the President, his Cabinet met in the President's study. This was the first meeting the President had with his staff since before his speaking tour. Much had changed in the nation since the last meeting and some of the Secretaries were new to their positions. Each of them had much to discuss with the President, especially Treasury Secretary Houston. The Coast Guard, Customs, and the Prohibition Bureau, all under his command, were stretched thin and overwhelmed by Prohibition enforcement.

Before the Cabinet members arrived, Wilson was put in a chair and propped up at the end of a desk. The President looked old, worn, and haggard. Half of his body was still crippled and his voice was weak and strained. Houston shook hands with him and sat down. Wilson put on a brave front and spent several minutes cracking jokes. Then there was a brief silence. Someone brought up the subject of nationalized railroads and discussed it at length. Wilson seemed to have trouble keeping his mind on the discussion. Then, Secretary of Labor Wilson and Attorney General Palmer began arguing over the deportation of suspected anarchists. Palmer argued that more deportations could have ended the mining strike, because many of the miners were immigrants. However, Secretary Wilson argued that it would only make matters worse. Dr. Grayson looked in the door several times during the meeting, as if to warn the Secretaries to keep the meeting short. The discussion dragged on for more than an hour. Mrs. Wilson, looking disturbed, finally came in and suggested that the Cabinet leave. Houston barely got a word in edgewise.[21]

Foreign Ships

When Prohibition first went into effect, the Treasury Department required all foreign vessels to seal their liquor stores when entering an American port. However, this caused some international problems, when French, Spanish, and Italian sailors began refusing to sign on for ships bound for American ports. Within the first couple of weeks under the new law, the entire engine room crew of an Italian liner left their ship at Genoa shouting "Never again!" after a dry visit to New York. British shipping companies also had difficulties finding crews bound for the US.[22]

Two weeks after the law went into effect, the Treasury Department reversed its policy. The Treasury decided to consider foreign ships as foreign territory and would, therefore, not interfere with the crews receiving their daily rations of wine and spirits. Spanish cruise lines endeavored to secure similar rights for their passengers, who strongly objected to being deprived of alcohol while stopping at American ports.[23]

The First Big Liquor Seizure

In early 1920, many ships still sailed into port with liquor aboard without making any attempts to hide it. But soon these ships would be the initial targets for seizure. One of the earliest examples was the steamer *Yarmouth*, which had sailed from New York for Cuba the day Prohibition took effect. The *Yarmouth* belonged to the Black Star Line, which was a shipping company owned and operated by blacks. For African Americans to manage such a feat in America during the 1920s was no small feat. Bear in mind that the Ku Klux Klan's membership was at its peak during this period, especially in parts of New York such as Long Island.[24]

The *Yarmouth* left New York with $4,800,000 worth of liquor only to return to New York Harbor two weeks later, allegedly because the ship sprang a leak and was sinking. Under orders from Washington, Federal Supervising Prohibition Agent James S. Shelvin put guards on board the steamer as it sat anchored near the Statue of Liberty. A few days later, the US Government formally seized the ship and Shelvin announced that his men would unload the liquor cargo and store it in bonded warehouses. Leo H. Healy, counsel for the owners of the *Yarmouth*, announced to the press that he would seek an injunction from a Federal Judge to restrain Agent Shelvin from interfering with the cargo.[25]

After looking at the ship's manifest, Agent Shelvin discovered that the ship was missing 500 cases of whisky. Officials of the Black Star Line claimed that the crew threw the cases overboard off the Virginia coast when the ship sprang a leak. Reverend Dr. R.D. Jonas, Secretary of the League of Darker Peoples, rushed to New York to explain what happened to the authorities. Dr. Jonas asserted that the owners were the victims of much undeserved criticism when they really deserved sympathy because the ship's misfortunes were not their fault. According to Jonas, the owners were the victims of a plot to steal the $4,800,000 liquor cargo and that only the bravery of the ship's black skipper, Captain Cockburn, an experienced sailor under the British flag, prevented the theft.[26]

The *Yarmouth*, Dr. Jonas said, left New York with a slight list to port. Another vessel followed the *Yarmouth* closely and when the ship was some distance off shore in a heavy storm, it had mysteriously sprung a leak. A white engineer aboard, who had been taken on at the last minute, rushed up to the bridge and informed Captain Cockburn that the boat was sinking and that there was nothing to do but board the lifeboats.[27]

The Captain drew a revolver and told the engineer, "You go back to your job and set the pumps going!" The engineer went back down below and the Captain followed him after sending out an S.O.S. as a precaution. After inspecting the leak, Cockburn suspected that someone had opened a seacock. The "sinking" ship still managed to reach port under its own power with its crew aboard.[28]

The legal action of Leo H. Healy and the story of Dr. Jonas were effective. After a conference in US Attorney Francis G. Caffey's office and a phone conversation with Prohibition Commissioner John F. Kremer in Washington, John J. Quigley, Assistant Federal Supervising Prohibition Agent, announced that the *Yarmouth* was free to sail to Cuba. On the day of the announcement, the ship was docked at West 80th Street, where it was taking on coal for fuel.[29]

A week and a half later, the *Yarmouth* finally left port with $4,000,000 worth of liquor, which meant that if the ship sold the missing liquor, the owners made a profit of $800,000. During the ship's stay in port, twenty agents worked in shifts to guard the vessel day and night. It cost the Government $200 a day to maintain the guard, totaling $4,200. As the *Yarmouth* raised anchor and moved slowly from the pier, the ten Federal Prohibition agents on duty gave sighs of relief and went rejoicing back to the Internal Revenue Office to await another assignment. Captain Joshua Cockburn was on the bridge when the *Yarmouth* departed. All 35 black crew members stood at the ship's rail to wave goodbye to their friends on the pier.[30]

Black Prohibition Agents

African Americans played a significant role on both sides of Prohibition. In 1924, Charles Dixon and William Harvey were black Prohibition agents. Acting on orders from Prohibition Director Merrick, the two went to a river wharf at the foot of Chapel Street in Newark, New Jersey. Smugglers expected a large delivery of liquor early that morning. Dixon and Harvey discovered a rum boat emerging from the shadows alongside the dock where three trucks were already waiting. The truck crews jumped aboard the craft and quickly transferred the cases to their vehicles. The boat then cast off and drifted into the stream.[31]

Agents Dixon and Harvey stood at the land end of the pier, blocking the exit with drawn revolvers when the three trucks attempted to leave. "Hijackers!" shouted the driver of the first truck. An automobile suddenly appeared behind the two agents. William Lillian stepped out of the car and took sides with the smugglers. When Harvey said that he and Dixon were Prohibition agents, Lillian refused to believe him. Lillian and Harvey grappled, and a general fight started as the others came from the trucks to help Lillian.[32]

"Get 'em on the boat!" one of the truckers yelled before the gang rushed Dixon down the wharf. The men put Dixon on a small boat and took him to the rum-runner in midstream. Word of the trouble reached the nearby police station and the reserves rushed to the wharf. The police found Lillian and Harvey still fighting. Dixon was nowhere to be found and the rum boat had disappeared.[33]

The police brought the two fighting men to the police station, where Harvey showed his credentials and was released. Lillian, on the other hand, was held by United States Commissioner George R. Sommer on $1,000 bail for the federal grand jury on a charge of violating the Volstead act. Later, Lillian was also arraigned before Acting Judge Guthrie in the Criminal Court on a charge of felonious assault, and was held on $500 bail for the Essex County Grand Jury. It is important to keep in mind that this happened three decades before the Civil Rights Movement of the 1950's and 60's. It was quite exceptional for black men to have such a high legal status and to receive protection from the law during a time when blacks could not eat at most restaurants or use public drinking fountains.[34]

Newark Police Headquarters sent out a general alarm for Dixon, as well as the trucks and the rum-runner. Some time later, police found one of the trucks abandoned in Newark, still loaded with liquor and out of gasoline. Detective Captain Frank Brex called Agent Harvey into his office and handed him the telephone. Dixon was at the other end of the line, reporting himself safe after rivermen released him at the Lister Company dock.[35]

Customs Raids

Customs officers immediately went to work seizing liquor on ships in port. In New York City during February, three men operating under Surveyor of Customs Thomas E. Rush seized 1,257 bottles of liquor hidden on incoming ships, mostly from Cuba. When the three men searched the Italian ship *Presidente Wilson*, they crew became hostile as the agents found several dozen bottles of cognac, which they placed on a table in the crew's quarters. The lights were suddenly turned off and the crewmembers threw the framework of an iron bunk onto the bottles, breaking several of them. The inspectors reached the light switch and turned on the lights, standing guard over the switch until reinforcements arrived. After the reinforcements arrived, they conducted a more thorough search and found 537 bottles of cognac and weapons concealed in the bunks.[36]

In October, a small force of Customs officers attempted to board another Italian steamship named the *Dante d'Alighieri*. However, the crew drew up the gangplank and the ship's officers refused to allow the inspectors to search the vessel because it flew the Italian flag. The Customs officers left when they heard that the captain was not aboard the ship. Soon, the Customs men returned with a force of sixty inspectors and eleven Coast Guardsmen. The captain of the ship allowed the men to search his ship. The inspectors found 175 bottles of undeclared champagne, whisky, cognac, and Benedictine hidden in the steamship, mostly in the crew's quarters. They also found a quantity of narcotics.[37]

Customs officers were also busy in Boston, where they paid more than one visit to the *Cretic* of the White Star Line. During the first raid of the ship, the Customs men found a large quantity of liquor. A few days later, the Customs officers returned and found an additional 200 bottles of liquor after one of the *Cretic's* crew grabbed a crowbar and attacked an inspector.[38]

Courtesy US Coast Guard Headquarters

Customs officials conduct a search for liquor.

The Navy and the Coast Guard

The longshoremen then joined the fight. The mostly-Irish longshoremen were still angry at the *Cretic's* Italian crew for the part they played in breaking the recent strike by loading and unloading cargo when the longshoremen refused to do it. Seizing whatever they could get on the pier, the longshoremen bombarded the crew of the *Cretic*. The fighting did not stop until Harbor Police, sailors from the destroyer *Susquehanna,* and Boston Police arrived.[39]

The seizure aboard the *Cretic* was one of the largest on record as of November 1920. The Customs men confiscated 600 bottles of wine and whisky valued at $5,000 plus four packages of morphine. The liquor was well hidden and it took over an hour for the inspectors to find it. The Customs men finally found the 600 bottles buried beneath piles of coal in the engine room and found the morphine under massive iron plates in the same room.[40]

The Coast Guard and the Navy had a love/hate relationship during the Prohibition years. One incident that did not help relations between the two services occurred in April 1920, off the coast of Florida. US Navy Submarine 4 was traveling on the surface 20 miles from Miami with its lights on.[41] The Coast Guard vessel fired a dozen rifle rounds and one six-pound round at the sub; fortunately, all of them missed. The sub's captain ordered his men to scan the water with a searchlight. A few moments later, another searchlight appeared from the Coast Guard cutter as it approached the submarine.

The captain of the S-4 called the Coast Guard vessel alongside and the two captains exchanged words. The officer of the Coast Guard vessel stated that the submarine had failed to stop when signaled and he had orders to fire on any vessel that did not comply.

Assistant Secretary of the Treasury Moyle claimed to the press that he had no report of the incident and that he did not believe that the commanders of Coast Guard vessels had orders to fire on any craft except in very unusual cases.[42]

Liquor-Filled Torpedoes

Smugglers quickly thought of creative methods to sneak rum into the United States. For example, rum-runners in the Detroit area figured out how to use torpedoes to smuggle whisky. An informant, who wished to protect his identity, told federal officers that electrically operated torpedoes loaded with whisky were being sent across the Detroit River from Canada. In May 1920, there were three different sizes in use: one that held 10 gallons, one that held 15, and one 20-gallon torpedo. They were made of copper with a propeller at the nose powered by electric batteries. The torpedoes submerged 100 feet and took five minutes to cross the river at a point east of Woodward Avenue. A red flag on one side and a white one on the other were the targets to which the operators guided the torpedoes. After the smugglers on the Detroit side caught and emptied the torpedoes, they filled them with water and launched them back to Canada. The informant also told the federal officers that a 50-gallon torpedo was under construction.[43]

****

Spring soon turned into summer and brought with it heated political debates to match the season. In June, the Republicans nominated Senator Warren G. Harding for President and Calvin Coolidge for Vice President. In July, the Democrats nominated Governor James M. Cox of Ohio to run for President with Franklin D. Roosevelt as his running mate. The main platform of the Democrats was the promotion of the League of Nations and the Treaty of Versailles. However, the American people were tired of foreign affairs, the war debt, and the high taxes paid during and after the war. In addition, businessmen were tired of economic controls.

As the campaign went on, the League of Nations began to look more and more like a sham. The French army occupied Frankfurt, Germany as France expanded its military alliances and all of the former Allies increased their armaments. Britain and France denied the Arab states their independence and small wars between Eastern European states continued, although these nations had signed the League Covenant. As a consequence, the American public was tired of foreign entanglements and rallied to Senator Harding's slogan, "Return to normalcy."[44]

In the summer of 1920, one only had to drive fifteen miles outside of Washington, DC to be in the countryside. Wilson's chauffeur drove the President's car for hours along the Conduit Road running toward Great Falls. The hills and reservoirs of rural Virginia were beautiful during that time of the year. As Wilson's car went slowly down country roads, children ran up to it and waved to him. Wilson rarely spoke; in fact, he was almost totally mute. He showed no interest in the Presidential campaign and did not give Mr. Cox any public endorsements that summer. He also believed that the majority of American voters still supported the League and the Treaty. Wilson also failed to address the millions of new women voters. During that summer, the number of eligible American voters doubled because women were given the right to vote under the new 19th Amendment.[45]

****

The campaign against rum smuggling was still not going well. In August, Assistant Secretary of the Treasury Shouse said that the Customs Service was "wholly inadequate" to meet the situation. He blamed the shortcomings of Customs on Congress' refusal to appropriate more funds to expand the service. Assistant Secretary Shouse argued that the only solution was a small army of men to patrol the coast and border territories. He stated that, although Customs agents had confiscated thousands of dollars worth of liquor from ships entering ports, vast quantities were still slipping in. Most of the liquor supplies did not come in through ports, but rather by the landings of launches and small boats in secluded spots along the Atlantic Coast. Larger seagoing vessels brought their liquor cargoes and then waited three miles or more from the coast for the smaller vessels, which picked up the shipments. US ships were not legally allowed to enforce Prohibition laws more than three miles away from the coast. Shouse argued that, although smuggling was a large problem across the Canadian border, it was nowhere near as bad as the smuggling problem along the coast.[46]

However, the problem of rum-running across the Canadian border was in reality just as bad, if not worse, than on the coast. A Canadian official, who wished to remain anonymous, stated to the press that the Prohibition law against smuggling was violated hundreds of times a day all along the border from Seattle to Maine. He doubted that the law could ever be successfully enforced without putting armed guards every hundred yards on the border from Vancouver to Winnipeg and every fifty feet the rest of the way across the continent. The Detroit rum-runners had a great deal of notoriety, but those smugglers were no more active than those in Maine, Vermont, and New York and all along the line of the St. Lawrence and the Great Lakes. Many of the roads from Canada did not have Customs checkpoints. Most of the Customs officers did not like the idea of being "whisky plotters" and enforced the dry laws only sporadically.[47]

Detroit circa 1920 Courtesy of National Archives

The unnamed Canadian official also stated that most of the liquor was smuggled across Lake Champlain by motorboat. There were no Customs or Coast Guard vessels checking for alcohol shipments. It only took the liquor-filled motorboats half an hour to cross the lake from Canada to either New York or Vermont. Once the smugglers arrived at their destinations on the US side, they simply carried the liquor a short distance and loaded it into a waiting car or truck, which could drive away without being searched.[48]

Smugglers were just as hostile to Canadian officers as they were to US law enforcement. For example, Constable Allan of the Windsor Police refused to take a bribe of £500 from rum smugglers on the border. In response, a gang of fifteen smugglers beat Allan senseless and restrained him with his own handcuffs. The smugglers threw the constable into a motorcar and began driving along a river road. After regaining consciousness, Allan jumped into a snow bank still handcuffed and almost blind from the blood in his eyes. He then staggered to the nearest telephone from which he called police headquarters. The Windsor police used Allan's information to seize the liquor at the local railway station. Stories like that of Constable Allan caused many Canadians to have doubts as to whether their police should get involved with enforcing this new American law.[49]

On October 11, officials from the Bureau of Internal Revenue made a statement to the press, indicating that the Bureau was considering the seizure of foreign vessels carrying alcohol. The Volstead Act provided specifically for the confiscation of any vehicle involved in a violation of the law. Technically, foreign ships were within American jurisdiction when inside the three-mile limit. This made them liable to confiscation any time contraband goods were found on board. The Internal Revenue officials also stated that the seizure of a few ships would end the activities of seagoing bootleggers.[50] Three days later, Byron R. Newton, Collector of Customs, denied the claim and assured the press that the situation had not yet reached the stage where the government was considering the seizure and sale of foreign ships. He claimed that he had not received word from Washington that the Bureau of Internal Revenue was considering seizure as a means to curb rum smuggling.[51] In contrast, the Prohibition law applied to American ships no matter what waters they were in—even on the high seas.[52]

Meanwhile, the attention of the American public was on the election. All through the summer, Wilson continued to say privately that Cox was sure to win. However, he ignored all requests to help the candidate until October. On October 27, with Election Day a week off, he received a handful of pro-League of Nations Republicans in the Green Room. He sat hunched over in his wheel chair under a portrait of Abraham Lincoln and did not stand when they came in. "I must apologize for receiving you like this," he said. "It is unavoidable and I guess you all understand."[53]

They remained standing around him as he began to read his statement as to why Cox should be elected. His voice was loud and strong in the beginning but gradually grew weaker and weaker. By the end of his short speech, he was whispering, "...I suggest the candidacy of every candidate for whatever office be tested by this question: Shall we or shall we not redeem the great moral obligations of the United States?" Wilson, breathing with difficulty, eyes closed, and trembling, was wheeled away. On Election Day, Harding won the most one-sided victory since the election of James Monroe one hundred years earlier.[54]

3

ATLANTIC CITY'S MYSTERY SHIP

President Wilson recovered his health sufficiently to follow the tradition of the outgoing President accompanying the President-elect to the inaugural ceremonies at the Capitol. On March 4, 1921, Wilson was notified that the President-elect was in the Blue Room awaiting his arrival. Alone, unaided, and grasping his old black-thorn walking stick, or his "third leg," as he called it, Wilson slowly made his way to the elevator. He met Harding in the Blue Room and greeted him in a gracious manner, hiding his pain. The ride to the Capitol was uneventful. Based on physical appearance alone, it was obvious which man was coming and which was going. On the right in the open convertible Wilson sat, looking gray, haggard, and broken. Harding appeared healthy and robust. Wilson interpreted the cheering from the crowds as belonging to Harding and looked straight ahead. It was the new President's day, not his.[1]

Wilson walked to the reception room in the Capitol, where he showed signs of pain as he signed some bills. Harding encouraged Wilson not to attend the inaugural ceremonies, so Wilson went straight to his new residence in Washington that his wife prepared. Harding's inaugural address was the first ever to be electronically amplified for the crowd, and was also the first to be broadcast over the radio and throughout the world.[2]

Immediately after being sworn in as President, Harding walked over to the Senate chamber to personally present the names of his Cabinet nominees. He was the first President since Thomas Jefferson to meet the Senate on his inauguration day. The senators greeted their former colleague with a round of applause. They held the impression that they would not be at odds with Harding— a former senator— as they had been with Wilson. Harding's message to the Senate emphasized cooperation between the three branches of government.[3]

Harding had a much different style of leadership than Wilson. Ever since Wilson delivered his war message, the iron gates of the White House had been locked, barred, and watched by armed guards. During Wilson's time in office, the White House had always been remote from the public. After Wilson's stroke, the building stayed mostly empty, with very few visitors. Although Wilson was admired for his intellect and strong leadership, he usually kept his distance from the American public.[4]

As soon as Harding returned from the Senate, the iron gates in front of the White House were thrown open. The open gates drew a crowd of curious onlookers. When the White House servants were closing the curtains in the East Room, Florence Harding insisted that they remain open. "Let 'em look if they want to," she said. "It's their White House."

In 1921, there was widespread economic depression in America (not to be confused with the Great Depression beginning in late 1929). So Harding insisted that the inauguration ceremonies be kept simple in order to honor his pledge to reduce federal spending. There was a small parade but no inaugural ball. The day after the inauguration, the lower floors and the grounds of the White House were open to visitors for the first time in years.

The Hardings loved to entertain guests, so the First Lady had the building redecorated both inside and out. She added more colorful interior decorations and flowers in almost every room. Gardeners planted thousands of bulbs on the White House lawns and birdhouses were placed in the trees. The First Lady hosted three garden parties for war veterans that summer and revived the traditions of White House teas, the "Easter Egg Roll" for children, and Marine Corps Band concerts on the lawn.

Although the Volstead Act had been in effect for more than a year, Harding drank and served liquor in the private rooms of the White House. He also liked to play poker. After becoming President, he played poker and drank with friends and members of the government from dinner until midnight at least twice a week. His administration would later be dubbed the "poker Cabinet".

The Senate was required to approve the President's Cabinet nominees, which normally took weeks of debate and background investigations. But when Harding presented his Cabinet choices to the Senate, they applauded and quickly approved them. (The Senate would eventually come to regret their impulsiveness.)

Harding designated Andrew Mellon as the new Secretary of the Treasury. Mellon was one of the richest men in the US. His father was a wealthy Pittsburgh banker, who used the family fortune to found the Mellon Bank. Mellon was a finance capitalist who invested his wealth in a vast array of industries. Until he was appointed to Harding's Cabinet, Mellon had little political experience and knew little about the Treasury

Department. The business and banking community was pleased with his appointment, while agriculture and labor were not; they believed he would side with the wealthy. They were correct. Mellon was not a popular person. He was very quiet, even in Cabinet meetings. Harding once dubbed him "the Sphinx." He rarely smiled and only shook hands with the tips of his fingers.[5]

Andrew Mellon accepted his new post with little enthusiasm. When Senator Philander Knox informed him that the position was open, Mellon replied, "I am not sure that the news is pleasing to me." Historian David Cannadine writes in his book, *Mellon: An American Life*, that it was likely Mellon took the post because his daughter, Ailsa, wanted to move to Washington. But aside from a fear of loneliness and the desire to live close to his daughter, Mellon also had business interests on the East Coast.[6]

Mellon, the man who would soon oversee the whole Prohibition enforcement effort, still owned many shares of Overholt Distillery stock. The *New York World* depicted Mellon as "the largest distiller of whisky in America," who made much of his fortune by selling booze. On top of that, Mellon owned millions of dollars in bank stock. Under the Federal Reserve Act of 1913, it was illegal for a member of the Federal Reserve Board to own any bank stock.[7]

Mellon had originally invested $25,000 in the Overholt Distillery in 1887, giving him one-third ownership of the company. By December 1918, his holdings in the company were worth $1.1 million. In 1921, Mellon and his brother Dick entered into an agreement with the Union Trust Company to acquire Overholt's property and remaining stocks of liquor, which the two brothers planned to sell to the Schulte Drug Stores for "medicinal purposes" in 1925. Mellon claimed that his distillery had ceased production of liquor more than three years before Prohibition went into effect. However, over the next ten years, rumors continued to spread that he made his money as a distiller and a bootlegger.[8]

Mellon's pro-business and anti-labor views were compatible with the President's and part of the plan to return to "normalcy." Harding's political platform of "normalcy" meant restoring low pre-war taxes, balanced budgets, a low national debt, limited government, and an international economy backed by the gold standard. The Great War had caused government spending to rise from $1 billion in 1916 to $18.5 billion in 1919. During that same period, the national debt rose from less than $2 billion to $26 billion. Interest rates were at 7 percent and the tax system was in chaos. Many wealthy people avoided paying the new income tax and the government imposed new taxes in a desperate effort to raise revenue. With the armistice in Europe came an abrupt halt to the demand for war goods. Two million demobilized troops returned home to find closed factories, liquidated businesses, failed banks, and widespread unemployment. Mellon witnessed this firsthand in Pittsburgh and commented that the crisis of 1921 was one of the worst he had ever witnessed.[9]

Prohibition enforcement would soon become an international issue. The European nations involved in the Great War were ravaged and their economies were in shambles. The Allies had run up a debt of $10 billion dollars to the United States during the war, but had no means to repay the loans. The Bolshevik Revolution and Civil War in Russia made matters even worse. These conditions made it especially tempting for Europeans to smuggle liquor into the US and make a quick profit.[10]

Mellon did not support Prohibition. While he was the Treasury Secretary, Mellon still took and served alcoholic drink. He also thought the dry laws were extreme and unenforceable. He believed the Treasury should focus on raising revenue, not detection and policing. During his tenure, Mellon tried his best to get the responsibility of Prohibition enforcement transferred to the Justice Department. Also, Prohibition agents were uninspired by the Chief of the Prohibition Unit, Roy A. Haynes, a former small-town newspaper editor and one of Harding's cronies.[11]

President Harding assigned Charlie Dawes to head the new Bureau of the Budget in an effort to cut governmental spending. In front of an audience of 1,200 government officials, Dawes explained how government spending needed to be reformed. He made his point by holding up two brooms and saying:

> "This may look like a stage play, but it's not, because things like this have to stop. Here is a Navy broom, made in accordance with Navy specifications. Here is an Army broom made in accordance with Army specifications. Now, the Army had 350,000 of these brooms in surplus. The Navy needed 18,000 brooms. It could have had the Army brooms for nothing but because they were wrapped with twine instead of wire, the Navy wouldn't take them as a gift. So the Navy went into the market and bought brooms at top prices."[12]

Dawes only volunteered to take his new post for one year. But during that year he cut government spending by more than a billion dollars.[13]

Graft

At the beginning of February of 1921, Byron R. Newton, Collector of the Port of New York, recommended the dismissal of eight Customs Inspectors for dereliction of duty of the baggage searchers on transatlantic steamships and piers. Newton's staff was also investigating 40 other Customs Inspectors in New York. Newton had launched an inquiry three weeks earlier that revealed that an international system of drug smuggling was pouring quantities of narcotics into the port. Police arrested a seaman who had $20,000 worth of cocaine. The police also discovered that most of the opiates were being smuggled from Germany.[14]

Mr. Newton denied reports of wholesale grafting. However, he did announce to the press that special agents of the Treasury Department working on the piers had evidence of passengers handing "gratuities" to inspectors, ranging from $1 to $300. The Collector also stated that inspectors had visited the homes and offices of passengers the day after their arrival to collect fees. He had this to say about the situation:

> "This is the hardest task I ever had to perform. Many men fundamentally honest have been drawn into this situation because of conditions and environments.
>
> "Passengers are forbidden to offer gratuities, but there is always a class in a hurry to get off the piers and they are willing to give an inspector $50 to $100 if he will rush their baggage through or not examine it at all...there are some who would be willing to give an inspector $500 or even $1,000 if they thought that it would induce him to pass their baggage without proper examination...
>
> "The smuggling of liquor is hard to guard against. Each steamship has a crew of from 50 to 250 men. You can use your imagination as to the result of this daily arrival from 'wet' ports."[15]

On February 8, 1921, the Department of Justice announced that no vessel of any nationality could enter a United States port or come within a three-mile limit of the coastline with intoxicating liquor on board. The Justice Department specified that ships transporting liquor from one foreign port to another were restricted from US ports. Customs authorities, however, argued that if agents enforced this new policy to the letter, no foreign passenger liners would be able to enter American ports, even with a sealed store of liquor. American shipping interests liked the idea. The American Mercantile Marine considered "dry" American passenger ships one of its main handicaps in competition for global shipping.[16]

The Islands

Bimini is a small island located 48 miles off the coast of Florida. In the 1920s, the island was British territory. William Jennings Bryan, the former US Secretary of State, and perennial Presidential candidate, had been living in Bimini for several years when Prohibition went into effect. Bryan, who was one of Prohibition's leading advocates, suffered great mental anguish as he watched flocks of American airplanes land on the tiny island to pick up liquor bound for the United States. Bryan went to New York in late April 1921 and gave a speech about the situation. He declared that Great Britain was permitting Bimini to become the base of a conspiracy against the Prohibition law. He told his audience that certain people in Bimini were making millions of dollars a year on liquor that was smuggled into the United States and suggested that the US Government make a formal protest to the British government.[17]

A month after William Jennings Bryan made his speech about a British Prohibition conspiracy, six steamers appeared off Atlantic City and New York loaded with liquor. Three of the ships were flying the British flag. The ships came from Nassau, Havana, and, of course, Bimini.[18]

Atlantic City

Atlantic City still managed to attract many tourists after the Prohibition laws went into effect. Obviously alcohol was still easy to purchase there because on the night of May 10, Prohibition agents made raids throughout the city and confiscated $75,000 worth of liquor. The agents who made the raids believed they were on the verge of exposing a gigantic smuggling plot, involving millions of dollars worth of foreign liquor and extending along the entire Atlantic seaboard. Customs agents informed the press that prominent men in many coastal cities were involved. The agents found sufficient evidence to make numerous arrests. After the raids in Atlantic City, undercover Customs agents began to secretly watch dozens of suspects from Maine to Florida.[19]

The agents soon learned that the "contraband booze fleet," hovering beyond the three-mile limit off of Atlantic City, numbered six vessels. Two steamers and one sloop, all flying British flags, were waiting off the coast for a week, unable to get local boatmen to unload their cargoes, despite offers of $1,000 a trip. On May 19, these three vessels were joined by three smaller vessels from Atlantic City. The three smaller vessels had just returned from Bimini, Nassau, and Havana, loaded with rye whisky, which had been shipped from the US on the eve of Prohibition and was now being sent back for sale at much higher bootleg prices.[20]

The "booze fleet" had $500,000 of liquor aboard its ships. The Coast Guard maintained a strict patrol between New York and Cape May, NJ The skippers of the "booze fleet" were unable to unload their cargo because of fear inspired by the arrests of Captain Harry Goukler and Eugene Johnson. The Coast Guard seized Goukler's yacht several days earlier, discovering fifty-one bottles of Scotch on board. Johnson had been arrested at the same time when agents found $75,000 of liquor in his boathouse.[21]

Two months later, the after-theater crowds were on the boardwalk at Atlantic City, when something in the distance drew their attention. A large steamer came within two miles of the shoreline and, after circling around, went back out to sea. While it was maneuvering, two small motorboats put out to sea and then turned their lights off.[22]

A few days later, the Coast Guard was on the lookout for what had been dubbed the "mystery ship," which had been in the area for at least a week. It did not carry the usual lights and refused to answer signals. The "mystery ship" was believed to have supplied a flotilla of motorboats disguised as fishing "smacks", which landed illicit cargoes at isolated points within a hundred-mile radius of Atlantic City. Federal agents stopped a truck in Ocean City and found $18,000 worth of fine whisky on board. The truck was on its way to Atlantic City after a crew loaded it with whisky at a landing wharf in Wildwood.[23]

While the hunt was on for liquor smugglers, the State Department received letters and phone calls from various embassies and diplomats protesting the seizure of foreign vessels within the three-mile limit. Foreign governments became very concerned about American interference with their shipping. According to the Volstead Act, a ship could not even pull into port to refuel if it had any liquor aboard. Also, the Coast Guard could seize any cruise ships that came within three miles of the coast if they carried alcohol, even if those ships closed the onboard bar and sealed up the liquor.[24]

On the morning of July 14, several scout planes left the Coastal Air Station in Cape May in search of the mystery ship. A naval steamer also left Cape May at dawn to run to the Northeast End Light vessel (a floating lighthouse), twenty-two miles off Cape May. This was the only lightship off the coast not equipped with wireless communications. Seagoing men believed that finding the "mystery ship" would clear up the pirate scare that had stirred sailors along the Atlantic Coast for weeks. Many sailors believed the ship had a pirate captain.[25]

Federal revenue officers and Prohibition agents joined forces to run down the liquor smuggler, who had been operating along the New Jersey coast. Because of the big cut in both forces, the men thought it best to combine. One federal officer stated to the press that there was no question the liquor was obtained from ocean liners. He said that all clues pointed that direction. The federal government made plans to quadruple its fleet of fast motorboats on patrol duty in an effort to trap the illegal carriers. Coast Guardsmen picked up rafts that were obviously from ocean liners with cargoes of liquor. The liquor-filled rafts were picked up by boats that answered given signals outside the three-mile limit, where no arrests could be made. Then, the cargo was again scattered among smaller, faster vessels.[26]

On July 20, the Coast Guard ordered the *Pocomoke* into Atlantic City because Customs officials believed it was the mystery ship. Those in charge of the *Pocomoke* said that the vessel came near the coast because it was leaking and seeking a harbor. Government officials said the vessel had left Nassau two weeks earlier with 1,000 cases of whisky, most likely from Quebec. When the inspectors boarded the vessel, its hold was found to be swept clean. None of the cargo was found and the leak was not serious. Some of the crew claimed they had thrown the whisky overboard in an easterly gale, and it had simply drifted ashore at various points along the New Jersey Coast. The *Pocomoke* had been an American vessel until an English syndicate purchased it and put it under the British flag. Nassau was its home port.[27]

Meanwhile, government agents along the Long Island Coast redoubled their efforts to find strange vessels reported at various times to be smuggling whisky. A three-masted schooner from the Bahamas managed to elude government sleuths and transferred a cargo of liquor to smaller boats just beyond the three-mile limit off Montauk Point, Long Island. The Coast Guard kept a close lookout for whisky smugglers both day and night. Residents of the area phoned the Westhampton Beach station with reports of suspicious craft at various points along the coast. However, the Coasties only spotted one of those vessels at that station when a three-masted schooner came within half a mile of the shore in heavy fog. The schooner altered its course and sped away rapidly; the Coast Guardsmen did not attempt to follow. The Guardsmen were aware that a large fleet of vessels was smuggling whisky onto the Long Island coast, where they could operate with impunity.[28]

This was in line with the findings of US Attorney Leroy W. Ross of Brooklyn. He learned that a schooner had unloaded contraband goods at that point and then brought most of the whisky was to New York City. In addition to the regular beach patrol at Westhampton, three launches were put into service to search for the smugglers. Commander B. L. Reed of the NY Coast Guard Division announced that if any vessels were being used for liquor smuggling in that vicinity they would certainly be caught, as the smugglers could not hope to elude the combined efforts of the Coast Guard, Customs, and Prohibition agents.[29]

On July 23, 1921, a Coast Guard officer received a tip that smugglers would attempt to bring liquor ashore that night. At midnight, a lighthouse at Newhaven Port, Long Island sent out the message that a small vessel had landed at a jetty and was unloading a cargo of whisky. Thirty policemen rushed to the spot in their patrol cars. The police drew their revolvers and charged the smugglers. Several of the smugglers dropped the kegs they were carrying and leaped into the sea. Others made frantic efforts to cast off and escape by using the boat's auxiliary engine. The plan did not work.[30]

In Atlantic City, the Coast Guard seized the *Pocomoke* a few days after the schooner was ordered into port. Captain Roy, the French-Canadian skipper, made no resistance. As the Coast Guardsmen seized the vessel, Federal Prohibition officers combed the city for traces of Captain Roy's cargo. The officers obtained a search warrant from US Commissioner Steelman early on July 23 and searched an Atlantic Avenue restaurant without finding any liquor.[31] Captain Roy proclaimed:

> "I never start a voyage on Saturday or Sunday, but after that I go with the first fair wind, papers or no papers. If there are any officials on board my ship when I get ready to sail, they can either go with me or jump. I left all my papers at the Philadelphia Custom House, but whether I get them back or not I am going to sail for Nassau just as soon as I get good and ready. I paid $22,000 for the vessel and she is mine."[32]

In response, Customs officials announced that they would remain on board the *Pocomoke* until the status of the mystery ship was settled. Even if Captain Roy did attempt to leave port, he would have had a difficult time—his entire crew, with the exception of one man, disappeared after he paid them off.[33]

ALCOHOL, BOAT CHASES, AND SHOOTOUTS!

Federal agents found evidence of at least two gigantic whisky-smuggling rings—one having headquarters in New York City and the other in Atlantic City operating with British vessels extensively between the Bahamas and Bimini and points along the Atlantic Coast. Coast Guard, Customs, and Prohibition agents combined to stop the smuggling and run down the conspirators. Persistent reports that the combined Prohibition force had been outwitted several times by smugglers had the effect of putting the government sleuths on their guard to make certain that the past performances of the smuggling rings were not repeated.[34]

The word spread among bootleggers along the Long Island coast that a fourth vessel, flying the British flag, was on the way from the Bahamas to Montauk Point, where it was expected to arrive on August 1 with 20,000 cases of choice Scotch and Irish whiskies and Jamaican rum. The word went out as a secret tip to the smugglers' customers but was somehow intercepted by government agents. The men of the whisky syndicate learned that government agents were aware of their plans and made every effort to get in touch with the craft and have it anchor beyond the three-mile limit off some other more secluded point along the coast. The craft likely had wireless communication and even if it did not, smaller boats were ready to be dispatched to give the warning.[35]

On July 25, twenty government agents were stationed in the vicinity of Montauk Point and several patrol boats were put on duty there day and night. Fishermen abandoned regular work altogether when the other three "booze" vessels began unloading their cargo. They found the handling of contraband goods far more profitable than fishing. The fishermen repeatedly denied to the press that they had seen or heard of any whisky runners along the coast. The most recent rum ship to anchor off Montauk Point kept nearly every fishing boat busy for four days. The whisky sold at about $45 a case in cash aboard the vessel and the fishermen received $15 a case for transporting the goods to shore, where it was transferred to trucks. These trucks remained hidden in the woods all day and drove to the water's edge at night, just in time to pick up their cargoes. Once the five-ton trucks were loaded, they headed to New York City and other nearby locations.[36]

Some fishing boat owners found the smuggling game so profitable that they became greedy and overloaded their craft. One man, whose vessel was only designed to carry the weight of five or six cases, took on twenty cases. The sea was rough and the boat was so far down in the water that the Captain was swept overboard and almost drowned. He lost ten cases of his expensive cargo. Many similar incidents happened in the area.[37]

After Coast Guard, Customs officers, and Prohibition agents seized the *Pocomoke*, several persons were put under surveillance. Federal agents told the press that they were closing in on those higher up in the liquor syndicate, men of wealth and influence. The agents believed that the directing genius of this organization, with members in many cities, was the president of a bank in one of the country's largest cities.[38]

Collector of Customs Elliott Repp of Atlantic City said that a mysterious three-masted schooner was waiting off Atlantic City. When the Coast Guard went out to the schooner in the afternoon they found it beyond the three-mile limit, making it untouchable. Repp also notified the press that a large steamer, which also had been waiting off Atlantic City for several days, weighed anchor on July 24 and disappeared. Before leaving, the ship signaled ashore to "lay down your money and come and get it."[39]

On the same day, police in New Haven, Connecticut made a raid at Lighthouse Point and arrested eighteen smugglers. The police caught the liquor runners unloading 300 cases of gin and whisky from the schooner *Jenny T*. The police were eager to learn about the financing of the deal that resulted in nearly $100,000 of liquor being brought in one boatload. Three of those arrested, Harmer Bronson, Pearl Sperry, and James Cherlone, were wealthy. Bronson was a wholesale liquor dealer and owner of a stable on the Grand Trotting Circuit. Sherry was the most widely known liquor dealer in Westville, and Cherlone was an Italian banker. Their combined wealth was over $1,000,000 (in 1921 dollars) and they used expensive cars to transport the liquor back to New Haven. The captured men faced a possible fine of $2,000 (the cost of two brand-new luxury cars) or two years in prison, or both.[40]

The New Haven police did not stop there. During the next day, while the 18 suspects were being arraigned in court, the police raided a small hotel run by Pearl B. Sperry Jr., son of one of the men rounded up at Lighthouse Point. They seized nearly a truckload of liquor as well as rectifying and bottling outfits. Sperry and his employee-turned-informant, Braxton Masick, were arrested for violating the Volstead Act.[41]

On the same day, a man named Michael Viglinicco of Philadelphia walked into a police station in Atlantic City, told the officers that he was guilty of illegally transporting whisky, and asked to be arrested. The police investigated his story and arrested him and five other men, two of whom were members of the police department.[42]

Viglinicco told the detectives that his employer had ordered him and another man to bring seventeen cases of whisky to Atlantic City in a truck. He was to deliver it to Dreamland Café in return for $1,020. The two men were not stopped by police on the way to the café and delivered their shipment successfully. While Viglinicco stood in front of the café waiting for his money, two policemen, one in uniform and the other in plain clothes, walked up to him and told him he was under arrest. Subsequently, they told him to get in his truck and "beat it." Viglinicco got in his truck, but only drove around the next corner where he watched the café. A man, whom he later identified to the police, drove up to the café and loaded the seventeen cases onto his truck. Viglinicco was outraged. He decided to turn himself into the police, thinking that he would be able to collect the $1,020. He thought wrong; instead, he wound up behind bars while the crooked policemen and smugglers kept the money.[43]

On the same day, government agents with search warrants visited half a dozen places in Atlantic City in a futile hunt for part of the cargo of the *Pocomoke*. Although the agents did not find liquor aboard Captain Roy's vessel, they did come up with a creative list of charges against him such as violating navigation acts, immigration laws, and federal health regulations. Late that afternoon, the US Marshal's office announced that they would formally seize the vessel on the charge of transferring an American registry to the British flag without permission of the Shipping Board.[44]

Business owners knew almost every move made by Customs officials almost immediately after the decisions were made. One official commented to the press, "This place is simply a human sieve of information. Start to do anything and you find that all your plans have been tipped off in advance." In response to the leaks, Customs officials obtained a batch of warrants in Trenton, NJ (the state capital) to make raids in Atlantic City.[45]

On July 27, 1921, Prohibition Commissioner Haynes announced to the press that he was practically powerless in his efforts to detect liquor ships beyond the three-mile limit. He suggested that the Prohibition Enforcement Unit needed to double the number of agents that operated on land. Haynes also doubted the wisdom of spending money on chasing smugglers at sea; he expected to have his agents simply wait on land to intercept them. During that year, the government was attempting to cut back on federal spending, so rapidly expanding the number of agents was going to raise the issue of funding. Haynes explained that the newly-expanded Prohibition Unit would easily pay for itself through fines and other penalties assessed against lawbreakers.[46]

Meanwhile in Boston, Harold D. Wilson, Chief Prohibition Officer for the New England district, told the press that former employees of the Internal Revenue Department were receiving large sums of money for their advice from an international rum-running syndicate, which operated all along the Atlantic Coast. The former inspectors and clerks guided the smugglers in all their movements using their knowledge of the habits of the Coast Guard and Internal Revenue Agents. The conspiracy included Boston, New Haven, other New England coast cities and cities further south. Up to that point, only one vessel suspected of being involved in the rum-running plot was found in Boston Harbor. When Internal Revenue Department inspectors visited the vessel, the steamer's cargo of alcohol, consigned to Africa, was 75,000 gallons short.[47]

Although smugglers were bringing thousands of gallons of high-quality alcohol into the US, the overall quality and standards of alcoholic beverages declined. Dr. Perry M. Lichtenstein, resident physician at the Tombs (a New York prison) testified before a Commission On Lunacy concerning the connection between alcohol and insanity. He stated that since Prohibition had taken effect, alcohol had caused more insanity than shell shock during the World War. Alcoholics drank poisonous substances offered for sale. Dr. Lichtenstein said the low-grade alcohol was absorbed through the lymphatic system and caused a toxic condition that deadens the nervous system and produced what was known as alcoholic psychosis.[48]

Disappearing Ships

During the Spring and Summer of 1921, a number of sailing ships had disappeared off the coasts of Virginia and New Jersey. A special correspondent of the Philadelphia *Public Ledger* asserted that the ships were, without a doubt, engaged in liquor smuggling. After unloading their cargoes, the ships were deliberately cast off because they were unable to return to port. In order to leave any port with liquor, a ship needed to have clearance papers. If a vessel was missing its liquor cargo when it pulled into a port, it faced the danger of being seized by Customs and the crew faced the possibility of arrest (even in foreign ports). Ever since stories began to appear in the newspapers about rum smuggling, those in shipping circles wondered how it was that the rum ships could leave the Bahamas or Bermuda and return without proper clearance papers from another port.[49]

ALCOHOL, BOAT CHASES, AND SHOOTOUTS!

The *Ledger* correspondent wrote that the profits of the trade were so large that smugglers bought old schooners and other sailing craft and sunk them, after the cargo was unloaded and sold. Afterward, the crews rowed ashore with a story of disaster. In some cases, the captains and crews divided the profits among themselves on landing and refused to give it up. Their employers had no legal recourse, because in order to prosecute the sailors, they would have had to disclose their own part in the smuggling.

****

In early August, the crew of the British schooner *Henry L. Marshall* was selling alcohol openly past the three-mile limit. Two boatmen seized the captain and first mate and brought them to Atlantic City. They were arrested on information provided by Coast Guard Captain John Holdzkom. Soon afterward, the crew of the Coast Guard cutter *Seneca* seized the *Marshall* and escorted the vessel to New York. There, US District Attorney William Hayward announced to the press that smugglers under foreign flags would no longer be protected by the three-mile limit. Hayward learned from Attorney General Daugherty in Washington that, under the Maritime Act of 1790, the US Government had the authority to seize vessels without a permit and their cargoes within twelve miles of the coast. The original three-mile limit had been set because that was the range of a smooth-bore cannon in 1790. The 1790 Act had been fashioned after the British Hovering Act of 1736, which set extended British jurisdiction to twelve miles from the shore.[50] Mr. Hayward made his announcement from the Ritz-Carlton, where he was staying. A few days later he made his headquarters in Atlantic City, which the federal government regarded as the center of rum smuggling activities.

A provision of the revised statutes against Customs violations, Sections 2866 and 2874, imposed penalties for a vessel unloading cargo of any character without a permit up to four leagues or twelve miles off the coast. Similar restrictions were placed on throwing cargo overboard with the intent of evading the law. The British Consul was present at the hearing but made no protest.[51]

When Hayward arrived in Atlantic City, he received a phone call from Special Assistant Prosecutor Burton L. Gaskill, telling him that the two men who brought in the captain and first mate of the *Marshall* were in his office and that he could interview them. Hayward said he would be there, but at noon he had still not shown up. Gaskill found out later that

Hayward was playing golf. In the afternoon, two Customs agents, who were working with Gaskill went to the hotel to see Hayward. He told them that he was on a vacation, did not wish to be bothered, and that they should take the matter up with the Federal Attorney at Trenton. When Gaskill did, the Trenton Federal Attorney promised to send a representative to his office, but no one showed up. Assistant Prosecutor Gaskill also provided the information to the federal authorities in Philadelphia. The Philadelphia official had the names of men higher up in the affair but took no action.[52]

The British were not silent for long on the seizure of the *Marshall*. On August 18, the British government sent Washington formal notice that it would not recognize the jurisdiction of the US past the three-mile limit fixed by international law. The British decided to await the outcome of court proceedings and the final establishment of the ship's registry before taking any further diplomatic steps. Records of the Bureau of Navigation showed that the *Marshall* had been sold several years earlier by Smith & Co. of Boston to William F. McCoy & Co., a firm of operators in Daytona, Florida. The McCoy Company obtained permission from the Shipping Board to sell the vessel abroad. Charles B. Albury, a British subject living in Nassau, Bahamas, bought the vessel and changed the registry from American to British.[53]

At a luncheon for the Committee of Allied Organizations Opposed to Federal Prohibition, Hudson Maxim gave a speech in which he said that a political and legislative aristocracy was being created along with a new parasite nobility and priesthood of religious and political "fanatical reformers and up-lifters". He continued:

> "Whatever the new priesthood wants, it gets from the political aristocracy. Any number of new offices and positions that may be exacted by the prohibition priesthood is readily granted by the political aristocracy. The result is we now have an army of prohibition enforcement agents, prohibition detectives, bung smellers and cellar weasels, far larger than any standing army that this Government ever had in time of peace prior to the World War."[54]

He went on to argue that Prohibition was no different than the Spanish Inquisition, except for the possible lack of physical torture.[55]

Dr. A.A. Brill, who followed Maxim at the conference, said in his speech that Prohibition "had its birth in small primitive towns among the ignorant and where life is primitive, where camp meetings started and where illiteracy is most rampant."[56]

To make life more difficult for US agents enforcing Prohibition, a Windsor, Ontario magistrate ruled that it was up to the US to arrest rum-runners on its side of the border, without the aid of Canadian officials. The Ontario Temperance Act did not ban the exportation of liquor to a foreign country. Magistrate Gundy, who made the ruling, went on to say that the United States was big enough to handle its own laws.[57] On the same day, Federal Prohibition Commissioner Haynes sent out memoranda stating that it was legal for anyone to manufacture 200 gallons of wine a year as long as that person obtained a permit from the government.[58]

****

While Prohibition forces tried to stem the tide of liquor into New Jersey, New York, and Philadelphia, Customs officials watched another British ship off the Massachusetts coast. The *Arethusa* was anchored off No Man's Land, an island outside the three-mile limit. Cellars all over the Boston area were stocked with good liquor from the converted fishing schooner. Gordon C. McMasters, Chief Deputy of the Prohibition field forces for the district, admitted to the press that he did not see how anything could be done about it. McMasters pointed out that he did not have either the floating force that could stand by to see if American citizens smuggled liquor ashore, nor the funds to charter boats to cope with the situation if they did. Strangely, on the same page of *The New York Times*, printed underneath that article, McMasters states that patrol boats were trailing the small boats making runs to the *Arethusa*. A recent court ruling made it necessary to indicate what the agents expected to find to in order to get a warrant. McMasters claimed that it was impossible for Prohibition agents to state what was to be found on the *Arethusa*.[59]

In the meantime, the *Arethusa's* crew built up a large wholesale and retail business offshore. The waters off New Bedford were never busier with vessels of all shapes and sizes, most carrying passengers. A newspaper reporter went aboard the *Arethusa* and found a regular bar room where he was able to buy liquor of almost any kind by the glass, the quart, or the barrel. Scotch sold for $6.25 a quart and champagne sold for $100 a case. Customers loaded the liquor into small boats tied up alongside. When the reporter asked a crew member how long they intended to stay, he replied, "As long as business holds good." He also stated that when the cargo on board was sold, there would be more. Although the *Arethusa* sold liquor openly, Wilfred W. Lufkin, Collector of Customs of Boston, told the press that he lacked definite proof of smuggling.[60]

During the same week in August, the Magistrate's Court at Windsor, Ontario ruled that the laws of the province, which was "dry" itself, did not prohibit the shipment of liquor for export. Within a few hours of the decision, 700 truckloads of whisky and beer arrived at Windsor and Sandwich for smuggling across the Detroit River and Lake Michigan.[61] Within a few days of the Canadian court decision, US Treasury Secretary Mellon temporarily suspended the Customs regulation prohibiting the movement of liquor from one foreign country to another through the United States. The ban on transporting liquor made up half of the Prohibition Act. In his own way, Mellon temporarily nullified the law that he was responsible for enforcing.[62]

Canadian rum-runners seemed to be trying to set a new smuggling record. Word made its way to Windsor, Canada that Michigan State Police, armed with rifles, had been mobilized to prevent the flow of liquor. In Canada, beer was hauled to the docks in Sandwich and Walkerville, truckload after truckload. Waterfront spectators watched as at least a dozen boats, filled with beer, left port every hour. The bustle along the waterfront continued in spite of reports that Michigan State Police, in high-powered motor boats, had run two liquor-laden craft ashore and seized their cargo. It was perfectly legal for Canadians to manufacture and export beer under the Ontario Temperance Act.

The smugglers planned to transport whisky in wholesale lots from Waterloo the following week. They transported beer into Detroit by water and in more than a dozen rail-car loads, disguised as hay. Smugglers mainly used fast motorboats that carried 2,000 cartons of beer. Each carton contained two-dozen pint-sized bottles. Every now and then, the smugglers used rowboats; however, that method quickly passed out of style after the Michigan State Police began chasing them in fast motorboats.[63]

While Secretary Mellon approved of allowing liquor to be transported internationally via the United States, the US District Court in New York did not. The Anchor Line brought legal action against the US Government to prevent agents from interfering with their shipments of liquor from Glasgow to Bermuda via New York. Judge Mayer dismissed the Anchor Line's case, thereby making it impossible to ship liquor across the US or to have it transshipped in any American port. The New York Court's decision contradicted the ruling of a Federal Court at

Detroit and the case went to the Supreme Court for a final decision. In the meantime, the rules against transporting liquor through the United States were still suspended.[64]

A Fiery Debate In Congress

On August 19, 1921, a fiery debate took place in Congress when the "dry" forces attempted to eliminate the Stanley amendment to the Campbell-Willis Bill, which legalized the manufacture of alcohol in private homes. The amendment denied the right of government agents to search a private house without a warrant and provided that agents could not obtain a warrant unless they had proof that those distilling the liquor planned to sell it. The "wets" planned to extend the provisions of the bill to cover motor cars and frisk searches.[65]

Senator Ashurst, who always voted in favor of Prohibition, surprised the Senate by declaring strongly that he would knock down any official who attempted to search his house or car without a warrant. Two other Senators immediately supported Ashurst. Senator Brandega of Connecticut stated that the Constitutional rights of citizens were far more important than Prohibition enforcement.[66]

The Senators made these statements under the nose of Wayne Wheeler, the chief counsel of the Anti-Saloon League, who always sat in the Visitors' Gallery when the Senate debated Prohibition legislation. Wheeler took careful notes of the speeches and recorded how each member voted. The statements of Ashurst and Brandega were mild in comparison with those of Senator Reed, who delivered a violent attack on Mr. Volstead, the author of the Enforcement Act. After stating that he was unaware of Mr. Volstead's ancestry, Reed said:

> "—I do know, however, that I have seen pictures of some conspirators of the past, the countenances of those who have led fanatical revolts, the burners of witches and executioners who applied the torch, and I saw them all again when I met the author of the Volstead Act for the first time the other day."[67]

Mr. Reed then attacked Mr. Wheeler, declaring that Wheeler had entered a private meeting of the Senate Committee, to which many members of Congress were not allowed, to urge those on the Committee to vote for the Anti-Beer Bill. Mr. Wheeler immediately circulated a statement denying the charge. Mr. Reed later interrupted the debate on another bill to declare that Mr. Wheeler was guilty of "deliberate, willful, cold-blooded, and malicious falsehood. And he knows it."[68]

Boom-Times In The Bahamas

By August 1921, a vast organization existed in the Bahamas for supplying liquor to American smugglers. Liquor exporters at Nassau had to construct new warehouses to store stocks of whisky, gin, and other liquor valued at £2,500,000. Families rented out rooms in their homes at four times the normal rent for the entire house for liquor storage. Schooners and motorboats left in large numbers every day for the Florida coast, New York, and other large cities. The ships left port empty in the Bahamas so that the clearance papers would show they carried no cargo. Once the ships left port, they loaded up about a mile offshore, usually at night. Over a period of forty days, at least 20,000 cases left Nassau for the United States.[69]

When Prohibition first took effect in January 1920, Nassau had been nearly bankrupt. However, soon afterward, the government imposed a moderate tariff on imported liquors, collecting the considerable sum of £170,000 sterling. Laborers, who had been glad to work for 4 shillings a day, now thought that they had done badly when they did not make £5 per day loading liquor offshore. Women, who had rejoiced in making a shilling a day at weeding, left the fields to make 8 shillings a day rolling barrels through the streets to the wharves.[70]

In 1913, Nassau had exported 515 gallons of whisky. In 1920, the total rose to 11,360 gallons. In 1913, Nassau had imported 2,215 cases of whisky. In 1920, Nassau imported 95,000 cases. Nassau's imports of brandy quadrupled and gin imports doubled in the same period. As far as the Bahamas was concerned, the liquor traffic was entirely legal. Vendors in the Bahamas sold the liquor to foreign traders and were not concerned with what became of it afterward.[71]

Nassau reflected the much larger trend of liquor smuggling into the US. The US Department of Commerce reported in September 1921 that the imports of whisky from January 1 to July 31 were three times as much as during the same period a year earlier, while the quantity of imported champagne had increased five times. During the first seven months of 1920, 38,000 gallons were legally imported into the US. During the same months in 1921, the figure rose to 111,000 gallons legally-imported, all for "medicinal purposes." US Government officials estimated that for every gallon brought into the country legitimately 100 were smuggled.[72]

ALCOHOL, BOAT CHASES, AND SHOOTOUTS!

Undercover Agent Gets Caught

Life for undercover Prohibition agents could be very dangerous. A newspaper reporter, who worked in New Orleans, interviewed one of the rum-running captains at a local café. Between taking puffs on his Cuban cigar and stroking his grizzled mustache, he told the story of two undercover agents who boarded his ship:

> "We were too smart for them geezers. They shipped two nice young dicks down to the port on an old Limey boat and the two men ditched the Limey and asked to ship on with us. That was their mistake."[73]

The captain had agreed to take them aboard as part of his crew. He noticed that when the two men were handling cases of liquor, one of the men winked at the other. The captain grinned and puffed on his cigar before he continued his story:

> "It was the day before we were to land, why I gave my cook careful instructions, most careful… 'Cook,' says I, after a little talkee-talkee. 'You knows what to do.' The cook—bless his old heart—just grins at me."[74]
>
> "Well," he sighed, "it was certainly one of them things you call a coincidence. Shortly after stowin' away their noon chuck them two dicks just got overtook by the sand man. They just slept and slept and I declare we couldn't do nothing to wake 'em up. Me, being a kind-hearted man, I didn't try so very hard. 'Let 'em sleep boys.' I says. 'They sure have worked hard this voyage, so let 'em sleep and whiles they wuz sleeping why don't we make port pretty as you please.'"[75]

The ship had landed and the crew unloaded the cargo of "hooch" as the two men slept and then headed back out to sea. When the two undercover agents woke up they had terrible headaches and found the ship far from land. The captain continued his story:

> "I nursed 'em a bit and then put 'em back to work. You know there's nothing like work to make a man feel good. If he is mad or disappointed or anything like that, why old General Work gets it all out of his system. Now I put them two dicks to work. I made them scrub all the decks. I got them to polish the brasswork and I found a job for them every time

they were silly enough to think they needed a rest. My prescription worked fine, for just as we sighted port they said they wuz entirely cured. I asked them if they'd like to ship for our return trip, but they both jus' told me to go to hell."[76]

The captain sighed again. "Now ain't that awful? No gratitude at all—none at all. They appeared to be mad, and then I lost my temper and kicked 'em off the boat, throwing their wages after them careful like, so they couldn't libel me and tie me up."[77]

4
THE PROHIBITION "NAVY" IS BORN

During the first two years of Prohibition, New York State went through three different Prohibition Directors: Charles O'Connor, Harold L. Hart, and E.C. Yellowley. In October 1921, the federal government appointed a fourth: Ralph A. Day. He was the owner of a business bearing his name, R.A. Day & Co., which manufactured cloaks and suits; he was also the director of the Capitol National Bank of New York. Day succeeded E.C. Yellowley, who became the national Prohibition chief. Within a few weeks of taking office, Day dropped more than fifty agents from the payrolls. He also immediately stopped agents from withdrawing liquor from federally-controlled warehouses. It was Director Day who had first brought to the attention of officials in Washington the disappearance of whisky from a warehouse. His investigation promised to unearth one of the biggest liquor frauds attempted since Prohibition went into effect.[1]

At the beginning of 1922, the federal government compiled a list of liquor-smuggling vessels operating in American waters. The list contained about twenty American and foreign ships. Compiling the list was difficult, because the owners of rum-running vessels changed the names of their ships frequently. Many smugglers kept two sets of clearance papers: one for Nova Scotia with a cargo of liquor and another for an American port in ballast. The rum-runners disposed of the liquor in some offshore location and then put into port in ballast, clearing from there.[2]

Smuggling On The Pacific Coast

Up to now this story has really only discussed smuggling on the East Coast and the Canadian border. There was also smuggling on the West Coast, but not on the same scale as off New York and New Jersey. The disparity lies in demographics and geography. In the 1920s, the West Coast was still sparsely populated. Also, it made little sense for European ships to travel all the way to California when they could sell the liquor off the East Coast of the United States. While it is true that Britain and France had colonies all over the globe, the liquor itself was distilled mostly in Europe and the Caribbean. Therefore, the Pacific route was a waste of both time and revenue. The Pacific Coast is also very rocky and dangerous to navigate in comparison with the East Coast.

Courtesy US Coast Guard Headquarters

CG 262 in San Francisco on Prohibition duty in the 1920s.

Some Japanese vessels smuggled imitation Scotch whisky into Oregon ports. Agents of Japanese steamship companies sent wireless messages to sea in order to protect ships carrying Scotch into port.[3] Another group of smugglers used a submarine to transport liquor from British Columbia to Seattle and California ports. The submarine had been built in the US, but was eventually turned over to the Canadian government, which later sold it as junk. A wealthy smuggler purchased the sub, had it restored, and then used it to haul large quantities of liquor.[4]

ALCOHOL, BOAT CHASES, AND SHOOTOUTS!

The former Navy Eagle Boat BOTHWELL transferred to the Coast Guard by the Navy Department. Built in Detroit, Mich., in 1919. Length 200 feet; beam 25½ feet; displacement 500 tons; material of hull, steel. Former station – San Diego, Calif.

Photo and caption courtesy of US Coast Guard Headquarters

On the morning of January 3rd, fishermen and Coast Guard lifesavers were surprised to find the coast near Westport, Washington strewn with bottles of rye whisky over a distance of two miles. As the surf beat its way in, more bottles were left on the shore. Strangely, most were unbroken and the seals on the stoppers were still intact. The Coast Guard quickly began an investigation and, after a few hours, found the answer: a battered and smashed launch, named *The Milk Maid*, was hurled ashore against the rocks. The Coast Guardsmen found the bodies of two men in the wreckage and learned that the vessel had 184 cases of whisky aboard, valued at $29,000 when it left Vancouver, British Columbia.[5]

The Pacific waters off Washington State were treacherous. Another pair of smugglers had encountered difficulties there. These men were on a powerful motor launch, speeding down the Pacific Coast. The launch was south of Seattle at night when the navigator sighted what he thought was a lighthouse. It was not. Because of his mistake, the launch was driven ashore against the rocks. The Coast Guard hurried to the rescue and found the two uninjured men. The launch was badly smashed and the intact cargo of whisky, valued at $15,000, was seized by the government.[6]

****

In January 1922, John Holly Clark, Jr., Assistant US District Attorney in charge of smuggling cases, told the press that he believed the most gigantic liquor smuggling ring had been smashed with the seizure of the *Marshall* and the ensuing arrests during the past summer. Crew statements and papers found on board the vessel led to the implication of several persons involved in a smuggling plot since January 1921. The vessels used had formerly been American schooners transferred to British owners, most of whom lived in the US, without citizenship papers. The new owners, of course, changed the registry of their ships to British. The *Arethusa* and the *Pocomoke* were also part of this ring. The *Pocomoke* had been seized, but the *Arethusa* was still sailing the high seas. Altogether, the three vessels smuggled about 15,000 cases of liquor ashore. Government officials believed the *Marshall* ring was broken up, at least in the New York area. The officials also believed that they had indicted all of the ring members except one, who stayed out of the country.[7]

The Assistant D.A. did acknowledge that it was difficult to keep schooners of this type from skirting the coasts and landing liquor. Fortunately, the men who brought the liquor ashore frequently got drunk or 'sore' and informed the government. Clark stated, "Experience shows that bootleggers in general are absolutely unprincipled and do not keep faith with each other." The crews frequently worked without pay for months and the men who brought the liquor ashore were frequently put off with promises. Clark continued:

> "...the entire system seems to be one of 'double-crossing,' which spells its own defeat...On the whole, I believe the amount of liquor which will arrive by the water route is not sufficient to cause any real joy to the hearts of the drinking men of the United States."[8]

After meeting with Prohibition Commissioner Haynes in Washington, DC, Prohibition Director Ralph A. Day of New York announced to the press that the two men discussed plans to use naval or Shipping Board vessels along the coast to catch rum-runners. Mr. Day said that he could not discuss the new plans to catch the smugglers until after their completion. He also stated that under the new Willis-Campbell Bill, the importation of liquor for medical purposes was banned.[9]

Smuggling In The South

By the early part of 1922, Washington officials figured that the South had become the main area of entry for liquor smuggled into the country. Prohibition officials decided to launch an intensive anti-smuggling campaign in those states. Several Prohibition agents under E.C. Yellowley were already in Florida, including Saul Grill, "the silent man", who had trapped hundreds of persons, from bankers to bartenders, in bootleg schemes. Prohibition Director Day declared that next to "home stills" the big problem in enforcing Prohibition was the flood of liquor from the South into New York. A considerable portion of New York's fine liquors, including hundreds of varieties of Scotch, landed first in the Southern states and were then shipped to New York by rail or boat.[10]

Frederick E. Walker was a very wealthy man connected with the Typhoon Fan Company in New York and various other enterprises throughout the eastern half of the country. After returning from a long business trip to New Orleans, Miami, and points in Georgia and the Carolinas, he reported his observations to Director Day. At the Waldorf-Astoria, Walker said to reporters:

> "I never thought it possible for smugglers to get so much liquor into the South as it appears they are now doing. Take New Orleans, for instance. Thousands of cases of liquor are being brought into that port, according to all reports…While the hotels in New Orleans are, for the most part, strictly observing the law, there are thousands of other places where liquors can be sold. The general agents under Mr. Yellowley who spent several weeks in New Orleans found the problem there much more difficult than in New York City, and it is quite certain that their efforts did not diminish by one drop the supply of 'wet' goods.[11]
>
> "But over in Miami, Fla., it is another story as regards the hotels. As you are being taken to your room in the

elevator the bell hop gives you the 'once over.' Even before you are well out of the elevator he is politicizing your liquor orders. Take me, for instance. I have been told that I even have the appearance of a Government Secret Service man, yet the bell hops in the hotels in which I have stopped there approached me for liquor orders before I had reached my room."[12]

A schooner, named the *Witch*, sailed into Miami in early 1922. It was, according to witnesses, an innocent looking craft. The papers of the *Witch* indicated that its cargo consisted entirely of tomatoes—1,000 crates of them. Florida was the land of tomatoes, but someone in Nassau decided to send thousands of tomatoes to that state anyway. The Coast Guard Cutter *Vidette* was off Miami as the *Witch* sailed into the harbor. The *Vidette's* captain was suspicious; he could not understand why anyone would send so many tomatoes into a state where they were so plentiful and grown year-round. So the skipper investigated and found fourteen small flasks of whisky, the crew's private stock. The skipper of the *Witch* murmured, "I told you so."[13]

The captain of the *Vidette* left the vessel and called Customs, who decided to come down and conduct a second inspection of the *Witch*.

"There are entirely too many tomatoes on that craft," said a Customs inspector. The Customs men ransacked the schooner from stem to stern, but could not find a drop of liquor aside from the crew's personal stash.[14]

"I still maintain these tomatoes are suspicious," said the Customs official in charge, as he climbed back into his launch. He ordered a third inspection. This time his men came with tack hammers and tapped the bulkheads. At first there were no hollow sounds. Then the Customs men did hit one that sounded hollow. The inspectors opened the bulkhead to find 650 bottles of whisky.[15]

Competition among liquor smugglers was so fierce in the South that the prices there were less than half of those in New York City. In addition to foreign liquor smuggled in by sea, Southerners transported large quantities of 'moonshine' whisky and Scotch whisky to the North by land, again forcing down the prices.[16]

A Small Fleet Of Wooden Boats

On March 5th, Prohibition Commissioner Haynes made an announcement that would hopefully mark the beginning of a new era for the Coast Guard. He announced that the Prohibition "navy" would be ready for operation in Atlantic coastal waters before the month was out. The Prohibition "navy" was made up of nine sub-chasers, which the Navy no longer wanted. These vessels had been repaired and given to the Coast Guard. The 110-foot ships were scattered at different Coast Guard stations. However, Prohibition authorities planned to base the main fleet at New York, with another strong squadron on duty in Florida's waters. While the Coast Guard retained the titles to the sub-chasers, the Prohibition Bureau bore the expense of their operation and kept enforcement agents aboard each craft.[17]

But the Prohibition "navy" did not form as quickly as Commissioner Haynes suggested. As of April 9th, only six of the vessels, scheduled to operate under the Prohibition ensign, had been transferred from the Coast Guard to the jurisdiction of the Prohibition Bureau;‡ those vessels were the *Hahn, Hansen, Johansson, Larsen, Newbury,* and *Taylor,* all sister ships.§

In an age of submarines, torpedoes, speedboats, and destroyers, the new Prohibition fleet was fragile and slow. All of these vessels had *wooden hulls*! They were built that way to save steel for the larger ships during the war. The vessels averaged about seventy-five tons displacement and were equipped with standard engines, having a maximum speed of fifteen knots. During the war, these vessels had been armed with 3-inch guns. (Three inches measured across the diameter of the gun barrel opening, or bore.)[18]

As soon as the ships were turned over to the Prohibition authorities, the latter began to pour questions into Coast Guard Headquarters, mostly by telephone, sometimes by messenger. Callers

---

‡ After the Coast Guard acquired the ships from the Navy, the ships then fell under the Prohibition Bureau. Coast Guardsmen maintained and operated the vessels but took Customs and Prohibition agents aboard to carry out missions. If it sounds confusing, it was, especially in disputes over who was in charge and who had jurisdiction. However, this confusing and chaotic arrangement would not last long.

§ 440 vessels were built during the submarine-chaser construction program of WWI. They were all completed by February 1919. Half of them were sent to Europe after the war. The other half were assigned to different uses after the Armistice. They were expensive to operate and maintain, so the Coast Guard decommissioned most of them after a few years of service.

bombarded Commandant Reynolds, Commander Moore, Commander Henderson, and Lieutenant Commander Hamlet with questions about vacancies aboard the "anti-bootleg navy". It was apparent that a liaison officer was needed to answer the many inquiries about the new "navy". Lieutenant Raymond L. Jack was assigned this task.[19]

In 1922, Coast Guard Headquarters was a little, old red brick building on 14th Street in Washington, DC. It was hidden away in the shadow of great hotels and the District of Columbia's administration building. Lieutenant Jack could be found on the third floor of the building from 9 to 5 on most days. One day, a young newspaper reporter, who happened to be in the Prohibition headquarters, overheard an inquiry addressed to Lieutenant Jack, so he wrote a story about "Admiral Jack Of The Booze Fleet," which brought fame to the young lieutenant. From one end of the country to the other, Jack was written up as the "Admiral of the Prohibition Fleet," the "Commander in Chief of the Booze Squadron," the "First Lord of the Prohibition Admiralty," and so on. Publications presented "Admiral Jack" to an interested public. He was portrayed as a mystery man, a "Flying Dutchman" sailing in search of elusive smugglers, a Prohibition "Sherlock Holmes" of the sea. In April, a news announcer on the radio told the public that at last someone had seen "Admiral Jack." He was six feet tall, his hair was black, and he had the face of a stern sea fighter.[20]

Lieutenant Jack smiled frequently, had an outstanding record in war and peace, and was very approachable. While the media told tall tales of "Admiral Jack," Lieutenant Jack continued to work at Coast Guard Headquarters as a member of the staff of Captain E.L. Reynolds, the Commandant of the Coast Guard. When a *New York Times* reporter asked Reynolds if Jack would command the "Booze Fleet," Reynolds replied that such a thing was not even suggested or contemplated.[21]

When interviewed by the same *Times* reporter, Jack stated that the Coast Guard had nothing to do with the command or the navigation of the "Booze Navy". That matter was left entirely in the hands of the Prohibition authorities. The "navy" was to be officered and manned by men who were being enlisted at the time, with preference given to former officers and seamen of the Navy and Coast Guard. Details of the fleet's organization were withheld from the public by the Prohibition Office. Jack also told the reporter that it would be a few weeks before the "Booze Navy" was ready for action. Prohibition authorities refused to comment on whether or not the fleet would operate as a unit or be scattered along the coast.[22]

ALCOHOL, BOAT CHASES, AND SHOOTOUTS!

The anonymous *New York Times* reporter was given access to some of the files at Coast Guard Headquarters and found several interesting stories to report. One happened off the New England coast not too long before the reporter's visit. A two-masted Canadian schooner had sailed down the coast and arrived off the harbor of Salem, where a few centuries earlier, alleged witches were burned at the stake and people who smoked on Sunday were imprisoned. One night, the schooner's crew loaded a launch with $50,000 worth of whisky and distributed it in the harbor, which was crowded with fishing boats. The Customs authorities in Boston got word of the Canadian schooner and contacted the captain of the Coast Guard Cutter *Tampa*. The cutter immediately left port to search for the smugglers.

The *Tampa* zigzagged up and down the Massachusetts coast for twenty-four hours. The officers had a good description of the schooner, its name, and its place of origin—the Bahamas. But the schooner could not be located; it had anchored 48 hours earlier near Salem.[23]

Dawn came and the lookout spotted a two-masted schooner that was sailing out to sea. The *Tampa*'s lookout peered three times through his looking-glass but found no name on the vessel. The *Tampa* changed course and steamed within hailing distance of the schooner.

"What have you got on board," the Coast Guard skipper shouted through his megaphone.

"Nothing, just ballast, and water ballast at that," replied the first mate of the schooner.

"What's your name?"

"Ain't got none," replied the first mate.

Then the *Tampa*'s captain noticed that there was nothing on the part of the bow where the name was supposed to be. He signaled the engine room and the cutter moved in closer. The skipper noticed that a piece of burlap, which matched the color of the schooner, was tacked over the name. The schooner's captain decided to make a run for it and rushed his vessel for the open sea. The schooner was under way before the *Tampa's* commander realized what was happening. The *Tampa* sped up and raced after the schooner. The schooner's crew ignored all commands to stop. The *Tampa's* gun crew fired a blank warning shot from the six-pounder on the forward deck. The skipper of the schooner knew the next round would not be blank; he slowed his vessel down and came to anchor. The *Tampa* towed the schooner into Boston Harbor, and the Coasties seized what was left of the schooner's $75,000 whisky cargo and arrested the crew.[24]

****

In the middle of April, Ralph A. Day, the Prohibition Enforcement Director of New York, announced his search for 100 ex-servicemen, who could shoot straight, for the Prohibition "navy" and patrol duty on the Canadian border. Day had a plan to reorganize the whole force of agents. He said to reporters, "We will shoot in every direction and anyone who tries to sell or smuggle liquor is going to get hurt. We will do everything possible to put the bootleggers out of business." The Canadian patrol would extend along the sixty-five mile border between Canada and New York. Half of the new force was to be assigned to this duty. Mr. Day planned to equip the agents with machine guns, motorcycles, and armored cars. He also stated that listening posts and blockhouses would be established along the border. The remainder of the new force would be used aboard the sub-chaser *Mehalatos*, the flagship of his new "navy".[25]

Drunken Smugglers

On the night of May 12, Coast Guard Patrol Boat 113 chased a ship, named the *Atalanta*, which was a 50-foot power boat with an armored superstructure. After a pitched battle between the two vessels near Atlantic City, the *Atalanta* managed to escape. However, the crew of another ship, the *Donnetta*, was not so lucky. Commander Blake of the Coast Guard Cutter *Seneca* stated that when his vessel pulled up alongside the *Donnetta*, he got "a gigantic whiff of alcoholic content which would have staggered a theater crowd." Crew members were on deck, drinking champagne from pitchers. After placing a few Coast Guardsmen on the *Donnetta*, Commander Blake took the vessel in tow, battling a northwest gale. The *Donnetta*'s cargo shifted and it listed dangerously to starboard as it trailed the *Seneca* up the bay at night. The Coast Guard anchored the *Donnetta* by the Statue of Liberty and sealed its hatches. When the *Seneca* pulled into port, the twenty-three captured sailors were "roaring drunk and obstreperous" and declared that no officer was among them. The *Donnetta* flew no flag and had no ships papers or officers, sufficient evidence to be charged with piracy in 1922.[26]

Assistant US Attorney Herman T. Stichman met the *Donnetta* down the bay and promptly conducted an investigation aboard the ship. He found 500 drums of Belgian alcohol of the highest proof, each containing 90 gallons; 7,000 cases of champagne, valued at $125 a case;

and 7,500 cases of Italian wines, Scotch whisky, and liquors, valued at $50 a case. In total, the cargo aboard the vessel was worth $1,420,000 (in 1922 dollars). Coast Guardsmen called it the biggest Prohibition prize captured since the dry laws went into effect two years earlier. The Coast Guard connected the *Donnetta* with a bootleg ring in Port Chester, NY, estimated to have assets of $10 million. Six members of the ring were indicted the day after the ship's seizure. The vessel was captured 60 miles southeast of Atlantic City, way past the new 12-mile limit. When a reporter asked Stichman if the US Coast Guard could board an American vessel, he replied, "that is an attribute of sovereignty."[27]

USCG Headquarters
The US Coast Guard Cutter *Seneca* in 1922

The *Donnetta*'s days of rum running were not over in 1922. The rum ship continued its trade for a few more years. The Coast Guard lost track of the ship on April 24, 1926. When they did find it, it was flying the "not under control" signal near the Delaware Breakwater. The ship received no help and had passed from sight under its own steam. For a few weeks, no one knew the whereabouts of the ship, but that all changed one day in mid-May. The Coast Guard Cutter *Seneca* was operating far from its base when the crew spotted the missing ship sixty miles off the coast. The *Donnetta*'s name was difficult to read on the hull, so Captain Blake ordered the *Seneca* to approach the ship for a closer look.[28]

As the *Seneca* came closer to the *Donnetta*, Blake noticed an unmistakable odor. Repeating his description from four years earlier, Blake said it "would have staggered a theatre crowd." When the Coast Guardsmen boarded the vessel, champagne was flowing freely. Members of the crew who were still sober enough to sit up, were sitting on the deck drinking it from large pitchers. One member of the crew wept because his cat had just had six kittens and he said that they would starve if he were arrested. No man aboard would admit he was an officer. Blake later told reporters that conditions aboard the ship "bordered upon piracy." He could find no ships papers aboard this ship that flew the American flag, and no one aboard had anything resembling credentials. Blake seized the ship and put some of his men aboard the captured vessel.[29]

The *Donnetta*'s steam engine was shut off and the ship was rigged up to the *Seneca*, which began puffing and tugging its way back to the home port. At Sandy Hook, the Coast Guard cutters *Wilsahickson* and the *Calumet* hooked their lines up to the *Donnetta*'s port and starboard sides and towed the ship into the windy lower bay.[30]

As the captured ship reached its anchorage, it was leaning thirty degrees to starboard and behaved as if it was as drunk as the crew. The ship had taken on eight feet of water in its cargo hold and was slowly sinking. The ship was the biggest Prohibition prize captured at sea in two years. One and a half million dollars worth of liquor were stored in the *Donnetta*'s five holds, all well battened down. Included in the cargo were five-hundred drums of Belgian alcohol of the highest proof, each drum containing ninety gallons; 7,500 cases of champagne valued at $125 a case and 7,500 cases of Italian wines, Scotch whisky and liquors valued at $50 a case.[31]

As they neared the port, the sobering crew seemed glad and put on their finest clothing. However, they were greatly disappointed to find out they would have to remain aboard for another night. Assistant US Attorney Herman T. Stichman boarded the ship for two hours, examining the cargo and questioning the crew. During the next day, the twenty-three crewmembers were arraigned before US Commissioner Garrett W. Cotter and released on $2,500 bond, with one exception. Fred McQueen, who was believed to have been the captain, was jailed for perjury for allegedly hiding the truth from the federal grand jury.[32]

Customs officials suspected that the ship's cargo was destined for Atlantic City, but refused to explain their evidence to the press. They also suspected that the *Donnetta* was part of the $10 million liquor syndicate operating out of Port Chester, NY.[33]

The *Donnetta* was not new to the rum trade. The ship was seized in 1921 at Pier 32 on the East River. Two hundred fifty drums of alcohol were found aboard, although the ship was supposed to be taking a cargo of flour to Constantinople. Deputy Surveyor William R. Sanders recognized the ship and remembered seizing it when it was named the *Javery*. Later, the *Javery* became the property of the Garland Steamship Company and the vessel's was renamed *Jeannette*. Investigators were not certain who owned the *Donnetta* at the time of the seizure.[34]

On the day the ship's crew went to court, the *Donnetta* sat anchored off the Statue of Liberty, still leaning to its starboard side. Customs men pumped water out of the ship continuously to keep it afloat. The eight feet of water entered the ship through a hole near the stern. The crew could not, or would not, explain how the hole got there.

Officials at the Brooklyn Army Base refused to let the ship dock there because the ship was sinking and also because the great quantity of Belgian alcohol aboard was highly explosive. Despite continuous pumping, the *Donnetta* lay like a drunken derelict under the raised arm of the Statue of Liberty. The 100-gallon drums aboard rolled with the movement of the water and guards with fire extinguishers remained on deck day and night.[35] Two days later, Army officials changed their minds and allowed the sinking ship to be towed to the base.[36]

In many cases, rum ship crews were released from jail within a few days or weeks. Unfortunately for the *Donnetta*'s crew, this was not the case. The men were convicted and remained in jail for months while they awaited an appeal. Louis Halle, the crew's attorney, argued at the US Circuit Court of Appeals that all charges should be dropped because the ship was seized beyond the twelve-mile limit. The Court agreed with Halle. After eleven months of imprisonment, the crew of the *Donnetta* was finally free.[37]

****

In the Spring of 1922, Congress debated naval disarmament. The House Sub-Committee on Disarmament came up with the figure of 67,000 sailors and twelve capital ships. The proposal sparked heated arguments in the House. Representative Gallivan, a Democrat from Massachusetts, argued that the new bill would produce a "toy Navy" and that the same Representatives, who argued for scrapping the Navy, looked on complacently while Congress voted millions to build the Prohibition Navy, commanded by the Prohibition Commissioner instead of the President.[38]

Gallivan went on to say that the border between the US and Canada had been unguarded for the past century.

> "But the Rum-running Navy, under command of Admiral Haynes and Real Admiral Wayne Wheeler, are supported by the gentlemen here who are ready to scrap the old navy of Jack Barry, John Paul Jones, Admiral Farragut and George Dewey will scrap the treaty of 1818 and transfer the naval operations from the Atlantic and the Pacific Oceans to the Great Lakes and the St. Lawrence River. Instead of the daily allowance of grog to the blue-jackets…we will have cold water and grape juice…to fight the rum-runners from Canada."[39]

While politicians in Congress debated over which service should get more ships, the Prohibition "navy" still had to carry out its mission. In late July 1922, the Prohibition "navy" was especially busy in the New York area. General Prohibition Agent John D. Appleby announced to the press that the Coast Guard and Customs were launching a new "hammering campaign," which was supposed to "close the door" on rum smugglers. Three rum vessels felt the first whack of the "hammer" on July 27.[40]

All three of the rum-running vessels—the *J.H.B.*, the small auxiliary sloop K10706, and the *Mosher*—were connected. The *Hansen*, a new addition to the Prohibition "navy" in New York Harbor, was on patrol when its crew spotted the *Mosher*. The *Mosher* seemed to be lying low in the water, as if it were overloaded with cargo. Captain Dizer drove the *Hansen* alongside the *Mosher* and hailed the vessel. One of the crew on the *Mosher* yelled, "For God's sake, come and take us off."[41]

The Prohibition and Customs agents went aboard with weapons drawn and the crew put up no resistance. Within a short time, the agents completed their search and found twenty barrels of whisky and 1,350 cases of liquor, some of which was 70 years old! There were eight men aboard; one of whom was Daniel Ludwig, who claimed to be the son of a member of the firm Ludwig and Gilbert, part of the Globe Line. Another crewmember, George Cox, told the agents his story, which was backed up by another crewmember. Cox claimed he had been hired as a mate on a fishing schooner sailing to Nassau. He traveled to Greenport, Long Island with Hudson, where they boarded a little fishing boat. The skipper then told them both go below deck and stay there until they were called. Five hours later, after the sloop sailed around Montauk Point, they came to a bigger schooner named the *Mosher*.

The skipper of the schooner ordered Cox and Hudson to board the other vessel. Once they boarded the *Mosher,* the captain ordered Cox, along with the others, to stand watch, but Cox told the captain he had shipped on as a mate. The captain turned to his cook and told him not to give Cox any food until he stood watch. He had nothing to eat the next day. The crew came after him and called him on deck. "You won't work, eh?" the captain asked, before he and another man knocked Cox down on the deck. As Cox hit the ground, the captain kicked him several times, giving him two black eyes. After the beating, the captain shouted, "Lug him aft and put him in the lazaret and let him stay there until he is willing to turn to."[42]

Cox finally gave in and stood watch, so he could eat. From that moment until he was taken off by the Prohibition agents, he was assigned the hardest tasks and told repeatedly by other crew members to keep his mouth shut. Unfortunately for the crew, Cox did not take their advice. By the time the Coast Guard caught up with the ship, he was all too willing to talk. As soon as he had the chance, he told the agents everything. Cox gave the agents detailed information on how the *Mosher's* crew unloaded its cargo into smaller boats and how the vessel was connected with the *J.H.B.* Cox gave an estimate of 100 barrels and 3,000 cases of liquor for the cargo, valued at $175,000, most of which was already ashore. The *Mosher* had been off the eastern end of Long Island since July 4 with its cargo from Nassau and Bermuda. The plan, Cox said, was to go to Newfoundland or a Canadian port after selling the cargo to buyers in New York.[43]

Meanwhile, the *J.H.B.* had run into a sandbar seven miles away from the *Mosher*. The Coast Guard Cutter *Hansen* spotted the vessel and sent a message to the Guardsmen at Point O'Woods, who came out to help the stranded vessel. After they pulled the *J.H.B.* off the sandbar, the Coast Guardsmen boarded it and found thirty-five barrels and 1,200 bottles of whisky, valued at $75,000. The Coasties telephoned Captain Byron L. Reed, who contacted the NYPD.

The police sent out the steamer *Manhattan*, which chased the K10706 through New York harbor. The police boat lost sight of the rum-runner until the next morning. When the *Manhattan* finally caught up with the K10706, the bow of the vessel looked battered, and it sat low in the water as if it were carrying heavy cargo. Two fishing lines were trailing from the stern. The *Manhattan* steamed up to the sloop, and the captain asked the two men aboard what luck they had.[44]

"The old boat is loaded down with our catch," one of the men replied. The police jumped aboard, discovering 250 cases of Scotch, Irish, and rye whisky. The *Manhattan* towed the sloop to Pier A, where a crowd of several thousand watched the unloading. The police took the two men, George Williams and his brother Edward, to Tombs Court, where they were arraigned and held on $1,000 bail.[45]

Customs agents immediately began looking for Ludwig and Gilbert. Neither was listed in the City Directory, nor were the officers of the Globe Line. The firm's office at 150 Broadway had been closed the night before. Another firm took over the vacant office. A representative of the new firm told the press that the Globe Line had left a week before and had their telephone service discontinued. Where they went or what became of the office staff or the boats the line claimed to operate were mysteries to him.[46]

5
A DRUNKEN SHOOTING SPREE

At the beginning of August, John D. Appleby, Prohibition Chief for New York and New Jersey, briefed the press on the expansion of the dry navy. Appleby's flotilla now had four sub-chasers and two motorboats, capable of thirty-five nautical miles per hour. Supplementing this force was a fleet of fishing "smacks" lying off the New Jersey coast. Each of the sub-chasers had a crew of fourteen and was armed with a gun that fired a one-pound shell. Two of the crew on each sub-chaser were Customs inspectors, which enabled the ships to stop and search ships as far out as twelve miles offshore. The smaller motorboats each had a crew of four or five, all of whom were Prohibition agents; they were armed with high-powered rifles and sawed-off shotguns. At the time of Appleby's announcements, Prohibition authorities were aware of five seagoing vessels, loaded with liquor, and lying outside the twelve-mile limit near New York City.[1]

Over the previous year, Customs agents had seized a large quantity of drugs and jewels, in addition to liquor. In the ports of New York, Customs agents had seized fifteen automobiles and a large number of vessels, ranging in size from a canoe to a large steamer. The agents made 600 arrests for liquor smuggling, but only 68 suspects were imprisoned, their sentences ranging from one day to three years.[2]

Prohibition agents patrolling off Fire Island told the New York Police Department that several large ships, loaded with liquor, were waiting outside the twelve-mile limit. The NYPD sent out both of its boats, the *Manhattan* and the *Blue Boy*, to look for suspicious vessels. The *Manhattan*'s crew spotted a small motorboat heading into New York Harbor at full speed. The speeding boat's crew refused to slow down after being hailed, so the *Manhattan* took off in pursuit. Unfortunately for the police, the motorboat disappeared into a bank of fog. The *Manhattan*'s captain radioed Lieutenant James Bannon, the captain of the *Blue Boy*, who took his vessel out to the Narrows and waited. Within a short time, the *Blue Boy*'s crew heard the noise of the rum-runner's engine. Lieutenant Bannon hailed the motorboat in the thick fog.[3]

"Oh, we're all right," one of the men replied. "We are revenue men out hunting for rum-runners."[4]

The lieutenant ordered the craft to halt, but was answered with roaring engines as the boat sped away. He then ordered his crew to fire a volley of warning shots, but that did not stop the speedboat. The *Blue Boy* took off in pursuit through the thick fog, guided only by the sound of the rum-runner's motor. The boat's motor went dead off Ellis Island and the *Blue Boy* steamed alongside. The boat was a forty-foot launch, named *B.NJ* and numbered K-3701. There were three men aboard and sacks of whisky in the bottom of the boat, which the police claimed they did not attempt to count, but estimated at 200 bottles. The police turned over the motor boat and thirty-five cases of whisky over to Customs authorities.[5]

When the smugglers were brought before US Commissioner Samuel M. Hitchcock, Assistant US District Attorney Falk said that sixty-five cases of whisky had disappeared while the boat was in police custody. He went on to say that the *B.NJ*'s cargo of 100 cases of Scotch had been taken off the schooner *Minnie Wallace,* thirty-five miles offshore.[6]

The police were not to get off easy for the sixty five missing cases of Scotch. US District Attorney Heyward demanded that Police Commissioner Enright start an investigation. Assistant District Attorney Herman L. Falk stated that, unless the missing liquor, worth $7,800, was turned in, he would ask for a warrant to search the *Blue Boy* and the Harbor Police Station at the Battery.[7] The next day, a statement by Commissioner Enright, a receipt from Customs for the captured boat, and letters written by the Assistant US Attorney, the Collector of Customs, and the Acting Collector appeared in the *New York Times.* Commissioner Enright told the newspaper that the police had brought the captured boat to Pier A. The desk sergeant at the Second Precinct immediately notified US Customs authorities. Within 30 minutes, two Customs House guards boarded the vessel. The Custom House officers remained on the boat until another Customs officer came to the station and wrote out a receipt for the vessel and cargo; however, the receipt was vague, reading that the K-3701 contained a "number of cases supposed to contain Scotch whisky." The receipt did not specify the number of cases nor did it verify that the cases contained Scotch whisky, which are important details to leave out when transferring custody of evidence.[8]

ALCOHOL, BOAT CHASES, AND SHOOTOUTS!

New York City Police Commissioner John A. Leach, on the right, supervises agents pouring liquor into a sewer in 1921.

The Customs authorities asked the NYPD to tow the vessel to the Barge Office, using the *Blue Boy*. Once the K-3701 reached the Barge Office, the Customs agents did not bother checking the cargo, because the vessel's hold was taking on water and already submerged in two feet of it. Even if the vessel were not sinking, the K-3701 was already in Federal custody and the agents saw no need to recheck the cargo. On the night of August 5th, three different agencies began an investigation of the missing liquor. Deputy Surveyor William R. Saunders took the statements of the three Customs officers who took charge of the vessel at Pier A. The US District Attorney's office notified the Customs House that they were beginning their own investigation. And John Clark, Heyward's Chief Assistant in the Civil Division, launched another probe into the matter.[9]

****

While the smugglers awaited their hearings, the *Hansen,* the *Taylor,* and the *Larsen* kept four large vessels under close watch about twenty miles off Fire Island. Captain George W. Tawes reported to John D. Appleby that all of the vessels were flying British flags. Captain Tawes and John D. Appleby Jr., the Prohibition director's 9-year-old son, went aboard one of the vessels at the captain's invitation. It was a fine yacht, worth between $300,000 and $400,000, with a liquor cargo worth $500,000 (in 1922 dollars). The rum ship's captain told Tawes that he was on his way to Nova Scotia, but had no manifest or bill of lading as proof. As the rum ships were well outside the Customs limit, the Prohibition agents were powerless to interfere with them. However, they did keep careful watch to prevent smaller boats from transporting the liquor to shore.[10]

A wireless message from the rum chaser *Larsen* to Acting Collector Stuart notified him that the crew of the *Larsen* had been unable to locate the *Minnie Wallace,* mother ship of the K-3701. The *Wallace* had weighed anchor and fled to safety past the twelve-mile limit.

About an hour later, Captain D.S. McDonald of the *Taylor* reported the presence of a rum pirate off the coast named "The Pelican". The Pelican and his pirate crew of eight men traveled in a very fast gasoline boat, about sixty feet long, and preyed on other rum smugglers.[11]

In one instance, the pirates drew alongside a smuggler's boat at anchor and a man leaped over the side to board the vessel. The pirate showed a large roll of bills and bargained for 200 cases of Scotch whisky. After the crew transferred the whisky to the pirate vessel, the "customer" pocketed the money and jumped back onto his own craft. When the rum smugglers attempted to stop him, they found themselves staring down the barrels of seven large automatic pistols, held by the other pirates. The Pelican was the first pirate reported operating out of New York. There were already many such reports of pirates off the Florida coast.[12]

Both Captain Tass of the rum chaser *Hahn* and Captain McDonald reported that they spotted large numbers of rum smugglers who could not be boarded because they sat outside the twelve-mile limit. In many cases, the rum-running captains had invited the Prohibition men aboard for a drink, while others of a more "hard boiled" variety stood at the rail and drank whisky to taunt the rum chaser crews. The smugglers had their own set of signals to warn each other of the approaching "dry" navy. At night, the rum-runners shot up flares as soon as they heard the noise of an approaching chaser.[13]

Deputy Surveyor Saunders announced to the press that the *Hahn, Hansen, Larsen,* and *Taylor*, manned by Customs men and Prohibition agents, were out looking for the *Minnie Wallace.* The *Wallace,* flying the British flag, had managed to escape the Prohibition fleet the night before. Saunders stated that the schooner would be seized, regardless of its location outside the twelve-mile limit, and used as a test case.[14]

Saunders said that he had investigated the disappearance of the sixty-five cases of Scotch on behalf of Customs. His inquiry showed that the four Customs agents aboard the *B.NJ* were in no way involved in the liquor's disappearance. Saunders also stated that the claims of the two smugglers about the 100-case cargo might have been false. He argued that rum smugglers, captured on other vessels, made extravagant claims about their cargo, either to be boastful or to discredit Customs men and the police. As far as Saunders was concerned, the investigation was complete and the Customs men were "clean."[15]

Assistant US Attorney John Holly Clark disagreed with Saunders. He declared that the story told by the two smugglers was true, finding no reason for them to lie. He argued that the "smugglers" were simply boatmen, hired out by bootleggers. Furthermore, it seemed unreasonable to Clark that the *B.NJ* would have traveled so far to get only thirty-five cases. Clark assured the press that his work was far from over, and he would exhaust every line of investigation to find out who stole the whisky.[16]

Shooting Spree

David A. Owens, one of the police of the NYPD Marine Division, cracked under the pressure of the investigation. Owens had previously gotten into trouble while on duty. His records showed that he had been suspended for intoxication; charged with assault, but acquitted; and charged for being absent from his post and reprimanded. In another incident, he had let a prisoner escape. The man subsequently killed himself by throwing himself in front of a train. Nonetheless, Owens was acquitted. He was also charged with failure to discover a burglary on his post, but was acquitted yet again. Finally, he was charged for being absent from reserve duty and fined a day's pay.[17]

A few days after the investigation started, Owens worked a full daytime shift. After work, he got drunk and staggered down 55th Street.

There were boys and girls on the street playing a game of tag, and they decided to include Owens in the game by tagging him. He was a good sport about it and played along. The children shrieked with laughter at his drunken attempts to catch them.[18]

With a broad grin on his face, Owens staggered into Francis' Restaurant, at 319 West 55th Street. After falling into a chair, he mopped the sweat from his brow with a napkin and looked at the menu, which he held upside down. The proprietor noticed that Owens was drunk and rowdy. For the short time he was actually in the restaurant, he was abusive and harassed the diners. Francis managed to get him out of the restaurant and slammed the door in his face.[19]

Angered by this, Owens kicked the door several times. When it seemed clear that he was not going to get back in, he moved along. His young admirers, who had been clustered at the restaurant window during his brief visit, gathered around and tried to tease him into another game. This time, Owens would have nothing to do with them. He shook them off angrily when they grabbed at his arm and staggered up the street muttering profanities.[20] Police Officer Owens then saw two uniformed "negro hallboys," as the *New York Times* described them, standing in front of the Stanwood Apartments on West 50th Street. One was the elevator operator and the other was the phone operator.[21]

"Want to fight?" Owens asked them. "I can lick anyone in the block, and I'm going to start now." He lunged at one of the boys, who blocked the blow before both of them fled into the building. Owens chased them, grabbing the phone operator, who managed to break free and hide under the stairs. The elevator operator ran and took cover in the elevator. As Owens started to leave the building, one of them poked his head out of his hiding place and the policeman turned. He drew his pistol and fired a shot, which hit the wall. As he stood in the front doorway, he fired another shot. Women screamed and children fled into their homes, while others ducked into basement areaways.** The cry of "Someone is shooting!" echoed throughout the block.[22]

Owens backed into the street, clutching his pistol, and started walking down the middle of the street toward Ninth Avenue. Halfway down the block, he bumped into a sixty-year-old waiter named Luce, who had just left his home opposite the Stanwood as the first shot rang out. Luce patted Owens gently on the shoulder and tried to take the pistol

---

** A basement areaway is an entryway/patio found in front of many 19th century townhouses and tenement buildings in large cities. These areaways are a few feet below street level and are accessed by a set of stairs leading from the sidewalk.

from him. The two walked side by side as spectators watched from covered positions and windows. Luce tried to persuade Owens to give him the pistol, and the effort seemed to be working, until Owens suddenly pushed the old waiter away and shouted, "You want to fight, too? You'll get it!"[23]

Owens raised the pistol and shot the old man. The bullet entered the right side of his chest and passed through his frail body. Luce sank to the sidewalk moaning, only a couple doors away from his home. As Owens stood unsteadily over the body of his fallen victim, a taxi driver who saw the whole incident drove to Ninth Avenue and informed Officer Green. Green made his way cautiously down the block and took cover behind a taxi. To avoid killing innocent bystanders, he intended to subdue Owens with his nightstick.[24]

Green waited for the right moment and walked up behind Owens, who was talking gibberish and waving his pistol around. As Green began running up behind the drunken policeman, Owens turned around and shot him in the forearm, sending his nightstick flying into the air. Although he was in great pain, Officer Green kept advancing toward Owens. As his right arm was hanging limp, Green reached around and grabbed his service revolver with his left hand. As Owens took aim to shoot again, Green dropped him with a bullet in the stomach. Owens rose on an elbow and attempted to shoot again, but the hammer clicked with no effect.[25]

At this point, a teenage boy picked up Green's nightstick and brought it down on Owens' head with a crushing blow. Green gave way to the pain and blood loss and slumped down on a curb. However, he mustered up some strength and, with the aid of others, managed to take Owens and Luce to Roosevelt Hospital in a taxi. Hundreds of people gathered at the scene afterward to hear stories of the NYPD Marine Division officer who went on a drunken shooting spree.

An angry mob gathered outside of Roosevelt Hospital while doctors operated on Owens and Luce. However, several police officers arrived and quickly dispersed the crowd. Shortly after the hospital staff wheeled Owens from the emergency room, he was arrested and suspended from the Police Department.[26]

****

The story of Owens' drunken shooting spree and the missing liquor was more than enough to fuel a public-relations fiasco for the NYPD. At the same time, US Customs and the Coast Guard were having public-relations problems on an international scale. The dry navy had chased the *Minnie Wallace* out to sea, where agents stopped the vessel thirty-five miles from the coast. The British government made it clear that they did not recognize US jurisdiction on the high seas and intended to send a formal protest if US agents made any arrests. After that date, the *Minnie Wallace* completely disappeared from the headlines. Most likely, the US took no action against the smugglers.[27]

Around the same time, the Naval Disarmament Treaty was becoming a reality. The US Navy scrapped the battleships *Virginia, New Jersey, Rhode Island, Nebraska,* and *Georgia.* These were the oldest battleships and probably would have been declared obsolete and disposed of regardless. As the Navy scrapped its battleships, the Prohibition navy continued to grow.[28]

New York Police Commissioner Enright made an effort to expand the NYPD's dry navy. As of September 1922, the total complement consisted of the high-powered launch *Blue Boy* and eight low-powered launches. Three of the launches were about to be condemned, and the remaining ones could only move at a speed of eight miles an hour, slower than a bicycle. To fight rum smuggling, Commissioner Enright submitted a request to the Board of Estimate to appropriate $77,500 for five high-powered motorboats and another $50,000 to establish an airplane auxiliary.[29]

Captain Gilbert's Cruise to Spain

Around this time, the mysterious Globe Line firm, which had quickly vacated its New York office several months earlier, made headlines once again. Before the Globe Line packed up its office at 150 Broadway, Mark L. Gilbert came up with a plan to place the shipping line under the Peruvian flag in order to camouflage its smuggling activities. Prohibition agents caught on to his scheme, and he was indicted for fraud against the government. Four officers from one of his ships, named the *Korona*, drafted a letter collectively, which was printed on the front page of the *New York Times* in late September 1922. The letter described the illegal activities conducted on and off the *Korona* to smuggle alcohol and accused the administration of New York City, US Customs, and the Prohibition Bureau of corruption.[30]

The letter stated that the *Korona* had originally been a Canadian vessel, purchased by the Globe Line through one of its "dummy" offices. It had a cargo of 6,000 barrels of molasses; 1,100 bags of sugar; 550 bags of rice; and 440 drums of alcohol, totaling 40,200 gallons and worth between $500,000 and $800,000. The Globe Line then arranged to have Greek merchants issue fake landing certificates for the alcohol, have it taken off the vessel at sea, and sent to New York City. The ship's papers were all sent without question through the Custom House and the Peruvian Consul General's office at New York. US Customs Inspectors gave the vessel a seaworthy certificate, and it was insured, even though the boiler was not seaworthy and the circulating pump rocker arm was cracked.[31]

Elmer H. Greenlaw, the *Korona*'s captain, had no license to operate or command a steam vessel. He arranged with the officers of the Globe Line to send wireless codes pertaining to boiler trouble when the ship passed the three-mile limit. These codes were to be used by smugglers to learn of the ship's position and move the alcohol to shore in smaller boats. On the evening of March 19th, the *Korona* pulled out of its berth at 131st St., on the Hudson River, and passed out to sea in the fog and rain. That night, the chief steward was awakened by voices coming from one of the staterooms. When he looked into the room, he saw three heavily-armed gunmen with orders to shoot anyone who might attempt to signal for help, stop, or leave the ship.[32]

As the *Korona* sat twenty-two miles off Block Island, the wireless operator sent out the captain's messages and the vessel was soon met by a tugboat. The tug's captain had a chart thrown aboard the *Korona* with instructions to proceed to Newport, R.I, under the cover of darkness, where the ship would unload its alcohol. The chief officer and the steward begged the captain to disregard those instructions, because the ship was cleared for Spain and re-entry into US waters would be an illegal act. The captain ignored the two men and soon the *Korona* returned to US waters. Two tugs and canal boats met the *Korona* at night. The crews worked feverishly to unload the cargo, but could not get it all off. In order to escape detection, the crew of the *Korona* weighed anchor and headed out, only to return the next night. Once the smugglers offloaded the alcohol, the gunmen left the ship. The crew sealed the hatches, raised anchor, and headed for Cadiz, Spain. The letter's authors claimed that a US revenue cutter was used to help transport the alcohol, known as "high spirited whale oil." When the alcohol reached Newtown Creek, eighteen uniformed policemen discarded their coats and caps to help transfer the alcohol from the barges to the waiting trucks.[33]

When the *Korona* was 800 miles out to sea, the rocker arm on the circulating pump broke and the vessel was towed to Bermuda. Captain Greenlaw cabled New York for advice, but received none. He then deserted the ship, taking his wife and chief engineer with him back to New York. Greenlaw was soon replaced by another captain, J.T. Fales. He had ran a liquor store until 1920 and held no certification for steam vessels. Soon Mark L. Gilbert and the Globe Line's senior staff arrived at Bermuda and arranged for the purchase of 2,200 cases of whisky and seventy-four barrels of liquor. Gilbert interviewed the firemen and sailors aboard the *Korona* and gave them $20 each to handle and unload the whisky whenever the captain gave orders. During the ship's stay at Bermuda, some of the crew became nervous. The cook, the baker, (sorry, no candle-stick maker) the first assistant engineer, and four firemen had deserted the ship. The new captain maintained absolute secrecy as to the ship's use and sailing date. The Globe Line feared that the US Consul in Bermuda would get wind of the plans and have US agents trail the vessel.[34]

    The captain received all of his papers from the British authorities and drove his ship out to sea. His destination was officially Cadiz, Spain, but the captain took another detour to Block Island, NY. The day after the *Korona* arrived at Block Island, a tugboat met the vessel to re-supply the ship. The tug's captain informed the *Korona*'s captain that the barges would be coming out the following day to pick up the whisky. The tugs and barges arrived on schedule. Each vessel had several gunmen aboard to prevent the *Korona*'s crew from deserting. One of the gunmen beat and knocked down one of the firemen[††] and threatened to throw him overboard. After the whisky was unloaded the following day, the *Korona* headed for Spain. The firemen mutinied and demanded $20 each, which Captain Fales paid them.[35]

    When the *Korona* finally arrived at Cadiz, Spain, the firemen and sailors demanded a payoff, but received none. The crew then left the ship and arranged to live ashore at the expense of the vessel. The captain cabled New York for funds, but received nothing. A man named Mr. Puga, who lived in Cadiz, gave the captain $1,000. After it was clear that the Globe Line had abandoned the *Korona*, the Captain and Mr. Puga agreed to sell the sugar and molasses aboard to pay the crew and send them home. The US Consul became aware of the plan and told Captain Fales to stop selling his cargo, but he refused. Even after selling the cargo, some of the crewmembers and officers had not been paid. Of course the abused and underpaid crew told the Spanish authorities that the alcohol had been landed in the US. The Spanish government then libeled the ship with a $31,000 fine for the missing cargo and the *Korona*

[††] On steam ships, the men who shoveled coal into the furnace were known as "firemen." The term also referred to enlisted sailors who operated engineering machinery.

was held in Cadiz' harbor.³⁶ The Globe Line went out of business at this time, supposedly due to the many bills the organization ran up.

When Captain Gilbert read the account of the disastrous voyage in the *New York Times*, he responded by writing his own account. He claimed that two of the officers who helped write the letter were actually Secret Service men, and that most of the account was wrong. Gilbert argued that his actions were no worse than what the US Shipping Board did openly by permitting liquor to be sold as soon as a US vessel passed the three-mile limit. The US ship *Martha Washington,* for example, was carrying 800 cases of liquor, but was not harassed by the Coast Guard or Customs.³⁷

The Return of Captain Gilbert

The rum ship *Homestead* was originally the USS *Lebanon*, which saw service in the Spanish-American War. After the US sold the ship to a South American government, it wound up in the hands of Captain Gilbert. With a tonnage of 1,321, the *Homestead* was one of the largest ships in the liquor business.³⁸

In 1925, Captain Mark Gilbert had been a fugitive for two years. His indictment concerned the rum ship *Korona* of the Globe Line, of which he was president. The *Korona* cleared from New York in March 1922 for Greece with 40,000 gallons of alcohol. Instead of going to Greece, the ship anchored off Narragansett Bay, where the cargo was transferred to a barge and brought back to shore. The ship then proceeded to Bermuda, took on a liquor cargo, brought it north and transferred it to another barge, which brought it to New York. The *Korona* continued to Spain, where it was seized. Gilbert was indicted in a US court and forfeited $2,500 bail.³⁹

Meanwhile, Commander Munter of the Coast Guard was busy at his headquarters in New London, Connecticut. The new expansion of the service had put him in charge of the important patrol area. Munter had seen the Coast Guard grow from a quaint force, back when it was still called the Revenue Cutter Service, to a virtual navy of over 20 destroyers plus over 300 smaller craft.⁴⁰

One day, Munter received a code message from Washington. He conferred with Lieutenant Commander F.H. Young, commanding Section Base 4 at New London, displaying a picture of the ship referred to in the message and said:

"If one of your little boats sees her let me know, and I'll send you a destroyer. Don't attempt to seize her with a patrol boat. There might be more than a 75-footer can handle."[41]

On February 5, Munter appeared at the office early. Something was clearly bothering him; there had been a stream of messages to and from Washington through the previous night. The destroyer *Jouett* had found the *Homestead* close to the shore, inside the 12-mile limit. Munter dispatched his flagship, the *Redwing,* to tow the *Homestead* to port.[42]

Mr. Dillon, the Collector of Customs at New London, knew Captain Gilbert. "He will try to escape," Dillon warned Ensign Marron, commander of the *Redwing*. "Watch him." Gilbert knew that Washington wanted him and his ship and that he was still under indictment for another charge of rum-running in 1923.

As the *Redwing* passed Southwest Ledge, the *Jouett* radioed the ship to seek shelter from rough seas and, therefore, postpone the mission. As the *Redwing* returned to port, the *Jouett* had engine trouble and was forced to abandon the rum ship. The *Homestead* put out to sea and escaped. Munter knew that Washington would not be pleased to hear about this mess, so he boarded a patrol boat and headed for the *Redwing*. He boarded the cutter as it entered New London Harbor. The ship's bow swung around seaward and headed for the *Homestead.*[43]

Munter gave the command, "Full speed ahead!" Soon the *Redwing* reached the area in which the *Homestead* was last seen. Of course, Captain Gilbert's ship was not there. The *Redwing* plowed on with a sharp lookout in all directions, until someone aboard finally spotted the *Homestead* at anchor. When Gilbert found out that an officer aboard the *Redwing* wanted to board his ship, he got under way immediately, dragging his anchor.

Munter spoke with Gilbert over the radio as he pursued his ship out to sea. Gilbert refused to be boarded and would not lay a course for New York. The gun crew aboard the *Redwing* fired three warning shots from the one-pound gun.‡‡ Munter informed Gilbert over the radio that he (Gilbert) would be responsible for any damage to life and property which might follow.

"Go ahead and shoot," Gilbert taunted, "You're firing at a defenseless British subject."[44]

---

‡‡ The ordnance fired from the gun weighed one pound.

The *Homestead* was flying a Costa Rican flag, not a British one. Coast Guardsmen climbed into two smaller boats aboard the *Redwing* and were lowered into the sea. When the boarding party reached the *Homestead* in the two boats, Gilbert refused to take their lines or help them board in any way. It was impossible for the Coast Guardsmen to climb up the side of the *Homestead* as rough seas tossed their tiny boats around like toys. The *Redwing* signaled for the boarding party to return.

"You're a bunch of Chinese pirates!" Gilbert shouted. "And if you come aboard I'll treat you as such."[45]

Commander Munter made no verbal reply. The *Redwing* fired a shot just off the hull and another cracked into the quarter. Seeing that his methods were not working, Gilbert lowered a whale boat in full view of the *Redwing*. Inside it was a rolled mattress, which he claimed was the body of one of his crew. The Costa Rican flag was brought to half mast.

"You've killed a man and wounded two others," Gilbert yelled.

"Will you head for New York?" Munter asked.

"I'm going to Havana!"[46]

At this moment, Commander Munter received instructions from Washington to bring in the *Homestead* irrespective of resistance. The Coasties fired more shots at the rum ship. The *Homestead* was an easy target after one of the shots disabled the steering gear and splintered the pilot house.

"Turn your guns the other way," Gilbert cried. "I haven't anything but a pocket knife."

"Will you be boarded or head for New York?" Munter asked again.

"I'm captain of this ship. We're bound for Havana and I'm going to take her there."[47]

Meanwhile, most of the *Homestead*'s crew, believing the ship would be sunk, had put off in two boats. Realizing that they would probably not be able to escape the Coast Guard in tiny boats on rough seas, the men returned to the *Homestead*. In all, the *Redwing* fired twenty shots, hitting the *Homestead* seven times. The rum ship stopped and sat dead in the water. However, Gilbert still refused to take a tow line or to drop a sea ladder.[48]

The *Redwing* was shorthanded and the crew had to wait for the *Seminole* for reinforcement. After the *Seminole* finally arrived from New York, the *Redwing* drew alongside the *Homestead*. The boarding party was prepared for a fight, as rumor had it that the rum-smugglers were armed with hand grenades. Fortunately, the crew gave up without a fight.[49]

The Coast Guard kept many of the details about the seizure secret, but there were vague reports leaking to the press that the Coast Guard captured the ship after it ignored warning shots across its bow. Several men aboard the steamer were rumored to be injured. It took the cutters nearly two days to tow the ship into port, where it was anchored off the Statue of Liberty.[50]

Aboard the *Homestead*, Coast Guardsmen found 12,000 cases of liquor and took twenty-eight men as prisoners. A guard was placed aboard the ship and the crew was not allowed to communicate with the outside world. A legal representative of the federal government told the press that he had heard the rumors, but not through official channels. He refused to give out any details on the seizure or explain the charges against the crew. Captain W.E.V. Jacobs, the Coast Guard's provisional commander of New York Harbor, went out to inspect the vessel accompanied by two Justice Department agents.[51]

During the capture of the *Homestead*, Customs officials announced that they had adopted a new system of dealing with rum-runners. They had arranged with the immigration authorities to question all captured rum smugglers about their citizenship or their legal right to be in the US[52]

During the bail hearing, Assistant US Attorney Francis A. McGurk brought up the fact that Gilbert had been a fugitive for two years. Gilbert's lawyer, Emanuel Tacker, said that he would probably apply for a writ of *habeas corpus*. McGurk argued that the *Homestead* was about twenty miles off shore, or at least within "one hour's steaming from shore" when seized. This would have put the ship within US jurisdiction. However, Gilbert's attorney told Judge Augustus Hand that he had a letter from Commander W.H. Munter of the *Red Wing* which stated that the *Homestead* was seventy-five miles out. Judge Hand set the bail at $50,000 (in 1925 dollars.)[53]

The confiscated liquor belonged to Great Britain's bootlegger baronet, Sir Broderick Hartwell. A few months after the liquor was seized, 2,000 cases of the liquor were released under a bond of $130,000 and shipped to Cuba. The ship itself was kept in port for previous violations of navigation and Customs laws. Gilbert was released on $25,000 bail on three indictments, including two Prohibition violations and one charge of mail fraud.[54]

6
CORRUPTION

At the beginning of October 1922, the Acting Internal Revenue Commissioner sent a telegram to Director Day. The telegram stated that six local Prohibition agents were to be suspended, pending an investigation of 5,200 missing cases of whisky and champagne. Using a forged Customs receipt, the agents had allegedly withdrawn the alcohol from the Republic Storage Warehouse on West 34th Street. This was the same warehouse Director Day had begun investigating a few months earlier. At the same time, a grand jury at New York's Federal Building was preparing to return indictments against thirty additional persons in connection with the warehouse-liquor plot.[1]

US Assistant District Attorney John Holley Clark conducted an investigation into the case and had reasons to believe that those involved in the fraud included a high Prohibition official, a former City Magistrate, several lawyers, warehousemen, realtors, and police officials. One Prohibition agent gave testimony against other agents in the department. It was right around this time that Director Day decided to resign.[2]

Zone Chief John D. Appleby and Commissioner Haynes were quick to lavish the outgoing director with praise. Appleby extolled Day to the press, describing him as "one of the best prohibition directors in the United States." Commissioner Haynes, who announced Day's resignation, stated that the New York branch of dry enforcement had never been "on such a high plane of efficiency," and that under Day, the New York office was in "excellent condition" and "so closely in touch with the Washington office at all times" that operations went more smoothly than a year earlier.[3]

Day spoke to the press in Washington the day after he resigned. He denied reports from Washington that there was friction between his office and federal officials. Before accepting his resignation, Commissioner of Internal Revenue Blair bombarded Day with questions about his private business affairs. Day claimed that the presence of US District Attorney Hayward in Washington was a mere coincidence as far as his resignation was concerned. He added that Hayward had gone to

Washington with him to discuss issues relating to the warehouse-liquor fraud. Day said, "The only reason for my resignation was the fact that I wanted to devote more time to my cloak and suit business."[4]

Despite his resignation, Day was not out of the woods yet. The day after he announced that his suit and cloak business was more important than enforcing federal laws, a man named H.L. Scaife made some damning statements to the press about him. Scaife stated that Director Day had borrowed $100,000 from an alleged bootlegger. Scaife also called for the resignation of Blair and Haynes for issuing false statements about the conduct of the New York office.[5]

Day appeared in the grand jury room of the Federal Building, but refused to testify unless he received immunity. Judge Rufus W. Foster subpoenaed Day to surrender R.A. Day & Co. books for inspection. He refused because his lawyer advised him that the subpoena was too sweeping. The judge soon issued a second subpoena calling for specific books, papers, and documents. Day did not produce those documents and claimed he did not receive the second subpoena until an hour after he was supposed to present the documents in court. After he received his second subpoena, he went straight to the Federal Building without his business records. Once again, he refused to testify before the grand jury unless he received immunity.[6]

Day denied to the press that he was intentionally withholding his books from the grand jury. He claimed that he had shown all the documents to the US District Attorney's office and given the fullest cooperation in the investigation of the 5,200 cases of missing liquor. When Mr. Day was scheduled for a contempt-of-court hearing soon after, he failed to produce the documents. Before he went to this hearing, he wrote in a press release that his legal difficulties were simply a matter of proper legal procedure. He also wrote that the Assistant D.A. had inspected his books and papers in his presence and with his assistance. He insisted that the investigation proceed "along orderly and proper lines" and that the subpoenas were "without any legal justification and…wholly improper under the law."[7]

The District Attorney's story was much different. Assistant D.A. John Holley Clark stated that Day had told the D.A.'s office that he and his books were at their service any time. However, when Clark tried to get in touch with him by phone to ask him to appear before the grand jury, his secretary told Clark he was out of town. A few days later, Clark got in touch with him, telling him to come down and testify and send his bookkeeper with the financial records. Day agreed. However, the following day, he called the District Attorney to say that he had important business and had to put the testimony off until the following day. Clark reluctantly agreed. When Day met Clark in the Federal Building, he told him he would not testify unless he had immunity. Day said his bookkeeper was out of town, and Clark could get no information concerning his whereabouts or when he would be back. Clark sent a subpoena to Day calling for all the firm's books. Day's attorney complained that the writ was too broad, so Clark sent out another subpoena, which was more specific. The subpoena server searched for Mr. Day all night, but could not find him. (He probably should have searched in the Day-time.) The next morning, when Day was supposed to appear at the Federal Building, his attorney told Clark that he would be in his office at 10:00 A.M. The subpoena was served at 11:00 A.M.[8]

For this hearing, Day had a different judge. Judge John C. Knox ruled that was not in contempt of court because the subpoenas calling for the records were "too sweeping." After the judge made his ruling, Day's attorney announced that he would present the documents to the grand jury only if the D.A.'s office issued a third subpoena. Assistant D.A. Clark said he would have another one waiting for Mr. Day in the morning, so that he and his missing bookkeeper could present the papers to the grand jury by 11:00 A.M.[9]

When the grand jury did look at Day's business records, they found that a man named Murray Garson loaned Mr. Day $100,000 while he still worked as the Prohibition Director. Friends of the former director claimed that Day's cloak and suit company was going to use the money for legitimate business transactions.[10]

****

On the same day Director Ralph Day announced his resignation, the Prohibition Bureau sent out a press release stating that the bootlegging ring in New York City had resorted to using sea and land planes. There were approximately 21 planes in total. The "land planes" operated between New York and Montreal. In case the planes were spotted by Prohibition agents, they were equipped with trap bottoms to dump their cargo into the Hudson River or the sea. The seaplanes operated between Montauk Point and Rockaway and were also equipped with trapdoors.[11]

The battle over jurisdiction continued between the United States and Britain. In October 1922, Judge John R. Hazel of the US District Court in New York made a ruling on the seizure of the *Henry L. Marshall*, which had been taken in August of the previous year. Judge

Hazel upheld the jurisdiction of the Prohibition navy past the three-mile limit. He also declared that any vessels unloading liquor cargoes to smaller vessels would be considered within the jurisdiction of the United States District Courts if they were within twelve miles of land. In the particular case of the *Marshall*, the court ruled that the vessel's captain and crew violated Prohibition and Customs laws by providing a false manifest, secretly landing liquor by smaller vessels, and failing to pay import duties. The British Foreign Office responded by informing the US State Department that Britain refused to permit the search and seizure of their vessels beyond the three-mile limit.[12]

Two days later, the British Embassy complained to the State Department about the seizure of another ship— the *Emerald*. A few days earlier, the Coast Guard Cutter *Hahn* captured the *Emerald* eight miles off the New Jersey coast with $50,000 worth of liquor aboard. Coast Guardsmen and Prohibition agents observed the *Emerald* unloading liquor onto small boats. The British argued that the small boats did not belong to the *Emerald*; therefore, the crew did not violate the recent policy of Attorney General Daugherty.[13]

The British ambassador stated to the press that his country had not taken any measures beyond the conversation with the State Department. The British refused to work out a treaty that would permit the US to search their vessels twelve miles offshore. The State Department told the press that the attempt to reach an agreement with the British was a closed case. Henry C. Stuart, the Acting Collector of Customs in New York, also refused to discuss the seizure of the *Emerald* with the press. He told reporters that "these matters are Government matters, and anything said must come from Washington, not from me."[14]

Nine days later, the American public read about the baffling outcome of the *Emerald* seizure. The Treasury Department, at the request of the State Department, ordered the Canadian schooner *Emerald* released. Although Secretary of State Hughes did not explain to the public how the seizure of the *Emerald* failed to conform to international law, *The New York Times* gave its own interpretation. According to the *Times*, Prohibition agents could not prove that the *Emerald* used its own boats to smuggle alcohol to shore. Therefore, the *Emerald* did not come within the territorial jurisdiction of the United States. This action set a new precedent, which flew in the face of the *Marshall* ruling from only two weeks earlier. If Prohibition agents were to use this action as a guideline, any rum-running ship that did not use "its own vessels" to smuggle liquor ashore was exempt from seizure.[15]

When Stuart released the *Emerald*, Customs vessels escorted the ship from Newark Bay to the Army Base in Brooklyn. There the crew reloaded the 1,000 cases of liquor that the Coast Guard had confiscated. After the crew finished on-loading the liquor, the Coast Guard escorted the *Emerald* to the area where it had been seized and released it.[16]

A few days later, a federal judge in Rhode Island released another British schooner— the *Marina*. A few months earlier, the Coast Guard Cutter *Hahn* captured the *Marina* two and a half miles off Block Island with 1,000 cases of liquor aboard. The vessel's captain argued that he had to allow his vessel to drift close to shore due to a heavy gale off Nantucket Light two days earlier. The jury bought the excuse and decided that the captain and crew of the *Marina* were not guilty. Even if the jury had found the captain and crew guilty, the Treasury Department would have freed the vessel under the new rule. The *Marina* left port two days later with its 1,000 cases of liquor, valued at $75,000.[17]

A week later, agents in fast government boats searched Rhode Island's waters for the *Marina*. Immediately after being released, the *Marina*'s crew unloaded a cargo of 775 cases of liquor to smaller craft in the Providence River and Narragansett Bay; an amount noticeably less than the 1,000 cases reported by *The New York Times*. A few days later, Prohibition agents reported that the vessel unloaded its "entire" cargo of 775 cases, leaving 225 cases unaccounted for. Not all of the 775 cases made it to the local speakeasies. On the morning of November 6th, Prohibition and Customs agents seized a vessel in New Bedford, named the *Pandora*, which had 145 cases from the *Marina* aboard.[18]

The State Department's new interpretation of international law stimulated the rum-running businesses of the Bahamas. During the week following the release of the *Marina*, US Customs officials learned that six British schooners were heading north from Nassau. All of the vessels were relatively small, but capable of carrying large cargoes of whisky. Prohibition agents learned through their sources that the six vessels were loaded with 100,000 cases of whisky, valued at $10,000,000. It was far more difficult for small craft to travel out to the twelve-mile limit rather than the renewed three-mile limit. Prohibition Zone Chief John D. Appleby of New York stated to the press that rum chasers spotted four or five liquor-laden schooners off the New Jersey coast during that same week. These smuggling boats were also from the Bahamas.[19]

On November 10, Treasury Secretary Mellon ordered the release of all foreign vessels seized outside the three-mile limit, where there was no evidence of communication with the shore by means of the vessels' own boats. Treasury officials estimated that there were about twenty vessels falling into this category, including the *M.M. Gardner*, the *Marion Mosher*, and the *Acadia*, which the Prohibition navy seized the day before carrying 557 cases. Secretary Mellon also ordered Customs to return the confiscated liquor cargoes to each vessel.[20]

Later in the month, the Treasury Secretary made life easier for alcohol vendors and US distilleries. Beginning on November 22, all persons accused of violating the liquor laws were entitled to post bail until a court found them guilty. Mellon also prepared an amendment to lower the cost of bail. At the same time, Prohibition Commissioner Haynes issued new rules governing the export of liquor to Canada, which imported liquor freely. Under the new rules, US manufacturers could export liquor to Canada as long as the manufacturer gave the government detailed information on the alcohol and its route.[21]

In late December 1922, Zone Chief John D. Appleby announced that the Prohibition navy had saved New York City from the rum-running fleets. Prohibition officials estimated that there had been anywhere from 100 to 300 smuggling vessels near New York only ten days earlier, but by December 21, the officials set the number at only six or eight.[22]

A terrible snow-storm hit New York and New Jersey on December 28. Up and down the coast, the storm drove small liquor-carrying vessels inland. As *The New York Times* stated it, the crews were caught between the "Volsteadevil and the deep blue sea." If the men stuck to their vessels, it meant almost certain death by drowning and if they reached shore it meant being captured by the Coast Guard.[23]

One rum-running schooner, named the *Jennie Bell*, ran aground off the mouth of the Shrewsbury River, near Sandy Hook, NJ Although the *Jennie Bell* had 510 cases of liquor aboard, the crew leaped from its decks into shoal water, managing to reach shore and escape. Soon after the schooner ran aground, Coast Guardsmen notified William R. Sanders, Deputy Surveyor in charge of the Narcotics Division of the Customs Service. The *Hansen*, of the Prohibition navy, went to the scene of the wreck where the crew picked up seventy cases of jettisoned liquor.[24]

Another vessel, named the *Madonna V.,* also came close to the shoreline during the heavy storm. In the middle of the night, the seas began to pound the British schooner to pieces. Coast Guardsmen attempted to launch lifeboats, but were unable to get anywhere in the raging northeast gale. Finally, the men were able to shoot a line to the disabled craft and evacuate the captain and crew of eight. The smugglers lost all 2,000 cases of liquor aboard as the storm crushed the vessel like a wooden toy. Case after case of Scotch whisky came tumbling ashore through the breakers, its shattered contents scenting the evening air. When the captain and crew reached the shore, the Coast Guardsmen detained them on the orders of Customs Collector Stuart; later, at the request of Customs, the men were transported to New York for interrogation.[25] The suspects told the Coast Guard that they were taking the liquor from Nassau to St. Pierre Miquelon, the lonely and sparsely-inhabited French isle which strangely seemed to demand schooner load after schooner load of Scotch.[26]

Courtesy US Coast Guard

This armored rum-runner ran aground. Note the Coast Guard cutter in the background.

Not far away, the motor boat *Fox* caught fire and the crew beached it on Sandy Hook, where the waves battered it to pieces, strewing the sands with 200 cases of liquor. No one was in sight when the rescuers arrived. The total value of the whisky that washed ashore that night from different wrecks was worth about $350,000.[27]

****

When John D. Appleby made his announcement to the press that the Prohibition navy was going to stop rum smugglers, he left out the important fact that this so-called "navy" only had one seaworthy vessel, the *Hansen*, which was supposed to cover both New York and New Jersey. The remaining patrol vessels were smaller craft that could not withstand rough seas. The day before New Year's Eve, the rum smugglers got a late Christmas present when the *Hansen* was stuck in port, supposedly for repairs. Although Prohibition headquarters and the NYPD did not find out about the *Hansen's* disabled engine until it was too late, the smugglers found out immediately. Fifteen vessels, filled with $7,000,000 of liquor, rushed toward New York City. By the next day, three vessels had already unloaded their cargoes. The Police Department had no vessels to interpose between the blockade runners and the harbor.[28]

Earlier it was mentioned that the crew of the *Hansen* had collected seventy cases of liquor from the wreck of the *Jennie Bell*. After the incident, Deputy Surveyor Sanders reported to officials at the Customs House that some of the liquor was missing. When the *Hansen* pulled into port, supposedly for "repairs," Customs agents went aboard to inspect the vessel. Two Customs Guards watched the crew as they stood on the pier during the inspection. The inspectors went aboard and found four cloth sacks containing bottles of liquor and two loose bottles in the crew's forward quarters. There was one case of liquor in a galley locker and six bottles hidden in the mess room. The inspectors found eleven bottles in the berth of the chief engineer and about fourteen cases behind barrels and in waste and rags. Customs immediately seized the contraband.[29]

Immediately following an argument between Prohibition and Customs officials, one of the men aboard the *Hansen* ordered his subordinates to dismantle and repair the engine. Chief Appleby did not learn about this ordeal until the next day. When he discovered that the *Hansen* was not at sea, he immediately called the captain. He ordered the ship to return immediately to sea, since it had been seaworthy enough to come into port under its own power. However, by that time it was too late. The crew was shorthanded due to the investigation, and the crew already began repairs on the engine.[30]

Following the Customs inspection, Captain George Dizer reported to Mr. Appleby, who suspended the *Hansen's* crew of eight men under charges after reporting to Prohibition Director Yellowley. Anyone familiar with maritime law knows that the captain is responsible for maintaining discipline and order among his crew, and is ultimately responsible for what happens on his vessel. But Captain Dizer, commander of the *Hansen*, tried to shift the blame to his crew—and it worked.[31] Both Customs and Prohibition officials absolved the captain of all blame. Dizer gave this version of his story to *The New York Tribune*:

> "We were working in a heavy storm. All the liquor that was salvaged was picked up with boat hooks and hauled on board. I had my hands full to keep the Hansen from going aground and for this reason I did not keep a personal check on the stock that was being salvaged.
>
> "I believed that the report and the stock turned over to the Customs Department was correct. What some of the members of the crew did while I was fighting the storm is a matter of which I had no knowledge. I was as surprised as any one when they found the liquor."[32]

****

Early in 1923, Customs acquired a new vessel, named the *Lexington*, which had been used for transport service during World War I. The vessel was 125 feet long and capable of a sluggish 17.5 knots. The press reported that the *Lexington* was to be equipped with rapid-fire guns fore and aft and also would carry two motorboats, capable of reaching a speed of 25 knots. The vessel was also to be fitted to carry a seaplane. Coast Guardsmen, under the direct supervision of Customs agents, would operate the vessel. In the newspapers, the *Lexington* was rumored to be the first of a new fleet assigned to the New York/ New Jersey area.[33]

The *Lexington*'s crew saw action almost immediately. A swarm of rum-running craft sought to overwhelm the Prohibition navy by sheer numbers. The Coast Guard crew captured the *Margaret B.*, loaded to the gunwales with whisky, while other Coast Guard vessels simultaneously captured three other rum-runners.[34]

As part of the synchronized effort, the Revenue Cutter *Surveyor* plowed into the swarming flotilla of little craft, scattering them in all directions. However, the *Surveyor* was too slow to catch them. The quicker smugglers sped toward shore and the larger, slower vessels escaped by reaching the three-mile limit before the *Surveyor*.[35]

The Coast Guard and Customs captured these vessels near the Highlands, on the New Jersey coast. However, a rumor swept through the area that smugglers had managed to get 35,000 cases ashore in one night. Prohibition officials held a news conference in the Highlands the next day to quash the rumor; however, they did admit that five Federal agents, who were assigned to that area, failed to keep watch that night.[36]

Zone Chief John D. Appleby said that the smugglers might have gotten some whisky ashore the previous night, but he ridiculed the figure of 35,000 cases. He argued that, in order to transport that many cases, smugglers would have had to load 140 trucks with 250 cases each or 1,500 cars with more than 20 cases each. "All of which," he said, "is such an absurdity that the story falls on its own weight." The Associated Press circulated the story, which bore an uncanny resemblance to the plot of a film then playing in the theaters titled, "One Great Night."[37]

There were so many rum vessels near the Highlands that the smugglers actually hung signs over the sides of their ships advertising their prices, in hopes of beating their competitors. The smugglers made no effort to conceal their activities and the local police made no attempts to stop the landings. Although the Prohibition officials denied that there was rampant smuggling in the Highlands, the Acting Customs Collector immediately dispatched the Coast Guard Cutters *Manhattan* and *Calumet* to the area.[38]

William D. Moss, Acting Federal Prohibition Director for New Jersey, announced the next day that he was recommending a federal grand jury investigation into the 35,000-case claim. He suggested that the Federal Court in Newark should subpoena anyone who claimed to have knowledge of that night's events and make them testify. Moss' sole object, he claimed, was to uncover the truth. He argued that "wet" propagandists duped the Associated Press reporters.[39]

Forming A Battle Plan

On January 19, 1923, officials from Customs, the Coast Guard, the Department of Justice, and the Prohibition Unit met at the office of the Collector of Customs in New York. The minutes of the meeting confirm that the smuggling situation in New York was alarming. The official report showed that there were about twenty rum ships anchored outside the three-mile limit near the city. Among them was the *Marion Mosher*, which obviously had not sailed to Canada after being released by the State Department on January 2.[40]

After a thorough discussion, the officials concluded that the only way to effectively stop the rum smugglers was to man the inlets of New York Harbor and patrol the coast as far as possible. However, the men also concluded that this was not feasible, because they lacked vessels of sufficient speed, tonnage and number, and the men to operate them. The only boat available for patrol duty on the day of the meeting was the *Surveyor*, which the Surveyor's Department used constantly inside the port, and occasionally outside the port. Since the *Surveyor* was tasked out to perform a variety of functions, it was available only occasionally for Prohibition duty. The Coast Guard had no boats available for Prohibition duty exclusively, and no vessels suitable to meet all the requirements that this type of work demanded. The Prohibition forces under Zone Chief Appleby had three small motorboats available—one in Fire Island Inlet, one in Jones' Inlet, and one in East Rockaway Inlet, on the South Shore of Long Island. These three boats were on fixed patrol in those areas and were incapable of offshore navigation.[41]

The men at the conference formed a plan that they believed would be adequate to handle twenty rum ships plus dozens of rum-runners. The plan called for twelve boats to patrol the coast from southern New Jersey to Newport, Rhode Island. In the plan, only one of the boats was to be seaworthy, and that boat was to patrol off the southern coast of New Jersey. One boat was to cover the coast from Montauk Point, Long Island, to Newport, R.I. Four large boats, supported by six smaller ones, were to prevent smuggling into the Port of New York. Neither the Collector of the Port, the Surveyor, nor the Coast Guard had the navigators to man these boats with operating crews. However, each agency did have men available to put on board these craft to act as searching and seizing officers.[42]

Still Lacking Resources

For several months prior to 1923, Customs officers were assigned to duty on six patrol vessels operated by the Prohibition service. The results were not satisfactory and the vessels were out of commission by January 1923. Although the duties of Customs increased greatly with the Prohibition Act, Congress refused to appropriate funds for the new Prohibition duties. Therefore, Customs had no vessels of its own. Realizing the futility of the situation, E.W. Camp of the Customs Division suggested to Assistant Treasury Secretary Clifford that Prohibition enforcement in US waters be turned over completely to the Coast Guard. Camp, arguing that the Coast Guard was far more capable of enforcing Prohibition with the resources it had available than either Customs or the Prohibition forces. He also pointed out that dual control of the rum patrols brought difficulties.[43] Assistant Attorney General Mabel Walker Willebrandt agreed with Camp's recommendations and sent her own endorsement of his plan to Assistant Secretary Clifford.[44]

Prohibition Commissioner Haynes, however, did not like either Willebrandt's or Camp's ideas. Haynes proposed using the Navy for

Prohibition duty and argued that the Coast Guard was inadequately manned and equipped to take over all of the work of smuggling interdiction. He wrote in a memorandum that the Prohibition Unit should direct all Prohibition enforcement, even on the water. Haynes disliked the idea of the Prohibition Unit being restricted to enforcement inland. The Prohibition Commissioner also did not like meetings between the different bureaus, like the one on January 19 in New York. He wrote in a memo:

> ...This Unit...is not in favor of absorption into any other service of its responsibilities which have been committed to it by law, and I fail to see what present good can result from the conferences at this time of the different branches of the service suggested by the Assistant Secretary.[45]

When E.W. Camp wrote his suggestion to the Assistant Secretary, the Coast Guard had 236 active and 41 inactive Coast Guard stations. The inactive stations were authorized by Congress but were closed due to a lack of funds. These stations were all connected by telephone. The Coast Guard had 95 vessels of varying classes, 75 of which were in commission. Forty-two of the vessels were equipped with radios. Most of the vessels also carried one-pounder guns, which the Prohibition patrol boats were not authorized to carry. The number of Coast Guardsmen at the time numbered approximately 4,600. Camp stated that the Coast Guard needed more equipment and that duties under the customs, navigation, quarantine, life-saving, and other laws were preventing the Coast Guard from focusing its resources on rum smuggling.[46]

7
PIRATES ATTACK RUM SHIPS

Chief Yellowley admitted to the press on January 20, 1923, that there was no "dry" navy and never had there been one. The Prohibition unit, he added, had a number of boats that agents used to chase rum-runners; however, he did not state exactly how many or where they were. During the previous week, *The New York Times* quoted several Coast Guardsmen and Customs agents who made the same claim. A high-ranking Coast Guard officer informed the press that when someone spotted a rum-runner, it was up to the Coast Guard to provide a cutter for Customs officers. The Coast Guard vessels were usually too big to follow the small rum-runners into shoal water. The only boat with that capability was the *Surveyor*, which could not handle the rough waters of the Atlantic.[1]

It turned out that the earlier report in *The New York Times* concerning the *Lexington* was "dry" propaganda. The former Coast Guard vessel was not fitted as a rum-chaser with guns and small motor launches. The Prohibition Bureau sent the *Lexington* to New York to be used instead as a boarding vessel. The Treasury Department in Washington was disgusted with the stories of rum-running and lax enforcement along the New York waterfront. The rank and file of Customs men were disgruntled because they performed the actual duties of apprehending rum-runners and then the Prohibition agents claimed credit for the arrests. The *Hansen* was the last of the six "dry" navy boats to be withdrawn from service. Several members of the discharged crew said that they were compelled to make money from bootlegging, because they were not paid their wages.[2]

A day after Yellowley admitted that there was no "dry" navy, Captain Byron L. Reed, Commander of the US Coast Guard's New York Division, reported to the Customs Collector that seventeen rum-running vessels were off the coast of New York and New Jersey. Three of the vessels were fairly large steamers. Among the fleet was the *Marion Mosher*, which the US Government had freed several months earlier.[3] Several days later, the federal government contacted Coast Guard stations throughout the country, notifying them that, thereafter, as officers of the Treasury Department, they would be expected to prevent smuggling. This order placed 3,000 more men in the Prohibition enforcement ranks.[4]

Courtesy US Coast Guard Headquarters

Captain Byron L. Reed, Commander of the New York Division and Captain of the Port of New York, showing the progress the Coast Guard made in law enforcement work.

A Dislike of the Press

Government officials were not happy with the public scrutiny of the Prohibition effort. Government finger-pointing and interdepartmental bickering were two results of the press reports on rum-running. Director of Customs Van Doren wrote about these problems in a memo to the Assistant Secretary of the Treasury, Edward Clifford. Van Doren wrote that there "is distinct hostility" between Prohibition officers, Customs, and other branches of the Treasury and concluded that Prohibition officers were the "aggressors." Van Doren disdained how the Prohibition Service freely resorted to publicity and how they "openly announced [their] intention of taking control of all activities of the kind." Van Doren wrote that this would lead to an "open rupture between branches of the Department." His memo recommended clearly-defined jurisdictions for the Coast Guard, Customs, and the Prohibition Unit, since those distinctions were lacking in early 1923. Van Doren suggested that the Coast Guard intercept rum-runners afloat, Customs cover the borders, including harbors, and Prohibition forces handle the interior.[5]

Assistant Secretary Clifford was not pleased with statements that Prohibition officials were making to the press. He requested, in a Treasury memo, that these officials stop talking to reporters. In fact, he did not want Prohibition officials to give any publicity to what they were doing. He wrote:

> ...I will see to it that the Customs Service and the Coast Guard officials say nothing. This matter can not be handled successfully by giving out information to the press.[6]

"Pirates" Attack the Mosher

A few weeks later, the *Marion Mosher* reached New Brunswick. The captain explained to the US Consul that pirates had stolen the 4,000 cases of liquor, worth $300,000. According to Captain Pettipass, his vessel had been off the coast of Long Island, on the way to New Brunswick, when a big steam trawler appeared with a crew of forty men, armed with a number of guns. The 40-man crew fired shots across his bow and brought his vessel to a stop. Then, according to Pettipass, the pirates came aboard and took every case of liquor. The transfer lasted about four hours. Meanwhile, the captain and crew watched helplessly, because the pirates bound them hand and foot. After the pirates were done, their captain supposedly told Captain Pettipass that if he saw the *Mosher* again, he would make him walk the plank. This was mistake number one of his story; anyone familiar with pirate history would know that walking the plank was largely a fictional punishment and was rarely, if ever, practiced by pirates during the "Golden Age of Piracy."[7]

Henry S. Culver, the US Consul at St. John, New Brunswick, did not buy Pettipass' Hollywood story. Customs agents had found several barrels of whisky from the *Marion Mosher* aboard the *Ada*, the *Ina*, and a few other vessels a couple of weeks earlier. Culver informed Pettipass that the crew of the *Manhattan* had spotted the *Marion Mosher* in the lineup of rum-runners off the New Jersey coast two weeks after the schooner had left port. Pettipass replied that it was not his ship the men spotted, but another one with the name *Marion Mosher* painted on it.

This was mistake number two in his story. Why would a smuggler want to paint a name on his vessel that had recently stirred up an international incident?[8]

While Pettipass told his fantastic tale, eleven other men were called by the federal grand jury to tell their stories. The grand jury indicted all eleven men from the Highlands for conspiracy to smuggle liquor into the United States. The charge was that the men tried to land whisky from the fleet of rum ships, anchored off Ambrose Channel Lightship. As of February 8, the men sat in prison with no court date set.[9]

****

Roy A. Haynes, the Federal Prohibition Commissioner, held conferences with various state officials and others involved in Prohibition. From what he heard at these meetings in Washington, Haynes devised a new strategy. The goal of this comprehensive plan was to clean up what he described as the three wet centers of the East coast— New York, New Jersey, and Pennsylvania. The plan placed the enforcement of the Volstead Act directly in the hands of the Federal Prohibition authorities in Washington. Federal Prohibition Directors assigned to each state would have less authority than before, and their new duties would consist largely of issuing permits to withdraw liquor from warehouses. Commissioner Haynes, with President Harding's approval, would have the power to choose the new directors, who would act directly under his orders. Under the new design, the political patronage system within each state was supposed to be eliminated. Under the old system, US Senators had control over those who filled the Prohibition posts. Now the choice was to be left to fewer people, who were supposedly above the spoils system.[10]

Haynes' plan called for sweeping changes in how Prohibition was enforced and who would lead the administration in New York, New Jersey, and Pennsylvania. Instead of having enforcement agents permanently attached to a district, personnel would be shifted from one area to another depending on the mission, much like the military.

Haynes' plan also created four new Federal Prohibition areas, which were to be administered differently from state Prohibition zones areas elsewhere in the country. These four new areas were: (1) Northern New Jersey and Southern New York, (2) Northern and Western New York, (3) Eastern Pennsylvania and Southern New Jersey, and (4) Western Pennsylvania. The idea behind these new zones was very logical: most bootlegging rings operated within a certain defined radius.

Under the new plan, an agent did not have to worry about jurisdiction when chasing a smuggler from Manhattan to Jersey City or from Atlantic City to Philadelphia. Agents in Northern and Western New York could focus on smugglers along the Canadian border while other administrators and agents handled the New York City area. Previously all of New York State had been considered one enforcement area.[11]

"Rum-running Is Doomed"

Prohibition Commissioner Haynes wrote a book in 1923, titled *Prohibition Inside Out*, in which he claimed that rum-running was "doomed."[12] The title of Haynes' book effectively sums up the contents of the book. Haynes describes both the organization of Prohibition forces in that year gives his opinion on how well the Prohibition Unit was doing at the time. He also describes in detail how rum smugglers and bootleggers operated.

During the fiscal year 1922, the Prohibition Unit, the Coast Guard, and Customs had combined to seize twenty-nine ships. Eighteen of those vessels were under foreign flags and were under the US flag. In addition to the rum ships, the combined Prohibition forces seized forty motorboats. Haynes writes that the press and bootleggers had grossly exaggerated Rum Row and that only a tiny trickle of liquor (1,500,000 gallons in 1922) was flowing into the United States.[13] The following are the words of the man who oversaw the entire Prohibition enforcement effort:

> It is virtually impossible to buy good whiskey from the illicit liquor interests in the United States to-day. What the bootlegger offers as high-grade imported whiskey or bottled-in-bond stuff is neither. In 95 per cent of the cases, or more, it is moonshine—not pure and simple, but watered, thinned down, adulterated, and fearfully doctored with chemicals, many poisonous, to give it color, a "kick," and a bead.
>
> The moonshine still is the bootlegger's chief source of supply. From what other source can he get his liquor in quantity? Surely not from the rigidly controlled bonded warehouses— they were eliminated at once. As to smuggled liquor, some, it is true, is brought into the country, but not one tenth as much as the illegal traffic would have us believe.
>
> When reports of huge smuggling operations are circulated, it should be remembered that the illicit liquor interests are conducting a great and elaborate propaganda

campaign to discredit law enforcement, and that the spreading of such reports is part and parcel of that campaign. No bootlegger, of course, is willing to admit that he can obtain only adulterated moonshine. Hence, fanciful tales of the wet wave sweeping in on our coasts, and other related falsehoods swung from mouth to mouth to hide the real and dangerous origin of the bootlegger has to sell.[14]

Pirates

There were pirates during the Prohibition years; however, sorting out the true from the false stories was no easy task when the victims were rum-runners. When a captain made claims that pirates came aboard his ship and stole all of his rum (it does sound trite), it absolved him of responsibility for where the rum wound up. "Pirates" became a legal loophole in the Volstead Act. While there was a clause against transporting and selling liquor, there was no clause in the Act against pirates plundering one's liquor and transporting it ashore. While piracy carried severe penalties in most places, punishment was not an issue if the "pirates" were fictitious. Claims of piracy were more credible if the merchandise aboard was legal. If a company was shipping legal cargo such as fruit or furniture, that company would have less incentive to stage a mock pirate raid.

Treasury agents had the duty of sifting through these sea stories. An unidentified person reported to Customs that pirates robbed the *McLaughlin*. A Treasury agent investigated the case and found that other smugglers verified the story. According to the story, on a Sunday night after midnight, the man on watch aboard the *McLaughlin* noticed the outline of a boat running without lights. The *McLaughlin*'s watchman informed his captain, who in turn hailed the trawler, which was coming dangerously close to his ship.[15]

"Watch out, you're running us down."

"Watch out," someone shouted from the trawler, "we're coming aboard."[16]

Without delay, more than twenty men, armed with revolvers, climbed aboard the *McLaughlin*. According to the report, the twenty-man crew of the *McLaughlin* realized the helplessness of their situation and put up no resistance. The pirates threw some of the men into the hold and locked the others in the cabins, making sure all of them were securely bound. The pirates transferred 4,200 cases of liquor (worth $400,000) from the victim ship to their trawler and left the *McLaughlin* adrift with the crew still bound. The strange part is that the captain of the *McLaughlin* did not pull into port to file a report with Customs. What is even more strange is that the agents were able to get such detailed information about what occurred, but could not find either vessel. The Treasury agents were also able to find out that after the pirates raided the vessel, the *McLaughlin* headed back to Nassau to pick up another cargo of liquor and that certain people saw the pirate trawler near Philadelphia trying to unload its cargo. Customs officials believed that this same crew of pirates may have raided the *Marion Mosher* two weeks earlier and another boat a month and a half earlier.[17]

A month later, in March of 1923, pirates struck again. Sailors spotted a vessel named the *Victor* off Ambrose lightship. Smugglers and agents knew the *Victor* as a rum-running vessel. The vessel was a seventy-seven ton schooner that had outrun the Prohibition navy on many occasions. A year earlier, Customs officials seized the vessel as it was anchored off 59th Street in Bay Ridge, NY and found 3,893 cases of Scotch whisky aboard. As a result, the crewmembers went to Federal Court facing charges of violating the Volstead Act. They all pled guilty and the US Government sold the *Victor* at an auction to Michael Rinaldo. After Rinaldo purchased the vessel, the *Victor* dropped out of sight for about a year.[18]

A few days after those sailors spotted the *Victor* off Ambrose lightship, the ship drifted in close to Barren Island (how appropriate) where the police spotted it. The Barren Island Police Department called William R. Sanders, the Deputy Surveyor of Customs, and reported the vessel as a derelict. Sanders and Customs Inspector Frank Thorp quickly boarded the Coast Guard tug *Hudson* and left Manhattan to inspect the drifting schooner. When the Customs men finally saw the vessel, they noticed several unusual things about it. The schooner was missing its sails, rigging, and lifeboats. When the agents went aboard, they found the tables set for dinner; food recently cooked and set upon the tables. The theory of the Customs men was that the *Victor* was the victim of pirates who had been reported raiding the rum-fleet just outside the three-mile limit. Customs confiscated the schooner once again and towed it to Manhattan, where it sat anchored off Battery Park, pending an investigation by Government officials.[19]

****

Meanwhile in New Jersey, political manure was hitting the fan. The former Federal Prohibition Director of New Jersey, Harold L. Hart, the former Secretary to ex-Governor Whitman, William A. Orr, and fourteen other defendants had to appear in court. The men were charged with conspiracy to defraud the government through the falsification of liquor permits. Thomas A. Felder, who acted as Hart's attorney, made a motion to dismiss the charges against all sixteen defendants. Felder argued that Hart had an unblemished reputation and had been "unjustly stigmatized by the indictment." He also argued the government had produced no evidence of any meeting between Hart and any of the other defendants, except Thomas M. Reddy, formerly his assistant, and Michael Lynch, former Chief Clerk. But then Felder slipped up and contradicted himself when he said:

> "I submit to your Honor that the prosecution has not shown so much as a wink, a nod or a gesture ever passed between Mr. Hart and any of these other defendants. I would go so far as to say that Mr. Hart never knew these other defendants before this trial began with the exception of Mr. Orr, whom he knew in a political way."[20]

Felder also argued that none of the evidence showed that Hart signed a single one of the stolen permits, only his rubber-stamp signature was on them. The prosecutor, Assistant US Attorney Maxwell S. Mattuck, argued that there was more than enough evidence for the jury to reach a verdict. Mattuck pointed out that drug companies made liquor withdrawals greatly in excess of their allowances, even when they were using the false permits from the office of the former Prohibition Director. Judge Francis A Winslow denied the motion to dismiss the case. The defendants were going to have to sweat it out.[21]

****

Atlantic City police locked up Mrs. Pearl Young, one of Zone Chief Appleby's investigators, on the charge of extortion. Appleby was furious that the police would lock up one of his investigators and made a special trip to Atlantic City to see that she was released. He made a statement to the press claiming that the Prohibition law was openly violated and gambling and "disorderly" houses flourished in that city. Mayor Edward L. Bader of Atlantic City was not happy with Appleby's remarks and expressed his displeasure to Senator Edge (also from Atlantic City). The Senator then contacted Prohibition Commissioner Haynes, who ordered Appleby to appear before a grand jury in Atlantic

City to give evidence of his charges or retract his statement. When reporters interviewed him, he denied that Haynes had ordered him to appear before the grand jury; however, he did say that if the grand jury wanted him to testify, he would do so, but could not give any firsthand information. His statements about Atlantic City were based on information from his investigators. If Appleby failed to substantiate his charges, Senator Edge planned to insist upon his dismissal on the grounds that he was unfit for the job.[22]

Within a few days, Haynes transferred Appleby from New York to Boston. Less than two weeks later, Appleby resigned from federal service. He announced plans to open law offices in New York City. He made a statement to the press about his resignation:

> "My work in the department, because of the steadfast support of my superiors and men, has been most pleasant. Commissioner Roy A. Haynes and E.C. Yellowley have especially supported me in all my efforts to uphold the law. Of course, we have not been able to accomplish all that we desired, and that is the one regret that I have in leaving the service."[23]

True to his announcement, Appleby did open up a law office, located at 1650 Broadway in Manhattan. A month and a half after Appleby resigned, he sent a business proposition to Prohibition Commissioner Haynes and forwarded a copy to the Secretary of the Treasury. In his letter, Appleby wrote that he would be willing to rent out seaplanes, sea sleds, speedboats, trucks, cars, and men to operate them for $50,000 a month. This Prohibition fleet for hire, he wrote, would patrol the coast from Maine to New Jersey. If the government wanted his privately-owned boats, vehicles, and planes to patrol the South, he would be willing to negotiate. It was very unusual for a lawyer to have all of this equipment at his disposal. Whether he owned this equipment is unclear. What is clear, however, is that Appleby failed in the public sector and now sought to make a profit in the rum war as a private contractor.[24]

Around the time of Appleby's resignation, R.Q. Merrick arrived to take his new post as Division Chief of the General Federal Prohibition Agents, in charge of New York State and northern New Jersey. Merrick had spent the previous eleven months as Prohibition Chief in Savannah, Georgia. He was definitely a busy man during his stay; his agents had confiscated thousands and thousands of cases of whisky from the

Bahamas in and around Savannah and the surrounding area. However, he admitted that thousands of cases still managed to get through the net of agents. While the agents in New York and New Jersey put confiscated liquor in bonded warehouses, agents in Savannah supposedly poured the confiscated whisky out, saving only enough to use as evidence. The rum-runners around Savannah had an advantage over the smugglers in New York and New Jersey. At high tide, there were many points around Savannah where boats drawing eight and ten feet of water could pull in and unload their cargoes, well concealed from the mainland. These ships, mostly schooners, carried 500 to 1,000 cases at a time. The smugglers hid the whisky in the undergrowth of the islands or in the marshes until it could be transported ashore by smaller boats. Once the liquor reached Savannah, distributors shipped it out in crates and boxes as commodities to various parts of the country. Although federal agents made seizures every day, great quantities still managed to get through to the interior on Pullman rail cars. Trainmen sold White Horse Cellar whisky for $5 a quart as far north as northern South Carolina, $5 to $10 cheaper than vendors were selling it up North.[25]

Smuggling brought prosperity. In dozens of towns along the coasts and borders, there were signs that rum-running was paying off. Hundreds of people who had been dirt poor before they took up the illegal trade now noticed a great improvement in their standard of living. Smugglers carried bigger rolls of bills than ever before and used their new-found wealth to buy automobiles, a definite sign of prosperity in the early '20s. They remodeled and painted their shacks, turning them into respectable houses, and bought items such as pianos, phonographs, and expensive furniture. Ironically, many men, who used to drink heavily, became sober and industrious after they entered the smuggling business.[26]

The rum pirates were no doubt encouraged by the political infighting within the Prohibition enforcement machine. While the Prohibition Bureau and Atlantic City politicians defended their images, pirates attacked another ship on the Hudson River. Early one morning, the Royal Mail Steam Packet *Orbita* was docked at the foot of Morton Street. A crew of eleven pirates aboard a launch pulled up alongside. The pirates boarded the *Orbita* and held the entire crew at gunpoint. Five pirates guarded the captives, while the other six made their way to the liquor. The pirates broke the seal, which Customs officials had placed on the door, broke the door open, and stole twenty cases of Scotch whisky. Just as the pirates lowered the last case of liquor into the launch, a watchman on the pier spotted them. Two other watchmen then ran up and the three men emptied their revolvers at the launch, which sped out of sight.[27]

The *Orbita* was legally allowed to bring its liquor into port due to a ruling made by Federal Judge Learned Hand (yes, that was his name) the previous Fall. Under Hand's ruling, foreign ships could bring liquors into American ports, provided they were kept under seal until the vessels passed beyond the three-mile limit. American passenger vessels suffered a drop in business due to the Prohibition Laws. In response, the American International Mercantile Company appealed to the Supreme Court to have the laws loosened for American ships. Congress did not include in either the 18th Amendment or the Prohibition Enforcement Act whether Prohibition applied to American vessels on the high seas or in foreign ports.[28]

Two days after pirates raided the *Orbita*, a speedboat pulled up to a wharf adjoining the Fort Lee ferry at 129th Street. There the crew unloaded forty cases of whisky from the Bahamas and put them in the back of a truck. Some of the bottles bore the labels of the United Fruit Line's steamship *Antilla*. Police spotted the six smugglers and the two parties began shooting at each other. The smugglers lost their nerve and surrendered. However, on the way to the police station, the transport truck crashed and the suspects escaped. The police shot at the unarmed men as they ran through the city streets in plain view of the local residents. Once again, the smugglers surrendered and the officers finally managed to transport them to the station. Amazingly, the smugglers were still allowed to post a $500 bail after shooting at police officers. The men denied any knowledge of the *Orbita* raid.[29]

****

On the same day, the fishing schooner *Eddie James* pulled into port at Halifax, Nova Scotia. When the crew went ashore, they had a very exciting sea story to tell to whoever would listen. While the liquor-laden *Eddie James* sat at anchor off the New Jersey coast near Highland Light, the crew had some visitors. A steam launch made its way from a large, powerfully built steamer and pulled alongside the *Eddie James*. Five seamen, "armed to the teeth," boarded the schooner and advised the captain that they wished to purchase some liquor. The captain agreed to a conference. The five strangers sat down in the cabin with the captain, his first mate, and supercargo (the man in charge of the ship's cargo). Suddenly, the five strangers started to fire their weapons indiscriminately, wounding the supercargo and driving the remainder of the crew to hiding places about the vessel. Two of the armed men held the frightened crew at bay, while the others passed all 600 cases of whisky over the schooner's side and into the launch. To add insult to injury, the pirates then robbed the captain of $8,000 in cash and kidnapped the wounded supercargo. As the pirates took off with their loot and captive, one of them yelled back that they would soon be back for more. Of course, the *Eddie James*' crew immediately raised anchor and put out to sea. On the way back to Nova Scotia, several storms tossed the fishing vessel around on rough seas.[30]

Prohibition and Customs officials told the press that they had never heard of the schooner *Eddie James* as a rum-running vessel, but did say that rum-runners identified pirates as their worst enemy. Pirates attacked well outside of federal jurisdiction and clearly operated outside of the law. While smugglers stood a good chance of recovering their alcohol and posting bail after a Coast Guard raid, their odds were not as good when dealing with pirates. The new Zone Chief R. Q. Merrick was very pleased to read about the pirate attack on the *Eddie James*.[31]

"It saves us a lot of work," he told the press. Merrick added that every time a pirate attacked a rum-runner, the risk level went up and the number of willing smugglers went down. According to reports he read in Savannah and at his new post, Merrick concluded that rum piracy was on the rise along the Atlantic Coast. He cited a big bootlegger in Savannah, who claimed that he feared 'liquor thieves' far more than federal agents. Rum-runners in the Highlands, NJ area began working on their pistol marksmanship to protect themselves against the pirates.[32]

While the pirates were busy shooting people and stealing rum, the press was wreaking havoc in the nation's capital. When the DC police arrested a man named Joseph E. Connor for selling liquor, they confiscated his list of customers. The next day, officials in Washington opened *The Washington Post* and read the names of about 500 patrons of bootleggers, arranged alphabetically. The list, published on March 12, ended with the letter *R*. Many prominent people in Washington, whose names began with subsequent letters, most likely did not sleep well that night. In fact, many of Washington's elite kept the wires busy on the 12th, trying to persuade the owner of the *Post* to prevent the publication of the rest of the list. While the police had managed to confiscate many such lists before, this was the first case in which the names and addresses were published in a newspaper. There were names on the list from the State Department, War Department, and Navy Department; soon Connor became known as the "State, War, and Navy" bootlegger.[33]

Many on the list quickly came up with alibis. Three Naval officers told Acting Secretary Franklin D. Roosevelt that, while their names were on the list, they had never purchased any liquor from the bootlegger. They told Roosevelt that the bootlegger had solicited them over the phone and was as persistent in his sales pitch as a book agent. The phone lines going into the State, War, and Navy buildings were busy all day with friends calling up those on the list. Practical jokers amused themselves by calling the officers and impersonating Prohibition officials, demanding that they show up in court the next day. Those connected with the Army's Judge Advocate General's office told officers, whose names were on the list, that federal Prohibition agents could not arrest them unless they found alcohol in their possession. (Although "possessing" alcohol was not a crime— buying, selling, manufacturing, or transporting it without a permit was.)[34]

Acting Secretary Roosevelt explained to the press that the Navy Department regarded the matter as one falling under civil authority and, therefore, out of the Navy's jurisdiction. He went on to say that, "if the sales had been made in naval territory that would be a horse of another color, and then the Navy Department would take up the matter and investigate."[35]

When reporters asked Secretary Hughes to comment on the appearance of names from the State Department, he simply smiled, saying he had nothing further. Acting Secretary of War Davis stated that the mere fact that the names of Army officers appeared in the paper did not "justify an interference detrimental to such officers or to the military services. Investigation, if one is deemed necessary, is up to civil authorities."[36]

Prohibition Commissioner Haynes was not in Washington at the time, and the Prohibition Unit, in the meantime, conducted no investigation. In fact, some of those listed had been out of Washington for several months and, in some cases, as long as two years.[37]

The rum-runners became bolder as 1923 went on. The rum trade off the New Jersey coast became an open market. There were so many rum ships clustered together that the customers went from one vessel to another looking for the best deal, causing the price of liquor to drop. Previously, at night, the cargo ships sat three miles or more off the coast with their lights off for concealment. In March 1923, fifteen tanker-sized rum ships sat three miles off the Highlands, their anchor lights blazing similar to those on lighthouses. The Coast Guard and Customs only had two vessels, which they shared, in order to chase the smugglers. The men aboard the *Porpoise* and the *Lexington* could clearly see the armada of rum ships at anchor with their lights ablaze, but could not board or search the vessels past the three-mile limit. The smaller vessels whizzed by the slow cutters as they brought the liquor to shore.[38]

The rum-runners were just as busy off the Long Island coast. At Riverhead, Long Island, fishermen, oystermen, and beachcombers abandoned their professions to make a small fortune unloading rum ships. Many poor fishermen became well-to-do bootleggers and refused to work as hired men, buying and selling on their own account. Men who used to drag rakes across beaches to find litter were now raking in cash. Until the Spring of 1923, ships usually landed their liquor according to a prearrangement with agents on the shore, who had cable or radio information on the ship's arrival date. The rum smugglers saw no need for maintaining such secrecy and held a public market off the Long Island coast, selling to all comers.[39]

As the rum smugglers grew bolder, they also became more dangerous. Smugglers drove big trucks through Riverhead to pick up cases of whisky at the waterfront. Each truck had a driver, a "fixer," and at least one gunman. The fixer's job was to supervise and pay the waterfront workers. The gunman's job was to fight off highwaymen. Several shootouts took place near Riverhead between gunmen guarding whisky trucks and ambushing bandits. For safety, whisky trucks traveled in convoys of three. Smugglers usually loaded the trucks at night, but recently began loading in broad daylight.[40]

Reverend Dr. James A. MacMillan of the Methodist Church at Sag Harbor complained to the press about the situation in his town:

> "I do not know for a fact that this town is the center of a great bootlegging traffic, but it is common rumor that boats come right up to the shore here, landing rum openly, and that it is carried away in motor trucks and that the whole thing is done brazenly, without interference from local or Federal officers. There is a general protest among good citizens here against this sort of thing..."[41]

On the night of March 22, 1923, there were five pistol battles between rum-runners, pirates, and highwaymen around Atlantic Highlands, NJ. It all started when a large vessel, carrying several hundred cases of Scotch, was heading in toward the Shrewsbury River. A truck was waiting on the banks nearby and all seemed well. There was a skiff moored in the middle of the river, directly in the path of the rum-runner, which looked empty.[42]

Suddenly, the rum-runner was ambushed, bullets flying at it from several angles. A man stood up in the skiff and commanded the smugglers to halt. Instead, the rum-runner's skipper used the full power of his engines to go forward as fast as he could. He was not sure if the men shooting at him were Prohibition agents or pirates, but he did know he was going to lose a lot of money if his cargo was taken, so he ordered his men to return fire. The skipper was not sure if his men killed any of the alleged pirates, but his vessel, crew, and Scotch whisky survived the shootout.[43]

The crew had some time to calm their nerves and count their lucky stars as the vessel made its way to the Atlantic Highlands Bridge. As they approached, the crew noticed more skiffs dotting the water. Once again, men sprang up from the skiffs and began showering the rum-runner with bullets. Then a swift motorboat, almost as large as the rum-runner, sped across the water and pulled up alongside. It was the pirates! The pirate vessel was faster than its rum-laden victim and armed with enough "artillery" to fight a small naval ship. According to the smugglers who escaped, the pirates captured the rum ship and sent the crew ashore in skiffs. When they got ashore, the pirates fired several warning shots at them to speed them along. The pirate captain then took command of his prize and escaped toward Sandy Hook.[44]

About an hour later, rum-runners delivered a small load of liquor to a large truck near the wooden seawall at Highlands Beach, just east of the Atlantic Highlands Bridge. After the crew finished loading the cargo, other men appeared and held them up. Men seated in cars parked nearby then fired a fusillade of bullets at the smugglers and their truck, which managed to escape with twenty-five cases.[45]

During the remainder of the night, there were two more gunfights between rum-runners and pirates, the last occurring near daybreak. These last two skirmishes occurred on the water just off Belford, NJ, only a few miles from Atlantic Highlands. An article in *The New York Times* speculates that the fighting could have been for control of the northern New Jersey bootlegging business. Many of the shooters were fishermen who had abandoned their nets and lines for guns, alcohol, and cash. However, not all were fishermen. Those who knew the details of the last fight off Belford believed the captains on both sides were familiar with naval tactics. When the night was over, several people were dead or wounded.[46]

Coast Guardsmen came in contact with some of these violent smugglers the next night. At 2 A.M., Boatswain's Mate Edward Butler was on patrol, when he came across a motorboat in Raritan Bay. He located the rum-runner from the sound of its engine and crept within close range of the blackened vessel before the "bottle fishermen" noticed. The rum-runner used both of its state-of-the-art Pierce-Arrow engines to speed away. The smugglers were about to leave the Coast Guard far behind when one of the engines blew out. As Boatswain's Mate Butler gained on them, the smugglers began to throw their cargo overboard. However, they gained no speed even after jettisoning their entire cargo of fifty-plus cases into the bay. Thinking quickly, the smugglers beached their boat near Atlantic Highlands and disappeared into the woods on the hillside. Although the men managed to escape, Butler brought the captured vessel along with any cargo he could recover to the Customs authorities in Sandy Hook, NJ.[47]

Boatswain Francis W. Downes was also on patrol that night, cruising in a powerboat. Just before dawn, he spotted another rum-running speedboat without lights off the Highlands. Downes fired across the bow of the boat, which sped past the Highlands and was quickly out of sight. On the way back to Sandy Hook, he spotted another motorboat running with no lights and sent a shot across its bow. The boat sped away, but Downes' boat was just as fast. Downes managed to trail the boat up to the Highlands where he heard a volley of bullets coming from the shore. Bullets splashed in the water around Downes' boat and the smugglers managed to escape.[48]

The demands of rum-running brought about rapid improvements in motorboats. In 1923, the fishing smacks that smugglers used only two years earlier had already been phased out and replaced by speedboats equipped with the most powerful airplane and automobile engines. To use an airplane engine in a small boat was a radically new concept. One has to remember that this was only two decades after the Wright Brothers struggled to get a powered glider off the ground at the beach in North Carolina. The airmail system was still being developed and the passenger plane was still a concept on the drawing board. The biplane, with an open cockpit, was still the most common type of plane. Coast Guardsmen were aware that, in order to pursue these smugglers, they would have to keep up with the rapid changes in technology.

Acting Prohibition Director Yellowley minimized reports of rum-running. In a statement to the Associated Press he said:

> "We have not even asked the Government for more ships to combat the activities of the so-called rum armada. I can get along very well with what I have at my disposal. The Government has the entire Atlantic coast efficiently patrolled

and while there are sporadic attempts at smuggling liquor, these are to be expected."[49]

In April, President Harding sent out a press release stating that he would soon launch a more aggressive campaign to enforce Prohibition. (This was the same President who served alcoholic drinks to his guests.) He sought to dispel the idea that federal authorities were not "exerting themselves to the utmost" to work with the Prohibition Enforcement Unit. Before Harding went on his vacation in April, he looked at a plan drafted by Navy officials, which called for the use of fifty Navy destroyers to chase rum-runners within the three-mile limit. Naval officers were generally against using war craft for civilian law enforcement; however, according to this plan, the Navy would lend its destroyers to the Coast Guard for a short time. There is no law against the Commander-in-Chief using the Navy for domestic purposes, and those that advised drastic action were confident that President Harding would approve the plan.[50] Federal Prohibition Director Roy A. Haynes backed the proposal. In addition to this plan, Haynes requested that the President order several government agencies to help stop rum-runners. The list of agencies included the State Department and the Department of Labor, unusual choices to be sure. Even odder, he included the Customs Service and Coast Guard on the list, those who already bore the brunt of the effort in 1923.[51]

On the same day, Senator Dial of North Carolina (D) had this to say about the enforcement situation:

> "It is worse than a farce, it is an outrage, that with the Shipping Board having something like 1,000 ships, to say nothing of the Navy, the Coast Guard and other government agencies that these rum-runners should be able to carry on this illicit trade."[52]

In March 1923, Andrew Mellon had been the Secretary of the Treasury for exactly two years. Mellon reported that labor was in strong demand, production in America's main manufacturing industries was at an all-time high, and rail traffic had surpassed all records. In 1923, many economic indexes reached levels that would not be equaled until the spring of 1929. This was the beginning of what would come to be known as the "Roaring Twenties." Much of the prosperity was due to factors beyond Mellon's control, such as the increasing use of automobiles and electricity, the real-estate boom, and the construction of highways and bridges, etc. But there were still large parts of the nation that did not benefit from the new prosperity, especially in the South and Midwest. However, millions of Americans were doing better than ever before, financially, and they gave credit to Mellon for bringing prosperity to a wrecked economy in such a short time. In a speech, Representative Simeon D. Fess claimed that Mellon was the greatest Secretary of the Treasury since Alexander Hamilton. Many people came to see Mellon as the administration's shining star and schools like Rutgers, New York University, Dartmouth, and Princeton gave him honorary degrees.[53]

8

MYSTERY OF THE SUNKEN RUM SHIP

In early April 1923, a heavy fog rolled over the Massachusetts coast. Coast Guardsmen patrolled the waters in an attempt to prevent rum-runners from sneaking in under the blanket of fog. Meanwhile in nearby Chatham, Massachusetts, the British freighter *Competitor*, carrying a cargo of liquor, went thirty miles off course in the fog and ran aground near Nauset. The crew of the *Competitor* waited aboard their ship for an entire day as it sank deeper and deeper into the sand. Coast Guardsmen from the Nauset Coast Guard station boarded the stranded vessel and searched it thoroughly for liquor, but found nothing. Most likely, the crew sold the cargo. That night, the vessel lay almost broadside to the beach, with its crew and the Coast Guardsmen still aboard awaiting assistance from a wrecking tug. As they waited, the seas grew rougher and the rising northwest winds added to the danger.[1]

In another incident, Captain Arthur C. Larkin, keeper of the Gay Head life-saving station, heard several short blasts from steamer whistles coming from several directions. After a short silence, he heard more whistling and the clanging of ships' bells. The steamers were about two or three miles apart, but the fog obscured them. The lifesavers got their gear ready and stood by for nearly an hour. When the mist cleared, Coast Guardsmen spotted a vessel in Vineyard Sound, off of Martha's Vineyard. The 150-foot steam trawler displayed a distress signal and its decks were awash. As the Coast Guardsmen scrambled to get rescue boats off the nearby beach, the ship rolled over, its boilers blew up and it sank.[2] A search of the area revealed no trace of the crew, but the Coast Guardsmen thought it was possible they had escaped in their own lifeboats. No one reported the crew landing anywhere on Martha's Vineyard. The Coast Guard also explored the possibility the theory that another vessel might have picked up the crew.[3]

The next day, the Coast Guard found the crew of the sunken mystery ship, floating dead amid barrels of ale. The ship turned out to be the *John Dwight*, which was a Navy ship during World War I. The Navy sold the ship to a rich yachtsman, and the new owner made a profit by using the steamer to salvage coal from barges sunk at sea. A week before the disaster, Captain John Carmichael, an old towboat owner from Jersey City, had arrived in Newport, R.I., where the ship was docked. He announced that there had been a temporary change in ownership and took charge. He brought an engineer and other assistants with him, and a few days later, more men arrived, bringing the crew up to eight or nine men. On the next day, the *John Dwight* left port without the captain announcing his destination. The rumor on the waterfront was that the vessel was smuggling rum to New York. The arrival of the crew of strangers reinforced that theory. [4]

The Coast Guard was baffled as to why they did not find the dead men or the floating cargo earlier. Seven of the bodies floating in the water had on life preservers and the other body was in a small boat. The man in the boat had made an ingenious fight for his life. There were neither oars nor oarlocks in the boat, but he made sweeps from strips of board torn from the inside of the boat and locks out of strips of canvas torn from a belt. The man most likely exhausted himself and fell to the bottom of the boat, where he drowned. [5] As for the other seven men, Captain Larkin and his crew, having hauled hundreds of dead from the waters there in past wrecks and marine disasters, said that they had never seen such terrible cuts and bruises on any previous casualty. All eight bodies were badly cut and mutilated, leading seafaring men to believe that there had been a battle between liquor smugglers and hijackers.[6]

Captain Carmichael was not among the dead. Coast Guardsmen and fishermen swept the seas and combed the beaches looking for him and any other possible victims. Fishermen, unsuccessful in their search for the victims, did, however, manage to find a great quantity of liquor. The searchers brought back dozens of barrels of bottled ale from the Frontier Breweries, Ltd., of Montreal.[7]

****

Several months later, the mystery of the *John Dwight* was still unsolved. One of the bodies the Coast Guardsmen found was that of James A. Craven of Lyndhurst, New Jersey. After the men found the mutilated body, it was placed in a tomb at the Cambridge Cemetery for six weeks, pending the outcome of the District Attorney's investigation. Massachusetts state authorities began an investigation a few weeks after the vessel sank. Divers located the hull of the vessel and examined it, but found no evidence to solve the mystery. In late May, federal authorities announced that James A. Craven had a bag filled with $100,000 in cash at the time of the sinking. After the vessel sank, searchers found the empty bag floating in Vineyard Sound.[8]

The Cambridge District Attorney indicted Thomas C. Craven of New York and others in connection with a multi-million dollar liquor plot. On the same day, a man who gave his name as Morton R. Craven went to the Cambridge City Clerk's office, changed the death record of James A. Craven, and received a permit to remove the body from the tomb. Six weeks earlier, morticians had laid out the eight bodies of the *John Dwight* for identification. A man, who claimed he was Martin R. Cronan of Cambridge, identified the body as that of his brother, James A. Cronan. "Martin" then had the body shipped to a Cambridge undertaker.[9]

On the day set for burial, the Cambridge police went to the undertaking room to take fingerprints and a general description of the body. They found that the hands were charred, making it impossible to take prints, the eye sockets were filled with white plaster, and the face had been painted over. Later, Martin R. Cronan admitted that he had made a false identification and requested a new death certificate. He said his real name was Martin R. Craven and that the body was that of his brother, James A. Craven. He said the reason for seeking a new certificate was to enable his brother's widow to collect $5,000 life insurance. Martin R. Craven had his brother's body buried without the knowledge of the District Attorney, who was still investigating the mutilation.[10]

Assistant Attorney General Joseph E. Warner believed that the *Dwight* had been involved in a big liquor running conspiracy based in New York City. By the end of June, the State of Massachusetts had still not solved the case, so the federal government became involved. The government's plan required sending an expert naval diver to the wreck, which lay 100 feet underwater. The government ordered the naval officers to find out why the *Dwight* sank, even if the hull had to be raised for examination. The possibility of successfully completing the mission came about unexpectedly with the appearance in the Sound of the USS *Falcon*, a mine sweeper from the Brooklyn Navy Yard. The Massachusetts State Police provided the naval officers with detailed information they collected in their recent investigation. The *Falcon* had four divers on board and was thoroughly equipped for salvage operations.[11]

As the *Falcon*'s crew was preparing to search the wreck, investigators on land learned an important fact from officers of the Merchants and Miners of Dorchester. The pilot, who witnessed the sinking, had previously reported having seen three men escape in the lifeboat. He changed his statement to say that he had seen five men with their heads above the gunwale, three rowing, one at the bow, and one at the stern. According to one of the *Dwight*'s owners in New York, there had been fifteen men aboard. Eight bodies were accounted for, but the questions as to what happened to the other seven bodies and what caused the ship to sink were still unsolved mysteries.[12] After the Navy divers finished examining the hull, the Coast Guard Cutter *Ossipee* dropped a mine on the *Dwight*'s hull and blew it up. The government did not release the results of the investigation to the press.[13]

****

A week after the Coast Guard found the abandoned *John Dwight*, the Coast Guard Cutter *Manhattan* was patrolling off the Long Island coast near Fire Island. The lookout spotted the outline of a schooner in the early dawn light. As the *Manhattan* came closer, Lieutenant Commander Ryan saw that the schooner had its sails up but was without lights. He called out "Ship ahoy!" several times but got no response. The name *Patricia M. Beman* was freshly painted on the stern of the 100-foot vessel. The schooner was moving only slightly and it was apparent that the vessel was dragging its anchor.[14]

The crew of the *Manhattan* turned its searchlight on the boat, Ryan spotted no signs of life. Ryan and several crew members boarded the vessel and examined it using their pocket flashlights. Ryan continued to call out in the hopes of waking one of the crew, but got no reply. He then went to the captain's quarters aft and knocked on the door several times. When he got no answer, he kicked the door open. He found the cabin deserted, with several pieces of clothing scattered around the room. The mate's cabin and the crew quarters were in a similar condition. There was food on the captain's table and enough provisions to last for another two weeks. Also, there was a 25-foot motorboat, in excellent condition, lashed to the forward deck.[15]

The schooner's deck showed evidence that the missing crew had engaged in a battle with liquor pirates. The Coast Guardsmen found bullet holes in the vessel and many empty cartridge shells on the deck. The shells were all .44 caliber and made in Britain. Ropes on the deck had been cut with a sharp axe, which was found on board. Belaying pins were removed from the rail and were scattered about the deck. There were still 1,000 unused rounds of the same caliber in the skipper's cabin, but no guns in the gun racks.[16]

After the *Manhattan* took the abandoned vessel in tow and docked it at the United States Barge Office at the Battery, in Manhattan, Ryan continued his investigation. He and his crew found no liquor; however, down in the hold, there was evidence that the boat, a Nova Scotia trading schooner, had carried a heavy liquor cargo. The hold was filled with empty whisky cases and burlap bags, each of which had once contained six bottles of whisky. A leaf torn from a pocket notebook also indicated that the captain had sold 3,918 packages of liquor, at $50 each, over two-and-a-half months. Other memoranda showed that the largest purchaser was "Ralph," but there was nothing to indicate whether "Ralph" was a man or a motorboat. There was no logbook aboard the schooner, but the last memorandum was dated five days before the *Manhattan* located the ship. One theory was that pirates killed the captain and crew and threw them overboard. Ryan expressed his belief that the *Patricia M. Beman* dropped anchor much further off shore but was driven in until its anchor held.[17]

Customs officials were divided over the fate of the crew. Some officials, who did not believe the pirate story, suggested that the crew had abandoned the boat after disposing of the liquor. The *Beman*'s papers showed its clearance from Nassau on December 17,[th] with 4,000 cases of liquor destined for St. Pierre and Miquelon Islands. According to the papers on board, the captain sold off most of his cargo. If the *Beman* pulled into port without its cargo, Customs would most likely have arrested the captain and crew.[18]

It is possible that the *Beman*'s captain sold all the liquor and had his men fire off rounds to scatter shell casings all over the deck. They may have not used the 25-foot motorboat on the forward deck, as that would have ruled out a pirate attack. Most likely, the captain and crew hitched a ride with their final customer and fired rounds at the *Beman* as they left in the smaller boat. The Coast Guard found neither bodies in the water nor blood aboard the ship, which definitely would have been present had the whole crew been killed. However, just because the captain and crew left the *Beman* safely does not mean that nothing suspicious happened to them elsewhere.

9

A LETTER FROM A SMUGGLER

One of the many rum ships off the East Coast in April 1923 was the *S.V. Istar*. One of the crew aboard that vessel wrote a letter to his wife, Jenny, in Greenock, Scotland. Since he was not able to mail the letter himself, he gave it to someone aboard the tugboat *Peerless* to mail for him. A couple of months earlier, the police boat *Blue Boy* had chased the *Peerless* past City Island and up the Long Island Sound. Although the *Peerless* was carrying 2,000 cases of liquor, it still managed to escape. When the *Peerless* came up alongside the *Istar* in April, the crews transferred 800 cases of Black and White Scotch to the *Peerless*, which then headed for New York City. As the *Peerless* made its way through the Narrows, the Coast Guard and Customs inspectors aboard the *Lexington* captured it. One of the captured men had the letter from the *Istar* in his pocket. The Customs inspectors seized it as evidence and gave it to John Holley Clark, the Assistant US District Attorney. Clark intended to use the letter as evidence that foreign vessels were helping Americans violate Customs, tariff, and national Prohibition laws. Here is an excerpt of the letter as it was printed in *The New York Times*:

> By the looks of it we will be a couple of months before we leave here for Greenock. We have only got rid of about 4,000 cases of whisky so far and it has taken us two months to get that out so you may well guess how long we will be. We still have 16,000 cases aboard and the weather is no good for the boats to come off as it is always blowing and we are laying about nine miles off the land. A boat loaded with fifty odd cases of whisky was lost on Tuesday night with the heavy seas. We are on watch all the time and we get called out at all hours to load the boats when they come alongside and I can tell you we are all fed up day after day with bad food and rotten meat to eat. The head ones aboard are trying to tell us we will be home in the beginning of May but it doesn't look like it. It wouldn't be so bad if we could go ashore once a week but we are penned up like convicts aboard here.
>
> It takes some doing to keep up one's spirits here. I wouldn't do a second trip in this ship for twenty thousand

pounds a month especially running whiskey. Sometimes I feel like getting drunk to cheer me up but I still manage to keep teetotal. So long as we get good weather homeward bound I don't mind if we are here another month but I know I wouldn't like to come through what we came through coming across here. I saw the 'Cameronia' coming into New York yesterday from Glasgow. I wish I had a chance of going home in her on Saturday.

Do you know Jenny I haven't had a bath since I left home as it is so cold in this ship I am feared (*sic*) in case I get a cold. I don't feel like one now until we get home as I haven't got a decent shift of clothes left to put on. I wish I was home, out of this ship, as what with drunken men and the smell of the drink, it near about knocks me sick. This is no place for anyone teetotal as they don't like me a bit because I won't drink with them.

I expect we will be going to Halifax in a fortnight's time and if she is going to come back here I am going to try and get out of her. The whole crowd may try and get paid off and sent home and I pray to God that we will. I think about it but if I am spared and well to come home I will tell you all about it. [1]

Prohibition Director Palmer Canfield reacted to this letter by announcing to the press that he and other officials would conduct an "official inspection" of the rum fleet just outside the three-mile limit. The headline in *The New York Times* stated, "Prohibition Chief To Visit Rum Fleet: Canfield Will Make Trip Outside 3-Mile Limit Thursday To Size Up Situation." Canfield was even considerate enough to let the rum smugglers know what day he would be visiting them.[2]

"One of the reasons for the trip," Canfield said, "is to view the rum fleet and size it up, if there is any fleet."[3] In April 1923, there were still some Washington officials that called the rum fleet a "myth." The myth-busting expedition began when the crowd of officials and reporters boarded the *Manhattan* and departed the Battery at 10 A.M. Aboard the vessel were Captain Byron L. Reed, Assistant US District Attorney Sanford H. Cohen, Representative Emanuel Celler, Samuel Wilson of the Anti-Saloon League of New Jersey, and twenty-five reporters. [4]

USCG Photo

Prohibition Director Palmer Canfield, Captain Byron L. Reed, plus other officials and reporters look for rum-runners.

The journey began under conditions of favoring tide and clear skies. As the *Manhattan* moved with a steady thump-thump over miles of water, Canfield took the opportunity to deliver a short speech to the press:

> "No longer will tame methods and spiritless activity and pusillanimity be sufficient or acceptable. Uncle Sam has to be a tiger and a bear at the same time. The smugglers smugly exhibit a super quintessence of audacity in setting at naught the one-hundred-year-old laws against smuggling.
>
> "While it is much exaggerated and greatly magnified, it is a grave indictment against the country that there is any smuggling. The people do not realize the menace that it constitutes because story books have always cast an atmosphere of glamour around pirates and smugglers. They forget that it is not merely a violation of the National Prohibition act but of the Internal Revenue laws and custom

laws that have existed for upward of a century and are a sacred part of our law structure.

"This smuggling cannot be eliminated with gondolas or canoes. It will require fast and swift eagle-winged boats. The boats must be armed—combatant boats. They must represent speed and force. They must be 'seven league' boats. The ocean bandits and the Viking smugglers will do like the Arabs— 'silently steal away in the night.'"[5]

About this time, the liquor fleet appeared on the horizon. There were six ships with an interval of about three-quarters of a mile between each vessel. The fleet was arranged in a battle formation, like a crescent with the tips pointing in toward the Jersey shore. There was not a single motor launch in sight, because, of course, the liquor fleet received advance notice of their visitors. The six ships rocked in the long sea swells as the *Manhattan* approached. Director Canfield was aft when the first of the rum ships came up directly ahead. As Canfield observed the fleet through his binoculars, the shutter of a movie man's camera clicked away, filming the scene. All hands aboard the *Manhattan* prepared to deal with the cutter, but it sheered off and headed for one of the schooners.[6]

The schooner turned out to be the *Katherine M.*, a two-masted schooner out of Nova Scotia. As the *Manhattan* got closer to the *Katherine M.*, a short, fat man rested his elbows on a rail and calmly looked at his vistors. He was smoking a short briar and, after deliberately looking the *Manhattan* over from stem to stern, removed the briar but did not answer any questions. The *Manhattan* slowly chugged around the stern and the crew discovered something.[7]

Moored at the side of the ship was a twenty-foot motor boat marked K-12208. The boat was new, with a $1,000 Sterling engine and a new coat of battleship gray paint. Two men were working on the engine. One was a huge Swede in oilskins and hip-length, red rubber boots. The second man was much smaller and was practically lost in his boots. He glanced up with a grin as the *Manhattan* came into sight. Ryan climbed to the bow of the *Manhattan* to ask these men what they were doing on Rum Row.

"We're lobster fishermen and we got a new boat," said the smaller man. "Last night we decided to give her a try out and the engine broke down and this ship picked us up."

Courtesy US Coast Guard Headquarters

The *Katherine*

"Sure you haven't any Scotch aboard?" Ryan asked. He then ordered the Swede to turn over a pile of life preservers at his feet and dislodge several pine boards resting against the side of the motorboat. Ryan could see no liquor, so he let them off with a warning and ordered the *Manhattan* to move on.[8]

The next vessel they came across was the *Catherine Mary*, a two-masted schooner out of Nassau. The three men on deck stood "like mummies" at the rail as the *Manhattan* went past slowly. When Ryan hailed the vessel, the men responded only with prolonged stares. Just as silent were the decks of the *Mary O'Conner*, another schooner from Nassau. The only response to calls from the *Manhattan* came from a small black dog, who barked furiously and raced over the coils of rope. The ship's deck was covered with a number of long wooden boxes painted a bright color. Ryan doubted that they contained either gasoline or water.

The next vessel was a 3,000-ton steamship, named the *Warszawa*, of London. This was a British "tramp" of the tanker type. The *Manhattan* passed the *Warszawa* and met the familiar *M.M. Gardner*, with eight men lounging on the deck. The crew of the *Manhattan* had seized the *Gardner* a year earlier for selling Scotch whisky. However, the State Department put pressure on the Treasury Department to release all vessels seized outside the three-mile limit; and so the *Gardner* headed back out to sea.

Ryan called out, "Any Scotch?"

"No Sco'ch."[9]

The *Manhattan* moved on and met up with the flagship, named the *Istar,* which now enjoyed some fame due to the confiscated letter. The *Istar* was a British yacht constructed in 1906. It was 250 feet long and could move rapidly. As the *Manhattan* got closer, it became apparent that the *Istar* had seen better days. The paint was falling off its sides in great blistering patches and the ship was dirty. The antenna attached to the mast showed that the ship had "wireless" and, as the *Manhattan* drew nearer, the radio operator of the *Istar* dashed out of his cabin and ran aft with a message for the skipper. [10]

Twenty-two of the yacht's crew, most in neat blue uniforms, stood at the rails. The skipper, a stocky man with a very red face, stood aft with a tall officer, either the first mate or purser, at his side. Captain Byron L. Reed picked up the long megaphone and hailed the *Istar.*

"How long have you been here?"

"Three weeks, sir," replied the first mate with a crisp salute.

"Well, stay here for a couple of days longer. The British Consul wants to come down and inspect you."

"Aye, aye!" the first mate answered with a smile.[11]

Later on, when reporters asked the British Consul General about his intended visit, he denied having any such plans. After Captain Reed was finished with the megaphone, Director Canfield took it and asked if he could come aboard the *Istar*. The skipper replied with a cordial invitation, but refused to allow reporters aboard. However, after talking to Captain Reed, Canfield decided not to go. He resumed his megaphonic conversation and the first mate climbed onto the *Istar*'s bow to hear better.

"What's your cargo?" shouted Canfield.

"Lemonade."

"How many men in your crew?"

"Fifty-three, sir."

"Would you like another?" shouted a reporter.

"Certainly, come aboard."

Courtesy US Coast Guard

The rum schooner *M.M. Gardner.*

"How many cases have you aboard now?" asked Canfield.
The figure on the bow doubled up in mirth.
"Now, now…there's some questions you must not ask."
"We hear you had 16,000 cases aboard yesterday, is that so?"
"Nope," replied the mate.
"Could you tell us if you have any Scotch aboard?"
"I could, but I wouldn't."
"How's business been?" asked the Prohibition Director.

"Rather slack."[12]

The well-publicized excursion made waves in Washington. On the same day the report hit the papers, President Harding met with his Cabinet to discuss possible solutions to the smuggling problem. After the Cabinet meeting, a White House spokesman said that the President and his advisors did not minimize the situation, considering it "grave." The Administration decided on stronger measures, but the spokesman told the press that it would be too early to outline the course of action.[13]

Federal Prohibition Commissioner Roy A. Haynes, however, still denied that the rum fleet was a problem. He argued that Canfield's trip only proved that stories about the rum-smuggling fleet had been greatly exaggerated. He stated that "instead of there being a liquor armada so large that ships could scarcely pass through it, it turned out that there were five boats of little or no consequence, and only one which amounted to anything."[14]

A few days later, the Treasury Department reported that the Prohibition Unit was quickly using up all its limited funds available for enforcing Prohibition laws. Without an additional appropriation from Congress, plans to expand patrols along the Atlantic Coast would not be feasible. Officials of the Prohibition Unit, Coast Guard, and Customs put their heads together in an attempt to form a plan, but came to no definite conclusions. The money Congress set aside under appropriations was barely enough to cover the work already being done. The White House entertained the idea of detailing naval vessels for Prohibition service without using the funds appropriated directly for Prohibition enforcement.[15]

Undeterred by a lack of funds, Director Canfield suggested in his report to Commissioner Haynes that seaplanes, a land force equipped with fast cars, and a fleet of ships operated by the Coast Guard were the solution.[16] One week after Canfield made his public and almost comical expedition, other Treasury officials made their own trip; however, this one was conducted in secret. The officials traveled aboard the *Manhattan* and noticed that the number of rum ships off the Jersey coast had increased from six to nine ships. The purpose of this visit was to gather as much information as possible on liquor smuggling. The officials were to present their findings to President Harding, Secretary Mellon, and other members of the Cabinet.[17]

President Harding and his Cabinet reviewed the findings of the Treasury officials and drafted a plan of action, involving Navy ships and personnel to pursue and capture American-registered ships and smaller craft smuggling liquor within the three-mile limit. The President submitted the plan to the Justice Department in order to confirm his legal authority to proclaim a national emergency and order the armed forces of the United States to break up liquor smuggling. After a Cabinet meeting, the White House announced that the plan would not threaten international relations and there was no thought of violating the three-mile territorial limit.[18]

One Cabinet member raised questions concerning whether the Executive Branch, without authorization from Congress, could transfer vessels and personnel from the Navy for duty with the Treasury Department and whether the expenses of those operations could be paid out of naval appropriations. In addition to questions of legality, there were objections from Navy officials. One objection was that Prohibition duty would shatter the morale and pride of the Navy. The Navy men also argued that the authorized strength of the Navy was insufficient to man the fleet. If the submarine-chasers and Eagle boats were put into Prohibition service, it would be necessary, they argued, to withdraw larger ships from commission that were required to round out the fleet. The Navy officers complained that Congress had cut their budget so drastically that they could only carry out normal naval operations through rigid fuel economy. If naval appropriations were diverted to Prohibition enforcement, the Navy would have had to curtail maneuvers essential to the fleet's battle efficiency. While the White House spokesman used the term "armed forces" in his statement, it was not clear if Harding planned to use the Army as well. [19]

Still Lacking Money, Fuel, and Ships

In May 1923, almost three and a half years after Prohibition took effect, the Coast Guard still lacked the vessels and funds to stop rum smugglers. A number of the vessels were out of commission and some of the stations (former life-saving stations) were closed or put on inactive status due to insufficient funds. The Coast Guard's appropriations fell under about a dozen subheads. The money for one subhead could not be transferred to another subhead without approval from Congress. In 1923, the Coast Guard could not secure Congressional approval for a transfer of funds, which led to an embarrassing situation for Admiral Reynolds. The Bureau of the Budget estimated that the Coast Guard would need $12,616,762 for 1923. Congress appropriated only $9,874,118. The Coast Guard estimated that it would need $1,063,200 for fuel and water, but Congress authorized only $760,270. This made it necessary for the

Coast Guard to be unusually strict with fuel, thereby limiting patrols. For a short period, Admiral Reynolds was not even sure if the Coast Guard would have enough fuel to continue operating throughout the fiscal year.[20]

Courtesy US Coast Guard Headquarters

The Coast Guard used five former Navy Eagle boats, such as the one pictured above, for Prohibition duty. These ships were: the *McGourty, Scally, Bothwell, Earp,* and *Carr.* Workers at Henry Ford's plant in Detroit built sixty of them for the Navy. None of them were completed before the Armistice of 1918. They were unpopular, even for routine patrols, because they had a tendency to leak oil and take on water; they also did not handle well on the high seas. Therefore, they generally remained in coastal waters. Most of them were out of commission by World War II.

In some districts, local officials criticized the Coast Guard for an apparent failure to stop rum-runners. Admiral Reynolds argued in a memo that this inactivity was not due to either neglect or lack of interest, but rather a shortage of fuel and budget restrictions. Congress appropriated only $800,000 for fuel the following year, meaning the Coast Guard would not be able to significantly increase its patrolling activities. Reynolds raised this issue in another memorandum for the Director of the Budget, from whom it was forwarded to the Secretary of the Treasury.[21]

While the Coast Guard was lacking fuel, Albert B. Fall, the Secretary of the Interior, was making huge profits by secretly leasing naval oil reserves to private companies. Secretary Fall convinced Secretary of the Navy Edwin Denby and others that the administration of the reserves should be turned over to him. In 1921, Fall secretly granted the Mammoth Oil Company exclusive rights to the Teapot Dome reserves in Wyoming. He also granted similar rights to the Pan American Petroleum Company over the Elk Hills and Buena Vista Hills reserves in California. In return for the leases, Fall received large cash gifts and "loans," amounting to $404,000.

In 1924, the Senate launched an investigation into this fraudulent sale of oil, meant for naval vessels. In what came to be known as the "Teapot Dome" scandal, Fall wound up in prison, but the Secretary of the Navy was cleared of all charges, even though his signature was on all of the leases. Harry F. Sinclair of Mammoth Oil Company and Edward L. Doheny of Pan American Petroleum Company were acquitted of charges of bribery and conspiracy. However, Sinclair spent 6 ½ months in jail for contempt of court and contempt of the US Senate.[22]

ALCOHOL, BOAT CHASES, AND SHOOTOUTS!

A cartoon by Clifford Kennedy Berryman depicting the Teapot Dome Scandal in 1924.

US Coast Guard
Force Available for Prohibition Duty As Of May 1923[8]

Atlantic Coast And Gulf Coast

Ships	Length	Headquarters
Ossippee	165'	Portland, Maine
Chicopee (Harbor Boat)	88'	Portland, Maine
Tampa	240'	Boston (on ice patrol)
Mackinac (H.B.)	110'	Boston
Acushnet	152'	Woods Hole, MA
Seneca	204'	New York
Gresham	205'	New York
Manhattan	120'	New York
Guide (H.B.)	70'	Philadelphia
Guthrie (H.B.)	88'	New York
Raritan (H.B.)	103'	New York
Hudson (H.B.)	96'	New York
Wissahickon (H.B.)	96'	New York
Lexington (H.B.)	122'	New York
Kickapoo	151'	Cape May, NJ
Apache	185'	Baltimore
Winnisimmet (H.B.)	96'	Baltimore
Arundel (H.B.)	100'	South Baltimore (out of commission)
Chattahoochee (H.B.)	88'	South Baltimore
Chenango (H.B.)	88'	South Baltimore
Chincoteague (H.B.)	88'	South Baltimore
Choptank (H.B.)	88'	South Baltimore
Chowan (H.B.)	88'	South Baltimore
Chulahoma (H.B.)	88'	South Baltimore
Manning	205'	Norfolk, VA
Mascoutin	151'	Norfolk, VA
Tioga (H.B.)	81'	Norfolk, VA
Four Submarine-chasers	110'	S. Baltimore (out of commission)
Pamlico (Inland Waters)	158'	New Bern, NC
Modoc	240'	Wilmington, NC (on ice patrol)

---

[8] Memorandum For General Lord, Director of the Budget, From Admiral W.E. Reynolds, Commandant of the Coast Guard. Washington, DC 3 May 1923.

ALCOHOL, BOAT CHASES, AND SHOOTOUTS!

Ships	Length	Headquarters
Yamacraw	191'	Savannah, GA
Seminole	188'	Temp. at New York
Saukee	151'	Key West, FL
Vidette (H.B.)	75'	Miami, FL
Tallapoosa	165'	Mobile, AL
Davey (H.B.)	92'	New Orleans, LA
Comanche	170'	Galveston, TX

Great Lakes

Ships	Length	Headquarters
Morrill	145'	Detroit, MI
Tuscarora	178'	Milwaukee, WI
Cook (sub-chaser)	110'	Grand Marais
Chillicothe (Harbor Boat)	88'	Ogdensburg, NY (out of commission)
Chippewa (H.B.)	88'	Sault Ste. Marie

Pacific Coast

Ships	Length	Headquarters
Tamaroa	151'	San Pedro, CA
Unalga	190'	Juneau, Alaska
Shawnee	158'	San Francisco, CA
Snohomish	152'	Port Angeles, WA
Algonquin	205'	Alaskan cruise
Bear	198'	Arctic cruise
Haida	240'	Alaskan cruise
Cahokia	151'	Eureka, CA
Mojave	240'	Hawaii (Alaskan cruise)
Arcata (Harbor Boat)	85'	Port Townsend, WA
Cycan (sub-chaser)	110'	San Francisco
Vaughan (sub-chaser)	110'	San Pedro, CA
Smith (sub-chaser)	110'	Kotchikan, Alaska
Golden Gate (Harbor Boat)	110'	San Francisco, CA
Guard (Harbor Boat)	67'	Friday Harbor, WA

10
THE GOVERNMENT ATTACKS RUM ROW

Secretary Hughes contacted the British Ambassador to request his nation's aid. More specifically, Hughes requested the negotiation of a mutual agreement by which the American and British governments would inform each other of the clearance of large cargoes prohibited under the laws of either country. The British government expressed its desire to cooperate with the United States; however, this was easier said than done. Although the British possessions in the West Indies fell under the control of the Colonial Office, a policy of issuing direct orders from London ran counter to the empire's evolving policies. The British government had been giving its colonies more autonomy. Canada, the source of much of the liquor, was entirely free to manage its own domestic affairs. Even in Crown colonies, where the Crown nominated many members of the legislative councils, the Colonial Office tried to interfere as little as possible. Therefore, when a situation arose, which could only be corrected by the alteration of local laws, the Colonial Office tried to persuade local authorities to act on their own initiative rather than compel them to do so. It was uncertain how far the British government was willing to go to enforce its authority, particularly for an unpopular cause.[1]

At the beginning of May, 1923, the Supreme Court ruled that as of June 10, both foreign and domestic vessels would be forbidden to transport liquor for "beverage purposes" within US territorial waters, either as sea stores or in bond. All vessels sailing for American ports, due to arrive after June 10th, would be subject to Prohibition enforcement. Newspapers of several foreign nations protested the ruling. Several countries had laws that made it mandatory for ships to carry liquor for their crews. However, there was a loophole in the new law— embassies and legations could still receive liquor under diplomatic seal or under the "baggage clause," which made diplomatic baggage immune from search and seizure.[2]

On the day of the ruling, the liquor fleet off the New Jersey coast began a general exodus. Shortly after the Coast Guard stopped and searched a small steamer bound for the rum fleet, the British tanker

Warszawa and the *Istar* headed out to sea. The federal government's plan was basically to starve the liquor fleet lying outside the three-mile limit. On the same day, Customs officials seized a tugboat and motorboat and charged the owners of the vessels with conspiring to violate the Prohibition law. Customs also made a charge of engaging in international commerce, where their license only authorized them to engage in coastal trade.[3]

The British were definitely not happy with the Supreme Court ruling. An editorial in one London paper suggested that Great Britain declare war on the US in order to enforce the right of its subjects to drink as much liquor as they wanted, wherever they wanted. Another suggestion was that Britain should retaliate by placing a ban on chewing gum, forcing American ships to dump their gum in the English Channel. The papers also raised questions on the new law's effect on "tramp" steamers. For example, a Spanish ship taking sherry to Cuba would be unable dock in Puerto Rico, and a ship bound from Vancouver to China could not stop in Honolulu or the Philippines if it carried even a single bottle of liquor.[4]

To make sure that the rum fleet was leaving, Director Canfield took another trip— this one by air. Canfield climbed into a plane at Miller Field, in Staten Island, NY. Lieutenant Robert Burt of the 102nd Observation Squadron took Canfield to an elevation of 1,000 feet, allowing him to see eighteen miles out to sea. The plane was in the air for twenty-five minutes. After landing back at Miller Field, Director Canfield, wearing an aviator's helmet, crawled out of the observer's seat and made this announcement to the press:

> "This is the beginning of the end for the rum fleet…To all appearances, the rum fleet has partly disintegrated. It looks as if they are fearful of the measures that have already been taken. The larger vessels have apparently left for parts unknown, and all we could see were a half-dozen sailboats. These seem to be all that remains of the fleet."[5]

The Philadelphia automobile raiders, who went to Sandy Hook, said they only spotted three schooners and one steamship. A week earlier, there had been a dozen ships outside the three-mile limit. However, many people in New Jersey did not buy the story. Many skeptics believed that the rum fleet was not leaving American waters, but only dispersing. One Prohibition official stated that the fleet split up because it was much more difficult to deal with the liquor ships separately than in fleets.[6]

The skeptics were correct. On May 4, the Coast Guard Cutter *Seneca* was on patrol near Jones inlet when the crew spotted the *Istar*. They observed a large gray seaplane, with no identifying numbers or letters, landing within 150 feet of the *Istar* and exchanging signals with the vessel. The smugglers were now using seaplanes to communicate with the bootleggers on shore. The *Istar* still had 14,000 cases aboard and was not going anywhere until the captain sold the rest of the cargo. The same was true of the *Warszawa*, which had 10,000 cases aboard. Instead of being clustered together, the ships maintained an interval of twelve miles. In reality, the rum fleet had not gone anywhere; the ships merely spread out, forming a 21-mile triangle.[7]

Sales of liquor dropped dramatically, because the operators of the small rum-runners feared capture by federal agents. But eventually, small boat operators devised new tactics to outwit the government boats. The smaller craft were to travel in groups of three to the liquor fleet, but only one was to take on a liquor cargo. The boats would then maneuver to lure the Coast Guard out in pursuit of one of the two that carried no liquor. The smugglers had already tried this plan and succeeded within the first week of the new federal crackdown.[8]

While the federal government tightened its grip on smugglers, the New York State legislature relaxed its grip. Only a few days after the Supreme Court ruling, the New York State legislature repealed the Mullan-Gage Act, which had incorporated provisions of the Prohibition Act into state law. This meant that state and city employees were no longer responsible for enforcing Prohibition. The repeal placed the burden of enforcement on about 250 federal officers, instead of the 25,000 state and local officers within the state.

A few days later, Federal Judge John C. Knox struck down a federal law that limited doctors to prescribing one pint of liquor for a patient every ten days. Since liquor was still legal as "medicine," he ruled, Congress could not restrict how much a doctor prescribed. And of course, doctors could prescribe liquor to treat any number of "ailments," including the effects of a day of manual labor or nervous strain. "Ailing" people, with prescriptions, were able to legally purchase liquor at their local pharmacies.

Rum-smugglers and bootleggers were overjoyed at this legal turn-around. They immediately planned to double or triple their sales in New York City. Liquor sales for the Spring of 1923 far exceeded those for the same period a year earlier. Federal officials told the press that they had every reason to believe that, during the next few months, even greater quantities of liquor would be smuggled in by boat, rail, and automobile. They based their conclusion on the number of ships leaving Nassau and other liquor ports and the increase in vessels planning to come from Europe. The rising demand for boats along the coast was also an indicator.[9]

Courtesy US Coast Guard Headquarters

Part of the "Prohibition navy" in port.

Although business seemed promising for rum smugglers in the Spring of 1923, life aboard the rum vessels could still be harsh. The British yacht *Yankton* carried about 9,000 cases of alcohol from Cuba to Rum Row, where the supercargo, Ernest Corn, had managed to sell off a good portion of the liquor between Miami and Boston.[10] After about three weeks, the *Yankton* pulled up to Montauk Point, where Mr. Corn and the remaining liquor went ashore in a smaller boat. He promised the *Yankton*'s crew that he would return with money and supplies. The ship still had rations for a few days. Those few days went by but Corn had still not returned. The crew went on reduced rations and soon ran out of fuel and water. They wound up stripping the cabin's woodwork to use as fuel. When the men ran completely out of food, they surrendered to Customs agents.[11]

The men said their pay was $30 a month and the captain's $40. At the quarantine station, the staff gave the hungry crew coffee and sandwiches. In between bites, the crewmen swore to never serve on a rum-runner again. The Cuban captain refused to make any statements, since there was no liquor aboard when the ship met up with Customs. The Coast Guard then transported the captain and crew ashore aboard the cutter *Guide*. When they reached the Customs House, agents interrogated them as the Cuban Consul looked on. Customs decided to turn the case over to the Federal District Attorney.[12]

The agents managed to pry a lot of information out of the crew. The *Yankton* had been part of one of the biggest bootlegging rings on the East Coast. The government kept the nineteen crewmembers aboard the ship until they could serve as material witnesses; they would not be defendants. Soon, US Commissioner Hitchcock approved warrants for the arrest of eight key players in the conspiracy, and the Coast Guard went on the hunt for a dozen smaller boats that had transported liquor from the *Yankton* to shore.[13]

The US Attorney's office claimed that the eight men had conspired to smuggle 80,000 gallons of Cuban alcohol into the United States. According to federal officials, the cargo aboard the *Yankton*, costing about $30,000 in Cuba, had a bootleg value in and around New York of about $3,000,000. Four indicted men promised to show up in Federal Court.[14] It turned out that only two of them actually appeared before US Commissioner Hitchcock. Agents arrested the third man in New Haven, Connecticut, and the fourth man had made it to Europe. Deputy US Marshals searched different cities for the other four.[15]

****

On May 23, government officials brought their complaints about the recent Supreme Court ruling to Treasury Secretary Mellon and suggested that the effective date of the new law be postponed. The officials, headed by Assistant Secretary Moss and Commissioner Blair of the Internal Revenue Bureau, had given up hope of writing around the Court's decision, realizing that there was no way to reconcile the conflict between the Prohibition Act and statutes of foreign countries requiring their ships to carry liquor rations for their crews. Although the US Government denied that foreign governments sent protests, the government did acknowledge that foreign capitals were watching the Treasury Department's every move with respect to the three-mile liquor ban.[16]

Three days later, Britain, France, Italy, Spain, and Holland made formal protests to the State Department. Some Treasury Department officials were in favor of regulations which would permit foreign ship owners to place wine rations for the crews under the control of the ship's doctor, who would ration them within American waters. However, Prohibition Commissioner R.A. Haynes was against the idea. He argued that allowing such an exception would be a violation of the Supreme Court decision.[17]

A few days after most of Western Europe protested the new regulations, Japan sent its own complaint to the State Department. Ambassador Hanihara stated that, although Japan had no law requiring liquor to be served as part of a crew's rations, the Treasury's new policy was extreme and would embarrass the Japanese steamship companies by inconveniencing their passengers and crews. The Japanese controlled a large share of the Pacific traffic, with lines running to San Francisco and Seattle and also through the Panama Canal to New Orleans and New York.[18]

Four days after Japan made its official complaint, dispatches from Canada declared that cargoes of Canadian beer and whisky were moving toward the international boundary on their way to New York State, due to the repeal of the Mullan-Gage Act. Canadian officials, stationed along the border, reported that rum-runners planned to flood New York with Dominion "hard stuff." Repeal of the New York State Prohibition law brought new blood and new capital into the business.[19]

A mosquito fleet of thirty to fifty small boats supplied Detroit and its suburbs with the equivalent of 50,000 to 65,000 pint bottles of Canadian beer every 24 hours. Smugglers transported beer across the Detroit River in barrels, kegs, and cases. In addition to the beer smuggled by the miniature rum fleet, there were occasional train shipments. The wealthiest operators on the Canadian side arranged for trains to carry their product through tunnels that ran under the Detroit River. The train cars were consigned to Mexico, but, of course, unloaded in the US. Smugglers estimated that about 19,000 bottles of beer came by train on a daily basis.[20]

National Archives

Rum smugglers make unsuccessful attempt to drive across Lake St. Clair, near Detroit.

In response to the massive flood of liquor into Detroit, Henry Ford, considering a run for the Presidency, had this to say:

> "Turn the Volstead act enforcement over to the army and navy. They haven't anything to do in peace time anyhow, but to go through a few drills and idle their time away cruising or maintaining the social relations at some isolated post. Why not give them something to do for the money we spend on them? Get them busy. Let them have a constructive job and they'll be happy." [21]

When a reporter asked Ford if he thought the Army and Navy could enforce the law, he replied:

> "Sure—absolutely. And they are the only men who can. They would surely put the rum-runners on the blink, too, if we turned the job over to them. Some of us would join the army ourselves to help enforce the liquor law. You would soon see just how popular the Volstead act is if you did that."[22]

A couple of days after Henry Ford made his statement, Coast Guardsmen aboard the speedboat P-103 captured a launch near Detroit, containing 100 cases and 20 kegs of beer. As the P-103 took the launch in tow, ten rum-running boats attacked the government vessel, ramming it twice in an attempt to sink it. The crew of the P-108 fired their shotguns and revolvers to repel the attackers only after their boat began leaking at the bow and stern. Barely afloat, the P-103 made it to port with its prize. After that incident, US District Attorney Earl J. Davis informed State Prohibition Director James R. Davis that Prohibition enforcement agents could use weapons to repel any attack by rum-runners. [23]

****

Meanwhile, the *Istar* and other vessels in the rum fleet off the New Jersey coast decided to take their business elsewhere. Federal agents arrested a man named William E. Burwell in New York. When they interrogated him, he told them he was the "second in command" of the Atlantic Coast rum fleet, which was now near Norfolk, Virginia. He went on to say that his organization controlled the fleet and that he negotiated the sales and delivery of the liquor. His liquor fleet was composed of the *Istar,* the *Cartona,* the *Strand Hill,* and the schooner *Mary Beatrice,* all operating under the British flag.[24] Representatives of the liquor fleet had been in Norfolk for the previous two weeks, making arrangements to move the cargo from the ships to shore and then to Washington, DC. During those two weeks, smugglers managed to get five or six thousand cases of liquor from the rum fleet to the nation's capital. The smugglers' overall plan was to deliver the entire cargo of the rum fleet to DC in time for the Shrine convention in June. The *Istar* alone had 33,000 cases aboard and managed to sell most of it.[25]

The rum smugglers adopted more tricks to evade capture by the Coast Guard. The rum ships sent out false messages by wireless, indicating that the rum fleet was heading for Bermuda. In reality, the ships moved slightly north. The type of men aboard the rum ships was also changing. Norfolk residents who had visited the fleet told federal authorities that what they saw astonished them. One visitor declared that at least one man aboard the *Istar* had held a seat in British Parliament, and that all he had come in contact with "bore evidence of excellent breeding and of wealth."[26]

Coast Guardsmen went out to get a closer look at the *Istar.* By the time they spotted the vessel, the crew had transferred all of its liquor to two other rum ships. The Coast Guardsmen noticed that the *Istar* carried a gun mounted on its aft deck, which they believed to be either a six-pounder or a three-inch rifle. Under international law, yachts were permitted to carry guns for saluting purposes, but those guns were normally one-pounders mounted on the forward deck.[27]

While the liquor fleet was at the mouth of the Chesapeake Bay, sending thousands of cases of liquor to Washington, Prohibition Commissioner Haynes made a statement to the press, asserting that the nation was drying up under Prohibition. He gave out figures to reporters to prove that liquor imports were only one and one-quarter percent of what they had been in 1913. He used figures on the liquor imports of Canada, the West Indies, and the Bahamas. He argued that if those places were importing less liquor, they were also exporting less liquor to the US. Canadian imports dropped to about 59 percent of what they had been in 1913. However, United Kingdom exports to the West Indies and the Bahamas showed an increase from 94,140 gallons in 1913 to 350,311 gallons for the first four months of 1923, or a rate of 1,050,933 gallons per year. The West Indies and Bahamas were importing more than ten times the amount they had ten years earlier![28]

Haynes did not let this painfully obvious figure stand in the way of his argument. He continued:

> "If the entire amount was smuggled into the United States it would equal less than three-fourths of one percent of the tax-paid liquor withdrawals for consumption in the United States for the fiscal year 1913, which amounted to 140,289,424 gallons."[29]

What Haynes omitted was the amount of liquor brought directly from England, France, Italy, Spain, Scotland, and any other country that had liquor and ships. He claimed that the stories of rum-runners delivering large shipments of liquor were fictional and used by bootleggers to sell their goods as "genuine imported stuff." He told the press that the rum fleet off the Virginia Capes had landed little liquor. He claimed that only two lots were ashore, and agents had already seized one and located the other.[30]

On June 10, the day the Supreme Court decision was to go into effect, the Coast Guard revealed its stronger, faster ships. The new fleet, operating off New York and New Jersey, was composed of the *Manhattan*, the *Seneca*, the *Seminole*, and the *Gresham*, plus eight speedboats. The Coast Guard had recently armed all four cutters with batteries of guns ranging from one-pounders to four-inch guns. The scouting work was to be done by the eight speedboats, which were capable of doing thirty knots and geared higher than any of the rum boats. Not only were the fast motorboats able to match the speed of the smugglers' craft, which the 15-knot cutters could not, they were also able to navigate shallow waters. A crew of five manned each speedboat, all of them well-trained in handling weapons. The cutters' crews consisted of about forty men.[31]

USGG Headquarters

Gun aboard the *Seneca*

The little fleet's instructions were to halt every American boat approaching or departing from the liquor fleets along the coast of New Jersey and Long Island. The first signal for a suspected vessel to come about was a single blank shot. If that did not work, the Coast Guardsmen were to use solid shot. The Coast Guard had begun using this method during the previous month and hit two rum ships. They fired at two ships, one British and one French, tearing away the riggings of both. Both of these incidents occurred at night. After the artillery hit each ship, the crews immediately raised anchor and moved rapidly out of range. As of June 10th, the shots had not led to any international complications. The Coast Guard had offered no apologies to the damaged ships, and their captains had not filed any complaints.[32]

As the Coast Guard adopted bolder methods, so did the smugglers. By late June 1923, bootleggers were ordering residents off the eastern beaches of Long Island when it was time to land their cargo. The residents obeyed the bootleggers, because they were aware that the smugglers recruited gunmen from Manhattan and elsewhere to protect their liquor convoys. The first people the smugglers ordered off the beach were residents of Riverhead, who were seeking relief from the heat on a Wednesday evening. (Homes did not have air conditioning yet.) The crew of a luxurious yacht, anchored about 700 feet off Pier Avenue, came ashore in a small boat and told men, women, and children to leave immediately. Some of the families with small children, who had planned to sleep on the beach all night, were upset but left rather than invite trouble.[33]

Before people left the beach, the smugglers aboard the yacht began to unload cases of liquor into small boats, which landed their cargo. Once the liquor was ashore, the smugglers loaded the cases onto trucks, which appeared just at the right time. Once the trucks were loaded, they left, each followed by a car full of armed men. The townspeople of Riverhead were so upset that most women were afraid to remain on the beaches after dark.[34]

Trouble On The Great Lakes

James L. Gordon, the Special Agent in Charge at Buffalo, New York, sent a bleak report of the smuggling activity on the Great Lakes to the Secretary of the Treasury. The Coast Guard did not have any seaworthy boats stationed on either Lake Erie or Ontario. Gordon reported that, during May and June, smuggling had increased at an alarming rate. Canadian laws protected the exportation of liquor from Ontario to the US. As a result, American saloon owners went to the Canadian distilleries and breweries in increasing numbers to purchase thousands of cases of liquor and beer. The owners also chartered vessels which carried the cases to the United States.[35]

In his letter to the Secretary, Gordon humbly asked for one vessel to patrol both lakes, because his agents had no means of pursuing the rum vessels. By his estimate, at least three vessels per day loaded liquor at Toronto and Hamilton and landed the cargo at unprotected spots along the American side of the lakes.[36]

Crackdown In Detroit

In July 1923, federal Prohibition and Customs agents began a crackdown on rum smugglers in Detroit. In one day, the agents seized 200 motorboats off Ecorse, Wyandotte, and Trenton in the down-river district. The agents seized the boats on the grounds that they did not comply with federal navigation laws, i.e. they did not have the required registration, navigation lights, markings, or equipment. They placed Customs seals on the engines, putting the vessels out of commission, towed them to docks along the riverfront, and placed them under guard.[37]

Waterfront lanes in Ecorse, the favorite routes for local rum-runners, were crowded with men who protested the authority of the agents to seize their boats. The officers had to fight off gangs several times. The most serious clash occurred when the agents found beer in a boat well. To prevent the agents from seizing the beer, saboteurs made three attempts to demolish the small wooden bridge leading to the well. A handful of federal agents held the bridge against an attempt to dynamite it and later dispersed a gang, armed with crowbars, who said they had been sent by the property owner to demolish the bridge. The agents also stopped a gang of men that attempted to set fire to the bridge.[38]

The actions of the Treasury agents were meant to make operations for the down-river rum-runners increasingly difficult. The boat owners were required to explain why their craft failed to comply with navigation laws and were warned by the authorities to register them. The Federal Prohibition Director for Michigan, James R. Davis, told the press that Treasury agents planned to run every unregistered boat out of American waters and penalize every vessel that did not show red and green lights at night. Davis also declared that all bootleggers brought into court would be held on $5,000 bail instead of $1,000. He claimed that most bootleggers in Detroit were broke and could not raise that amount of money. He added that he expected to expand his force in Detroit to fifty agents.[39]

****

Around the same time the Treasury agents cracked down on rum-runners in Detroit, another rum fleet appeared off the New Jersey shore. The fleet, comprised of twelve ships, was anchored twelve miles off Ocean City. Some of the ships flew the message, "Come and get it." Captain R.C. Weightman of the Coast Guard Cutter *Kickapoo* reported sighting a British yacht, carrying 4,000 cases of whisky, valued at $200,000, twenty-five miles southeast of Five-Fathom Light. The Coast Guard planned to conduct training maneuvers off Cape May in August, but put those plans on hold with the appearance of the liquor fleet. Competition among the bootleggers was becoming so fierce that they were selling liquor door-to-door, offering Scotch whisky for as little as $50 a case.[40]

Byron L. Reed, commander of the New York/ New Jersey district, ordered his men to use solid shot on any rum-runners that opened fire on Coast Guard vessels. He gave this order in response to a report by James Ahearn, commander of the cutter *Seminole,* just back from a three-day patrol of off the New Jersey coast. Ahearn reported that one of the smugglers they had encountered threatened to "fill them with lead." He also reported that the rum-runners, mostly of British, French, and Norwegian registry, spanned a stretch of thirty-five miles.[41]

One of the vessels off the New Jersey coast was the French rum-runner *Mulhouse,* anchored twelve miles offshore. Coast Guard officer Christopher Benham boarded the ship and asked to see its manifest. The skipper of the *Mulhouse* handed him a blank piece of paper, adding that he would not divulge the nature of his cargo. Benham learned from the crew that the ship was carrying 35,000 cases of liquor. It was obvious that the ship was carrying a heavy load because it was awash amidships.[42]

Several days after Benham paid his visit to the *Mulhouse,* the rum-ship's skipper reciprocated by visiting Benham at the Townend's Inlet Coast Guard Station, 24 miles north of Cape May, NJ. When he reached the station at 2 A.M., he offered Benham $2 a case if he would turn his back and allow the smugglers to land 35,000 cases of liquor on the lonely stretch of sand. The visitor assured Benham that he would be a millionaire in less than a year if he would "get in the game." Benham replied that he would rather be poor all his life than violate his oath as an officer.[43]

At the end of July, the federal government's legal experts reached a decision on the plan to use the Army and Navy for Prohibition enforcement. They were convinced that existing laws were squarely against such a utilization and that the traditions and sentiments of the American people were also opposed to such a practice. Mabel Walker Willebrandt, the Assistant Attorney General, prepared an opinion on the subject, which Attorney General Daugherty planned to present to President Harding as soon as he returned from his speaking tour.

Secretary Weeks and Secretary Denby had already asserted that it was doubtful if a precedent existed for such a use of the Army and Navy. [44]

The legal experts found that one of the earliest opinions on the subject was the declaration of James Madison in *The Federalist*:

> The Constitution does not say a standing army should be called out to execute the laws. The militia ought to be called out to suppress smugglers. Ought this to be denied? If a riot should happen the militia are proper to quell it, to prevent resort to another mode.[45]

The experts also cited a law enacted by Congress during the Civil War banning Army and Navy officers from civilian law enforcement duties. They also cited the Anti-Posse Comitatus Act, which was first contained in the Army Appropriation Act of 1878:

> From and after the passage of this act it shall not be lawful to employ any part of the army of the United States as a posse comitatus or otherwise, for the purpose of executing the laws except in such cases and under such circumstances as such employment of said force may be expressly authorized by the Constitution or by an act of Congress. And any person willfully violating the provision of this section shall be deemed guilty of a misdemeanor and on conviction thereof be punished by fines not exceeding $10,000 or imprisonment not exceeding two years or by both such fine and imprisonment.[46]

It is interesting to note that the 1878 Act does not completely rule out the possibility of using the Army and Navy, but simply states that only the Constitution or Congress could authorize it. By citing the preceding passage, the Justice Department actually shot holes in its own legal argument. Many Prohibitionists argued that, since there were such widespread violations of the 18th Amendment, the use of the Army and Navy was necessary, and Congress had the authority to pass a bill that would assign Prohibition duties to those branches of the military.

While the US Government was wrangling over legal issues on Prohibition enforcement, Secretary of State Hughes was in London trying to strike an agreement with the British. Hughes proposed that Great Britain allow the Americans to search their vessels twelve miles off shore, instead of three. Lord Curzon, of the House of Lords, condemned the proposal. Most people thought Curzon's opposition would immediately kill the proposal; however, the British government diplomatically gave it to an interdepartmental committee, headed by Ronald McNeill, Undersecretary of Foreign Affairs. Shortly thereafter, press dispatches from London reported that the committee's report was also unfavorable.[47]

As the British government shot down the American proposal, one of its citizens, named Sir Broderick Hartwell, circulated a business proposal inviting people to invest in his liquor-exporting business. Hartwell had a distinguished record as a veteran of both the Boer and World Wars. His circular promised a 20 percent profit on all money invested in his whisky exports within a sixty-day period. His advertisement stated that he would ship 5,000 cases of whisky over the following four weeks and 10,000 cases a month after that. Payments for the whisky were guaranteed once the cargo reached a point twenty miles offshore, although he did not specify whose shores.[48]

11

THE PRESIDENT'S UNPLEASANT TRIP

In 1923, Congress and President Harding were not getting along, so he decided to bypass Congress by rallying the support of the American public. He planned to do this by going on a 1,500 mile, two-month speaking tour called the "Voyage of Understanding." On June 20, the President's train left Washington's Union Station as a Navy band played a dance tune. The train was made up of ten cars, the last of which was named the *Superb*. The party of 65 persons on board included 10 Secret Service agents, stenographers, 22 Washington correspondents, five photographers, newsreel cameramen, and several technicians from the telephone company to arrange for the long-distance relaying of the President's messages.[1]

Above all else, Harding promoted the idea of a World Court. The World Court was supposed to work like an international version of the US Supreme Court, where international disputes could be resolved by a panel of judges. After World War I, most Americans wanted nothing to do with foreign affairs. Congress voted against joining the League of Nations a few years earlier and there were too many pressing issues at home for most Americans to be concerned with international law.

One of the President's stops was in Denver, Colorado. He was the central figure in a motor car procession through the heart of the city and its residential section. As Mr. and Mrs. Harding toured ten miles of Denver's streets in an open car, they were greeted by cheering crowds, waving flags and handkerchiefs. When they arrived at Denver's Municipal Auditorium, the audience of 12,000 rose and made the President know he was welcome.[2]

After the applause died down, Harding stood in front of the microphone, which would bring his message to the entire nation. He told the audience that he wanted rigid enforcement of Prohibition. Harding said that the Eighteenth Amendment was here to stay and would never be repealed. He condemned the New York State Legislature and Governor Smith, for the recent repeal of their state Prohibition act. He used the term "nullification" to describe their actions. At the time, the legislatures of Massachusetts, New Jersey, Wisconsin, Illinois, Connecticut, and Rhode Island were considering similar measures.[3] Harding appealed to the individual states to do their part to help the federal government enforce Prohibition and argued that repealing state law enforcement acts would not increase states rights. The audience gave a lukewarm response, but there was enough applause to give the President some encouragement.[4]

After making publicity stops at various points across the nation, the President and his party boarded the refurbished troop transport ship, *Henderson*, for the 1,000-mile voyage to Alaska. The *Henderson*, commanded by Captain Allen Buchanan, carried 21 officers, 460 sailors, 72 Marines, and a Navy band. During the war, the ship had been one of the first to carry American troops to Europe. At one time, the ship had caught fire at sea and been abandoned. For this reason, a few believed that the ship was bad luck.

As the ship departed Tacoma for Alaska, those on shore sang "God Be With You Till We Meet Again" and batteries from the Army post fired a 21-gun salute. As the ship followed the mountainous Canadian coastline, the routine on board was pleasant for Harding and his entourage. The Navy band played three concerts a day with group sing-alongs of popular tunes. In the evenings, Harding and the other guests watched movies in the salon. The President stayed in a room normally reserved for a Marine Colonel; his wife had an adjoining suite. For Secretary Herbert Hoover, however, the trip was a nightmare voyage. He recalled the following details twenty-eight years later:

> As soon as we were aboard ship he [Harding] insisted on playing bridge, beginning every day immediately after breakfast and continuing except for mealtime often until after midnight. There were often only four other bridge players in the party, and we soon set up shifts so that one at a time had some relief. For some reason I developed a distaste for bridge on this journey and never played it again.[5]

While in Alaska, Harding received bad news daily through wireless messages. The price of wheat had dropped to a very low level, which was going to hurt the Midwestern economy. The talk of Henry Ford for President in 1924 was growing stronger. While Harding was eating breakfast at the Curry Hotel at Anchorage, he learned that Magnus Johnson, the immigrant candidate of the Farmer-Labor party, had beaten the Republican candidate by 60,000 votes in the special Minnesota senatorial election. Johnson stood for everything Harding was against: a redistribution of income, public ownership of railroads, the soldier's bonus, a curb on the Supreme Court, and government aid for farmers. He was also against all foreign entanglements, especially Harding's World Court proposal. Johnson's victory was significant because Harding won that state by 360,000 votes three years earlier. The *Boston Herald* concluded in an editorial that the President's overwhelming popularity in 1920 had been wiped out and that he would be defeated for reelection.[6]

As the *Henderson* traveled south along the Alaska coast, a Navy seaplane delivered a long, coded message to the President from Washington. After reading it, Harding almost collapsed. For the rest of the day, he seemed half-stunned, often muttering to himself. He retreated to his stateroom, asking Hoover to join him. When Hoover entered, Harding asked him, "If you knew of a great scandal in our administration, would you for the good of the country and the party expose it publicly or would you bury it?"

"Publish it, and at least get credit for integrity on your side," Hoover answered.

Harding replied that it might be "politically dangerous."[7]

Skeletons In The Closet

When Hoover asked for an explanation, Harding replied that it had to do with some rumors of "irregularities" centering around Jess Smith in connection with cases at the Department of Justice. When Hoover asked for more details, Harding clammed up and never mentioned the topic again. Jess Smith was part of the "Ohio Gang," cronies who Harding rewarded with political appointments. Another member of the "Gang" was US Attorney General Harry Daugherty. Smith had an unofficial position at the Department of Justice, working as a secretary and sidekick of Daugherty. The two men shared a house at 1509 H Street, halfway between the White House and the Department of Justice, and had an "intimate friendship." Daugherty called their house "The Love Nest."[8]

A bootlegger named Bill Orr frequently carried suitcases full of liquor to "The Love Nest." Daugherty and Smith stashed it in an old wall safe in the front room. Smith sold liquor permits to George Remus, known as the "King of Bootleggers." Remus purchased permits for 250,000 cases of liquor from Smith. Remus also made occasional payments of $50,000 to Smith (totaling $250,000 to $300,000), for immunity from prosecution. Smith deposited the money with Gaston Means, a Bureau of Investigation employee, who kept it in an underground safe in his backyard.[9] Despite Remus' frequent bribes, he had been arrested in October 1921. Smith took another large bribe from Remus and assured him that he would go free on appeal. After more than a year of legal proceedings, Remus had gone to prison for two and a half years.

The President had tried to subdue an uncooperative Congress by having Daugherty's Bureau of Investigation agents spy on senators, in an attempt to blackmail or intimidate them. The plan backfired and sparked a Congressional investigation. Gaston Means told the Senate that Jess Smith had given him orders to spy on the Senators. Smith became paranoid, because he had become an enemy of both the King of Bootleggers and a number of US senators. He wound up shooting himself in the head in a hotel room shortly before Harding went on his Voyage of Understanding.

To make matters worse, the First Lady had finally caught the President in an affair with his long-time mistress, Nan Britton. Mrs. Harding had ordered Gaston Means to have his agents spy on Nan Britton, who recently had given birth to the President's daughter. As if this list of scandals was not long enough, members of Harding's "poker Cabinet" were involved in the Teapot Dome oil scandal.

The Voyage Continues

The message Harding received on the *Henderson* could have been related to any of these scandals. However, he destroyed the letter after receiving it. Hoover noticed that Harding became more nervous as the Voyage of Understanding continued. The impressive scenery of Alaska did little to put the President in a better mood. On the way back to the mainland, the *Henderson* collided amidships with the destroyer *Zeilen*. After the first grinding crash, there was the cry of "All hands on deck!" However, the President remained lying on his bed with his face hidden in his hands. When Major Brooks came down to check up on him, Harding asked what had happened. Brooks replied that the ship had been in a collision and that all hands had been ordered on deck. "I hope the boat sinks," Harding said as he lay there, his hands still covering his face.[10]

The following day in Seattle, Harding delivered a speech to a crowd of 60,000. As the hot summer sun beat down on him in the crowded stadium, he seemed confused and his face showed exhaustion and pain. When he spoke about his voyage off the coast of Alaska, he hesitated several times, slurring his words and referring to Alaska as "Nebraska." Halfway through the speech, he dropped his manuscript and held on to the lectern to stop himself from falling. Hoover, who was sitting just behind Harding, picked up the pages from the floor and handed them back to the President. It seemed as if Harding was going to end his speech early, but he did manage to finish after struggling a great deal.

That night, Harding suffered from what Surgeon General Sawyer diagnosed as acute indigestion from crab meat. Harding's doctors told him to rest, and another member of the party, Doctor Joel Boone, told Harding that he was suffering from heart trouble. The President's speaking engagements were cancelled and his train proceeded directly to San Francisco. When he arrived, Harding refused to use a wheelchair and walked very slowly from the train to a nearby limousine. Reporters noted that the President looked "old and worn."

The following night, Harding's temperature rose to 102 and his pulse to 120. He was rapidly developing bronchial pneumonia. The next day, Tuesday, he seemed better, and by Wednesday he was well enough to sit up in bed, eat solid food, and read newspapers. His temperature was back to normal and his pulse rate had dropped below 100. By late Thursday afternoon, Harding felt well enough to return to Washington.

The First Lady had dinner with Daugherty in San Francisco, who was in town but would not visit the President. After dinner, she returned to her husband and read him an article from the *Saturday Evening Post*. The article said that Harding was following a good, steady course as President. Of course he enjoyed the article and asked her to read the whole thing. When she finished, the Duchess (as the First Lady was called) went to her room across the corridor. Harding remained in a half-seated position with his eyes shut, propped up by a couple of pillows. Harding's nurse went for a glass of water to give him with his night medicine. As she exited the bathroom, she saw his face twitch sharply and his mouth drop open. Then, his body slumped and his head fell to his shoulder. The President was dead.

Dr. Sawyer diagnosed the cause of death as a cerebral hemorrhage, but the other doctors disagreed. The Duchess refused to let the doctors perform an autopsy or make a death mask. After some debate, the five doctors signed a bulletin that said the death was due to some "brain evolvement, probably an apoplexy," and also that during the day Harding showed every indication that he was about to recover.[11]

Many Americans believed the theory that Mrs. Harding had poisoned the President. Some of this speculation comes from the fact that the Duchess spent her remaining years living with Dr. Sawyer. After Harding's death, she devoted the next few weeks to sifting through his papers and burning box-loads of letters that she did not want anyone to see.[12]

A Night At Plymouth Notch

The day before Harding died, Calvin Coolidge had been on vacation at his father's house in Plymouth Notch, Vermont. Photographers took pictures of him as he climbed atop a bench, holding a hatchet, and chipping away at a cavity in a tree, so it could be cemented. Coolidge had shed the jacket of his three piece business suit for his tree surgeon work. Mrs. Coolidge was photographed raking leaves. The photo of the two working in the yard appeared in newspapers the following day. After spending the next day doing more chores, Coolidge went to bed early.

The Vice President's hometown only had one telephone, which was located at the general store. After Harding died, one of his secretaries sent a telegram. It took several hours to get through. Telegraphers relayed the message to White River Junction, Vermont, and then to Bridgewater, eight miles from Plymouth Notch. When the telegrapher at Bridgewater received the message, he called the one telephone in Plymoth Notch. The general store was closed, because it was late at night, so no one answered the phone. Wilfred Perkins, the Bridgewater telegrapher, went to a boardinghouse and woke Erwin Geisser, a stenographer, the Vice President's chauffeur Joseph McInerney, and newspaperman William Crawford. Together they went to Plymouth Notch in the Vice President's limousine. Other newspapermen at the Ludlow Hotel received the news and rushed to the Coolidge house.[13]

The Crawford party arrived first and Coolidge's chauffeur knocked on the door. John Coolidge, Calvin's father, woke up first. Since the house did not have electricity, he lit a kerosene lamp and went to see who was knocking at such a late hour. When John Coolidge answered the door, he heard the news and called upstairs to his son. After everyone in the house heard the news, Calvin and his wife returned to the bedroom, where they washed, dressed, and knelt by the bed to pray. Finally, they went downstairs, where Coolidge dictated a message of condolence to Mrs. Harding.[14]

Coolidge received a telegram from Attorney General Daugherty, urging him to take the Presidential oath immediately. Coolidge went across the street to the general store, woke the owner, and used the telephone to call Secretary of State Hughes, who told him that a notary could administer the oath. Conveniently, Coolidge's father was a notary. When he returned home, the family, staff members, and reporters met in the downstairs sitting room.[15]

The Coolidge family home was like many other American homes of the time; it not only lacked electricity and a telephone, the house also had no indoor plumbing or central heating. The "sitting room" was small for a living room (14' x 17') with an eight-foot ceiling. A worn carpet covered the floor, and the light from an oil lamp revealed a wood stove and a rocking chair. In this simple room, John Coolidge swore in his son as President using the family Bible. Paintings and drawings of the scene appeared in all of the nation's newspapers and were replicated and sold by the hundreds of thousands.[16]

The modern Presidency would have been completely alien to Calvin Coolidge. He was the last President to spend hours greeting tourists in the White House lobby. He was the last President to have only one secretary and no other aides. He did not know how to drive a car. He took his first automobile ride when he was 32 and thought that the new contraptions would not amount to much. At his White House office, Coolidge had no phone on his desk. There was a phone booth outside of his office, which he never used.[17]

Coolidge had a reputation for being silent. He told no stories, made no jokes, and rarely laughed. When he shook hands, the shake was brief and businesslike. Warmth and good fellowship were alien qualities to Coolidge. Cartoonists of the 1920s depicted him as a cold, distant man. Most importantly, he only showed half-hearted support for Prohibition.

After Coolidge took office, Andrew Mellon tried to reapply himself to the Prohibition effort. Although he was still opposed to the futile law, he was growing weary of criticism from the "drys" that enforcement was lacking. Mellon reluctantly decided to increase his efforts, especially since it seemed unlikely that the Justice Department would take this burden from him. The Secretary was convinced that the Prohibition Unit was weak from top to bottom, starting with Roy Haynes' poor leadership down to the lowest-ranking agents, whom he viewed as the dregs of the Treasury Department. So Mellon slowly began to reorganize and expand the Prohibition enforcement effort.[18]

12

RUM SMUGGLER TELLS ALL

Rum smugglers and pirates did not stop their business due to a change in administration. Around the same time Harding died, the schooner *J. Scott Hankerson* left Yarmouth, Nova Scotia, loaded with Scotch whisky. The ship's clearance papers indicated that the ship was bound for Nassau, but it went no further south than Massachusetts.[1] While the *Hankerson* sat off the Massachusetts coast, the crew sold large quantities of liquor to smaller rum-running boats.[2]

The short trip was profitable, but the *Hankerson*'s men had entered dangerous waters. Pirates attacked another rum schooner from Yarmouth. That other ship was anchored at sea, having disposed of part of its cargo. A motorboat approached and the schooner's crew, believing that customers had arrived, allowed several men to come aboard. After coming aboard, the men drew their revolvers on the captain and crew, who put up no resistance. The pirates escaped unscathed with $18,000; and the victims sailed back home. The easy success of the pirate raid encouraged the pirates to pay a visit to the *Hankerson*.[3] One of the crewmembers told the press what happened next:

> "The pirates came up to us in a motor boat about five o'clock on Monday afternoon. Our crew, with the exception of the cook, were all on deck at the time. The pirate boat came alongside and two men, the only ones we could see on her then, came aboard and asked for our skipper, Captain Arthur Moore. As the Captain was going down the companionway, one of the strange men shot him in the back. Our skipper yelled to us to come and help. Just as we started aft, seven men who had been hidden on the pirate boat swarmed aboard us. They were armed to the teeth with guns and revolvers. They drove me and my three men toward the forecastle, where we were forced to remain until the pirates were ready to leave the ship."[4]

The crew listened helplessly to revolver shots. Fortunately, the captain also carried a pistol and returned fire. At least one of the pirates clutched a wound as he escaped. When the shooting ceased, the crew rushed up on deck and chased after the pirates as they dropped over the side into their motorboat. The crew found their captain in the cabin with seven bullet wounds in his body. He was seriously wounded in the back, side and arms. The pirates also shot off four of his fingers. The cook also suffered from gunshot wounds.[5] Fortunately, Captain Moore had heard about the other pirate attack and went ashore to put $15,000 in a bank. When the pirates attacked his ship, they only got away with $35.[6] The captain was near death and needed to be taken to a hospital immediately. The cook also needed treatment for his wounds. The *Hankerson*'s crew knew that if they pulled into an American port, Customs officials would seize the ship and arrest everyone aboard; so they sent the two wounded men ashore on a Gloucester fishing boat. When the wounded men and the story of the attack reached shore, the Coast Guard Cutter *Tampa* left Boston immediately to search for the pirates.[7]

The night after the incident, fishermen found an abandoned 35-foot motorboat off Jeffries Bank, which showed signs of a scuttling attempt. Investigators believed that this was the boat of the pirates that attacked the *Hankerson*. Unwittingly, the pirates left the hull number (K12113) intact, which is like leaving the original license plate on a "getaway" car.[8]

Federal agents and Gloucester police found out that one of the trigger-happy pirates was Carl Voss. Within a week of the *Hankerson* incident, the authorities arrested Voss, charged him with attempted murder, and held him on $10,000 bail in the District Court. The agents quickly learned the names of everyone involved in the two attacks. Several of the pirates who lived in Gloucester were smart enough to flee and had been missing since the *Hankerson* attack.[9]

Meanwhile, the Coast Guard was still busy chasing rum-runners off Long Island. Now that the Coast Guard had fast speedboats, smuggling was more difficult. One rum-runner's sides were awash with cases of whisky when federal agents appeared from opposite sides of Jones Inlet. To avoid being captured with liquor, the crew threw the entire cargo overboard. Later that night, when most people were in bed, an armada of wooden boxes drifted onto the beach. A few people, who were up late on that August night, saw the boxes drifting to shore and went to see what was in them. Peering inside, they were delighted to see bottles of Scotch. Like wildfire, word spread throughout the resort, and tired businessmen rushed out of their beds and down to the beach. Residents and visitors, who found one or several of the bottles, showed no desire to help Prohibition enforcement by turning in the contraband.

R.Q. Merrick, New York's Divisional Prohibition Enforcement Director, ruefully admitted to the press that he had no idea what had become of the 200 cases, containing 2,400 bottles of Scotch.[10]

****

Much like the residents of Long Island, the British continued to make a mockery of the Prohibition Act. On August 30, 1923, *The Daily Express* (a British newspaper) hailed Captain Leonard St. John Claire as the ace of whisky traders. Over the previous year, he had sold more Scotch whisky to New York than any other individual. Claire bought his whisky in Nassau, where it cost £5 a case, and sold it to the bootleggers at £8 a case. The American consumer then paid about $10 a bottle for it.[11] Captain Claire gave an interview to the press about his business and said the following:

> "I am not a smuggler. I am a legitimate trader. I sell goods that are in demand, just as you might in Maidstone marketplace, only my marketplace is the high seas. I have made twelve trips from Nassau with whisky during the past year, and I have never been nearer than eighteen miles to the American coast; and, what is more, I have never seen a preventive man.
>
> "There seems to be no limit to the money to be made by bootlegging. One man I worked with bought a ship with borrowed money and in eighteen days made a profit of £12,000 and paid for his ship. A half-caste who began with a small fishing 'hooker' now has a mansion, a yacht, a Rolls-Royce and a schooner for whisky-running. Another man cleared £10,000 in an eight days' out-and-back whisky run.
>
> "Everybody in Nassau is in the whisky business— even priests and police bandsmen. One of the vessels I commanded and took out laden with spirits was formerly the yacht of Henry Ford, who makes cars and is an ardent prohibitionist. He was anxious to know how the yacht was used. Nearly 2,000,000 cases of whisky were run into New York alone during the last twelve months, yet one preventive vessel, if it was alive and wanted to do so, could stop the whole business.
>
> "When the capture of a shore-running boat is to be made, it is always known in advance. I have had men come aboard me and say, 'Well, Captain, I have to be caught today; so I want only a small quantity of stuff over the side.' A

runner, when he is caught, debits his fine against his profits. His boat is put up for sale by the authorities, and he buys it cheaply under another name, because no one else bids against him.

"It is a great country. Whisky runners come aboard me and sample my cargo and bid for it as though I were a floating spirit store. No preventive man dare touch me, for I fly the British flag and keep miles outside the coastal area limit."[12]

Not to be outdone, Sir Broderick Hartwell of London was still openly advertising for investors to put their money into his liquor business. American travelers brought back copies of his circular, promising a 20 percent profit every sixty days from liquor shipments to America. Sir Broderick had been a Lieutenant Colonel in the British Army and at one time the Inspector General of the Constabulary of Jamaica, so he was very well-connected and respected within the empire. R.Q. Merrick described Broderick's plan as the boldest attempt yet to supply liquor to the bootleg trade. Merrick made a complaint to the State Department, which, in turn, made a formal protest to the British government. The British House of Commons discussed the issue but took no action against Sir Broderick.[13]

The British government's refusal to take action against Broderick Hartwell encouraged competition by other British entrepreneurs. Two men from Gravesend, England issued circulars asserting that they were demobilized officers of the British Navy. Their circular promised a 25% profit in 45 days, or 100% within four months without any shadow of illegality.[14]

The good times did not last long, however. Hartwell was no longer his cocky self in April 1925. For the previous few years, he had taunted the Coast Guard and the US Government in several newspaper interviews for their lax enforcement. He gave off an air of infallibility and legitimacy and told reporters that what happened to his liquor once it reached American shores was none of his concern. He argued that he was a "legitimate" businessman who sold his goods on the high seas, where it was perfectly legal, or so he claimed. He even posted advertisements in newspapers promising investors that he would double their money within a few months. What he failed to mention is that it was illegal to unload cargo before it reached the port indicated on its shipping papers.

As the mastermind of a large smuggling syndicate, Hartwell did not go out on rum ships; he coordinated the shipments and took payments at his office in London. In February, he suffered a staggering loss when the Coast Guard captured the *Homestead* and confiscated 12,000 cases of his liquor. Hartwell broke from his office routine in March 1925 and sailed with his seventh and largest shipment to America. The Coast Guard and Customs intercepted most of the liquor cargo as rum-runners made a dash from his ship to the shore. By April, he sent the following cable message to his London offices:

> "Visit discloses appalling situation. Over 30,000 [crates] seized in small vessels. Aranda only just escaped. Balance goods transferred three schooners. At present safe, but cannot reach or communicate.
> "Few thousand unloaded, but resulting funds paid out for chartering vessels. No funds available unless three schooners land goods. At present impossible owing intensive campaign.
> "Returning soonest possible. Communicate to inquirers. With deepest regrets."[15]

This telegram was reprinted in several newspapers, including *The New York Times*. The Treasury Department used the letter and the seizures to make the claim that rum-running on a large scale was a thing of the past. According to one official, reports showed that only minor shipments eluded Prohibition agents and Coast Guard ships.[16] The negative publicity was bad for business. Exports of liquor from England dropped significantly after Hartwell's cablegram reached his London offices. Although Hartwell's associates refused to comment on his message, many in the liquor exporting business viewed shipments to Rum Row as an increasingly risky business.[17]

Several days after Hartwell's dismal telegram, he sent another one giving more details. The Coast Guard seized 32,000 out of his 61,000 cases. He sold 6,000 cases but used the profits to buy coal, food for his crew, etc. As of April 27, he had 23,000 cases available for sale. His newest message stated in part:

> "When we shall be able to dispose of the goods is problematical and the risk of further seizures is, I am told, very great.
> "Unless the balance of the cargo is successfully landed, I personally shall be left absolutely stranded. Of course, it is obvious a big loss of capital is inevitable and that

every contributor has the right to sue me for non-fulfillment of my guarantee.

"I can only repeat that owing to the disasters I have detailed I lost everything and any such action would only have the result of hampering my endeavors to save something for my contributors from the wreck, and I am the only person who can do so under the circumstances."[18]

By the end of the year, Sir Broderick still had not recovered from his losses. On December 30, 1925, his creditors estimated that he owed $1,250,000. Since the rum-running nobleman had not made any offers to pay off his debts, his British creditors passed a resolution that he be declared bankrupt and that a trustee should be appointed to handle his affairs. Coast Guard and Prohibition officials were ecstatic at the news of Sir Broderick's financial downfall and they took credit for putting him into bankruptcy.[19]

****

Before President Harding had gone on his trip in late June, he asked Daugherty's opinion on using the Navy and Army to enforce Prohibition. Attorney General Daugherty, who bought liquor from bootleggers and issued thousands of illegal liquor permits to George Remus, finally formed his legal opinion, three months after Harding's request. By that point, however, Daugherty's opinion was not worth much to Harding; he had been dead for a month and a half! According to Daugherty, the President had no authority to use the Navy or the Army to enforce Prohibition without authorization from Congress. Congress could not approve such a measure unless an emergency existed, and in Daugherty's opinion there was none.[20] He released this opinion around the same time the US Department of Commerce reported that smugglers had brought $20,000,000 worth of liquor into the US during the previous year.[21]

The Attorney General, for those who do not know much about the position, is the chief legal officer of the US Government. The Attorney General's duties are to advise the Executive branch on legal questions, represent the government in legal controversies, appear personally in court in important cases, and supervise the prosecution of criminal cases. The Attorney General also heads the Department of Justice and supervises its administration, directs special matters relating to national defense, oversees federal penitentiaries, supervises US

Attorneys and US Marshals, and approves abstracts for lands acquired by the government for civil and military uses. The Attorney General is not a judge and his legal opinions are just that— opinions. His legal opinions may be taken very seriously because of his powerful position, but his opinions do not equal a decision by the judicial branch of the government. A President can choose whether or not to follow the Attorney General's legal advice.

Calvin Coolidge, not greatly excited about Prohibition to begin with, announced that he accepted the "ruling" of Attorney General Daugherty as final; he would not use the US armed forces to suppress liquor traffic. The White House also informed the press that the President did not even intend to ask Congress to give him the authority to use the Navy and Army. Despite his current stance, according to a White House spokesman, Coolidge could visualize that a time may come when it would be desirable to use naval vessels to prevent smuggling; however, Coolidge did not want to put an additional burden on the federal government.[22]

Over-tasked Coast Guardsmen began to grow weary of Prohibition enforcement. In October 1923, forty Coast Guardsmen deserted the Fifth District, which extended from Sandy Hook to Cape May. The defections were due to low pay and the dangers of guarding the coast against smugglers. Surfmen received $60 a month and $30 for subsistence. One Captain told *The New York Times* that:

> "When the men entered the service, they were hired to save lives and property from the ships in trouble along the coast, but now they want us to stop rum-runners, who if they are caught do not hesitate to take a shot at you with a high-powered rifle."[23]

In late November, Coolidge recommended that Congress appropriate $20,000,000 for specially-designed Coast Guard craft plus another $8,500,000 for maintenance and wages. These figures were based on a plan that the Treasury Department put together, which included increasing the number of officers from 209 to 353; warrant officers from 396 to 716; and enlisted men from 4,051 to 7,122. The Treasury's plan called for twenty cruising cutters, to cost about $11,000,000; 200 cabin cruising motorboats, costing $7,650,000, and 100 small speed boats, costing about $1,000,000. Most of these vessels were to be stationed on the East Coast and the Gulf of Mexico.[24]

13

THE REAL McCOY

The expression "the real McCoy" comes from a rum-runner in the 1920s named William McCoy. McCoy's imported liquor had a reputation for quality, which was becoming increasingly rare as bootleggers diluted their liquor, or in many cases sold American liquor with foreign labels to get a higher price. Instructions had been broadcast from Florida to Maine to watch out for him, because federal officials regarded him as one of the chief factors in the flooding of New Jersey and Long Island with West Indian liquor. McCoy was also under indictment in Federal Court. Howard Estabrook, special agent of the Treasury Department in New York, had been on the lookout for McCoy for five months. Estabrook found out that McCoy's ship was named the *Tomaka* (formerly the rum ship *Arethusa*) and that the vessel was lying off Seabright. He contacted the Coast Guard and the men of the cutter *Seneca* went searching for the "real McCoy."[1]

The *Seneca*'s crew spotted the *Tomaka*, which was sitting at anchor, and radioed the *Lexington* for support. The *Lexington* was about half an hour away; however, the Customs agents aboard the *Seneca* did not want to wait that long. The *Tomaka* was outside the three-mile limit. However, that did not stop the Coast Guard and Customs from searching the vessel. When the agents boarded the *Tomaka* under the direction of Special Agent Lynch, they wound up in a big fistfight with the smugglers, resulting in some black eyes and a few bloody noses. The Customs agents withdrew and reported the incident to Lieutenant Commander Perkins of the *Seneca*.[2]

The *Tomaka*'s crew raised anchor and the ship turned to head out to sea. The *Seneca* followed and the *Lexington* maneuvered into position to give support. Lt. Commander Perkins used a megaphone to warn the smugglers that he would fire upon them if they did not stop. Captain Downey of the *Tomaka* ignored the warning and his ship moved on. The *Seneca*'s three-pound guns fired two shots across the *Tomaka's* bow. The *Tomaka*'s crew returned fire with a machine gun mounted on the forward deck. However, the machine gunners ran for cover when the shells came close enough to spray water on the deck.³ Perkins then yelled through his megaphone, "If you don't heave to, we'll blow you to hell." Captain Downey finally surrendered and brought his vessel around.

Aboard the US Coast Guard Cutter *Seneca*

This time, a much larger crew of Customs and Coast Guardsmen boarded the *Tomaka*. As the agents boarded the schooner, the *Tomaka's* crew disassembled a machine gun and threw it overboard. They tried to do the same with a second machine gun but ran out of time. The ship's papers showed that the *Tomaka* had taken on a load of 4,200 cases of whisky in Nassau; however, after the agents arrested the crew, they only found 200 cases aboard. Before the crew loaded the whisky at Nassau, Treasury agents had secretly marked each case to keep track of the liquor. The agents were pleased to see that all 200 of the cases had the secret Treasury markings, which indicated that the *Tomaka* likely had not stopped at another port to replenish its supply.⁴

The Customs agents found William McCoy hiding under a bunk in the cabin. When they searched him, they found $60,000 in one of his trouser pockets. In addition to McCoy, the agents arrested Captain George Downey and seven crewmembers, who each carried $1,000 to $2,000. On top of that, the agents found another $30,000 stashed away in a small safe. The Coast Guard towed the ship, liquor, cash, and prisoners to the Barge Office pier at the Battery in Manhattan. All nine prisoners, under heavy guard, were kept in a special room to await questioning by Edward H. Barnes, Assistant Solicitor of the port. McCoy, who had been hiding under a bunk a few hours earlier, was now bold and defiant. He admitted that all of the cash aboard the ship was from liquor sales, but argued that he sold all of it outside the three-mile limit, making the transactions legal.[5]

By seizing a vessel outside the three-mile limit, the Coast Guard and Customs were treading on thin ice. The British Embassy and the US State Department both denied that there was any kind of agreement about seizures outside the three-mile limit. Prohibition Commissioner Roy A. Haynes said that he did not know of any order issued from Washington for the seizure of the vessel. Coast Guard officials told the press that they had received no general order in regard to seizures. One Coast Guard official stated that the *Tomaka* was seized because there was evidence that the schooner had contraband liquor aboard and had contact with the shore by means of its own smaller boats. He argued that such a seizure would be legal. Because of possible international complications, most government officials were very guarded in their comments to the press.[6]

The very next day, *The New York Times* printed an article saying that the Treasury Department ordered the seizure after agents found evidence that the *Tomaka* had been in contact with the shore. Coast Guard records also showed that the vessel had fired repeatedly on Coast Guard cutters. McCoy was arraigned in three Federal jurisdictions. When McCoy appeared at the hearing before the Assistant Solicitor, he said:

> "I have no tale of woe to tell you. I was outside the three-mile limit, selling whisky, and good whisky, to anyone and everyone who would buy. Up until three years ago, I lived with my parents in Daytona, Fla., and I built high-class yachts. I built one for Frederick Vanderbilt and another for Maxine Eliot. Then in 1921 my parents died. Shortly after this my bulldog died. That was the last tie to my affections in Daytona, so I decided to go out to sea.
>
> "I bought a yacht of British registry, stocked her with booze at Nassau, put the liquor under seal and brought her to various American ports. The most profitable port was New York. I would dock at this port, then go up Broadway and scout for pleasure parties desiring to take a little excursion trip. I later formed the British Transportation Company, Inc., with headquarters at Daytona. I bought two yachts, put them

under charter to various parties, specifying that they stay outside the twelve-mile limit if they intended to peddle liquor. The *Henry Marshall*, sister ship of the *Tomaka,* was manned by a crew and officer with little discipline, who ran liquor off Atlantic City. Owing to the fact that there was little discipline aboard, these men were arrested in a drunken condition at Atlantic City and I as owner of the yacht was indicted for conspiracy.

"I think I should have surrendered then, but, having heard weird tales of the treatment accorded bootleggers, I stayed away from prohibition authorities. The captain of the *Henry Marshall* was a cheater and, after his arrest, I decided to go into business for myself.

"It was from the Ocean Trading Company of Halifax that I bought the *Tomaka.* I put her under British registry and manned her with a British captain, mate, engineer and four sailors. I ran the vessel for a year outside of the three-mile limit selling liquor only of a high quality and giving every one a square deal."[7]

After meeting with representatives of the Collector of Internal Revenue, Assistant Solicitor Barnes ordered $68,000 of the confiscated money to be returned to McCoy. The government gave the money back to him in a large burlap sack. The British Vice Consul Leonard Parrish was present at the hearing, but refused to comment on the case, explaining that he would follow the preliminary investigation and report to the British Consul General. A cable from London showed that the British government was still waiting for an official report.[8]

Although federal officials knew that the Coast Guard had seized the *Tomaka* six miles off the coast, the US Government was still confident of its position. The Department of Justice had voluminous records on the ship from the time it first entered the liquor trade as the *Arethusa.* McCoy's bail was $15,000, which he could have pulled out of his burlap sack and handed to the court, leaving him a substantial amount to live on for a few years. One of the federal courts ordered that McCoy's crew be held without bail as material witnesses. The US prosecutors argued that the *Tomaka* violated the "hovering statutes," the American Tariff Act, and Customs laws.[9]

The *Tomaka* seizure caused some worry along Rum Row. Several of the rum vessels moved a few miles farther from the shore. Smugglers closely followed the newspaper accounts of the negotiations between the United States and Britain on an extension of the three-mile limit. Rum-runners were not too concerned about traveling a few extra miles; they were used to conducting business twelve to fifteen miles off the coast. Also, the smugglers had better, faster boats in 1923 than they did a year earlier.[10]

The year 1924 began with the British and American governments fighting over whether the schooner *Tomoka* was registered as a British or Canadian ship. William McCoy had good luck in one of his federal court appearances. US Commissioner Hitchcock discharged McCoy and eight members of his crew from any further proceedings on a charge of having landed liquor on the New Jersey Coast. The defendants were then arraigned before Federal Judge Hand, who increased their bail from $5,000 to $7,500 at the request of Assistant District Attorney John Holley Clark. Clark explained that the authorities in New Jersey wanted the defendants so they could answer a charge of contempt of court for failure to answer questions in admiralty proceedings against the *Tomoka*. The bail amount was literally pocket change for McCoy.[11]

The eight sailors refused to cooperate after being called to testify in forfeiture proceedings. The defense argued that their testimony might tend to incriminate them, despite the fact that they might have testified with immunity under Section 30 of the Prohibition Act. When they refused to testify, Judge Hand held them in contempt and they appealed their case to the US Circuit Court of Appeals. A month later, the US Circuit Court of Appeals upheld Judge Hand's decision.[12]

14

MERRY CHRISTMAS!

In December 1923, Attorney General Daugherty delivered his annual report to Congress. His report showed that a large part of the Justice Department's work was related to the Prohibition Act. Mabel Walker Willebrandt, the Assistant Attorney General in charge of Prohibition cases, reported a steady increase in the number of cases brought to court. From June 30, 1922 to June 30, 1923, the Justice Department had prosecuted 49,021 criminal cases, plus 4,109 civil cases relating to alcohol; the number had increased by 15,889 over the previous year. The federal courts could not keep up with the increase and had to appoint additional judges to relieve the congestion in court.[1]

Daugherty could only give a partial estimate of the amount of liquor smuggled during the year. However, he provided figures from official data at Nassau, Bahamas and Glasgow, Scotland to give some idea of the magnitude of the smuggling. Nassau ships alone had carried 1,300,000 gallons of alcohol to the US and ships that left from Glasgow had carried 147,915 gallons to American waters. Keep in mind that these figures came from only two ports and cover a small fraction of the liquor smuggled into the country. Daugherty's figures also omit alcohol smuggled by land from Canada and Mexico.[2]

In December, the battle between rum-runners and enforcement agents was on. The Prohibition blockade attempted to cover land, sea, and air routes. Ships heavily laden with alcohol reinforced rum fleets anchored off Long Island and New Jersey. To the North, a mild December and the absence of snow permitted fleets of motor vehicles, full of liquor, to drive across Canada's open border. In Pennsylvania, where there were wide open saloons in several large cities, the product was mainly domestic and consisted of beer carted out from breweries careless of their federal licenses to brew "near-beer." West of Pennsylvania, in Cleveland, Toledo, Milwaukee and Chicago, those who planned on celebrating the holidays with liquid holiday cheer relied on the Great Lakes' smugglers for their supply. In Baltimore and Washington, DC, rum-runners were active on the Potomac River and in Chesapeake Bay, where fleets of small motorboats darted out to foreign ships anchored off the Virginia Capes. In addition, bootleggers on land were smuggling moonshine distilled all over the South.[3]

From Nassau, Cuba, and the West Indies rum-runners were attempting to sneak by the scattered Coast Guard vessels on the Florida and Gulf coasts. On the Mexican border, there were 1,500 miles of sparsely settled border in between the cities of Brownsville, El Paso, Nogales, and San Diego. Across those largely unguarded areas, smugglers were transporting European liquor as well as Mexican brandy, tequila, and Chihuahua beer. On the West coast, the Pacific smugglers drew upon the legally wet territories of Mexico.[4]

Photo and Caption Courtesy US Coast Guard Headquarters

"THE WEAPONS TO MAKE THE OCEAN DRY: SQUADRON OF CAPITAL SHIPS OF THE DRY FLEET, Anchored Off Atlantic City To Stop The Flow Of Illegal Cheer At Christmas."

Off the New Jersey coast, the ships of Rum Row were trying desperately to land thousands of cases of liquor before Christmas. In addition to Coast Guard vessels, the New Jersey State Police were stepping up patrols on land, especially where the smaller boats could make their landings. "Bottle fishermen" paid a Great War aviator, named "Monte," $150 a trip to fly along the Row three times a week. He charted the locations of the mother ships for the benefit of the small craft, which otherwise might not have found the large ships at night. As of December 10, Monte reported that there were sixteen ships off the New Jersey coast and another six off Fire Island, New York.[5] Assistant Attorney General Willebrandt read about the large rum fleet in *The Washington Post* and wrote a letter to Treasury Secretary Mellon urging him to do more to stop it.[6]

Meanwhile, a squadron of New Jersey State Troopers, equipped with a fleet of fast patrol cars, patrolled about 150 miles of highways and byways near the secret liquor landing points on the ocean front. Within a 24-hour period, the troopers seized six trucks and automobiles and about 400 cases of whisky. The troopers' first stop was at a landing in Keyport.[7]

The tiny harbor was dark and quiet. A gray shadow rode at anchor 100 yards offshore. A bright light flashed from the shadow and disappeared. Five minutes later, another flash came from the same location. Then, an even brighter flash came in response from a deserted building ashore. The floating shadow was a spotter boat signaling that all was safe in the harbor, and the watchman in the building was signaling that all was right ashore. The roar of a powerful engine followed these signals and, in a few moments, a boat with no lights headed to the landing. A crew of men sprang from the shadows to meet the boat. The crew silently unloaded the cargo, piling all thirty cases on the dock. The little craft sped away before the state troopers could reach them. However, the officers did manage to seize the liquor and an automobile with a New York license plate, which the smugglers were loading with liquor after it appeared by the wharf.[8]

The troopers went from wharf to wharf, searching inlets, creeks, basins and bays. They waited for hours, sometimes in an abandoned warehouse, or hidden by swamp grass and driftwood, or other times on the bare sands. The mysterious light signals from sea to land and back again were constant. At a shipyard in Keyport, an old woman answered the sea signals by turning the lights on and off in the window of a two story bungalow. Her ship finally came in. But, the 48-foot speedboat had engine trouble, which caused a delay. About twenty or more youths in army shirts and sea boots hid their automobiles, waiting in an uptown lunch room until the cargo landed. They were supposed to transport the booze to Trenton and Newark, but the troopers got several of them before the night was over.[9]

In mid-December the ships of Rum Row were stretched out over a distance of 25 miles near the New Jersey coast. Because competition was so fierce and there was so much cargo to unload, the rum ships engaged in a price-cutting war. Instead of buying from the most convenient ship and paying standardized prices, the customers went from ship to ship looking for the best deal. There was only one Coast Guard cutter patrolling Rum Row at the time, and it took two hours to go from one end to the other, so the shoppers simply had to time their purchases right to avoid getting caught.[10]

ALCOHOL, BOAT CHASES, AND SHOOTOUTS!

The main obstacle to liquor sales was actually rough seas, a particularly common problem in the winter. On December 14, a gale and heavy seas forced most of the liquor fleet off New Jersey and New York to weigh anchor and head further out into the ocean. No rum-runners dared to venture out on the rough seas that day.[11] However, as soon as the weather cleared up the next day, all 18 ships headed back to their old positions. Before noon, the lone Coast Guard cutter patrolling the area turned eastward and headed for a point opposite Jones Inlet. The rum-runners hailed the departure of the cutter as the signal for a dash to the liquor fleet. Along the shore, owners of small boats started their engines and emerged at the same time, as if in a race. On the shore, observers with looking glasses counted eighteen speedboats, which hurried out to Rum Row. The speedboats drew alongside the liquor ships, whose decks were unusually busy. The crewmembers loaded the smaller boats without delay; however, the speedboats had to wait for nightfall before returning to the shore.[12]

In response to the anticipated liquor rush, Sheriff Joseph Holman of Ocean County, New Jersey, had deputized fifty men to stop smugglers to the south of Toms River. Sheriff Holman had a difficult time finding enough men willing to work as deputy sheriffs in the bootleg war. Most people considered the duty too dangerous.[13]

A newspaper reporter named James C. Young went out to witness the Christmas rum fleet himself. The number of rum ships off the New Jersey coast increased from eighteen to twenty-five almost overnight. Some of the ships carried over a million dollars in cargo. Captain Blunt of the sloop *Bessie Smith* told Young that it would not be much trouble to get aboard a rum-runner and learn how things were done. Of course, the captain pointed out, a man must first be willing to take his chances. Young asked the captain what those chances might be. The captain replied that there was always the risk of getting shot, disappearing, or drowning in rough seas. A few days earlier, a small boat had gone out with two men. The two men later returned to shore as floating corpses, after they drowned, accompanied by twenty cases of liquor.[14]

James C. Young was a daring reporter, so he decided to visit the rum fleet in spite of the captain's warning. Young and Captain Blunt agreed to a start time for their trip. At the designated hour, the four men (Captain Blunt, Eddie the engineer, Johnson the young cameraman, and James Young) met at the boat's dock in Shrewsbury, New Jersey. The boat was built for adventure, a five-ton sloop with a long bowsprit and a weather-beaten look. Captain Blunt inspected the boat with a sailor's eye, while Eddie went below to start the engine. The engine was as worn as the rest of the schooner, so starting it required some coaxing. Eventually, the engine did start and the boat headed down the Shrewsbury River to the sea.[15]

It was a gray morning with low clouds that seemed to merge with the water in the distance. Captain Blunt, however, seemed certain that it would not rain. The Shrewsbury River was an interesting place for anyone curious about rum-runners. Any river pilot could point out the bootleggers' headquarters in a certain hotel, and a little further on a fleet of speedboats were tied to a convenient dock. Nearby, there was the yard where builders assembled the boats, capable of thirty miles an hour even with fifty cases aboard.[16]

As the *Bessie Smith* made its way into the bay, Captain Blunt described the contest between the smugglers and the Coast Guard as a game that required wit and daring. The captain believed that the smugglers had the advantage, but admitted that the Coast Guard made the "game" more difficult. Eddie, who was standing at the wheel, shook his head as he listened to the discussion. Eddie did not like the Coast Guard and had little use for them. His face had a three-day stubble of black and gray, his skin was like leather, and he had a penetrating eye. He was just the sort of man who would bring the whole rum fleet up the bay and tell the Coast Guard and Customs to go to hell.[17]

As the schooner passed Sandy Hook, the men saw the Coast Guard station that caused the most trouble for smugglers. It was a trim establishment with a look of discipline and efficiency. Eddie did not care for it and used the language of a sailor to express his disapproval. As the *Bessie Smith* got closer to the rum ships, the schooner began to pass empty whisky cases, bearing Scotland's best-known names, floating in the water. The four men began to place nickel bets on what brand case would show up next. James Young's brand, White Horse, appeared so often that all bets were soon off.

Eddie frequently looked through his binoculars. "There's a rum-runner ahead," he said. The other men looked into the distant gray without seeing anything. It took a few minutes for them to spot the smudge on the horizon. As the *Bessie Smith* kept chugging along, the distant dot began to look more like a ship. Eddie then spotted another rum-runner, a schooner this time, a few points to starboard. Farther out, there was yet another.[18]

"What's that?" the captain asked while pointing. It was a white ship moving across the horizon. The captain looked through his glasses and saw that it was a Coast Guard cutter. "Young fellow, I wouldn't go aboard no rum boat with that cutter lying around," said the captain.[19]

"But they can't bother a peaceable American citizen for paying a friendly call to a peaceable British citizen; can they?" replied the reporter.

"You don't know what they are likely to do," said the captain, "brass buttons make a man mighty proud."

This was not reassuring to the reporter and cameraman. They had momentary apprehensions about being shot or thrown overboard, but did not think about the risk of getting arrested. As the *Bessie Smith* got closer to the first rum vessel, the men saw that it was a dirty old ship. It was riding high at both ends, so the two newsmen said that it must be almost out of liquor. Eddie replied that liquor does not weigh as much as gold and that one could not tell if a ship is sold out. The captain and Eddie brought the small boat alongside the rum ship. The men aboard the ship stood by the rail and stared down at the *Bessie Smith*'s motley crew. The rum ship's crew looked like an ordinary lot of sailors. The captain was a fat, red-faced man, wearing a blue shirt without any collar and a makeshift blue uniform. He looked like an elevator man in a second-rate office building, but he waved in a friendly manner and answered the hail of Captain Blunt.[20]

"Better sheer off and come back in ten minutes; that blarsted cutter is waiting."

"How much for Scotch?" asked someone aboard the *Bessie Smith*.

"Twenty-three dollars a case, and all you want," replied the fat captain.

The men aboard the *Bessie Smith* discussed what they were going to do next. The captain was dead against boarding any rum-runner with the Coast Guard cutter nearby. Eddie made the suggestion that they continue on to the next schooner. As they approached the next schooner, Eddie pointed out the whisky piled on deck, stacked chest-high, and covered in straw wrappers. The schooner's captain was a big man, six-foot-two, with a wind-and-sun burned face. He was leaning over a rail as the *Bessie Smith* came alongside.

"Can we come aboard?"

"That's your risk; the cutter is waiting," replied the captain.[21]

The four men aboard the smaller boat again discussed what they were going to do next and agreed to move on to the next schooner. By this time, they were twenty miles out, daylight was running out, and dark clouds indicated heavy rain. The men saw ten rum ships scattered around them and the common report indicated that there were ten more. As they approached the next schooner, the men aboard the *Bessie Smith* dropped a dory over the side. James Young, Eddie, and Johnson jumped into it and shoved off. The men were tossed around on the heaving sea, while Eddie rowed the tiny craft over to the nearby rum ship.

When the men were alongside the ship, named the *Sea Witch,* its crew peered down at them, without even waving a hand in greeting. The *Sea Witch* was a new eighty-ton schooner, freshly painted shiny black, with a white rail. The vessel had eight men on deck, about half of them Scandinavian and the others Canadian.

The three men in the dory climbed a rope up the side of the *Sea Witch,* one at a time, as the ocean tossed their tiny boat around. Once aboard, the *Sea Witch*'s crew continued to scrutinize the three men closely. The reporter and photographer did not look like their usual customers. In turn, the two men thought about this as they remembered all the stories they had heard of men who never came back from the rum fleet.[22]

The supercargo was a whale of a man from the East Side of New York City. The reporter told him that a certain New York club was running short on Christmas liquor and needed to be resupplied. Fortunately, the supercargo bought the story. The men then discussed what liquors the *Sea Witch* had in stock and haggled over the price per case. Thirty dollars was too high, the men of the *Bessie Smith* argued, because they already had a quote of twenty-three dollars from another ship. The supercargo told them that he would have to ask the skipper and went forward.

The skipper was even bigger than the supercargo, by about fifty pounds. He did not like the looks of the three customers. He asked them where they came from and why and how soon they planned to go back. However, all of the questioning did not change their story. The men managed to haggle a price of $25 per case for one hundred cases. James C. Young complimented the skipper's ship, and he let his guard down, almost smiling. Soon they were discussing all the complexities and phases of rum-running. The captain invited them below, which was very unusual. As the men went down the cabin stairs into the lair of the rum-runner, the supercargo gave them a surprised look because customers rarely went there. The captain's quarters were very comfortable. The cabin was equipped with easy chairs and a table. The men drew up to the table and got down to business.

"How much liquor do you really want?" the skipper asked.

"Well, we might take a hundred cases off tonight if that cutter doesn't get us."

"Oh, the cutter. She can't see what's going on after dark. But why don't you take it for now and get a flying start at dusk?" [23]

The men told the skipper that the *Bessie Smith* was not built for flying starts. He in turn asked them why they would be willing to risk a hundred cases of good liquor in a slow, old boat. This led the men to confess that they were new to the smuggling trade.

"I thought so," answered the captain. "By the way, you must be a little cold after your trip. Have a bite— and something to drink." He did not wait for a reply. "John," he called, and a cabin boy came in, "bring us a bite and— what'll you have?"

"Oh, anything you say, Captain; whatever you are drinking."

"Two cups of tea, John."[24]

There was a painful pause and the skipper finally smiled. "Maybe you would prefer something else," he said, "I only drink tea myself. Never touch anything stronger."

The men were baffled that a rum-runner drank tea and they asked him why.

"Oh, I couldn't take chances," he explained, "and besides, I don't care for it. I'm here on business, you know, and there is no rum-drinking on this ship. If anybody wants to drink they can go ashore and get it. I won't have it aboard." The captain's sandwiches were excellent and so was his hospitality. He gave the men some of his insight into rum-running:

> "This is a game just like any other," he said. "There is big money in it and we are taking the risks. But business is pretty dull now. These cutters [of the Coast Guard] scare away chance customers. Only the professionals will take the chance. You are the first man I have had aboard today. Tonight we will fill a dozen boats and I look for a big holiday trade. Five thousand cases aboard now, and I hope to sell out in time for another trip to the Bahamas before Christmas.
>
> "Trouble getting it?" he continued, "None whatever. It is coming over from England by every ship. Why not? If your country passes foolish laws that its citizens do not respect, why shouldn't we have the benefit? There is nothing criminal about rum-running, as I see it; just a game between us and your revenue men. I wouldn't be mixed up in this business if it was crooked. I am not that sort of a man; always been on the level and kept my word. There is no funny business on this

ship. Now, you, I fancy, have a big sum of money in your pocket. Well, it is safe. You can leave it there on the table and come around for it next week, if you like. It will be right there."[25]

The three men looked at the captain and believed him, but asked about certain intimidating men on deck. The captain replied that he needed to be prepared for trouble.
"Do you have much of it?" the reporter asked.
"Well, there is more of it in the newspapers than anywhere else," emphasizing "newspapers" quite strongly. The men were about to tell the captain the truth when the supercargo came down.
"If you fellows want that whisky, you had better take it and beat it, because we have some other boats coming out soon." The men broke up their interview and made their escape, pleading that the Coast Guard cutter could turn up. The men climbed into the dory and made their way to the *Bessie Smith*. Once aboard, the men traveled twenty miles back to shore and past a Coast Guard station without seeing a single Coast Guard cutter on patrol.

****

New speed boats, equipped with airplane engines, landed $250,000 worth of liquor on the night of December 23, near Atlantic City. Scores of small boats carried the liquor to secret caches for temporary storage, as it was impossible to get enough autos over the dangerously slippery roads for immediate distribution. The smugglers timed their operations with a heavy rainstorm and mist that provided low visibility seaward in the early evening. They moved back and forth without any detection by Coast Guard vessels. There were some accidents, however. In their rush to land the liquor, the swiftly moving boats, without lights, sometimes collided with each other.[26]
According to members of Atlantic City's liquor ring, the cargoes brought in on that one night contained enough liquor for all of the holiday trade and well beyond the New Year. The new speedboats, which the smugglers used to transport the liquor, could reach fifty miles per hour. The operators purchased them from the larger ships of the rum fleet. Each boat was equipped with an airplane engine, ranging from 400 to 600 horsepower. Captain Creese of the Cold Spring station at Cape May said the new boats would make the Coast Guard vessels look like "a race between a thoroughbred horse and a crippled old nag."[27]

Another Conspiracy?

While patrolling on a Sunday night off Fire Island, the Coast Guard Cutter *Seminole* came across a thirty-ton motorboat, numbered 7909, with six men aboard. Two bright lights, which burned fore and aft, caught the attention of Philip Scott, commander of the *Seminole*. The men made no effort to escape, and one of them said that the engine was disabled and they needed assistance. Federal agents went aboard the craft and searched for liquor. After they failed to find any, the agents went through the pockets of the six men. One of the men was Robert Graham Fothergill, an Englishman living at the Waldorf Hotel under the name Graham. Fothergill had $46,356 on him and a memoranda book listing the names of men in all parts of the country. The agents believed that the names in the book were those of bootleggers. Fothergill asserted that his predicament was all a mistake and he could prove himself innocent. The agents arrested the men, and the Coast Guard transported them to the Barge Office, where they were charged with conspiring to violate the Volstead Act.[28]

When Fothergill stood before M.P. Andrews, solicitor to the Collector of the Port, he admitted that his full name was Robert Graham Fothergill of London, owner of the steamer *Wrack*, which had sailed from Nassau over a month earlier. He also said that the *Wrack* was under lease and might have been loaded with liquor— "a member of the fleet of seventeen rum-runners in Rum Row," he stated. Fothergill was paroled for a further hearing later in the week. Customs indicated that they believed all six men aboard had been in touch with the liquor fleet and that Fothergill collected the $46,356 from the sale of the *Wrack's* cargo. The charge against the crew of "going foreign," in that the motorboat was outside of the twelve-mile limit, was withdrawn. The *Seminole's* commander acknowledged that the disabled craft could have drifted out that far.

For those readers not familiar with the Waldorf-Astoria Hotel, it was (and still is) a very luxurious and expensive hotel, in New York. When reporters interviewed Fothergill in his room at the hotel, he said:

> "It's all a mistake. There was no intention to violate any law. It was not to have been anything but a little pleasure jaunt. Our boat was loaded with passengers, all friends, and we were not engaged in smuggling operations of any description. If I had been out to buy liquor, I don't think it would have been necessary to carry any such sum as $46,000.

As a matter of fact, from what I hear I think one-eighth of that amount would have bought enough to swamp our boat.

"We were out on a jaunt and our engine broke down. We lit night distress signals and the boat that came to our assistance arrested us, and that's all there is. I think the authorities made a mistake and I am quite sure they realize it."[29]

After Christmas, Fothergill appeared before Assistant Solicitor Edward Barnes once again. Barnes asked Fothergill why he was carrying $46,356 in his pockets at the time of his arrest. Fothergill explained that he always carried large sums with him, both in America and England. He said that he had no banking connections in the US and explained that he was a ship's broker. Barnes asked him if he was going out to the *Wrack* when the cutter *Seminole* found them. Fothergill replied that he was not, which was most likely true, since he had already collected his money. He insisted that he and his crew were simply going out on a pleasure trip.[30]

15

Nineteen Twenty-Four

On January 23, 1924, Secretary Hughes and Sir Auckland Geddes signed a treaty at the State Department between the United States and Great Britain. The treaty recognized that the territorial waters of the US were three nautical miles from the low tide mark, but there was a catch. The treaty also stated that:

> It is provided that this right of seizure may be exercised within the distance from the coast that may be traversed in one hour by the vessel suspected of endeavoring to commit the offense. Where a transfer from one vessel to another is contemplated, it is the speed of the latter vessel which is to determine the distance from the coast with which the seizure may be made.[1]

Captain Byron L. Reed told the press that he believed the new treaty would stop smuggling, provided that the search limit of "an hour's steam" was applicable to all types of vessels engaged in rum-running. Captain Reed said, if this were the case, the Coast Guard would be able to seize speedboats forty miles off the coast. Reed saw little use for a twelve-mile limit, because most of the rum fleet's ships were already anchored about fifteen miles off shore.[2]

Britain had no anti-liquor laws. There were several British officials who publicly denounce British liquor smugglers, but it is difficult to know how much of that condemnation was just diplomatic posturing. The main criticism of the new treaty, among the British, was that it was impossible to determine what a ship's maximum speed was before capturing it. If a ship could do only eight nautical miles per hour, then that was the farthest distance the Coast Guard could go out to board it.[3]

****

After the treaty's approval, Sir Broderick Hartwell sent out circulars advertising his fourth Scotch shipment to the United States. He still offered a twenty percent profit to investors within sixty days. The British and US governments were aware of Hartwell's circular and had no doubt that his offer was bona fide. He even included his street address in the circular—31 Haymarket, London—because he knew that his end of the business was entirely legal—at least in England. Broderick made arrangements with an American syndicate to ship 1,000 cases of Scotch each month to a point twenty-five miles offshore, where Americans could purchase it. [4]

Busy British workers continued to load ships with liquor and investors anxiously waited for cablegrams announcing that their cases had safely reached their destinations. Those who had already invested in Hartwell's enterprise received certified checks amounting to a 100 percent profit or better. Sir Broderick Hartwell continued to solicit investors in England, Wales, Scotland, and Ireland through the English Post Office. His circular stated, in part:

> I can offer you an opportunity of making 20 per cent on your capital every sixty days. I am shipping a fourth cargo of whisky abroad within the next few weeks. A portion of my shipment has already been arranged for, but I have still space for several thousand cases to fill my cargo. I have arranged with an American syndicate to take from me at least 10,000 cases of high-class Scotch whisky monthly.
>
> This syndicate has deposited with me United States gold bonds to the value of £10,000 (roughly $43,000), as a guarantee that the goods purchased will be paid for in cash on their arrival at a point twenty-five miles off shore.[5]

Sir Broderick referred to his plan as the "legitimate purchase and resale of British goods," and assured his prospective investors that the export of whisky from Britain was perfectly legal, helped British trade, increased employment, and swelled the national revenue.[6] Contrary to Hartwell's assurances of legitimacy, some members of the British Parliament were probing to find ways to stop Hartwell. One Member of Parliament asked Prime Minister MacDonald if it were possible to strip Hartwell of his titles and military honors and raised the point that Hartwell's operations were being subsidized by public funds. Mr. MacDonald replied that he would be glad to stop Hartwell's export business, which the House of Commons replied to with cheers. Another Member proposed asking the Underwriter's Association to stop insurance policies on Hartwell's cargoes while Viscountess Astor (of the famous Astor family) proposed applying a big export tax on the liquor shipments.[7]

At the same time that Hartwell was advertising his next shipment, one American company found a legal loophole they could exploit to sell liquor that otherwise would have sat in storage. The previous methods of removing impounded liquor were either to purchase liquor permits illegally or just steal it from warehouses. However, Julius Wile, Sons & Co., figured out a different approach. Before Prohibition took effect, the company had imported 9,000 cases of liquor, valued at $1,000,000. In early 1924, the company argued that hospitals and druggists were not willing to pay high enough prices, so they sent all 9,000 cases back to Europe. The great thing about this plan is that it was completely legal. Once the liquor reached Europe and cleared Customs, the liquor could be loaded onto another ship and sent right back to the US, eventually selling at higher prices and at a much faster rate than it would have in a bonded warehouse.[8]

US District Attorney Hayward stated to the press that hospitals were not rejecting the liquor because of its price but because hospital chemists had found that confiscated liquor was unfit for human consumption. Mr. Hayward made public the results of an analysis that showed that bootleg "Scotch whisky" contained diluted grain or re-distilled denatured alcohol, glycerine, a dash of creosote, and artificial "smoke." Smugglers bottled this concoction with labels and caps closely resembling those of a well-known brand. According to Hayward, Prohibition officials found smuggled rye whisky, gin and champagne to be synthetic, containing such ingredients as denatured alcohol, fusel oil[***], soap, bark oil, juniper, and coloring matter.[9]

The Plane! The Plane!

The government assigned very few airplanes to the task of enforcing Prohibition. In early 1924, the Coast Guard had no aircraft for anti-smuggling operations. The Navy was struggling to do routine work after massive cutbacks. The Army Air Service had not been ordered to patrol for Prohibition. In 1924, there was no check on a pilot's

---

[***] Fusel oil [G. Fusel, bad liquor.] "A clear, colorless, poisonous liquid mixture of amyl alcohols, obtained as a by-product of the fermentation of starch-containing and sugar-containing plant materials and used as a solvent for fats, oils, resins, and waxes and in making explosives and pure amyl alcohols." — *Webster's II New Collegiate Dictionary* (New York: Houghton Mifflin Co., 1999.)

bootlegging activities; neither he nor his machine was licensed. There was also no law compelling aircraft registration. Most bootleggers acquired their planes from the US Government, which sold them at bargain prices as surplus war equipment. Sometimes the planes passed through several hands before reaching the rum-running class. However, some of the planes came directly from federal sources.[10]

Since the rum fleet's ships were always on the move, bootleggers on land hired pilots to fly a "rum-spotter" out to sea. The rum-spotter knew which ship he was looking for and used a pair of powerful binoculars to locate it. After finding the rum-ship, the spotter charted its position, brought the information back to shore, and passed it on to the smaller boats.[11]

During the winter of 1923-24, there were at least a dozen flying boat accidents offshore due to bad weather and mechanical problems. One of these flying boats was a common sight over New York, where it seemed to be doing a good business carrying sightseers. However, nearly all of the pilot's customers came from the rum-spotters, who paid from $200 to $300 for each trip off Sandy Hook.[12]

One afternoon, the plane with its pilot, mechanic, and spotter did not return. A general alert was sent out. The Navy sent out planes to scan the sea. Radio men sent wireless messages to ships to be on the lookout for the plane. As it turned out, a sudden storm and a misfiring engine had caused the trouble. Once the plane was over the rum fleet, the spotter tried to signal one of the schooners. At that point the engine stalled and the little plane came down on the waves, which were kicked up by a fierce wind. The rum fleet's vessels pulled anchor and moved out a few miles to safer water. Apparently, nobody saw the plane come down nor had they heard the frantic signals for help. Night fell, and the men on board grew cold and hungry. They dared not smoke, for in trying to fix the engine, they had flooded it with gasoline. The gasoline had seeped down into the hull and there was no way of knowing where it lay ready to ignite. The men were deathly ill with the constant pitching of the waves, and remained belted to their seats throughout the night. By morning, the waves were pounding the water-logged plane into wreckage that might sink at any moment. The rum fleet was nowhere in sight.[13]

All that day, they saw nothing but the sun and sea. The waves rolled over the wings and constantly drenched the men. They were so thirsty that they drank the oily, rusty water from the radiator. They managed to crawl out on the upper wings and fastened undershirts to either end as a distress signal. Toward sundown, a single smokestack appeared over the horizon and then moved on. Other ships followed that ship, but it was too dark to be spotted. The stranded men had no flashlight and stood a fair chance of being run down by a larger craft. They spent that night wide awake and watching.[14]

In the morning, still half asleep from exhaustion, a small boat bumped into the plane and a hoarse voice shouted profane greetings. The three men climbed into the boat and were soon aboard a nearby rum-runner.

"Any chance of putting us ashore?" asked the pilot.

"Not a chance in the world. I've got a juicy cargo here, m'lad, and can't take the risk. At that, maybe we can send you back in one of the launches."[15]

Later in the day, a small craft pulled up alongside, and soon all hands were transferring cases from the schooner to the motorboat. The three stranded men helped the others and thus found favor with the captain, who agreed to put them ashore. The captain took a chance and put them in his small rowboat, which his crew members used to bring them to Long Beach, Long Island.[16]

At various points along the coast, there were aviators with small flying boats who would take the risks of flying a rum-spotter for $50 per trip. The pilots argued that there was nothing dishonest about it and pretended not to know what was going on. In January 1924, a pilot boasted that he was making three runs a week off Atlantic Highlands, NJ, for which he received $150 a trip. He was doing well until he decided to start his own smuggling business. He flew his flying boat out to a rum ship and packed his plane with a dozen cases, all his small craft could hold. He then attempted to take off, but found out that his overloaded machine could not get into the air. He spent the night taxiing into port. His plane was ruined, and he wound up abandoning it and swimming to shore.[17]

Another man, attempting the same feat with his flying boat, managed to make it back to a dock. A group of strangers met him. One of the men stuck a gun against his ribs and told him they would take care of his cargo and plane. The men marched him several hundred yards down a country road and permitted him to go free. When he finally turned back to look, the hijackers sped past him in a car and he saw that they had set fire to his plane.[18]

A New Commandant

Admiral Reynolds had amazingly avoided being singled out or publicly scrutinized during his tenure as commandant. Although dozens of rum ships sat off the coast and the flow of liquor into the US did not cease, the media and public seemed to blame everyone but him. What makes this even more amazing is that Reynolds managed to walk away unscathed after the Congressional inquiries following President Harding's death. While large numbers of high-level government officials testified before Congress either on their failures to enforce Prohibition or their roles in violating that law, Reynolds managed to fade into the background. This would be the equivalent of the General of the Army avoiding a Congressional hearing on why the US was not winning a ground war.

Courtesy US Coast Guard Headquarters

A candid photo of Admiral Reynolds.

On January 11, 1924, President Coolidge appointed Frederick C. Billard as the new Commandant of the Coast Guard. Billard, thirteen years younger than Reynolds, was forward-thinking and not afraid of publicity. During his tenure, he aggressively sought to improve and expand the Coast Guard. Billlard was born in Washington, DC in 1873. He was appointed a cadet in 1894 and received his early training on the Practice Ship *Chase*. He was appointed a Third Lieutenant in the Revenue Cutter Service in 1896 and a Captain in 1912. During the Spanish-American War he served on the Cutter *Corwin*, which was attached to the Pacific Fleet. From 1900 to 1905, he was navigator and instructor on the Practice Ship *Chase*. From 1906 to 1911 he was aide to Captain Worth J. Ross, the Chief of the Revenue Cutter Service. In 1918, he was given command of the USS *Aphrodite*, operating in the European theater. This was the first American war vessel to pass through the Kiel Canal, in Germany, after the Armistice. In 1919, he became Admiral Reynolds' aide until President Coolidge appointed him Commandant in 1924. While he served as Reynold's aide, he also served as the Superintendent of the Coast Guard Academy.[19]

One of the first things Admiral Billard did as Commandant was appear before Congress to ask for funding for a bigger and better Coast Guard. Much of Billard's testimony before the House Committee on Interstate and Foreign Commerce discussed the details of hiring more officers and enlisted men. Billard also requested 20 old destroyers and two mine sweepers from the Navy yards for Prohibition duty. The following are excerpts from that hearing:

Edward E. Denison (Illinois): Is the Coast Guard engaged in this work now?
Admiral Billard: We are engaged in it to the best of our ability and facilities, taking into consideration all the other important work we have to do. In other words, we are doing the best we can with it.
Mr. Denison: Now, let me ask you, just for information, as to how you proceed, Admiral. Are any of the Coast Guard vessels armed?
Admiral Billard: They are all armed, all the seagoing ships; yes.
Mr. Denison: I mean with heavy arms?
Admiral Billard: They are armed with 4 and 5 inch guns.
Mr. Denison: Now, what is your procedure when you start after a ship that is trying to land liquor? Do you try to capture it? Do you capture it if you can?
Admiral Billard: They try to capture the craft, yes.
Mr. Denison: What do you do when you capture it?
Admiral Billard: The boat is taken in and turned over to the Collector of Customs. He turns it over to the proper judicial authorities.

Courtesy US Coast Guard Headquarters

Coast Guardsmen man a 5-inch gun.

Mr. Denison: And he turns the men over with it?

Admiral Billard: I understand so. Our connection with it terminates when we have delivered it to the Collector of Customs.

Mr. Denison: If a Coast Guard vessel should start after one of these vessels carrying contraband, do you not have the authority, and use it, to shoot at them if they do not stop when you command them?

Admiral Billard: What our ships do is, they blow the whistle repeatedly, and when they are satisfied that the boat has heard the warning but refuses to stop, they fire a shot across her bow. That is the established custom of the sea.

Mr. Denison: That is a pretty good warning. Then what do you do?

Admiral Billard: Then they will fire another shot, and if she doesn't stop then, they will fire at her, quite properly, I think—I know. It so happens that when the shots begin to drop in pretty close proximity, the craft comes to heel usually...[20]

Admiral Billard then told the Congressmen that there was a fleet of rum ships about 30 or 40 miles off New York and that the Coast Guard only had two or three cutters there. These cutters were only capable of a slow ten knots. He added that the Coast Guardsmen were out in those waters day and night in all kinds of weather, making desperate efforts to do their duty, despite lacking the necessary equipment. Mr. Denison then raised the subject of the twelve-mile limit.

Mr. Denison: Now, they are outside of the 12-mile line, as I understand it, this rum fleet?

Admiral Billard: Of late, I understand, they have been laying off pretty well. Of course, under existing treaties they only have to remain outside the 3-mile line.

Mr. Denison: I have understood that the 12-mile treaty has been agreed upon.

Admiral Billard: It has not been confirmed by the Senate. It has been signed by representatives of the Governments, but of course will not be in effect until it is ratified by the Senate.

Ashton C. Shallenberger (Nebraska): And they can come up to the 3-mile limit?

Admiral Billard: They would have the right to under international law.[21]

After more discussion on the details of international treaties and an old US statute that would allow the Coast Guard to search vessels beyond the 3-mile limit, the hearing moved on to the subject of violence at sea.

John G. Cooper (Ohio): Admiral, have any of your men been fired on by the rum-runners?

Admiral Billard: There have been some cases, as I recall now, where some of our men in launches have been fired on by these rum-runners whom they are pursuing.

Mr. Cooper: Have any of them been wounded or killed?

Admiral Billard: No; none of our men have been killed, and I do not recall any of them ever being wounded.

Mr. Cooper: You take it, then, that the rum-runners as a rule are pretty desperate characters?

Admiral Billard: That is the impression I have, and our reports indicate a change in the general characteristics of those gentry, that they are much more desperate characters now than was the case at first. In other words, that a bad element of those coastal communities have gone into this thing now.

Mr. Cooper: Evidently they would not hesitate to kill?

Admiral Billard: No; I do not think so.[22]

Courtesy of US Coast Guard Headquarters

The crew of the rum-runner *Linwood* set fire to their vessel after being pursued by a patrol boat in order to destroy the evidence. In response to such acts, Admiral Billard described rum smugglers as "desperate characters" before a House Committee.

The House Committee also looked over two letters in support of Billard's request for additional funding, one from President Coolidge and the other from H.M. Lord, Director of the Bureau of the Budget. Both letters requested $13,853,989 in addition to the normal annual budget, which was approximately $10,000,000.

****

On February 17th, Attorney General Daugherty submitted a report to President Coolidge summarizing the previous four years of Prohibition. The report stated that the Federal Courts had handled more than 115,000 cases related to alcohol. By 1923, the average number of Federal Court cases tried on a given day, relating to Prohibition, was 119. Eighty percent of the cases resulted in convictions and brought in $15,726,593 in fines. Also, the number of cases rose dramatically during those years, from 29,114 in 1921 to 49,021 in 1923. The number of pending cases also rose dramatically in those two years— 10,365 in 1921 versus 23,052 in 1923.[23] Daugherty's report also discussed the magnitude of rum-smuggling in the United States:

> Though the number of boats of the Coast Guard assigned to the work is small, and the equipment inadequate, they have already done an admirable piece of work and will be a large factor in helping rid our coast of this gang of law violators.
> Up to Dec. 1, 1923, there had been 354 boats seized. In most instances forfeiture proceedings have been brought and about half of the boats have been sold. Approximately 250 of the boats are registered as American, the others are distributed among the various nations but the largest number are British. Most of them have been seized during the last two years.
> Southern Florida reports sixty seizures, Massachusetts 22, Southern New York 28, Eastern New York 18, Western New York 12, New Jersey 20, and Northern Ohio 10. But the eastern district of Michigan, which lies along the Detroit River, leads the list with 105 seizures. The center of operation is at Detroit, where a strenuous effort is now being made on the part of both Federal and State authorities to keep out Canadian liquor which has been pouring across the border in all sorts of small craft.
> Out of the thirty-four judicial districts having boundaries on the water, nine report no seizures. The failure of some of these districts is hard to understand when rumors of operation in their vicinities are heard quite frequently. Among those which reported no seizures are Northern Illinois (principal seaport, Chicago), Maryland (principal seaport, Baltimore), Southern Alabama (principal seaport, Mobile), and Maine (principal seaport, Portland).[24]

A few days later, the Coast Guard issued its own official report on liquor smuggling. According to that report, liquor smuggling had increased greatly over the winter. In late February 1924, there were 158 liquor-vessels off the US coast. During the last three months of 1923, the amount of whisky shipped to the US from Scotland had been estimated at 415,703 gallons in bulk and 26,755 cases. According to the Coast Guard, merchants shipped 104,241 cases of whisky, plus 415,965 gallons in bulk from Europe since January 1922. From Canada had come 57,365 cases plus 9,000 more from Miquelon. The Coast Guard estimated that it had intercepted only five percent of the smuggled liquor.[25]

Although the Coast Guard was becoming more efficient at detecting and capturing rum smugglers, local judges cancelled out much of that effort when the cases reached the courtroom. Captain Philip Scott wrote a letter complaining about his frustration to Captain Byron L. Reed, Commander of the New York Division. Captain Reed, in turn, forwarded the letter to the Attorney General. What triggered this particular complaint was an incident that had occurred on February 8, 1924. On that day, men aboard the Coast Guard Cutter *Seminole* captured the motor boat K-8940 at the entrance of Jones Inlet, Long Island. When the men first captured the vessel, Lieutenant Carleton Smith raised a corner of the tarpaulin and saw that the boat was filled with cases of liquor. The Coast Guardsmen took the three men aboard as prisoners and seized sixty-five cases and three bottles of liquor, all marked Scotch whisky. None of the cases or bottles was opened, but one case was leaking when the Coast Guardsmen removed it from the boat. The liquor leaked on the main deck, and later on the wardroom deck, where the men stored the cases. According to standard procedure, Lieutenant Smith gave Edward J. Bishop, the master of the K-8940, a receipt for the confiscated liquor. The Coast Guardsmen searched all three prisoners and found that Bishop was carrying an account book, showing that he had been rum-running for at least eight months. The book held his receipts, disbursements, and the number of cases landed. It also contained entries indicating that he had bribed government employees, including members of the Coast Guard, to assist in his operations.[26]

A month later, the case went to court before a US Commissioner in Brooklyn. Before the proceedings began, the Assistant District Attorney told Lieutenant Smith that he had no case. The Commissioner blamed Lieutenant Smith for unlawfully interfering with the Constitutional rights of a law-abiding American citizen and dismissed the case on the grounds that there was no evidence. He told Smith that he should have broken open one of the seized cases, opened and tasted a bottle, and then brought that bottle along with him to court. Captain Scott wrote in a letter:

> ...I have been reprimanded by Headquarters for expressing my honest opinion of the results and effects of the patrol off [the] New York entrance, and it is with some temerity that I again voice an opinion matured by close observation extending over a period of five months. I have come in from recent patrols encouraged with the belief that

good had been accomplished; I have gone back with the knowledge that most of the captures of the last patrol were ahead of me, released for the most part with nominal fines…If justice has been done here, then it were well for the Coast Guard to pause and consider that the large increase in force requested to enable it to enforce the law will be of absolutely no use.[27]

In early 1924, the Coast Guard consisted of 29 steamers and 129 sailing vessels, which varied in size from 70 to 9,000 tons. In opposition, the smugglers had an inshore fleet of several hundred motorboats and small vessels, plus the use of a few aircraft. A Coast Guard report stated that the bulk of the smuggling organization was based in New York City. New York was the headquarters of a large syndicate that owned and operated a fleet of nearly 100 craft, large and small. When the report was written, the Coast Guard had captured a total of 149 vessels, mostly small ones; 30,847 cases of liquor and 8 ¾ pounds of narcotics. Keep in mind that these figures cover four years of enforcement.[28] In response to these reports, the House Appropriations Committee recommended $13,850,622 to enable the Coast Guard to recondition twenty old Navy destroyers and buy 323 fast motorboats for use against rum-runners.[29] Congress approved the proposed budget and the increases in personnel and vessels in the Act of April 21, 1924. The Coast Guard's annual budget skyrocketed from $9,904,936 in 1923 (which was actually less than the preceding years) to $24,423,745 in 1924.[30]

Come Hell or High Water

Forces of nature were a much greater deterrent to rum smugglers than any fleet of government vessels ever were. Usually if there was a bad storm, rum smuggling came to a halt. This was definitely the case on March 11, 1924, when the entire Atlantic seaboard was swept by the worst storm in many years. Though only five people died in the storm—three in New York, one in Baltimore, and one in Providence—a considerable number of people were injured by large flying objects such as trees and signboards. The 80 mile-per-hour gale ripped the roofs off of houses and sent debris flying through the streets.[31]

Washington was almost completely isolated for hours. The storm blew all of the overhead telephone and telegraph wires down from west to south. The naval wireless stations in Washington, Arlington,

Annapolis, and Philadelphia had to suspend operations, and naval communications were seriously hampered. Trains arriving at the capital from distant points were two to six hours late.[32]

There was heavy snowfall in New England and as much as seven inches of snow in Lynchburg, Virginia. New York had only a light snowfall, but suffered much material damage within the city and along the Long Island shore. The waves everywhere passed the old high-water marks, undermining and carrying bungalows out to sea, flooding cellars and roads farther inland, and wrecking dozens of light vessels in the inlets. Along the New Jersey coast, the storm reached a velocity of 83 miles per hour and tore the roofs off of many houses.[33]

The British Royal Mail Liner *Orduna* was in port in New York during the storm. The US Government had been at work for many months to build up a case against the ship. Federal agents of the Narcotics Division had bought drugs and liquor from crewmembers on its previous trip, but the time had not been ripe for the seizure.

One would think that after the widespread destruction of the storm, US Government agents would temporarily suspend anti-smuggling operations to focus on other things. However, this was not the case. The morning after the storm, agents disguised as workmen went aboard and renewed their acquaintances with stewards and storekeepers. The agents made purchases on the first two days and then arranged to see all of the available liquor. When the undercover men showed up at the arranged time, the *Orduna*'s crew showed them 700 bottles of ale and 600 bottles of whisky, plus other types of liquor. Agent Oyler, who was more interested in the narcotics end of the deal, purchased 2,500 grams of morphine.[34]

While the undercover operations were in progress, the agents kept District Attorney Hayward and other men at the Federal Building informed by telephone. Shortly after midnight on the second night of the operations, Hayward and the other men went to the foot of Morton Street, where the *Orduna* was docked. There they waited for the signal, indicating that some of the crew had left the ship and passed liquor and drugs to agents.[35]

Hayward and his men went aboard. After identifying himself, Hayward personally conducted the search of the *Orduna*, which took two hours. The agents arrested seven men, all of them stewards and storekeepers; they also seized the ship. Since the craft was a British Royal Mail ship, the seizure caused quite a stir in steamship circles. Hayward made an official announcement of the seizure on the following afternoon. He told the press that he would file a libel against the *Orduna* as quickly as his staff could prepare the papers and that the government would demand a bond of not less than $3,000,000 for the vessel's release. He said that the Treasury Department asked him to make the seizure on three counts— violations of Customs laws, the Federal Narcotics Act, and the Prohibition law. However, Hayward went on to make more accusations against foreign ships and said:

> "I am convinced from evidence I have before me that every liner which comes into our harbor, without exception, is allowing liquor and narcotics to be sold freely from the ships. Either there exists the lowest possible state of discipline, thereby constituting a menace to passengers, or else the head officers (or even the steamship lines themselves) are in collusion and are sharing in the profits of this illicit traffic...the Government of this country did everything in its power to prevent annoyance or serious interference with the routine of foreign ships by permitting liquor to be carried as medical stores under certificate of the Public Health Officer...
> "It has been the worst breach of faith that I have ever known in all my official life. In the instance of the Orduna it is perfectly clear that the bootlegging on a large scale was carried on. They have had quantities of beer which never were included in the medical permits. They have been constant smugglers of narcotics. I expect to report all of these facts to Washington with a recommendation that all privileges and courtesies heretofore granted for the purpose of maintaining goodwill be revoked and that we be allowed to stand squarely on the laws of the United States and make the laws apply to foreigners as well as to our own people."[36]

A few hours after the press conference, Assistant District Attorney John Holley Clark, accompanied by other federal officials, made another raid on the *Orduna*, breaking open the seals of storerooms and liquor bars. They found no additional liquor. The officials interrogated Captain Warner of the *Orduna* in his office on the ship. He told them he had traveled the seas for many years, but had never encountered the difficulties he had experienced in American ports since the beginning of Prohibition. Captain Warner said that he had issued orders for the liquor stores to be sealed on reaching the three-mile limit and presumed that the crew followed his orders.[37]

District Attorney Hayward kept his word and filed a libel in Federal District Court against the *Orduna* on March 14th. His libel stated that, "each and every time the *Orduna* arrived in the port of New York, from January 16, 1920 to the date of the libel, she was used in smuggling intoxicating liquors and narcotics." Also, Hayward made the charge that the owner and master of the vessel evaded paying $100,000 in taxes by not reporting their liquor cargoes, making the owners liable to a penalty of twice that sum. Federal Judge Augustus N. Hand set the bond at $1,000,000, not the requested $3,000,000. The Royal Mail Line posted the bond and the ship left port the next day.[38]

An hour after these proceedings took place, two of the seven arrested crewmembers pleaded guilty in Judge Edwin L. Garvin's courtroom to smuggling liquor. Two made complete confessions and another gave a statement implicating others. The Court assured the prisoners who pleaded guilty that they would receive consideration if they assisted the authorities in catching men higher up in the organization. Counsel for the Royal Mail Line filed a general denial of the government's allegations. At the same time, the British government asked its Washington Embassy for a full report.[39]

Before the court session began on March 15, the other five prisoners also pled guilty. Judge Edwin L. Garvin remanded them to the Tombs and promised them leniency, if they cooperated with the Government. In the other courtroom, Judge Hand dismissed the Prohibition charge, because the authorities failed to arrest the commanding officer, Captain Walter P. Warner. Therefore, the trial proceeded on charges of violation of the Customs and Narcotics laws.[40]

One of the prisoners was Charles Dawe, who was a small-statured, sallow-faced Englishman. He had worked aboard the *Orduna* for three years as the assistant to Cort, the ship's storekeeper. Dawe testified that the *Orduna*'s crew had smuggled liquor into port on about fourteen trips during that period. The average number of cases sold was about 80, and at times, the ship sold as many as 120 cases to smugglers who came to the ship's side at night in motorboats.[41]

In Judge Hand's courtroom, counsel for the Royal Mail Line assured the court that Captain Warner would be in court at the next session. Judge Hand left the date of the next session open with the understanding that it would be during April, when the *Orduna* returned to New York. None of the men testified that any responsible officer of the *Orduna* or any official of the Royal Mail Line was aware of the sale of liquor or narcotics.[42]

The New York Consulate of the British Embassy reported back to the government concerning the *Orduna*. The report cleared the Royal Mail Line of any ties with the smuggling activities carried on by the crew. The British Ambassador told the press that he would not take any action in the matter unless his government told him to do so.[43]

The Big Punishment

In consideration of the assistance that the seven men had given the District Attorney, Federal Judge Edwin L. Garvin imposed fines of $25 to $100 on each. (They could have paid their fines off by selling two cases of liquor each.) Judge Garvin said that if some of them could not pay their fines within a few days, he wanted them to write him. He promised that if they could not pay, he would remit their fines. Garvin said that the penalties were light because it was expected that the seven would consider themselves "missionaries to spread the word throughout the British merchant marine that it is a serious matter to bring liquor into American ports."[44]

Several months later, Judge Hand dismissed the libel proceedings against the *Orduna*. Assistant US Attorney John Holley Clark filed a complaint listing forty-five reasons the government should confiscate the ship. Of those forty-five counts, Judge Hand overruled all except six, which related to failure to declare that liquor was aboard the vessel. The Judge stated:

> "In my opinion the vessel must be in possession of the guilty person with consent of the owner, or his agent, to be subject to forfeiture. The point is that either the owner or his agent must have some intention to smuggle goods or violate the statutes before its provision for forfeiture shall apply.
>
> "That a vessel or vehicle should be forfeited because of the conduct of a trespasser or persons having no right of possession would seem a most unnecessarily harsh interpretation of the statutes never adopted by any court. If the liquor was smuggled on by members of the crew with the consent of the master the situation would be quite different from that disclosed by the libel."[45]

A 50-Mile Boat Chase

In March 1924, the Coast Guard was busier than ever. By the middle of that month, there were twenty-eight large rum ships in the New York/ New Jersey area. In the early afternoon of March 15, the Coast Guard Cutter *Gresham* spotted the tug *Albatross*. The Coast Guard had seized the tug only a few months earlier for rum-running and it looked like the men aboard the vessel were about to give a repeat performance. From four and a half miles away, the Coast Guardsmen watched as the *Albatross* moored alongside the Norwegian steamship *Strudsholm*.[46]

The *Gresham* headed for the *Albatross*, which immediately put on steam and headed for the open sea. During the chase, the cutter and the fugitive tug darted a zigzag course; however, the *Gresham* soon closed the distance. Within an hour, the Coast Guardsmen saw the crew of the *Albatross* dumping cases of whisky overboard. The *Gresham* fired a six-pound shot across the tug's bow. In response, the tug sped up and the men aboard began throwing cases overboard even more frantically. As the *Gresham* got closer to the *Albatross*, its crew picked up two cases from among the hundreds that were floating around, and held them as evidence. The cases contained Scotch whisky and were sealed with foreign Customs seals; the markings showed that they had been shipped via Antwerp.[47]

Late in the afternoon, the *Gresham* fired a second shot as the gap between the two racing craft closed. This also failed to stop the *Albatross*, so the *Gresham* fired another six-pound shot. The shot whizzed close by the pilot house and frightened the skipper, who ordered the *Albatross* to stop and then waited for the *Gresham* to come alongside. By this point, the *Gresham* had chased the tug for fifty miles and its crew had thrown 3,000 cases of whisky overboard.[48]

As the Customs agents on the *Gresham* boarded the tug, the captain and crew of the *Albatross* made their hostility quickly apparent. They would not answer any questions and the few comments they made were very unfriendly. The tugboat's skipper, Captain Conway, was the most antagonistic of the lot and flatly refused to give any information. In response, the Coast Guardsmen locked him up overnight in the *Gresham's* brig. Some of the *Gresham's* crew manned the tugboat as the cutter took the vessel in tow. During the night, the cutter steamed leisurely back to port and arrived off Quarantine at noon. Once in port, the *Albatross*' crew posted bail.[49]

The men were arraigned before Federal Commissioner Stanton in Hoboken, NJ. The *Gresham*'s officers testified that they captured the *Albatross* nineteen miles from shore, which led counsel for the defendants to contend that the capture was illegal. The *Gresham's* officers also admitted that they found no liquor aboard the tug. The Court gave the defense two weeks to file briefs.[50]

More Plans For Expansion

In March 1924, five Navy vessels were tied up at Philadelphia to be converted and turned over to the Coast Guard. The Coast Guard revealed plans for expansion that were supposed to put the rum-runners out of business. Captain William V.E. Jacobs announced that the Coast Guard would soon assign fast naval craft to each of the rum vessels stationed outside the twelve-mile limit. The Coast Guard Cutters *Gresham, Seneca, Manhattan,* and *Hudson* were scheduled to take strategic positions off Sandy Hook and act as pivots, from which the other vessels of the dry fleet would operate.[51]

Captain Jacobs pointed out that the House had already appropriated $12,000,000 to fight smuggling and predicted Senate approval in a few days. Jacobs also said that the plans called for thirty 72-foot launches, capable of a speed of eighteen knots, each equipped with one-pounders (a type of naval gun) and Lewis machine guns. There would be another group of thirty boats, 36-feet long, capable of more than thirty knots, to be used for patrolling near the shore.[52]

Courtesy US Coast Guard Headquarters

A former Navy destroyer in dry dock as it is refitted for Coast Guard Prohibition Duty.

In reality, the plans were even bigger than what Captain Jacobs revealed to the press in March. By early April, Congress appropriated $18,000,000 for the Coast Guard to acquire 300 vessels and hire 5,000 recruits. The nucleus of the force was to consist of twenty destroyers, which Congress authorized the Coast Guard to buy from the Navy. The plan was to select twenty ships from the destroyer squadron lying out of commission at Philadelphia. Coast Guard officials inspected these ships and drew up plans for their reconditioning. The other vessels would be smaller, but the Coast Guard did not have any set plans on how the service would acquire these vessels.[53]

Reporter Spends A Week Aboard The Seminole

James C. Young, the same reporter who had written about his ride on a rum-running boat in December, spent a week aboard the Coast Guard Cutter *Seminole* in May 1924. The cutter left port in bad weather. The wind howled as the rain washed in a torrent across the deck. It was pointless to look for rum-runners in such harsh weather, so the *Seminole* spent the first night at anchor.[54]

Young passed the night in the wardroom, listening to tall stories about rum-runners and other things. Young also had a chance to get well acquainted with Philip Scott, commander of the *Seminole*. With 28 years of service, Scott was the kind of man a visitor would expect to meet at the helm of a cutter. Scott viewed the difficulties of the rum patrol as a minor matter, because he had encountered every sort of problem known to the Coast Guard. He found relaxation in studying Latin classics from original texts and composing his own rhymes. He was in the middle of reading *Caesar's Gallic War* when Young interviewed him. After telling the reporter that they would have to wait for the weather to clear up before chasing rum-runners, Scott spoke in detail about why he thought Caesar was the greatest man who ever lived. As Scott talked about the historic figure, rain poured on the deck above and pounded on the portholes. Finally, a bell indicated that it was 12:30 AM and time for the crew to change watch. The tired reporter then went to sleep.[55]

When Young woke up in the morning, heavy rain, wind, and high seas still pounded the cutter. The *Seminole* remained anchored all day and did not head for Montauk until after dark. The sky finally cleared and a silver moon shed light upon the Atlantic as the *Seminole* went down the Main Ship Channel, then into Ambrose, between the two blinking lines of buoys, past the pilot ship, the lightship, and into the open Atlantic.[56]

Lieutenant Rae B. Hall explained to James C. Young how to take a star sight. After the lieutenant's explanation, Young was even more confused; however, he did learn, at least, that a star sight is something a mariner uses when he has nothing else to navigate by. The lieutenant explained that first he found a star, then figured how far it was from the star to the horizon, and then determined the distance back from the horizon to the ship. After completing that process, a mariner could tell where he happened to be, providing he chose the right star and did his math accurately. By the time Young understood the process somewhat, it was time to hit the rack again. He wrote in his article that "it cramps the soul to sleep aboard ship."[57]

When he woke, Young was disappointed to see an overcast sky with rain clouds hovering low. Scott told the reporter that the weather conditions were excellent for rum-running. The commander was soon proven correct as the men on the *Seminole* spotted a possible smuggler. The fugitive boat came out from the protection of Montauk Point late on that rainy Sunday afternoon. For an hour, the rum-runner raced along the horizon, appearing as a dark smudge sandwiched between the foggy sky and dark water. The boat's skipper may have believed he was below the *Seminole's* line of visibility, but he was wrong. The men aboard the Coast Guard cutter were still able to spot him with a looking-glass.[58]

The confident smugglers pulled up alongside a loaded rum ship, twenty miles off Montauk Point. As evening came, the small vessel hid on the opposite side of the rum ship to avoid detection, but it was too late. As the *Seminole* maneuvered toward the two ships, the small boat quickly broke away. The time for stealth was over as Scott ordered full speed ahead.[59]

Daylight was running out as the two ships raced across the Atlantic waters. The *Seminole's* speed was no match for the rum-runner's, but the six-pound guns were. The guns could hit a target accurately from three miles. During the pursuit, Scott kept asking his crew if the smugglers were within range. The answer was "no" every time. The *Seminole* got within four miles of the rum-runner, with only about twenty minutes of daylight remaining. Scott knew that it was then or never.[60]

"Put up your sights as far as they will go and then tilt the barrel some more," Scott ordered.

The boatswain barked the order to the gunner. He and his crew did a lot of tricks with the gun, then passed back the word that the gun was ready.

"Fire when ready," said Scott. The boatswain barked the order to the gun crew in a way that showed he liked that particular order. As the gun went off with a loud bang, there was a shower of paper wadding and the smell of gunpowder. Every eye aboard watched for the splash. For

James C. Young, it seemed like an eternity before the shell sent up a geyser a hundred yards behind the rum-runner. The splash indicated that the gunners had stretched the range a mile or so and almost hit the fugitive with the first round. [61]

The rum-runner's skipper turned toward the Coast Guard cutter and struck his colors. The *Seminole* slowed down and the Coast Guardsmen waited for the boat to come alongside. The craft was 40 feet long with a 500-case capacity, specially-remodeled for rum smuggling. The former cabin was entirely covered over; a forward hatch provided a ready means for quick loading and unloading. The boat was painted battleship gray, giving it a formidable look. There were three men aboard. Two said they were New York taxi drivers. The three claimed that they were looking for a lost boat. When the Coast Guard searched the vessel, they found no liquor; however, they did find evidence that someone aboard had communicated with liquor smugglers. The Coast Guard took the three men into custody and seized the boat. [62]

As the *Seminole* patrolled the coast, with three alleged smugglers locked up in the ship's brig, Young and Scott spent another evening discussing Caesar. There were six rum ships off Montauk Point and seventeen more off the Highlands in New Jersey. During the night, the *Seminole* passed three of the ships near Fire Island, NY. Their average cargo was worth $10,000,000. [63]

On the following morning, a tiny schooner emerged out of the gray. Its sails were out and it was moving very slowly due to the lack of wind. On spotting the Coast Guard, the schooner turned away from the cutter. The skipper of the suspect vessel started his gasoline engine and put out to sea. After burning up many shovelfuls of coal, the *Seminole* came within hailing distance of the fleeing schooner. Soon, the men on the *Seminole* dropped a smaller boat over the side and sent a search party. The old captain of the schooner was sitting at the wheel and grinning as the Coast Guardsmen knocked off cover hatches and ransacked his ship. The crew found no liquor and he gave them a derisive wave as they left his boat. [64]

The *Seminole* left the schooner and spotted a small boat leaving a rum ship; the small craft headed straight for the open sea. The boat realized this was a poor way to escape, as the cutter soon caught up in the small boat's wake. The captain realized his tactical mistake and came about, heading for the cutter. As the boat came alongside the *Seminole*, the Coast Guardsmen saw that this was no ordinary rum boat; it had brass fittings, wicker furniture, and mahogany-finished cabin. [65]

The man at the helm seemed even more out of place than the boat. The six-foot tall man with military posture sprang onto the *Seminole*. He was well-dressed and apparently well-bred, with an English accent. The man seemed anxious as Scott asked him what he was doing in the area. He replied that he was visiting from Canada, and had just come out for a look at the rum fleet, so he would have a tale to tell his folks back home. Scott did not buy the story and sent some men aboard to search his vessel. They found no liquor. They did, however, find a memorandum book with two cablegram entries, one to the Bahamas and another to England. When Scott questioned the man about his book, he became even more nervous. The ship's officers decided that he was a shore agent for the rum-runners, so they locked him in the ship's brig with the other three prisoners and confiscated his boat.[66]

The *Seminole* now had two confiscated boats. Scott decided to use both of them for his mission instead of bringing them directly to port. Scott knew that he would have more success catching rum-runners using smaller, faster, unmarked boats than he would with the big, slow cutter. The *Seminole*, along with the two confiscated boats manned by Coast Guardsmen, headed for Rum Row. After a few miles, they passed the *Andora*, a 5,000-ton steamship, flying the Norwegian flag. The *Andora's* crew leaned curiously over the side and waved as the three vessels passed by. The *Andora* was heavily laden, and the crew most likely did not realize that some of their ship's papers were aboard the *Seminole*, taken from the first three prisoners. Many of the rum smugglers did not realize how much the Coast Guard knew about their activities. The Coast Guard recorded the arrival, departure, and approximate cargoes of the rum ships with as much care as the movements of merchant ships. However, although the Coast Guard knew the *Andora* was carrying and selling liquor, it was over twelve miles off-shore, and the Coast Guard could do nothing about it. The *Seminole* and its two smaller vessels moved on.[67]

It became rainy and windy again as the *Seminole* approached the *Glasgow*, a big steam yacht, about twenty miles off shore. No one was outside to greet the Coast Guard. The *Seminole* then visited the *Rask*, which had "London" prominently painted on its bow. The *Rask's* crew was friendly and turned out in force to grin and wave at the Coast Guardsmen. It was a wash day and there was an odd assortment of laundry hanging from the rigging of the ship, including a little blue dress for a two-year-old girl.[68]

The *Seminole* moved on and approached the *Catherine and Mary*, a schooner that the Coast Guard knew carried tons of narcotics.

No one on the drug ship stirred when the *Seminole* passed by. Since the *Catherine and Mary* was also outside the limit, the *Seminole* could again do nothing. Night came and the sea was running high, so the *Seminole* and the two smaller boats headed for New London, Connecticut. As the wind howled in the ship's rigging, the lights of the rum-ships and the *Catherine and Mary* were clearly visible. The *Seminole* anchored off New London and the crew endured another stormy night.[69]

Most of the next day was devoted to arraigning the prisoners. Two of the men from the rum cruiser went free and the third was held in light bail. The more important suspect went to New York to face further examination. The following day brought more wind and rain. James C. Young went with some of the Coast Guardsmen aboard the boat that they had recently confiscated from the lone Englishman. They brought a machine gun, a rifle, and pistol for each man, and "enough ammunition to sink the whole fleet off Montauk." Armed to the teeth, they drove out of New London Harbor as the waves tossed them around.[70]

The rum-runners did not stir. The undercover vessel patrolled the waters off Fisher's Island, hearing only the ringing of bell-buoys and seeing only fog. The men heard a report that there would be rum-running around the island, and the fog provided excellent cover. Only blind luck would help the men find any smugglers, but they had no such luck. After a few miserable hours aboard the small boat, they headed back for New London. By that time the boat was half full of water and the men were cold. Even with the harsh conditions, some of the men, including Young, managed to doze off.[71]

After one of the crew shook Young from his sleep, he looked up to see the white hull of the *Seminole*. For the *New York Times* article he wrote, "Never was any ship so welcome to afflicted man." Young scrambled up the ladder of the *Seminole* and went below into the warm, dry wardroom. The table was set with white napkins and a mess steward was arranging the silverware. While Young enjoyed the relative luxury of the wardroom, he heard more stories about the rum-runners.[72]

In one of the stories, the men of the *Seminole* encountered a motorboat with six men aboard and a broken-down engine. The Coast Guardsmen took the men onto their cutter and began to ask questions. One was an Englishman, wearing the latest London fashion. The well-dressed English captain objected to the Coast Guard searching his vessel, but that did not stop them. When they searched the vessel, the Coast Guardsmen found the captain's table covered with piles of money, more than most of them had ever seen. In the Englishman's pockets, there were banknotes ranging from $100 to $1,000 in a surprising quantity. It took an hour to count his wealth— $46,500 in total. Scott confiscated the money and held the six men as prisoners. Later, they obtained their release and also got their money back. The Englishman, as it turned out, was the master of a rum cargo, intercepted while going ashore to deposit some of his money.[73]

The Coast Guard had many methods for dealing with smugglers. One of the most effective measures was seizing their capital. In practically every case, the smugglers recovered their money in court, but still experienced financial distress and loss of time. Rum pirates were also proving to be an asset to the Coast Guard's efforts. Pirates made rum smuggling far more dangerous and proved a greater deterrent than the Coast Guard. In response to this dual threat, the men who owned the cargoes had offices in New York, where they accepted orders and payments. The owners then wrote out orders of their own for the master of the rum ship to deliver a certain number of cases. Young listened to more stories of rum pirates and smugglers as the *Seminole* fought its way up the coast against a gale, bound for New York and dry land.[74]

Flying Boats And The Grand Scheme

In May 1924, the King of England signed the treaty authorizing the US to search and seize all vessels within an hour's steaming distance of the American coast.[75] The treaty virtually abolished the three-mile limit. Many called it a 12-mile treaty, although for faster rum ships it actually meant a 15 to 18-mile limit. While the smaller speedboats were capable of 40 miles an hour, it was not wise to take those boats out on the high seas. The larger ships, which crossed the Atlantic, still moved at the relatively slow speed of 18 miles an hour or less. Some government agencies believed that the new treaty would reduce smuggling to a minimum, but that was not the case. As a precaution, the rum ships had been staying out beyond the new treaty limits for over four months.[76]

The rum-runners planned to deliver large shipments of liquor to New York before the Democratic Convention in June. The ships came from England, France, Italy, Spain, Bermuda, the Bahamas, and other places. Some carried 30,000 cases of whisky; others carried half that quantity. When the ships came to anchor at Rum Row, they were prepared to lay off shore for two or three months.[77]

New York bootleggers planned to use seaplanes in increasing numbers. They had experimented with the planes during the previous year for spotting ships, and found them to be very useful. Smugglers made inquiries and offers to several airplane companies in the first few months of the year. In several cases, the smugglers specified that the aircraft be flying boats, with engines guaranteed to function steadily for a twenty-mile flight out over the sea and back again. They asked for seaworthy hulls capable of remaining afloat on the waves and able to carry enough liquor to make the trips profitable. In May, airplane companies were conditioning at least a dozen flying boats, old and new, for service with the rum fleet. The latest flying boats were designed specifically for rum traffic, with waterproof hulls and wings with a powerful lifting capacity. Their prices ranged from $20,000 to $50,000.[78]

During the bad weather of early Spring, which halted rum-running for several days, many of the rum-ship captains, supercargoes, and agents came ashore, where bootleggers entertained them lavishly. One night, a schooner captain accepted an invitation to come ashore and met a liquor broker and the New York agent of a foreign liquor company. They talked freely about the treaty and laughed when a reporter asked them if the treaty would be effective. The captain responded:

> "The ships have been recognizing it practically for four months now, and if the prohibition people tell you the truth, they will admit that the stuff is coming ashore, barring weather, in greater quantities than ever before. Before leaving England I met a former pilot who was trying to bring liquor over in boats. He would equip each boat with seaplanes, so that, anchored fifteen miles offshore, he could have sent the stuff not only to New York but far up the Hudson and on occasion to Philadelphia and Baltimore. He was especially keen on flying direct to Newport, because you know the rich people there and at Southampton buy their booze in thousand dollar lots. They must have it. They entertain so much, you know.
>
> "Of course you know that you have at least five big liquor rings handling most of the business in New York. These big syndicates sell to smaller rings, which in turn dispose of it to others. The big syndicates buy up the stuff in Europe far in advance. They charter the ships through their own agents or order the stuff to be delivered in whole cargo lots off the treaty limit. Then they handle it themselves. They either hire their small speed boats to go out and bring it in or else they maintain a fleet of small craft and also a complete hauling service such as motor cars, trucks, and moving vans. One big concern is using a floating grain elevator.
>
> "When you speak of a $20,000 flying boat, it means little or nothing to the bootleg ring, because they are financed

up in the millions. One outfit, I'm informed is backed as high as $30,000,000. It can well afford to maintain a whole aerial fleet if it will serve a purpose." [79]

The bootleggers laughed at the twelve-mile treaty, because a flying boat could fly twenty miles out over the water, land near a vessel, take aboard cargo, and get away before the Coast Guard could come anywhere near them. Spotter planes also could warn the smaller craft when a Coast Guard cutter was approaching. After the planes warned the smaller craft, the boats could scatter and leave decoys to lead the Coast Guard on a futile chase.[80]

One night in May, a fleet of small boats was almost within gun range of the Coast Guard cutters standing by the rum ships off Atlantic Highlands, NJ. The cutters had their smaller boats lowered, ready for a chase. When the Coast Guard vessels went out to pursue the liquor-laden boats, it seemed as if the smugglers would not escape. One rum craft lagged behind the others and the Coast Guard stopped it. When they inspected the boat, the Coast Guardsmen found, to their disgust, that the boat was loaded with empty fruit cases.[81]

Captain R.Q. Merrick, enforcement officer in charge of the New York Prohibition agents, asserted that captures on land were increasing monthly. He said that when the smugglers used aircraft in large numbers, his agents observed and trailed them to find where the liquor was being landed. The Coast Guard appropriation bill, then in Congress, also provided for aircraft. Rear Admiral Billard, the Commandant, told the press that the aircraft would be useful in their work. The aviation wing would begin as a very small force, he said, and increase as the smugglers used more planes.[82]

Bootleggers expected that some smugglers would be arrested and considered those losses when fixing prices. In New York, the bootlegging industry functioned like a stock exchange. Bulletins with daily prices, quotations, remarks, and suggestions circulated among the trade every weekday. That is why the smugglers were willing to deal with the conditions of the 12-mile treaty. Investors placed bonds guaranteeing payment for the liquor aboard the fleet off New York, and had similar guarantees for the next big shipment due before the Democratic Convention. Also, smugglers signed contracts with syndicates in most large cities in the western part of the United States. A representative of New York's largest syndicate agreed to talk to a *New York Times* reporter on the condition that he remain anonymous. He gave this insightful statement:

"What if the Coast Guard does use aircraft? The twelve or fifteen miles limit is better than three miles actually. The flying machines have a greater radius in which to fly. We will bring the stuff ashore at night. We do all our hauling from fleet to shore at night, anyway. As the surface craft now operate, if we start toward Keyport, NJ, for example, and find a police boat coming toward us, we simply turn around and run toward a Long Island port. Now, that is much easier than when we were operating three miles off shore, because it gives us a larger area. The prohibition people say it makes the gamut longer for us to run. It works both ways, you see. The larger the area the less chance for discovery. And we have proved to our own satisfaction that even when discovered we have better chances of getting away." [83]

The rum-runners typically worked from midnight to dawn. However, the Coast Guard was still able to detect surface craft and flying boats, even in fog and mist. One rum smuggler explained how this was possible:

"In some instances they might trail us by our exhausts if we are using sea-planes. But they, too, must carry riding lights, else stand a chance of being run down in the dark. And a collision in midair would be fatal to both sides. As for shooting our fellows out of the sky, we're willing to take a chance. We have scores of ex-service men willing to take that chance. And I do not believe the Coast Guard can find enough airplanes to carry searchlights and scan the entire area from midnight until dawn. That is where the larger area between land and Rum Row gives us the advantage.

"There are as many brains working to defeat prohibition as to support it. New innovations are being developed constantly. The Coast Guard and marine police have already found that machine gun bullets do little or no damage, because the fast speed boats running the stuff to shore are sheathed in steel so that the bullets cannot penetrate.

"They are equipped with the strongest engines built, airplane motors, often two, three and sometimes four, usually one held in reserve in case an engine fails. These speed boats can travel as fast as thirty knots. The law enforcement agencies have been unable to match such speed. By the time they have made requisition for them, and the boats are made available, we shall have still faster machines and aircraft."[84]

ALCOHOL, BOAT CHASES, AND SHOOTOUTS!

Some of the speed boats used foreign engines; others used Liberty airplane engines.††† Empty, the boats were unbeatable; loaded, they were also very profitable. In areas where the liquor ring did not control the mosquito fleet, boat owners charged $150 to $300 per trip. The cost of getting liquor ashore had doubled since the 12-mile treaty went into effect. The bootlegger had even more to tell the reporter:

> "The shifting fortunes in our trade are caused by the liquor market. If times are bad, as they have been since the first of the year, you will find a certain clique cutting prices, and where there is price-cutting you will find watered liquor, vile home-made stuff, new whisky from Europe. These people will refuse to pay graft for protection where graft is due and protection is badly needed. Those are the fellows who sooner or later are caught; and most of them prove to be anything but gentlemen. Few of the real ones are caught.
>
> "Rum-running is great fun. Some of us take our wives along. You see, it is pretty lonesome for the women folks, staying alone from midnight until dawn. And they always worry for fear we will stop a bullet or have a wreck. So they go along with us when there's room.
>
> "There are usually three or four ships plying far offshore. We call it the second line of defense. The prohibition agents think they are mother ships to supply the small schooners in Rum Row. They are mistaken. Those fellows out there are doctoring liquor. They bring over a third of a cargo of new whisky or old stuff, as the case may be. Then they make three bottles out of a good one.
>
> "You are getting two kinds of whisky in this country and most of you don't know the difference. The new Scotch is from three nights to six weeks old. It isn't fit to drink, but it tastes good. An American syndicate is buying it up as fast as it is made. They ship it into Germany, where arrangements have been perfected for putting this stuff in bottles and under old labels to make it look like the real goods.
>
> "Your saloons and restaurants are selling new Scotch and most of it is half water at that. I'll explain why good stuff costs money in this country. Take Scotch, for example. It sells in England for $27 a case wholesale for the old, cured stuff.

---

††† The Liberty L-12 engine produced 400 horsepower. It was originally designed and manufactured for aircraft and tanks during WWI. After the war, the government sold thousands of surplus Liberty engines to public buyers.

The new Scotch costs only $12 a case. The big syndicates buy 10,000 to 50,000 cases of old Scotch. The pikers get only the new stuff.

"The syndicates sell to other and smaller rings for from $23 to $25 a case in lots of 500 to 1,000 cases. Then they in turn sell to smaller rings of 'brokers' for from $35 to $50 a case in lots of 50 to 100 cases. This is also sold through brokers and salesmen. They have their business cards and offices, telephones, and in many instances cable addresses. There are seventy-three bootleggers in one New York office building within half a mile of prohibition enforcement headquarters.

"The brokers do a lot of business on credit. They trust their customers. Lawyers are the best customers. They buy a lot for clients. Doctors come next. They buy for themselves and patients. For the most part, the real liquor and wine coming into the United States is being consumed by the rich people. They are willing to pay any price for the good stuff. Why sell to others?" [85]

****

Although the Department of Justice managed to avoid the unpleasant task of Prohibition enforcement, the department's reputation suffered as many attacks as the Treasury Department. In the Spring of 1924, the Bureau of Investigation's reputation had never been worse. Federal prosecutors uncovered evidence that the Department of Justice was conducting illegal surveillance operations. Attorney General Harry Daugherty and the Bureau of Investigation's director William Burns were also involved in the widespread violation of Prohibition laws that would force them out of office and implicate Republican Party patronage networks.[86]

After Daugherty had resigned, President Coolidge appointed Harlan Fiske Stone to take his place. Coolidge picked the New York judge in an effort to restore the government's image. Stone was a Republican who was part of a Wall Street partnership, with an upper class background. These characteristics distinguished Stone from Harding's political lackeys, known as the "Ohio Gang." Stone, in turn, searched for an acting Bureau director to fill the vacancy left by William Burns. Stone ignored the political patronage system and hired an unlikely candidate.

The candidate, named John, had entered government service when he was only sixteen. He attended both college and then law school at night, while working days at the Library of Congress and then as a mail room clerk at the Department of Justice. John attempted to join the Bureau of Investigation several times as a special agent, but was turned down. He finally received a job offer from Attorney General A. Mitchell Palmer to investigate labor organizers, socialists, pacifists, and communists. Soon John's excellent memory and clerical skills got him promoted to the division's chief administrator. He devised a system that permitted his clerks to sort surveillance information from paid informants and played a big part in getting many people deported. However, Federal judges overturned many of the deportation rulings on appeal and condemned Palmer's raids as illegal. Palmer wound up resigning in disgrace.[87]

When any Washington bureaucrat is involved in a scandal, usually there are two likely outcomes: either that person will resign and disappear from public life or get promoted. John miraculously managed to avoid getting fired, despite working directly with Palmer and carrying out his orders. At the time Stone interviewed the new candidate, John was a thin 25-year-old. Normally, a 25-year-old would be lucky to get a job supervising a small business, never mind a government agency. He was a lifetime resident of Washington, DC; therefore, he had never voted or joined a political party. The press portrayed the new candidate as professional, modern, and politically unbiased. His friends described him as a "clean" man, more concerned with gathering evidence legally than 'getting the goods.' That candidate's full name was John Edgar Hoover.[88]

As the acting Director, J. Edgar Hoover made such sweeping changes in the Bureau that Stone confirmed his permanent appointment by the end of the year. Hoover's reputation for hunting communists worked in his favor, because anti-immigrant and anti-radical views were in vogue at the time. Borrowing the ideas of municipal reformers, he reorganized the staff of special agents into a scientifically-trained national police force. Hoover looked to the Prohibition Bureau for examples of what *not* to do. Therefore, if the Prohibition Bureau accomplished nothing else in the long run, it opened a national discussion on what role federal agents should play in a modern state and how they should perform their duties. In the early years of his new career, two of Hoover's expressed goals were to separate federal police work from the political spoils system and to avoid getting involved in political matters.[89]

J. Edgar Hoover was the Director of the Bureau of Investigation for the next fifty years. He began reforms in 1924 that provided a stark contrast to Prohibition Bureau policies. He limited recruitment to white men, most of whom had college and postgraduate degrees and many of whom had served in the military. The Bureau conducted rigorous training and maintained strict regulations on dress, conduct, and investigative procedures. The new dress code distinguished the agents and visually marked the beginning of a new era in federal law enforcement. The Bureau rotated agents in and out of Washington on a regular basis, with no agents left at any one post for too long. (Hoover obviously saw himself as an exception to that rule.) He also demanded and received discretion over his own budget. That reform, in and of itself, made the Bureau much less open to Congressional scrutiny and therefore more autonomous than the Prohibition Bureau.[90]

16

"Stop shooting, this is a police boat!"

In early 1924, the New York City Police Department was still patrolling the waters of New York in search of rum-smugglers. On the night of January 19th, the police boat *Manhattan* (not to be confused with the Coast Guard Cutter *Manhattan*) spotted the tugboat *Capitol No. 1* off Governor's Island with only one light visible on its tail mast. The police aboard the *Manhattan* ordered the vessel to stop and the men aboard the tugboat responded by shooting their pistols. The police then used their machine guns, firing a number of shots across the tugboat's bow. People at Governor's Island, Ellis Island, and the Battery heard the crackle of small arms fire. Many rushed to the waterfront to see the naval engagement, but the ships were both obscured by darkness.[1]

Meanwhile, the *Manhattan* gained on the tug, which put in at Erie Railroad Pier 22, at the foot of Chambers Street. The helmsman of the *Capitol* had barely pointed his craft toward the pier when he found himself headed for an Erie boat leaving the same location. The police aboard the *Manhattan* were close enough to hear half a dozen shouts of warning by the men aboard the tug. The Erie boat and the tugboat were hardly a boat's length apart and a collision seemed inevitable.[2]

However, the pilots of both *Capitol No.1* and the Erie boat changed their courses just in time to avoid an accident. When the tug pulled alongside the pier, seven men jumped off and ran toward the street. A few minutes later the police boat also reached the pier and two of the policemen raced after the fugitives. At the same time, Captain McCormack, Patrolman Edward Beban and Charles Francis, the police boat's wireless operator, started to board the liquor boat. As they climbed over the side of their own boat, they heard a shuffle of feet on the deck of the tug, followed by a loud splash. The police believed that a man had jumped or fallen overboard. The three police found two men on the tug's deck, making hasty preparations to leave.[3]

The police engaged in a hand-to-hand fight with the two men on the slippery deck and finally managed to overpower them. Meanwhile, the police, who chased the other suspects on foot, caught up with and arrested all four. After the police placed all six prisoners under guard at the pier, they searched for the man who went overboard, but found no one. The police found no weapons on the prisoners and concluded that they dropped their firearms overboard when their capture was imminent. Under a hatch on the *Capitol No.1*, the police found 1,500 cases of liquor, worth more than $100,000. The police later turned the captured men over to federal authorities. United States Commissioner Hitchcock held them in $2,000 bail each for a hearing before Edward Barnes, Assistant Solicitor of the Legal Division at the Custom House.[4]

In February 1924, the *Manhattan* was the flagship of the New York Police Department's Marine Division, but that distinction was to soon change. The new flagship, sitting at Pier A at the Battery, had yet to be officially commissioned. The new vessel was a 55-foot speedboat, capable of 45 miles an hour. The *Manhattan*, by comparison, was big and slow, measuring 75-feet, and capable of only 20 miles an hour. In addition to the new vessel, the New York Police Department added five 35-foot boats, capable of 25 miles an hour. In 1920, the *Manhattan* had been fast enough to catch most smugglers, who were using row boats, sail boats, and boats with weak engines. However, by 1923 the *Manhattan* was far too slow to catch the average rum-runner. The police had to outwit or outshoot them because their boats were just too slow for any other tactics. The new flotilla of patrol boats, capable of only 25 miles an hour, was still too slow to catch most speedboats.[5]

The "captains" of the *Manhattan* were Patrolmen David Byrne and James Ward. Byrne held an unlimited tonnage pilot's license and Ward was licensed to pilot big steamers into the harbor. Though both were only patrolmen, they each had the full command of a crew of ten men for 24 hours out of every 48. The crews they commanded frequently included a sergeant, who could not challenge a single order that Byrne or Ward gave. In February 1924, the NYPD had about twenty men who were qualified seamen, but Byrne and Ward were the only two police with their particular qualifications. The two skippers were respected by their crews and also known by name in the smuggling community.[6]

The New York Police Department patrol boats chased and captured many smugglers. In this way, the NYPD greatly augmented the efforts of the Coast Guard and Customs. When it came to fighting rum-smuggling, the police in New York had a few advantages over the Coast Guard and Customs. First of all, the NYPD's police officers patrolled the entire city, unlike the Coast Guard and Customs officers, who stayed near or on the water. The officers knew their "beat," or patrol areas, very well. The police officers became familiar with the people who lived and worked on their patrol routes and, therefore, had a very effective way of gathering intelligence about criminal activities. In this respect, federal agents were at a disadvantage in comparison to the "neighborhood cop." Also, the NYPD had the advantage of being able to pursue suspects from water to land or vice-versa, unlike the Coast Guard. Usually when smugglers reached the shore and started running, the Coast Guard could do little except ask for assistance from the local authorities.

One of the many boats chased by the NYPD was the power yacht *Monon*. The *Monon* was an expensive vessel (valued $100,000), trimmed with mahogany, and powered by an 800-horsepower engine. It had accommodations for fifteen passengers and ample space for cargo. The police had been on the lookout for the yacht for about a week, when it flashed by them in the darkness at a speed of 40 miles an hour. The men aboard the *Manhattan* spotted the boat in the Narrows and signaled two other patrol boats, which started off at full speed in an effort to head off the *Monon*. The *Monon* changed its course and dodged behind a passing lighter. Instead of continuing up the bay, it circled a ferryboat bound for Staten Island. The *Monon* then headed up the East River. Meanwhile, the pursuing police boats opened fire with their machine guns.[7]

The *Monon*, disregarding the bullets, headed for a pier at Roosevelt Street in Manhattan. Once there, the men jumped ashore and disappeared. The abandoned yacht drifted away and police found it near the Brooklyn Bridge. Amazingly, the yacht had no holes in it, despite being showered with bullets for nine miles. However, the police did find a quantity of whisky aboard.[8]

In another incident, Police Launch 4 was cruising off Princess Bay, Staten Island, when the officers aboard spotted rum-runners speeding toward the shore with all lights out. The police launch set out in pursuit and followed the vessel for twenty miles. After other warnings, the police fired in the air, but the smugglers ignored them. After the officers began to shoot at the craft, the smugglers returned fire with their pistols. The police fired at the fuel tank with a machine gun, causing the tank to explode. One of the four fugitives leaped to his feet with his clothing ablaze. After he plunged into the water, his three companions followed him. The powerboat sped on until it grounded on a reef off Keyport, New Jersey. The flames burned away all identification marks. The police could find no trace of the four men and believed they had drowned. They towed the charred boat back to New York, having discovered only two cases of whisky aboard.[9]

World's Fastest Police Boat Chases World's Fastest Rum Boat

In May of 1924, the *Gypsy* was the world's fastest police boat, capable of a maximum speed of 45 miles per hour. Smugglers thoroughly studied the *Gypsy* and ordered shipbuilders to construct something faster. The builders produced a $50,000 speedboat, named the *May*. The police heard about the *May* and kept it under constant watch. One night, a policeman watched four men board the *May* at its moorings in the North River, in New York. After a few minutes they cast off. Within a minute, the telephone rang at the Harbor police station at the Battery. [10]

"The May has left its moorings," said the voice on the phone.

Police Captain Richard O'Connor immediately notified Sergeant Luke Grace, pilot of the *Gypsy*. Several other policemen climbed aboard and the *Gypsy* set out in hot pursuit of the smugglers. The men on the *Gypsy* failed to intercept the *May* on the way down the river and lower bay. Convinced that the *May* had passed them, the *Gypsy* turned out to sea to visit the rum fleet. [11]

The *Gypsy* made a wide circle around one large rum ship which lay at anchor fourteen miles out, but found no boats around it. The *Gypsy* then made a second pass around the ship, but still found nothing. Two hours later, Captain O'Connor saw the glint of lights from the portholes of another rum ship through his looking-glass. The *Gypsy* headed for that vessel and circled it, but the rum ship appeared to be doing no business. The police then headed for the third and last of the rum ships within a reasonable distance of New York Harbor. There were no small craft around it. [12]

Captain O'Connor ordered the *Gypsy* to turn around, and the police boat visited the other two rum ships again. The ship's crews kept themselves hidden as the police came around a second time, but the waters around the ships were still free of smaller boats. The *Gypsy* headed back for New York. The boat made three excursions in the directions of lights, but accomplished nothing. [13]

This continued for eight hours before the *Gypsy* turned back. It was still dark, but the early morning light was breaking on the horizon as the *Gypsy* approached the Narrows. Suddenly, a light appeared near Fort Wadsworth on the Staten Island shore. It glared for about three seconds and then went out. [14]

"Somebody just lit a cigarette on a boat over by Fort Wadsworth," Captain O'Connor said to the pilot. "Make for it." A few minutes later, the police spotted a long, gray speedboat through the mist. "I believe it's the *May*," he called. "Put on full speed." [15]

At the same moment, one of the men on the *May* saw the *Gypsy* and the race started. The *May* headed directly for the East River. In a few minutes, the boat's nose was high out of the water. The *May*'s engines roared as it created a huge, foamy wake. The smugglers had a half-mile head start and kept that lead in a dash across the bay. However, as they passed Governor's Island, it became clear that the police were catching up. As the two boats raced along the misty river, the roar of their engines broke the early dawn quiet and their wakes rocked the nearby boats.[16]

The *May* cut close to one of the piers of the Brooklyn Bridge and the *Gypsy* followed. The *May*'s crew began to throw dozens of cases overboard, and soon the waters between Brooklyn and Manhattan were filled with bobbing cases of liquor. Captain O'Connor could not use his revolver or his voice to stop the fleeing boat. The roar of the engines drowned out his voice. His pistol was still holstered as he held on tightly with both hands to keep from flying out of the boat or falling onto the deck.[17]

The *Gypsy* hit a case of Scotch whisky, which made a loud crashing sound, sending pieces of wood and broken glass flying everywhere. The men aboard the *May* threw case after case overboard as they passed under more bridges along the East River. The *Gypsy* continued to gain on the *May* and was only a few yards behind. The *May*'s pilot attempted to trick the police. He headed for the west side of Ward's Island and tried to turn suddenly to the right, hoping to pass the east side of the island. This might have worked, because Ward's Island is very narrow.[18]

However, the boat was going too fast to pull off the maneuver, and the *May* crashed into the island. The speedboat glanced off a submerged rock and shot out of the water like a dolphin. The boat fell on its side and skidded along the rocks and sand. It almost cleared the beach when a large rock tore the boat to pieces. The rock snapped the bow off, broke the vessel's ribs, and smashed the engine flat. In addition, some of the pipes bent and wrapped around the rock.[19]

The crash sent the men flying into the air like rag dolls, tumbling among the rocks and sand. One man lay motionless, while the others staggered to their feet. There was a blast behind them as the waves created by the shock swept over the superheated engines. Steam shot into the air with a great roar.[20]

The *Gypsy* wound up going to the west of the island, because the police pilot thought it was too dangerous to follow. Captain O'Connor thought that he had been outwitted until he heard the explosion. The policemen landed on the beach and easily rounded up the fugitives, who were too injured and dispirited to make an escape. This was the maiden voyage of the *May*. Within less than ten hours, the $50,000 speedboat went from being a mariner's dream to a pile of twisted metal and broken wood. The *May*'s lost cargo was worth between $30,000 and $50,000. The police retraced their route and managed to recover twenty floating cases of liquor. Throughout the rest of the day, scores of men in rowboats and launches salvaged cases of Scotch whisky down the East River and in the upper bay. [21]

Several months later, the *Gypsy* chased another worthy opponent, named the *Cigarette*. The *Cigarette* was well known both among rum-runners and police. The boat was sixty-five feet long, equipped with two airplane motors, and capable of a maximum speed of 45 mph. One night in November, the police boat *Gypsy* was patrolling down the lower bay near Norton's Point. There was a full moon, but a thick haze covered the water. The police aboard the *Gypsy* spotted a boat with no running lights moving stealthily through the Narrows. Sergeant Pat Lee hailed the vessel but got no response. As the police boat started to speed up in pursuit, the other boat did likewise. [22]

The world's fastest police boat could not match the speed of the *Cigarette* and gradually slipped farther and farther behind. The *Gypsy* followed the *Cigarette* up past Fort Hamilton and through the Narrows. The *Cigarette* followed the Brooklyn shore, heading for Bay Ridge. By the time the *Cigarette* was off Bay Ridge, the *Gypsy* was too far behind to catch up by using speed alone. [23]

The *Cigarette*'s crew feared to proceed up either the East or North River and turned the vessel around, heading toward Staten Island. The *Gypsy* headed off the *Cigarette* and met the fugitive craft close to Stapleton. The *Cigarette* came to a halt and then turned swiftly. The *Cigarette* then charged ahead at full speed, attempting to ram the *Gypsy* amidships and cut it in half from the side. Sergeant Lee, anticipating this maneuver, ordered the man at the wheel to send it hard over. The Sergeant stood waiting for the impact with his pistol ready. The *Cigarette* crashed into the *Gypsy* near the stern and water poured in through the large hole. As the two boats came together, Lee and his men jumped aboard the *Cigarette*. After a brief struggle, the police subdued the four-man crew. [24]

The *Gypsy* was still taking on water, and Sergeant Lee, fearing that the launch would sink before any answer came to his distress signals, used the *Cigarette* to tow his boat to Pier 3 in Staten Island.

Halfway there, a fireboat appeared and gave assistance. When the boats reached Pier 3, the police boat *Manhattan* and the fireboat worked their pumps on the *Gypsy* to keep it from sinking. When the police searched the *Cigarette*, they found more than 200 cases of Scotch whisky. The police locked up the four members of the *Cigarette* crew at the police station in St. George.[25]

The following day, Inspector Michael Sweeney supervised the unloading of the *Cigarette's* cargo at Dead Man's Basin at the Barge Office. As the men offloaded the cargo around noon, two speedboats tried to pass into the North River through the harbor's thickest traffic. They were passing the Statue of Liberty at full speed when Sweeney spotted them heading for the Hudson River.[26]

Sweeney commandeered a new $18,000 speedboat belonging to a friend, Edward Reilly, a marine engineer. On a recent test run, the boat had attained a speed of 48 mph. Inspector Sweeney took two Customs Guards with him and took off in hot pursuit. Near Fifteenth Street, the two boats, *Man of War* and *Rose Marie,* were forced to separate to pass a lighter. Reilly's speedboat quickly caught up with the *Man of War.* The Customs guards jumped aboard the vessel while Inspector Sweeney continued his chase after the other boat. The three crew members of the *Man of War* surrendered immediately and the Customs guards found 300 cases of liquor aboard.[27]

Inspector Sweeney caught up to the *Rose Marie*, which tried to land on the New Jersey side of the river. Sweeney overtook the boat off Fiftieth Street and the crew surrendered, offering no resistance. He then ordered the boat to steer towards the Barge Office to join the *Cigarette* and the *Man of War.*[28]

"Stop shooting, this is a police boat!"

At midnight, on July 13, 1924, Police Launch No. 3., with Lieutenant Glavin aboard, left St. George, Staten Island to patrol the waters in the area. Until he boarded the launch, Glavin had been a desk lieutenant at the St. George Police Station. Deputy Chief Inspector Cornelius F. Cahalane had just assigned him to take charge of the Marine Division. The launch passed through the upper bay, went through the Narrows, and then moved down the lower bay to a point off Tottenville, S.I. After patrolling for several hours off the Staten Island shore, the police saw no craft that looked like rum-runners.[29]

The police boat then pulled off shore and headed out toward Ambrose Channel. Near the bell buoy off South Beach, about a half-mile from the entrance of the Narrows, Lieutenant Glavin thought he heard the chugging of a motor ahead. Since the police could see no light, they concluded that a rum-runner was attempting to sneak in under the cover of darkness. Sergeant Green, the commander of the launch, ordered full speed ahead. As was customary when chasing a suspected boat, the police launch turned off its lights and headed toward shore to cut off the suspected rum-runner. The men on the launch were all on the alert, trying to locate the fugitive.[30]

Off Quarantine and close to the course of the police launch, they were spotted by the Coast Guard Cutter *Surveyor*, commanded by Frank Johnson. The Coast Guardsmen thought the police launch was a rum-runner and gave chase. Johnson fired two shots across the bow of the launch. When those shots failed to stop it, a crewmember of the *Surveyor* fired three more shots. Lieutenant Glavin fell to the deck and cried out in the darkness, "I'm shot!"[31]

Sergeant Greene ordered the vessel's lights to be switched on and rushed to the side of the wounded lieutenant. Green then shouted to the *Surveyor*, "Stop shooting, this is a police boat!" The police boat stopped and the *Surveyor* came alongside. The two boats exchanged identities and then rushed Glavin to the Quarantine pier at Fort Wadsworth. In response to a phone call from the fort, an ambulance rushed from Staten Island Hospital. By the time it arrived, Lieutenant Glavin was unconscious. When he arrived at the hospital, Doctor George Montgomery found that one of the bullets had entered Glavin's left shoulder, the second his left groin, and the third the lower part of his back.[32]

Surgeons operated on Glavin and removed two of the bullets; they postponed removing the bullet from his groin until the following morning. While the wounds were very serious, the doctors said that Glavin had a chance to recover, provided he did not have blood poisoning.

Deputy Surveyor William R. Sanders, who made an investigation for the Customs authorities told the press:

> "At the time of the shooting it was not known that the suspected boat was a police launch. Our boat was running with lights and the police launch was running without lights. Naturally our men thought it was a bootleggers boat. The men on the Surveyor hailed the police launch, but it didn't stop. Two shots were fired in the air and it kept on. Three more shots were fired at the boat and unfortunately they wounded

> Lieutenant Glavin. Our boats make a practice never to run without lights inside the harbor." [33]

Lieutenant Glavin had been a member of the Police Department for thirty years. He spent fifteen of those years on Staten Island and the other fifteen in Manhattan and Brooklyn. He was fifty-five years old and lived with his wife and two daughters in Tottenville, S.I. A week earlier, he had discussed his long police service with his family and told them that he was considering retirement.[34]

17

SECRETARY MELLON IN THE HOT SEAT

In May 1924, Governor Gifford Pinchot of Pennsylvania spoke before a crowd of 3,000 men at a general conference of the Methodist Episcopal Church. His topic was the enforcement of Prohibition and Treasury Secretary Andrew Mellon's role in Federal corruption. The following are excerpts from his speech:

"Enforcement of the law is the greatest moral issue before the American people. Never before in our history has disregard for law and disobedience for the Constitution been so general, so dangerous, and so openly paraded. The moral forces of America have stood too long on the defensive. It is time for them to attack.

"I have repeatedly pointed out how the law can be enforced. In brief, give the Treasury Department the will to enforce the law, take the enforcement service wholly out of politics, and use the full power of the law through the permit system. When these three things are done, and well done, the law will be enforced. Until they are done, it will not.

"The failure of the Federal enforcement service is sometimes claimed to mean that the Eighteenth Amendment has failed. It means nothing of the sort. We are infinitely better off now, with all deductions made for wretched enforcement, than we were before. This law has not failed. What has failed is the enforcement of it.

"The Secretary of the Treasury opposes any investigation. I am sorry, for official opposition to being investigated is always unwise. He has publicly defended conditions which our whole people know to be scandalous in the extreme. He has publicly denounced the proposal to let in the light. There remains but a single remedy, and that is to let the light in, fix responsibility for the facts disclosed, and let public opinion prescribe the cure...

"Mr. Mellon's opposition to the investigation of the enforcement service will direct public attention and the attention of the investigating committee to the fact that Mr. Mellon was part owner of many thousands of barrels of Overholt whisky when the Eighteenth Amendment went into effect; to the fact that as late as March 31 of this year he was, on the authority of Senator Reed of Pennsylvania, still interested in the proceeds of this whisky when sold; to the ten illegal withdrawals of whisky, comprising more than 42,000 gallons, made from the Overholt warehouses near Pittsburgh, which led to indictments, and to the fact that the indictments were quashed and the men responsible were never punished.

"It will call attention of the committee- and if it does not, I will- to the ghastly break-down of the Federal enforcement service in Mr. Mellon's own city, in Mr. Mellon's own State and in other States, and to the degradation of public morals and the increase of human misery which that break-down has caused.

"I do not know whether it is legal for a man who has been in the whisky business for forty years to be at the head of the law enforcement, but I do know that it is wrong.

"I do not know whether it is legal for a man who has had, during his entire official life, a pecuniary interest in large quantities of whisky to be at the head of law enforcement, but I do know that it is wrong.

"Understand me clearly. I have no personal feeling either for or against Mr. Mellon. I am not questioning Mr. Mellon's ability as a financier. I am not talking about investigating the taxation of Mr. Mellon's investments, about which I know nothing, nor the Income Tax Bureau, nor anything else, except the failure of the Federal enforcement service. In that, as Governor of Pennsylvania, I am vitally concerned, and for that Mr. Mellon, as Secretary of the Treasury, is directly responsible.

"What our people and our Government need most of all is a return to first principles. Fall, Denby, Daugherty and the Federal enforcement service have taken from us much of our former confidence in the Government. The truth alone can restore it...

"I am a Republican, but I am not here to talk partisan politics. I am here to ask every one of you and the millions you represent, whatever your political faith, to unite in a common effort for righteousness in public life, for law enforcement, and for obedience to the Constitution of the United States." [1]

Pinchot got his wish two weeks later when Gaston Means testified before a Senate committee, called the Brookhart committee. Means, a former Department of Justice agent, told the committee that Secretary Mellon was involved in the wholesale withdrawal of liquor from bonded warehouses to assist banking institutions in liquidating "frozen" assets. Means went on to say that Andrew Mellon had entered into an arrangement with Rex Sheldon, which involved the sale of liquor withdrawal permits. After Sheldon received his commission, the proceeds from the liquor withdrawals were to be applied to wiping out the Republican National Committee's deficit. Means said that Mellon had admitted this to H.K. Scaife, a former agent of the Department of Justice, but later denied that he had done so.[2]

Senator Wheeler, who asked most of the questions on behalf of the committee, prompted Gaston Means to tell what he knew about the whisky situation in Pittsburgh. Means replied that he had made an investigation, under the direction of Jess Smith, in connection with the withdrawals of whisky from the Overholt Distillery. His instructions had been to determine the quantities of alcohol being withdrawn for both legitimate medical uses and other illegitimate purposes.[3]

At this point, Means created a stir in the committee room by stating that his investigation had led him to Motor Square Hotel and roadhouses in or near Pittsburgh. He claimed they were owned by either Mellon or the Mellon interests. He added that the Motor Square Hotel "ran wide open" and was "protected by town officials and State officials." Means told the committee that he had bought whisky at the hotel's bar.[4]

"They not only were guilty of selling whisky; there was no crime short of murder that they wouldn't commit there," said Means. "I don't want to go into the lewd side of it and tell about the dancing that I saw." He added that, at the time of his investigation, the Motor Square Hotel was so popular that a long line of automobiles seeking parking spots impeded traffic.[5]

Secretary Mellon responded to the charges by writing a letter to Senator Brookhart. The following are excerpts from that letter:

> ...There has been no intimation to me, directly or indirectly, that any campaign fund would be or has been benefited in any way by the issuance of the permits.
> The applications were handled on their merits and strictly in accordance with law...

Mr. Means again raises the question of my connection with the Overholt Distillery Company. My interest in the company was explained in detail in the Senate on March 31 last.

Since 1916 the Overholt Company has not manufactured any liquor. Prior to my becoming Secretary of the Treasury all of the assets of the company were transferred to a trust company with no authority to operate but only to dispose of the assets in accordance with law and distribute the proceeds. Since that time the trust company has sold or disposed of no whisky whatsoever excepting fifty-two cases to a drug company as permitted by the Volstead act.

...In addition to being a manufacturer of whisky, the Overholt Company was a warehouse, holding whisky belonging to other persons. After the passage of the national Prohibition act, whisky was released from the warehouse only on the production of the permits provided for by the regulations...

Mr. Means states that banks, particularly the line of banks with which I was formerly connected, have large loans secured by whisky certificates; that these banks are, therefore, interested in realizing on what Mr. Means calls "frozen assets," and therefore, in "bootlegging."

Since prohibition none of these banks has made or held any loan whatsoever on the security of whisky certificates. Since the collateral cannot be realized upon, and therefore loans secured by such collateral would not be sound loans for a bank to make. I question whether such loans exist in this country to any material extent.

...Mr. Means states that I had some arrangements with Rex Sheldon for the issuance of wholesale drug permits, conditioned upon contributions from the holders of these permits to the Republican campaign fund. Mr. Sheldon once did come to see me, but, as I recall, not in connection with permits. I understand that his request, about which there was nothing unusual, was not granted by the official of the Treasury to whom I have referred him.[6]

Two weeks later, a Federal Court issued a subpoena for Secretary Mellon and his secretary, Arthur Sixsmith, to testify at the trial of Gaston Means and his former secretary, Elmer W. Jarnecke. Means and Jarnecke were charged with conspiring to violate the Prohibition laws. Government witnesses had testified that they used graft money to purchase whisky withdrawal permits. The money from the liquor sales was used to repay a $1,700,000 loan that Mellon had made to the Republican Party to finance a campaign against Henry Ford.[7]

In his testimony, Means stated that Secretary Mellon had tried to prevent the prosecution of a Prohibition agent accused of taking part in a conspiracy that involved the use of forged permits and resulted in the withdrawal of $1,000,000 worth of whisky from a Pittsburgh distillery. "In this case," said Means, "a number of men were indicted and convicted. Among those indicted were three prohibition agents, one named Homer. Mellon tried to prevent the prosecution of Homer. My investigation in this case was one of the reasons for the indictment against me in today's case here." [8]

Andrew Mellon finally took the witness stand on June 26, 1924. Thomas B. Felder, counsel for the defense, questioned Mellon about John W. Hubbard, a Trenton steel manufacturer, who had testified that he gave Means $15,000 for legal withdrawal of whisky and complained to Mellon that Means had kept the money and did not deliver the liquor.[9]

"Did you own an interest in the Overholt Distillery Company at Pittsburgh?" asked Felder.

"I did, but the business has been liquidated," answered Mellon. The Court would not permit Felder to question Mellon on the extent of his interest.

"Do you know about the release from the Overholt Distillery of 2,950 cases and 49,000 gallons of whisky to a man named Goodman?" asked Felder. In response, Special Assistant Attorney Todd objected and Judge Wolverton upheld the objection. Felder argued that the question was of great importance, because Means had been dismissed from the Department of Justice and indicted due to his investigation into this alleged release of forged permits. Felder told the Court that Means found forged withdrawal permits for whisky in the Mellon National Bank in Pittsburgh, put up as collateral for a loan by a man named Goodman.

"Isn't it a fact that the forged permits used by Goodman were found in the Mellon National Bank?" asked Felder.

"Not to my knowledge," replied Mr. Mellon. "At the time of the Brookhart committee investigation into the Department of Justice I made inquiries of the banks in Pittsburgh and was informed that they had had no whisky permits as collateral for loans for as far back as 1915."[10]

Captain H.L. Scaife, formerly of the Department of Justice, sent a letter to Mellon a few hours after he testified. He also sent a copy to *The New York Times*, where it appeared the next day. The following are excerpts from that letter:

...In 1922 I determined to force to a public issue the graft and corruption which existed in Washington, and in April of that year I resigned from the Department of Justice as a protest and laid before Congress the facts in regard to the failure to prosecute war graft cases. On Aug. 15 of the same year I wrote you a letter calling attention to the corruption then existing in connection with the enforcement of prohibition laws...

Eventually, notwithstanding the official whitewashing in notorious cases and the official statements then being given out that millionaire bootleggers were in the past, on Dec. 8, 1922, President Harding delivered his message to Congress calling attention to widespread violations, official corruption, individual demoralization and the rending of the moral fibre of the republic through contempt for the law.

In refutation of the claim that your Old Overholt distillery went into liquidation before you became Secretary of the Treasury, I wish to call attention to Pro-Mimeograph 3005 of the Commision of Internal Revenue, showing that on Sept. 5, 1922, A. Overholt Company was designated by the Treasury Department as a concentration internal revenue bonded warehouse.

Your reported statements were made under circumstances which afford you protection and immunity, but in view of the high official position you occupy, I protest against your denying statements which you and I know to be correct.[11]

18

PIRATES ATTACK A FRENCH STEAMSHIP

In July 1924, pirates had attacked the French steamer *Mulhouse* off the New Jersey coast. The *Mulhouse*'s captain filed a report at Halifax, and a US Government agent investigated the captain's claims. The Treasury agent discovered that the captain was telling the truth and that pirates were attacking other ships in the area. Forty pirates had boarded the *Mulhouse* and stole 15,000 cases of liquor. They left 1,200 cases of liquor aboard to keep the steamer from entering US waters. Two days later, the pirates attacked another ship and stole 9,000 cases of liquor. As of July 15, the agent had not yet forwarded the results of his investigation to the Treasury Department. The investigation was on the initiative of local government officials in anticipation of a request by the State Department for information in order to satisfy possible French demands.[1] Although some details of the investigation were classified, the agent was still able to give the press a good account of what happened:

> "Piracy is rampant among the liquor ships off New Jersey and Long Island. Of course, we can't do anything about it because the ships attacked are too far out. There have been a number of raids on ships anchored off Montauk Point, but they are anchored out beyond our jurisdiction, so what can we do?
>
> "We ran into one of these pirate bands coming into port just after the raid on the French steamer, and just before the attack on the second vessel. They probably were part of a piratical crew that boarded the French ship and practically cleaned it out.
>
> "They had one of the finest and fastest boats I have ever seen in these waters. It was a motorboat, about fifty feet long, and was driven by three Liberty motors. I believe it could make a speed of thirty-five or forty miles an hour.
>
> "We suspected she was a rum-runner. There were five of us on my boat and we didn't suspect there were fifteen aboard the other ship when we boarded her. We saw four men in the pilot house when we climbed upon her decks.

"The men in the pilot house tried to induce us not to go below, stoutly maintaining that their boat carried no liquor and that there was nothing below. We went down anyway, and in the hold of the motorboat we found eleven other men and an elaborate collection of handcuffs, rifles, pistols, knives, and clubs.

"They were a desperate-looking lot of men. Some of them were young and athletic. Others were seasoned men. They looked ready for any kind of job. When we asked them about the firearms and the other suspicious weapons, they claimed that they were dumped there by unknown persons when the motorboat was tied up at the dock. We found no evidence on which we could hold them, so [we] let them go. It was the next night that the second piratical attack on one of the liquor ships resulted in the robbery of 9,000 cases of whisky.

"Our report shows that the pirates went aboard the Frenchman with a cleverly laid scheme. Their ship pulled alongside the French steamer. A member of the pirate band shouted to one of the men on the Frenchman that he wanted to buy some champagne and whiskys. The Frenchman asked the other boat, supposedly a rum-runner, to send its order aboard.

"Two of the pirates went aboard with the order. While the Frenchmen were looking over the order, the other pirates swarmed on the deck of the French steamer, carrying rifles, pistols, and handcuffs. They quickly lined up every man in the Frenchman's crew and snapped handcuffs on them. Then they marched their prisoners below decks where the Frenchmen were held while the ship was looted." [2]

Virtually all rum ships carried foreign flags, and in the previous few months, several governments complained to the United States that pirates had robbed their vessels of huge sums. The Treasury Department's stance was that there was no reason why the US should protect the safety of crews carrying liquor to be sold to smugglers. The law of piracy was fixed in the United States Revised Statutes and regulated by international treaties. Any pirates seized on the high seas could be brought before the courts of the nation whose vessel seized them and punished by the laws of that nation. Section 5370 of the United States Revised Statues states that:

Every person who upon the high seas or in any open roadstead, or in any haven, basin or bay, or in any river where the sea ebbs and flows, commits the crime of robbery in or upon any vessel or in or upon any of the ship's company of any vessel or the landing thereof, is a pirate and shall suffer death.[3]

Another section of the statutes states that every member of the crew of a vessel engaged in acts of piracy is a pirate and liable to the death penalty. With these harsh punishments in the statutes, one might wonder why anyone would be willing to take such a risk. The answer lies in the legal loopholes. If one of the pirates were captured, the agents who seized him would have had to take him to the United States or have him taken as a prisoner to the nation from which the rum ship had cleared. Under the Customs laws, a ship entering an American harbor was required to register. A rum ship could not do this without agents seizing its cargo. Therefore, it was very unlikely that a shipmaster would have brought his vessel into port to testify against a pirate.[4]

Captain Bernard H. Camden, executive officer of the New York District of the Coast Guard stated that he was certain a great volume of cash changed hands in Rum Row, despite the recent trend of paying land agents for the liquor and bringing the receipt to a rum ship. Captain Camden gave his insight to *The New York Times*:

> "Is it any wonder that rum ships are held up? They are isolated and poorly protected, and most of the liquor sales are made at night. Have you ever stopped to consider the amount of cash that might be accumulated aboard one of these vessels? Supposing a vessel carries 5,000 cases of liquor. This, sold at $40 a case, would bring $200,000 cash.
>
> "These rum-runners are men of desperate character, and the fact compels the Captain to be most cautious when he is making any money transactions with them. Early in the days of rum-running several masters were cheated by rum-runners who, in the darkness, paid them with counterfeit money.
>
> "When one of the runners draws up to the rum ship and makes fast, only one, or perhaps two, of its crew are permitted by the armed guard to come aboard the vessel. Once aboard, the rum buyer must go straight to the cabin to make arrangements with the Captain. Pirates have been known to visit a vessel two or three times, sizing up the strength of the crew and gaining the confidence of the Captain. On the third visit they have attacked.
>
> "Concealed in the rum boat there might be ten or twelve armed men, most of them underworld characters to whom the thought of murder is not distasteful. The head of the

crew comes aboard, bringing with him a companion, and together they barter with the Captain alone in his cabin. The Captain thinks he knows them and is not suspicious. However, at a given signal, the two attack the Captain, and before he knows what happened they have beaten him into unconsciousness.

"The discharge of a revolver may be the signal for the waiting members of the rum-runner's crew to hop aboard. Brandishing revolvers and knives, they climb over the rail very much in the way that the pirates did centuries ago. It is an easy matter to waylay a few sleepy sailors, unsuspicious for the most part, and the whole crew are taken below and handcuffed.

"They may be kidnapped and taken ashore, or they may be carried off to another ship. In some cases they have been left to free themselves as best they might." [5]

Two weeks after pirates attacked the *Mulhouse*, the French Consulate in Halifax, Nova Scotia, started its own investigation of the attack. According to the *Mulhouse*'s captain, the pirates had stolen 33,200 cases, more than double the figure he had reported to the US Treasury Department two weeks earlier. When the *Mulhouse* docked at Halifax, Captain Ferrene reported that on June 24 thirty pirates boarded his vessel and imprisoned the crew for ten days. While the crew was imprisoned, the pirates transferred the liquor to eight schooners. The captain reported the names of all eight steamers to the authorities and also informed them that the pirates boarded the steamer from a speedboat of New York registry. James Frazer, who represented the owners, estimated the value of the stolen liquor at $500,000. The cargo included brandy, whisky, champagne, and wine. [6]

The owners of the vessel declared that they had instructed the captain not to stop en route from Canada to Bordeaux; therefore, they were not part of a conspiracy to break any law. Because they were conducting what they claimed to be a legitimate business, the owners demanded protection under French law. The Maritime Tribunal of Brest, France reviewed the case and decided to take action. Captain Fournier instructed Comissaire Legrande of the St. Georges district, Paris, to conduct a special investigation. The French police suspected that the pirates had planned the raid in Paris and that prominent persons were involved in the crime. The French government requested that the US Government assist in finding the pirates and, once arrested, extradite them for trial in a French maritime court.[7]

On September 16, four men entered a police station in Paris near the Opera House. Two of them were French traders making shipments to the United States. The third man was a detective. The fourth man, who the other men held tightly by the arms, was Captain Max Jerome Pfaff, an American citizen who was born in Germany. He gave his address as 219 East 196th Street, New York.

"We charge this man with robbery on the high seas," said the traders, while the captain violently defended his innocence. Pfaff told the police that the other men were mistaken and produced papers to back his claim. His accusers, however, were so positive of his guilt that the Police Comissaire decided to hold the captain under police supervision, although they did not immediately arrest him. A telegram dispatched to Brest brought confirmation of the charges and the police arrested Pfaff the following morning.[8]

Earlier, Pfaff had arrived from London via Antwerp and Brussels. Since leaving London, a detective had been following him the whole time. Police hoped that Pfaff's arrest would help them learn the identities of the other pirates.[9] The police transferred Pfaff to the naval barracks jail in Brest, where he awaited his trial. Pfaff faced a possible sentence of death by hanging. The preliminary hearing was set for the following Friday; however, P.G.E. Gide, of the Paris and London Bar Association, acting for the defense, requested a postponement to further review his client's case before entering a plea of not guilty.[10]

The French law of 1825 still governed cases of piracy on the high seas. The penalty for conviction was death by hanging. There had been no trial under that law since 1871, when a Greek privateer was tried at Toulon, convicted, and executed. The Admiral commanding the Brest region appointed the tribunal, which was composed of a naval officer with the rank of captain, two lieutenants, one naval engineer, and three judges attached to the local civil courts.[11]

Pfaff's attorney stated that he planned to enter a plea of not guilty and challenge the competency of the tribunal. If the tribunal overruled these measures, he would offer an alibi to prove that Pfaff was in Halifax when pirates boarded and looted the *Mulhouse*. In the proceedings, Pfaff was entitled to admit that he smuggled contraband liquor into the United States and could have demanded a trial in a US court. The defense also could have argued that the *Mulhouse*'s owners were liable to the American courts. Pfaff declared that he was unwilling "to be made the goat" and said he would implicate men "higher up" in America, as well as well-known firms in Great Britain.[12]

Mrs. Pfaff told *The New York Times* that her husband was a lawyer, not a pirate. She stated that he had studied law in Chattanooga, Tennessee, and was licensed to practice in New York State, although he had no office there. She added that her husband was not a "captain," nor was he working at sea in any other capacity. She claimed that he had simply gone abroad on a business trip.[13]

When the trial began on September 27, Captain Fournier grilled Pfaff for twelve hours. The tribunal conducted the examination in strict privacy, in the presence of Pfaff's attorney. Afterward, Gide told the press that his client had repudiated the accusation of piracy, but had given many interesting details concerning the smuggling of liquor into the United States.[14]

Three days later, Pfaff emerged from the courthouse smiling, after the tribunal questioned him for another nine hours. Pfaff pleaded not guilty and declared he could provide an alibi. He argued that it was not necessary for him to commit piracy, because he had unlimited credit with a big Canadian bank, enabling him to purchase contraband whisky without the use of "Captain Kidd" methods. He told the court he was prepared to produce documents, which would show that, on three different occasions, the Canadian bank had given him letters of credit for £25,000 in order to purchase whisky in England for smuggling into the United States.[15]

"What whisky houses in London were supplying you?" asked Commandant Fournier.

"I am saving that for another day," responded Pfaff.[16]

Pfaff told the court that a man imprisoned in Montreal, awaiting trial on charges of piracy and rum-running, was behind his arrest. He declared that the man had pirated his boat, the *Lutzen*, carrying 20,000 cases of whisky. Pfaff told the Commandant that "this was just a little matter between rum-runners, and I don't see why French justice should bother about it." As to the charge of being an instigator of the alleged piracy, even though he was not actually present, Pfaff told the court: "You will know all about the instigators before this case is finished. I am not going to be made the goat." [17]

The interpreter had some difficulty translating "goat" to the Commandant. Fournier told Pfaff that he was anxious to have the entire truth brought out and would send a commission to Canada to obtain affidavits from persons whom Pfaff claimed had seen him in Halifax the day pirates had looted the *Mulhouse*.

The prosecution based its case on a confession Pfaff allegedly had made traveling on a train between Southampton and London earlier that month. Although Pfaff denied the "confession," special detectives filed three affidavits with Commandant Fournier, describing the details of his conversations with them. These were the same detectives who had trailed him since his departure from the London. Pfaff declared that he knew no more about the *Mulhouse* piracy than any other smuggler off the American coast. In order to expedite the legal proceedings and to shorten Pfaff's time in jail, the defense announced that it would commission a firm of New York lawyers to obtain affidavits at Halifax to prove his alibi.[18]

On October 1, Pfaff withstood another ten-hour examination before Commandant Fournier. When the smoke of the courtroom battle cleared, Pfaff succeeded in having the original charge of piracy dropped, along with the possible death sentence. The prosecution now charged him with the lesser offense of "complicity in organizing piracy on the high seas." The prosecution also agreed to allow Pfaff to post a $35,000 bail. The abandonment of the major piracy charge was the result of testimony by James Kimpton, an American citizen living in Paris. Kimpton was the *Mulhouse*'s supercargo and testified that Pfaff was not among the men who boarded the vessel and stole the whisky.[19]

Following Kimpton's testimony and the substitution of the lesser charge, Pfaff again pleaded not guilty and continued to deny any knowledge of the *Mulhouse* incident. He explained that his "confession" in regard to the *Mulhouse* had merely been some remarks made to traveling companions aboard a train after having too many drinks. Pfaff protested that he did not have the slightest intention of running away from France and even planned for his wife and daughter to come to Brest to stay with him during the trial, if he could get out of jail. However, Pfaff did not post his $35,000 bail and returned to the naval jail that evening.[20]

At the close of the day's session, Commandant Fournier told an Associated Press correspondent that the evidence indicated that more than 150,000 cases of whisky, brandy, and wine had entered the US along the shores of Maine, Massachusetts, Connecticut, and New York during June. Fournier also told the correspondent that he had the names and addresses of men higher up in the whisky ring in New York and these would come out during Pfaff's trial. He also had the address of the meeting place in New York, where brokers for whisky firms met agents of whisky rings and closed six-figure deals daily.[21]

"These men have unlimited financial backing," Commandant Fournier said. "One of the strongest banks in Canada is shown as financing many of their deals." Fournier said that if the US sent a

Prohibition agent with the proper credentials, he would share the information with him. Commandant Fournier called upon the owners of the *Mulhouse* to produce bills of lading for the vessel's cargo, the ship's log, and its insurance papers. He also demanded that Captain Ferrero, commander of the *Mulhouse*, come to Brest to tell the story of the pirate attack.[22]

The Commandant was especially interested in obtaining the vessel's insurance policy. He wanted to know whether the *Mulhouse* was insured for a cargo of fish, as the captain claimed, or a shipload of liquor. It seemed likely that the preliminary investigation of Pfaff would drag on for weeks, perhaps months. Attorneys Pierre Gide and M. Legouasguen argued that French Naval Justice could not keep an American citizen in jail indefinitely at the request of a French firm, which, they asserted, admitted to breaking American laws.[23]

Fournier found another puzzling matter in the affidavits. According to the sworn statements, although the Coast Guard Cutters *Manhattan* and *Kickapoo* had come within hailing distance of the *Mulhouse* twice, supposedly while the pirates were raiding and unloading, they had not intervened.[24]

Pfaff complained bitterly about the unsanitary conditions of the arsenal jail, built under the direction of Jean Baptiste Colbert in the early eighteenth century. "This jail may have been all right in 1700, but it is getting a little bit damp now," said Pfaff. Commandant Fournier allowed Pfaff to have a long talk with a correspondent, during which he said:

> "I am caught in a fight between master smugglers. These people don't care how long they keep me in jail as long as they collect their insurance and don't have to pay their shareholders any dividends. Why was it these people were insured against piracy? They must have been expecting it."[25]

When the US Government received the information from France concerning Pfaff and the list of names he had provided, the Justice Department revealed some details of its own probe. US agents had been conducting an investigation that involved Pfaff and Alexander Adelman, who figured more prominently in the operations. However, the agents had no definite information on William McCoy (a.k.a. the "real McCoy") who Pfaff also named in court. Federal Attorney William Hayward assigned F.A. McGuirk to conduct a further investigation based on the information Pfaff gave in Brest. The Justice Department's investigation revealed the existence of a New York and Canadian gang of pirates, who sometimes seized ships and, at other times, faked piracies to collect insurance on stolen cargoes.[26]

Alexander Adelman's attorney, Bernard M. Reich, told the press that his client had nothing to do with Pfaff. Reich went on to claim that Adelman was a wealthy resident of Montreal, where he owned a wholesale clothing house and was also engaged in the rubber business. He said that, although his client had gone to Europe several weeks earlier, he expected to hear from him in a couple of days regarding Pfaff's allegations.[27]

Reich's representation of his client's background was slightly overblown. In fact, Adelman owned a little tailor shop on Clarke Street in Montreal. Over the preceding weeks, his neighbors had not seen him very often. Adelman had been so busy over the previous two years that he seemed to have put down the needle for good. He did not flaunt his wealth, but when he was home, a stream of expensive, fast cars stopped by. Adelman was frequently away for weeks at a time. When reporters asked his neighbors about his whereabouts, they answered only with smiles.[28]

According to Prohibition Director R.Q. Merrick, the federal investigation showed that Pfaff and Adelman were members of a gang, operating out of Canada, with its headquarters in New York City. The gang shipped liquor from St. John, New Brunswick, presumably for the Caribbean, and discharged the cargoes off Long Island. Pirates had seized one such cargo off Long Island from the schooner *Lutzen*. However, the *Lutzen*'s crew was soon selling the "stolen" liquor off Atlantic Highlands, NJ. Investigators said that Adelman's part of the work had been to arrange the sales offshore. Pfaff arranged for the transportation of liquor ashore. The agents believed that Adelman was part owner of the Sidney Wine and Spirit Company of Montreal, a large shipper of liquor, which happened to own the *Lutzen*.[29]

Commandant Fournier's statement that a leading Canadian bank financed the operations of the rum-runners off the coast of the United States caused no excitement in Montreal. People in that city had already been talking about it for months before Pfaff's case had become a public spectacle. In 1924, there were only twelve large chartered banks in Canada, all closely associated through the Canadian Bankers Association. It was very rare that news reflecting on the management of any of the banks wound up in print. At least five of these Canadian banks had branches in New York. Any advances the banks made to rum-runners through those branches would be liable under American law.[30]

Tall Tales

In this increasingly complicated story of conspiracies, mock pirate attacks, and insurance fraud, it is often difficult to tell the real pirate stories from fabricated ones. A year earlier, John M. Isaacs had signed an affidavit describing a pirate attack on the *Lutzen*. According to Isaacs, the schooner left St. John, New Brunswick, on October 9, 1923, headed for Havana with 4,100 cases of Scotch whisky. A few days after leaving Canada, the schooner came to anchor off Bay Shore. The following day, Isaacs claimed, a gang of men, stowaways or boarders from one of the hovering speedboats, confronted the crew with pistols and herded them below as prisoners.[31]

A man who said he was "Captain Ford," threatened to "drill holes through anybody making trouble" and only allowed the prisoners to go up on deck for exercise and air. Captain Ford took the schooner to a point off Atlantic Highlands, all the while expressing his disappointment at the small cargo. He announced that he would sell every case and planned to take the vessel and prisoners to Buenos Aires. The day after the *Lutzen* arrived off Atlantic Highlands, a fishing schooner, named *Plymouth*, came alongside and bought forty cases. Captain Ford jeeringly displayed the money he received to the prisoners. On the following day, Ford supposedly sent a man ashore to inform customers of a change in the schooner's position. Over the next twelve days, Captain Ford sold 2,300 cases of liquor to visiting speedboats, while his men kept the prisoners under guard. According to the affidavit, Captain Ford taunted the prisoners with thousand-dollar bills. The next morning, a dozen boats came alongside and Ford sold the remaining cargo. The *Lutzen* then sailed for Bermuda, where the pirates put the prisoners ashore, and then supposedly headed south.[32]

Meanwhile, the Sidney Wine and Spirit Company had become "alarmed" over the missing *Lutzen*. The firm's attorneys informed the authorities in Ottawa and Washington, requesting help in finding the craft. An airplane flew out of New York City several times in search of the vessel. On October 23, the pilot reported sighting the *Lutzen* off Atlantic Highlands. He reported that the schooner had been repainted and renamed the *Lyon*, which matched the information in the Isaacs affidavit.[33]

There are several aspects of this story that destroy its credibility. First of all, Isaacs did not know whether the pirates hid themselves on the *Lutzen* or came by speed boat. Second, a pirate would not hold a ship full of captives for two weeks so close to the US coast. If the captives were really being held against their will, they would have posed a risk to the pirates, especially with the Coast Guard and Customs patrolling the area. Captives also need to eat, drink, and carry out certain bodily functions. Why would pirates take on these unnecessary burdens when they could have simply held the crew at gunpoint and stole the liquor? The answer is: they most likely would not.

Isaacs' affidavit also stated that "Captain Ford" had taunted the crew with $1,000 bills. This was very unlikely, because smugglers were generally not making cash transactions at sea in 1923. Customers made the purchases at a land office and brought a torn playing card or some other type of receipt with them to pick up the liquor. Also, $1,000 bills were as almost as rare outside of bank vaults in 1923 as they are today.[‡‡‡] The average smuggler could not have used a $1,000 bill because most businesses would not have provided change for such a large denomination. Also, a smuggler could not have deposited a $1,000 bill without bringing the attention of the police or the Internal Revenue Service. Keep in mind that in 1923, $1,000 was more than enough to buy a new car.

A year after the incident, Captain Samuel Ford faced piracy charges in a Montreal courtroom. However, the New York Prohibition Office knew that Ford had ties to Alexander Adelman and Max Jerome Pfaff. Both Adelman and Pfaff were connected with the Sidney Wine and Spirit Company, which owned the vessel that Ford had supposedly attacked and stolen. Captain Walters, a co-defendant of Ford's at the *Lutzen* trial, wrote an affidavit stating that Pfaff had offered him $10,000 to pull off the *Mulhouse* piracy. However, Walters turned the job down because it was too dangerous. One only has to connect the dots to see that the *Lutzen* and *Mulhouse* piracies were both staged.[34]

On examining the evidence, Fournier told the press that Pfaff had traveled to Europe to purchase £75,000 worth of whisky in England. The Commandant also learned that the liquor Pfaff purchased had just landed in the US within the past day or two. Pfaff was hurrying home on the ship *Leviathan* when the three men apprehended him and brought him to the Paris police station. Pfaff was anxious to arrive in time to take delivery of the liquor cargo. Adelman received the entire shipment and Pfaff feared that he would lose his entire share of the profits.[35]

[‡‡‡] The Treasury and Federal Reserve discontinued the use of bank notes over $100 in 1969 due to a lack of use. Although bank notes of $1,000 were issued until 1969, they were not printed after 1945.

"My share of the profits amounts to $35,000," Pfaff told the Commandant.

"Just cable Adelman to deposit that amount with the French Consul General in New York and I will let you out on bail immediately," Fournier replied.[36]

One of the witnesses at Captain Ford's trial was a New York bootlegger named Frank Hoffman. He testified that the activities of the Coast Guard cutters along Rum Row were mostly for show. A few of the Coast Guardsmen, he said, might have been serious about trying to make a name for themselves, but the majority of the officers were "in on the game." He claimed that a $10,000 bribe was enough to buy protection for a year, but the man who paid the bribe could make over $50,000 in that same year. Hoffman explained that when bootleggers used trucks to transport liquor cargo, traffic policemen on motorcycles either went along with them or telephoned ahead to clear the way. The average cost of police protection was $3 a case.[37]

On October 24, Commandant Fournier listened as the affidavits of the *Mulhouse*'s officers and crew were read aloud to the court. All of the affidavits stated that Phaff was not among the pirates who boarded and looted the ship. Martin Legasse, general manager of the company that owned the *Mulhouse*, gave the names of the schooners that took part in unloading the big whisky cargo. He declared that the first schooner to reach the *Mulhouse* was the *Petara*, commanded by William McCoy. The others, he testified, were the *Clarke Gorcum*, the *Quacco Queen*, the *Tessie Aubrie*, the *Mary Bradner*, the *Genevieve*, and the *Catherine Marie*.[38] Two weeks later, Pfaff got out of prison on a bail of 5,000 francs.[39]

Pfaff boarded a ship, named *President Harding*, bound for New York. The United States Lines, which had been somehow involved in the mock piracies, happened to own the *Harding*. While the *President Harding* crossed the Atlantic, the ship encountered the four-masted British schooner *Veronica*, which had been missing for six weeks. The *Veronica* shot up flares as a distress signal and the captain of the *Harding* responded by sending his ship's boats out to help. The schooner's captain reported that pirates had raided his ship and that it was "adrift"; however, the details of the story did not add up.[40]

The *Veronica's* captain reported to Captain Paul Greening of the *President Harding* that pirates raided his ship on November 15. He also reported that, after raiding the *Veronica*, they stole the compass magnets and put the chronometer out of order. Here is an excerpt from a message Captain Greening sent to the United States Lines via wireless telegraph:

> The Veronica requested a tow. They attempted to lower a case of liquor to the ship's boats. The President Harding was delayed two hours on account of rendering assistance to the Veronica, which, to all appearances, was seaworthy and had a large crew in good health, who were satisfied to remain on board. Believe Veronica broke from moorings during recent gales. Owners acknowledged report.[41]

A tugboat towed the *Veronica* into port at Halifax, Nova Scotia on November 21. The schooner's captain and the two supercargoes refused to talk about what happened, but the mate, J.T. Tweedle, was willing to tell his version to the press. He said that fifteen men had boarded the ship on October 24 off Montauk Point, under the pretense of buying liquor. When the men were aboard, they drew revolvers and subdued the crew. After the pirates took charge, they proceeded to sell the liquor cargo to smaller craft until nearly all of it was gone. Tweedle went on to say that the pirates confined the officers in the chain locker and forced the crew to assist in disposing of the cargo. He also claimed that the pirates locked the entire crew in a compartment every night and kept them under guard until morning.[42]

Then, according to the *Veronica*'s mate, after three weeks the "pirates" left the ship. As they left, they crippled the engines, smashed the compass, chronometer, and other instruments. After that, the pirates went over the side, leaving the ship an aimless hulk. The mate claimed that the ship drifted about and the officers had been unable to take their bearings. When the *President Harding* conveniently happened to come across the "disabled" vessel, it was 100 miles off of Cape Sable, Nova Scotia.[43]

After assisting the *Veronica,* the *President Harding* soon arrived in New York. Once Max Pfaff set foot in New York he denied that he had offered to tell US Government officials the inside story of the bootlegging industry. He also added that he would file a civil suit for damages against those responsible for his arrest. He told reporters:

> "I know nothing about bootlegging or the people engaged in it. I am a lawyer and intend to return to my practice. I am innocent of the charges brought against me and can prove that I was in Halifax on June 24 when the attack was made on the Mulhouse...I was never near the steamship Mulhouse in my life. The French officials acted without authority in arresting me as they did." [44]

ALCOHOL, BOAT CHASES, AND SHOOTOUTS!

Max Pfaff was not the only one to change his story. J.T. Tweedle re-told his story to the press a few months later, changing some major details. In February 1925, he told this version of the story:

> "...While lying off Montauk the crew grew rebellious and demanded more money for overtime. They were given a 50 percent increase in wages if they would stick to the ship. Speed boats then came alongside and took off 4,500 cases, mostly of whisky, and a few came aboard with another man to arrange for the sale of the remaining cargo. It was agreed that a schooner be chartered for this work.
>
> "Three days later launches approached bearing men who declared they were the buyers of the remaining stock. They asked for a drink and when I led them to my cabin I found myself covered with four revolvers and was then thrown into No. 2 hold, bound and blindfolded, where I remained two days without food or water before I was released and ordered to take some soundings and work as a navigator for the pirates. My next surprise was when the pirates' mate told me a United States revenue cutter [a Coast Guard cutter] had been sighted, but for reasons I can only hint at the cutter cleared off."[45]

In this version, Tweedle said that the pirates had held them for three days and then released the crew. The crew then informed the *Veronica's* captain what course he should take and told him that the pirates intended to follow the ship with their machine guns ready.[46]

These accounts of the alleged pirate attack are far too inconsistent for the story to be true. The vessel's captain said the attack happened on November 15, while Tweedle claimed that it occurred on October 24. In one account, the pirates held the ship captive for three days, in another, three weeks. Tweedle's later account does not mention anything about the pirates sabotaging the ship's engine or equipment, which conflicts with his original version.

According to the *President Harding*'s captain, the crew had appeared to be in good health and wanted to remain aboard the *Veronica*. This scenario would be highly unlikely after three weeks of captivity and forced labor by armed pirates. Another unbelievable aspect of the story is the idea that the *Veronica* was adrift and the officers and crew had no idea which direction to go. The *Veronica* was a four-masted schooner, so even if the engine was not working, the ship could have used its sails. If the "pirates" sabotaged the rudder, the crew could have maneuvered the sails to steer the vessel. According to Tweedle's first account, the pirates smashed the navigational equipment. However, anyone trained in basic navigation knows how to find direction using the sun and the stars. The schooner was about 100 miles off the North American coast. Even in the highly unlikely scenario that a ship full of sailors did not know how to use the stars to navigate, they could have just headed in the opposite direction of the sunrise and followed the sunset later on in the day. Several newspapers printed these ridiculous accounts and most likely there were many people who believed them. However, these inconsistent stories were just fabrications to cover up insurance fraud and provided a way out of paying investors their dividends.

19

ALIENS, NARCOTICS, AND A BULLETPROOF BOAT

At the beginning of 1924, the British four-masted schooner *Rask* sailed from England with 20,000 cases of Scotch whisky, worth about $1,000,000. After sitting off the coast for six months, the *Rask* was anchored fifteen miles off Ambrose Lightship carrying only about 2,000 cases of whisky. The captain came up on deck one morning and saw signals flying from the *Bessie*, another vessel in the liquor fleet, asking for medical assistance. The *Rask*'s physician, Ralph Folkes, responded. He found that Ralph Conrad, one of the crew, was dying from injuries caused by an exploding gasoline engine. Conrad needed to go to a hospital immediately, but getting him to shore from a rum-ship, without putting him on a rum-runner, was going to be a challenge. The problem was solved with the appearance of the *Elsie B.*, an American yacht with Matthew Hanson and Lou Richards on board. Three days earlier, Hanson had received a summons for smoking on the deck of a Staten Island ferryboat and was on his way to the First District Court.[1]

After being signaled by the *Bessie*, Hanson brought his yacht about and agreed to take the seaman ashore, accompanied by Folkes and Philip Smith, another crewmember. The *Elsie B.* headed for Rockaway Point, and as it was rounding the point, the thought occurred to Hanson that Folkes and Smith, being foreigners, had no right to land on American shores without the proper documents. At the same time, the lookout of the Rockaway Coast Guard station spotted the *Elsie B.* and hailed it. A crew put out in one of the speedboats, assuming that the vessel was smuggling liquor. When Captain G. Moran, commander of the station, learned about the injured man, he called an ambulance for him from Rockaway Beach Hospital and detained the other four men.[2]

Moran recalled headlines in *The New York Times* concerning the recent capture of thirty-one Italian immigrants attempting to land near Rockaway on a small boat. To be on the safe side, Captain Moran took the four men before Edward Barnes, Assistant Solicitor of Customs, who released the two Americans and ordered the two British citizens be escorted back to their ship.[3]

A week later, the Coast Guard captured Hanson and Richards again, after firing a shot across the *Elsie B.'s* bow. There were 200 cases of liquor aboard the yacht. When the Coast Guardsmen checked Hanson's pockets, they found two letters written by crewmembers of the *Rask*. One of the letters had a stamp and was not opened. Since the other was unstamped, the Coast Guardsmen opened it. The letter was written by Robert W. Wylie Jr., a seaman on the *Rask*, and was addressed to his father at Glasgow, Scotland. It read:

> Just a line to let you know all is well and dandy. Don't write any more as we are nearly empty and shall soon be home. We are having fine weather and have only about 2,000 cases, which we will discharge in two days if all goes well. I hope you and the family are all right as this finds me well, and if I get all my bonus and the wages due me I'll not forget to bring some presents home.
>
> There are so many sales here and things are four times cheaper than at home. Well, parents, this is a very exciting life out here. There are boatloads of Chinese, Italians, Greeks, &c., all waiting to be smuggled into the States. There are also a couple of steamships with opium, heroin, morphine and cocaine, all of which is being smuggled in every day.
>
> There is a seaplane that comes out and loads nineteen cases which it carries on each trip, making over six trips daily. There is a launch nearby and I must close. With love and kisses to all.[4]

Hanson and Richards appeared again before Assistant Solicitor Barnes, only a week after he released them. Hanson admitted buying 200 cases of liquor from the *Rask*. He said the usual price was $15 a case, but he had gotten a discount because he assisted with evacuating the wounded man a week earlier.[5]

In response to the confiscated letter, Special Agent Van Doren told the press that he would ask Washington to use Coast Guard cutters and naval destroyers to visit and inspect all foreign boats in the rum fleet outside the twelve-mile limit. Van Doren also stated that, if the Coast Guard officers found the statements in Wylie's letter to be correct, they would forward a report to the State Department. The State Department, in turn, would make representations to the various countries whose ships were lying in Rum Row.[6]

Beach Mob Fights Over Liquor

During the night of July 24, smugglers brought ashore 2,000 cases of liquor, leaving them on the sands of Rockaway Beach, NY. Piles of cases stretched over half a mile of beach. Bootleggers were supposed to arrive at night to load them into trucks and drive them away; however, the trucks failed to arrive as scheduled. When vacationers came out of their bungalows for an early morning swim, they shouted with glee and awakened the entire waterfront. By 6 A.M., the beach was covered with tourists dragging cases to their bungalows on the beach.[7]

When Police Sergeant Masterson of the Rockaway Beach Precinct saw the melee, he immediately telephoned the reserves. Hundreds of summer residents were milling about and fighting over cases of whisky. Men, women, and children dragged out cases and hustled them into automobiles. Whenever two or more persons attempted to seize a case, they fought each other with their fists and shouted profanities. Even after the police reserves arrived, scores of the mob persisted in struggling for the liquor. Of the two thousand cases originally left on the beach, only two hundred wound up in police hands. Of the hundreds who stormed the beach, the police arrested only four.[8]

Customs Agents Fire 600 Rounds At A Rum-Runner

A few days after the beach incident, Customs agents Lyons, Geary, and Dureck were patrolling off Montauk Point early one morning in a speedboat named the *Shark*. The agents were running without lights when they spotted a speeding yacht headed straight for them. As the yacht approached, the agents increased their speed to 25 knots in preparation for a chase. Special Agent Lyons yelled through a megaphone, "Heave to, Customs officers!"[9]

The yacht increased its speed and headed directly for the Customs patrol boat, which turned hard to port to avoid being rammed. The Customs agents responded by firing three magazines of ammunition from their Lewis machine gun. The yacht attempted to ram the Customs boat three times and, although the *Shark* was traveling at a speed of 33 knots, the yacht began to leave the agents behind. During the yacht's third ramming attempt, Special Agent Lyons emptied his eighth 'pan' of bullets, which could penetrate half an inch of steel from half a mile.

Agent Geary turned the wheel hard to starboard to dodge the yacht. Agent Lyons, still manning the machine gun at the stern, flew overboard as the *Shark* made a sharp turn. [10]

Agents Geary and Dureck threw out a 130-foot lifeline and circled Lyons twice before he managed to grab hold. Meanwhile, the yacht had disappeared. As the two agents were about to pull Lyons out of the water, Geary yelled, "There's another one over toward Cornfield Lightship!" Leaving Agent Lyons hanging on to the lifeline, the other agents brought the *Shark* up to 35 knots, dragging Lyons across the water. After being dragged several hundred yards, he climbed aboard the patrol boat. The *Shark* chased the second yacht for four miles and the agents fired 600 rounds before it stopped.[11]

The agents discovered that their captured vessel was the *Williams 18,* a $150,000, eighty-six foot yacht, famous for its speed along Rum Row. When the agents boarded the vessel, they noticed that most of the bullets had found their target, filling the steel-plated hull with holes. There were so many holes that the vessel was half full of water, and the 800 cases of whisky, many of which were also full of holes, were afloat. However, the Customs boat was still able to tow the *Williams 18* to the Battery. Customs searched for the other yacht the next day, but saw no sign of it. Judging from the condition of the *Williams 18,* the agents assumed the other yacht had sunk.[12]

Peter J. Sullivan, in charge of the Customs Marine Patrol, broadcast a general alarm up and down the coast after the Montauk fight. Two weeks later, the Deputy Collector at New London, Connecticut told Sullivan that a craft matching the description was tied up at a dock at Mystic. When agents Lyons, Geary, and Proschak came up from the New York office, they found the vessel abandoned. The boat had originally been a US Navy torpedo boat, valued at $100,000; it had been converted into an armor-clad rum-runner named the *Com-an-Go.* The boat was protected by heavy steel plates. A steel deck roofed a hold with a capacity of at least 400 cases. The bulletproof steel cabin contained a duplicate steering wheel.[13]

On the return trip to New York, the Customs agents were able to bring the *Com-an-Go* up to a speed of thirty-three knots. At the Barge Office, the Customs men pointed out more than sixty dabs of fresh gray paint on the hull, covering dents that looked like bullet holes. The vessel contained no liquor. It also had no navigation papers or license number. However, marine records showed that a license had been issued for a boat of this type to Philip Kobrin, who lived on 116th Street in Manhattan. When the agents went to his apartment, he was not there. His wife told the agents that her husband had never owned a boat and had been working at a produce firm in the Harlem Market for twelve years.[14]

Customs agents liked the sturdy war vessel and planned to use it for future operations. They were not willing to part with their prize easily. The agents told the press that if anyone claimed the vessel, that person would be charged with attempting to ram and sink a government boat.[15]

The adventure of the Customs shootouts with the two yachts and the seizure of the *Com-an-Go* made headlines. William B. Shearer, formerly a special expert of the Navy Department, was stunned when he picked up the newspaper and read about the vessel he had designed during the war. The original name of the *Com-an-Go* was the *Sea Hornet II*. Shearer designed the vessel for an attack on the German submarine base at Zeebrugge.[16]

Courtesy US Coast Guard Headquarters
An armored rum-runner.

Shearer declared that while the government had used the boat from time to time, he had never received a penny for expenses. The boat had cost him between $30,000 and $40,000 to build and had been launched several years earlier at City Island shipyards in the presence of a number of distinguished Navy and Army officers. When Shearer designed the *Sea Hornet*, he had hoped the Navy would order a large number of them. He designed this particular type of vessel as a small, fast craft, which could be sent against the enemy in large numbers. The vessel's low profile allowed it to get close to its target. The *Sea Hornet* was built to be bulletproof. When the Customs men seized it, they pointed out that the hundreds of rounds only made dents in the steel sides. The fifty-eight foot vessel had originally been equipped with three rapid-fire guns and a 600-horsepower engine.[17]

While the boat was being built, the United States Coast Artillery Corps had become interested, wanting to use it for coastal defense. The *Sea Hornet* made test runs along the Atlantic coast and, after running about 5,000 miles, traveled up the Potomac to Washington. John Hays Hammond Jr. had just perfected a radio control for torpedoes, allowing an operator to control them from an airplane 8,000 to 9,000 feet away. Shearer talked with Secretary of War Weeks, who approved his plan to test Hammond's device on the *Sea Hornet*.[18]

The government sent the torpedo boat to Boston, where a staff was to conduct the tests. Everything was ready when a telegram came from Edwin Denby, then the Secretary of the Navy, announcing his decision to cancel the experiment. Denby did not explain his decision to Shearer. Not long after, Lieutenant Moffet of the Army Air Service came to Boston with a communication from Secretary Weeks, approving a trial of the one-man torpedo boat. Servicemen conducted the experiment off Boston between Marblehead and Plymouth. The confidential Navy report on the experiments proved Shearer's claims to be true. (At least that's what Shearer told *The New York Times*.)[19]

Shearer's negotiations with the government were still not over. He was about to put the *Sea Hornet* out of commission at a Boston shipyard when the Chief of the Army Air Service asked to use the boat. The Army Air Service was about to conduct bombing tests at Langley Field and wanted to use the *Sea Hornet* as a rescue boat, in case any of the pilots or mechanics fell into the water. Shearer took the boat to Fortress Monroe, a distance of 655 miles, and turned it over to the Air Service. After the bombing tests, the government sent the vessel up to New York.[20]

Mr. Shearer then went to Washington and visited Major General Mason M. Patrick, Chief of the Air Service. Shearer showed the general a letter from the War Department in which the government agreed to reimburse him for his expenses in taking the boat to Virginia; he presented the general with a bill of $3,400. General Patrick told Shearer that he was very sorry but the Army's aviation section had no money and could not pay him. Shearer became angered by this and decided not to have anything more to do with the boat. He then took the boat to the Bayonne shipyards of the Submarine Boat Corporation and left it there. Later, General Patrick sent Shearer a letter thanking him for the use of his torpedo boat. The government had placed a libel against the boat and sold the boat for $400 at a US Marshal auction in the Spring of 1923. That was the last Shearer had heard of the boat until he read about its encounter with Customs.[21]

Subs and Blimps

In August 1924, a large German submarine, operating off Cape Cod, flooded the Massachusetts coast with German beer and French wine. US Attorney Robert O. Harris reported this phenomenon to the Collector of the Port and turned over the information to local Customs officials for investigation. The reports of the submarine off Cape Cod coincided with reports from New York that airplane pilots had spotted "mysterious" submarines in the Hudson River.[22]

Federal officials told the press that the government maintained an air base at the tip of the Cape, and they would use airplanes to search for the sub. The same officials also said that it was feasible for a submarine to cross the Atlantic to run foreign liquor through the American blockade. The successful trips of the freighter *Deutschland* and the submarine U-53 during the war were sufficient proof, the officials argued. Rum-smugglers also had the financial resources to equip and maintain freight submarines, which in some cases cost less than transatlantic steamers.[23]

In addition to airplanes, the government used blimps to observe Rum Row. A week after the submarine sighting off Cape Cod, the naval dirigible (or blimp) *Shenandoah* was returning at night from Narragansett Bay to its Lakehurst, New Jersey hangar. To avoid lightning, the *Shenandoah* flew twenty miles off Point Judith on the Rhode Island shore. The powerful searchlight in the control gondola revealed three rum-runners, piled high with cases of liquor.[24]

The three boats scattered at once. The skippers most likely had heard stories about marine patrols using machine guns, and desperately tried to escape the spotlight. To the amusement of the men in the blimp, the three boats could not escape the glare of the light no matter how hard they tried. The *Shenandoah* was able to keep the fleeing boats in sight for miles. Had the dirigible been under orders from the Prohibition authorities, the Coast Guard would have had no trouble finding unlighted boats at night.[25]

20

A NEW FLEET

On August 12, 1924, President Coolidge signed commissions for sixty-five men. They were the first group of 150 temporary officers whom the Coast Guard planned to use for its expanding fleet. Rear Admiral Frederick C. Billard, Commandant of the Coast Guard, and Lieutenant Commander Stephen S. Yeandle, the Admiral's aide, had picked the appointees from a list of more than 1,000 applicants. Many of those selected were World War veterans with outstanding naval records. Others had formerly served in the Coast Guard. The plan called for the temporary officers to be spread throughout the fleet, thereby allowing the regular commissioned officers to command vessels against the rum fleet. The Winslow Bill, approved in April, authorized the commissioning of officers, 400 temporary warrant officers, and 2,240 enlisted men. The warrant officers were to be recruited from the enlisted ranks.[1] Meanwhile, in Philadelphia, there was unusual activity and rigid censorship of all news covering a section of the League Island Navy Yard, as the Coast Guard made preparations for its September campaign to sweep the rum fleet from the Atlantic. More than 1,000 secretly-mobilized men worked all day to prepare the destroyers, mine-sweepers, and speedboats for the hour when they would put out to sea, forming an armed barrier along the coast against the illegal traffic of liquor, narcotics, and aliens. Another 1,000 men were expected to join the force later.[2]

Mechanics put finishing touches on the vessels that would allow them to withstand the rigors of sea patrol. Gun crews drilled at the quick-firers aboard the destroyers as men with air-hammers drove in rivets. Below decks, engineer recruits were getting acquainted with their engines and boilers. Twenty World War I destroyers, some with stars on their smokestacks, indicating the number of German submarines the ship destroyed, made up the battle-line of the new Coast Guard fleet. The secondary squadron was composed of two mine sweepers, while scout work and near-shore duties would be handled by a mosquito fleet of 300 small craft. The Coast Guard planned to have twenty-four bases along the coast, with three additional recruiting stations.[3]

All the destroyers were capable of 25 to 30 knots and mounted main batteries of three or four-inch quick-firing guns, with one-pounders and machine guns as auxiliaries. To lighten the load for increased speed, workers removed the torpedo tubes and Y-guns for hurling depth charges. The Coast Guard attempted to censor the press in an effort to keep their plans from becoming known to spies of the smuggling interests. No civilians were allowed near the section of the yard where the fleet was arming. Obviously the censorship did not work all that well, because all of the information in the preceding paragraphs was taken from a *New York Times* article printed on August 14, 1924.[4]

At a conference at the Fifth District Headquarters in Asbury Park, New Jersey, Admiral Billard, Captain Maxson, and Captain M.W. Rasmussen discussed the fleet's future plans with the press. Captain Rasmussen said that the Coast Guard would reopen four of its stations at Spring Lake, Bay Head, Long Beach, and Wildwood as bases from which the refurbished ships could strike at Rum Row. He disclosed that a large number of the ships and forces being mobilized at the Philadelphia Navy Yard would be assigned to service off New Jersey. Admiral Billard predicted that with the Coast Guard's increased forces and funding, rum-running off the New Jersey coast would be completely different. Captain Rasmussen predicted that rum-running would be "wiped out entirely."[5]

Admiral Billard wrote enthusiastically about the expansion program in a letter:

> ...I am proud to say that the Coast Guard is going full speed ahead with the enlargement program and the personnel are working under a high pressure unprecedented in the entire history of the Service, not excluding the period of the World War...I do not hesitate to express to you my profound conviction that when the Coast Guard has put through its enlargement plan and has the additional vessels and personnel that Congress has authorized, the Service will reduce the smuggling of liquor into the United States from the sea to an almost negligible quantity.[6]

Courtesy US Coast Guard Headquarters

"THREE CRACKING GOOD DESTROYERS"

The Coast Guard's refurbished Navy destroyers were twice as large as the average Coast Guard cutter and more than three times the size of most of the vessels in the Coast Guard's inventory. The above illustrations were taken from a Coast Guard publication circa 1924. The vessel shown at the top is the *Porter*. The *Porter* was 310 feet long and had a beam of 29 feet 11 inches, a maximum draft of 9 feet 4 ½ inches and displaced 1,090 tons. The ship was built in Philadelphia in 1910 and was attached to Destroyer Force Division Two under the command of Lieutenant Commander Stephen S. Yeandle, USCG.

The vessel pictured in the lower half is the *Conyngham*. The *Conyngham* had the same dimensions as the *Porter* and was built in Philadelphia in 1916. The ship was attached to Destroyer Division Three under the command of Lieutenant Commander J.A. Starr.

The ship pictured in the left insert is the *Jouett*. The *Jouett* was 293 feet long with a beam of 26 feet 1 ½ inches. It had a maximum draft of 8 feet 4 inches and was built in Bath, Maine in 1912. The *Jouett* was also attached to Destroyer Division Three and commanded by Lieutenant Commander Henry Coyle.

Note: The editors of the Coast Guard publication added the teddy bear to the illustration for entertainment purposes. The teddy bear played no part in selecting or refurbishing the former Navy destroyers, nor did he help shape the Coast Guard's policies on Prohibition enforcement.

ALCOHOL, BOAT CHASES, AND SHOOTOUTS!

The Floating Cabaret

Sanford Jarrell, a reporter of *The New York Herald Tribune*, wrote an article describing a ship he claimed to have visited. He claimed the vessel was completely fitted out as a cabaret ship, with a bar, a ballroom, an Alabama jazz band, and other entertainers. He wrote that the ship was anchored well beyond the 12-mile limit, with its lights ablaze in defiance of US Prohibition enforcement. Jarrell also wrote that various private yachts were anchored nearby while the owners sipped drinks on the liner at prices ranging from $1 to $2.50. On the liner's poop deck was a crude reproduction of the Statue of Liberty.[7]

About a year earlier, a man had approached Coast Guard officials with stock to sell for a floating bar, very similar to the one allegedly in business off the coast. He did not attempt to sell the stock to the Coast Guard officers, but he did want to find out whether such a scheme could be operated within the law.[8]

Rear Admiral Billard issued orders to search for the palatial floating barroom, which was supposedly off the Long Island coast. Jarrell reported that the vessel was flying a British flag. If the vessel were to be found within "an hour's steaming" from American shores, the Coast Guard planned to board it, in accordance with the recent treaty between the US and Britain. The cutter *Seneca* and other Coast Guard craft kept close watch for any vessels traveling to and from the liner. Under the law, boats that visited a rum-runner could be seized, but the law applied mainly to those vessels suspected of bringing liquor ashore. However, those laws did not cover boats transporting visitors to a floating bar. Officials in Washington, however, believed that the floating bar's patrons would be inclined to bring a bottle or two back to shore. If they did, then they and the boats that carried them would be liable under the transportation clause of the Volstead Act.[9]

Wayne B. Wheeler, general counsel for the Anti-Saloon League, said he did not believe such a vessel could carry on its trade very much longer. First of all, argued Wheeler, the ship was probably violating Revenue laws. He also argued that Great Britain would use its influence to stop British ships from conducting such a business.[10]

"There are two other good reasons why I think she will not operate long," added Mr. Wheeler. "Storms and seasickness are one, and the other is the high cost of the so-called enjoyment, which can manifestly draw only upon a limited class."[11]

W.V.E. Jacobs, Captain of the Port, US Coast Guard, doubted the existence of such a ship. He stated that the existence of such a ship might be possible, but not probable. He could not believe that his men, who patrolled the waters from Cape Cod to Cape May, could have overlooked it. However, if it were true, he said that the Coast Guard could arrest anyone crossing the international limit in a small boat for "going foreign." The penalty was a fine and a reprimand. If the boaters had "gone foreign" and happened to be near Rum Row, they could have been charged with trafficking and faced harsher punishments. Captain Jacobs proposed the theory that the members of Rum Row had become so bored by the monotony of doing nothing but collecting large sums of money, that they had established a floating cabaret. Here, the rum-runners would have a chance to spend some of their money and stage parties where their bootleg clientele would supply the guests, which meant women.[12]

Captain Jacobs suggested that, if there was such a vessel, it might have been the *Von Steuben*, formerly the *Kronprinz Wilhelm*, a German raider early in the war. However, that ship was sitting at Curtis Bay at Baltimore after being sold by the US Shipping Board for scrap metal. Another theory was that the ship was the former *Friederick der Grosse*. However, a representative of the United American Line, said that that ship had sunk under the name of *City of Honolulu*. Another theory was that the whole story would turn out to be a publicity stunt for a movie that was about to be released in the theaters. Meanwhile, when reporters canvassed boatmen and yacht clubs along the Long Island shore, everyone interviewed claimed ignorance of the ship's existence. However, boatmen were usually "ignorant" of liquor secrets until they knew to whom they were speaking.[13]

The Coast Guard Cutter *Seneca* spent an entire day searching for the "floating saloon," but found nothing. Captain B.H. Camden, Executive Officer of the New York District, remained on call all day in order to pay a personal visit to determine if the ship was violating the international liquor treaty. Captain James Blaikie, master of the *California* of the Anchor Line, told reporters that he had passed Fire Island the day before and saw no ship matching the description of the floating saloon. He joined the ranks of those skeptics who were unable to see how such a ship could support itself with so few customers. If there were more customers, Blaikie could not figure out how they traveled to the ship unobserved. He also reported that he had sailed through what was normally Rum Row without seeing a single rum ship.[14]

Eugene Blake, commander of the *Seneca*, arrived at New London, Connecticut after a forty-hour search for the floating saloon. He called the reported vessel "somebody's brain child." He was at a loss to explain the mysterious craft unless it was the steamship *Arakaka* from Liverpool, an 8,800-ton vessel. The men aboard the *Seneca* had been watching the *Arakaka*, first off New York Harbor and then off Montauk Point, but it did not match the description of the notorious ship. Blake reported that the *Seneca* had scoured the waters from Fire Island to the New Jersey shore and 100 miles south, steaming twenty miles out, without finding a trace of the mystery ship.[15]

A week after Jarrell's article appeared in *The New York Herald-Tribune*, a publicity agent of Universal Pictures Corporation sent an advertisement signed "Captain of the Twelve-Mile Limit Café" to various newspapers. The flyer claimed to "clear the mystery" of the floating cabaret described in Jarrell's article. The ad read in part that if "you want to see this ship, its rollicking crew and its unusual equipment, go to the manager of your favorite motion picture theater and ask him to put on the picture 'Wine.'"[16]

Robert H. Cochrane, Vice President of Universal Pictures Corporation, explained that the advertisement was designed to borrow from the publicity generated by Jarrell's story. Mr. Cochrane added that the advertisement had been inspired by a rumor that Universal might have "planted" the ship that Jarrell found off Fire Island to boost the picture. Since the ship in "Wine" and the Fire Island ship had some similarities, Cochrane stated, it would be good advertising to "take advantage of a piece of good fortune." The movie had been made in California a few months earlier, and Cochrane claimed that the ship used in the movie was not the mystery ship. Meanwhile, the government ships still found no traces of the floating saloon.[17]

The management of *The New York Herald-Tribune* continued to uphold the authenticity of Jarrell's report in public. Behind the scenes, however, the newspaper launched its own investigation. John A. Wilbur and James Zegel, Prohibition agents at Bay Shore, provided valuable information to R.Q. Merrick, Divisional Prohibition Chief at New York City. Up to a point, the investigation seemed to confirm Jarrell's story, but it soon became apparent that he had never visited the floating saloon.[18] When the agents questioned Jarrell closely he insisted, at first, that every detail of his story was true. However, he gradually began to weaken and admitted "embellishment." The agents gave him every opportunity to prove his story was true, but Jarrell could not do so. Still insisting that his story was fundamentally true, he left the office promising to return and straighten out the matter. Instead of returning, Jarrell sent back a written confession that his article was false and resigned from the newspaper staff.[19]

21

INTO THE LION'S DEN

While the Coast Guard was expanding its fleet, the Customs Marine Patrol did more than its share of Prohibition enforcement. Officials in Washington decided to expand the Customs Marine Patrol to check the flow of liquor until Congressional appropriations bore fruit. The new patrol had started on April 11 and expanded quickly, as Customs seized hundreds of boats. In late August 1924, Captain Peter J. Sullivan of US Customs reported what the Customs patrols had accomplished during the previous five months. Over that time, Customs had captured 300 rum boats, seized cargoes worth $2,000,000 and assessed fines and penalties of more than $100,000 in the half of the cases that went to trial.[1]

The jurisdiction of the newly-expanded Customs patrol was the coastline of Connecticut, New York, and New Jersey. Captain Sulllivan told the press that the patrols were initially like "shooting at the moon." Their first patrol boats went only 22 miles per hour, and these patrols were to be disbanded after three months. However, Washington was so pleased with the results that they channeled more money into it. With new boats and new facilities, the patrol began to bottle up Montauk Point and Atlantic Highlands.[2]

When Customs first began their patrols, smugglers had landed at Montauk, driven the natives off the beach, and proceeded to land their liquor undisturbed. The situation was just as bad at the Highlands, Sullivan stated. As the patrol boats gradually decimated the rum-runners in those areas, the rum traffic moved elsewhere. Along with the success of the Customs patrols came an increase in their duties. The men stayed out day and night for weeks at a time. Sullivan and his executive officer, Frank Thropp, set an example by not having taken a vacation in five years.[3]

"We will match our men against any unit in the country," said Sullivan. "They know the game, know what to do, and it's not eight hours with them. They eat on the boats, sleep on the boats, in fact, we can hardly keep 'em off the boats."[4]

Captain Sullivan stated that the patrol's greatest accomplishment was not any single capture, but the gradual suppression of small speedboats. He cited Jones Inlet, the entrance to Freeport, Long Island, where liquor traffic was only one twentieth of what it had been before the Customs crackdown. Customs agents observed the smugglers' patterns and used that knowledge to capture them. For example, rum-runners almost never landed at the same place twice; usually they had four or five "drops," or secret ports of entry, made the round, and then made a new set. Runners never went out without having decided which "drop" they would make coming in. Bootleggers signaled from the shore to indicate if the coast was clear. Originally these signals were flares and bonfires, but the smugglers had progressed to using flashlights of different colors, signaling in Morse code.[5]

The New "Secret" Campaign

Meanwhile, the Coast Guard made every attempt to censor public knowledge of the new "dry fleet" and the impending anti-smuggling campaign. The destroyers *Jewett* and *Cassin* managed to make their way to New York waters before the newspapers found out. However, the press did report on August 30 that the warships were engaged in speed trials and a "shakedown" cruise off the coast in order to determine the effects of four years of sitting at anchor.[6]

Smugglers interpreted the Coast Guard's tightening censorship to mean that the new vessels were beginning to assume their scheduled stations in full strength. Reporters managed to find out that four converted destroyers were on their way to New York, with four more headed to New London, Connecticut. These fighting units were to be supplemented by scores of well-armed patrol and picket boats. Of these boats, the larger seventy-five-foot boats were equipped with powerful wireless radio sets.[7]

In the middle of September, a number of bootleggers were in a crowd that witnessed the Coast Guard's launching of a fast motorboat at Freeport, Long Island. The boat was the first of 475 that the government planned to use against smugglers. The boat was 36 feet long, 9 feet wide, and capable of 25 knots. Captain F.T. Ford told the press that the Coast Guard would use 300 boats of this type, plus another 175 boats with a length of seventy-five feet. The government contract called for the completion of all of these vessels within the next six months.[8]

Government officials in Washington were aware of the active rum-running off the New England coast and planned a vigorous anti-smuggling campaign. Assistant Secretary of the Treasury Moss, Assistant Attorney General Mabel Willebrandt, and Admiral F.C. Billard mapped out the plans. The patrol fleet arrived in New England waters in mid-September. At the end of October, Lieutenant Commander S.S. Yeadle, who directed the movements of the New England patrol, briefed the press on the dry fleet's progress. In one month, the Coast Guard captured four ships, seven smaller boats, and 103,000 cases of liquor off the New England coast, not to mention a large number of prisoners.[9]

One of the Coast Guard cutters off the New England coast was the *Tampa*. In mid-October, the *Tampa*, plus a squadron of 30-foot speedboats, moved into position for a raid that was to take place a few days later. For five days crews were on watch, eating at irregular intervals, and getting little sleep when they could. One machinist, in charge of machine-gun equipment, stood duty for 48 hours straight. During the night before the raid, the *Tampa* lost contact with two of the smaller boats. However, they reappeared as the action began. One boat ran into a whale and nearly capsized. At the break of dawn, Lieutenant Commander Yeandle gave the word to start the roundup.[10]

Daylight exposed two steamers, three three-masted schooners, ten smaller schooners and a large number of powerboats. The rum-runners scattered north, east, and south, throwing hundreds of cases into the sea to lighten their loads. The Coast Guard captured as many fleeing craft as the size of their squadron permitted. The skipper of one of the fastest boats raced away as the Coast Guard sprayed his vessel with machine gun rounds. The bullets shattered every window in the cabin and began to rip through the partitions when he surrendered. The Coast Guardsmen found guns on most of the captured vessels, but none of the smugglers returned fire.[11]

****

One of the ships the Coast Guard captured was named the *Marjorie E. Bachman*. The *Marjorie* was anchored just off Bird Island Flats, where Customs officers, following the Coast Guard fleet, took command of it. Aboard the ship, the Customs men found 850 cases of brandy, whisky, and champagne.[12] When the captain of the *Marjorie E. Bachman* went to Federal Court two days later, his lawyer stated that the Coast Guardsmen who boarded his vessel had sold 150 cases of champagne over the side of the ship, sent another 150 cases to the *Tampa*, and took nearly $1,000 in cash from members of the crew. Captain Harry Richie's lawyer also added that the defense would ask for the Coast Guardsmen's extradition to Canada on charges of piracy unless the men returned the 300 cases of liquor, plus the money and personal effects they supposedly stole from the schooner's crew. Judge Morton ordered the Coast Guard to return the money, unless the US Attorney could prove that it was part of the ship's money.[13]

However, these charges did not prevent Captain Richie and his crew from being indicted before the federal grand jury for conspiracy to violate the Tariff Act of 1922 and the Volstead Act. Lieutenant Commander Yeandle countered the piracy charges by declaring that the liquor smugglers, having failed in their attempts to place spies in the Coast Guard, sought to publicly attack the character of Coast Guard officers in order to undermine public confidence. He added:

> "They are endeavoring to place spies in the service on sea and land. Only last week four men tried to enlist in the Coast Guard Service, but when the time came to take their fingerprints they departed, leaving their clothing behind. When spies succeed in getting in they try to corrupt members of the organization."[14]

Into the Lion's Den

Saul Grill was an experienced Prohibition agent who had previously laid a trap that led to the arrest of a large number of persons in the $80,000 New Jersey beer conspiracy. Grill teamed up with Prohibition agents W. E. Dunnigan, Norman Nichol, and Arthur Sleator for a new case. From time to time, the four agents posed as bootleggers. They met the owner of a British trawler, named the *Frederick B.*, in New York City. They carried on negotiations at elaborate dinner and theater parties. The investigators used confiscated champagne and other liquor to convince the trawler's owner that they were prosperous Pennsylvanians. They made an offer to buy 25,000 cases of whisky at $22 a case, and the owner accepted the terms.[15]

In August, the *Frederick B.* set out from Halifax to a point off the New Jersey coast under the name *Bernard M.*—which was also the name of Alexander Adelman's attorney. The agents still needed to hire a rum-runner to get the liquor from the ship to the shore, so they employed a smuggler who owned a small motorboat. The smuggler agreed to pilot the boat himself. Prohibition Agents Nichols and Sleater, along with two Customs inspectors, went out on the motorboat to the trawler. They bought $1,000 worth of liquor and agreed to repeat the trip and purchase even more.[16]

The undercover agents then directed the rum-runner to head for Long Branch. The trip took an hour and a half, making it impossible for the federal authorities to proceed against the British trawler under the "one hour steaming from shore" provision of the liquor treaty. The agents made up excuses as to why they could not purchase more liquor as they had promised earlier. They told the rum-runner that they had encountered a problem and would buy more liquor when the trawler made the next trip.[17]

When the *Frederick B.* arrived off Monmouth Beach, New Jersey, in late September, the agents were once again prepared to do business. They arranged with another rum smuggler, who owned a speedboat, to transport liquor from the trawler. Nichols and Sleater, with two Customs inspectors, went out to the trawler one evening aboard the speedboat. The rum-runner had guaranteed a speed of thirty knots on the condition that his clients pay him $1,000 to insure against loss, if captured. The Prohibition agents not only agreed to pay $1,000, they also offered a bonus.[18]

The men pulled up alongside the *Frederick B.*, purchased 25 cases of liquor, and instructed the rum-runner to head straight for Long Branch. They made the trip in 42 minutes. Since the Prohibition agents wanted to land in under an hour, they waded ashore. While it was less common to use this approach, the rum-runner thought that the men were simply avoiding piers and other landings where they might be discovered.[19]

The agents hurried to a telephone to notify the Coast Guard in Manhattan about the trawler. However, a Coast Guardsman on duty at Long Branch thought they were smugglers and arrested them. The agents had difficulty convincing him that they not rum-runners. He became persuaded only when he checked on the telephone number the Prohibition agents used and listened to their conversation. The agents then returned to the rum-runner and ordered the smuggler to head for the Battery in Manhattan. The smuggler hesitated, because he knew the Battery was swarming with Coast Guardsmen, Customs agents, and New York Police. However, the undercover agents assured him that they had "fixed" the Coast Guard and marine police.[20]

The skeptical rum-runner reluctantly steered for Manhattan. He interrogated the men the entire trip as to how they had managed to "rig the customs men and the police." He had difficulty buying their simplistic story, but continued on his course. The bootlegger was so nervous as he approached the Battery that he nearly crashed into a ferry. Sweating profusely, he steered his boat up to the dock at the Barge

Office and fumbled with the hawsers to secure it. Customs inspectors in uniform, Coast Guardsmen, and other government officials were on the pier. They went about their business, hardly taking notice as the smuggler unloaded his cargo onto the dock. The agents paid the rum-runner his bonus and he set off without any interference. As the rum-runner headed down the bay, he waved his hat at the agents and shouted, "I've got to hand it to you." [21]

The liquor cases landed at the Battery provided enough evidence for the government to seize the *Frederick B*. The Coast Guard Cutter *Manhattan*, under the command of Oscar Vinge, set out to capture the trawler. The *Manhattan* arrived with the seized vessel the following morning. Vinge ordered the master of the *Frederick B*. to drop anchor off the Statue of Liberty. A Customs guard boarded the ship and the Coast Guard notified the US Attorney's office. Assistant US Attorney John Holley Clark went aboard the liquor ship and questioned the master and other members of the crew. There were 5,500 cases of whisky and a large quantity of grain alcohol on board. Clark found evidence that the *Frederick B*. had sold 400 cases of whisky and announced to the press that he would start libel proceedings against the ship the following Monday. Clark also stated that the *Frederick B*. was one of a fleet used by an international ring of American, Canadian, and British bootleggers to smuggle more than $1,000,000 worth of liquor into the United States.[22]

When the trial went to court, Assistant US Attorney Francis S. McGurk charged that someone had tampered with the witnesses. McGurk failed in all his attempts to establish that the *Frederick B*. was selling liquor offshore. The witnesses all appeared to be ignorant of the trawler's activities. William J. Martin, counsel for the defendants, responded to McGurk's charges of tampering by stating that the District Attorney's office was far more guilty of that charge. Commissioner Boyle, who presided over the case, advised McGurk to confine his questions to the facts on which he hoped to base his case. Boyle said:

> "If you have to depend on seafaring folk to make out your case of bootlegging, you probably never will prove anything. As a matter of fact, I don't think you will get anywhere with these witnesses." [23]

In commenting on the case, Assistant US Attorney Clark added that the rum-runners had established a commercial information service. He stated that a lawyer in Manhattan found out about the seizure of the

Frederick B. several hours before the US Attorney's office. He added that the government had not yet discovered how smugglers sent information from sea to land.[24] The entire crew of the *Frederick B.* stayed aboard the ship with their liquor instead of going to prison. Although they were aliens, they soon posted bail and were able to roam about New York freely. The US Government held the trawler pending the outcome of the libel action filed against it.[25]

Britain's Rum-Running Knight

Baronet Sir Broderick Hartwell had made great progress in the liquor trade by late 1924. Although he had been in the "export" business for barely a year, his shipments toward the general direction of the United States added up to $1,320,000, based on distillery prices. When one takes into consideration that Scotch cost four times as much in New York as in England, that figure increases to $5,000,000.[26]

Although Sir Broderick was not the largest figure in the liquor exporting business, he certainly was one of the most interesting. He was a fourth generation baronet. His family tree included an admiral and a general in the British military. His father was the Consul General for Naples and Southern Italy. One of his uncles was Sir Francis Hartwell of Crimean War fame. Another uncle, Admiral Arthur Paget of the Royal Navy, who served with Admiral Sir Frederick Bedford, was Broderick's godfather.[27]

Broderick's life had been somewhat of an adventure even before he took up liquor exports. As a boy, he spent five years in Jamaica while his father held an official post there. When he was 19, Broderick was secretary under his father at the British Consulate in Naples. He then went off to Ceylon, where he tried tea-planting for two years. He joined the British Army at the outbreak of the Boer War, serving as an officer. After the war, he resigned his commission and purchased a schooner. When he set out to explore the Pacific Ocean, his ship was wrecked. After losing his ship in the Pacific, Broderick traveled the world and engaged in various financial adventures in London. When the Great War broke out, Broderick joined the army again and fought at Gallipoli in 1915. He was wounded at that battle and sent home.[28]

What also made Sir Broderick unusual in the world of smugglers was that he conducted his business openly. He maintained an office on one of the busiest streets of downtown London and had a list of one thousand stockholders spread throughout England and many other parts of the world. He also advertised his business and mailed out circulars to 100,000 persons in England.[29]

One American reporter was intrigued by Broderick and decided to pay him a visit. The morning after Donald Lawder of *The New York Times* arrived in London, he rang the bell at Broderick's office at 31 Haymarket. Sir Broderick was extremely polite, but not pleased to learn that Lawder was a reporter. "I have had quite enough publicity," he said, as he gestured toward a stack of press clippings. "Not that I have anything to hide. My business is quite legal, I assure you." [30]

Lawder: It's all true then? All this about stockholders and big dividends and thousands of cases of liquor sent to our rum row. You are actually and openly helping others to violate our prohibition laws.

Broderick: Certainly it's true. I am engaged in a legitimate business. I am violating no law of your country nor of my own. I am simply buying whisky and wines from distilleries and selling them on the high seas to whoever may buy them. That the liquor lands on American territory eventually is none of my concern.

Lawder: But you find America a most profitable market and you are pretty sure your liquor eventually does land there, aren't you?

Broderick: Certainly. I take care to see it does land there. At least within twenty-five miles of there—the legal limit is now twenty miles. What happens to it afterward is none of my concern. I don't see why they are making all this fuss about it. Look here. You say you have prohibition in the United States. In the first place you haven't prohibition. You have a prohibition law, but your people don't enforce it. Your officials don't enforce it. No one seems to care about enforcing it. Why should I look after that? That's your business.

Later on in the interview, Lawder asked Sir Broderick about the risk of seizure.

Broderick: There is absolutely no risk of loss. Absolutely no risk...My ships never go within the radius where seizures are allowed under the new treaty between Great Britain and the United States. In fact, they never go within five or ten miles of where they may be seized. So much for that. Then, I sell my goods for cash against delivery on the high seas. My agent on the ship receives a check for the entire cargo before a single case is transferred off the ship. If a case of whisky falls into the sea in the transfer from one ship to another, as sometimes happens, that loss is borne by the American importers. Furthermore, my cargoes are insured at Lloyd's against marine disasters. The coverage is complete. There is absolutely no possibility of loss.

After answering a few more questions, Broderick concluded the interview by asking the reporter a question:

"Here is a clipping from The London Daily Mail of March 8, 1924. It is headed 'From Our Own Correspondent' and the date line is that of New York City. Here is what it says: 'Revenues totaling £38,160 ($172,904,000) have been lost to the United States on liquor landed by rum-runners on waters adjacent to New York in the two years since the so-called Rum Row came into existence. These figures were given by Mr. Edward Barnes, Assistant Solicitor to the Collector of the Port of New York, who says that a careful check by the Coast Guard shows that 2,460,000 cases of 14,460,000 gallons of liquor have been landed from Rum Row. The revenue from each gallon would normally be £2.13 ($11.66).

"Now will you please tell me," Broderick continued, "how your Coast Guard was able to arrive at those figures? It is a natural presumption to consider the Coast Guard is stationed to stop smugglers from landing goods. But in relation to whisky it appears it not only made a careful check of the number of cases landed in New York City during the period of two years, but that it actually notified the Collector of the Port of this fact. I cannot understand it.

"I am not decrying American public officials nor American public servants; don't misunderstand me. But a shipload of liquor is a rather bulky affair. It must be landed somewhere. It must be carted from the landing place to some warehouse. And it must then be redistributed from that warehouse to its ultimate customers. How it gets there is none of my business. But I don't see how they can check it so accurately.

"Of course," he laughed, "I don't expect you to be able to answer that."[31]

****

ALCOHOL, BOAT CHASES, AND SHOOTOUTS!

In late November 1924, Romaine Q. Merrick, Prohibition Enforcement Chief for the State of New York and Northern New Jersey, reported that the Prohibition blockade off Long Island had sprung a leak. Merrick sent a report to Washington that an enormous quantity of liquor was coming from the general direction of Montauk Point. Since the Coast Guard had begun its fall offensive against rum-running, the average number of truck seizures was two or three per week in Long Island. During the third week of November, however, Prohibition agents seized eleven trucks, carrying 1,100 cases of liquor. Merrick added, "There is a big leak somewhere near Montauk Point, and the amount of liquor coming in through Long Island is increasing so rapidly that conditions [are] begin[ing] to look like they did last Winter."[32]

After Merrick made a trip to Washington to report on the situation, he went "away for a rest" and was replaced by W.H. Walker, Acting Divisional Enforcement Director. D.H. Blair, US Commissioner of Internal Revenue, ordered an overhaul of the Prohibition Enforcement Unit in New York State. Commissioner Blair aimed to take politics out of Prohibition enforcement and to make appointments and promotions based on efficient performance. The following is an excerpt of a statement Blair made to the press:

> "R.Q. Merrick, the local director, is a good man. He is doing the best he can to enforce the law and the Eighteenth Amendment. He has done some very efficient work up-State, where he has closed up a number of breweries operating in violation of the Constitution and Volstead law. I believe, however, that enforcement of the statutes relating to prohibition should be transferred to the Department of Justice. It does not belong in the Treasury Department." [33]

A week later, Samuel Wilson, Assistant Superintendent of the Anti-Saloon League of New Jersey, filed a request with Assistant Attorney General Willebrandt for a federal investigation of the Coast Guard and Prohibition Enforcement Unit from Montauk Point to Cape May. Wilson submitted detailed recommendations for an investigation of all federal, state, and county authorities in the metropolitan area, asking that a Special Assistant Attorney General be assigned to the task along with a staff of Department of Justice investigators.[34]

Samuel Wilson filed his demand in response to a recent court case in which the Hudson County Grand Jury had returned indictments against twelve defendants, charged with conspiracy and bribery to furnish official protection for the landing of millions of dollars' worth of liquor along the New Jersey shore. When reporters asked if his demand for an investigation of the Department of Justice and the Coast Guard indicated his belief that they were corrupt, he answered, "I believe there is room for inquiry into all the enforcement forces. That includes the Department of Justice and the Coast Guard."[35]

22

REPORTER VISITS RUM ROW

The Coast Guard did not stop the flow of liquor by the end of 1924, but it did change how rum-smugglers operated. James C. Young, the same *New York Times* reporter who visited Rum Row twice over the previous year, paid another visit in December 1924. Young wrote that there had never been such a blockade during a time of peace as the one the Coast Guard maintained from Delaware Bay to Cape Cod. However, the volume of liquor smuggled and the prices smugglers charged had hardly changed over the course of the year.[1]

Rum-running had altered unbelievably during 1924. The rules had changed and amateur smugglers became scarce. Bargain days along Rum Row were over and, instead of waiting three miles off the coast, rum ships waited thirty or fifty miles out. The waters were more dangerous for smugglers; the Coast Guard did not hesitate to fire and hijackers were on the waters in record numbers.[2]

Young went to visit Rum Row with the same smugglers he traveled with a year earlier. Captain Blunt and Eddie took Young on the same route, traveling down the Shrewsbury River to go out to sea. As the men felt the December cold, Eddie told the reporter about the desperate measures smugglers had adopted with the tightened blockade. Smugglers were running their speedboats aground at the beach in the middle of the night. Then, a half-dozen men plunged waist-deep into freezing water to carry the cargo ashore.[3]

As the men traveled down the Shrewsbury, they made a stop at a place the locals called the bootleggers' hotel. Young noticed several craft with low profiles, painted battleship gray to blend into the sea. The smugglers were proud of their boats and even allowed the reporter to go aboard one for a closer look. The boat Young looked at was capable of 35 miles an hour. The speedboat's two 350-horsepower engines were built overseas and sat deep. There was room for two hundred cases aft in the $5,000 boat. While $5,000 seemed like a risky investment for a boat that was likely to be seized or sunk, this type of boat paid for itself in three trips.[4]

The smugglers all admitted that the Coast Guard had done its job in trying to stop the trade of Rum Row. Certain smugglers told Young that the Coast Guard had driven them to distant points and devious routes. The colorful fleet of rum-runners that once sat a few miles off Ambrose Lightship had disappeared. Only one or two rum vessels cruised in Fire Island waters, far from shore. A large fleet sat off Montauk and an even larger fleet was anchored southeast of Asbury Park, New Jersey. The Asbury Park fleet was broken up into two flotillas, the first thirty miles from shore, the second ten miles further out. By the estimates of rum-runners, they were loaded with cargoes worth millions.[5]

The Coast Guard's presence had expanded greatly since Young made his previous visit. During the previous December, there had been only two Coast Guard cutters that regularly patrolled Rum Row. A year later, there were four cutters, four destroyers, ten submarine-chasers, and a flock of smaller boats. All of these vessels were well-armed and did not hesitate to shoot. Rum Row's casualty list was six dead and many wounded.[6]

The smugglers also told Young that big business had taken hold of rum-running. Free trade for the small boat owner was a thing of the past. In December 1924, rum-running was an organized traffic in which capital controlled the source of supply, meaning the "little man's" business was no longer welcome. Those on rum ships viewed ten-case orders as a nuisance because there was a chance that the amateur smuggler would be caught and tell his story to government officials. Twenty-five cases was the smallest order the rum ships would take, and even those orders were filled grudgingly.[7]

Rum schooners, or masted-sailing ships, were near extinction in the rum trade. Warfare waged on land and sea had driven them out. The smugglers told Young stories of schooners boarded and men murdered, because they had stuck to the trade. In one particular case, rival smugglers boarded one vessel, stole its food, water, money, and liquor, and then smashed the ship's compass and wheel.

As a result of this fierce competition and the influence of big business, virtually all of New York's Christmas liquor in 1924 arrived from Europe in lots of 10,000 to 50,000 cases. These large cargoes were carried largely in Norwegian ships under British charter. The rum-running syndicates controlled from one to a half-dozen ships each and had cargoes en route in a steady stream.[8]

Within a year's time, the actual method of transaction had also changed. The days of cash sales on board had ended. Fear of seizure by the Coast Guard or hijackers had driven money from the trade. Rum Row had resorted to an old method devised by the Bank of England. In earlier times, the bank identified its patrons by matching notched sticks with them. The smugglers of 1924 used a slightly different version. They took a playing card and cut it into a sort of jigsaw puzzle. One half of the card remained aboard a rum-runner and the other was sold ashore. Each card had its own pattern and represented a certain number of cases, from 25 up to 1,000. There was a design for every sale. Smugglers cut the cards abroad and shipped the necessary halves to the US. The supercargoes aboard the ships had further means of identifying the cards, such as invisible ink. One syndicate used green markings.[9]

If a man went to sea with half of a two-spot of spades, representing a hundred cases, and the Coast Guard drove him back, he could turn in his card for the full cash value. If the Coast Guard seized the card, the owner would have to bear the loss. These card pieces had cash value in the smuggling world and could be used as currency along the New Jersey and Long Island coasts. There were several cases in which the owners lost their cards and the finders profited from their loss.

****

On February 2, 1925, Attorney General Stone gave a public report on liquor smuggling during 1924. According to the Justice Department, 332 foreign ocean-going vessels had smuggled liquor into the US during that year. Out of that number, 307 flew the British flag, 10 flew the Norwegian flag, four flew the French flag, and the remainder displayed the flags of various other nations. Most of these vessels had engaged in no other business and operated as rum ships for several years. Others engaged in the traffic only casually. They all remained at a safe distance off the coast. The Justice Department found that there had been fleets of liquor vessels constantly anchored off the Atlantic and Pacific seaboards and in the Gulf of Mexico. There had been as many as 63 vessels anchored off the US coast at the same time. As a general rule, foreign vessels brought the liquor conveniently close to the American shore and small American boats completed the journey.[10]

A number of foreign smuggling bases were in full operation. The main British bases were Halifax, Lunenburg, Sydney and Yarmouth, Nova Scotia; St. John's, New Foundland, Bermuda, Nassau and the islands of Bimini and Gun Cay, British West Indies; Victoria and Vancouver, British Columbia, and Windsor and Belleville, Ontario. Other important bases were St. Pierre and Miquelon Islands (French); Havana, Cuba; Hamburg, Germany and Antwerp, Belgium. Practically all of the foreign liquor vessels sailed on fraudulent clearance papers.[11]

During 1924, the United States Government entered into treaties relating to liquor smuggling with six foreign countries— Great Britain, Norway, Denmark, Sweden, and Italy. These treaties authorized the Coast Guard to seize foreign vessels engaged in liquor smuggling within a certain prescribed distance of the US coast. Between May 22, the effective date of the first liquor treaty, and the end of the calendar year, the US Coast Guard, Customs Services, and other enforcement agencies had seized sixteen rum ships. Thirteen of these ships were British, one Norwegian, one French, and one Italian. One large vessel, the British steamer *Quadra*, was seized on the Pacific Coast.[12]

President Coolidge and his Cabinet briefly considered the Attorney General's report. Coolidge asked Stone to elaborate on this report, which was based on information gathered by field agents of the Department of Justice. A White House spokesman told the press that President Coolidge had not considered further plans for tightening up Federal forces against liquor smugglers.[13]

Five Years of Prohibition

High-speed boat chases, shootouts, and pirate attacks were only part of the much larger picture of rum running. Looking back on these five years of drunkenness and lawbreaking, one can observe several historical trends. Many of these trends run parallel to modern ones and some are a repeat of very old ones. Several of the big issues relating to Prohibition enforcement have been debated since the days of the Founding Fathers; Americans had been smuggling and illegally distilling alcohol for a century and a half before the Eighteenth Amendment became law.

The New York State legislature's attempt to nullify the Prohibition Act was taken from an old political playbook. In 1787, delegates at the Constitutional Convention debated over a state's rights to nullify an unpopular federal law. Most of them were also strongly opposed to the idea of a strong federal government intervening in the affairs of individuals.

The issue of search and seizure of vessels on the high seas, another big issue in the 1920s, helped trigger the American Revolution and the War of 1812 when the British searched American ships. In the 1920s, the roles were reversed as American officials searched and seized British ships.

Another issue that has caused heated debates since the days of Jefferson and Hamilton is the size of the military. Many of the Founding

Fathers were opposed to a large Navy because they believed a big fleet of ships would, in one way or another, cause diplomatic disasters and possibly war. During the early 1920s, the US Government signed the Naval Disarmament Treaty with several other world powers in an effort to maintain peace. By scaling back on the size of the Navy, the logic went, the United States and other nations could avoid another world war. However, while America reduced its Navy, it increased the size of the Coast Guard by several hundred vessels. The prediction of the Founding Fathers was correct in the case of Prohibition. During those years, foreign embassies sent endless complaints to the US State Department over the Coast Guard's actions.

While the US Government scaled back on the size of the Army and Navy, it drastically expanded the size of federal law enforcement agencies. The Coast Guard alone added over 1,500 men to its force. The Prohibition Bureau, which did not exist before 1920, had over three thousand employees by 1924. US Customs, the Narcotics Bureau, and the Bureau of Investigation all multiplied their budgets and manpower several times over in the early '20s. The Coast Guard changed completely from a quaint force of a few steamers and rescue boats to a virtual navy of over twenty destroyers and hundreds of small motorboats.

Only ten years earlier, federal agents were few and far between. In the early 1920s, these agents became a common sight, whether conducting raids on speakeasies, stopping smugglers at the borders, rounding up suspected communists in big cities, or chasing smugglers at sea, the long arm of Uncle Sam was growing longer.

The war on alcohol escalated as it dragged on. The government poured more and more money into the problem and increased federal forces exponentially. Politicians who supported Prohibition told the American people early on that the war on alcohol would pay for itself through fines and seized property. As Prohibition dragged on, the smugglers became more organized, wealthier, and better equipped. Both sides raced to build faster boats with better weapons. However, the smugglers were making a profit while the US Government was draining the federal budget.

One positive outcome of this smuggling race was a dramatic improvement in technology. Cars and boats attained speeds unheard of only a few years earlier; planes were redesigned to land on water and carry cargo—all in an effort to avoid capture.

Courtesy US Coast Guard

As Prohibition dragged on, encounters between smugglers and Coast Guardsmen became more violent. In this 1924 photo, there are at least nine crew members aboard the cutter *Seneca* prepared to fire their rifles at the tiny K-13091. Keep in mind that the Coast Guard ship was also equipped with naval artillery. Such an overwhelming show of force against civilian vessels was almost unheard of before Prohibition, except in wartime.

Prohibition enforcement overwhelmed the court systems at the federal, state, and local levels. There were simply not enough judges to hear the cases. Although judges dismissed many of the cases, the prisons overflowed with violators of Prohibition laws. The legal system cancelled out much of the Coast Guard's efforts as many of the smugglers walked free with small fines or were released by the State Department after foreign ambassadors protested. As more people went to prison for liquor-related charges, smugglers and law enforcement agencies became more violent and more desperate in their means to achieve their interests. Criminals also became more violent against one another to maintain their competitive edge. Like the gangsters in big cities, the liquor syndicates at sea were not afraid to use violence to crush un-welcome competition.

The criminal syndicates also followed the examples of tycoons like Rockefeller, Carnegie, Mellon, and Morgan to consolidate their power. The liquor syndicates did not want independent rum-runners in business for themselves; they wanted to buy out and/or intimidate their competitors into working with their organizations. Ultimately, the smugglers created a regulated smuggling market with fixed prices, much like certain tycoons cornered and "fixed" the finance, steel, and railroad industries.

By 1924, it became apparent that the Coast Guard could not stop the flow of liquor into the United States, not even with a fleet of 300-plus vessels. Politicians bickered in Congress over who to blame, whether or not the law was futile, and what to do next. No matter what side a politician took on the issue, there were millions of Americans who were strongly opposed. The Anti-Saloon League was a very vocal and powerful group. There were many Senators who moved to repeal the law soon after it went into effect. However, to save face and avoid the wrath of the 'drys,' many Senators voted to maintain the status quo.

Part II: 1925-1930

National Archives

23

Crazy Sea Stories

Rum Row was busy in 1925, but still one of the loneliest places in the world for a crewmember, so crews deserted frequently. The food and water were terrible and so was the pay. So "shanghai" gangs, or men who kidnapped other men and forced them to work on a ship, had plenty of work to do for the first time in many years. A letter from one such unfortunate man arrived at Police Headquarters in New York City in February. The post mark indicated that it was mailed from Grand Central Station. It read:

> I have been drugged and held captive on a ship. I can see High Bridge through a crack in the side of the ship. I threw a bottle in the water with a note in it. Please notify the police and my wife, Mrs....[1]

Police looked into the matter and discovered that the man who signed the crumpled paper had disappeared from Brooklyn, leaving his distraught wife behind. The police were unable to locate the man or the ship he claimed to be on. How the message traveled from a bottle in the river to Grand Central Station is unknown.

In the US District Court, two American sailors filed an action against a rum vessel that was recently captured, charging that they were shanghaied and kept prisoner. The two sailors claimed that they signed papers to voyage on an ordinary ship. They were then taken with several other men in a motor boat to a point off Rockville Centre, Long Island. When they asked questions about where they were going, the two were told to keep quiet. Soon they were forced onto a weather-beaten, unkempt schooner. When the motor boat left, they found out they were aboard a rum ship. Under threats, the two men were forced to work with little food or water. After the Coast Guard captured the ship, the two men retaliated against the rum ship with legal action.[2]

James C. Young, the same reporter who visited Rum Row several times over the past years, decided to investigate this phenomenon. As part of his investigation, he visited a shipping master's office, located at a corner on South Street in Manhattan. Young walked up the long, rusty, iron stairway on the outside of the building to reach a red door. When he opened the door he saw an old office with a brass railing at its counter. Behind the railing sat a grizzled shipping master who hired sailors. Young asked the old man if men were being shanghaied to Rum Row and he replied:

> "The thing has been done, they say, and probably true. Rotten ships, bad skippers, bad food and no water. That worries the crews for the most. It is harder and harder to get water from shore, because the Coast Guard keeps strict watch. Bad enough to get away with a load of liquor, let alone trying to carry out casks of water.
>
> "Yes, the crews desert. I heard of one ship where they quit in a body and defied their officers to stop them. Took to the boats and came ashore. Every week we have sailors turn up here without kit or papers looking for a berth. They must come from somewhere. I asked one chap if he wouldn't like to go out on a rum ship and he turned white at the idea.
>
> "Well, I didn't mean to say anything about that, but you have caught me. The fact is that I have heard of a standing offer from the agents of rum ships to sign on men at a premium for us and the men, too. But I haven't taken any of that money. It wouldn't do me any good. The real seafaring men detest rum ships and would not go aboard. And they wouldn't feel very friendly to an agent who sent them out by a trick.
>
> "I have been told about a Portugee (*sic*) down the street who takes out men every week. Just loafers, you know, and scalawags running from the police. By the way, if a man is in trouble Rum Row offers him his best chance. I am told that the trails of many men badly wanted have ended here at South Street. They get away to Rum Row and safety. No questions are asked out there, and if a man has money he can buy a comfortable berth to almost any country.
>
> "Shanghaiing? Well, there is a lot of talk about it. I heard of a case last week where a man was drugged in one of

those newfangled speak-easies that are run as drug stores. They said along the street that a shanghai gang had got him, stole his money and shipped him to sea. But you couldn't prove it, could you? The man is gone, and who could trace him? If you have an enemy and want to get rid of the man, just say some shanghai gang put him aboard a ship."[3]

Captain Tweedie's Story of Rum Pirates

In February 1925, a British sea captain returned to London and told the local newspapers about his experiences with rum pirates. He served as first mate aboard the rum-runner *Veronica*, carrying about $700,000 worth of whisky and champagne from Bermuda to New York. This is his story:

> "I had no intentions of becoming a rum runner. When I joined the *Veronica* at Bermuda I signed the ship's articles agreeing to cruise to Melilla, in Morocco. That was the way the ship's paper's read. But after a few days out orders came to change the course to Madeira and then head for Bermuda. The next orders instructed us to proceed to the coast of the United States and take up a position twenty-five miles south of Montauk Point and wait for the real operators to come out via motorboats.
>
> "While lying off Montauk the crew grew rebellious and demanded more money for overtime. They were given a 50 per cent increase in wages if they would stick to the ship. Speed boats then came alongside and took off 4,500 cases, mostly of whisky, and a few days later a London representative came aboard with another man to arrange for the sale of the remaining cargo. It was agreed that a schooner be chartered for this work.
>
> "Three days later launches approached bearing men who declared they were buyers of the remaining stock. They asked me for a drink and when I led them to my cabin I found myself covered with four revolvers and was then thrown in to No. 2 hold, bound and blindfolded where I remained two days without food or water before I was released and ordered to take soundings and work as navigator for the pirates. My next surprise was when the pirates told me a United States revenue cutter had been sighted, but for reasons I can only hint at the cutter cleared off."[4]

Captain Tweedie told the press that when the pirates left three days later, the released crew informed the *Veronica*'s officer what course he should take and that the pirates intended to follow the ship with machine guns ready. A British vessel soon met the *Veronica* and towed it to Halifax. Captain Tweedie made his way back to England on another ship.[5]

Life in the Late 1920s

Part II of this story takes place during the second half of the 1920s. During this time, the Rum War escalated beyond belief. But, before launching into this part of the story, it is important to get an idea of what was going on in America at the time. Good history books about the late 1920s tend to be few and far between. However, one that goes into great detail is Gerald Leinwand's book *1927: High Tide of the 1920s*, which includes many fascinating details. At the time, America's wealth was as great as that of all of Europe (including Russia) combined. Americans had more spending cash than ever before. More than half of America's 118 million people lived in cities, commercial transatlantic telephone calls were a new phenomenon, and a third of households owned a radio. Millions of Americans made their first-time purchases of such gadgets as fans, electric irons, toasters, vacuum cleaners, heating pads, refrigerators, coffee percolators, washing machines, waffle irons, and dozens of other items powered by electricity.[6]

These purchases were largely made possible by installment buying, the precursor of the credit card. As the 1920s roared on, the credit bubble grew bigger and bigger. More than 85% of furniture, 80% of phonographs, 75% of washing machines, and most refrigerators, radios, sewing machines, pianos, and vacuum cleaners were purchased on installment plans. Also, millions of Americans bought stocks on margin, another form of credit. Over the short term, credit made life sweeter for average Americans and enabled them to live a lifestyle they could not otherwise afford.[7]

Advertising as an industry grew at an incredible rate. Manufacturers spent over a billion dollars to advertise their products on the radio, in newspapers and magazines, through direct mail, on billboards, and elsewhere. These ads were effective in reaching the average American, who went to the movies once every other week, plus the 25% of Americans who were fortunate enough to listen to the radio for an hour a day.[8]

The automobile was quickly changing American life. In the United States, there was one car to every five persons and construction crews were rapidly building paved highways. By 1927, one could drive on paved highways from New York to Kansas; however, most of America's roads remained unpaved. When it rained, the carriage-like wheels of the average car could easily get stuck in deep mud. Americans were driving Fords, Buicks, Cadillacs, Chevrolets, Chryslers, Dodges, Lincolns, Oldsmobiles, and Pontiacs. Also popular were the Auburn, Chandler, Essex, Hudson, Hupmobile, Packard, Pierce-Arrow, Rickenbacker, Studebaker, and Stutz. Some families lacked indoor plumbing yet still owned cars.

In 1927, half of the cars on the road were Model-T Fords. The ten million Model-T's were mostly black, with the exception of a few brown ones. When Ford introduced the Model A at the end of 1927, it was a smash hit. A million people tried to see the new phenomenon on the first day. American drivers, who were used to hand-cranking the Model-T to get it started, were amazed at the electric starter. The gas tank was forward of the dash, which displayed a speedometer, gas gauge, and ammeter. What made the Model-A so spectacular to the American consumer was that it came in different colors—red, yellow, green, and blue.[9] The automobile did not replace other forms of transportation overnight. Despite the growing popularity of the automobile, trolleys were almost still as common in the late twenties as they were a decade earlier. Horses pulling carts, even in big cities, were also still a common sight.

The average American had a very limited education in the late '20s. Only 64% of America's youth attended school during that period. The average student finished school permanently by seventh grade. Only two Americans out of 100 went to college and only half of that two percent graduated. Movie producers and advertisers took this data into consideration, trying to find common ground between the average American and those with college degrees. Newspaper advertisements aimed anywhere above the reading comprehension of an eighth-grader cut readership in half.[10]

Rural America was becoming more modernized than in the first half of the decade, but still far behind the cities. Two-fifths of rural households had telephones and only 9% used electric lighting, as opposed to 85% of city homes. Most country homes were still using kerosene lamps for light. Eighty-three percent of farm households had no bathrooms and eighty-five percent had no sewage disposal. Kitchens generally used ice boxes instead of refrigerators. For those who don't know, an ice box is a large, insulated metal cooler that has a space to hold a block of ice. Ice trucks and wagons would make the rounds daily to deliver ice to those who still had no refrigerators. Half of country homes had no cupboards or ceramic dishes. Instead, pots, pans, and tin dishes were either hung on the wall or lay on kitchen tables, reminiscent of pioneer days. Since country stores carried a very limited selection of goods, farmers frequently ordered from catalogues and paid on installment plans.[11]

While farm animals still did more work than machines in rural America, reliance upon these animals was rapidly declining. The horse population declined from 20 million in 1914 to 15 million in 1928, while the number of tractors on farms increased from 80,000 in 1918 to 853,000 ten years later.[12]

Prosperity?

America's economy was booming in the 1920s, but the living conditions and wages of the average person were nothing like those depicted in nostalgic movies. Corporate profits rose faster than wages and unemployment was growing rapidly. In 1927, four million people were unemployed, compared to one million only four years earlier. The unemployment rate was just as bad as during the recession following World War I, only a few years earlier. In some factories, women and children as young as fourteen worked a 70-hour week. Approximately two million boys and girls under the age of 15 worked in textile mills, beet fields, and cranberry bogs. The average family's income was $2,550, barely enough to live on.[13]

In 1927, there was evidence that consumer spending was falling. Wages and salaries in manufacturing grew very little although manufacturing output kept increasing. Americans cut their spending on durable goods such as refrigerators and other large appliances. There was a sharp drop in automobile sales. The real estate market, which began to collapse in 1926, continued to decline through the late '20s and into the Great Depression. State and local governments also cut their spending, meaning less jobs and less money flowing into the economy.[14]

ALCOHOL, BOAT CHASES, AND SHOOTOUTS!

The federal government attempted to bail out the failing economy as early as 1927 by using its surplus revenue to reduce the national debt and cut interest payments. The Federal Reserve Board adopted an easy money policy, lowered the discount rate from 4% to 3.5%, and purchased government securities on the open market. These moves by the Fed encouraged stock market speculation and disguised the signs of impending financial doom.[15]

A Bigger And Better Rum Fleet

On the night of February 6, 1925, the Coast Guard began an armed motor patrol from Seaside Park to Highland Beach, NJ, covering 38 miles. The patrol, commanded by M.W. Rasmussen, Superintendent of the Coast Guard's Fifth District, included six patrol cars, each carrying four Coast Guardsmen. Each car was to keep in contact with Coast Guard headquarters at Asbury Park. Rasmussen told the press that he would be able to contact and dispatch any of the six vehicles within twenty minutes to meet any party of smugglers within his jurisdiction. Any of the patrol cars could request backup if necessary.[16]

On the same day Rasmussen began his motorized shore patrol, the Coast Guard spotted the largest liquor fleet assembled in a year 42 miles off the New Jersey Shore. The armada of rum ships moved slowly northward, in search of anchorage. A rusty old 3,000-ton steamer led the procession. Behind the steamer were smaller steamers, freshly painted in battleship gray, several schooners, and a converted yacht. Cases of liquor were piled high on the decks.[17]

A few miles away were two large flotillas of Coast Guard vessels, including cutters and speedboats. They had cleared their decks and were ready to intercept any smaller boats attempting to smuggle liquor ashore. Coast Guardsmen believed that the ships they saw were only a small part of a much larger fleet, which stretched out beyond the horizon.

A dozen seventy-five foot Coast Guard cutters went out to escort the rum ships if they steamed within the jurisdiction of the Fifth District. The cutters stayed within four or five miles of the rum ships. Later, thirty-six picket boats came out to intercept rum-runners from the shore. These fast boats were capable of 35 to 40 miles per hour in calm seas.[18]

Adventures of the World's Fastest Police Boat

The Coast Guard had help from local police in fighting rum-runners. In early 1925, the world's fastest police boat was the *Gypsy*. The boat, powered by two 250-horsepower engines, was definitely an effective weapon against rum-runners. Sergeant Patrick J. Lee, who had worked in the NYPD Marine Division for two years, commanded the speedboat. Lee had spent twenty years with the New York Police Department. Before joining the marine division, he had arrested many river pirates while patrolling West and South Streets in Manhattan. The police assigned to rum patrols worked in 24-hour shifts, followed by 24 hours off. Sergeant Lee and his crew had been so successful over the previous two years that most of his "days off" were spent arraigning smugglers in federal court.[19]

In early February, Sergeant Lee took some rare leave time to attend his mother's funeral, but he soon went right back into action. Little did he know he would soon be joining his mother in the afterlife. While patrolling near Fort Wadsworth at dawn, Lee spotted a suspicious craft headed for Kill Van Kull, the narrow body of water between Staten Island and New Jersey. The crew of the suspect craft got nervous and the boat sped away. As the police boat passed the St. George ferry terminal, the officers began firing their pistols at the other boat.

Sergeant Lee climbed out on the bow of the *Gypsy* to get a better shot at the craft ahead. Water sprayed up and coated Lee with a layer of ice. He complained of the chill and his crew pulled him back into the cabin. Seeing that Lee was suffering from hypothermia, the crew gave up the pursuit and sent him home. A week later, he died of pneumonia.[20]

Although Sergeant Lee's death was a great loss, the New York police still had a war to wage against smugglers. Three weeks after Lee's death, the *Gypsy* was patrolling in the lower bay when the crew heard shots coming from a Coast Guard cutter. A speedboat raced by in the early morning darkness without running lights. The *Gypsy* chased the boat at full speed.[21]

The fleeing vessel, named the *War Bug*, was a seventy-foot vessel equipped with two 450-horsepower Liberty engines and one 300-horsepower Fiat engine. The speedboat rounded Governors Island and headed for the Narrows, but the Coast Guard intercepted it. The *War Bug* turned its bow toward Newark. The *Gypsy*'s crew opened fire on the craft with a shotgun as it headed for the North River. The *War Bug* was loaded down with a liquor cargo and unable to shake off the police as they continued to shoot at them. As the boat passed 135th Street, flames shot up as an explosion came from the *War Bug*'s engine room. As the smugglers slowed down, the *Gypsy* came alongside. Patrolman Matthew Thomasson leaped from the deck, but miscalculated the distance, crashing against the stern and disappearing into the ice-cold river.[22]

The *Gypsy*'s searchlight swept the surface of the water. After Thomasson reappeared, his fellow officers hauled him aboard. The police then boarded the *War Bug* with drawn pistols and arrested the crew as the boat burned. The police smothered the flames with extinguishers and took the three prisoners, the *War Bug,* and its 200 cases of liquor to the Barge Office.[23]

US Commissioner Henry S. Rasquin, assigned to the Eastern District of New York City, made a trip down to the Southern District at 2 AM to set the bail of the three rum runners. He let each of them out on $1,000 bail. Commissioner Rasquin's actions raised suspicions among those in the legal profession. It was very unusual for a commissioner to go to another district at 2 AM to set bail for rum smugglers. In response, Assistant US District Attorney Herman L. Falk went before Commissioner John N. Boyle and obtained warrants for the arrest of the three defendants in case they failed to appear in court that morning. Falk said that the facts offered no explanation for the action of Commissioner Rasquin.[24] In his defense, Rasquin told the press that he acted in accordance with the usual custom.[25]

Shoot First, Ask Questions Later

On April 1, Randolph Ridgeley Jr., commander of the Coast Guard in Atlantic City, issued orders to "shoot first and ask questions afterward" if any suspected craft refused to halt. Ridgeley took this action after receiving instructions from Washington to wage vigorous warfare on smugglers. As part of the new program, the Coast Guard painted the cutters and picket boats of the "dry" navy dark grey and removed the hull numbers. The command to "shoot first" resulted from numerous incidents involving smugglers and the improvements in rum-runners. In 1925, many rum runners could travel 45 miles per hour, leaving the government boats behind. The smugglers had stopped trying to run liquor into the inlets of Atlantic City and began landing it directly on the beaches in small boats.[26]

Officials in Washington were quick to deny that they had given instructions to "shoot first and ask questions afterward." Lieutenant Commander Stephen S. Yeandle, aide to Admiral Billard, said that there had been no departure from the regulations set by the Act of 1799:

> "Under this old law, which governs Coast Guard officers in prohibition cases as well as others with which they are concerned, the rum hunters are required when pursuing bootleggers afloat to give warning before they open fire. The regulations provide that before opening fire they must give a warning blast of the siren and throw a warning shot into the water. If the vessel that is being pursued does not then stop, the commanding officer may shoot at it or into it, in the language of the law."[27]

Before the end of the month, Ridgeley's men put his directive into practice. He received a tip that fifteen rum smugglers in two small boats were trying to land a cargo near Margate, NJ. The informant said that two trucks were on shore and would soon transport the liquor inland. Captain Ridgeley assigned two officers and four enlisted men to support the Coast Guardsmen that were already on their way to Margate. His men also started up an armed seaplane recently added to the Atlantic City fleet. While the plane took off on its mission, four more Coast Guardsmen sped for Margate in an automobile.[28]

When the plane landed on the water, two small boats were alongside Margate landing. The boats were empty and fifteen men were busy carrying cases to the nearby trucks. At the sight of two Coasties wading ashore from the plane, eleven of the smugglers escaped inland. One of the two boats got away quickly, but the other lagged behind. The Coast Guardsmen, armed with machine guns, ordered the boat to stop. After the fleeing smugglers ignored the order, the two men showered the boat with bullets, hitting one of the men aboard. The two men in the boat jumped overboard close to shore and escaped. While the boat sank, the Coast Guard seized the two trucks, loaded with 187 cases of liquor. Captain Ridgeley sent word out to all local hospitals to look for a man with a gunshot wound.[29]

24

UNCLE SAM CHOKES THE RUM FLEET

By the spring of 1925, the Coast Guard's new Prohibition fleet was almost fully operational. A year earlier, Congress appropriated $12 million for the construction of a bigger, better dry fleet numbering near 400 vessels. Congress also authorized 4,000 additional men to operate the fleet. Most of the vessels were newly-built on special designs. The destroyers, left over from World War I, were not new, but modified. They would be used as long-distance scouts and as "mother ships" for smaller Coast Guard vessels. The destroyers kept all of their wartime equipment and armaments aboard, with the exception of torpedoes.[1]

The new vessels fell into three categories: patrol boats, picket boats, and 100-foot patrol boats. There were 203 patrol boats, which looked like yachts, measuring 75 feet in length. Twenty-five of these boats were assigned to the Pacific, 25 to the Great Lakes, and 153 to the Atlantic.[2] On the forward deck of each was a one-pounder gun with a range of five to ten miles. There were also machine guns and rifles aboard. Each of these carried a crew of eight men, who lived on board, commanded by a warrant officer. The boats operated from land bases over a range of twenty-five to thirty miles.[3] In addition to the patrol boats, there were 105 picket boats, measuring 36 feet in length. They used small gasoline engines for work in rivers and inlets. Normally manned by a crew of three, these boats carried machine guns, rifles, and pistols.

There were ten of the 100-foot patrol boats, which were to be used as the "trouble-shooters" in the busier areas. Their function was to handle emergencies and to aid the smaller craft when they were in trouble. These boats carried three-pounder guns, and were powered by a pair of 150-horsepower diesel engines. Unlike the Coast Guard's earlier vessels, these were constructed of steel, not wood.[4]

Captain Quinton R. Newman, Chief Engineer of the Coast Guard, gave this insight into the design of the new fleet:

> "In designing these boats, we had to give thought to several important considerations. One of course, is speed. But seaworthiness and dependability are even more important. The rum-runner may not use his launch more than once or twice a month; hence he can sacrifice other things for speed alone. But these boats of ours will be at sea most of the time, and must be able to face any weather and stay out indefinitely. We also took pains to see that the patrol boats were provided with comfortable living quarters for the crews; for you can't get good service unless the men are able to rest when off duty. For these purposes I think the boats will stand up against any others in existence. Several of them have survived tough experiences already."[5]

Coast Guard officers would not tell the press how fast these new vessels could go, but they did admit that some of the rum-runners were faster. The Coast Guard planned to offset the disadvantage of speed with their long-range guns. The Prohibition fleet did not include submarines or airplanes; however, the Coast Guard planned on experimenting with planes for reconnaissance and for dealing with speedboats.[6]

In addition to granting money to build a new Prohibition fleet, Congress authorized the Coast Guard to take over and use, after legal action, the boats that were confiscated on account of capture. These confiscated vessels would help greatly in surprising and capturing smugglers.[7]

The new fleet was equipped with radios made by the Western Electric Company. These radios operated on a special frequency that the rum-runners had great difficulty picking up. The radios had a range of 50 miles for "telephony" and 100 miles for "interrupted continuous wave telegraphy."[8]

Surveillance

Surveillance work made up a significant part of the Coast Guard's campaign against smuggling. The Coast Guard had its own intelligence network which kept tabs on the operations, persons, and vessels in the rum-running trade. Coast Guard and Justice Department agents kept track of over 300 vessels, keeping detailed descriptions of the vessels themselves and their activities. Usually when a rum ship left a foreign port, a full report went out to all Coast Guard units.[9]

Even though the Coast Guard could not board a vessel outside of the set limits, there was no law against following a vessel. In one case, a rum ship, anchored at a safe distance from shore, was awaiting smaller craft. Nearby, however, was a Coast Guard cutter, keeping watch day and night. At night, the cutter cast a searchlight on the ship, scaring away all potential customers. When the rum ship steamed away, the Coast Guard followed it for several hundred miles and kept a searchlight focused on its decks every night. After that terrible experience, the ship did not return to Rum Row.[10]

The Offensive Begins

Treasury Secretary Mellon decided to coordinate all of the Prohibition units under a single leader. He chose retired Brigadier General Lincoln Clark Andrews to take charge of Prohibition agents, Customs, and the Coast Guard. Andrews, a disciplinarian, was a graduate of West Point who served in the Army for 30 years. He was the assistant to General H. H. Bandholtz, in charge of the military police in Paris after the Armistice. Almost immediately after receiving his new appointment, Andrews launched a new offensive against Rum Row.[11]

On May 5, business for Sir Broderick Hartwell and other smugglers went from bad to worse as fifty Coast Guard vessels prepared for their biggest offensive yet. Admiral Billard mobilized the fleet from different stations along the coast. The cutters, fast launches, destroyers, and sub-chasers made an imposing, threatening array lying out from Piers 17 and 18 at Staten Island.[12]

After taking a tour of different Coast Guard stations and cutters along the East Coast, Lincoln C. Andrews directed a new "starvation and surveillance" offensive against Rum Row. Assistant Secretary Andrews reorganized the personnel in response to rumors that several Coast Guardsmen were involved in liquor smuggling. A few hours before the offensive, an amended order came down from Washington. The men formed up on the pier and were reassigned to new vessels. The crews grumbled as they were shifted around. Almost no one remained on their original ship. Many of the men had been with the same crew since the beginning of their enlistment and now had to work with complete strangers.[13]

The assembled fleet consisted of ten cutters plus forty smaller vessels. Those cutters were the *Gresham, Mojave, Redwing, Seminole, Seneca, Tallapoosa, Yamacraw, Manhattan, Ossippee,* and *Acushnet*. Each of the cutters was equipped with two six-inch guns, two anti-aircraft guns, four one-pounders, plus machine guns.[14] All of the vessels were stocked with food and supplies for a four-day patrol and were scheduled to be resupplied by cutters, which would run back and forth from the blockading line to the bases at Stapleton, Atlantic City, and Greenpoint.[15]

At 9:45 P.M., only a few hours after the men had been reassigned to new vessels, 35 of the vessels left port. The officers of the ships did not receive the details of their mission until they were out at sea. The instructions were coded and wired to the cutter *Seneca*, which acted as the flagship. Every effort was made to keep the Coast Guard's movements secret until they reached their assigned positions. The ships were to patrol a course approximately fifty miles long, extending from New Jersey to Long Island. In addition, other patrols covered the New England coast.[16]

The Smugglers Retaliate

The Coast Guard reported that no liquor had been landed since the "starvation" campaign began a few days earlier. Lieutenant Commander Yeandle, aide to Admiral Billard, told the press that smugglers were retaliating against the Coast Guard in large numbers. The smugglers interfered with operations everywhere they could by sabotaging vessels and attacking Coast Guardsmen.[17]

The Coast Guard put men on watch to protect their ships while in port to prevent sabotage. A saboteur caused thousands of dollars in damage to the destroyer *Jewett* by inserting a small piece of steel into the ship's steam turbine. The crew did not discover this problem until the ship was out to sea and the machinery began to malfunction. Parts of the turbine were reduced to powder and the destroyer barely made it back to port.[18]

Explosions on Coast Guard vessels became frequent. One of the fleet's ships exploded and sank at Atlantic City, supposedly because of an "accidental gasoline explosion." However, Lieutenant Commander

Yeandle stated that there was evidence to prove that it was an act of sabotage. In another incident, two men were blown overboard by an explosion. One of them died and the other was permanently disabled.[19]

One ship was scuttled at its dock. Smugglers wrapped chains around Coast Guard propeller blades, causing much damage when the crews started their engines. The bearings of one of the best vessels in the fleet were ruined when a saboteur poured ground glass in the gears. In addition, rum-runners intentionally interfered with Coast Guard vessels as they pursued other smugglers; in some cases, they actually rammed the government's boats.[20]

Coast Guard officials told the press that the rum smugglers were out to kill those who attempted to interfere with their operations. Boatswain Pearson, attached to the Atlantic City base, was kidnapped by bootleggers. They bound and gagged him and took him to the outskirts of town. When the captors realized that they had the wrong man, they let him go.

Assistant Treasury Secretary Andrews and Admiral Billard were fully aware of the gravity of the situation as the list of casualties grew on both sides. Rum agents called Coast Guard Headquarters in Washington, DC to offer bribes. When the officials turned the bribes down, the smugglers branded them as crooks and accused them of letting other rum boats through the lines. In one instance, a caller told Lieutenant Commander Yeandle to make himself "scarce" around New York after he turned down a bribe offer.[21] Not only were officers and enlisted men threatened, but also members of Coast Guard families. The smugglers also began their own propaganda campaign to demoralize the crews of the patrol fleet.

Smuggling rings hired their own spies, who infested Coast Guard Headquarters and tried to steal orders and read official papers in the hopes of learning of the fleet's movements. Some liquor salesmen even had the audacity to invite officers and enlisted men at headquarters out to dine.[22]

Victory?

On May 11, 1925, Coast Guard officers announced that they had broken up Rum Row by driving away two steamers and four of the eight schooners which had been sighted south of Sandy Hook. Three Coast Guard picket boats returned to Staten Island and reported that only four schooners were visible. The missing rum ships headed south under a cover of heavy fog to avoid the patrol boats. Captain John Bryan, commander of the Staten Island base, speculated that the rum ships were heading for Atlantic City or further south.[23]

Many Coast Guardsmen believed that they had won a complete victory over Rum Row. Certain officers stated that not a single boatload of liquor had been smuggled ashore in the past day, despite heavy fog. The New York Police Department's marine patrol verified that statement. The NYPD had been cooperating closely with the Coast Guard during the strengthened blockade. Neither the police boats nor the patrolmen at the waterfront spotted any smuggling, or so they claimed. The failure of the rum smugglers to get through the blockade in the fog and rain (ideal smuggling weather) was enough proof for many Coast Guardsmen that the tide had turned in their favor.[24]

Both in New York and Atlantic City, Coast Guard officers announced their plans to starve the rum crews out. The Coast Guard ships blockaded Rum Row in both directions, meaning the rum ships ran low on water, food, and other supplies until they were forced to leave. The Associated Press reported that some of the whisky ships had returned to Nova Scotia with their decks piled high with unsold liquor cases.

Although the Coast Guard's blockade had disrupted the rum fleet, there were still thirty rum ships off the coasts of Connecticut, Rhode Island, and Massachusetts. Fourteen patrol boats left New London, Connecticut to follow these ships. Some of the ships headed out to sea, while others cruised up and down the coast in an attempt to shake off the patrol boats. Several rum-runners attempted to sneak out of New London under the cover of fog, but made it no farther than the inner line of the blockade.[25]

Grand Plans

Coast Guard Headquarters planned the war on rum smuggling much like a wartime naval blockade, but without using mines and torpedoes. Coast Guard Headquarters in Washington had a gigantic map showing the positions of rum ships on the Atlantic Coast. Ships on the map were represented by black-headed pins, which were moved as radio dispatches told of their movements. Admiral Billard planned to send Coast Guard cutters to escort rum ships after they left Rum Row. The cutters had orders to follow the ships until they reached the next district, where other Coast Guard ships would meet the smugglers to continue the surveillance and harassment further along the coast. Billard also mobilized patrol boats in the South and on the Great Lakes for a more extensive rum patrol.[26]

The rising prices of liquor were proof that the blockade was effective. Since the new offensive began a week earlier, only two boatloads of liquor were landed in New York City. The price of Scotch whisky rose from $7 a bottle to $12 due to a short supply. Retail liquor sellers found real, uncut Scotch almost impossible to obtain, although synthetic or doctored whisky was plentiful.[27]

On May 12, Assistant Treasury Secretary Andrews announced that the current blockade off the Atlantic Coast was "only a minor engagement" and would be followed by "real naval liquor warfare." He went on to say:

> "The warfare going on now is not in any sense a big drive. It is a test. We want to see how the rum-runners will defend themselves against this treatment. Then we will take the offensive against whatever move they make, and so on, until it seems that we can operate against them in a really successful way.
>
> "When that time comes, then you will see real naval liquor warfare instead of the minor engagement going on."[28]

Differing Opinions

Treasury Secretary Mellon was pleased with the new offensive against the East Coast's Rum Row. He expressed his pleasure at the cooperation between the Coast Guard, Customs, and the Prohibition Bureau. He stated that the attack on Rum Row would be the most successful in history and that its moral effect in cowing lawbreakers would be long-lasting. The grand strategy of the Treasury Department was to smash liquor smuggling by sea, and then shift more resources to crushing bootleggers on land. Distillers were already using industrial alcohol and corn liquor to keep up with the demand. The government's stance, including President Coolidge's, was that if public opinion could be swayed in favor of Prohibition, the public would put pressure on judges and district attorneys to adequately punish offenders of the Volstead Act. Coolidge wanted to see the fight kept up unceasingly through the summer and was willing to ask Congress for more funds if the present force was too small.[29]

Obviously, there were many Americans who disagreed with the rum blockade and the tightening federal noose. One of the most outspoken critics was W.H. Stayton, founder and executive head of the Association Against the Prohibition Amendment. He was strongly opposed to the federal government's new plan to share part of the fines and proceeds of ships seized with informants:

> "This disgusting scheme links the Republican Party and the present Administration more closely with the Anti-Saloon League. The dry league is directly responsible for the introduction of a similar system in the State of Ohio. A reign of terror, graft, corruption and lawless acts followed. Rural dry agents and judges were paid from the fines collected for liquor law violations. The more arrests and convictions, the more money the judge and agent shared.
>
> "This system resulted in the framing of innocent persons and the imposition of unjust fines. It also resulted in the conviction of scores of rural dry agents operating in Ohio...
>
> "The increased activity of the Coast Guard in concentrating its ships off rum row is futile and a waste of money. In the old Revolutionary days the entire British navy was sent to these coasts to stop smuggling. The immediate result of this action was the making of real sailors out of the American smugglers. History repeats itself. The vigilance of the Coast Guard will make skillful seamen out of the rum-runners. The so-called successful bottling up of rum row is nothing less than a farce."[30]

Commander Yeandle Visits Rum Row

A week after the tightened liquor blockade began, Lieutenant Commander Stephen S. Yeandle, aide to Admiral Billard, went on a three day inspection cruise of Rum Row. He traveled aboard the Coast Guard cable ship *Pequot* from Nantucket, Massachusetts to Barnegat, New Jersey. When he returned from his trip, he reported his observations to the press:

"We left New London about 3 o'clock last Wednesday afternoon and went directly out to the rum fleet off Montauk Point, which was the nearest one to our starting place. As soon as we started out we began to pick up the patrol boats and destroyers of the Coast Guard cruising back and forth. There had been no advance information to the personnel that we were coming, and I was very much pleased to see how efficiently the men were on the job. We saw some of the fastest boats between New London and Montauk—pursuit ships that can make forty or fifty miles an hour, and keep up with the fastest rum-runners in the business.

"South of Montauk Point, which used to be a hotbed of liquor ships, because the rum runners could land stuff from there either on Long Island or Connecticut and take it thereafter either to New York or Boston, we saw only four rum ships. Each was surrounded by Coast Guard vessels, and if anything had happened enough additional Coast Guard ships could have been brought up quickly to make ten for each liquor ship...

"Two of the liquor ships left the Montauk area about the time we arrived and one, left afterward. The captain of the remaining vessel shouted to us that he intended to remain 'until hell froze over.'

"We left Montauk late Wednesday night and cruised north, finding destroyers running up and down the coast according to plan and watching for any new arrivals or departures under cover of darkness. They all had their searchlights working, and the whole surface of the sea was lighted up.

"On Thursday morning, which we spent in the area south of Nantucket, we found only three liquor ships there, although a short time ago we had reports of thirty-one being in that area.

"One of the ships we saw on Thursday was south of No Man's Land, another was south of Block Island, and the third was south of Nantucket. A notorious French rum steamer was one of these. We were informed by the Coast Guard men guarding her that she had several hundred thousand dollars worth of champagne on board, besides some Scotch whisky and liquors.

"As we steamed up close to the Frenchman, her crew lined the side, and began shouting to us in English. Despite the French flag they were sailing under, it was apparent that most of them were from the east side of New York—pretty tough looking specimens they were. They didn't know our old cable ship was a Coast Guard boat, and they began offering us champagne at bargain prices, $25 to $35 a case for wine, and as low as $20 a case for whisky. They offered to trade a case of champagne for a carton of cigarettes, and even invited us to come on board and have all we wanted to drink. We told them 'nothing doing.'

"Another ship in the Nantucket area flying the British flag but with American faces and voices predominantly in the crew, offered us 500-case lots of whisky at $20 a case...

"We stopped off the Long Island coast on Friday morning and the picket boats from the inshore patrol came out to see who we were, showing they were right on the job. Having inspected the situation out at sea, we decided to spend Friday seeing whether every precaution was being taken to keep the rum-runners from shore bottled up in the innumerable inlets of the Long Island coast...

"On Friday afternoon we left Fire Island and went straight out to sea for the last part of our job—an inspection of the 'old New York Rum Row.' In the old days there were sometimes 100 or more liquor ships in a string between Nantucket and Barnegat, you would sometimes find as many as seventy off New York City, and you would always find from twenty to thirty. This area covers about 1,600 square miles, which we traversed back and forth, talking to Commander W.J. Wheeler on his flagship Mojave, commanding the New York squadron, and the men on his cutters, destroyers and picket boats.

"Instead of the forty ships reported off New York at the beginning of the blockade we found only five. The Coast Guard men said that not a case of liquor had been landed from the New York Rum Row since the beginning of the blockade. The men on board the liquor ships here were very glum looking and seemed ready to quit. Three of the eight ships we had sighted between Montauk and Barnegat left this morning, incidentally after we started to New York Harbor. We spent Friday afternoon and night cruising between Long Island and Barnegat.

"On our return to New York this morning we lay off Ambrose Lightship and sent a small boat ahead with some of our civilians to see if they could run the blockade into New

York Harbor. They had hardly started when a patrol boat stopped them...

"We came back to New York convinced that we had broken up the rum fleet, but also aware that we have made a harder job for ourselves. With the supply of liquor decreased the price on shore naturally will go up, and there will be even greater temptations for rum-running at greater distances than in the past. With radio and airplanes to send messages between shore and rum ships 200 or 300 miles off shore, they may arrange rendezvous and try to slip through our lines at widely separated places. Therefore we will continue to patrol the coast indefinitely."[31]

Some People Are Never Satisfied

On the day after Commander Yeandle delivered his dazzling report on how the Coast Guard smashed Rum Row, a Senate committee came to the conclusion that Prohibition enforcement had practically collapsed. Senator King of Utah, a member of the committee, stated that the time had come to transfer Prohibition enforcement from the Treasury to the Justice Department. In great contrast with Yeandle's observations, King delivered this scathing report:

"We had our investigators go through the prohibition unit and report back to us some typical cases indicating inefficiency, misadministration and, in some instances, what looked like corruption...

"It seems generally conceded that there has been a general breakdown of the law. It is a very big problem and the committee has not yet decided what its future course will be...

"At the meeting today I insisted that there is one thing Congress should certainly do at the earliest opportunity and that is transfer this whole business of prohibition enforcement to the Department of Justice, where it belongs..."[32]

On May 19, only two weeks after the tightened blockade began, Captain John Bryan, in command of Coast Guard Base 2, proclaimed the complete defeat of rum-runners operating to and from Rum Row. After the cutter *Ashunec* returned from a fifteen-day patrol, Captain Bryan said to the press:

"The bootleggers are licked. There are fewer boats in Rum Row now than ever before. They're starved out. The Ashunec did not see a boat to chase and did not fire a single shot in the entire fifteen days. Even the boat there now [the German ship *Walter Holterman*] is expected to leave because she is being watched so closely she cannot do business with anyone..."[33]

A day later, Captain W.V.E. Jacobs, commandant of the Coast Guard's New York Division, reported that nine vessels had appeared off New York and New Jersey and that rum-runners had landed more than 1,000 cases on the north shore of Long Island during the previous weekend.[34]

A Very Expensive War

While Admiral Billard and Lincoln C. Andrews were directing an escalating war on Rum Row off New York and New Jersey, a Senate committee released its findings on the costs of Prohibition enforcement. Senators King, Watson, and Couzens declared that the evidence pointed to a breakdown in the enforcement system. The committee estimated that there were at least 250,000 persons in the United States whose duties included Prohibition enforcement. Included in that figure were: 100,000 uniformed police officers; between 15,000 and 20,000 municipal detectives; 10,700 sheriffs with at least three times as many deputies; between 8,000 and 10,000 marshals and constables; 10,000 judges; 2,500 Coast Guardsmen; 10,000 prosecutors; and another 55,000 law officers enlisted under other titles. There were also the Department of Justice investigators, postal inspectors, the Customs Service, state constabulary organizations such as the Texas Rangers and state troopers, and, in many of the states, independent Prohibition enforcement units. Their salaries averaged $2,000 a year, bringing the total to $500,000,000 for salaries alone.[35]

Although the newspapers were saturated with articles on the Coast Guard's new attack on Rum Row, there were few in Washington who believed that the blockade had stopped rum running. The fleet had curbed liquor smugglers and made rum-running even more dangerous, but there was 10,000 miles of American coastline to protect. Even with 20 destroyers and over 300 smaller craft, the Coast Guard would have been stretched very thin in an attempt to cover the entire coastline. The

Coast Guard had one destroyer for every 500 miles of coast line, one patrol boat to every 45 miles, and one picket boat to cover every 100 miles. However, because the Prohibition fleet had to concentrate its vessels in one area to be effective, much of the coastline went completely unguarded. Operating and expanding the Coast Guard was also becoming very expensive. Congress appropriated over $12 million during the previous year for ships, materials, and armaments, plus another $9,500,000 to operate the fleet.[36] Even if the Coast Guard did somehow manage to acquire enough vessels to patrol the entire American coastline, rum runners would still have broken the blockade with airplanes, submarines, and, of course, bribery.

During the strengthened blockade, seaplanes were making frequent flights from the Gulf of Mexico to various points inland. One seaplane had a carrying capacity of 2,000 pounds and made deliveries along the Mississippi River. The pilot knew where to land by looking for previously-determined code signals. Keep in mind that this was in 1925, when commercial aviation was new. There were still no commercial passenger airlines or direct flights across the continent. In fact, it would still be a couple of years before Charles Lindberg made his famous trans-Atlantic flight. Planes crashed with alarming frequency and there was no system of air traffic control as we know it today.[37] However, wealthy men in the liquor business were optimistic about the use of aircraft and invested many thousands of dollars to build an air fleet. By using planes in greater numbers, the interior of the country could become "wetter" than before.

Coast Guard Shoots at a Harvard Boat

On the night of May 28, 1925, the Atlantic City Chamber of Commerce met and discussed the rough methods of the Coast Guard. Samuel P. Leeds (the chamber's president) and others at the meeting told stories of rowdy treatment and indiscriminate shooting when the Coast Guard ordered boats to halt.

To make matters worse, another shooting incident occurred on the following morning off the Massachusetts coast. Two Harvard boats, named the *Pep* and the *Patricia*, were on their way to the varsity crew's training quarters at New London. Both boats were well-lit. While the boats were off Nantucket in a heavy haze, the students aboard heard a siren. Seeing no vessel and thinking that the siren was a fog horn, both

Harvard crews maintained their speed. What they did not know was that the siren came from a Coast Guard patrol boat.[38]

Shots whizzed by the boats before the students realized what was happening. A solid shot came over the bow of the *Pep* and another fell six feet astern. The Harvard men stopped their engines and hove to. Out of the mist came the gray patrol boat, its crew at the rail with revolvers at the ready. When the Coast Guardsmen asked them about their business, they replied that they were on the way to Red Top, where they would stay until after the Yale race. The disappointed Coasties accepted the story and sheered off with a reluctant apology.

By the afternoon, the Harvard boat returned to Cambridge and the crew members told others what happened. The *Pep* was leaking when it docked. Because the Coast Guard was firing blindly into the haze, only luck, they said, saved them from death or injury and prevented their boats from sinking.[39] Senator Walter E. Edge was furious at these incidents and sent the following telegram to Treasury Secretary Mellon:

> Many and insistent protests have reached me of totally unjustified practices and treatment on the part of members of the Coast Guard against innocent citizens, pleasure yachting along the New Jersey coast. Indignation of the citizens expressed at meeting of Chamber of Commerce last night. (*sic*)
>
> No citizen wants to interfere with vigorous efforts to enforce obedience to the law and recognize some annoyance to the innocent will result. Apparently, however, there is little, if any effort to discriminate. The reckless use of firearms, if not curbed, may result in unfortunate casualties. Signals to stop are frequently misinterpreted by the amateur boatman, and every care should be used to relieve the consternation now apparent among pleasure seekers and yachtsmen spending the summer at the shore.
>
> The vacation season is opening and for the next three months there will be thousands of pleasure craft using our inlets and harbors. They are neither bootleggers nor rum runners and ordinary courtesy and discretion should be used to prevent a reign of terror among them.[40]

Assistant Secretary Andrews immediately fired back with a letter to Senator Edge. He stated emphatically that the Coast Guard crews were required by law to stop and inspect any suspicious vessel. The law also required the Coast Guard to give signals for the boats to stop. If the boats did not stop, Andrews wrote, the Coast Guard was compelled to fire across their bows. Rum runners never stopped when pursued by a patrol boat. Therefore, he argued, every time a boat refused to stop, the Coast Guard assumed it had a load of liquor aboard and was justified in shooting at it. Andrews added that the tactics of the Coast Guard were absolutely necessary and that the Treasury Department could not modify them.[41]

The argument between the two men attracted much public attention. It was the first clash of its kind waged in the open involving a prominent Republican politician. Stricter Prohibition enforcement was a key Republican platform in the 1920s. Senator Edge denied that he was attempting to use his political influence, contending that he was merely representing his district.[42]

Less than two weeks after the Harvard shooting incident, another well-known, powerful man made a furious complaint to the Treasury Department. Charles T. Fisher was the vice-president of the Fisher Body Corporation, maker of car bodies for Cadillac. He complained that men aboard a government patrol boat fired at his three sons several times while they were aboard a launch in the Detroit River. One of the shots, he said, went through the boat, and several bullets passed near it. The three boys were on a pleasure ride and said they heard no commands to halt and did not stop until one of the bullets passed through their craft.[43]

Senator Couzens sent a letter to President Coolidge requesting that he issue an executive order to stop indiscriminate shooting by agents and Coast Guardsmen. In his letter, he mentioned the Fisher boys and told Coolidge that he intended to bring the matter up in the next session of Congress. Couzens recommended long prison sentences for the agents who fired at the boat.[44]

The Senator also sent a letter to Assistant Secretary Andrews in which he said he felt sure that Andrews was "interested in stopping this sort of thing." He asked Andrews to take steps to prevent additional shootings. In his letters, Couzens included clippings from Detroit newspapers telling about the shooting. He forwarded a copy of an affidavit made by the Fisher boys to the President, plus letters from Mr. Fisher, Charles L. Barnowsky of the United Motor Sales Company, and another person who witnessed the shooting.[45]

A few days after the Fisher shooting, the Coast Guard's stance became more lenient. Admiral Billard wrote a letter and sent copies to commodores of yacht and motor boat clubs and to editors of yachting magazines. Here is an excerpt:

> ...As it may reasonably be presumed that yachtsmen and owners of bona-fide pleasure craft are not engaged in smuggling liquor from the rum fleet, this office, after mature consideration, has issued orders that vessels which may be plainly recognized as yachts or as craft used solely for pleasure be not stopped, boarded or searched for the purpose of ascertaining if they are smuggling liquor unless they be found communicating with or hovering about rum ships, or unless other particularly suspicious circumstances require that they be stopped, boarded, or searched.
> This action by the Coast Guard is virtually placing yachtsmen and amateur motorboat men on their honor not to attempt to smuggle liquor into the United States...[46]

Coast Guard officials told the press that Admiral Billard's letter represented voluntary action by the service and was not the result of any protest, including the well-publicized letters of the two Senators. Officials also indicated that the Coast Guard would not loosen up its activities and that extreme measures would be followed when "necessary."[47]

President Coolidge Goes On Vacation

In June 1925, President Coolidge became greatly annoyed by reports that coastal resorts from Florida to Maine were overflowing with liquor. He planned to go on summer vacation in Massachusetts, then known as the one of the "wettest" zones in the United States. Thousands of other visitors planned to visit the north shore of Massachusetts that summer and Coolidge did not want them to find rum flowing freely and openly in roadhouses and bungalows.[48]

The President met with Assistant Treasury Secretary Andrews for half an hour to discuss the new master plan of the nation's Prohibition enforcement. This plan was to include attacks on bootleggers in the larger cities on the East Coast and reorganization of the state enforcement units on July 1, ten days away.[49] Andrews gave out orders almost immediately. The day after his meeting with the President, a fleet of fourteen new high-power motor boats arrived at Boston for Prohibition duty. In addition, three destroyers and a seaplane were on their way to patrol near Swampscott, Massachusetts, where Coolidge would spend his vacation.[50]

Dick Jarvis, head of the Secret Service, arrived at Swampscott before the President. Lieutenant Edgar Allen Poe Jr., who commanded a special detachment of Marines, reconnoitered the area. In addition, a detail of special police from the town watched the approaches to Little's Point and kept traffic moving on Puritan Road [how appropriate]. Before the President arrived, a great number of visitors invaded the town to get a glimpse of the President's summer home; however, the security detail managed to keep onlookers away and kept the traffic moving.[51]

The tightened Coast Guard blockade was not very effective. Rum Row was still plainly visible from Swampscott on July 6. The President and his guests could clearly see the rum ships from the piazza of his estate, named White Court. Coolidge sent a message to Treasury Secretary Mellon regarding this phenomenon. Mellon, in turn, ordered the Coast Guard to dispatch more patrol boats to the area. Before the President's arrival, the favorite spot for landing liquor was at Little's Point, right next to White Court. A private driveway connected Little's Point to White Court and other cottages nearby.[52]

Smugglers kept a cache of liquor in a cottage next to the President's summer home. Federal officers stormed the cottage and seized $30,000 of whisky. This move brought about wholesale arrests, including the arrest of Swampscott's Chief of Police. All involved, including the police chief, were indicted for violating the Volstead Act.[53]

The Coast Guard managed to sweep most of the rum ships from the Swampscott area; however, bootleggers were still bringing liquor into the town from Boston. President Coolidge wanted to see the North Shore rid of Rum Row before his return to Washington. Andrews assured him that he would concentrate the Coast Guard's vessels in that area for the next few weeks. In addition, he promised the President to carry out more raids on land against bootleggers in Swampscott and in the Boston area. President Coolidge planned to study the outcome of the crackdown near his summer home. If the attack on smuggling was not successful, Coolidge intended to recommend a bigger budget for Prohibition enforcement.[54]

Despite Coolidge's order to sweep rum ships from the Massachusetts coast, three rum ships soon reappeared near Boston. The British schooners *Grace and Ruby, Montclair,* and the *James W. Parker* appeared on July 17 after the Coast Guard had chased them away two weeks earlier. The Coast Guard destroyers *McCall*, *Beale*, *Patterson*, and *Cummings*, plus the cutters *Acushnet* and *Ossipee* and dozens of smaller patrol boats were still in those waters.[55]

By the next day, however, the Prohibition fleet pushed the three ships out to sea and Rum Row was no longer visible from White Court. The rum schooners headed in the direction of the Grand Banks and it was rumored that they would land their cargoes in Nova Scotia. William Callahan, Swampscott's new police chief, made an eighty mile trip along the coast and reported that it was entirely 'dry' and that he saw no liquor ships.[56]

25

MISCONDUCT

A few weeks after the great liquor offensive began, six Coast Guardsmen were found guilty by court-martial of smuggling liquor into New York and sentenced to serve six months each. Three others were sentenced to serve 90 days each for intoxication. Nineteen Coast Guardsmen in all were confined to the Richmond County Jail awaiting courts-martial for various offenses. In connection with the smuggling charges, there were reports that a few of the crew members had been bringing liquor in before the blockading fleet began its operations, storing small quantities on Manhattan piers.[1]

Around the same time, a Coast Guardsman named Carl Meyers emerged from an Atlantic City saloon and fired his pistol at pedestrians. After being arrested, Meyers admitted to the police that he had fought in the German army in 1917 and that he was not a US citizen. However, that did not prevent him from enlisting as a Coast Guard petty officer at Cape May and serving on Patrol Boat 103, which had been engaged in the rum blockade.[2]

At the Staten Island base, a high percentage of the blockading fleet's crewmembers were near the end of their enlistments. Few of them intended to reenlist. Among the 90 men aboard the destroyer *Porter*, about 30 percent refused to reenlist. The crewmembers gave several reasons why they did not want to continue their service. The main complaint was that the strenuous patrol duty required by the tightened blockade cut into the men's shore leave. Men on the smaller vessels pointed out the dangers of chasing rum-runners through shallow shore waters.[3]

Lieutenant Commander Stephen S. Yeandle, aide to Admiral Billard, said that the Coast Guard had been receiving much unjust criticism since the new blockade began only a few weeks earlier. After arriving in New York, Yeandle went on a three-day inspection tour of the blockade from Nantucket to Barnegat. He then stated to the press:

> "The Coast Guard men have been condemned as grafters, prohibition agents, bunglers, and so on, but the men I saw on the revenue cutters, destroyers and patrol boats over the 370 miles we covered were a pretty clean, average set of young American boys. They are about the same type as the boys who enlist in the Navy and Marine Corps, and every ship is commanded by officers who have spent years in the Coast Guard service. Most of the skippers in the war zone now have been in the service at least twenty years.
>
> "Despite all the criticism I have seen in the newspapers of the poor seamanship of the Coast Guard, the ships I saw last week were handled very well indeed. Of course, a little bungling and poor seamanship is inevitable, and this is just the end of our breaking-in period for the new men, and for the new equipment we took in after Congress authorized the increase of the Coast Guard to meet the rum-running situation."[4]

Commander Yeandle also gave an interview to the Associated Press in which he stated that the rum-runners had a billion dollar budget while the Coast Guard had to do its job with only thirty million dollars of equipment. He pointed out that there were 385 foreign liquor boats of all types which had been pouring liquor into the US with the help of an intricate land-based organization. Against this massive number of vessels, the Coast Guard had 16 cutters, 20 destroyers, 203 seventy-five foot patrol boats, plus 103 thirty-six-foot picket boats. However, Yeandle's numerical argument was not a strong one; if one adds up the numbers, the Coast Guard was equipped with 342 vessels to the smugglers' 385. The Coast Guard was also equipped with an assortment of naval artillery to compensate for a lack of speed or numbers.[5]

Coast Guardsmen Escape From Jail

Several months after the courts-martial, four of the Coast Guardsmen broke out of the Richmond County Jail in Staten Island. The men, who occupied adjoining cells on the third floor of the jail, obtained a metal file, a heavy wrench, and rope. One of the prisoners sawed through his cell bars, then aided the others in doing the same. The men cut two bars in each of the cell doors, making openings just big enough to squeeze through.[6]

After escaping from their cells, a second door still remained between the escaping men and the utility hall. They sawed through this with ease and then made their way up an unguarded staircase. After breaking its weak metal grating, the men forced open a skylight to reach the roof. They tied the rope to the skylight grating and repelled down the wall. Since there was no fence or wall around the jail, they were free once their feet touched the ground. At no time during their escape did they encounter a guard.

There was another man, named John Farrell, who attempted to escape with the others but when they tried to pull him through the small opening in his cell door, he cried out in pain. The sawed metal bars cut him from his shoulder to his thigh. One of the men, named Elias Jelando, knocked him unconscious with a wrench to keep him quiet and left him behind. Soon, a guard found Farrell and the jail sent out a general alert.

An hour later, a policeman found Jelando on a trolley car near the St. George ferry terminal. When he went back to jail, he bore the additional charges of escape and felonious assault. Two of the others took a taxi to the ferry terminal, arrived in Manhattan, and went to the Broad Street Hospital to treat their rope burns. After the treatment, the two simply walked out of the hospital and disappeared into the crowded streets of the city.

Disgruntled Coast Guardsmen

On June 1, 1925, nine Coast Guardsmen attached to Base 2, Staten Island, NY, quit the service. One hundred more Coasties planned on doing the same a month later when their enlistments were over. The nine men from Base 2 had served two years and said they were not re-enlisting because they had not had enough shore liberty since the tightened blockade began. After spending 21 days at sea, they had only received 48 hours shore leave. Those who had served on small boats said their lives had been endangered by machine-gun fire from rum runners and that they had to chase whisky boats into shoal waters, where there was a serious risk of running aground.[7]

A day later, five more Coast Guardsmen from the cutter *Seneca* quit. The *Seneca*'s crew said that ten of their members almost lost their lives a few days earlier. As part of a new strategy, the *Seneca* had to prevent rum ships from communicating with one another. A high sea was running when the captain of the rum ship *White* hailed the captain of the rum ship *Himmelman* to come aboard and split a bottle of champagne. When the *Himmelman* lowered their skipper over the side in a small boat, the *Seneca's* captain tried to stop him from reaching the other ship. He immediately sent out ten of his own men in one of the cutter's lifeboats. The rough seas tossed the men around as they rowed their tiny boat between the two rum ships.

The Coast Guard crew was unable to reach the spot before the *Himmelman's* captain climbed aboard the *White*. To make matters worse, the *Himmelman* bumped into the lifeboat and damaged it. When the Coasties rowed alongside the *White*, the crew of the ship threw boxes at them and insulted them, while the two captains drank their champagne on deck with great bravado. The Coast Guard tried to stop the *White's* captain from returning to his own ship, but he was transferred in a small boat early the next morning.[8]

Although these transfers were made in plain sight of Coast Guard vessels, and despite reports of great liquor cargoes landing near Atlantic City, Coast Guard officials still claimed that none of the rum runners had been able to run the blockade there.[9]

In addition to hazardous duty and very few days off, Coast Guardsmen were also being denied insurance policies. Some insurance companies had refused to issue policies to Coast Guardsmen on the grounds that chasing rum runners was an extra-hazardous occupation. This was yet another reason why some servicemen were refusing to re-enlist. Officials at the Staten Island base told the press that the Coast Guard would easily be able to replace the men who left the service with two years of sea duty experience.[10]

Liquor Found Aboard A Navy Transport Ship

The US Navy transport *Beaufort* was a small cargo carrier that was used to transport naval supplies and passengers to ships and bases along the Caribbean. It kept a regular schedule of runs between Norfolk, Virginia, and the West Indies, stopping frequently at "wet" ports. An enlisted sailor's wife tipped off US Customs that the *Beaufort*, heading for Hampton Roads, Virginia, was carrying liquor worth more than $5,000. Milton M. Vipond, Assistant Collector of Customs at Norfolk, hurried to the Navy base and informed Rear Admiral Roger Welles,

Commandant of the Fifth Naval District. Captain Wilbert Smith, under the orders of the Admiral, led a raiding squad of Marines, searched the vessel, and detained everyone aboard the ship. The sailors made a wild attempt to throw the cases and jugs overboard; however, the Marines salvaged practically all of the contraband and took it to the administration building on the base. While the ship was being searched, all telephone lines out of the naval base were kept under surveillance and the gates were closely guarded. In total, the Marines found forty cases of liquor. Admiral Welles immediately ordered a Board of Inquiry to investigate and fix responsibility before beginning court-martial proceedings.[11]

The raid of the *Beaufort* created quite a stir in naval circles, extending far beyond the Hampton Roads base. Captain Smith, whose Marines made a thorough job of inspecting the ship, had been transferred to the War College in Newport.[12] Two months after the raid, Navy Secretary Wilbur ordered the court-martial of Commander D.W. Fuller (captain of the ship) plus two other officers and three enlisted men. Fuller, who denied knowing about the liquor, was charged with negligence. The others were charged with illegal possession of liquor. None of the *Beaufort*'s passengers was included in the charges.[13]

Several months later, Commander Fuller and Lieutenant Clarence Baker were cleared of the charges by court-martial with the approval of Navy Secretary Wilbur. However, two lieutenants and two enlisted men were found guilty. All of them lost promotion points. The enlisted men had to pay a fine of $40 a month for a year, while the officers, who earned more, had no fines to pay.[14] This amount might not seem like much today, but it added up to over $400 each, which was a quarter of the average American's annual salary in the 1920s. In 1925, $400 was enough to buy a brand new Model T Ford.

26

Nineteen Twenty-Six

In early January 1926, the freighter *Alegrete* was steaming slowly up the New Jersey coast in heavy fog when the lookout spotted a plane wreck in the water. The ship maneuvered close to the wreck and sent out two small boats. The men searched the plane carefully and found two pairs of goggles. They then rowed around for nearly an hour looking for survivors. When the search failed, the crew rigged a block and tackle and hauled the plane aboard. Captain O. Barboza Lima looked over the wreckage and noticed that it had no identification marks and the engines had no numbers. The *Alegrete* continued its trip and brought the wreckage to a dock at 43rd Street in Brooklyn.[1]

Rumors circulated among rum-runners that the plane was used for rum smuggling. A bootlegger's seaplane had left Atlantic City on New Year's Day and had not been heard from since. A woman visited the wreckage at Bush Terminal in Brooklyn and identified it as the plane her husband, Charles R. Warren, and another man named George Hand, had departed in more than a week earlier. She told the press that her husband had purchased the plane a few months beforehand. Hand and Warren took off from Brooklyn. After the engines began to malfunction, they landed near Atlantic City. From there, they departed for Florida. When asked if her husband was flying for business or pleasure, she replied, "Well, it was sort of a business trip."[2]

Although many people believed that the two men were dead, someone phoned Commander Randolph Ridgely at the Atlantic City base to inform him that they had been picked up shortly after the crash and that they were with friends. Mrs. Warren claimed she knew nothing of her husband's fate.[3]

The rum schooner *Waldic* spotted the two men after they crashed and took them aboard. However, the men were stuck aboard the vessel for several days because no one wanted to risk approaching the ship under the watch of the Coast Guard. Eventually, the *Waldic* turned the men over to the Coast Guard Cutter *Kickapoo*. From there, the two were brought to Coast Guard Base No.9 at Cape May, NJ, where they were detained and questioned about rum-smuggling.[4] However, since there was no liquor aboard, the Coast Guard did not have enough evidence to detain the men for smuggling.

Andrews Loses His Morale

Soon after the plane crash, Assistant Treasury Secretary Andrews and US Attorney Emory R. Buckner addressed several hundred ministers at the old John Street Church in New York. The two were there to discuss the progress of Prohibition enforcement. This particular talk was just a little over seven months after Andrews launched his great liquor offensive, which included the tightened blockade in the Northeast. After Buckner told the ministers that there were not enough agents and courts, Andrews rose and said:

> "Addressing you ministers, I feel that I would like to bare my soul and lay my burden on the Lord...You think it is up to me to enforce prohibition. I can't do it. I am only a policeman. I have had to tell my people to stop making general arrests and to hook up with the District Attorneys and find out whom to arrest.
>
> "It is small wonder that some of our Coast Guardsmen yield to the rum-runner's temptings when they sometimes capture the same rum boat as many as seven times, and it and its crew are as often bailed out to resume their rum running. The rum-runner tells them everybody else is doing it, and that all he will have to do is look the other way and receive $1,000 or more."[5]

Lieutenant Commander Yeandle, stationed at Washington, DC, also spoke to the group. He praised the Coast Guard and said that the older members were loyal. Rum smuggling, he declared, would go on as long as people were willing to buy it. He talked about rum spies who watched every movement of the Coast Guard, drilled holes in unguarded boats and stole others. When he invited the ministers to go out on any night for a look at Rum Row and possibly a rum chase, Andrews rose and said he would "bet six to one" that no minister would ever be found on a Coast Guard cutter on a winter's night.[6]

More Coast Guardsmen Go To Jail

On January 30, eight Coast Guardsmen stationed at Atlantic City were convicted of smuggling liquor in Coast Guard cutters. In addition to receiving dishonorable discharges, they were each sentenced to serve one year at the naval prison in Portsmouth, New Hampshire. After receiving word that the findings of the recent courts-martial had been approved by Washington, Commander Ridgley held a formation including all of the personnel at the Atlantic City base. He then read the names of the eight men and the sentences imposed.[12]

The convicted men had spent the previous month in the brig of the US Steamship *Pickering* and were transferred to a destroyer, which took them to Portsmouth. After announcing the sentences, Commander Ridgley told the massive formation that they "could not put anything over on him" and that they "could not get away with any acceptance of bribes from liquor smugglers or participation in any way with such lawbreaking."[7]

During the previous eight months, five other Coast Guardsmen had been found guilty on similar charges and received equally harsh punishments. The testimony of witnesses at the various courts-martial, held on the *Pickering*, involved several civilians. One of the charges against the Coasties was that they had loaded a cutter with a large quantity of whisky and landed it on the Mullica River, in southern New Jersey. Further testimony indicated that the crew of another Coast Guard boat took bribes of $300 each, and that smugglers from Atlantic City traveled to Rum Row aboard Coast Guard cutters.[8]

Corruption

In the spring of 1926, Game Warden Hamilton Everingham of Toms River, New Jersey, arrested several men for shooting more ducks than they were allowed to by law. When Everingham was arraigning the men before Justice of the Peace Potter in West Creek, a Coast

---

[12] Boatswain Oscar Pearson; Jan Butler, chief boatswain's mate; William C. McPhail, chief boatswain's mate; Marvin A. Turner, chief motor machinist's mate; Louis K. Knewstep, motor machinist's mate; Robert S. Ada, motor machinist's mate; Boatswain Frank J. Cassidy and Henry D. Sterling, chief boatswain's mate.

Guardsman telephoned Sheriff John Grant to tell him that there was a bottle of liquor in Everingham's car.

The sheriff drove to West Creek while the warden was still in court and found a bottle of whisky in Everingham's vehicle. Instead of arresting him, Sheriff Grant told him about the telephone conversation. Everingham claimed that the bottle had been "planted" by a Coast Guardsman and told the sheriff about the alleged rum-running activities of the Coast Guard which had come to his attention.

Grant then called Superintendant M.W. Rasmussen of the Coast Guard's Fifth District. A few weeks earlier, Sheriff Grant went to the town of Tuckerton and obtained an affidavit from a resident who swore he had delivered eight cases of liquor to a restaurant in the area. The witness said that Coast Guardsmen of the Shipbottom Station landed the liquor on the beach paid him $25 to deliver it.[9]

A couple of weeks later, Sheriff Grant made a raid in Waretown and arrested a man named Eugene Danley, who had eight gallons of liquor in his possession. According to the sheriff, Danley said that the Coast Guard delivered and sold the liquor to him. A few days later, Danley accompanied Commander William J. Wheeler and Superintendant Rasmussen from Washington, DC to a Coast Guard station where he identified the men who sold him the liquor.

Sheriff Grant told the press that virtually the entire force of Coast Guardsmen from Barnegat to Cape May would be removed and a new force would be sent to man these stations. Undersheriff Walter Brower told reporters that twelve of the twenty-three enlisted men, plus and officer, signed confessions that they had received bribes ranging from $200 to $1,000.[10]

Soon, eleven Coast Guardsmen were arrested, fourteen were transferred, and two men were demoted in the Fifth District. Commander Wheeler had found evidence of corruption in stations at Ship Bottom, Little Egg, and Bonds. The Coast Guardsmen's confessions implicated five bootleggers representing three syndicates operating through Atlantic City to Camden and Philadelphia.[11]

Chief Boatswain's Mate J. Edward Falkenburg, commander of the Shipbottom Station, along with ten other men, were tried by court-martial in August. Falkenburg confessed that a Coast Guardsman received a $30,000 bribe for aiding rum runners. Captain M.W. Rasmussen, Superintendant of the Fifth District, testified that Falkenburg also admitted receiving $100 for transporting eight cases of liquor across

Barnegat Bay in a Coast Guard boat.[12] Rasmussen added that Falkenburg had reported no liquor seizures between March 1925 and June 1926, which implicated that he had been involved in rum-running for over a year.[13]

Machinist Mate First Class Leroy Rider and Surfman Frank L. Thompson were called to the witness stand to corroborate Falkenburg's confession. Both men refused to answer questions on the ground that it might tend to incriminate them. Both of them allegedly accompanied Falkenburg the night he transported liquor.[14]

On August 23, the court-martial proceedings against the eleven men were postponed indefinitely without making its findings public. The court submitted the evidence to the Board of Review in Washington, thereby removing the embarrassing case from the news headlines.[15]

Expensive Gridlock In The Senate

In the spring of 1926, Congress and the nation were still divided over whether or not to continue Prohibition. Senator Edge (Republican) of New Jersey introduced a joint resolution that would allow voters to express their opinions on Prohibition by ballot in the Congressional elections of 1928, two years later. Simultaneously, in the House, the "wets" began another assault on the government's handling of the Prohibition problem. Representative Linthicum, Democrat, of Maryland stated that appropriations for enforcement amounted to $33 million annually, plus another $53 million to expand the Coast Guard and other government machinery. Of the $33 million figure, $14.5 million paid for the Coast Guard's Prohibition enforcement duties, $10.6 million went to the Treasury Department, and another $6 million went to the Justice Department.[16]

The costs of maintaining and expanding the fleet were put in a different category. During the fiscal year 1926, the government spent $19.2 million dollars for new Coast Guard vessels and also to repair old ones. During the next fiscal year, Congress allotted $3.9 million for additional ships and repairs plus $37.5 million for 25 torpedo boats transferred from the Navy to the Coast Guard.[17] It is important to remember that these figures are in 1925 dollars. Today, those same figures would amount to billions of dollars. These expenses were just a portion of Prohibition costs. Mr. Lithicum added that these figures did not include Border Patrol, Customs, and the money that individual states were spending on enforcement. To make matters worse, Lithicum added:

> "I am told that of the 175 Coast Guard employees in the Narragansett service, seventy-five are under arrest. Two crews of the Coast Guard have gone over to the enemy entirely. From Cincinnati it is said that a great Pullman train carrying forty policemen and twenty prohibition officers left for the Atlanta prison. The great service known as the Coast Guard Service has been so injured through the efforts to enforce the Volstead act that no longer is it an honor to be a member thereof."[18]

In July of 1926, Assistant Treasury Secretary Andrews made a trip to Europe. His goal was to reach an agreement with Britain, France, and Germany to prevent liquor from being shipped to the United States. By this point, Andrews was growing weary of fighting a futile war against rum-running and many of his colleagues believed he would resign in the fall.

Andrews was particularly angry over Congress' failure to pass the Goff Bill, which contained modified search and seizure provisions, and the bill setting up the Prohibition Unit as a separate bureau in the Treasury Department. Another bill whose rejection disappointed him was the one that would have permitted him to utilize the services of retired military officers as agents of the Prohibition Unit.[19]

Administration officials made every effort to persuade Andrews to stay in office for another year, arguing that retiring at that point would hurt the cause of law enforcement. They also argued that his departure during a period of transition might impair the efficiency of the organization which he had built up.

Before Andrews left on his European trip, he held a long conference with Acting Treasury Secretary Winston. After the meeting, neither of the two men would make any statements to the press on Andrew's retirement, allowing the impression to remain that the rumors were true.

Andrews drafted his resignation, which was to become effective on September 1, 1926, and handed it to Treasury Secretary Mellon. He also recommended John F. O'Ryan of New York as his successor. However, after further consideration, Andrews decided to postpone his resignation. The announcement of his retirement at that time would have been an official acknowledgement that the administration's Prohibition policies were failing. Since the mid-term elections were around the corner, the general consensus among Republicans was that it would be better for Andrews to wait until after November to resign.[20]

Walton A. Green, the chief of undercover Prohibition investigators and a close friend of Andrews, did not wait for November. He resigned in early July. Prohibition Administrator Eugene C. Roberts, Jr. made an official announcement that he would retire when Andrews did. Roberts met with Andrews in early July and told reporters, "My boss seemed a disgusted man. He's all through with the service, and would have relinquished his office last week if he could have had his way."[21]

On the day these announcements made the press, seven new rum ships appeared near Boston. Six schooners and one steamer, the largest number in nearly a year, stretched from Cape Ann to Cape Cod. The all-too familiar names of these ships were: *Beatrice, I'm Alone, Mary Jane, Ocean Maid, Fred Himmelman, Sunner,* and *Petrel.* These heavily-laden rum ships sat anchored about 80 miles from Boston Lightship. The Coast Guard had two destroyers, four cutters, and dozens of patrol boats in the area to deal with the nuisance.[22]

Andrews Plans a Counterattack

Although Andrews did not foresee himself remaining in office much longer, the former Army general planned a final offensive in true military fashion. He announced to reporters:

> "I have not resigned and will not consider such action until the task of organization under the grants made recently in Congress, is completed. I think I can finish that work early in September."[23]

Armed with $29 million in funds, a ground force of 4,500 officers, and a naval force of more than 5,000 men and 400 vessels, Andrews was prepared to launch the biggest "dry" offensive yet. The ground forces were composed mostly of former military men. Their objective in the new campaign would be to eliminate the sources of liquor, as opposed to simply chasing bootleggers, breaking up speakeasies, and raiding warehouses. Under centralized command, these federal officers would target the following:

1. The diversion of industrial alcohol into bootleg channels.
2. Breweries, which were only allowed to make "near-beer," but still made real beer.
3. Smuggling across the Canadian and Mexican borders.
4. Bootleggers who did not pay taxes on their smuggled liquor.
5. Drug stores and physicians, with the goal of curbing liquor prescription abuse.
6. Corruption in local police departments relating to Prohibition.

On the naval front, the Prohibition fleet was to be strengthened by the addition of larger, more efficient ships. Andrews planned to add thirty-six ships, each measuring 125 feet in length. These vessels would be able to cross the ocean if necessary, unlike the small patrol boats. Five more former Navy destroyers were being reconditioned for Coast Guard service to add to the twenty destroyers already on Prohibition duty. Thus, within a few months there were to be seventy-one seagoing fighting ships, 200 patrol boats, 105 picket boats, and fifteen miscellaneous boats, totaling about 390 vessels. These vessels were assisted by the Coast Guard's regular fleet, whose primary duties were in other fields. The regular fleet was also in the process of being enlarged by ten cutters. Also, the Coast Guard planned to add five planes in addition to the one already in service.[24]

In addition to the new vessels and planes, the Coast Guard began using a new device that could locate ships by radio signal. The radio direction finder was invented several years earlier, but it was not until the mid-1920s that the new gadgets could be operated on small patrol boats.[25]

Andrews often expressed the opinion that if he could dry up New York, drying the rest of the country would be easy. On July 15, he began his intensive campaign to dry up the city by sending 150 additional agents. A month later, forty Customs inspectors were sworn in as federal Prohibition agents and were immediately assigned to a special harbor patrol. While they were assigned exclusively to Prohibition duties, the inspectors retained their Customs rank and the right to search and seizure. Before this new Customs team was assembled, the search for liquor aboard liners had been conducted by the same men who were assigned to inspect all luggage and cargo. Therefore, only a fraction of their time had been available for Prohibition work. They began their work at once, using converted rum-runners until eight specially designed, 36-foot speedboats were manufactured and delivered from Detroit.[26]

Andrews was aware that large quantities of liquor were being brought into New York on liners and carried away in small boats at night. Jurisdiction-wise, this particular type of violation was best dealt with by Customs. The Customs patrol was to operate from the Barge Office, in the East, North, and Harlem Rivers. The United States Customs 417, a 93-foot converted auxiliary schooner, was assigned to act as a repair ship for the new fleet. The forty inspector-agents were to work with the regular Coast Guard patrol and the marine police patrol.[27]

Massachusetts

On November 3, 1926, *The Boston American* newspaper printed a story describing how six Coast Guard boats were transporting liquor from Rum Row. A federal investigation led by Commander William J. Wheeler revealed that not only were Coast Guard boats carrying rum, but also that some of the officers aboard were part owners of Rum Row vessels. Commander Wheeler made a series of secret investigations and returned to Washington with his reports. In addition to smuggling in the Boston area, Wheeler's assistants uncovered a liquor trail leading to Providence, Rhode Island.[28]

A confession of one of the Coast Guardsmen involved was printed in *The Boston American* and *The New York Times*:

> "My boat and three others in our patrol running out of bases would spend four days on Rum Row. After we left port the skipper would tell us the name of the boat we were to unload or assist in getting the booze off into speedboats.
>
> "When we got out to Rum Row the *George and Earle,* one of the best known rum runners that comes into Rum Row, would greet our skipper. On one occasion seven speedboats from Plymouth came up alongside the *George and Earle* and we helped unload 1,300 cases of liquor off this ship to the speedboats. On this particular load our skipper got $1,500. Our crew numbered eight, counting the skipper. The crew got $300 to split among seven, while the skipper had a grand for himself.
>
> "Believe me, things were rosy. After we got through work we would celebrate. Night after night our crews have

been so drunk that we did not know whether we were in Rum Row or someplace else.

"I have known occasions when a Coast Guard boat would accompany as many as seven speedboats from Rum Row into Plymouth Harbor to see that they were escorted safely in. We unloaded an average of 1,500 cases a night, so you could see all the boys were fixed pretty good financially."[29]

The Coast Guardsman blamed the "leak" on friction between the men over pay. The men did not see why they should unload the liquor for free for one of the officers on base when they could have divided $300 to $500 among seven men for a night's work. This would have given each man between $40 and $70, enough to pay a month's rent.

The radio operator aboard the rum-runner *I'm Alone* was an undercover agent for the Department of Justice who secured evidence against the Coasties. The informant had his suspicions all along, and said, "I was always suspicious of that boat because one day I saw one of the crew taking pictures of our patrol boat unloading the *George and Earle*."[30]

Andrews was furious over stories of how the Coast Guard sold out to bootleggers and rum-runners. Two days after the Coast Guardsman's confession made the papers, Andrews stated that:

"Bootleggers who need advertising for their home-made foreign liquor must start these stories. They have got to make it appear that liquor is getting in to shore and presumably from abroad. All this so-called Rum-Row liquor is home-made. We haven't sighted a rum ship off the coast anywhere recently."[31]

In one of the most drastic overturns in the history of Prohibition enforcement, Treasury Secretary Andrew Mellon accepted the resignations of both Lincoln C. Andrews and Roy A. Haynes on the same day, May 20, 1927. Andrews resigned from his post as Assistant Secretary of the Treasury in charge of Prohibition enforcement. Haynes resigned from his job as Acting Prohibition Commissioner. Mellon appointed Seymore W. Lowman, former Lieutenant Governor of New York, to fill Andrews' position and Dr. James M. Doran, Chief Chemist of the Prohibition Unit, to fill Haynes' position. Lowman was to begin his new job on August 1, assuming jurisdiction over the Customs and

Prohibition bureaus, plus the Coast Guard. Doran took charge of the Prohibition Bureau immediately.[32]

Administration officials expressed their hopes that the resignations of Andrews and Haynes would end the factionalism in the Prohibition Bureau, which had tended to lessen the efficiency of enforcement. Haynes, a former officer of the Anti-Saloon League, had been at swords' points with his superiors at the Treasury Department for years. To make matters worse, the Anti-Saloon League frequently criticized Andrews on his dry enforcement policies publicly.

Dr. Doran, the son of a reverend, was born in Grand Forks, North Dakota, in 1885. He was educated in the public schools of Minnesota, graduated from the University of Minnesota in 1907, and did postgraduate work at George Washington University. He entered government service as a chemist in the Bureau of Internal Revenue and became head of the Industrial Alcohol and Chemical Division in 1920. In 1926, Doran became head of the Technical Division of the Prohibition Unit.[33]

Dr. Doran had specialized in chemical studies of alcohol and had published several scientific papers on the subject. A man with his knowledge could have made an incredible amount of money working for an illegal liquor syndicate. However, Doran was a Prohibitionist and decided to forego the opportunity to become wealthy in order to fight what he saw as an evil. He had a record as a staunch "dry" and had advocated militant enforcement before Congressional committees.

Seymore Lowman, now in charge of Prohibition enforcement, brought a wide experience in politics, business, and law practice to the job. He was born on a farm near Elmira, NY. His father was Pennsylvania Dutch (German) and his mother was of old New England Yankee stock. After teaching at a rural school, Lowman perfected his shorthand and went to work in the Elmira law office of Francis E. Baldwin, long an active leader in the Prohibition party.[34]

For nearly twenty years, Lowman exercised a directing hand in the affairs of the New York State Republican Party. He held the office of City Chamberlain in Elmira for seven years, and in 1908 was elected to the lower State Senate, where he served six years. In 1924, he was elected Lieutenant Governor of New York, where he served alongside one of New York's most colorful, influential, and powerful Governors—Al Smith.

Lowman led the fight that made Elmira "dry" under the New York Local Option law, which preceded the adoption of the 18th Amendment. He also led the fight in the New York Senate for the ratification of the "dry" amendment to the US Constitution and helped put through the Mullan-Gage Enforcement Act, the state's version of the 18th Amendment. (The Mullan-Gage Act was repealed in 1923.) After being appointed, Lowman gave reporters some insight into his plans on Prohibition enforcement:

> "...The great problem, as I said before, is to find for enforcement work in the Prohibition Bureau skilled men who will withstand the temptations that beset enforcement officers. I am going to do all I can to help develop a Bureau of Prohibition force that will be as efficient and trustworthy as are the forces of the Customs Bureau and the Coast Guard. If that can be done, satisfactory enforcement should follow.
>
> "Whether it can be done is something nobody knows. The temptations are 'opportunities' in the language of crooks. Many crooks, naturally, try to get into the service. We have worked out what seems to be a perfect system for checking up on personnel, and we hope it will yield results..."[35]

27

The West Coast

In the 1920s, California was sparsely populated compared to the East Coast. Although there were rum ships off the California coast in the early 1920s, large smuggling syndicates were more attracted by the bigger populations living along the Atlantic and Gulf coasts. Bigger populations, of course, meant more potential customers. Today it is hard to imagine California as ever having been sparsely populated. Now the state has an unbroken chain of large cities and suburbs stretching from San Diego to north of San Francisco, covering a distance of more than 500 miles!

There are logistical reasons as to why the West Coast's population was much less than the East Coast in the 1920s. One has to keep in mind that before the completion of the transcontinental railroad in 1869, traveling to the West Coast from other parts of the nation was a nightmare. The option of traveling all the way to the West Coast by train had only been around for about fifty-some years in the 1920s. Before railroads, or even decent roads and bridges for horses and wagons, the trip was extremely dangerous. To travel to the West Coast by ship was not much better. The Panama Canal was opened in 1914, and before that, there were two really unpleasant options. The first option was to sail all the way around South America, through very hazardous waters. This option took a few weeks. The other option was to sail to a point in Central America, say Nicaragua, get off the ship and travel on land and on shallow rivers through insect infested jungles, where malaria was common, then get on another ship to complete the journey. The East Coast had been steadily growing in population since the 1600s. The population of the West Coast did not start to really grow until the Gold Rush of 1849, approximately 200 years later.

The statistics illustrate the large population gap between the East and West Coasts. In 1925, for example, the entire Pacific Coast had a population of 6.5 million, approximately the same population as New

York City during the same year. The population along the East Coast was approximately 47.5 million.[1] Although the population grew quickly on the West Coast during the 1920s, the population only reached 8 million by 1930, as compared to 50 million on the East Coast during the same year.[2]

In pure logistical and financial terms, it made more sense to risk running the blockade in the East than to sail all the way to California, Oregon, or Washington State. Delivering liquor from Europe or the Caribbean to the West Coast meant a loss of time and money for the shipping companies. To reach the Pacific from the Atlantic, a ship had to either sail all the way around South America or go through the Panama Canal, which was controlled by the United States. Both routes had great disadvantages. Sailing all the way around South America wasted a lot of time and money; however, if passing through the Panama Canal, a ship had to bear the scrutiny of the US Government, which is exactly what rum ships sought to avoid. The extra days or weeks it took for ships to reach California meant higher fuel and labor costs, in addition to the extra time it took to sell the product and return to port to restock. A combination of increased costs, slower returns on investments, and a smaller market kept most rum ships in the Atlantic and the Gulf of Mexico, despite the threats posed by the Coast Guard.

The tight blockade of the Atlantic Coast drove a portion of the rum fleet to the Pacific Coast. Federal officers admitted that smugglers were landing large quantities of liquor in California and that the price of Scotch whisky dropped from $9 a quart to $4.[3] Some estimates valued the whisky landed in and around San Diego at more than $200,000 over a two day period.

The Coast Guard Cutters *Tamaroa* and *Vaughn* were unable to deal with the five rum ships off Southern California, carrying approximately $3 million worth of liquor. The rum ships and smaller rum-runners were all faster than the Coast Guard cutters. The cutters could only manage a ridiculously slow speed of 13 knots, which frequently brought shouts and laughter from the rum-runners, and much embarrassment for the Coasties.[4]

On the night of May 4, the Cutter *Tamaroa* found the Pacific rum fleet off Santa Rosa Island, California. When daylight came, the officers aboard spotted five large freighters, their decks piled high with cases of whisky. Hovering around the ships was a score of fast motor launches, most likely from San Pedro. After spotting the Coast Guard, the speed boats immediately began racing toward San Pedro, while the rum ships began weighing anchor.[5]

The ships headed in different directions. The *Tamaroa* followed one of the ships for 106 miles when it gave up the chase. When the cutter returned to Santa Rosa Island, the crew saw that some of the liquor ships had returned. Again, the cutter gave chase, following another ship until it was in Mexican waters. When the *Tamaroa* returned from the second futile chase, it ran into another group of rum ships. Short on provisions and fuel, the cutter was forced to go back to its home port of San Diego, leaving the *Vaughn* to single-handedly fight California's Rum Row.[6]

Every day, smugglers were delivering whisky valued at $10,000-$20,000 to San Pedro. Law enforcement authorities in the area frankly admitted that the liquor would continue to pour in as long as there was a complete lack of speedboats for rum patrols. Rum smugglers were also landing liquor north and south of the harbor. Orange County authorities asked for federal aid to block liquor landings at Laguna, Newport, and other points on the Orange County coast.[7]

In San Diego, good quality Scotch whisky was available in unlimited quantities at $45 per case, delivered to any address within five miles of the local waterfront. Gin, champagne, brandy, and other alcoholic beverages were available at the lowest prices since the beginning of Prohibition. The five vessels off the coast managed to unload half a million dollars of cargo in less than two weeks.[8] This relative lack of enforcement was also present in the Gulf of Mexico and on the Florida Coast, mostly due to a lack of patrol boats. The tightened blockade off the northern Atlantic Coast was still relatively effective.[9]

For the Atlantic blockade, the Coast Guard pulled as many men and as much equipment as could possibly be spared from other sections of the country. This mobilization removed most of the cutters from the West Coast and all of the cutters from Hawaii. Since there was not a single boat available to patrol the waters of Hawaii, ships filled with liquor and narcotics easily unloaded their cargo into sampans (small, flat-bottomed boats) before they reached port.

In August 1925, Captain W.C.E. Jacobs, former commandant of the New York Coast Guard district, headed west to take up his new post in San Francisco. Jacobs, known as the man who "smashed" Rum Row in the east, would be given command of the territory stretching from the Oregon line to the Mexican border. Within his new area, he had full authority to use armed vessels to wage a merciless war on smuggling.

Bootleggers and rum-runners off the California coast were somewhat nervous when they heard the news of Captain Jacobs' transfer. Known as one of the "hardest hitting" officers in the Coast Guard, he supervised the crushing blockade of 1925, which resulted in the dispersion of Rum Row. Jacobs now planned to turn his guns, literally, on the Pacific rum fleet.[10]

1926

In 1926, *The New York Times* sent inquiries to its correspondents all up and down the West Coast regarding rum-running and bootlegging. According to the reports, the illicit liquor trade there was definitely flourishing. San Francisco had its own Rum Row off the Golden Gate, bearing some Canadian Scotch, though the supply had been reduced, and other high-grade liquor from Havana and Asia. In addition to that, gin was being freely manufactured in the city and delivered anywhere on telephone order. "Jackass" brandy was being made in former industrial plants, and there was a thriving trade in California grape wine. All of these drinks were available in unlimited quantities in open barrooms and cafés, especially in the lower-class sections of San Francisco.[11]

The Prohibition Enforcement Division of Northern California, which also had jurisdiction over Nevada, was the chief enforcer in that region. The Coast Guard there had a "mosquito fleet" of rum chasers, but confined its activities to seizing rum-runners and its fleet of "feeder" boats. City and county authorities helped by making frequent arrests under the state liquor law and providing squads of police for raids when federal authorities requested help. There were only forty federal agents in the Northern California district, and they confined their activities to fighting smugglers on land, leaving the fight against rum-running on the water completely to the tiny Coast Guard force.

Los Angeles enjoyed moonshine from the foothills and plenty of high-proof liquor imported from overseas for movie stars and other wealthy patrons who did not object to high prices, and, of course, the liquor smuggled in from Mexico. In both Los Angeles and San Francisco, federal and local Prohibition enforcement efforts were ineffective and there was a general sentiment that the Prohibition law should be modified.

In Washington State, the old ways of the Appalachian mountaineers were copied and moonshining in Washington's hills became a highly-perfected industry, producing whisky at $10 a quart for those who could not afford the Canadian brands. Canadian whisky came across the border by land, via the Puget Sound and by airplane. As in Los Angeles, federal authorities were hopeful for real Prohibition enforcement, given sufficient resources and manpower. However, Seattle's chief of police had his doubts and said that easing the law would improve the situation there. [12]

Bank-Financed Bootleggers

June 1926 was definitely a bad month for Prohibition forces on the West Coast. Exacerbating the bad publicity was a man named William D. Davidson, who described himself as ex-bootlegger William Caine. Davidson testified before the House Alcoholic Liquor Traffic Committee in Washington, DC, where he gave the inside story of how half a dozen banks financed bootleggers. He appeared at both day and night sessions at the invitation of Representative Fiorello LaGuardia of New York, the only "wet" member of the committee. Davidson told the committee that he lived in Los Angeles but refused to state where he was staying in Washington because he "didn't want to be bumped off."[13]

Davidson accused Assistant Treasury Secretary Andrews of failing to act on evidence of the dry law violations, including bank transactions which he had told Andrews about. Davidson also stated that Samuel McNab, federal district attorney at Los Angeles, and a Mr. Frith, Prohibition administrator of Southern California, failed to take action after he told them his story.

Asserting that he had worked for about five years in the wholesale end of the bootlegging business in various parts of the country, Davidson told of various transactions with the following banks: the United States National Bank branch in San Diego, California; the Northwestern Bank in Portland, Oregon; the Royal Bank of Canada; and a branch of the California Bank in Los Angeles.[14]

Davidson angered the wrong people. Within 24 hours of his testimony, the San Francisco police department sent a telegram to Washington asking for the arrest of Davidson, also known as Cain, for passing bad checks. The police said that in 1923, he passed a bad check for $4,600 on a San Francisco bank after endorsement by a restaurant owner, who had to stand the loss. Frank M. Buckley, the vice-president of a Vancouver bank, one of the accused banks, added that Davidson's stories about banks aiding rum-runners were "wholly imagination." Although Davidson's credibility may have been destroyed, the accusations against the banks were now in the open.[15]

The Pacific's Rum Fleet Grows Larger Than Ever

At the end of June 1926, sixteen British, Belgian, Panamanian, and Mexican rum ships sat off San Diego. This was a greater number of rum ships seen in one spot on the West Coast than ever before. The ships had a combined cargo of 95,000 cases of Scotch and gin, valued at $4,750,000, which they planned to land in time for the 4th of July.[16]

The entire Prohibition fleet of the Southern California Coast was concentrated in the area. To stem the flow of liquor into San Diego, the Coast Guard mobilized the cutter *Vaughan* and the fast patrol launches 253, 254, 256, 257, 258, and 261. Among the larger rum vessels were: the Nova Scotian fishing schooner *Marion Douglas*, reported to have brought a cargo of 25,000 cases of Scotch whisky; the *Stadacona*, with 10,000 cases, anchored near Bishop Rock; the *Chasiana*, with 8,000 cases; the *Malahat*, 9,000 cases; the Belgian steamship *Federalship*, formerly the *Gertrude*, loaded with 15,000 cases; *Prince Albert*, 10,000 cases; the Panamanian steamer *Packadada*, 3,000 cases; *Principio*, 11,000 cases; and a Mexican steamer with 4,000 cases.[17]

The rum fleet operating near San Diego was actually larger than the sixteen ships sitting off the coast at that time. The Coast Guard estimated that there were more than forty ships bringing liquor from British Columbia to that city. The fast launches that brought the liquor ashore from the larger vessels were making enormous profits. The men aboard these boats were buying the liquor for $10-$15 a case and making $3,000-$4,000 every trip.

Many of the rum-runners were very fast compared to the Coast Guard's patrol launches. The only way the Coast Guard could capture them was to corner them in the harbor or hope their engines would break down during the pursuit. The smugglers also perfected a communication system that impressed Coast Guardsmen. In several cases, fast launches loaded with liquor broke down near the shore. Almost immediately, rescue rum-runners came speeding out to meet the distressed vessel and saved the cargo from seizure.[18]

Prohibition Administrator Is Investigated

On July 22, 1926, a federal grand jury at San Francisco began investigating the activities of Ned M. Green, Federal Prohibition Administrator for Northern California and Nevada. The investigation was an outgrowth of an extensive inquiry carried out by the intelligence department of the Internal Revenue Division. The principal charges against Green included: criminal misconduct in office, protection of bootleggers, padding of government expense accounts, misappropriation of seized liquor, and being intoxicated in public. Acting Treasury Secretary Winston announced on July 24 that Green was suspended.[19]

When Assistant Treasury Secretary Andrews left for Europe on a diplomatic trip, difficulties had increased in the Prohibition Unit. Andrews had gone to London to negotiate a new liquor treaty with Great Britain. Since Andrews had no authority to appear in a diplomatic capacity abroad, he was seeking to reach a "gentleman's agreement" with the British. Andrews planned to use this agreement to cut off the flow of liquor from British territories.[20]

When told that he would be suspended, Green said, "I should have been suspended long ago." Federal agents visited him in his room at the Hotel Whitcomb after he was suspended and demanded the liquor in his possession. "You can take anything in the room you want," he said, smiling. He then handed over a variety of liquor, which almost filled a bureau drawer.[21]

"Some of that stuff may be pre-Volstead stuff and some of it may not," he said. "Don't tell anybody; but it isn't anybody's business. It isn't against the law to have liquor in your home or offer it to your guests." Ned Green was correct— it was perfectly legal to have liquor in your home and serve it to guests, as long as you did not transport, manufacture, or sell it without a permit. Green said he welcomed the indictment and trial because, he declared, it would show that he had not been in possession of governmentally-controlled liquor and had not been guilty of misconduct.[22] He elaborated by telling reporters:

> "I have had liquor in my hotel room, but it has been sent to me by persons unknown to me. I frequently find liquor which has been left in my room and in my offices. Friends who have called on me in my room at the hotel have accepted my invitation to drink. My friends know that I drink very seldom and that I won't drink alone. If visitors call on me, I

offer them a drink; I won't be a 'dead head' and I join them in the drink even if it gags me. I have nothing to fear or to be ashamed of in this tempest.

"I have had under my control liquor valued at more than $2,000,000. If I was crooked I could order a barrel or two sent around to the homes of friends. But no one can accuse me of having broken that trust. I am doing what I came out here to do, stopping liquor at the source. Why don't they investigate that angle of it?"[23]

Green showed reporters two dresser drawers in his room filled with bottles of assorted liquors.

"There's my answer to the Government charges. There's the liquor they say I keep in my room. I drink it. I've served it at parties here, parties that men and women attend. Those charges are true, and any time the investigators or the members of the United States Grand Jury want to come here and see it they're welcome, and they can taste it, too, if they want to."[24]

After being in session only three and a half hours, the federal grand jury returned an indictment against Ned Green. The charges against him were that he had misappropriated governmentally controlled liquor and had been guilty of misconduct in office. US District Judge Frank H. Kerrigan fixed the bail at $5,000, which a bonding company immediately posted.

The indictment contained ten counts. Several of the counts involved only one or two bottles! The most serious count involved ten bottles. In total, Green was being investigated by a federal grand jury over one case of liquor. For this, the jury was considering charging Green with a felony. Prior to this investigation, Green was considered the leading choice to succeed Andrews as Assistant Treasury Secretary.[25]

In late December 1926, Green was acquitted and reinstated as Prohibition Administrator for Northern California and Nevada.[26] He had completely forgotten his previous admissions of guilt and said the following in a signed statement:

"The prompt verdict of the jury after a trial of nearly three weeks has demonstrated the utter falsity of the charges brought against me…

"While it is not my personal desire to continue to act as Prohibition Administrator, my future plans are indefinite until I have had the opportunity of either conferring or communicating with my chief.

"For the present it is sufficient to say that I am happy beyond words that my chief now knows his confidence in me has neither been misplaced nor betrayed."[27]

Pushing The Limits

In early March 1927, the steamer *Federalship*, suspected of being a rum-runner, was "loafing" along the coast near San Francisco. The ship operated out of British Columbia and cleared from that port for Tahiti with a liquor cargo. The ship was obviously not bound for Tahiti. The Coast Guard cutters kept a watchful eye on the ship and sent messages back to the San Francisco base.[28]

The *Federalship* was an old boat by 1927. The ship, originally a Belgian ship named the *Gertrude*, was sold in Vancouver in 1926 by a very disgruntled crew to compensate for their lack of pay. The Federal Shipping Company, a private company of Vancouver, purchased the vessel. The company registered the ship as a Panamanian vessel and chartered it to the Canadian-Mexican Shipping Company.[29]

In 1926, the *Federalship* had a very busy year. A Treasury Department report showed that during the early part of the year, the ship delivered liquor off the California coast to several boats from shore. On June 4, the vessel cleared from Vancouver, British Columbia, with another liquor cargo. The master declared the cargo was destined for John Douglas & Co. in La Libertad, Salvador. An investigation disclosed that there was no such firm at that location. On September 3, the vessel returned to Vancouver empty and the Canadian customs authorities imposed fines for making a false declaration. On October 10, the vessel cleared with a liquor cargo consigned to John Douglas & Co. at La Libertad, and thirty barrels of beer, consigned to the Rainier Brewery, address not given. It made no sense whatsoever to deliver barrels of beer to a brewery. An investigation showed that the Rainier Brewery was located at San Francisco. The secretary at the brewery, of course, said that they did not order beer. The only other company that went by the same name was located at Kamloops, British Columbia, 250 miles inland from Vancouver.[30]

The *Federalship* proceeded down the coast, anchored first near San Francisco and then off Los Angeles. On October 21, a Coast Guard cutter spotted the ship near Point Arena, and on the following day it was found 120 miles west of the Farallon Islands, which are off the coast near San Francisco. On January 4th, the ship was seen about 180 miles from San Pedro. The American Consul in charge at San Salvador reported on December 4 that the ship had not entered the Salvadorean port during October or November.

In 1927, the *Federalship* continued the same scheme. The ship returned to Vancouver and departed on February 23 with a liquor cargo supposedly bound for Buenaventura. Captain S.S. Stone, skipper of the *Federalship*, noticed that an American Coast Guard boat was following him as soon as his ship entered neutral waters. Stone took his ship 70 miles west and then south, way out of American jurisdiction. Off the Columbia River bar, the Coast Guard Cutter *Algonquin* began trailing the rum ship, relieving the other patrol vessel. Many times during the trip south to a point 270 miles off the Farallone Islands, the *Algonquin* darted in front of the *Federalship*, repeating this maneuver in spite of Stone's protests.[31]

Soon, the Coast Guard Cutter *Cahokia* joined the *Algonquin* in the pursuit and signaled for the *Federalship* to stop. When the ship did not stop, the *Cahokia* fired two blank shots. The cutters ordered the rum ship to heave-to, and when the *Federalship* refused to obey, the *Algonquin* fired a blank warning shot and then a six-pound solid shot between its masts. The *Algonquin* followed with another solid shot, which struck a hatch. Realizing that the Coast Guard meant business, Captain Stone immediately surrendered.[32]

The Coast Guard Cutter *Cahokia* towed the *Federalship* into San Francisco Bay. The cutters *Algonquin* and *Smith* were at each side, while several other government boats trailed along to make sure that no one touched the rich prize. Members of the *Federalship*'s crew, young, well-dressed men, leaned against the rails nonchalantly and ate oranges.[33]

Stone later claimed that he was 325 miles off the Farallones when the Coast Guard seized his ship and took him into custody. The officers of the *Cahokia* took command of the vessel and brought it into San Francisco Harbor under convoy with its million dollar liquor cargo. When he arrived at the city, Captain Stone and his nineteen crewmembers were held incommunicado for two days and then indicted by a federal grand jury on charges of conspiracy to prevent enforcement of laws of the United States. Even with all of the evidence stacked against him, Stone maintained that he was destined for Buenaventura, Columbia, and insisted his ship never went within the twelve-mile limit of the American coast. He also boldly claimed that his ship never had communication with the American coast. He insisted that there was no evidence that his cargo was meant to reach the United States, nor did the federal indictment make that specific charge.[34]

One of the men aboard the *Federalship* was William Bowen, who was from a wealthy bay district family and a fugitive from justice facing murder and conspiracy charges. He had been a fugitive for almost two years, under indictments which followed the famous "Battle of Moss Landing," in July 1925 in which Deputy Sheriff Rader was killed and Sheriff Oyer was wounded by machine gun fire. Bowen faced a murder charge in Monterey County and charges of conspiracy to violate the Volstead Act in San Francisco. He was taken from the *Federalship* and held on the *Cahokia* to be turned over to the authorities.[35]

The seizure of the ship raised legal questions about jurisdiction on the high seas. The *Federalship* was approximately 300 miles out to sea, far beyond the limits of any international treaty. The ship flew the Panamanian flag. Many in the legal profession raised the question of whether the Coast Guard would have taken such an action against a British or Japanese ship on the high seas. For example, would Great Britain, the world's most powerful empire in the 1920s, tolerate American ships going into neutral waters and seizing any vessel upon suspicion of illegal trading or conspiracy to violate an American law? No. History has shown repeatedly that Britain would not stand for it, especially in the case of Prohibition.[36]

As W.H. Metson, a prominent attorney of the time, stated so eloquently:

> "We are a powerful nation, and in this seizure we first enquire whether a ship far out on the high seas floats the flag of a strong warlike nation. Finding it flies the flag of a friendly but humble State, we send out our dog of war and loose with thunderous roar its round shot on the weak. This is as oppressors have always done."[37]

No one really questioned the charge that the *Federalship* was a rum vessel or that its mission was to violate American laws. However, many questioned the right of the American government to seize the ship of another nation on the high seas without making specific charges.[38]

Ernestino de LaGuardia, Consul General of Panama at San Francisco made the following statement to the press about the seizure:

> "I should not doubt that my Government will make protest and that it may even demand damages. My country has shown its entire willingness to cooperate with the United States Government in making liquor treaties. We have provided that a vessel known to be an habitual rum-runner shall lose her Panamanian registry. We have also agreed to let the United States seize and search vessels within an hour's cruising distance of the coast, generally accepted as twelve miles out.
>
> "We believe, however, that the Federalship has not violated any of this agreement in any manner. She has a legitimate crew, a legitimate destination, and she kept away from the mainland of the United States. The Government of Panama is not interested in the crew or the cargo; its sole interest is in the ship, which appears to have been going peaceably along its way, legally entitled to protection at the hands of the Republic of Panama. It was hailed and fired upon by American vessels, and brought into San Francisco. I believe this procedure was illegal..."[39]

After sitting in jail for a month and a half, the captain and crew finally heard Judge George M. Bourquin's decision:

> "This seizure was sheer aggression and trespass, like that which contributed to the War of 1812, is contrary to treaty and not to be sanctioned by any court and cannot be the basis of any proceedings adverse to the defendants..."[40]

After the judge declared the defendants not guilty, they were released from the county jail. The defense attorneys told the press that they would demand that the Coast Guard tow the ship back to where they had seized it. On April 30, 1927, the Department of Justice ordered the release of the vessel. Assistant Treasury Secretary Andrews was very upset by the decision, but did not criticize the Justice Department. Instead, he made a public statement condemning Panama's intervention in the case. He also argued that the only thing Panamanian about the ship was its flag. A Canadian corporation owned the vessel and its cargo. In addition, the officers and crew were all Canadian.[41]

Lincoln C. Andrews was not about to let a decision by the Justice Department or a federal court decision stand in his way. On May 2, he ordered Acting Collector of Customs Henry E. Farmer to detain the *Federalship*. The telegram from Washington stated that the ship must be detained "until such time as the present negotiations with Panama have reached fruition." The telegram did not give any direction on what to do with Captain Stone and his nineteen crewmembers, who were preparing to steam out of port.[42]

On the following day, Judge Kerrigan, of the Federal District Court, ordered Customs and Coast Guard officials to release the ship and its $1 million cargo. The court order forbade officials to interfere with the ship's departure.[43] And so the ship steamed out through the Golden Gate with its 12,500 cases of liquor. The Coast Guard Cutter *Shawnee* followed closely in the ship's wake with orders to see that not a single bottle was dropped overboard. The *Federalship*'s attorneys received a government check for $413.50 to cover perishable food stores, which the government removed after the seizure.[44] A year later, in the spring of 1928, the *Federalship* was off the California coast again. The ship, renamed *La Aguila*, was now carrying $2 million worth of liquor.[45]

28
The Dwyer Conspiracy

In mid-January 1926, an informant called the office of US Attorney Emory R. Buckner and left a message about an ocean-going tug named the *Rescue*. The informant said that the tug had been transporting liquor from the rum ship *Tilley*. The *Rescue* was one of many boats owned by the largest rum-running syndicate in existence, controlled by William V. Dwyer. Soon, a federal grand jury subpoenaed a bondsman of four men arrested during the previous month. Since the men were connected with Dwyer, the grand jury used them to find more information on the boat. In addition, a guard was posted day and night at the pier off Jefferson Street, along the East River, where the tug frequently unloaded its cargo.[1]

Following the tip to Mr. Buckner, Coast Guardsmen were on the lookout for the tug. One night, Cutter 2326 spotted the *Rescue* as it was steaming through the Narrows. The cutter ordered the tug to stop, but received no answer. The Coasties then fired their one-pounder across the *Rescue*'s bow. The smugglers ignored the warning shots and raced at top speed toward Manhattan. The Coast Guardsmen then opened fire with their machine gun. At that moment, the engine died on the Coast Guard boat and the tug sped away into the darkness.

The police marine patrol heard the shots and spotted the tug. The *Rescue* continued to steam up the East River and rammed head-on into the pier at Jefferson Street. Twenty men leapt ashore and escaped. The police managed to catch four who lagged behind. When the police boarded the tug, it was sinking; the crew had thrown the seacocks open in an effort to destroy the evidence. Patrolmen dove into the icy water to close the valves and keep the tug afloat. Later, the tug was taken to the Brooklyn Army Base under its own power and unloaded. Captain Wunsche of the NYPD Marine Division told the press that the boat plus cargo were worth $1 million, qualifying it as the biggest seizure his department had yet made.[2] A few months later, a federal judge decreed that the *Rescue* would be turned over to the Treasury Department to be used for Prohibition enforcement.[3]

Charles A. Smith was a mariner formerly employed by William V. Dwyer, who was charged with operating a $40 million rum ring. On July 13, 1926, he testified against his former boss before Federal Judge Julian W. Mack and a jury. On the witness stand, he told the court that uniformed New York City police officers were present at the unloading of about two hundred loads of liquor cargo, which had been brought in from Rum Row for Dwyer and landed at North and East River piers from February 1923 to March 1925. Uniformed police, Smith added, were regular visitors to Dwyer's offices at 395 Broadway.[4]

Twice, according to Smith, cargoes were unloaded at the Bellevue Hospital pier in the presence of several patrolmen, whom he had seen talking with William Gallagher, one of Dwyer's co-defendants. On one or two occasions, Smith said, the Weehawken and Hudson County (New Jersey) police, plus the railroad police helped unload liquor from speedboats at the fire-damaged Erie Railroad pier in Weehawken. Smith testified that Dwyer had paid him $200 for each of his trips, totaling about $40,000. Only five cargoes out of 200 were seized.[5]

Amazingly, Charles Smith landed a job working for the Treasury Department and still held his job while he was on the witness stand. Smith was tasked with painting and repairing a Treasury boat which he had recently brought to New London, Connecticut, to put in dry dock. While he testified, the Treasury Department paid Smith $50 per week to compensate him for his lost time.[6]

On the stand, Smith described many trips. He described how he brought four boats in to Weehawken in broad daylight. He telephoned Dwyer, who told him to take the boats up the Hudson River and return to Weehawken at 9 PM for unloading. He told stories of several chases, captures, and escapes, and of how Dwyer always told him which route to follow. On one occasion, Smith asked Dwyer about the police boat *Gypsy* and another rum-chaser. He quoted Dwyer as saying, "They will not be anywhere near you tonight."[7]

From time to time he mentioned the names of each of the ten defendants in the case as having been connected with some rum-running venture. Other piers Smith mentioned were: Pier 32 on the North River; Pier 33 on the East River; under the Manhattan Bridge; a North River pier which he could not identify; and a pier at Edgewater, NJ.[8]

Smith said that he got most of his liquor from the *Ellias B.*, the *Catherine Moulton*, and the *Strudholm*. He had used many rum runners for his trips, including: the *Dorothy*, the *Dick*, the *Mary*, the *Rosemary*, the *Toxaway*, the *Vee*, the *Helen*, the *Tina*, the *War Bug*, the *Robert C. Clowry*, the *Andora* and others. His cargo ranged from 300 to 750 cases. Smith never had a permit to transport liquor and never paid any Customs duties. In addition to William Gallagher, Smith said he frequently met with two men named Joe Cody and Walter Wieder on the various docks. He identified "Red" Rairden, another defendant, as supercargo on the *Ellie B*.[9]

Coast Guardsmen Take the Stand

A few minutes after Charles Smith got off the witness stand, two Coast Guardsmen, named John Hubbard Reeder and Robert Sanderson, took the stand. They identified Smith as the man on the *Robert C. Clowry* who offered bribes. In telling of the rum ship's seizure in March 1925, Warrant Officer Reeder said he smelled liquor when passing windward of the vessel early in the evening and boarded to investigate. He found 5,000 cases of champagne in the hold. Then, accompanied by Chief Sanderson, he went into the cabin with Smith and two other men.[10]

There was a stack of money four inches thick on the table. The first bribe the smugglers offered the Coast Guardsmen was $10,000. After they refused that offer, the bribe went up to $25,000, plus a house, a job paying $150 a week, a car, and a ring. Sanderson's testimony matched Reeder's. Under cross-examination, Chief Sanderson, who spoke with a strong Scottish accent, kept the courtroom smiling with his good natured retorts. He explained that when they first boarded the vessel they were far out to sea. Had it come to an open fight, he and Reeder would have stood no chance against the *Clowry* crew. They discussed the bribe for five hours with Smith, pretending they were interested, and all the while the ship was getting closer to port. Finally, at 2 AM they came near Quarantine, where they signaled for help. Reinforcements from shore completed the seizure.[11]

Customs Inspector Michael F. Sweeny and Customs Guard Arthur J. Kenney also took the stand and told of the pursuit and capture of the *Rosemary* and the *Man of War*. Sweeny testified that Smith offered him a $10,000 bribe. Kenney identified Smith as having been on the *Rosemary* at the time of the seizure.[12]

Following the testimonies of the Customs men, a former Coast Guardsman named Paul Lewis Crim took the stand. Crim served only a few months in the Coast Guard, from September 1924 until January 1925. He said he first met Dwyer one month after entering the service and spoke with him on Broadway, across the street from Dwyer's office in the Loew's State Building. Dwyer ensured that Crim served on the CG 203, whose commander was Edward Gallagher, another defendant in the trial. Dwyer always directed that the CG 203 continue to patrol Rum Row and protect the rum runners out there.[13]

When the two men met the second time, Dwyer gave Crim $100 to buy clothing. If he wanted more money, Dwyer told him, he would have to smuggle some rum himself. Crim asserted that Dwyer told him to talk with Gallagher about using the Coast Guard boat as a rum-runner. After agreeing on the plan, Crim and Gallagher let four other crewmembers in on the plot, leaving only a machinist mate and the cook out of the loop.

The men completed their planning with Dwyer on December 27, 1924 and the patrol boat took on a supercargo at Sheepshead Bay, where it docked for fuel. They headed for the schooner *Elias B.*, anchored thirty-five miles southeast of Ambrose Light. Vessels they hailed en-route were afraid to tell the Coast Guardsmen where the rum ship was. When they finally reached the schooner, Crim testified, the supercargo went aboard to make arrangements. The CG 203 then cast off and circled the schooner to throw a nearby Coast Guard destroyer off the trail. The men took 700 cases of Perfection Scotch aboard the patrol boat and landed it at the Christopher Street pier in Manhattan. The crew also received two cases of champagne for their own use. Two days after the delivery, Dwyer gave Crim $700 for his services. The CG 203 made another run on New Year's Eve.[14]

After Crim was discharged from the Coast Guard, he became Dwyer's personal chauffeur until he got into an accident that almost killed his boss. During that period, he frequently helped unload rum boats. On one occasion, a man named Tony Cassino, another defendant in the trial, paid him $45 for such services. Crim also told the court about his trips to a cutting plant. "What is that?" the prosecutor asked. "That is a place where they make three cases out of one case," Crim replied.[15]

Crim said that after he stopped working for Dwyer, he did not see him again until January 1926, when Dwyer visited his home and told him that the rum ring was about to be indicted. He advised Crim to hide because the authorities had his address. This occurred three weeks before the sealed indictments were opened. Dwyer received his advance information from someone who worked at the office of US Attorney Emory R. Buckner. Crim took his advice and moved with his wife to an apartment in Harlem and then to the Bronx, where he worked as a superintendent.

The day before the trial began, two city detectives and a government agent walked into his office. He recognized one of the detectives and gave no resistance when they told him he was wanted downtown. The police took him to the station and booked him as a fugitive. From there he went to the office of Attorney A. Bruce Bielaski, who worked for the government's Prohibition forces. Crim remained there for five hours and signed a prepared statement. Finally, he was allowed to leave and told to return in the morning.[16]

Crim hurried to the Fifty-fourth Street Club to find Dwyer, but could not find him. He returned later in the evening with his wife and met with Dwyer. When he asked what happened, Crim told him that he had been arrested and would have to testify before a grand jury in the morning. He also told him about the statement he had made, which Dwyer did not seem too worried about. When Dwyer learned that Crim did not know what his legal rights would be before the grand jury, he immediately sent for Louis Halle, one of the defense attorneys involved in the trial. According to Crim's story, Dwyer, Halle, he, and his wife all met in a car. Halle advised Crim that his best move would be to flee to Canada because he could not be extradited in a liquor case. Halle added that they would beat the case and that everything would "blow over" in a year or two.[17]

According to the plan, Mrs. Crim would stay in New York and join him later on. In the meantime, they could correspond through the Hockey Club in New York and the Back River Jockey Club in Montreal. Finally, Crim agreed to go. After a long trip by car and train, Crim arrived at the Mount Royal race track in Montreal, which Dwyer was a part owner of. He had two days of peace in Montreal, but then the same government agent who had visited his office a few days earlier appeared at the track. He showed him a letter from Crim's wife and he agreed to return voluntarily.

Strangely, when Mrs. Crim took the witness stand a week after her husband, it took her four attempts to identify Louis Halle. The first three men she pointed to in the courtroom were bald, while Halle had a full head of black hair.[18]

Another Coast Guardsman, Chief Boatswain's Mate Joseph Tilton, testified on the same day as Crim. He commanded the CG 2210 in March 1925, when it captured the SC 217, one of the alleged Dwyer boats. He described the crew's attempt to burn the boat and sink it while it was being towed to port.[19]

Tilton's story matched that of Reginald Rigg, who was crewmember of the SC-217 and was arrested at the time. Rigg spend an entire morning facing a barrage of questions from five defense attorneys. The defense attorney brought up the fact that for two months Rigg had been receiving $150 a month through Bielaski. Rigg stated that the government paid him for serving as an engineer on the 996, but later admitted that the 996 was not owned by the government during the first month he was paid and that he received his money for "standing by."[20]

Rigg refused to admit that his employment depended on his testifying for the government, but admitted signing a statement for one of Bielaski's men. Finally, when he was asked if he did not know that his employment as an engineer was because of his usefulness as a witness in the case, he replied "maybe."[21]

Rum Smuggler Joins the Coast Guard

On July 17, 1926, Judge Julian W. Mack and the jury listened to yet more damning testimony, this time from former Warrant Officer John D. Weishaar, Petty Officer Bendt Bendtsan, and several other Coast Guardsmen. After Paul Crim finished his testimony, Weishaar took the witness stand and testified that he went to see Mr. Gallagher in the Loew's State Building in January 1925. William Gallagher was named in the indictment against Dwyer, but was never arrested and was a fugitive at the time of the hearing. Weishaar said that Gallagher sent him to the Marine Garage, headquarters for the liquor boats, where he met E.C. Cohron, another defendant. He told Cohron that he was looking for a job as a rum-runner, but had no experience in that area. Weishaar quoted Cohron as saying, "You need not be afraid of the Coast Guard in the harbor. If they shoot at you they will only shoot in the air. But outside it is survival of the fittest."[22]

Scotty Clyde, another defendant, told Weishaar that he would receive $100 for each successful trip and sent him out to Rum Row in command of the SC 217. Weishaar made two unsuccessful trips in search of the schooner *Elias B*. The Coast Guard then seized his vessel when he made contact with the French schooner *Laurel*. Wieshaar was taken to the Custom House. After he was released, Weishaar immediately reported to Dwyer, who told him that things would be fixed up and sent him to see an attorney, who told him that it would not be necessary to report back to the Custom House. A few days later, the SC 217 was back at the Marine Garage.[23]

The third trip, which Dwyer gave Weishaar instructions for in person, resulted in the landing of 1,200 cases of whisky from the German steamer *Falkenhurst*. As the smugglers landed at a pier near the foot of Canal Street, Weishaar saw a Coast Guard boat and a speed boat named the *War Bug* unloading at the same time.

Weishaar also gave an account of his last trip on the SC 217, during which he went to the schooner *Haverstrudle* off Martha's Vineyard. His story matched the one Reginald Rigg told on the stand earlier in the trial. Like Rigg, he also identified William J. Maloney, a defendant, as the supercargo on the *Haverstrudle*. Weishaar informed Dwyer that he wanted to leave the boat because it was leaking, luck aboard was bad, morale was low, and they were not making any money. Dwyer sent him money and urged him to finish the trip. On the return trip, the SC 217's supercargo told Weishaaar to avoid the Long Island Sound because the wrong Coast Guard boat was on patrol. Cohron paid Weishaar $300 after he returned with 1,800 cases of whisky.[24]

Weishaar made another trip for Dwyer on another boat named the *Gold Star*, but the Coast Guard foiled his plans. When he returned, he told Dwyer that he was not making enough money and thought he would like to join the Coast Guard. Dwyer told Weishaar that he would be able to help him. In May 1925, Weishaar was appointed as a Warrant Officer and stationed at Cape May. Weishaar once again visited Dwyer's New York office, where he told him that he could have him transferred to New York. He told the court about this discussion:

> "I said to him, 'You must have a lot of pull to be able to do that.' And he said he was having lunch with the boss tomorrow. I asked who the boss was, but he didn't tell me. He just said it was 'the big boss from Washington.' Then I asked him if he was paying all the high commissioned officers in the Coast Guard, and he said 'not all, only some,' and that some

took presents for their wives and some were just good sports."[25]

Weishaar was convicted in a general court-martial during the previous April for accepting bribes from rum-runners. When Assistant US Attorney William E. Stevenson attempted to bring out the details of the conviction, defense attorney Benjamin Spellman objected on the grounds that the government was stealing his thunder and assured the court that he would do everything he could to discredit Weishaar in his cross-examination.

Spellman brought out the fact that Weishaar had been sent to the Navy brig at Portsmouth, New Hampshire to serve a three-month sentence. However, after three weeks, he was released, his sentence remitted. He then visited the office of A. Bruce Bielaski. Weishaar told the court that he had been receiving expense money from Bielaski for two months, including $250 to visit his sick wife in Phoenix, Arizona. Weishaar denied that Bielaski obtained the remission of his sentence and claimed it had been done by his Coast Guard base commander, E.S. Edison, and Commander Weaver, Inspector General of the Coast Guard. He insisted that his conscience alone moved him to testify against Dwyer.[26]

The last witness of the day was Petty Officer Bendt Bendtsan, who was difficult to understand because of his foreign accent. Bendtsan had been in the Coast Guard for two and a half years and testified that he met Dwyer through a shipmate named Olsen. Dwyer told Bendtsan that he would be able to recognize his boats because all of them carried dories on their sterns. Dwyer then gave him $200. He continued to meet Dwyer every week, receiving $50 per visit, until November 1925, when he received more than $2,000. Bendstan did not tell the court what he did in return for the weekly payments.[27]

Mr. Bielaski Takes The Stand

A. Bruce Bielaski was a Special Assistant US Attorney General. Assistant Treasury Secretary Andrews assigned him the task of overseeing Prohibition enforcement. When Benjamin Spellman asked for Mr. Bielaski, he wanted him to bring all his records, memoranda, and accounts showing the government's financial transactions with private sources. Judge Mack told Spellman that he could only question Bielaski about money he, or the government, paid to witnesses in this case.

Bielaski said that he did not bring his records on the Dwyer case because they were so intermingled with other records and were in both New York and Washington. His frequently gave one word answers on the stand and showed no willingness to volunteer information.[28]

Bielaski testified that the Treasury Department paid him $1,100 a month, which for most Americans in 1926 was half a year's salary. He also had the privilege of drawing additional funds to pay witnesses in Prohibition cases. The government money, he said, was most often paid in checks, but occasionally paid in cash.

"How much money have you paid Charles Augustus Smith?" asked Spellman.

"Smith has received $550 since May 26, 1926," replied Bielaski.

"And is he still on your payroll?"

"No, on the Government's payroll."[29]

Bielaski added that Weishaar was a paid government witness and had received $250 for traveling expenses. He also recommended Weishaar for reappointment in the Coast Guard, although he knew he had been discharged for accepting bribes. Reginald Rigg, he added, was also a paid government witness.[30]

Drama In The Courtroom

On the morning of July 22, Smith appeared more nervous than during his earlier testimony, especially as Judge Mack and Mr. Buckner examined his military service record. On the witness stand, Smith stuck to his original story and denied that he had enlisted in the Navy more than once. He also denied that he had ever been convicted of a crime and received a dishonorable discharge, as his service record showed.

Then, to Smith's complete surprise, a woman who claimed to have once been married to Smith appeared in the courtroom. She entered the room on the arm of Jack Wolff, counsel for the defense, and sank into a chair at the side of the counsel table. With trembling hands, she toyed with her handkerchief. Spellman pointed at the woman and shouted at Smith:

"Were you married to this woman in 1914?"

Smith quickly glanced at the woman, who stared back at him. Then, looking at Spellman, he replied, "No."

"Weren't you married by John G. Toby, a Justice of the Peace, to this lady at Portsmouth, New Hampshire?"

"No, sir, I wasn't," Smith answered.

"Weren't you married to this lady on December 22, 1914?" Spellman asked again.

"No, sir, I was in Liverpool, England, at that time."[31]

Spellman then read from the marriage record, which identified the woman as Mary Agnes Carroll of Portsmouth, N.H., who had, at the time of her alleged marriage to Smith, worked as a waitress at the Portsmouth Navy Yard. Smith previously had testified that he had only been married once, to another woman, who obtained an annulment on the ground that Smith had gotten her so drunk that she was unaware that she was marrying him.

Miss Carroll, who divorced Smith for desertion, was too weak to walk to the witness chair. She took the oath where she sat and gave her testimony from her seat near the counsel table. She said that she knew him as "Harry," one of his known aliases, and that she had not seen him since he left her a decade earlier.

During the cross-examination of Smith, he denied that he had signed the records brought from the Navy Department at Washington. Buckner asked Smith if he would be willing to be fingerprinted. Smith replied that he did not think that it was necessary.

"That is a fine idea!" shouted Spellman. "We have the fingerprints of the man who signed these enlistment papers, and you say you did not sign them. Will you be fingerprinted?"

"No," said Smith.

"Do you refuse because to do so might incriminate you?"

"I don't know what you mean."

"I mean, do you fear it might convict you of perjury?"

"No, I have no reason. I don't care to be fingerprinted now."[32]

Judge Mack directed that Smith be fingerprinted. At Buckner's suggestion, a fingerprint expert from the police department was sent for.

Navy Lieutenant Paul Dingwell personally carried Smith's service record from Washington, DC. He read the record aloud in court, which stated that Smith had enlisted in 1912 and again in 1917. Smith was court-martialed in 1913 for bad conduct. In 1918, Smith had three general courts-martial and was sentenced to five years in the brig. The sentence was then reduced to a three-year and two-year sentence, to be served concurrently. He only served ten months of his sentence at Portsmouth Prison. In 1919, he was again dishonorably discharged.

When Buckner showed Smith the signature to his 1912 enlistment, he said he had not written it. When Buckner asked him to write his signature several times on a piece of paper, the signature seemed very similar to the one on the enlistment paper. The enlistment paper also gave an exact description of Smith, including scars and tattoos.

After lunch recess, Mr. Buckner announced that the chief witness had vanished. The judge summoned Bielaski to court and he took the stand only long enough to say that he had seen Smith at his office shortly before 1:30 PM. He told Buckner that Agent William J. Kelly accompanied Smith as he visited the Bielaski office. As Smith and Kelly were leaving, Bielaski called Agent Kelly back into his office, leaving Smith outside. He walked off and did not appear in court. Bielaski's agents and a US Marshal soon found Smith and brought him to the Ludlow Street Jail.[33]

The Closing Arguments

On July 23, 1926, Herbert C. Smyth, attorney for the defense, summed up his argument. He stressed that Dwyer and his co-defendants were charged with conspiracy, but, he argued, bringing in a single cargo of liquor by one, or even all of the defendants, did not constitute conspiracy. Judge Mack interrupted to say that if any two defendants agreed to break the law, he would consider it a conspiracy. Smyth argued that if the jury disregarded Smith's testimony there would be no credible evidence of conspiracy. He added:

> "When Bielaski gets his contract with prohibition enforcement and gets a bigger salary than that of his chief, bigger than Mr. Bruckner's salary, he, a lawyer, seems to forget what is due in performing his duty. If any attorney in private practice should do as Bielaski has done he would be hauled before the Grievance Committee of the Bar Association, for it amounts to nothing less than bribery. Yet the Volstead act fanaticism has so seized upon him that he is oblivious to all else.
>
> "Bielaski is an attorney, yet he offered a witness in this case bigger pay than the man had been getting, and this was done under the guise of giving the witness employment. Take the case of Smith—the Government , through Bielaski, paid him $500 a week. For what? He was supposed to do some

work on a Government boat. But what does an attorney have to do with ships? That pay to Smith was merely a bribe in order to make out a story that would spell conspiracy. In the same way Rigg was paid for doing practically nothing and Weishaar was taken to a quiet hotel in Brooklyn and kept there all day to tell his story."[34]

In defense of Smith, Spellman made this closing argument:

"Smith is the Government's prize package in this case. He is the one who sold the gold brick to Bielaski. His testimony is an index to that of the other scoundrels who took the stand for the Government. The invisible government of Bielaski meanwhile has been paying them under the guise of remunerating them for real work, and your money and the people's money was being used for that purpose.

"It seems that the United States is willing to buy testimony and bribe witnesses. But there is something in this case that nobody but Bielaski knows. Either Smith has sold the Government a gold brick, or he was covering up someone else."[35]

Referring to Smith's disappearance from Bielaski's office, Spellman added:

"But the cloak of charity has been thrown around this man Bielaski, who conducts the invisible government from his law office at 120 Broadway. Does anyone believe that Bielaski told Smith to 'beat it'? Oh, no! Because Bielaski is a mighty man. No one must speak ill of Brutus."[36]

The Verdict

The jury began deliberating at 11:45 AM and delivered its verdict twelve hours later. The jury only spent six of those hours actually deliberating; the jurors spent the rest of the time on meal breaks and reading testimony. The courtroom was filled with people as the jury came in at 11:00 PM. Dwyer and Cohron were guilty; their six co-defendants were acquitted. Judge Julian W. Mack sentenced the two men to two years in prison, the maximum under the law. He fined Dwyer $10,000 and Cohron $5,000, both laughable amounts considering how much money they made. The judge said that throughout his twenty-four years on the bench he had never presided over a case in which the evidence of guilt was clearer. He added, "The facts cry out to heaven of wholesale violation of the law in every way. There is no shadow of doubt of the existence of the conspiracy alleged."[37]

The acquitted men shook hands with Dwyer and Cohron and gave their condolences, while the two convicted men smiled and congratulated those who had been found not guilty. The acquitted men were:

- Edward Gallagher: former Coast Guard officer, alleged to have protected rum boats and to have used a Coast Guard cutter for landing 1,400 cases of liquor.
- George Clyde: said to be Cohron's partner in the Marine Garage, where much liquor was allegedly landed.
- Arch M. Eversole: owner of the rum-runner *Augusta* before it was seized with liquor aboard.
- Walter Wieder: said to have been on various docks at four liquor unloadings.
- John J. McCambridge: said to have been seen seventy-five times in Dwyer's offices.
- William J. Maloney: said to have been a supercargo on one of Dwyer's rum boats.

After Dwyer's trial, Charles Smith was indicted by the federal grand jury for perjury. With all of his earlier bravado and confidence gone, Smith pled guilty and asked for leniency. Judge Julian Mack, completely out of patience with Smith, sentenced him to sixty days in Westchester County Penitentiary.[38]

More Lies Exposed

During the trial, Bielaski testified that he was the "personal representative" of Lincoln C. Andrews in his official capacity as Secretary of the Treasury in charge of Prohibition enforcement and that he had been appointed a Special Assistant US Attorney General. Representative Fiorello H. LaGuardia of New York told the press that Bielaski was lying:

"I have had so many inquiries and such a flood of protests as to the status of A. Bruce Bielaski since he testified in a recent trial that I have looked into the matter and can find no record of any payments to him during the past fiscal year as for salary as an officer or employee of the Department of Justice or the Treasury Department.

"I believe it will be a source of gratification to a great many taxpayers to know that this man is neither an official nor an employee of the United States Government. I know, of course, that there is no position authorized by Congress to pay $1,000 a month for the work Mr. Bielaski testified he was doing.

"It does appear, however, from vouchers in the accounts of the Disbursing Clerk of the Treasury Department that Walton A. Green, chief prohibition investigator, has, during the past fiscal year, made numerous payments to Mr. Bielaski aggregating $15,000, as for confidential information and assistance, such payments evidently having been made from funds advanced to Mr. Green under the appropriation for securing evidence of violations of the Narcotic and Prohibition acts, pursuant to the provision in the act of Jan. 22, 1925.

"No doubt the vouchers will show that Mr. Bielaski acted in the capacity of an informer and received a sort of piece-meal payment. Similar work is paid for by the Police Department and is generally known as stool-pigeon work.

"I am quite sure that the next session of Congress will prevent further abuses of public funds in such manner. At least it is well to have the situation cleared and the status of people who claim to be important Government officials established."[39]

Mr. Dwyer's Short Stay In Jail

After the guilty verdict, Dwyer went to the Tombs jail in Manhattan where he awaited release on appeal. Meanwhile, he ate heartily, smoked cigars, and told reporters that both the food and tobacco were cheaper than on the outside.[40] Within a few days, Judge Mack ordered that he be taken from the Tombs every Monday, Wednesday, and Friday to receive medical treatment, and not remain out of the jail for more than four hours on any given day.[41]

Benjamin Spellman presented the petition for the order, which was accompanied by certificates from a dentist and a podiatrist. The dentist certified that he had been treating Dwyer for a fractured jaw he received in an automobile accident and had found it necessary to remove fragments of the bone and several teeth. The podiatrist claimed that Dwyer's right heel needed treatment.[42]

With the chief witness in the case convicted of perjury and Bielaski exposed as a fraud by Congressman LaGuardia, Dwyer's odds at an appeal were much better. On August 21, not even a month after hearing their guilty verdicts, Dwyer and Cohron were freed on bail. Dwyer paid $50,000 in bail and Cohron paid $25,000.[43]

Gallagher Runs From Agents

William H. Gallagher, alias William Cavenaugh, once president of the Dominion Warehouse Company, was still wanted by the government for his role in the Dwyer conspiracy. When he failed to appear in court, he forfeited his $10,000 bail and was declared a fugitive.

On the afternoon of August 25, Agents William Thibideau and Harry Cook were walking up Broadway. When the men reached 40th Street, Thibideau grabbed Cook's arm and shouted, "Look! Bill Gallagher!"[44]

Thibideau pointed at a stocky man who stood with three or four others. The agents approached the group cautiously. Cook walked ahead of Thibideau, and, as he came abreast of Gallagher, he seized his wrist and announced, "All right, Bill, there's a warrant out for you. You're under arrest."[45]

At first, Gallagher offered no resistance. When Thibideau stood in front of him, he extended his arm as if to shake hands. As Cook released his grip on his sleeve, Gallagher punched Thibideau in the jaw, causing the agent to stagger backward. He followed his punch with a kick to Thibideau's stomach. The agent dropped. Gallagher fell down while kicking Thibideau, but was soon back on his feet.

As he began running away, Gallagher collided with an old lady, knocking her into a gutter filled with rain water. Cook chased Gallagher across Broadway toward 42nd Street. Within a few steps of the subway kiosk, outside the Knickerbocker Building, Cook saw two uniformed policemen and yelled to them to stop Gallagher. One of the patrolman reached for his nightstick and hit Gallagher on the head. Gallagher dropped. When he regained consciousness, he was in handcuffs.

Amazingly, he was still able to post a $40,000 bail after attempting to flee from police.[46]

29

The Plot Thickens

A few months after the Dwyer trial, there was a new trial in the US District Court in New York, with Judge Francis A. Winslow presiding. Eighteen men were charged with conspiracy to import liquor. The alleged ringleaders were among those arrested with William Dwyer. Edward and Frank Costello, Edward and Frank Kelly, plus fourteen others[13] were placed on trial in early January 1927. The indictments charged a series of offenses dating back to October 1923. Included in the charges were: the loading and unloading of several craft running between St. Pierre and New York, New Jersey, and Connecticut; bribery of Coastguardsmen; and the importation of thousands of cases of liquor.[1]

The first witness examined was William R. Newman of Freeport, formerly a dentist's assistant. Newman was under indictment, yet testifying for the government. Newman said he met Edward Kelly in Freeport in 1924. Kelly told Newman that he had several ships operating between Canada and the Long Island shore, but he had problems with his supercargoes because they drank too much. Newman accepted a job at $75 a week. He was assigned to the ship *Integral*, which had 8,000 cases aboard.

Later, he worked on the schooner *Vincent White*. He left the ship after a run from Lunenberg, Nova Scotia, and on the next trip down from Canada, the schooner got lost on its way to Rum Row. Newman went to Curtiss Field, near Mineola on Long Island, and hired a seaplane to take him out over Rum Row. It took two flights to spot the lost ship, but once he found it, the seaplane landed on the ocean and Newman went aboard the ship. As a bonus, he gave the seaplane captain a case of liquor. A Mr. Merrill, in charge of the Curtiss fliers, confirmed the story and said, "Our

---

[13] The others were Daniel J. Keleher, Richard Ellis, Michael Doherty, Philip J. Coffey, Frank J. Corson, C. Hunter Carpenter, William Bleet, Frederick J. Lewis, John Lowins, Tony Melillo, Frederick B. Miller, James P. O'Connell, and William Pump.

planes are like taxicabs in that it is none of the driver's business what his passenger is about. The hiring of the seaplane in that case was merely a matter of business."[2]

Newman explained the elaborate book-keeping done aboard the *Vincent White* and the businesslike methods followed. The "contact" boats, onto which the liquor was transshipped from the schooner, were identified by serial numbers on dollar bills. The home office in New York gave him a list of numbers. When a contact boat came alongside, the captain of the smaller boat presented a dollar bill. If it had a serial number that matched one on Newman's list, the liquor was delivered in accordance with specifications on the list.

Newman testified that he continued to smuggle liquor until June 1925, when the Coast Guard escalated its war on Rum Row and the *Vincent White* went back to Canada. At Lunenberg, he met Kelly, who told him to take the schooner to a point between Yarmouth, Massachusetts and Boston, where a cargo of liquor was to be put aboard a Standard Oil steamer. (Standard Oil was owned by the Rockefeller.) However, on the way south, the vessel became fog-bound and he had to return to Lunenburg.[3]

On cross-examination, Newman admitted that he had become an agent for A. Bruce Bielaski, chief undercover Prohibition agent in New York. Nathan Burkan, one of the counsels for defense, then asked Newman why he had gone to work for Bielaski. Newman answered that he felt he had been cheated of several hundred dollars by the Kellys and he thought he saw a chance to earn enough for the support of his family by becoming a dry agent.

"How much money did you get from being a spy?" asked Mr. Burkan.

"I received $250 a month," Newman answered.[4]

Newman added that he would send his former associates and even his own brother to jail if he found that they were still in the rum business. He said that after he had worked for more than a year for the Kellys as a supercargo, he had been fired because of a dispute over wages. In frustration, Newman wrote a letter to Lincoln C. Andrews, Federal Prohibition Administrator, described his background and asked for a job as an agent for the government. Andrews referred the case to a subordinate and eventually, Newman was hired as one of Bielaski's staff.

ALCOHOL, BOAT CHASES, AND SHOOTOUTS!

Former Coast Guardsman Testifies

On the following day, a former Coast Guardsman testified in the Costello and Kelly case. William R. Hughes was a machinist aboard the Coast Guard boat 126 who was arrested as a smuggler. He pleaded guilty to the charges and was discharged from the Coast Guard. Hughes testified that boat 126 frequently went out to Rum Row in September and October 1925 to communicate with the *Vincent A. White*. He said that on one occasion, the skipper of the patrol boat and the cook boarded the rum ship and later came back drunk with the ship's supercargo, Tony Melillo, and that the 126 was ordered to put into Greenport so that Melillo could meet up with a customer to arrange a pick-up. However, a fist fight between the skipper and the cook stopped the trip.[5]

In October, Hughes said, the same boat went out to another rum ship, named the *Arcolo*. The supercargo, Mike Doherty, rowed over to the Coast Guard boat and suggested that it take ashore 300 cases of liquor. Patrol boat 188, came up and its skipper told the skipper of the 126 it would "be suicide to take the stuff ashore" as the destroyers were watching the patrol boats.

Hughes added that on one occasion, when there were destroyers present, patrol boat 126 kept its small one-pound guns loaded so they could be fired and thus give the appearance of being in a chase if interrupted. However, at the time, Coffey was on the 126 and was being taken out to the *Vincent A. White*. Later, Hughes said, they all went back to Greenport. There, two men went around the docks to see who was moving liquor so they could collect the usual fee paid the Coast Guard per case. Unfortunately for them, no liquor was coming in and they got nothing.[6]

On October 22, with Nicolas Brown in command of patrol boat 126, the crew learned that the small boats, which had been taking the liquor off the *Vincent A. White*, couldn't find the ship and were coming in empty. The schooner was far off its course and Brown put out to find it. They located the ship and put it back on the proper course so the rum-runners could get to it. Brown then signaled to the ship that many fishing boats were in the vicinity and ready to offload liquor.

Under cross-examination, Hughes disclosed that he had pleaded guilty to charges against him. He added that he began working for Prohibition forces (on the civilian side) during the previous October. He said he was a confidential agent and worked for a "Captain Saltman" and not for Bielaski.

Brown took the stand late in the day. He was yet another of those originally indicted but had their charges dropped after turning government witness and pleading guilty. Brown said he lived in Boston and that on the first day of his patrol work he ran out to the *Vincent A. White*, and, after a conversation, acquired a case of whisky.

"What happened next?" the prosecution asked.

"I don't know what happened to the rest of the men; personally, I got drunk," said Brown.[7]

Brown was arrested in Boston during January of the previous year and was released on bail. While he was free, Bielaski's agents seized him and carried him aboard the Coast Guard Cutter *Seneca*. There, he and other men involved in the smuggling were put in irons and confined in the *Seneca*'s brig. The cutter put to sea and was gone a week.

"The place was like a madhouse," Brown testified. He continued:

> "I was almost out of my head. We were shackled with double irons and kept in confinement the whole week. The hatches were battened down and the air was foul. They fed us rotten meat and gave us rotten water. Sometimes someone would look in to see if we were active. We were not allowed to communicate with our friends."[8]

At the end of the week, Bielaski sent a radio message to the cutter. He wanted to know if Brown would confess. Brown caved in and agreed to confess. "You were anxious to get away from the *Seneca*?" the attorney asked before the court.

"I'll tell the world I was," replied Brown. Brown was taken to the Battery in Manhattan, where he was brought into Bielaski's office. After he told Bielaski that he would plead guilty, he received much different treatment. He went home to Boston after that.[9]

Brown's testimony corroborated that of Hughes– that he had traded cigarettes for meat with the rum-runners on the row, that he had received $1,180 from Philip J. Coffey, one of the defendants, and that he had given a bribe of $1,000 to Samuel Briggs, the executive officer at the New London base. Brown also confirmed that his boat, the 126, was used to ferry supercargoes from the shore to rum ships. He admitted that he was drinking or drunk every day and that the rum-runners frequently turned over cases of champagne, whisky and ale. On one occasion, he carried 350 cases of liquor ashore.

"I drank a great deal that day," Brown said. "I got drunk, but I didn't pass out until I reached the buoy at Montauk Point. Next morning, I woke up at 9:30 and Coffey came to the boat and told me I was a fool to bring in the liquor because if I was going to get drunk when I did that sort of thing I would spoil the whole game."[10]

Another witness, Frank J. Stuart, also a former Coastie who pleaded guilty and turned government witness, had been in command of boat 129. His criminal career, which lasted two months, landed him in jail and brought him several thousand dollars in bribes. Stuart explained that he became corrupt because of the hardships of duty and the "rotten conditions" he found there. Just before Labor Day 1925, he testified, he had accepted a bribe of $2,000 from Philip J. Coffey for allowing several fishing boats to land the liquor in Fort Pond Bay, near Montauk.

Stuart told the story of how he captured the *Dawn,* a ship on which there were 200 cases of liquor. His patrol boat took the *Dawn* in tow, but the wind and tide were against him and the heavier vessel swung to shore and ran aground. Stuart cut loose after salvaging the liquor. He ordered his men to fire several shots into the stranded *Dawn* and the boat caught fire and sank. Then, boat 129 ran into Fort Pond Bay, landed the liquor, and the crew sold it for $3,000, which was divided amongst them.[11]

Steven was captured on New Year's Eve in Philadelphia and taken to the Coast Guard base in New London, where he "came clean." He signed a confession and was sentenced to six months, but was released after serving twenty-eight days when Prohibition Administrator Andrews sent a telegram.

Due to the level of corruption involved, Federal Judge Winslow took the unusual step of confining the jury to a hotel. It was the first time in ten years that a federal jury had been sequestered during the trial and before the case was given to it for deliberation.

On January 12, 1927, Samuel Briggs took the stand as a witness. Briggs had formerly been a high-ranking Coast Guard officer at the base in New London, Connecticut. He was a sandy-haired young man who was slight, pale, and wore glasses. He admitted to accepting two $500 bribes from a rum-runner, which he claimed to have turned over to his superiors. He then told the court about his connections with members of the ring. He included in that account Lincoln C. Andrews, head of the government Prohibition forces. Here he is referred to as "General Andrews" because he was a retired general.[12]

On November 16, 1925, Briggs testified, he received a phone message from a man named "John Davis," *a.k.a.* Phillip Coffey, the paymaster for the rum ring. On the following day, Briggs met Coffey at the Mohican Hotel in New London for lunch. The following is an excerpt from Briggs' testimony:

Attorney Nathan Burkan: "What took place at that luncheon?"
Briggs: "Coffey explained to me that previous to this – sometime prior to this—two men had come to New London; they were presumably government agents. One of these two men I was introduced to as a Mr. Wilson. During the discussion at the luncheon, Coffey told me not to worry about these two men, Wilson and that associate of his; that this Mr. Wilson was General Andrew's personal representative—personal agent—and that they had the schooner Athenia and the cargo was owned jointly by his people—the Coffey people—and General Andrews, or General Andrews representative; and explained that after all expenses, overhead, etc., had been paid General Andrews' share of the transaction would amount to approximately $2,000."
Burkan: "They were going to give General Andrews $2,000?"
Briggs: "Yes; but he told me, he explained that after they once got started they planned to make a trip each week, and where there were fifty-two weeks a year it would be approximately $100,000 that General Andrews would be receiving."
Burkan: "This was a proposition that they were to put up to General Andrews?"
Briggs: "Now, sir, as I understood it, the proposition had already been made through Mr. Wilson."
Burkan: "They had put the proposition up to Mr. Wilson?"
Briggs: "As I understood it."[13]

When Andrews heard the allegations, he not only denied them, but refused to take them seriously and laughingly remarked that his only connection with rum rings was "to put them all in jail."

ALCOHOL, BOAT CHASES, AND SHOOTOUTS!

Distrust Within the Coast Guard

A man named Martin T. Moran also testified at the federal trial on what it was like to be in the Coast Guard in 1925. During that year, Moran was the skipper of Coast Guard boat 188. Frank J. Stuart, commander of another Coast Guard vessel, approached Moran and tried to recruit his services for the rum-runners. Stuart had testified already, having pleaded guilty to the indictment against him. Stuart admitted he had accepted $2,000 from Philip Coffey. Moran said Stuart suggested that he (Moran) join in the plan to allow fishing boats to run in from Rum Row in exchange for bribe money, but Moran declined the offer.[14]

Moran did not report the bribe offer to his superior officers immediately. When he was asked on the witness stand why he delayed, he said he feared that the officers might also be involved with the rum ring. One defendant at the trial (heard by Judge Winslow at the Federal Building in New York in January 1927) told Samuel D. Briggs, executive officer at the New London Coast Guard base, that Lincoln C. Andrews was in a scheme whereby he was to receive $2,000 a week through cargoes landed from the *Athena*. Briggs also took the stand, where he defended his action in taking $1,200 in bribes and turning the money over to Bruce Bielaski.

The Jury Deliberates

Nathan Burkan, as counsel for the defense, summed up his closing argument by devoting the greater part of his time attacking the government witnesses, whom he described as "rats." He spoke bitterly against Bruce Bielaski, chief of undercover Prohibition agents in New York, and the methods Bielaski used to accomplish his goals.

Bielaski, who had offices at 120 Broadway, was, according to Burkan, a "mysterious and invisible power who employs as agent hijackers, pirates, crooks and bribe takers."[15] He pointed out that a number of the government's witnesses in this case were named as co-defendants with Costello and others in the indictment, and also that, almost without exception, these men had admitted that they were on Bielaski's staff. Lowering his voice to almost a whisper, Burkan said to the jury, "The depraved character of the witnesses and the foul use of money in this case by the government make it an insult to your intelligence to have to pass judgment upon it."[16]

Assistant US Attorney Horace Hitchcock, who, with Assistant US Attorney Willam E. Stevenson, had conducted the prosecution, defended the government's method of obtaining evidence and presenting it through witnesses who had confessed. He added that the procedure of turning suspects into government witnesses was not a new technique, and that it was customary to pay such witnesses as special employees, or informers pending the trial of the case.

Judge Winslow, in his instructions to the jury, said the first charge in the indictment was conspiracy to violate the Prohibition law, the second charge was conspiracy to smuggle in merchandise not invoiced with Customs officials, and the third charge was conspiracy to facilitate the transportation of the allegedly smuggled goods. He stated that only one of the overt acts named in the indictment need be proven to reach a guilty verdict. He added that the acts need not have been performed within their jurisdiction in order to establish guilt, but that it was only necessary to prove that the conspiracy originated in that district.

After listening to testimony for two weeks, the jury began deliberating at 3:30 PM. At 11 PM, they were still nowhere near a verdict and sent word to the judge that they wished to retire to the Hotel McAlpin for the night. The judge granted permission for the jurors to leave with instructions that they report their verdict first thing in the morning, should they reach one that night. The defendants seemed depressed as they saw the jury leaving. A few relatives and friends in the corridors tried to cheer them. The jury sought no instructions after retiring to deliberate.[17] After being out for twenty-four hours, the jury acquitted eight of the defendants and reached no agreement on the other six defendants; so every defendant walked free when the trial was over.[18]

Bielaski's Operation Ruined

The fact that neither Frank Costello, nor any of the other thirteen others tried with him were convicted caused a great stir in New York's Federal Building. Bielaski's operation had a terrible track record. During the previous two years, 94 men were indicted as "higher-ups" in liquor smuggling rings, but only two had been convicted, and the cases of those two (William V. Dwyer and E.C. Cohron) were being reviewed by the US Circuit Court of Appeals.[19]

While the Costello trial was still underway, Judge Winslow was also hearing another case that was damning for Bielaski. That separate trial dealt with a government-run speakeasy known as the Bridge Whist Club. Ralph W. Bickle, an agent of Bielaski, operated the speakeasy at 14 East 44th St. The speakeasy was meant to be a trap set for those violating the Prohibition law; however, when the public learned that the government was running a Manhattan bar, the outrage went all the way to Congress.[20] Bielaski resigned two months after the Costello case and returned to private law practice. His under-cover office at 120 Broadway was closed soon after that.

30

The Mysterious Envelope

In May 1926, a Nassau, Bahamas constable named George Pinder had a very interesting story to tell. He told the British Vice Consul that he and four other officers seized the three-masted schooner *Tillie* several weeks earlier. They had heard that the schooner was carrying alcohol from the steamship *Eker*. When the *Eker*'s captain refused to pay the $100,000 duty on 33,000 cases of liquor aboard, British officials decided to seize the ship.[1]

Constable Pinder was aboard the *Eker* as a government ship was towing the seized vessel to port. However, when the towing hawser broke, the crew seized Pinder and tied him up. After an hour's chase, the *Eker* escaped and headed for Miami.[2] From Miami, the ship went to Charleston and then to New York. Once the ship reached New York, Pinder managed to make it to shore and headed back to Nassau. The *Eker* boldly entered New York Harbor and sailed up the Hudson River. Customs inspectors stopped the ship as it was passing Yonkers, New York. The ship had been in service for 36 years and was badly in need of repairs. The inspectors noticed that the weather-beaten ship reeked of alcohol, even from fifty feet away. They found that the ship's water tank on the upper deck contained about 300 gallons of grain alcohol. In addition, a huge tank below deck in the aft part of the ship was filled with 25,000 gallons of grain alcohol. The total value of all the liquor aboard was $1 million.[3]

After Customs agents seized the ship, they took the twelve crewmembers into custody. The *Eker*'s captain, however, was not present. After a thorough search, the agents found a memorandum book which listed $20,000 in bribes paid out to ensure the ship's safe arrival at Yonkers. The book contained entries such as "Pd. Cops $8,500, pd. pro. agt. $1,000," and with ditto marks under the "Pd.," the following: "Red, $5,000; Pay Off $20,000; Cop, $125; Capt., $2,500; Ferry, $250."[4]

354

Before the Customs agents seized the *Eker*, an unmarked envelope filled with $9,500 cash "appeared" on the desk of Captain Hugo O. Wunsche of the NY Police Department's Marine Division. Wunsche told this story to reporters:

> "I did not sleep at the Marine Division headquarters as usual Monday but went on duty there at 7:50 A.M. Tuesday. I went into my office and cleared up my desk. That is, I attended to all mail that was waiting for me, and left my desk clear of papers. I then went to a storeroom at the water end of the house, taking with me my clerical assistant. We made a sort of inventory of some old goods there.
>
> "I returned to my desk at 9:35 A.M., and was surprised to see on top of my desk a long, white envelope, face down. I picked it up. It was sealed and had no mark on it. With my clerical assistant as a witness, I opened the envelope and was astonished to find inside, wrapped in two sheets of foolscap paper, nine $1,000 bills and five $100 bills. There was no mark of identification to be found, other than a Boston water mark on the paper, which seemed like a legal size, larger than an ordinary sheet of writing paper.
>
> "Policemen have been in and out of the office as usual, I supposed, so I immediately questioned the desk Lieutenant and all the policemen around the place. They all said they had seen no one enter or leave my office.
>
> "My desk is near a window, in fact, within easy arm's reach of the window, which, I noticed upon my return was lowered from the top. Outside the Marine Headquarters runs a little stringpiece or ledge, along which a man might walk. A man on that ledge might easily have placed the money on the desk. I am utterly at a loss to account for the presence of the money in my office, and I can make no conjectures, as the matter is under investigation."[5]

Captain Wunsche added that there were no signs of footprints on the ledge or fingerprints on the window. He said he tried three times to phone Deputy Chief Inspector West of the Marine Division, but could not reach him. Then, he said, he went to Police Headquarters and turned the money over to Commissioner McLaughlin. The Commissioner, in turn, gave his own statement to the press, which contradicted Wunsche's statement:

"Prior to the report of the finding of the memorandum book aboard the steamship Eker we were investigating the matter—starting Thursday afternoon—of the envelope left on the desk of the captain of the Marine Division...

"Captain Wunsche at 3 P.M. Thursday walked into his office at the Marine Division headquarters and found the envelope. He called in two men and then opened it. He at once got in touch with Deputy Chief West and told him. West went to Wunsche, and after conferring with him they came to this office. Chief Inspector William J. Lahey was placed in charge of the investigation and questioned West and Wunsche."[6]

To make these conflicting stories even more suspicious, US Attorney Emory R. Buckner did not hear anything about the matter until Saturday, after the *Eker* story had reached the press. No one outside of the police department knew about the envelope until two days after the *Eker* seizure. Wunsche told the press that he found the money on Tuesday morning, while the Commissioner said he found it on Thursday afternoon. Wunsche said that one man witnessed him opening the envelope, while the Commissioner claimed there were two witnesses. Wunsche said that he could not contact Deputy Chief Inspector West; the Commissioner, on the other hand, stated that Wunsche not only contacted West, but came with him to the Commissioner's office. Wunsche speculated that a man could have walked on the ledge outside of his window and simply reached in, dropping the money on the desk. However, Wunsche shot that ridiculous scenario down by stating that there were no footprints on the ledge or fingerprints on the window. He also pointed out that the window was open from the top. If someone were actually crazy enough to climb a ledge on the outside of a police building in broad daylight, they would at least open the window from the bottom to gain access to whatever room they were breaking into. Overall, the story made no sense. Wunsche was not going to get off easy with his unbelievable fabrication—the investigation was soon taken up by a federal grand jury.[7]

On the first day of the hearing, Captain Wunsche spent more than two hours before the grand jury while his staff sat in the ante room under subpoena. Two days later, the jury members visited police headquarters at Pier A and noticed that Wunsche's desk was not next to the window as he claimed, but across the room. Some of the jurors climbed on the ledge outside of the window to see how difficult it would be to throw an envelope to his desk from that position. They came to the conclusion that it would have taken a very lucky shot to throw the envelope across the room and have it land squarely on the Captain's desk.[8]

Policemen at Marine Headquarters took newspaper men through the place and insisted that it was the "greatest mystery" to them how the money got on the desk. Lieutenant William O. Jones said he was on desk duty when the money was "found" and had been on all that morning. Although Jones had a clear view of the office from his desk, he had seen no one enter. However, he added that he was "busy writing" during that time and not watching the office continuously.[9]

The mysterious envelope caused the New York Police Department great embarrassment. By January of 1927, Deputy Chief Inspector West still did not know who put it there, and if he did, he did not tell anyone publicly. Police Commissioner McLaughlin was not pleased with West's performance, so he demoted him to captain and transferred him to the Fifth Street Station in Manhattan. West's salary was reduced from $5,500 to $4,200. If he had remained a deputy chief inspector for six more days he would have completed five years at that pay grade and would have been able to retire on pension due to that rank. His retirement pension dropped by $650 a year, enough to buy a new Model A Ford in 1927.[10]

Meanwhile, federal agents managed to find and arrest the *Eker*'s missing captain, Bernard M. Reaves. He was already under a $7,500 bond pending an appeal from a conviction in the federal court at Norfolk, Virginia, on a liquor charge. The agents arrested him and he was again charged with smuggling.[11]

George Pinder returned to Nassau and was rewarded by the Bahamas government for refusing to take a bribe. He then returned to New York to testify in the trial of George J. Hearn, the *Eker*'s shipping agent. Constable Pinder, a tall black man, told his story in court. He boarded the ship to ensure that it was anchored closer to Nassau the following day. The *Eker*'s captain pulled out a revolver and told Pinder that he had $2 million worth of cargo aboard and did not want to be delayed. He ordered Constable Pinder to go below decks. Pinder, refusing to comply, knocked the captain down. The crew attacked Pinder and one of the men knocked him unconscious with the butt of their pistol. When he recovered, the *Eker* was at sea. Pinder was forced to work. After the ship landed 38,000 cases of liquor at Edgewater, New

Jersey, he was given money to return home. During the eleven days the ship was at Edgewater, no one interfered with the unloading of liquor and a policeman came aboard for a friendly visit.[12]

The British Government sought to have the captain and crew of the rum ship returned to Nassau to face various charges, including shanghaiing, failure to pay customs duties, and assault. Sir Esme Howard, British ambassador, sent a letter to Assistant US Attorney Herman Stichman asking for the extradition of the twelve defendants.[13]

When Constable Pinder finally faced his former captors in court, he was visibly nervous. When he was asked to identify the men of the crew, he walked slowly about the room and pointed out all but one. He also told the court that the men threatened his life constantly while he was aboard the ship.[14]

A few days later, Captain Reeves and seven of his crew were sent to the Tombs prison in Manhattan without bail to await a decision on extradition. Three other crew members forfeited their bail by not returning to court.[15] Captain Reeves was soon extradited to Nassau on charges of kidnapping and failure to pay export duties, amounting to $200,000.[16] He wound up serving eighteen months in a Nassau prison.

Chief of Police and Mayor Are Indicted

By December 1926, Assistant US Attorney Stichman still did not come up with an explanation as to how the mysterious envelope full of money wound up on Captain Wunsche's desk. However, after the eight-month investigation there was plenty of other blame to go around. In connection with the *Eker*, Stichman indicted the mayor of Edgewater, New Jersey, Henry Wissel and the town's police chief, James A. Dinan. He also indicted a New York Harbor Patrol Police Sergeant, a US Customs inspector, two Edgewater detectives, plus twenty-seven other defendants in federal court. Stichman told US Commissioner Garrett W. Cotter that the mayor had allegedly accepted $50,000 in bribes and that Police Sergeant John J. Lowery of the NYPD Marine Division had accepted $20,000 from rum-runners.[17]

George Cutley, who represented Mayor Wissel, Chief Dinan, and the Edgewater detectives, announced that his clients had no intention of appearing in New York's federal court. Cutley said that his clients had not received any official notice of their indictment, no attempt had been made to arrest them, and that they would fight extradition from New

Jersey to New York. In response, US Attorney Emory R. Buckner told the press that no warrants would be issued unless the men failed to appear for pleading.[18] A week later, the men still had not appeared at the federal court, so Judge John C. Knox issued bench warrants for the arrest of the mayor, the police chief, and for fifteen of the other defendants. The ones not included in the warrants, including police sergeant Lowery, appeared in court to plead not guilty.[19] Despite their defiant talk, the mayor and police chief turned themselves in to a US Marshal and each posted $2,500 bail while awaiting their trial date.[20]

A big break in the case came in November 1926. In Chicago, Edward Ritz, a New Jersey Customs Inspector, testified before a US Commissioner that Cecil M. Kinder, wholesale bootlegger and owner of the *Eker*, told him that he (Kinder) had paid more than $50,000 to Edgewater's mayor for protection privileges. For this bribe, Kinder was allowed to land 46,000 cases of whisky in New Jersey. Kinder, a Chicago millionaire and alleged head of a $10 million Bahamian whisky smuggling ring, was before the US Commissioner in proceedings to have him extradited to New Jersey to stand trial on smuggling charges.[21]

Several months earlier, Customs Inspectors Edward Ritz and J.L. Solieri posed as representatives of Edgewater's Mayor and tricked Kinder into admitting he paid large sums of money to practically all of Edgewater's police to keep them quiet on his smuggling operations. When Assistant District Attorney James G. Cotter confronted the police chief with evidence accusing him of corruption, he had a heart attack, which he survived. When Kinder returned to Chicago in late October, he was arrested for smuggling liquor from England and the Bahamas into the United States.

When he was arrested, Kinder said, "Well, you've put one over on me, but if I am stuck in this matter the whole Administration will be stuck with me." And so it was. Kinder was one of fifty indicted in New Jersey in the smuggling operation. Clifford Kinder, Cecil's brother, was also indicted.[22]

The Mayor, Police Chief, and Cohorts On Trial

Mayor Henry Wissel, Police Chief James A. Dinan, and seventeen other defendants[14] arrived at the US District Court in

---

[14] The other defendants were Alexander F. Flannery and Edward Pickering, Edgewater Detectives; Edward A. Ritz, US Customs Inspector at Union City, NJ; Police Sergeant

Manhattan at the beginning of February 1927. They were charged with conspiring to violate Prohibition and Customs laws. Before the jury was selected, Cecil Kinder and D. Turner of Chicago pleaded guilty to the same indictment. Another man, named Maurice Borden, a.k.a. Tony Murphy, from Newport, Rhode Island, also pleaded guilty. Following its custom, the US Government intended to use these men, one of whom was allegedly the leader of the conspiracy, as witnesses.[23]

The government had difficulty in selecting a jury because so many of those interviewed were strongly opposed to the Volstead Act. Some of the jury candidates were surprisingly frank. One told Assistant US Attorney Herman T. Stichman, who led the prosecution, that a member of his family had been running liquor in from the North since the beginning of Prohibition. Another admitted that he had financial interests in the liquor business. Mr. Stichman thanked them for their honesty and excused them.[24]

The indictment dealt specifically with the attempt to land $2 million worth of liquor at Edgewater from the steamship *Eker*. Of the thirty-three defendants named in the indictment, six had not been arrested, four had jumped bail, and three had pleaded guilty. The ship's captain, Bernard Reeves, was serving a sentence of eleven months in prison for kidnapping Constable Pinder at Nassau and keeping him aboard the ship against his will.[25]

One of the key witnesses in the trial was DeWitt T. Turner. On the witness stand, he confessed to the following:

> "On the Friday after the Eker arrived at Edgewater in April last, I paid Mayor Wissel in the power house office $4,500. The following day I paid him $4,000 more. He asked me how everything was going along and I said 'very nicely.' The following week I saw him three times. Our talk was just about as on the two previous occasions when I paid him money. On the last three occasions I have referred to, however, I paid him $5,000 twice and $4,000 once..."[26]

John J. Lowry of the NYPD Marine Division; Eustace R. Smith, Paul Demontreaux and James Baldwin, owners of the Edgewater Boat Repair Yards; George Rosenbaum of Newark, Henry Gertner and Louis Smith of New York City, and John Cambel, Henry Ennis, Archibald McDonald, William G. Ross, John Shelvin, James Smith, and James Thompson, members of the *Eker*'s crew.

When asked to identify the mayor in the courtroom, Turner immediately pointed to him. Mayor Wissel, a large, fat man with a belligerent chin, stood up and stared hard at the witness as Mr. Stichman announced: "Identifying Mayor Wissel."[27]

When New York Police Captain Hugo Wunsche took the stand, it seemed that the public would finally find out how the $9,500 wound up on his desk. He had testified under questioning by Mr. Stichman that Patrol Boat 5, skippered by Sergeant John J. Lowery of the NYPD Marine Division and one of the defendants, was the only police boat patrolling the Hudson River along Post 7, which ran from the Battery to the city line on the north, on April 25 and 27th. The money was found on the captain's desk on the morning of April 27. He testified that Lowery could only come into his office at the Battery when he himself was there.[28]

Mr. Stichman asked the witness three times if he had found a sum of money on his desk on the morning of April 27, and each time objections by Mr. Steuer and others on the defense counsel were sustained. Just before Captain Wunsche left the stand, Judge Meekins granted a motion by Mr. Steuer to strike all of Wunsche's testimony from the record. Wunsche, who obviously received a bribe but tried to cover his tracks by turning in the money, was not even a defendant in the case and walked away scot free. Sergeant Lowery escaped conviction because a key witness could not identify him in the courtroom.[29]

The trial lasted less than a week, which is very unusual considering the magnitude of the scandal. The jury found fourteen of the defendants guilty of violating Customs laws. No one was found guilty of violating the Prohibition Act. Judge Isaac Meekins asked the crew of the *Eker* to stand, and, when asked, all of them stated that they were not US citizens. He sentenced each of them to a year and a day in Atlanta Penitentiary. The sentence was to take effect on June 3 "provided they could be found," which meant that if they left the United States they would not have to serve their sentences.[30]

Paul Demontreaux and James Baldwin, alleged owners of the Edgewater Boat Repair Yards, told the court they were not owners but employees at $50 a week each, and that they were married with children. Judge Meekins suspended their one-year sentences and paroled them for two years. Eustice R. Smith, who admitted he was an owner of the yards, told the court that he received "only" $3,500 for his part in the rum deals. The judge fined him $1,000 with no jail time. United States Customs

Inspector Edward A. Ritz was sentenced to a year and a day in the Atlanta Penitentiary.

The Mayor and Police Chief Are Sentenced

When Mayor Wissel first heard his guilty verdict, he bowed his head in his hands and appeared to be either crying or sighing deeply. He hid his face and seemed on the verge of a breakdown.[31] On the day of his sentencing, five-hundred of Wissel's fellow townspeople showed up at the courthouse with a petition for leniency. Some of them were so overcome with sympathy for their mayor that they openly wept. Judge Meekins sentenced Wissel to a year and a day in Atlanta Penitentiary. If his fellow townspeople had not presented such a big petition, and if the mayor had not told the story of how he moved up from being a poor truck driver to the director of a corporation, he would have received two years instead of one. The judge told the courtroom that he had fully intended to impose such a sentence.[32]

Police Chief Dinan of Edgewater was also sentenced to a year and a day in Atlanta. Edgewater policemen Alexander F. Flannery and Edward Pickering received suspended sentences of nine months each in the county jail. They both had to report to a probation officer monthly. Cecil N. Kinder and DeWitt T. Turner, two of the main players in the conspiracy, received eighteen months each in Atlanta Penitentiary. Cecil's brother, Charles, who had pleaded guilty before the trial, was sentenced to six months in the county jail.[33]

Mayor Wissel, Police Chief Dinan, and Customs Inspector Ritz were all released from prison on bail pending appeal. Detectives Flannery and Pickering's, whose nine-month sentences were suspended "during good behavior," also joined in the appeal. The court of appeals set aside the guilty verdict on all five of the men based on instructions Judge Meekins gave to the jury. During the original hearing, the jury deliberated for several hours and returned to the courtroom twice for instructions. When they came back the second time, Judge Meekins told them:

> "A jury may arbitrarily set at defiance law and reason and refuse to convict the accused by returning a verdict of not guilty. When a jury does that the guilty escape no matter how plain the guilt. To set aside law and reason may be in the power of the jury, but such defiance is not within the jury's

right. The jury is as much bound by the law and by their conscience as is the Court.

"I cannot instruct you directly as to what your verdict should be, for it is your function to decide the question of fact in this case. However, I consider it my duty to say to you that, in my opinion, upon the evidence offered in this case, you should find no difficulty in returning your verdict."[34]

On appeal, Judge Manton, stated in his opinion that "a trial judge may advise and he may persuade, but he may not command, unduly influence, or coerce a jury in a criminal case."[35] Manton's decision, concurred by Judges Augustus Hand and Learned Hand, overturned the verdict and directed a new trial.

31

Defeat and Denial

The last few months of 1926 were definitely not inspiring for anyone involved in Prohibition enforcement. One prominent case, involving the 196-ton British trawler *Frederick B.*, came to a very bad end after two years of legal battles. The agent responsible for the seizure was Saul "the silent man" Grill, who had disappeared in 1926. Two years earlier, he and his fellow Prohibition agents posed as bootleggers throughout the investigation. Saul Grill threw lavish parties where champagne flowed freely and convinced the trawler's owner that he was a successful bootlegger and rum-runner. Mr. Grill then went to Canada where he arranged for the purchase of a large liquor cargo.[1]

He agreed to ride in a boat to meet the *Frederick B.* at sea. After the agents took liquor aboard from the trawler, they rushed to shore. Under the rum-running treaty between the United States and Great Britain, a rum ship could be seized if it were less than an hour's steaming distance from shore. The agents headed for the nearest point of land and waded ashore to touch land in under an hour.

The Coast Guard seized the trawler fourteen miles off Monmouth Beach, NJ. The Coast Guardsmen found five thousand cases of Canadian Club whisky, valued at $350,000. Assistant US Attorney John Holley Clark went aboard after the seizure and questioned members of the crew. He soon made this public statement:

> "I consider this one of the most important seizures since the negotiation of the liquor search treaty. It will probably be followed by other large seizures. We have evidence against leading bootleggers in the United States and Canada. There is also a Canadian bank involved in the case. The liquor ring deposited funds also in American banks."[2]

Two other ships, the *Sagatin* and *Diamantina*, also seized in October 1924, carried liquor cargoes worth approximately $2 million. The US Court of Appeals eventually ruled that the seizures of those two ships, both more than 12 miles off shore, were illegal. In the *Frederick B.* case, Judge Francis A. Winslow followed the precedent set by the Court of Appeals and ruled that the seizure was illegal. Judge Winslow explained that while the treaty between the US and Britain might be all right as long as the two nations were in agreement on such action, it was not a law and did not mean that selling liquor beyond the twelve-mile limit represented a Prohibition violation.

The case represented a complete loss for the government and a serious blow to Prohibition enforcement. The indictments against twenty members of the *Frederick B.*'s crew were dismissed. Judge Winslow ordered that the liquor be returned to the trawler and that the ship be granted safe passage out to sea. Two Coast Guard vessels escorted the ship well beyond American waters.[3]

Denial

Near the end of November 1926, Commander Addison of the Cape May Coast Guard base told the press that there was no rum fleet off the New Jersey coast carrying holiday liquor.

> "Our patrol boats have been cruising along the Jersey Coast from Atlantic City to the Five-Mile Light during the past week, and to date I have received reports of only one rum-runner. This boat is anchored 200 miles east of Cape May. If the thirsty ones are depending on a supply of liquor from off-shore, they will have to look to other sources. Beginning the first of the week we expect to be operating three airplanes, which will serve as a point of contact between the base and the patrol boats.
>
> "If the general opinion is that a fleet of rum boats has arrived off the New Jersey coast, I will stand ready to disprove it by taking a reporter on one of the patrol boats out to rum row to see how empty and false the report is. As far as I am concerned, I believe that this holiday season is witnessing the greatest dearth of rum boats all along the Atlantic Coast of any season since the prohibition law went into effect."[4]

After Christmas, Admiral Billard, Commandant of the Coast Guard, publicly expressed his indignation at photos in various newspapers showing rum-runners aboard a ship busily unloading Christmas liquor for New York City. Billard declared that Rum Row no longer existed and that his official reports showed that right before Christmas his vessels had spotted only three or four possible rum ships off the entire North Atlantic coast. He added that these ships were too far out to capture and did not come to shore. He gave particular attention to a photograph taken in Raritan Bay, showing men taking boxes from the deck of a ship and loading them onto a small boat:

> "This picture is an absolute fake, pure and simple. It was staged right in New York Bay; that is, in Raritan Bay. We have an affidavit by an observer on another vessel, anchored nearby, describing the whole performance when a load of empty boxes was piled up on the four-masted schooner Richard T. Greene, anchored in the harbor, and photographs taken showing the passing of these empty cases over the side and into a small motor boat. Any one at all familiar with the sea can tell at a glance that the picture was faked; that it was taken in a quiet, peaceful harbor.
>
> "Near this fake rum ship may be seen the hull of another vessel lying peacefully at anchor. As a matter of fact, the Coast Guard in New York knows the two vessels well, because, in carrying out the anchorage regulations, it has had occasion to move them out of the channel several times..."[5]

In January 1927, reports of the Canadian Department of Commerce and showed that Canada had exported $20 million of liquor to the United States. This figure did not include $5 million worth of ale, beer, and gin. During December, when Commander Addison and Admiral Billard officially declared that Rum Row no longer existed, Canada shipped an estimated $1.4 million dollars of liquor to the US.[6]

A year earlier, the US and Canada had signed an anti-smuggling treaty. While it was illegal to import liquor into the United States, it was not illegal to export liquor from Canada to the United States thanks to a 'joker' clause included in the treaty. That clause stated that Canadian customs officers could not refuse clearances to rum-runners provided they appeared capable of making the journey to the American port designated in their papers. While there may have been fewer ships on Rum Row, rum traffic on Lake Erie and Lake Ontario was booming.[7]

During January, Treasury Secretary Mellon did something extremely unusual for a man responsible for the nation's Prohibition enforcement— he pushed a bill that would authorize private corporations to acquire and sell medicinal liquor. Lincoln C. Andrews announced that if the bill failed to pass, his next step would be to consider plans to allow distillers to manufacture "medicinal" liquor to replenish dwindling supplies. When the bill reached the House of Representatives, it provoked hostility among many dry Congressmen. Representative Blanton of Texas argued:

> "Everybody knows prohibition enforcement is hampered because [it is] placed in the hands of the present Secretary of the Treasury. He doesn't believe in prohibition. He is largely interested in distilleries and in ownership of stock in bonded warehouses which he cannot dispose of under the present system except for medicinal purposes.
>
> "What is medicinal whisky, anyway? Hundreds of doctors are making a business out of whisky prescriptions. Dr. Mayo of Rochester, Minn., one of the country's greatest surgeons, has held that whisky for medicinal purposes is needless...
>
> "Ninety-nine out of every 100 persons who get whisky on prescriptions get it for beverage purposes, and all this law is for is to provide a market for liquor that cannot be sold. They tell you it's to be a private corporation, but it says in the bill that a Government official or employee may become a director. And I imagine the Secretary of the Treasury will be the Chairman."[8]

Mr. Hudson of Michigan asked, "Is it not true that this bill is the opening wedge for putting the Government in the liquor business?"

Mr. Blanton replied, "It is the opening wedge for men all over the United States to get all the liquor they want."[9]

Rum Row Is Gone, Again

Despite his earlier pessimism and his talk of resigning, Lincoln C. Andrews was still the Assistant Treasury Secretary in the spring of 1927 and still in charge of Prohibition enforcement. He summed up his rosy view of the overall situation in a *New York Times* interview in March:

"Rum-running by sea has not ceased but it has been greatly reduced and we now look forward confidently to a day, which I think is not far ahead, when there will be no smuggling of liquor in commercial quantities into the country.

"During the last six months we stopped at the source a flow approximating 15,000,000 to 20,000,000 gallons of alcohol a year that probably had been getting into the hands of bootleggers for synthetization. We have the machinery at work to eliminate the permittees who divert alcohol and hope someday to accomplish it...

"We are getting cooperation abroad. The executive agreement made with the British Government last year has been of great help in curbing the smugglers. I might say that the agreement does not call for the help of a foreign Government in the enforcement of our laws. What it calls for in the main is cooperation in the enforcement of the laws of both countries. For smugglers usually violate the laws of countries from which they smuggle as well as those into which they carry illegally their goods. We went to London on the invitation of the British authorities, who have done splendidly in carrying out the understanding we arrived at. They have stopped ship after ship by driving the vessels out of illegal operations, and they are seriously prosecuting offenders on evidence frequently supplied by us. That is as much as we can ask.

"The Cuban authorities likewise have been cooperating with us under a treaty ratified several months ago. Since then very little liquor for smuggling into the United States has gone from the Port of Havana. We have under way an arrangement with the Canadian Government similar to the one with the Home Government. Treaties or agreements have been or will be arranged with other Governments."[10]

A Very Mixed Message

The medicinal whisky bill, a very bizarre plan coming from Mellon and Andrews, was shot down in Congress. On March 14, Andrews and Mellon sought to bypass Congress by calling their own conference of American distilleries. The purpose of the conference was to work out some system by which medicinal liquor could be manufactured under permit.[11]

At the same time, thirty-three new "long-legged" Coast Guard cutters were almost ready for service, having been assigned to patrol from the North Atlantic to the Virginia Capes to Maine. The new cutters were called "long-legged" because they had diesel engines and had a much wider cruising radius than any other craft used in the patrol of Rum Row. They could stay out for two or three weeks. These steel ships were each armed with a three-inch gun. The new vessels were 100 to 125 feet long, as opposed to the earlier models, which were 75 feet. The extra size made it possible for the crew to be more comfortable and to carry more provisions for a longer cruise. The new ships would make it possible for the Coast Guard to maintain surveillance on rum ships for longer periods of time.[12] The thirty-three boats were identical in all respects and could cover a 4,000-mile radius without refueling. Each would be manned by one officer, one radio operator, and thirteen petty officers and junior enlisted men.[13]

Americans Keep Voting For Dry Candidates

Since the repeal of Prohibition, the overwhelmingly popular opinion is that it was one of the most ridiculous laws ever passed in the United States. People look back in hindsight and wonder how the law remained in effect for as long as it did while most Americans were seemingly against it. In this case, what Americans said and what they actually voted for were two different things. By 1927, eight years had gone by since the Eighteenth Amendment was passed and ratified by the states. After 1920, there had been quite a few elections where Prohibition was one of the main issues.

In 1919, when Congress sent the Prohibition amendment to the states for ratification, 46 out of 48 states approved it. Only two states, Connecticut and Rhode Island, did not. However, those two states did not vote against it, they just did not bother to vote on it. No other Constitutional amendment had previously been ratified by such a large majority of the states.[14]

Eight years after the 18th Amendment was passed, there had been four Congressional elections. By 1927, Congress had become drier and drier, voting in favor of new Prohibition measures every year by an overwhelming majority. The wet vote was approximately 15 percent in Congress— not enough to form a real opposition. The same phenomenon applied to the gubernatorial races. In 1927, only five states— New York,

Maryland, Rhode Island, Connecticut, and Wisconsin— had "wet" governors. Most of the state legislatures were also "dry" in that year. Four of the state legislatures were split on the issue and only one state, Maryland, had a "wet" legislature.[15] Meanwhile, millions of Americans were still buying and drinking massive amounts of liquor. US Customs estimated that Americans purchased $40 million of liquor during that year.[16]

32

A Man Walked Into an Inn

During early March 1927, sea captain Browne Willis staggered into an inn. He had been shot twice in Van Cortlandt Park, in the Bronx, NY. Fortunately for Willis, the bullets lodged in his left arm and nowhere else. He told Bronx detectives that he was attempting to separate two unknown duelists and was caught in the crossfire. Willis was transported to the Jewish Memorial Hospital, where federal authorities took charge of his case.[1]

At the time of the shooting, Willis was already under $15,000 bail on a rum smuggling charge. In addition to that charge, he faced a new charge of "spiriting" away fourteen witnesses, former members of his crew, who were under subpoena to appear before a federal grand jury. Authorities believed that Willis' shooting was part of an elaborate scheme which brought about the disappearance of the witnesses from a waterfront hotel.

The operations for which Captain Willis was indicted were notable for their boldness. During the previous New Year's Eve, Captain Willis, in command of the steamship *Clara*, landed 1,800 cases of liquor in broad daylight at a North River pier. The quantity of liquor landed was not large, but authorities believed that Willis and his crew were part of a huge Canadian liquor ring.[2]

Willis' New Year's cargo landing did not go well. Authorities seized the cargo, but the captain and crew managed to flee. While the search was being made for Willis, agents rounded up members of his crew as witnesses. Willis, meanwhile, was caught in Boston, where he was placed under $15,000 bail to appear in a New York court.

The whole investigation was guarded with secrecy due to Willis' notorious reputation. He was cited in many bootleg reports, and in charges of gun-running and miscellaneous smuggling before Prohibition. However, he had never been convicted for any of the operations he had been suspected of. Among the many charges against him was one of scuttling, or sinking, his ship at Hampton Roads, Virginia, in order to destroy alcoholic evidence. A conviction on this charge would have carried a maximum sentence of life imprisonment.[3]

Because of his many crimes at sea, one would expect Willis to look like a storybook pirate captain, but he was the complete opposite. As the *New York Times* stated, Willis was the "personification of dignity" and the "typical old line sea captain, with trim gray goatee and almost majestic bearing."[4] He had remarkable skill in eluding charges, despite the lack of goodwill of the crews which served under him. In the Virginia case two of his engineers gave the most damning testimony against him at a preliminary hearing.

A few days before Willis was shot, the grand jury met in the Federal Building in New York and not one of the fourteen witnesses showed up. US Marshals and investigators were put on the trail and the next day they found the waterfront hotel where all fourteen had been registered the night before. However, the trail ended there, and the men were gone.

The Justice Department's agents who arrested Willis on June 11, 1927 told reporters that they believed he was the owner of the steamer *Trader*, also known as the *Turner*, which was seized in the Narrows a few days earlier. Aboard the ship were 12,000 cases of liquor and 7,500 gallons of Scotch malt. The agents captured Willis in Boston when he arrived as a passenger aboard the Holland-America liner *Veendam*. They found two pistols and a dirk (a long, straight-bladed dagger) on him at the time.[5]

The 322-foot long steamer *Trader*, a.k.a. *Turner*, became a rum ship in the 1920s and was one of a fleet of whalebacks built at Superior, Michigan around 1892. The old ship had also gone by the names *Blue Hill*, *Presidente Estrada*, *Yuma*, and *Cabrera*. Captain McDougal of Duluth, Minnesota designed the ship to carry iron ore. Freshwater sailors knew the whalebacks, a few of which continued to travel the Great Lakes, as "pigs" because of their shape. By the 1920s, shipbuilders were no longer making these ships.[6]

The *Turner*, a 2,194-ton vessel of American registry, was classified as a pirate ship under international maritime law. When the Coast Guard captured the ship in the Narrows, between Staten Island and Brooklyn, it was carrying a liquor cargo worth $350,000. The US Government held the ship's captain, Thomas E. Kirk, and the crew aboard as prisoners, and they were kept under watch as the ship sat anchored near the Statue of Liberty.[7]

The Coast Guard had been trying to catch the *Turner* for quite a while, but it managed to evade them along the New Jersey and Long Island coasts. Customs records indicated that the *Turner* sailed from Halifax, Nova Scotia on June 6 under the name *Trader*. Apparently, the name *Trader* was painted out and *Turner* was painted on its bow and stern while the ship was en route to New York. Because of the many unauthorized name changes, the vessel was officially classified as a pirate ship.

US Commissioner Garret W. Cotter released twenty-six of the thirty-five crew members who were arrested on June 19 following the seizure. Their attorney, Louis Halle, pleaded that they should not be held as there was no proof that they had knowledge of the liquor aboard the ship. Assistant US Attorneys Herman T. Stichman and Robert Watts asked that all the men be held on charges of conspiracy to import liquor into the United States. However, that motion was denied.[8]

On the morning of January 25, 1928, members of the federal jury, selected for the Willis conspiracy case, left their homes thinking they would be back in time for dinner. However, at 4:30 PM, they found out that they would be held incommunicado, unable to see their families or attend to personal or business affairs for two weeks or more. The jurors threw a fit and began yelling. They did quiet down eventually, but when Judge Morris retired to his chambers, the jury burst out in louder clamor than ever. The jurors complained of family or business affairs that would become badly complicated by a two week's absence without prior warning.

Later on, the judge allowed the jurors to briefly visit their families under the escort of deputy US Marshals. After saying farewell, the jurors were confined to the Hotel Martinique when they were not in court. On the first day of jury duty, the members were ushered into Judge Morris' courtroom, where they learned that Captain Willis, Max Gordon, and three others were about to go on trial for conspiracy to violate the Prohibition law. Judge Morris of New Hampshire was sent to New York to help relieve court congestion.[9]

The Trial

Captain Kirk was the government's chief witness in the Willis conspiracy trial. On the stand, he told the court that he had been a sea captain for twenty-eight years, and that he commanded the *Trader* when it sailed into New York harbor with a liquor cargo hidden under scrap iron. After further liquor smuggling ventures not connected with the *Trader*, Kirk finally came to take the $7 a day job from the government as its witness. He was disgruntled because his fellow conspirators failed to pay him his full wages.[10]

Kirk gave an ultimatum to Louis Halle, chief defense counsel in the case, just before going to the prosecution. He told Halle that he would not testify if the other defendants just paid him the $700 he was due. He quoted Halle as telling him that other "squealers" had been shot, an excellent way to convince a key witness not to testify. On cross examination, Kirk stated that he did not fear for his life.

Kirk brought four of the five defendants into his testimony. Captain Willis, Kirk said, approached him at Halifax to take over the boat at St. Pierre, Miquelon, where it had gone to complete its cargo onload prior to sailing for Japan with scrap iron. There, he relieved Captain Bickford, who testified for the prosecution on the previous day. He discussed the route with Max Gordon, and was instructed to take orders from Al Contendo and "Lefty" Clayton, also defendants, while at sea.

These two, he testified, told him to sail straight to New York, where he was to go straight up the harbor into the East River and dock at the third open pier he came to on the Manhattan side. It was at this point, he claimed, that he realized that he was smuggling liquor. He then ordered the name *Turner* to be painted over the real name of the vessel as a disguise.

When it was brought out in cross examination that Kirk had known he was violating the law, he replied that he was not an American citizen. Halle then pointed out that according to Boatswain Leonard T. Jones, the Coast Guardsman who led the capture, Kirk said he wished he had run away and shot the pursuing Coast Guardsmen "full of holes." However, Kirk denied he had said this.[11]

Under cross examination by Joseph Shalleck, counsel for the defendant Contento, Kirk confessed to his illegal activities. Kirk admitted that he had smuggled liquor into the US since the venture of the *Trader*. Shalleck also asked Captain Kirk if he had ever killed a man.

"Yes," Kirk replied, "in subduing a mutiny on the high seas. That was legalized killing permitted by British law in case of necessity at sea."[12]

Captain Willis told a different story about the *Trader* venture. He claimed that he had never known that Kirk had taken command of the vessel and had never hired him for that purpose. Willis said that Captain Bickford, another government witness, had remained in command with Kirk aboard as supercargo. Willis also claimed that the liquor was intended for Vera Cruz, Mexico, and the scrap iron for Japan. Under his orders, the ship should have continued on to Vera Cruz at the time Kirk brought it to New York. Without naming names, Willis said that there had been a conspiracy between someone on the *Trader* and a relative in the Coast Guard, and the attempted landing at New York was made in order to obtain prize money for the capture.[13]

Assistant US Attorney Kerwin attacked the plausibility of Willis' story on cross-examination. Scrap iron is a heavy cargo and requires a lot of extra fuel to transport. Kerwin argued that to carry the scrap iron from the southern coast of the United States to Canada, then back to Vera Cruz, and again back to Newfoundland and then across the Atlantic and through the Suez Canal to Japan, would have resulted in a heavy loss, and could hardly be considered a creditable explanation of the ship's journey.

The government rested its case shortly before 4 o'clock and the defense motions to dismiss the charges were denied. The jury reached its verdict at 11:30 PM. Captain Willis and Max Gordon were found guilty of conspiracy to violate the Prohibition law. They were sentenced to two years each in the Atlanta Federal Penitentiary and fined $1,000 each. James "Lefty" Clayton was sentenced to eight months in Westchester Penitentiary. Al Contento and Donald Kent were acquitted by the jury.

Captain Kirk was released from jail before the trial as a reward for agreeing to testify for the government. He was not charged with any crime and there was nothing to stop him from resuming his career as a rum-smuggler.

33

Canada Opens the Floodgates

Prohibition in Ontario, Canada came to an end on May 15, 1927. Ontario is the part of Canada that covers the border from New York State to Minnesota. During the previous year, G. Howard Ferguson was elected Premier of Ontario on the platform of ending Prohibition. More specifically, his party sought government control of liquor sales.[1]

When the news was broadcast via radio and printed in newspapers that Ontario liquor stores would open on May 16th, Americans flooded into Detroit from every direction. Hotel rooms were sold out from Windsor, Canada to Niagara Falls, 300 miles away. Since many of America's streets were still unpaved, Detroit's streets were filled with dusty and mud-splattered cars bearing license plates from dozens of states. Some Americans drove a thousand miles just to enjoy a legal, high quality drink after seven years of Prohibition. However, at the last minute there was a disastrous hitch. The Ontario Liquor Commission announced that it had not yet completed arrangements to open government stores and the sale of alcohol would be postponed for another two weeks. A farmer from Salina, Kansas said in response:

> "Gosh, here I have been driving a week on the worst roads I ever saw, dodging the Mississippi flood and taking my vacation early so as to be on hand for this party, and they are not even ready. How can I wait around here? My crops need tending now and I've got to get back home. Guess I'll have to look up a bootlegger and hold my party anyway."[2]

Under the new law, the government would have a monopoly over liquor sales, both foreign and domestic stock. No private businesses would be allowed to sell liquor, meaning that no bars or restaurants would be allowed to serve alcohol. Liquor could only be consumed in hotel guest rooms or residences after buying it from a government store.

The Ontario government insisted on getting every dollar of profit in the business. Those who purchased the liquor from government stores and then resold it would be considered bootleggers, but only if they sold it in Ontario. The sentence for the first offense of bootlegging was six months in jail without bail. The sentences were more severe for repeat offenders.[3]

Under the new laws, the government kept track of each customer's purchases on their liquor permit. Quebec had a similar law at the time, which allowed a buyer to purchase one bottle or package of hard liquor at a time. In contrast, there was no limit as to how much liquor one could buy in Ontario. A man could fill his entire vehicle with cases of liquor and drive away legally. The Ontario law allowed customers to drive vehicles filled with liquor into the United States and had no penalties for selling liquor south of the border.[4]

American tourists could buy liquor permits immediately upon arrival in Ontario, valid for thirty days, renewable each month for a $2 fee. In anticipation of the coming liquor flood, Ontario's government printed one million blank permits, expecting to make a $2 million profit within the first year on permits alone.[5]

At first, the government entertained the idea of keeping the stores open for a limited number of hours every day, but officials decided that it would only drive more business to bootleggers after hours. Stores in large cities, such as Toronto, would stay open until midnight.

Ontario's government sought not only a huge profit from a liquor monopoly, but also sought to put an end to bootlegging within the borders of that province. Bootleggers had become a menace in Ontario and forcing them to make their sales elsewhere made sense. What did not make sense was restricting where people could drink. One thing the new laws did not take into account was the demand for places where people could meet, be entertained, and get drunk. So, while the law was well thought out to crush illegal sales of liquor within Ontario, it did nothing to address the problem of speakeasies.

In the first week after Ontario ended its Prohibition, smugglers brought 40,000 cases of liquor into Detroit alone. By June 3, the liquor supply failed to keep up with the demand, so Ontario's government placed limitations on purchases. A customer could now only buy one case of liquor at a time and twenty-four quarts of beer at a time. Of course, there were many repeat customers. In a futile, token gesture,

Assistant Treasury Secretary Andrews added fifty men and a few speedboats to the patrol on the Detroit River.[6]

British liquor exporters turned their attention away from the Caribbean and began sending more of it to Canada. In the first seven months of 1927, British merchants sent 511,980 gallons of liquor to Canada, up from 345,475 gallons during the entire previous year.[7]

Official reports from the Dominion Department of Trade and Commerce showed that Canadian liquor was reaching Florida in large quantities. Since Canada did not prohibit liquor exports to the United States, most Canadian rum-runners had nothing to hide and declared to their customs officers exactly where they were taking their shipments. In fact, when ships were in Canadian ports loading up with liquor, they were no longer rum-runners— they were legitimate cargo ships carrying goods legally. On the Canadian side, shipping companies no longer had to pay bribes to police or load their cargo under the cover of darkness. They could now load unlimited amounts of liquor onto their ships in broad daylight without having to worry about doing jail time. During the fiscal year 1927, which in Canada ended in March, merchants legally shipped out more than $24 million of liquor. Of that amount, $22 million of liquor was declared to be destined for the United States.[8]

In August, Assistant Treasury Secretary Seymour Lowman[15] declared that Detroit presented "the most critical condition in law enforcement in the country." Lowman made Michigan its own enforcement district, separating it from Ohio. He told the press that his new plan would plug the hole in the border which allowed rum to flow in from Canada. While local Detroit officials welcomed the federal help, the consensus was that nothing would make Detroit dry. Police Commissioner William P. Rutledge told reporters that "Detroit cannot be made dry in thirty days or thirty years."[9]

Citizens of Detroit complained that federal Prohibition officers were using their guns way too often and Detroit's representatives in Congress made protests in Washington. During that month, charges were pending against two federal officers for running down two men aboard a motor boat without stopping to give aid.[10]

Lowman held conferences with Coast Guard Commandant Admiral Billard and Prohibition Commissioner James M. Doran in August to form a plan to stem the tide of Canadian liquor. Lowman

---

[15] There was more than one Assistant Treasury Secretary in 1927.

decided that the liquor patrol on the border should be given over exclusively to the Prohibition Bureau. Customs Collector Ferguson at Detroit was to be relieved of his work. Sumner C. Sleeper, recently in charge of the dry patrol in Maine, would take command of the region stretching from Buffalo to Lake Huron. Included in Lowman's plans was an expansion of the Prohibition patrol from 200 to 400 men, supplemented by a large number of Coast Guard patrol boats, especially speedboats.[11]

By 1930, the situation had not improved for those hoping to stop smuggling across the Canadian border. In that year, there were 1,000 separate smuggling roads from Canada into the US. The opportunities to smuggle liquor by boat were even more numerous. The Strait of Juan de Fuca, near Seattle, Washington, has 100 miles of coast and is only fifteen miles wide between Vancouver Island and the Olympic Peninsula. Liquor came through in tramp steamers, coal barges, and in sacks tied to the bottom of rowboats. Small boats made their way across the Niagara River into New York. Most small towns in Ontario on Lake Huron had at least one rum-running boat, which operated openly. An airplane crash in 1930 revealed a large smuggling ring transporting liquor by air from Canada.[12]

In the St. Lawrence Gulf, south of Newfoundland, are the small French islands of St. Pierre and Miquelon. They had a population of only 4,000 in 1930, yet about $4 million worth of liquor was shipped there yearly from Canada. From there, the rum was smuggled into the US. The legal Canadian exports of liquor amounted to about $30 million per year.[13] Although the United States Government put pressure on Canada to criminalize liquor exports, the Canadian government could not ignore the great amount of revenue generated by the liquor trade. There was very little motivation for the Canadian government to pass unpopular laws from another country onto its own people.

Escalating Violence

Although business was easy for rum-runners on the Canadian side of the border, it became increasingly dangerous on the American side. The Treasury Department, which had received much public criticism for lax enforcement, decided to escalate the Rum War on the Great Lakes. One example of the escalating violence happened near Buffalo on October 23, 1927. The Coast Guard spotted a suspected rum-runner at the lighthouse off Sturgeon Point in Lake Erie. When the cabin cruiser refused to stop, the Coast Guard riddled it with bullets. The smugglers ran the prow of their boat into a dock, damaging the hull. Two men managed to jump ashore and escape.[14]

The remaining man aboard was Willard Goff, 21 years old. He was alone on board when the Coast Guard shot him. Somehow he managed to escape and make his way back to Canada, where he was picked up by a motorist and brought to a hospital. When the Coast Guard seized the boat, they found 318 cases of ale. Goff told the hospital surgeons that he had been beaten over the head by hijackers and it was not until the following day that they discovered the bullet wound. [Not a very thorough examination on the doctor's part.] Goff became unconscious and died the next day.[15]

34

Bravery in Action

On February 20, 1927, a gale came from the Atlantic that ravaged the northeastern United States. During high tide on that morning, huge waves of thirty or forty feet smashed against some parts of Long Island and the New Jersey Shore. Sea water swept away piers and jetties, tore up boardwalks and sidewalks, knocked down houses and bungalows, tossed boats like toys, submerged railroads, highways, and streets and drove thousands of people from their homes and communities.

Atlantic City was hit very hard by 80-mile per hour winds, which caused the beach to flood and swamped twenty blocks of the city. In Staten Island, two policemen were injured and two nearly drowned while rescuing residents from flooded bungalows along the South Shore. In many other places, police, firemen, and civilians made daring rescues using rowboats to get people out of their homes.[1]

Freezing weather made the storm even worse by turning it into a fierce blizzard. Phone, power, and telegraph lines snapped under the weight of the ice. Sandy Hook, NJ, where a key Coast Guard station was located, lost communication with the outside world. Rough seas caused many ships to be stuck out at sea to ride the high waves.

Some of the worst scenes of damage were at Long Beach, Long Island where the gigantic waves were so powerful that they picked up fourteen houses and carried them out to sea. The Long Beach boardwalk was badly damaged and the streets of the town were so severely flooded that residents could not reach the rest of Long Island by automobile.

Rum Ship Wrecked

One casualty of the storm was a rum ship. At 2 AM off Bayville, Long Island, a two-masted schooner named the *W.T. Bell* ran aground in the storm. The 40-year-old ship was stranded about 100 feet from the summer estate of Winslow S. Pierce, lawyer and financier. The Bayville Fire Department responded to distress signals from the ship and got them ashore before daybreak by using a "boatswain's chair" rigged up on the ship with some lumber, rope, and block and tackle. The townspeople of Bayville took in the almost-frozen men, gave them dry clothing and warm drinks and food. The men thanked them and told the good Samaritans that they would go out to take a look at their ship.

Several hours later, they had still not returned. Some of the townspeople went out to see if they were attempting to save their vessel, but the crew was nowhere to be found. The waves were still pounding the schooner against the shore. Several adventurous men got a boat and went out to the stranded ship only to find that there was no one aboard. However, they did find that the schooner was fully loaded with twenty-five-gallon kegs, stamped "blended whisky, Newfoundland."

The news got out to everyone except the police. On the following morning, residents of Bayville spent several hours throwing kegs overboard and allowing the tide to carry them close to shore. Dozens of men waded out in the freezing water to guide the kegs ashore.

The free-for-all did not last for long. Soon, two gangs of bootleggers from Oyster Bay got news of the liquor. They came with trucks and started removing the barrels efficiently. Unloading liquor was, after all, their full-time profession. But they did not bother the townspeople who wanted a keg for their personal use. During the course of that day, 200 kegs, containing about 5,000 gallons, were gone. By nightfall, much of the liquor was removed, or so most people thought.[2]

The county police took charge of the boat later in the evening, sending away anyone who remained in the area and standing guard with machine guns to prevent a raid by bootleggers on whatever was left. During the next few days, Prohibition agents discovered that small craft were busily picking up floating kegs of malt extract, which bootleggers used to make "night club scotch." The agents notified William Sanders, Surveyor of the Port, who dispatched the Coast Guard Cutter *Manhattan* to unload the wreck. As the old wooden ship was being pounded to pieces, agents and Coast Guardsmen unloaded 339 sixteen-gallon kegs of extract, worth $216,690 wholesale. The malt extract was taken to the Brooklyn Army base, where it was supposedly poured into the river, or at least that was the official story.[3]

ALCOHOL, BOAT CHASES, AND SHOOTOUTS!

Coast Guard Patrol Boat Fights the Storm

Illness had sent Edward S. Cronin to the Chelsea Marine Hospital in Boston several days before the storm. His illness turned out to be a stroke of good luck because his shipmates wound up sailing out into the storm. The blizzard had been blowing for thirty hours when the 75-foot Patrol Boat 238 dropped its two anchors in hopes of riding it out. As the ship sat anchored off Provincetown, Massachusetts, the blinker flashed a message ashore that its engines and radio were disabled. At 5 PM, the towerman at Highland Station caught the distress signals. He shouted the message to his commander, who telephoned and radioed Base 5 in East Boston.

Two cutters and two destroyers left the harbor and headed straight into the gale-force winds. The crews of these vessels worked strenuously for hours to force their ships through 50 miles of rough seas. Meanwhile, the shore crews of the Highland, Peaked Hill, and Race Point Stations gathered on the beach with guns and breeches buoys,[16] ready to shoot the life-saving devices to their fellow Coasties.[4]

The blinker light stopped its signals. The men ashore hoped it meant that the vessel was no longer in distress. The men strained to see the boat in the fierce snowstorm. The vessel was still there at 3 AM, being tossed about by colossal waves. A steamer came past, possibly a passenger ship. The Coast Guard station signaled frantically in hope of drawing the steamer's attention to the patrol boat. In 1927, radio communication aboard ships was very new and expensive technology, so most ships were communicating through light flashes, flags, horn blasts, etc. The steamer most likely did not see the signals and moved on. Or, the steamer may have had passengers aboard and would not risk the lives of its passengers by going so close to shore.

Soon afterward, before any rescue craft appeared, the PT 238 was no longer in sight. The sea had snapped its anchor cables and rushed the boat to the beach at High Head, where it slammed down and rolled over. Then, the waves picked the boat up and hurled it again and again, smashing it to pieces. Men who saw the wreckage said that the only thing

---

[16] A breeches buoy is a crude rope-based device used to rescue people from wrecked vessels. This device resembles a round personal flotation device, or 'life saver,' with leg harnesses attached. It was shot from a large gun or propelled by a rocket to reach from ship to shore, or vice-versa.

to come ashore in one piece was the gun, which was mounted on the fore-deck.

Soon, two bodies washed up on the beach. The waiting rescue team grabbed them before the waves pulled them back into the Atlantic. Boatswain's Mates Raymond Clark and Charles Freeburn were dead. Throughout the morning, the men of Highland Station struggled to save whoever may have survived. Unfortunately, all six of the other men aboard the patrol boat died.[17]

The bigger ships, which made a bold effort to rescue Patrol Boat 238, did not escape undamaged. The *Paulding* reported back by radio that several of its boats and its small antennae had been carried away. The destroyer *Jouette* had been forced to lie-to while an overheated bearing was repaired.

The Fearless Ensign Duke

On the night of July 4, 1927, Coast Guard Ensign Charles L. Duke was patrolling New York Harbor on the tiny launch CG 2327 with a crew of two men. The new German liner *New York* was anchored off Quarantine, where it stopped for a Customs inspection. Another vessel, hiding behind the German ship, did not stop. Ensign Duke noticed the same dirty, salt-caked ship creeping along the Bay Ridge shore earlier. The ship turned out to be the British freighter *Greypoint*, renamed the *Economy*. Running two dim lights, the freighter proceeded past Quarantine, up the Narrows, and toward the upper bay. Duke was suspicious. He said in a later interview, "It had that rum-runner look. You'd think they would be wise and paint their boats, but they always pick out the worst old tubs for their rum ships. I can tell one almost every time."[5]

Ensign Duke was no rookie. He served in the US Navy during the Great War. During that time, he was assigned to destroyer duty in Europe. After he was discharged in 1921, he joined the staff of the *Washington Star*. He remained in the newspaper business for four years, leaving it to join the Coast Guard. His first assignment was aboard the cutter *Gresham* with the rank of ensign. Duke received his commission

---

[17] Those six men were: Cook Alexander Clarence of Greenville, S.C.; Coxswain Leo Kryzabowski of South Chicago; Fred McCausland of Portland, Maine; Mechanic Joseph Maxim of Dorchester, Mass.; Chief Mechanic's Mate Cornelius Shea of Roxbury, Mass.; and the skipper, Boatswain Jesse K. Rivenback of Oak Bluffs, Mass.

while the Coast Guard was going through a great expansion and in need of officers. Later, he was assigned to the floating headquarters at Stapleton, Staten Island.[6]

Duke steered his launch in the wake of the suspicious freighter and got close enough to read the ship's name, *Economy*. He hailed the vessel and told its captain to heave to, but was ignored. From the zigzag course the ship was taking, Duke figured the pilot did not know New York Harbor. He hailed the vessel again, and this time got an answer. "I'm going to dock at Greenville," someone yelled from the ship. "If you want me, you can find me there. I don't intend to stop now."[7]

In response, the ensign sped through the waves in his little boat until he was alongside the freighter's bow. He fired two warning shots with his pistol, but the freighter kept going. Battling 40-mile winds, the tiny Coast Guard launch was poking its nose into every wave, showering the men inside with cold saltwater. Duke, now thoroughly drenched and cold, stood up on the bow while his two-man crew maneuvered the launch closer to the freighter. The waves tossed the tiny boat around as it got closer to the ship, nearly colliding with the side.

While both vessels were still moving, Duke grabbed the freighter's rail and climbed aboard. He knew how defenseless he was, with only a few bullets in his pistol and a flashlight. He had no idea how many men were aboard or what weapons they had. Bluffing, he turned to Chief Boatswain's Mate Madsen and said in a loud voice, "If I'm not out of that pilot house in two minutes, you turn the machine gun on them."[8]

Madsen knew the launch had no gun, but he nodded and acknowledged the fake order loudly. Searching the dark ship with his flashlight, Duke cautiously entered the deckhouse. A burly seaman appeared and said, "Where do you think you're going?" Duke answered by hitting him in the head with the butt of his pistol, sending the big man to the deck unconscious.

There was one more flight of stairs to the bridge and Duke was in a rush to reach the captain. If the boat reached a pier, the crew could have easily escaped. As he reached the bridge, he found six men huddling in corners. In the cabin he found the captain, who was intent on reaching the New Jersey shore.

"You'll stop this ship or I'll pull the trigger," Duke told him as he pressed the pistol against the captain's ribs. The captain was stubborn and argued with Duke. He claimed that he did not know he had already passed Quarantine. Ensign Duke asked where his Customs stamp was and why the boat reeked of alcohol. He ordered the captain to reverse his course so that Prohibition authorities could seize the ship near the Statue of Liberty.[9]

The captain disregarded the order and the ensign poked the pistol against his ribs again. Duke grabbed the wheel himself and swung the ship around. The ship jolted as it ran aground in ten feet of water. Wasting no time, Duke herded the six men on the bridge together and ordered them below decks. The Coast Guard launch was not equipped with a wireless radio. (At the time, wireless radios were new and expensive technology.) So, Duke ordered his two men to speed to the Statue of Liberty to get some help. A suspicious looking speedboat was circling the *Economy*, most likely pilots who were waiting to tell the captain where to land the liquor.

While Duke was looking for something to barricade the door with, a young seaman begged him to be lenient on his captain. Duke, the former newspaper writer, found little use for words on this day. He smashed his flashlight against the boy's face, giving him a black eye and gashing his forehead.

Meanwhile, the two Coast Guardsmen were speeding to the Army barracks at Bedlow's Island. When they reached the Statue of Liberty after midnight, the soldiers refused to let them use the telephone. They had to cross the river to the Barge Office where help was sent at once. Instead of going to Robbins Reef, where the boat ran aground, the Coast Guardsmen went to Weehawken and followed the west shore until they found the *Economy*.

The cutter *Calumet* arrived on the scene at 2 AM, but could not get close in the shallow water. Patrol Boat 122 went aground on the mud flats and Patrol Boat 143 came very close to running aground. It was not until 6 AM that the first help came to Ensign Duke. He did not get off the ship until four hours later, when guards had been sent aboard to watch the crew. He went back to Staten Island, where he reported to his commanding officer at 11 AM. Lieutenant Commander E.D. Jones told the press:

> "He looked as unruffled as if he were just coming down to breakfast after a sound sleep. His uniform was bedraggled from the salt water, and he needed a shave. But you would never have imagined that that man had been on duty continuously for twenty-six hours."[10]

Commander Jones told him to hit the rack and allowed no one to disturb him before 5 PM. When he awoke, he told the story to reporters as he sat next to his pretty, blue-eyed wife, whom he had been married to for fifteen months. "I wish he wouldn't do things like that," she said. "It's kind of risky, jumping on boats like that, all alone."[11]

The *Economy,* also known as the *Greypoint,* remained stuck in the mud for a few days. It turned out that there were actually 22 men aboard— Duke captured them almost single-handedly. The vessel was carrying 3,000 fifty-gallon drums of alcohol, worth $500,000.[12]

****

About a month after Ensign Duke made his daring raid, another Coast Guardsman showed his bravery in action. The New York Police Department had received tips that led them to believe that the former property of the Downey Shipbuilding Corporation, on Richmond Terrace in Staten Island, was a rum-running base. The vacant property had not been used as a shipyard for about a year and more than one rum-runner had used it as a safe landing base without the knowledge of anyone connected with the property.[13]

Rookie Patrolman Ferdinand Dauria, of the St. George Precinct, was on bicycle patrol near the property on the night of August 12. At 1:30 AM he saw four covered trucks moving in the direction of the gate to the property. When he saw them enter the gate, he followed them and noticed a large group of men standing around on a pier. Just off shore was the ship *Ansonia.*

Officer Dauria knew that he could not capture them all single handedly, so he rode his bicycle to the Elizabethport ferry and telephoned headquarters at St. George. He then returned to watch the men on the pier. Soon, Captain George Ferrie and a team of ten patrolmen and two detectives were en-route. Also on the way were the Coast Guard picket boat 3321, the police boat *Gypsy,* and police patrol boat 4 from Manhattan.

When Captain Ferrie's team arrived, they moved in on the men with pistols drawn. The smugglers did not put up a fight. However, the police found out that the *Ansonia* had not been able to tie up to the pier, because of the low tide, and was steaming down the Kill van Kull tidal strait. The ship had gone too far out to be stopped from the shore, so the police just rounded up the dock workers and brought them to the precinct station.

The police had reason to believe that someone had told the *Ansonia* that the police were on the way. While the ship was plowing down the Kill van Kull, the Coast Guard and police boats were speeding toward Mariner's Harbor on the lookout for any suspicious vessel. In a desperate rush to escape, the *Ansonia* crashed head-on into a barge, cutting twenty feet off the barge's bow and throwing the one man aboard into the water. He was able to swim to shore, but the freighter did not bother stopping to help.

Boatswain George K. Lomis, aboard picket boat 3321, spotted the *Ansonia* off New Brighton, Staten Island. He swung his boat around to the freighter's portside amidships. The picket boat's bow was high above the water and the heavily-laden rum ship's deck was not much higher.

While both vessels were moving alongside one another, Lomis leaped, caught the rail, and swung himself onto the freighter's deck. With a pistol in hand, he mounted the bridge, where four men were waiting for him. When he asked them who the captain was, they replied that they did not know. Unable to get any information, Lomis turned to the man at the wheel and ordered him to steer the ship to a point near the Statue of Liberty. The helmsman obeyed. At that moment, one of Lomis' crew members appeared on the bridge for backup. Lomis told him to watch the men and make sure the man at the wheel followed orders. Lomis then went and searched the rest of the ship alone. After finding men scattered all over the ship, he herded the entire crew on the main deck. When he asked who the captain was, the crew again pretended not to know.

The *Ansonia* hit a sandbar just before reaching Robbin Reef Lighthouse, but was able to pull off under its own steam. After the ship had been brought to anchor, Lomis sent his picket boat back to Staten Island with information about the capture. He also sent word to Customs officials, who boarded the Ansonia later in the day. There were between 7,000 and 10,000 cases of liquor, worth $500,000, aboard the ship, which was anchored alongside the *Sebastopol*, captured the day before with a cargo worth $300,000.[14]

Shootout With Customs Agents

Like the Coast Guard, US Customs received fire from both smugglers and politicians. The fire from smugglers, of course, was less complicated to deal with. The job of Customs officers during Prohibition was no less dangerous than that of the Coast Guard. One incident that illustrates this point happened during November 1927. Three Customs men— John McAdams, Robert Ennis, and Thomas Lanning— had received a tip that smugglers were landing goods at Pier 99 at the foot of West 55th Street in Manhattan.[15]

On the night of the 17th, a warehouse was on fire two blocks away from the pier. The Customs agents figured that the smugglers would seize the opportunity to bring in their goods while the neighborhood's attention was focused on the fire. At 11 PM, the three men hid in the shadows of the pier and waited three hours before they heard the sound of motors. The agents saw two launches approach the edge of the pier and circle out into the river a few times.[16]

When the launches finally tied up alongside the French freighter *Caracoli*, dozens of men left the small boats and entered the ship's side. McAdams and his fellow agents tried to move in on the pier undetected, but were spotted by lookouts who gave the alarm and began shooting. Bullets flew between the three agents and the smugglers, who were clustered around the liquor at the stern. The smugglers jumped over the side of the ship and into the launches tied up alongside. The agents did, however, capture the last two smugglers as they prepared to jump over the side.[17]

After the excitement was over, Agent Ennis felt blood running down his face. A bullet had grazed his temple. Fortunately, the wound was not serious and he was able to return to work the next day.[18]

35

A Bad Year For Customs

On January 8, 1928, Representative LaGuardia made public his most recent letter to Secretary Mellon. In the letter, LaGuardia reiterated his previous claims that passengers on steamships were using cancelled Customs stamps to smuggle liquor ashore. He recommended an additional 750 Customs guards for the Port of New York and similar increases in all other ports.[1]

The New York Congressman said that he had turned his evidence over to the Collector of Customs and had refused to give it to New York's Prohibition Administrator because he had no confidence in that office. LaGuardia also claimed that smugglers had been in contact with the Prohibition Unit. On the day he met with Customs officials, there were 200 steamers and 44 sailing vessels in port with only 100 Customs men to check them. He added that the pay of Customs guards was "disgracefully low" and should be raised immediately.[2]

Within a day, the Coast Guard released its data on New York's liquor seizures for 1927. During that year, Customs, the Coast Guard, and marine police seized a total of forty six ships, only one less than the year before. Those seized ships carried between 1.2 and 1.5 million quarts of liquor. Much of the seized liquor was whisky malt. This figure of seized ships completely discredited any claims by government officials that New York's Rum Row was gone.[3]

New York Prohibition Administrator Maurice Campbell told reporters that he knew nothing about the tabulation of liquor seizures. Although previous administrators had taken an active role in planning with Coast Guard and Customs officials, Campbell's attitude about ship seizures at sea was that they were outside of his province and he knew nothing about them.[4]

In response to LaGuardia's report, Assistant Treasury Secretary Lowman visited New York to personally investigate the situation. While Lowman admitted that some liquor may have leaked in because of the small number of Customs officers, he discounted the idea that there was wholesale smuggling at the port. Oddly, Lowman made no plans to visit Prohibition Administrator Campbell.[5]

Campbell did not increase his activities against smuggling after LaGuardia's report and did not launch any kind of investigation. Customs, on the other hand, placed additional guards on liners in the port. As a result of this increased effort, Customs men seized 260 bottles of cognac after they were passed through a porthole of the French liner *Paris* to a barge lying alongside. The *Paris* liquor seizure occurred on January 14th, one day before the eighth anniversary of Prohibition. On that day in New York City, officers arrested six men and seized $14,000 worth of liquor, two trucks, and a barge—very small numbers when you consider the scale of rum-running and bootlegging in New York.[6]

The day after Prohibition's eight-year anniversary, Lowman returned to Washington and he officially concluded that smuggling was rampant in New York because of the inadequacy of the Customs force. Fifty million dollars worth of diamonds were slipping into the country each year via an international smuggling ring. Lowman added that "some" liquor was being smuggled into the port, but he found no evidence of a conspiracy between Customs guards and smugglers. He argued that New York was no longer the main entry point for liquor into the US because most of the liquor now came in through the Canadian border. Official Canadian reports disclosed that $23 million dollars worth of liquor crossed the border during 1927.[7]

To make matters worse, robberies were on the increase at the docks. Lowman declared that it was impossible for Customs authorities to deal with the situation with their tiny force. He told reporters he would recommend an additional 450 Customs guards for the New York district and an additional appropriation of $480,000. At the time, the Customs force of that district included 437 men. However, those men were also tasked with guarding the docks in Jersey City, Yonkers, Brooklyn, the Bush Terminal, and the Erie Basin. Anyone familiar with those sites today, some of which are now abandoned, would realize the massive scale of ship, rail, and truck traffic that came through those ports and the impossible task Customs men faced in screening it for contraband.[8]

****

In July 1928, Federal Prohibition Commissioner James M. Doran announced that the Coast Guard had broken up Rum Row. While he did not reveal the source of his figures, he stated that in 1927 more than 14 million gallons of liquor had been shipped from foreign ports to the United States and that the quantity shipped during the fiscal year of 1928 had dropped to about 5 million gallons. However, he omitted the amount of liquor shipped to Canada, the Caribbean, and Mexico, which was obviously bound for the US.[9]

The searches conducted by Customs men on passenger liners were very unpopular. In August, Representative Emmanuel Celler sent an angry letter to Assistant Treasury Secretary Lowman, whom he mistakenly addressed as the Prohibition Commissioner:

> Once again custom agents insultingly examined visitors to the French Line pier on the departure of the S.S. La France. This is a repetition of the frisking and the slapping of thighs of visitors to the French Line pier. I, for one, will not stand idly by and allow, without vigorous protest, this rank indignity to become a custom. With rare tact you single out the French Line as the recipient of your attention. I predict that our State Department will soon hear from the French Government.
>
> What right does your patrol presume to frisk promiscuously, and without reasonable suspicion, these victims, forcing women to open their handbags and discard their wraps, compelling men to loosen their outer garments? Permit me to offer my sincerest congratulations upon the success of your gargantuan effort: two bottles discovered, 2,000 citizens outraged. The mountain labored and brought forth a mouse. Once again our Constitution has been gloriously upheld![10]

Lowman countered by writing that Customs men actually seized twenty-six bottles from seventeen visitors and six from three crewmembers of the *France*. The number of visitors aboard was approximately 1,000, not 2,000. One Customs guard asked a woman if she had anything concealed in a coat she was carrying. She kicked him. Another man threatened to hit him with his cane. Part of Lowman's written response said:

> I have read with some amazement that "a mountain labored and brought forth a mouse." After the examination of the visitors to the Ile de France, a newspaper reporter called on

me and wished to know whether any special orders had been given with reference to the matter, and I told him that no such orders had been issued, but that it was perfectly legal for Customs agents to examine visitors to foreign vessels when they are landing again, for the purpose of finding out whether they carried any diamonds, narcotics or other merchandise that was being illegally brought into the country. The Customs Bureau, as you know, does not make the laws but we are charged with the duty of enforcing them.[11]

Mr. Celler replied by telling reporters:

"Apparently Mr. Lowman now admits the search is for liquor. Originally he fell back on the excuse that it was for the detection of smuggled diamonds and narcotics. The whole business is stupid and senseless, and naturally breeds sullen resentment of the citizenry. Furthermore, the practice is confined to the French lines. How about the other lines?

"This insulting examination on the piers is part and parcel of the general plan of the Republican Party to discredit New York. It will undoubtedly have the unforeseen effect of piling up huge majorities for Governor Smith. It is in line with the wire-tapping activities of the prohibition department, the contemplated use of poison gasses in padlocking proceedings, the shooting of innocent citizens like J.H. Hansen along the border by Coast Guardsmen and Mrs. Willebrandt's hippodrome methods in examining witnesses in the night club proceedings."[12]

36

Buffalo

At the end of March, 1928, Coast Guard officers in the Niagara frontier area were busy preparing for the most intensive drive yet against rum smugglers. Canadian liquor flowed in almost uninterrupted across Lakes Erie and Ontario and the Niagara River. Every day, rum runners loaded up at Port Dalhousie, Chippewa, Port Colborne, Fort Erie and Bridgeburg. Every night, the heavily-laden vessels chugged their way through ice floes to land their cargoes at secluded spots on the American shores. Each morning, the tired smuggling crews were back in their Canadian ports, their pockets full of US dollars.[1]

A small but efficient Coast Guard unit tried its best to fight the tide of liquor, but with little impact. While the Coast Guard managed to capture an occasional rum boat, for each capture there were dozens of boats that made it to their destinations along the 200-mile Niagara border. Occasionally, Customs stopped trucks loaded with smuggled Canadian liquor on waterfront highways. But hundreds of other trucks rolled on to the East Coast, where they successfully delivered their liquor.

The Coast Guard transferred Commander Martin W. Rasmussen to Buffalo from Atlantic City to lead the new campaign against smuggling. He made plans for a patrol fleet of 250 boats to drive rum-runners from local waters. His plan also included the use of airplanes to spot rum-runners and to watch loading operations in Canadian ports.

The campaign also included a system of radio communication never before used in anti-smuggling operations in the Buffalo area. Coast Guard boats were stationed in Lakes Erie and Ontario and the Niagara River near the loading bases of the rum-runners. Messages were flashed to the Coast Guard units as the smuggling craft left their docks. The fleet of Coast Guard craft was backed by boats used by the Customs patrol and the fleet of automobiles used by Customs and Immigration units. Rasmussen predicted that the result would be either the end of rum-running through captures of the bolder operators or courts-martial of Coast Guard officers who let the smugglers slip through the net.[2]

The smugglers were unfazed by the Coast Guard's saber rattling. On the Canadian side of the Niagara River and lower Lake Erie, many new rum boats were being built. Some were nearly ready for launching; others needed paint and hardware; and some were awaiting motors that were being built in American factories. Brewers and distillers had the largest orders ever for Canadian ale and liquor, mostly for export. Every day, train cars full of liquor were unloaded at the docks and then returned back to the breweries and distilleries to be reloaded.

Library of Congress
Buffalo, NY, Lafayette Square, circa 1925

Armored Rum-Runners

Meanwhile in nearby Toronto, Ontario, the smugglers were preparing a fleet of armored rum-runners. Previously, rum boats on the Great Lakes stood little chance against the American patrol boats, many of which were armed with machine guns. The new smuggling boats were bullet-proof (against small-arms fire) and faster than the government boats. The fastest rum patrol boats had a speed of thirty miles an hour, while the new armored rum-runners had a speed of about forty-two miles an hour. The men who operated these craft were expert lake sailors and mechanics.[3]

These fast new boats were powered by 450-horsepower engines and had extremely sharp bows, much like a modern speedboat. The boats were designed to carry large loads and sit low in the water, making them harder to spot and harder to shoot at. The steel in the new rum-runners was 1/8 of an inch thick and much thicker in some places to protect the crew. These forty-foot long vessels were built with an all-steel pilot house, with bullet-proof windows and steel hatches, which, when raised, gave protection to the pilot. For the crew inside, the cargo aboard gave them added protection from any rounds that managed to penetrate the hull.[4]

By early May, bootleggers of three states and Ontario were assembling a rum fleet larger and faster than anything assembled before in that region. Undaunted by the threats of local Coast Guard officials, the smugglers went ahead with their schemes to outwit the vast Coast Guard fleet, the vanguard of which had already begun to arrive in Buffalo. The rum smugglers coordinated to withdraw their boats from the Niagara River, where operations were conducted in the open, and concentrated their activities at Port Colborne and other ports along the lake front to Port Dover, forty miles away. Port Colborne became the new headquarters of the liquor ring, whose business was growing so rapidly that its business totaled several million dollars a year.[5] Due to the ice blockage of the local harbor, many boats had been operating out of Port Maitland, west of Port Colborne; however, when the ice thawed, the boats returned to Port Colborne and their operations began from there.

ALCOHOL, BOAT CHASES, AND SHOOTOUTS!

****

The government announced that the beginning of its new campaign against the Great Lakes smugglers would begin on May 21, 1928. On that day, the first vessels of the Coast Guard fleet, brought from the Atlantic Coast earlier in the month, would begin their activities on Lake Erie. Five of the largest Coast Guard cutters to ever operate on inland waters left the Black Rock channel entrance at Buffalo, where they had been blocked in by ice with ten other boats of the fleet since their arrival from New York. They moved up the Niagara River to take their stations along the river and at the outlet of Lake Erie. These 75-foot long cutters were propelled by two engines of 200-horsepower. They carried crews of eight men each were each equipped with machine guns and a one-pounder gun, which could blast holes in any of the new armored craft.[6]

In addition to the small patrol fleet already there, the district would also receive seventy additional boats as part of the plans laid out by Commander Rasmussen, Customs Collector Fred Bradley, and Assistant Treasury Secretary Seymour Lowman. In total, there would be 84 boats in the Buffalo area to fight rum smugglers.[7]

During the following month, thirty rum smugglers were arrested near Buffalo, ten boats were seized and twelve automobiles confiscated. Rum runners in the area were abandoning the use of large boats and resorting to rowboats to cut down on losses to the patrol. The large number of rowboats seized in June was clear proof of the new trend.[8]

In early July, Coasties shot at a private yacht named *Ticker*, which happened to have a couple of VIPs aboard. In response to the public outcry at yet another seemingly indiscriminate shooting, Lieutenant Wolf, commander of the Buffalo district, announced that there would be no investigation of the incident unless he received specific orders from Washington:

> "There is nothing that can be done. The *Ticker* is a typical rum-running craft, and when she was sighted Boatswain Burch fired two blanks, the signal to heave-to. When the signal was disregarded he opened fire with his one-pound cannon. In doing so he was entirely within his rights, in fact, he was obeying orders."[9]

Aboard the craft was Frank G. Raichle, law partner of Assistant US Attorney General William J. Donovan. Oops! Those aboard said the Coast Guard cutter fired without warning, several shells striking near the yacht, which flew an American flag and the flag of the Buffalo Yacht Club. During his conference with Lieutenant Wolf, Raichle asked that orders be issued to not fire on yachts or other craft until they were identified. Raichle told the lieutenant that if he did not comply with his request, he would bring the matter up to Washington officials. Raichle did not have to bother bringing up the matter with Washington officials, because the story was soon in *The New York Times*. He told *Times* reporters that if the Coast Guard did use signal guns, they were fired from a distance of at least two miles away, when the cutter was a mere speck on the horizon. At that distance, he said, the gun could not be heard unless there was a favoring wind.[10]

A few months later, a similar, but more tragic encounter occurred in Lake Ontario, six miles east of the Niagara River mouth. Coast Guard boat 2364 came across a suspicious craft that was cruising in the dark without lights. The unlit craft, named the *Bug*, ignored the Coast Guard's command to halt, so one of the Coasties opened fire with a machine gun.

One of the rounds hit the boat, glanced off, and tore through a cabin window to strike a man named Carl Anderson in the back of the head. He died as the bullet tore his skull open. The other man aboard, Edmund Sahr of Niagara Falls, was shot in the shoulder. He survived. After Anderson was killed, the *Bug* continued to plow through the water until Sahr crawled over his friend's dead body to shut the engine off. Sahr later told reporters that when the Coast Guard boat came alongside and found one of them dead and another wounded, they told him to stay in the craft and that they would get a doctor, which is highly unusual, considering that the duties of the Coast Guard include rescuing people at sea, administering first aid, and transporting casualties to shore. So either Sahr fabricated his story, or the Coasties left him there to die by bleeding to death.[11]

Sahr waited for an hour and then waded ashore and went to a nearby farmhouse. The farmer who owned the house took Sahr to a nearby doctor, who gave him first aid. They then transported him to the hospital and the police were notified. There, Under-Sheriff Irish and police Lieutenant Patrick Carmody took Sahr's statement. Sahr admitted that the boat was running without lights and that they did not stop when signaled to do so. Irish told reporters that a search of Anderson's clothing revealed several Canadian Customs clearance papers for ale and a bill of lading dated a couple days earlier for a consignment of 200 cases of ale. There was no contraband aboard the boat at the time of the shooting, but, Irish added, he did verify that the *Bug* cleared from Niagara-on-the-Lake during the previous night with 200 cases of ale aboard.[12]

Some readers may read the previous paragraph and begin to think that the shooting was justified. Yes, the evidence is overwhelming that the two men were engaged in rum-running, but does that justify the use of deadly force? No one claimed that the two rum smugglers fired weapons at the Coast Guard nor even *had* weapons in their possession. It is true that there was, and still is, a maritime statute that states that the Coast Guard may fire on a vessel that does not stop after being signaled to stop. The Coast Guard followed a policy of literally shooting first and asking questions later, and many people died or were seriously injured unnecessarily. It is true that many of the men the Coast Guard shot at were committing a felony, but would a court of law have sentenced a man to die for transporting and selling liquor? No. Fortunately, the rules have changed greatly since the 1920s and law enforcement officers may only shoot at a fleeing felon if that person has committed a dangerous felony and poses a risk to public safety. This is known as the "fleeing felon rule." Smuggling or selling contraband items would not fall into that category. During the first half of the 20th century, many unarmed people were gunned down by police as they fled the scenes of their crimes. The Coast Guard's policies during the 1920s were nothing but an extension of that policy to the coasts and waterways of the United States.

37

I'm Alone

One of the most notorious rum ships of the late 1920s was named *I'm Alone*. The ship operated mostly in the waters off the northeastern United States and, like many other vessels of the early 1900s, used a combination of sails and propellers. The captain, John T. Randell, was a daring if not completely reckless man. Captain Randell had a few unpleasant encounters with the Coast Guard during his brief career as a rum smuggler. One of those encounters had a spectacular, yet disastrous end that made the front pages of countless newspapers in several countries.

Captain Randell was a grizzled sea captain hardened by war. During the Great War (World War I), he received the Distinguished Service Cross after a sea fight. He achieved the rank of Lieutenant Commander in the British Navy. He also received the *Croix de Guerre* with two palms for his battle service, and, since the war, had distinguished himself as an Arctic explorer. In the summer of 1928, he commanded the schooner *Morso* to the so-called Barren Lands of the Arctic. When reporters asked him how he earned the Distinguished Service Cross, he replied, "Oh, I got into a mix-up off the coast of Norway, captured a couple of German ships and sank two or three more."[1]

Randell's brief career in rum-running was, without a doubt, a very bold one. His boldness, which served him well in the Royal Navy, proved disastrous in his battle of the wills with the US Coast Guard. The 49-year-old captain was born in Trinity, Newfoundland, and lived in Liverpool, Nova Scotia with his wife and two children. He had been a Canadian citizen since 1899. A master mariner, he carried a master's "C.O. and C." license, issued in England. Randell first learned about the *I'm Alone* two and a half years earlier when he read about the ship as a rum-runner in the newspaper. The firm of Robin, Jones, & Whitman of Lunenberg, NS bought the notorious rum-runner in the spring of 1928.

ALCOHOL, BOAT CHASES, AND SHOOTOUTS!

On November 10, 1928, the ship docked at St. Pierre and took on a cargo of approximately 1,400 cases of assorted liquors from the Great West Wine Company. Before clearing from St. Pierre, an employee of the wine company gave Randell a dozen torn halves of dollar bills. His instructions were to take his ship to a position thirty miles south of the Trinity Shoals light buoy off Louisiana. He was to deliver his cargo to the person who presented the other half of one of the dollar bills.

Soon, he cleared from St. Pierre for Belize, British Honduras, and took a detour to the buoy off Louisiana. Before he could unload his cargo, the Coast Guard Cutter *Walcott* spotted his ship and began to follow it. After 48 hours of being watched, Captain Randell decided to leave the area and go to Belize. He remained there for one or two days and cleared for Nassau with his entire liquor cargo still aboard.[2]

Of course, Randell did not take his ship to Nassau like his papers said and he went back to the same spot off the Louisiana coast. On a moonless night, a large motorboat came alongside. The skipper of the boat presented the missing half of one of the dollar bills and Randell delivered his entire liquor cargo to him without asking any questions. The *I'm Alone* then returned to Belize and took on another load of liquor, this time 2,600 cases. He returned to the same buoy and was met by a man in a motorboat who had the other half of the second dollar bill in the sequence. This time, the liquor cargo was loaded onto three different boats that came on different dates.

Captain Randell returned to Belize on March 6, 1929 and cleared with another cargo a week later. This time his ship's papers said he was going to Bermuda. He did not go to Bermuda, but went again to the buoy off Trinity Shoals, this time with a cargo of 2,800 cases. On the morning of March 20, Randell anchored at a spot he believed to be fourteen miles off shore. Shortly after daybreak, the *I'm Alone*'s crew spotted the Coast Guard Cutter *Walcott*. After the rum ship tried to flee, the cutter soon caught up.

The *Walcott*'s skipper ordered Randell to heave to. Randell replied, "Captain, you have no jurisdiction over me. I am on the high seas outside of treaty waters. I cannot and will not heave to."[3] The cutter then fired three or four blank shots and proceeded toward a tank steamer nearby. Soon, the cutter returned with the flag signal for "heave to." Randell replied with the flag signal for "no." The cutter came close and the cutter's commander said over the megaphone, "Captain, will you heave to?"

Randell answered, "No, you have no jurisdiction over me or my ship on the high seas."

"I would like to come on board and have a talk with you," the Coast Guard skipper announced.

Randell described what happened next to reporters:

"After talking with him through the megaphone for a few minutes, I decided to let him come on board. He came alongside after I had stopped my engines, with his gun crew ready to fire. I told him that I could only allow him to get on board if he came unarmed and not to have one of his guns trained on my ship in the meantime.

"We stopped and the captain of the Walcott came on board and talked with me for probably an hour and three-quarters, during which time he said to me, 'Captain, you made a mistake this morning.'

"I replied. 'What was that, sir?'

"He said, 'You threatened to shoot me or anybody that came on board.'

"I replied, 'Captain, nothing was further from my thoughts. I did not say such words. I can give you my word as an officer and a gentleman that I did not even think of such a thing or say it, and I can swear to you upon everything that I hold sacred that I did not say those words or have any intention of saying them.

"I said, 'Do you believe me? Will you take my hand and say that you believe what I said?'

"He replied, 'Yes, I believe it was just a mistake when you told me I could shoot if necessary.'

"We shook hands and the Captain left. That was roughly around 11:30 A.M. March 20.

"We then proceeded on southerly course at a speed of about seven and one-half knots. About 2 P.M. the Walcott again came up and said, with signals flying, 'Heave to, or I will fire.'

"I replied to him by megaphone that I had no intention of stopping and that he could fire if he wished.

"He said, 'I will give you a quarter of an hour to make up your mind.'

"We still kept on going and a few moments after the time expired the Walcott commenced firing. I do not know the number of shots fired. Several shots passed through our sails and rigging, and one shell passed through the flag which was flying from the time the cutter came up at first.

"After firing with his four-pounder a certain number of shots, he opened fire from his quarter ports with a machine gun, or a quick firing rifle. I presume these bullets had been waxed, as one hit me on the right leg just below the hip and partly paralyzed it.[4]

"I then noticed that he had some trouble with his four-pounder, as she misfired. He then dropped astern. We then proceeded on our course with the cutter trailing us until after dark. We were still making a southerly course.

"During the day of March 21 we headed south and cast all day and at evening we took down our sails and headed for a position about eighteen or twenty miles east of Alacran Reefs off the Mexican coast. By the morning of the 22nd the wind had increased to a moderate gale, a rough sea running.

"About 7:30 A.M., March 22, we saw another cutter approaching from the southwest. I was then in a position...about 215 miles south by east, roughly, from the entrance to New Orleans.

"When the second cutter came up we recognized her as the Dexter. She, after a conference with the Walcott, came up flying the signals, 'Heave to or I'll fire at you.'

"I replied by semaphore[*] and megaphone that I did not consider that he had any jurisdiction over me or my ship on the high seas, and that he could fire if he wished. He then commenced to fire shell after shell, first to my rigging and sails, and then opened fire from the bridge with several quick firing rifles. After about twenty shells had been fired, several of which hit the ship in various places, I semaphored to him after he had called to me and again said, 'Now will you heave to?' that he might fire and sink my ship but I refused to heave to.

"He then opened fire again both with rifles and guns, cutting my rigging adrift and shell after shell plunged into the ship through our bulwarks, smashing both my bulwarks to pieces and one shell went into the side of the ship.

"He again called to me 'Will you heave to?' I replied again in the negative.

---

[*] Semaphore is a system of signals in which two hand-held flags are used to indicate different messages.

"He then commenced firing, smashing our fore boom, firing through our main mast and shell after shell came on board, smashing our windows, engines and occasionally hitting the hull below the water line. I roughly estimate that about sixty or seventy shots struck the vessel.

"During all this time, the men kept firing closer and closer with their rifles, cutting through the cabin house, through the ports in the cabin and around myself and my men gathered aft. None of my men was struck except by splinters, which were flying all around as shell after shell hit the vessel.

"The engineer reported to me then that the water was over the engine-room floor and that the vessel appeared to be settling down. I immediately gave orders to stop the engines and clear away the dories, which although they were of no use, would be something for my men to cling to in the heavy seas.[5]

"By the time my boats had been put over the side, which was roughly ten minutes, the vessel's forward decks were level with the water. I told my men to jump into the water and cling to the dories and throw overboard anything that would help to float them. I believe I was the last to jump from the ship. My bow was then about twenty feet under water and her stern about ten feet in the air and she was beginning to dive.

"From that time I have no recollection of what happened to the other men except, when swimming toward the cutter Dexter, I felt myself losing strength and gripped the cabin doors, which had floated off. I remained on the doors until I had regained my strength and then began swimming toward the Dexter.

"At this time I heard some of my men who were clinging to the door shouting to the Dexter, 'Throw a life line to that man, he is drowning.'

"He had evidently been drawn down by the suction of the vessel and was weighted down with heavy clothing. This was my man, Leon Mainjoy. I then reached the side of the cutter and three of my men were alongside at the same time. I called to the men aboard the cutter to throw lines to them as they were drowning, and two men were apparently in bad shape.

"The cutter threw a small piece of signal halyards and as we were on the windward side I fully expected that we would all go down because we were all trying to cling to this small line. A few minutes later they threw large lines and took my men on board one by one, and myself as well.

"During this time one sailor, Edward Fouchard, was clinging to one of the broken dories. They put out a boat from the Dexter and saved him. I then learned that my other men were safe on board the Walcott but that Mainjoy was unconscious and they were trying to resuscitate him.

"We were all taken on board the cutters just as we jumped from the vessels, some of us without any more clothing than a shirt and trousers. The people on board the cutter treated us very well and gave us dry clothing and allowed us to remain on deck during the day.

"To my surprise, on going below after supper I was told that I would have to submit to leg irons. I remarked to the captain that I did not consider that I was a prisoner of war and had no intention of doing anything rash. But he assured me that it was his orders, and as such I told him I could only submit to force.

"After that we remained in custody down below until yesterday, Saturday, when we were allowed to come up on deck, and we were kept in irons until this morning, when we arrived alongside the dock in New Orleans..."[6]

Chesley Hobbs, the *I'm Alone*'s chief engineer gave a similar account, describing the incident as "worse than war":

"They peppered us with a three-inch gun, rifles and rapid-fire machine guns. They cut the ship all to pieces, and even shot away our lifeboats. They started to shell us at five minutes after 8, and at four minutes past 9 the ship was gone. When I stopped her engines the flywheel was in the water. We had no boats and threw pieces of dories over the side to cling to in the water."[7]

He added that the Coast Guard stood by while the men swam desperately for their lives:

"They [the Coast Guardsmen] claimed that they were afraid of being drawn down by the suction of a sinking ship, but that's only a bluff. We were flying the British flag and they riddled it with shell-fire. We were not given any dry clothes. I took mine off on deck and dried them. We were sent below and put in irons at night with an armed guard watching us."[8]

When the crew arrived in New Orleans, the patrol boats touched at four different docks before finally casting anchor in the middle of the river below the city. At one dock, the Coasties offloaded the body of Leon Mainjoy, a French citizen of St. Pierre Miquelon. At another dock, the Coast Guard brought ashore three prisoners, handcuffed together and wearing leg irons. The *Dexter* brought four more prisoners to a dock further down river, also in handcuffs and leg irons. All of them were rushed away in taxicabs to the Custom House. After that, the captain and crew of the *I'm Alone* were locked up in New Orleans' Third Precinct Police Station.[9] The captain and crew were released from jail the next day on bail, pending a hearing during the following week.

Federal officials and the crew of the sunken schooner agreed that the ship was flying the British flag. They also agreed that the ship was 200 miles off the coast when it sank, after a two-day pursuit. They also agreed that Captain Randall told the Coast Guard officers that they could sink the ship but not seize it. The two parties, however, did not agree on exactly where the chase began. During the bombardment of the schooner, the two Coast Guard cutters fired more than 120 rounds of three-inch, high explosive shells.[10]

Interestingly, the US Government decided to press charges against Captain Randell and his crew for their alleged rum-running activities a few months earlier along the East Coast. Specifically, Customs authorities told the press that the affidavit filed against the crew charging conspiracy to smuggle liquor was based completely on Captain Randell's signed statement. Unless the statement was supported by other evidence, it seemed likely that the court would dismiss the charges.

The sinking of the *I'm Alone* created quite a stir in Washington, because it was flying a British flag at the time. Keep in mind that in the 1920s Britain had the world's largest navy and an empire covering approximately a quarter of the Earth's landmass. In the 1920s, the British Empire was *the* world power. In London, newspapers reported the story with headlines like "British Seamen in Manacles," "British Flag Fired Upon by American Coast Guard," and "British Subject Killed."[11] Sir Howard Esme, the British Ambassador, visited the State Department soon after the incident. He told William R. Castle Jr., Assistant Secretary of European Affairs, that if the facts were as they were reported in the press, it could be a serious case.[12] One British official stated:

> "The thing I regret most in the whole affair is that your Coast Guard officers put the sailors in manacles and took them ashore in chains. England has not done anything of that sort for generations with the exception of the days of extreme violence. It is the sort of thing that English people most resent. That apparently needless humiliation of their fellow countrymen is apt to be more galling than the accidental loss of one life in a sea scrimmage or the fact that a chance shot of the Coast Guard hit the British flag."[13]

Since 1924, the British House of Commons had been periodically debating the merits of continuing the ship liquor treaty, which Britain entered into reluctantly, mostly for diplomatic reasons. Until the treaty was negotiated, Britain had never allowed the modification of the three-mile international limit. After Britain entered the agreement, other nations quickly followed, which meant that the Coast Guard could stop ships from several nations outside of the previous three-mile limit.

The Treasury Department strongly defended the actions of the Coast Guard. Treasury Secretary Mellon told the press that the Coast Guard's actions were justified by the Tariff Act of 1922, which authorized enforcement officers to board vessels within four leagues of the coast. He defended the sinking of the ship more than 200 miles offshore by claiming that the pursuit began within the twelve-mile limit and that the pursuit was continuous. If either of those two points were not true, the Coast Guard could have been held liable for damages. He argued that shelling the ship was authorized because Captain Randell would not allow the Coast Guard to board his ship and because he supposedly waved a pistol.[14]

The Commandant of the Coast Guard also defended his men. After declaring that the schooner was a "notorious rum-runner," Admiral Billard publicly stated:

> "Its [the *I'm Alone's*] record was well known to every Coast Guard officer on the Atlantic and Gulf Coasts. In the past five years we have had dozens of records of our vessels spotting it, but it had always been too fast for them. This time all the Coast Guard craft along the Southern coast had been on the lookout for the ship and the two patrol boats proved its equal in speed."[15]

A few days after the incident, the British Ambassador learned that the *I'm Alone* was registered as a Canadian vessel. Vincent Massey, the Canadian Minister, visited the US State Department and requested the information that the British ambassador had previously sought. Although the British government transferred the matter to Canada, because of the ship's registry, Britain still had strong interest in the case. Canada was part of the British Commonwealth and the ship was flying the British flag when the Coast Guard shot it to pieces, sinking the schooner. In addition, France became involved because the man who drowned was a French national.

The results of Montjoy's autopsy at the Marine Hospital were kept secret. The secrecy stirred speculation that he might have been struck by the fragment of a shell or the splinters of the wreckage as the *Dexter* fired 70 to 100 rounds into the schooner. Edward Grace, attorney for the crew, declared that if it could be shown that the cutter first signaled the *I'm Alone* outside of the twelve-mile limit, he would consider charging the Coast Guardsmen with murder.[16]

Getting the Last Laugh

On April 9, 1929, Canadian Minister Massey delivered a note of protest to Secretary Stimson regarding the Coast Guard's sinking of the *I'm Alone*. He spoke to Stimson for about twenty minutes, and, when he emerged, told reporters that he had left the note but would shed no light on the conversation he had with the Secretary.[17]

On the same day, Attorney General Mitchell announced that he was dropping the conspiracy case against Captain Randell and his crew because of "insufficient evidence." However, he stated that the Coast Guard had every right to pursue and sink the schooner. The captain and crew of the *I'm Alone* were released at the request of US District Attorney Edmond E. Talbot. Federal Commissioner Reginald H. Carter Jr. immediately signed the papers to dismiss the charges, the whole procedure taking less than five minutes.

"Thank the Lord, that's all over," Captain Randell said after his release. "I'll probably go back to the sea, but not as a rum-runner."[18]

38

Florida

Red Shannon was a big, red-faced, jovial Irishman whom Coast Guardsmen knew as the "king of Miami rum-runners." Shannon had run more liquor into Miami and South Florida than any other single rum-runner. His contemporaries agreed that he was well supplied with "Irish brass." Although he made a lot of money in his ventures, the real thrill of his business came from the battle of wits in which he repeatedly outsmarted the Coast Guard.

One afternoon, Shannon and a Coast Guard officer sat in the cabin of a rum ship. His speedboat sat alongside. When one of his helpers announced that his boat was ready for the trip, Shannon turned to the Coast Guardsman and said, "I am starting for Miami. Come, on, let's have a race."[1] Before the officer could board his own craft, Red had enough of a lead to out-distance the patrol boat in the 42-mile race across the gulf stream to Miami.

In early February 1926, Lincoln C. Andrews visited Miami on an inspection tour of the Southeastern District. As Andrews was being ferried out to a cutter aboard a smaller patrol boat, they encountered the notorious red-haired smuggler. He was making a mad dash down the channel in his super-powered speed boat, loaded with liquor, as he saw the government officials.

Shannon recognized Andrews aboard the Coast Guard boat, but did not turn back. Instead, he sped his boat across their bow, thumbed his nose at the "dry czar," and chuckled as he threw liquor overboard. Before the Coasties recovered from their shock, Red Shannon was speeding out of the range of their small arms. On that day, the press buzzed with the news of how a rum-runner defied the nation's Prohibition chief. Coast Guardsmen swore to get the redheaded one who dared to embarrass them in front of "the big boss."[2]

A month later, the Coast Guard finally did catch Shannon. When he raised his hands to surrender, one of the Coast Guardsman shot him.

Shannon made it to the hospital, where he learned that he would not survive his wounds. "It's all in the game," he told reporters as he lay dying.[3]

Commander Porcher of the Miami Coast Guard Base told reporters that "Red Shannon played the game squarely and on his nerve. He was a dead game sport."[4] Following Shannon's death, five Coast Guardsmen were arrested for manslaughter. Six eyewitnesses testified that he was shot while he had his hands in the air. Assistant Secretary Andrews made a statement declaring that the Coast Guardsmen would be defended by a US Attorney in federal court, since a report to his department showed that they acted "in the line of duty."[5]

A Desperate Sea Battle

In 1927, the Florida coast was plagued by counterfeiters, rum-runners, drugs, and alien smugglers. Chicago gunmen and other similar characters were recruited to aid the Florida smugglers. Coast Guard officers regarded the Florida coast as one of the most dangerous places for law enforcement officers. More than 100 vessels engaged in liquor and drug smuggling had been seized between January and September. Most of the contraband was obtained in the Bahamas. The Florida syndicates were well financed and equipped, served by men who were determined to stick to their trade until they were either dead or in jail.[6]

Three years earlier, the rum-runners off Atlantic City were the bane of the Coast Guard. They were bold and violent, going to any extremes to land their cargoes. However, the Atlantic City gangs handled mostly liquor and kept clear of other forms of smuggling. The Florida smugglers, in many cases the same smugglers who hovered off the New Jersey shore a few years earlier, smuggled drugs in addition to liquor because it was more profitable. In practical terms, drugs also took up less space aboard a ship and weighed less than kegs of alcohol. A large bag of heroin or marijuana sold for the same price as many cases of liquor, and was much easier to conceal.

The Florida bootleggers also had alliances with skilled counterfeiters. The Treasury Department traced fake money circulating in Florida and the West Indies to gangs that had originally come to Florida for the liquor trade. The gangsters in Florida had their own intelligence service and were in every respect one of the best organized bootleg rings with which the government had to deal with since the beginning of Prohibition. Chicago gunmen in Florida had repeatedly attempted to shoot government agents.

A couple of these dangerous Florida rum-smugglers left Miami on the evening of August 6th aboard the V-13977, a 40-foot long boat. Horace "Tommy" Alderman was aboard as master and Robert Weech as engineer and general assistant. When they reached Bimini, they took on a contraband cargo and headed back to Florida. Soon, Alderman spotted Coast Guard vessel 249. He did not change his course and made no attempt to escape. When warning shots crossed his bow, Alderman stopped his engine and the CG-245 came up alongside.[7]

Aboard the Coast Guard cutter was Boatswain S.C. Sanderlin, commanding; Boatswain's Mate First Class Laurence Frank Tuten; Boatswain's Mate Second Class John A. Robinson, Frank Lehman, Victor A. Lamby, H.M. Caudle, and J.L. Hollingsworth. Robert A. Webster, a Secret Service agent, was also aboard. He was heading to Bimini to talk to a man who had information on counterfeit $20 and $50 bills, which had found their way into Florida banks.[8]

As the two vessels came together, Sanderlin, Lamby, and Webster were in the pilot house, and Robinson was asleep below. The others were topside. Sanderlin boarded the rum-runner and found several sacks of whisky. When Sanderlin was calling in his report by radio, Alderman shot him in the back, killing him almost instantly. Lamby, who was unarmed, ran to the armory, which was located in the cabin. Trying not to get shot, he jumped for the engine room hatch, but was not quick enough.

Alderman stepped out of the portside pilot house door and shot him. The bullet pierced Lamby's right side, struck his spine, and paralyzed his legs. He dropped to the lower engine room platform and crawled forward between the engines to seek cover. Alderman quickly returned to the pilot house and took Sanderlin's pistol. He fired a shot into the deck just to see if it worked.

Agent Webster, in the meantime, jumped to the stern of the V-13977. Alderman appeared at the starboard pilot house door of the CG-249, aimed both pistols at the men aboard his rum-runner, ordered "hands up," and called for his assistant. Before Weech could get aboard the CG-249, Robinson grabbed a wrench from the deck of the rum-runner and threw it in the direction of Alderman's head. The wrench missed and Robinson dived overboard to avoid being shot.[9]

Alderman then ordered all hands to stand on the stern sheets, but there was not enough room for everyone. Webster, Tuten, and Hollingsworth were forced to stand in the cockpit. At this point, Weech had joined Alderman aboard the Coast Guard cutter.

"I have two of them and I will kill the rest of the ----- with their own guns," Alderman yelled.[10]

While keeping his pistols aimed at the Coast Guard crew, Alderman ordered Weech to break all gasoline lines aboard the CG-249. Alderman then stepped aboard the V-13977 and positioned himself near the forward engine room hatch. Weech went below and ordered Lamby, who was laying there paralyzed, to tear out the gasoline lines. Lamby replied that he could not move his legs and was helpless. Weech kicked him and beat him with his pistol and again ordered him to tear down the gas line or die. Lamby replied that he could not physically do it, even with the death threats. To avoid receiving more of a beating, he reached up to the wrench board and handed a wrench to Weech. The wrench was the right size for the pipe fittings, so Weech proceeded to tear down the gasoline lines between the vacuum tanks and carburetors, causing five gallons of gas to run into the engine compartment.

When Weech returned to Alderman to report that the engine room was now flooded with gasoline, Alderman told Weech to order Lamby on deck. Weech replied that Lamby could not move. Alderman ordered Weech to kill Lamby with his pistol, but he objected. Alderman then ordered Weech to set fire to the boat and burn Lamby to death. Weech, for some strange reason, had no ethical issues with torching a man instead of just shooting him. So he tossed a match and threw it below. Miraculously, neither the gasoline nor the more combustible fumes ignited.

Alderman then told his captives that he was going to kill them one at a time and ordered them to get on their knees and say their last prayers. Agent Webster suggested to Alderman that he should not kill so many people over a little liquor and should give them a lifeboat and a chance to get ashore. Alderman replied:

"You big pot-bellied slob, I am going to kill you first. You are one of those sneaks and snoopers who go around and get the goods on good men."[11]

Boatswain's Mate Tuten suggested that it would be a good idea to start the engine of the V-13977 before setting the Coast Guard cutter ablaze. Alderman replied that he would tend to that and that he wanted no suggestions from the Coast Guard. He ordered Weech to start the V-13977's engine, but he could not get it started. Alderman called him on deck, gave him one of his pistols, and told him to keep everyone covered while he went into the engine room.

The engine fired up and Alderman returned to the deck to begin his murders. At this moment, the engine backfired and stalled out again. Weech went below and started the engine, only to stall out again. Alderman looked down the hatch to see what was wrong. Seizing the opportunity, Webster and Tuten rushed Alderman, followed by Hollingsworth, Caudle, and Robinson, who had climbed back aboard. Webster grabbed Alderman's right arm, but was not quick enough. Alderman shot him dead.

Tuten had Alderman by the left arm but could not prevent him from firing with his left hand twice, hitting Hollingsworth in the shoulder and head. Hollingsworth rolled overboard. Robinson stabbed Alderman four or five times with an ice pick and Caudle pried the pistol from his left hand. Lehman, who had picked up a boat scraper, slammed his makeshift weapon against Alderman's head, knocking him unconscious. Alderman then received the beating of a lifetime.

Caudle then went after Weech by entering the engine room through the after hatch. Weech headed for the forward hatch. Caudle grabbed him by the leg and crawled on deck with him. Robinson, who was also near the hatch, knocked Weech over the head and rolled him overboard. Weech swam to the stern of the CG-249 and Tuten, Robinson, and Lehman boarded the cutter to get him.

At this point, the mooring fasts broke and the two boats drifted apart. The three Coasties lowered the dinghy, towed the V-13977 alongside, and made it fast again. Amazingly, after seeing these two men shed the blood of their shipmates, the Coast Guard brought the murderers to shore alive. How tempting it must have been for the whole crew to just throw Alderman and Weech overboard and watch them "accidentally drown."

Lamby died on August 11th. Webster and Sanderline were dead and Hollinsworth barely survived his gunshot wounds. Alderman and Weech were taken to Idlewild under heavy guard and placed aboard Coast Guard vessel 248 in double irons.

****

James C. Young, reporter for the *New York Times*, had written several in-depth articles on rum-running during the 1920s. Over the years, he spent time on rum ships, at the docks, and on Coast Guard vessels to get the inside scoop. In the spring of 1929, he traveled to Florida, where he interviewed Coast Guard officers on their campaign against rum-running.

The illegal liquor trade had come a long way since Prohibition went into effect in 1920. By 1929, rum-running had grown exponentially. It was highly organized and well-funded. Smugglers used state-of-the-art communications equipment and used their unlimited funds to build better boats and airplanes to get their cargo where it needed to go.

When Young made his visit to Florida, a Coast Guard officer showed him a large chart (nautical map) of Florida. The chart included the Keys and adjacent islands. Shipping lanes were indicated by curving lines and the grid squares were shaded with different colors to indicate smuggling activity. The white squares indicated very little or no smuggling, dark blue indicated moderate activity, and red showed the worst sections.[12]

The entire southern end of the state and the sea over to the western edge of Cuba were red. The officer explained that Florida has hundreds of miles of coastline with hundreds of inlets, bays, and islands—all excellent hiding places. The Coast Guard's campaign against smuggling was organized along the lines of wartime coastal patrols. Or, as Young so eloquently put it, "In this game of speed and guns, of men and ships, the Coast Guard has been organized as if by a war board of strategy."[13]

The scouting line was anywhere from twenty to a hundred miles off shore. The patrol boats on scouting duty were the fastest 36-footers in the service. They could remain at sea for a week and withstand terrible storms. Closer to shore were the older, slower craft, backed up by a fleet of 20-footers armed with rapid-fire guns. There were also a few cutters patrolling the area, which had a tendency to appear at the worst times for smugglers.

The Coast Guard's Florida patrol was commanded by radio from a central base ashore. Rum-runners, to their credit, also had radio operators on land and had their own maps showing where the Coast

Guard patrols were tightest. The two parties watched each other and maneuvered accordingly. They intercepted each other's messages and, most likely, read each other's code with equal ease. Deception played a big part in the rum war, each side attempting to throw the other off course with false messages. These messages have caused the Coast Guard to wind up patrolling the wrong areas while liquor slipped through. On the other hand, the Coasties' false messages have delivered numerous rum-runners right into their hands.

While the Coast Guard patrolled off the Florida coasts, the liquor syndicates had men ashore and in scout ships monitoring the movements of government vessels. The scout ships were sometimes empty, serving as decoys. When the scouts found an area that was unguarded, they immediately sent encrypted radio signals out to guide the rum-runners. While the rum blockade was much like a wartime blockade, there were far more limitations in a peacetime setting. A wartime blockade stops most, if not all, vessels from reaching a given coast, with the intended goal of crippling that nation. The Coast Guard's mission was much different during the Rum War. The goal was not to devastate the US economy; it was only to prevent certain goods from being smuggled ashore. It is important to note that there were hundreds of other vessels in the Atlantic and the Gulf of Mexico carrying on legitimate business, so stopping every ship was not a realistic option for the Coast Guard. To make matters worse, there were airplanes overhead keeping track of the Coasties and also smuggling liquor, completely unchecked.[14]

The island of Bimini is only 90 miles from Florida. Fast boats made the trip in only a few hours. A cargo purchased in Bimini for $1,000 was worth $2,000-$3,000 in the US. However, navigating at night, with no lights, in a speedboat, past the Coast Guard, and through shoal-studded waters was not a task for amateurs. The fact that cargoes arrived almost every night in Florida says a lot about the skills of these men. Many writers of the time romanticized the exploits of the smugglers by comparing them to the pirates and privateers who sailed those same waters two centuries earlier.

Unlike in the North Atlantic, smugglers tried to avoid using large ships off of Florida. Up north, large cargo ships were necessary to weather the storms and rough seas. Of course, smaller, faster boats usually carried the liquor ashore to places like New York, Atlantic City, Boston, etc. However, in the calmer waters off Florida, smaller vessels could make trips to the islands without having to remain at sea for days or weeks at a time. Large cargo ships were easier to spot and incapable of outrunning the Coast Guard. The rum syndicates, being experts in risk management after years of costly mistakes, decided to minimize that risk by cutting back on rum ships.

Rum boats large enough to carry 500 cases ran close to selected reefs off the Florida coast and dropped their goods overboard in sacks. Within half an hour, they started heading back to whichever port they came from. Rum-runners with smaller boats waited for the next night when there was no moonlight before going out to look for the sacks. The men used grappling hooks to fish the liquor-sacks from the shallow sea bed and brought it ashore. A liquor connoisseur could tell the quality of the liquor by the mud on the label. The best bars of Miami seldom offered a brand without a label that showed signs of having been in the sea.[15]

The system was not foolproof, however. In one case, the Coast Guard confiscated a map showing the various spots to find liquor in the shoals— a 1920s treasure map, if you will. Other members of the rum ring had no idea the map was missing and continued to dump sacks of liquor bottles at those same spots. Eventually, the rum smugglers abandoned those points to ones farther out and found that the Coast Guard knew exactly where to look for their cargoes.

Not all smugglers off the Florida coast were part of a liquor syndicate. There were quite a few who operated on their own, even in 1929. They were the real daredevils. Independent rum-runners did not have any intelligence network or radio signals to rely on. They had to rely on their eyes and ears, chugging along in old fishing boats. Many of these independent rum-smugglers were not the typical criminal type. Quite a few of them considered themselves honest men who were tempted away from their previous jobs by the easy money of transporting liquor, which, in their view, should not have been illegal to begin with.

Prohibition created opportunities for wealth that did not exist a decade earlier. The average man or woman slaved away working long hours only to earn $1,500-$2,500 a year. However, that same man or woman could earn the same amount from a couple of liquor runs, needing only a small boat to get to and from the offload point. Also, liquor was socially acceptable, far more than narcotics.

One man who made a fortune during Prohibition was a wounded war veteran from England who settled in Bimini. During World War I, he was gassed and maimed. The "Major," as he was called, moved to the tropical island soon after the war. When Prohibition became law in the United States, the Major quickly realized that a very lucrative market was right at his feet. He made the first runs to Florida himself in a motorboat, earning money faster than he expected. With the money he earned, he purchased more boats until he owned a small fleet of about a dozen rum-runners. The Major then became a wholesaler of rum and wound up as the boss of Bimini's liquor trade. In 1929, he was still a secretive figure and the public did not know his identity. However, reporter James C. Young learned that the Major had earned over $3 million in the rum trade by 1929. Almost every liquor boat of Bimini paid their tribute to the Major before heading to the United States.[16]

39
Detroit

In May of 1928, a *New York Times* reporter made a trip to Detroit to investigate the claim that Detroit was the "rum capitol" of the United States. The reporter, Charles A. Selden, interviewed Detroit's mayor, John C. Lodge, who said:

> "Of course, there is some liquor in this city, but neither I nor anybody else can tell how much. Any estimate must, from the nature of the case, be a guess. I am not frightened because some guesses are in terms of millions."[1]

The mayor made no apologies for Detroit, the city of 1.5 million people, for being a "wet" city. He was elected during the previous fall without making any promises on Prohibition enforcement. Lodge's opponent, Mayor Smith, hoping to stay in office, openly declared against enforcing the liquor law. After his election, Mayor Lodge said that there should be no "fanaticism" in running the city. The popular translation of "fanaticism" in Detroit applied to Prohibitionists, who often took a fanatical, crusading approach to their cause.

At first, Selden did not come across evidence that Detroit was the "rum capitol" because the city's wetness was very well-concealed. His luck changed when he met a certain city official who was eager to demonstrate that Detroit was indeed the liquor capital of America. Seldon visited the unnamed official's office, who telephoned another official while Seldon sat there, "There's a man here from New York who wants to know how wet Detroit is. What do you say to a little speed-boat trip to show him that New York has nothing on us?"[2]

They met with the other city official for lunch at a Detroit club, where they drank liquor, and then met at a law office in a downtown skyscraper, where they drank more liquor. The three men then boarded a speedboat and began traveling up the Detroit River. They skirted Belle Isle, which had Detroit's most beautiful park; rounded Peach Island, which belongs to Canada, and made port at the Canadian customs wharf on the mainland at Riverside to visit a brewery.[3]

Breweries and distilleries could operate legally in Canada, so the reporter and his escorts did not have to knock on a back-alley door and utter a secret password to get in. The brewers were very hospitable. They set up a table with some chairs and rolled out a keg for their guests. They gave their visitors souvenir bottle openers to help them remember their brand of beer and told them the places in Detroit where it was sold exclusively and where it was sold in competition with other Canadian beers. The brewery produced 2,500 cases, or 60,000 bottles a day. Eighty percent of the beer was shipped to Detroit. The brewers pointed out the new construction on the property and explained that they were enlarging the plant in order to triple their output. This brewery was one of 83 breweries in Canada. In addition to that, there were more than a score of distilleries, all operating within Canadian law.[4]

The men again boarded their speedboat and proceeded to another Canadian point, opposite Fighting Island, where drinks were sold freely at a bar. Soon, they slowed down in front of a row of boat houses built out on the edge of deep water on the Ecorse shore, an outlying part of Detroit. The boat houses appeared innocent, but reeked of beer and liquor.

"Where will we stop first?" asked the man at the wheel.

"Let's go to Boyd's place," replied the official.

The man turned the wheel hard and ran alongside a landing platform outside a green door, which opened up without any delay and without any inspection of the visitors to see if it was safe to admit them. Inside was a fully-equipped bar with all of the traditional furnishings and the wide variety of drinks that American saloons carried in the days before Prohibition. The bar even had the time-honored free lunch to go along with the drinks.

Two things were different from the typical pre-Prohibition bar at Boyd's place– a gambling room in the back and the many attractive women who roamed the place freely. This was only one of many such places in that long row of boat houses. When the men crossed the road to the land side of the resort, they found similar places.[5]

The men made their return trip after dark. As they sped upstream, they spotted an occasional lantern being swung from the end of a wharf or the roof of a warehouse, and lights being flashed on and off from high windows in waterfront buildings. Some of these signals indicated the location of customs officers. Several fast boats crossed their bow and disappeared into the darkness along the Detroit shore. Generally, these boats carried only their own loads, but several had good-sized barges in tow.

There were many other ways to smuggle liquor besides running it in by motor boat. Ferries running between Detroit and Windsor carried 20 million passengers a year and approximately one-million automobiles. Most of the traffic was made up of those who lived in Canada and worked in Detroit, but there were many Americans who went to Windsor by ferry to do their own bootlegging.[6]

The Canadian liquor law made such trips simple and inexpensive. The law forbade open bars or selling liquor with meals at hotels and public restaurants. Canadian citizens could purchase liquor at government liquor stores, with the understanding that the beer, wine, and liquor would be consumed at home. An American tourist could also buy liquor legally if he paid a $2 fee and showed some evidence that he was registered at a hotel and occupied a room. There were Canadian hotels that made a lot of money by selling false hotel receipts to visitors so that they could buy liquor. Equipped with the right documents, anyone could go to a Canadian liquor store and stock up. Thousands of Detroit residents made periodic trips and did exactly that.

In mid-1928, the Customs Collector at Detroit had a force of only ninety men for his patrol. These men were rotated in three eight-hour shifts daily, so there were rarely more than thirty men on duty at one time. These thirty men were stretched extremely thin and had to work on land and man the patrol boats. The Detroit Customs district covered the Detroit River and St. Clair Bay; therefore, the thirty men were supposed to cover seventy miles of waterfront. The Customs men had a fleet of twenty boats, most of which they confiscated from rum smugglers. Of course, with such a small number of men on duty at a time, they could only use a few patrol boats at one time. The few patrol boats were also greatly outnumbered by rum-running vessels.[7]

In 1925, the United States and Canada entered into a treaty whereby each country would help the other to intercept smuggled liquor and drugs. When the treaty first went into effect, the Customs Collector at Detroit asked the collector at Windsor to notify him immediately by telephone of every boat clearing from Canadian customs to Detroit with a liquor cargo. At first, the Canadians made many phone calls across the river, but little came of them. All the rum-runners had to do was cruise up and down on the Canadian side or circle the islands until dark, then make an easy run the American side. Soon, the Canadian customs men did not bother calling their American counterparts.[8]

Courtesy National Archives
Detroit in the 1920s

The outnumbered Customs men in Detroit did have *some* help. There was the Detroit police department, which had a reputation for being very lax in Prohibition enforcement. The department had "clean-up" squads, ranging in size from two to ten men. There were only six of these "clean-up" squads to a precinct and there were fifteen precincts, so ninety of these small teams had to enforce prohibition in a city of 1.5 million. However, these squads also had the duties of suppressing gambling and prostitution, which in themselves were overwhelming tasks. In addition to the Detroit police, there was the federal Prohibition unit for Michigan, which had seventy-five men to cover the whole state. Fifty of the federal Prohibition men did most of their work in Detroit. During the eight-month period from October 1927 to May 1928, these men seized and destroyed liquor and liquor-making apparatus valued at $2 million. This sounds like a lot but it was only a drop in the bucket when compared with the liquor that was not seized or destroyed.[9]

Slipping Away In The Night

On August 18, 1928, the fleet of approximately two dozen rum-runners, anchored for several days at liquor export docks on the Canadian side of the Detroit River, was nowhere to be seen. Canadians who passed the docks that morning were amazed to find no boats riding at anchor, with the exception of one dilapidated craft that was disabled. During the previous night, the rum fleet lay at anchor, loaded to capacity with cases, sacks and half-barrels of hard liquor and beer. By the next morning, not only were the boats gone, but so were much of the liquor stocks at the export docks. Where they had gone was a mystery.[10]

Two weeks earlier, the Canadian provincial government seized somewhere between half and two-thirds of the liquor stocks of the Erie Transit Corporation and the Interstate Transit Corporation on the grounds of illegal possession. American Customs officials denied that more rum than usual had crossed the border. Their view was that the Canadians had hidden the liquor somewhere on their side of the river.

Alarmed by the impending doom of their smuggling operations, exporters from all of the Detroit-area border cities gathered in Windsor, Ontario. There they tried to figure out ways to save their industry from a Canadian-American joint effort to destroy their business. Of prime concern was the recent ruling of Magistrate W.A. Smith of Windsor that storage of beer and liquor in export warehouses was in violation of the Ontario Liquor Control Act. Magistrate Smith's decision, if upheld by higher courts, could have stopped the exportation of millions of dollars of liquor each year. Smith gave his ruling on the day before the Windsor export meeting, when he fined a rum-runner $200 and confiscated his boat for illegal possession of liquor.[11]

Corrupt Agents Arrested

The many newspaper reports about Detroit did not go unnoticed. A few months after *New York Times* reporter Charles Selden made his trip to that city, there was a general crackdown on Customs men on both sides of the border. On November 30, 1928, the United States and Canadian governments moved to crush the racket along the Detroit River, estimated to be a $50 million-a-year industry.[12]

Liquor seizure on the Detroit River — National Archives

While US Customs officials were arresting eleven Border Patrol inspectors on charges of accepting bribes and conspiracy to aid in the smuggling of liquor, Canadian officials were issuing orders to close thirty liquor export docks in border cities. US District Attorney John R. Watkins described the action as a "general house-cleaning" and told reporters that he estimated fifty inspectors would be dismissed before the investigation ended. Watkins estimated that half the liquor brought across from Canada was smuggled in with the help of Customs officials. The average procedure was for the rum runner to arrange with the patrol for a free night when his boat and crew could work in safety. The average bribe for a "free night" was $500. Sumner C. Sleeper, chief of the Border Patrol, said one agent went undercover for six weeks and accepted bribes along with other patrol inspectors totaling $1,500, all of which were marked and turned over to the Collector of Customs as evidence.[13]

Sir Henry Drayton, chairman of the Ontario Liquor Control Board, and W.D. Euler, Minister of National Revenue, issued orders to close export docks on the Canadian side to centralize the liquor export business in ten large docks to be strictly supervised by Customs officers.

After The Crackdown...Another Crackdown

On June 1, 1929, on the Detroit River, two Customs officers were in a patrol boat when they spotted a rum-runner. They sped after the boat and quickly began to catch up when one of the bootleggers aboard raised a machine gun and began firing. The rounds splashed in the water all around the Customs boat. The officers emptied their pistols at the man, who did not stop shooting until he reached Canadian waters. Fortunately, neither of the officers were hit, and, not surprisingly, the bootlegger got away unscathed. Pistols are not generally accurate past 50 meters and even less accurate when fired from a speeding boat bouncing on the water.[14]

According to a report by Carey D. Ferguson, Detroit's Collector of Customs, this was the first time in history that bootleggers used machine guns against officers on the Detroit River. The use of machine guns could have been a response to the new Jones Law, which provided five years imprisonment and a $10,000 fine for bootleggers. Ferguson announced to reporters that Customs officers would respond in kind.[15]

On June 10, Federal heads of Prohibition enforcement met at Detroit and devised plans for a new campaign against Canadian liquor smuggling.[19] The men planned to mobilize the greatest armed force ever assembled in Detroit to curtail the flow of liquor. Assistant Treasury Secretary Lowman stated that the 100 miles of border between Lake Erie and Lake Huron was the "sore spot" of the country and that 85 percent of the liquor coming in from Canada entered through Detroit. At the same time, the administration in Washington was seriously considering sending Marines to Detroit because previous measures had proven ineffective.[16]

The Detroit plan included an immediate increase in Prohibition, Customs, and Coast Guard units; the acquisition of more automobiles and speedboats for Prohibition and Customs units; more cutters for the

---

[19] Those attending the conference were Seymore Lowman, Assistant Secretary of the Treasury; James M. Doran, National Prohibition Commissioner; Bernard Wait, Chief of Special Customs Agents; Thomas E. Stone, Michigan Prohibition Administrator; Thomas H. Brennan, Mr. Stone's assistant; Commander Rasmussen; Walter S. Petty, Detroit's Assistant Collector of Customs; and a Mr. Norwood.

Coast Guard; and a system for coordinating the three units under the direction of E.R. Norwood. Lowman announced that he had ordered every available Customs officer to the Detroit area:

> "There will probably be several hundred additional men available within the next two days. We are here on the smuggling problem. The Canadians are pushing us pretty hard these days, but I do not think things will get out of hand. Liquor from Canada was less in 1928 than in 1927. The history for 1929 has yet to be written. We are after the criminals now and, under the Jones law, they can be properly dealt with when convicted."[17]

President Herbert Hoover, who had only been in office for a few months, gave a speech in which he expressed hope that communities along the border would do their best to help the Treasury "end the systematic war that is being carried on by international criminals against the laws of the United States."[18]

Dr. James M. Doran, National Prohibition Commissioner, emphasized that the key to success was to have the Coast Guard, Customs, and the Prohibition Bureau under a single command for this campaign. In mid-June, Doran proclaimed, "We need only adequate numbers of men and boats, responsible authority, unflagging zeal. All of these needs are about to be supplied. For the first time I have the means at my command to stop the Detroit smuggling."[19]

By late June, two-hundred additional men arrived in Detroit to bolster the Prohibition force, and the government was mobilizing more. These two-hundred men were hand-picked for their good service records, supposedly. Smugglers did not operate as openly or as easily as before along that particular stretch of the Detroit River. Meanwhile, locals grew anxious about the increased violence between the law and rum-runners.

Detroit had little reason to believe that this campaign would work. The people of the city had seen earlier Prohibition efforts amount to nothing. The hundred miles of water between Huron and Erie gave the advantage to smugglers. The international boundary is broken by indented shores and stream outlets, not to mention islands and shoals, marshes and rocks. To make matters worse, American patrol forces were not allowed to cross an invisible line in the center of the river. Rum-runners simply waited on the Canadian side waiting to make the four-minute trip across the Detroit River. Belle Isle at the north and Grosse Ile at the south are fairly large landmasses, and the rum-runners used them to their advantage. In the 1920s, Belle Isle was, and still is, a large island-park approximately 1.5 square miles in area. Grosse Ile was an exclusive summer resort with many expensive homes. Liquor syndicates used some of the large homes in Grosse Ile as warehouses, especially during the winter, when the town was deserted and covered in ice and snow. When the Treasury Department decided to launch its campaign against Detroit smugglers in 1929, one of the city's high police officials was awaiting trial on the charge of guiding rum cargoes across Belle Isle.[20]

Ninety percent of Canada's export liquor was destined for the United States. The Canadian government collected approximately $8 million a year in excise taxes on liquor exports to the United States, so the government was making a huge profit from smuggling. However, exporting liquor from Canada was not considered 'smuggling' until the cargo reached US waters (or land). Two years earlier, $23,772,829 worth of Canadian liquor was cleared for export to the United States. Add to that figure foreign liquors such as Scotch whiskies and French wines that made their way through Canada and into the US, valued at $7,439,741, and the figure totaled over $30 million.[21]

Prohibition enforcement officers admitted that most of the liquor exported to the US was successfully landed. In 1929, Commissioner of Customs E.W. Camp reported that during the previous two fiscal years 46,594 cases of beer plus 6,644 barrels of beer and 16,560 cases of whisky were confiscated on the Detroit border, where Customs and the Coast Guard were most active. This made up only 3.5 percent of the beer and 1.2 percent of the spirits which cleared Canadian customs for the United States. Camp reported that Prohibition forces did not confiscate more than five to ten percent of Canadian liquor nationwide.[22]

Two grand jury investigations had brought out some of the implications of Canadian liquor smuggling. The Buffalo investigation uncovered a $10 million international liquor ring and led to the indictment of dozens of Canadian distillers and brewers. In Detroit, a grand jury found that corruption was rampant in the US Border Patrol. The jury estimated that rum-runners paid over $2 million a year in bribes to agents. The Border Patrol had to be completely reorganized after the indictments and forced resignations of federal agents.

As law enforcement tightened its grip on the Detroit area, smugglers were forced to rely on their wits more than ever. Buying liquor across the river in Windsor, Ontario was the easy part. Anyone could legally purchase as much liquor as he could afford. When a representative of a smuggling ring purchased liquor for export, he usually named a fake consignee in the United States. The buyer then used a forwarding agent, or rum-running boss. These men worked openly on the Canadian docks.

After the buyer made arrangements with the boss rum-runner, he would normally return to the United States and wait for a notice telling him when and where his cargo would arrive. The smarter importer, however, did not go through the trouble of visiting Windsor. He would simply make a phone call or send a letter, in some cases doing no more than waving a handkerchief on the waterfront. The Canadian distillers and boss rum-runners had agents in Detroit to "drum up" business, so they were known as "drummers." Until the summer of '29, purchasing a liquor cargo in Detroit was relatively simple and easy.

Deliveries of rum shipments to Detroit were usually on time. Although the buyer was responsible for moving his goods, he could not do it safely himself because the longshoremen wanted their percentage. Finally, there were the shore carriers, with trucks and cars, who transported the contraband to points near and far with great efficiency.[23]

As the liquor made its perilous and expensive journey, its prices went up. A case of liquor worth $30 in Windsor, Canada cost $40 when it landed across the river and $50 delivered. Each bottle in the case was worth $95 at the local speakeasy. There were various fees that cut into the profit, e.g. shipping and handling, bribes, etc. Rum traders complained that the business was no longer as profitable as it was a few years earlier and wondered aloud how they would maintain their expensive cars if the government actually meant its threats of a Detroit crackdown.

The big men of the trade had banking connections and influence that allowed them to smuggle liquor by the boatload without interference. One such rum trader operated his own bank as part of his smuggling business, which helped with credit arrangements and collections. The really wealthy men of the trade created the biggest obstacle to enforcement. They had the means to arrange shipments in ways that the average smuggler or bootlegger could not. For example, they would arrange to have freight train cars move from the United States, through Canada, and back to the US. While the freight cars passed through Canada, the legitimate cargo was switched out for cases of booze. The American car seals were preserved and restored to escape detection by Customs. It was impossible for Customs men to inspect every car, case, and bale, so hundreds, if not thousands, of carloads of liquor made their way across the country without interference.

One part of the government's planned crackdown on Detroit smuggling was closer scrutiny of the city's banks and seeking more cooperation with the railroads and Canadian officials. To Canadians, the sale of whisky for export was no different than the sale of any other legal product— it was completely legal. Once a week, Canadian officials in Windsor supplied a list to US Government officials in Detroit showing the liquor exported to American buyers in the previous week, all of which had been safely landed.

In June 1929, Commissioner Doran was planning to begin a regular patrol of the 100 miles between Huron and Erie. The river would be plotted into squares of feet and yards with men and boats assigned to them. The planned patrol would be on a 24-hour watch, commanded via radio communication.[24]

The Smugglers' Revised Tactics

The ferrymen, longshoremen, and carters had their own defined spheres of influence, but united in their fight against the Prohibition law. Enforcement officials estimated that more than 5,000 men were working against them around the clock. At least three communities along the Detroit River were centers of the rum trade. The days when a rum-runner could simply cut across the river whenever he wanted were gone. Smuggling into Detroit had become more sophisticated and complex. Rum rings made preparations and set up safeguards. The fast, expensive motorboats gave way to cheaper rowboats equipped with outboard motors. It was better to make frequent trips in a smaller, cheaper boat than risk losing a large cargo in a bigger, more expensive vessel. The rum-runners had their own underwriting syndicates to pay the costs of capture and trial plus excellent lawyers, bondsmen, and political defenders.[25]

The liquor traffic across the Detroit River became so profitable that there were men on the lookout 24 hours per day on both shores. They took note of each new face and every moving thing. No rum-runner headed for the opposite shore until one of his colleagues signaled for him.

The smugglers also resorted to kidnapping. On June 18, a photographer for *The Border Cities Star* named Horace Wild decided to go on a river cruise. Accompanied by his 18-year old son and two newspaper men, Wild was traveled by boat along the Amherstburg waterfront, taking photos. A score of rum-runners became angry when they saw that Wild was capturing their illegal activities on film. He caught them in the process of stowing their cargoes in preparation for the night's run.[26]

As Wild's boat steered north, four automobiles, loaded with men from the export docks, followed the boat by driving along the waterfront. When Wild and his son alighted at a private dock, a group of a dozen men captured them. An hour later, the kidnappers freed both of them, but only after they removed the film from his camera.

****

Like anywhere else, Detroit's smugglers used decoys. In one case, a boat that looked the part of a rum-runner went calmly downstream, inside the Canadian line. The rum patrol could not help but notice and when the boat was about to cross into American waters, half a dozen Prohibition boats were immediately in pursuit. The boat sped up and tore off down the river, leaving the patrol boats in his foamy wake. When the patrol boats finally caught up, the runner's papers were in order and, aside from the smell of alcohol, his boat was empty. During the pursuit, other boats carrying liquor sped across the river and landed thousands of cases. In 1929, hundreds of thousands of cases came from Canada every month, approaching 500,000 cases in the busiest months.[27]

While the government was drawing its plans for a huge Detroit Prohibition offensive, the rum syndicates were devising their own plans. On June 12, rum-runners from Buffalo to Mackinaw met secretly at Ecorse. They worked out plans for a system where their traffic would be diverted to Lake Erie or Lake Huron whenever the Coast Guard patrol and other Prohibition units were clustered on the Detroit River.[28]

At the local boat wells, there were signs that new plans were underway. Speedboats, the preferred smuggling craft for several years, were being offered for sale at low prices because they were no match for the latest patrol boats. Tugs of 60 to 80 feet were being rebuilt and large motors were being installed on them to give them more speed. The tugs could withstand the conditions of the Great Lakes and had sufficient speed for their purpose. Rum-runners told reporters that smuggling on the Detroit River had practically ceased for two or three days while the bosses were drawing up a new battle plan.[29]

On the night of June 13, many of the speedboats and tugs of the lower Detroit rum fleet cleared from the Amherstburg sector. They headed for Port Colborne and Bridgeburg and other ports along the north shore of Lake Erie. They were moving their operations to the Buffalo sector, where the Prohibition forces were weakened by the transfer of patrol boats and officers to the Detroit area. Other rum crews headed to Frieau, Port Stanley, and Port Dover on the Canadian side, from where they could smuggle to Erie, Pennsylvania, Conneaut, Cleveland and other northern Ohio points.

Within a couple of weeks, however, the rum-runners were landing their cargoes at docks in the heart of Detroit in broad daylight. An armed gang of a dozen men transferred the liquor from the boats to their automobiles, threatening any dockworkers who came too close. They worked on a schedule, regular landings being made at 7 AM, 10:30 AM, and noon. Acting Customs Collector Walter S. Petty told reporters that the smugglers were able to break the dry blockade because a picket boat's crew disobeyed orders and left their patrol area and returned to the Customs Border Patrol base to "refuel." However, once the glaring breach made the newspapers, dozens of Customs Border Patrol inspectors swarmed the docks.[30]

The Canadian government carefully avoided any entanglements with smuggling on the Detroit-Windsor border, even after many front-page stories of blazing guns, shot-riddled speedboats, and hijackings by men dressed up as law enforcement officers. Unofficially, however, Parliament Hill had strong views on the subject and did not like being blamed for the rampant smuggling. The Ontario Police Deputy Commissioner, Alfred E. Cuddy, had investigated the border activities and was convinced, amazingly, that no Canadian boats or citizens were smuggling liquor across the border. Cuddy reported that he was inspecting the liquor docks when he saw a speedboat pull out from the

Canadian side in broad daylight. The boat headed straight for the American shore with approximately fifty cases, unloaded the cases, and returned to Canada all within a few minutes. Canadian officials argued that such open traffic could not be carried on without the approval of American officials and that it was pointless to blame Canada for not stopping liquor traffic when the Americans were doing so little themselves.[31]

The pressure on the Canadian government did not come solely from American "drys." Canada also had a large number of "drys" who were angry at their government for not doing more to help the American Prohibition effort. The news from Detroit inflamed many Canadian religious and temperance groups, who bombarded Parliament with petitions asking that liquor clearances to the United States be denied. These formal protests were mild compared to angry telegrams and letters that were pouring in on the ministers of the Crown from every province, accusing the Canadian government of fearing the liquor syndicates and harboring armed thugs who attacked law officers of a friendly nation.[32]

To be fair, the US Prohibition forces were severely outnumbered by smugglers, both in manpower and craft. When the Coast Guard or Customs did make a seizure, it had the effect of temporarily shaking up the local smugglers and somewhat curtailing their business. On a foggy day in early July, a Coast Guard cutter captured one of the larger rum boats operating out of Amherstburg headed for Lake St. Clair. The boat contained 500 cases of beer and forty cases of whisky. After the seizure, most rum-runners temporarily suspended their operations in the area. However, rowboats with outboard motors, known as "skipjacks" still managed to get through the river blockade.[33]

Ecorse

On the southern fringe of Detroit is a town called Ecorse. The town became a significant economic force in the area when its first steel mill opened in 1923, but that was not the only reason. In the summer of 1929, it was one of the main ports of entry for Canadian liquor. The thriving, multicultural suburban town seemed like any other river town during the day. Two out of three people walking its streets spoke different European languages and the storefronts reflected that ethnic diversity.

By night, the town was much different. Its dark roads were ideal for smugglers. Trucks emerged from alleys and sped away, well-stocked with cases of liquor. On the river and ashore, boat and truck engines hummed as lookout-men closely scrutinized any passers-by. To the northwest in Detroit, the lights from the big plants lit the sky. Sparks flew up from gigantic smokestacks and when furnace doors were opened, the light from the fires could be seen from a great distance. Closer by, the lake boats passed. The river was narrow at Ecorse, only four minutes across to Canada by motorboat. Narrow, winding lanes ran from the one thoroughfare down to the river. At night, the entrances were completely dark and occasionally large trucks emerged out of the darkness in a rush, giving bystanders a jolt.

The river also became a no-man's land after dark, where any moving silhouette, noise, or flash of light could have meant danger. In the summer of 1929, with stricter enforcement, both sides resorted to shooting with the slightest provocation. Prohibition boats sometimes operated in the disguise of rum-runners and rum-runners also sometimes posed as Prohibition agents. To identify friend or foe on the river at night required keen senses.[34]

There were three classes of rum-running boats in Ecorse: fifty-footers that did 35 knots when loaded, the "flat tubs" barely able to make ten knots, and the small powerboats that quickly zipped across the river and back. There were about 500 boats of all types operating out of Ecorse. By day, the rum-runners sat tied up to docks for everyone to see. Anyone who doubted the use of the boats would only have to smell the scent of alcohol emanating from it or see the broken cases nearby, bearing labels such as Golden Wedding, Old Crow, Haig & Haig.

The two-mile waterfront of Ecorse had many secret tunnels and hidden docks. Before Prohibition, the town had few piers or warehouses. It was easy for the rum rings to rent or buy property and convert it to their purposes. Prohibition agents raided one old, dilapidated house in Ecorse that smugglers had converted into a warehouse. The cellar door opened almost at river level and the smugglers dug the earth and built a small, concealed dock where rum boats could land their goods. In another case, an underground channel penetrated several hundred yards inland, leading to a house that no one suspected.

The 1929 crackdown on smuggling made it very risky to store smuggled liquor around Ecorse. Smugglers preferred to load trucks and cars directly from incoming boats. This method required accurate timing and coordination. Once the craft touched the shore, dozens of workers were usually ready to offload the cargo, taking only a few minutes to finish the task. A force of guards and lookout men protected the cases of liquor until the trucks started their engines and sped off into the night. Despite the best efforts of law enforcement, the system of signals, maneuvering and docking, of unloading and then speeding the cargo away in trucks was amazingly effective. Thousands of cases came through Ecorse nightly.[35]

Strengthening the Great Lakes Prohibition Fleet

In August, the Coast Guard increased the size of its fleet in the Great Lakes by adding eight 75-foot cutters, bringing the total number of that type of vessel up to nineteen. Sixteen smaller patrol boats made their way to the Great Lakes via the Erie Canal, bringing the total number of Coast Guard vessels on the lakes up to 100. The new fleet would operate only on Lakes Ontario, Erie, and Huron.[36]

With the exception of the nineteen cutters, all vessels operating on the Great Lakes would be armed only with Navy rifles and Army revolvers. The 75-footers, which operated a good distance from shore, carried machine guns, rifles, revolvers, and one-pounders. Assistant Treasury Secretary Lowman referred to the one-pounders as "signal guns" for warning rum-runners. Lowman also announced to reporters that he had banned the use of machine guns on smaller Coast Guard and Customs boats operating along the Detroit River and close to the shoreline in order to minimize the danger of shooting citizens on land.[37]

Captain R.M. Chiswell, Assistant Commandant of the Coast Guard, told the press that only ordnance heavier than the one-pounder had been or would be removed from the Coast Guard cutters on the lakes. Coasties had already removed the three-inch and five-inch guns mounted aboard the *Seminole* and stored them in order to comply with the Rush-Bagot agreement with Canada.[20] Captain Chiswell explained the partial disarmament:

---

[20] The Rush Bagot agreement of 1817 stipulated that the naval force to be maintained upon the lakes by the United States and Great Britain "shall henceforth be confined to the following vessels on each side: On Lake Ontario to one vessel not exceeding 100 tons burden, and armed with one 18-pound cannon. On the upper lakes to two vessels not exceeding the like burden each and armed with like force, and on the waters of Lake Champlain to one vessel not exceeding like burden and armed with like force."

"Our orders directing the stripping of heavy ordnance from boats ordered to lake duty was misconstrued by some of the officers in the field. In some cases steps were taken to remove machine guns and all ordnance from Coast Guard boats. Those orders have been rescinded. The big boats will keep their one-pounders and machine guns. The smaller craft will carry rifles and revolvers."[38]

By the end of September, the big crackdown on Detroit's rum-runners ran out of steam. The Customs Border Patrol was letting more liquor get across from Ontario. In August 1929, almost as much liquor came from Canada as in August 1928, right before 23 members of the patrol were arrested for taking bribes and 90 percent of the rest were dismissed. In November 1928, when the patrolmen were arrested, nineteen bootleggers were indicted, of whom only six were captured. The rest fled to Canada.[39]

40

Raiding a Fortress

On September 19, 1929, the rum ship *Shawnee* arrived in port at Halifax, Nova Scotia with holes from gunfire. Captain John McLeod, master of the vessel, made a formal protest to the Canadian government through an attorney. According to McLeod's story, the *Shawnee* encountered Coast Guard Boat 145 at night a week earlier, twenty-six miles off New York. The vessel was flying the Canadian ensign and fully-lit. The 75-foot Coast Guard craft, however, was unlit.[1]

According to McLeod, the Coast Guard began firing, without warning, at his unarmed ship from a range of 100 yards, and fired the last round from four yards away—point blank for a naval gun. One of the shots passed through the stern, coming within four inches of the muffler and tearing the asbestos lining off. Another struck the rail on the wheelhouse.

He told reporters that it was remarkable that his ship did not sink, explaining that if one of the shots hit the muffler, his ship most likely would have burst into flames. If the shot had passed through the wooden hull one plank lower, the vessel would have sunk. The shell McLeod was referring to passed clean through the wooden hull, leaving a large hole on the starboard side, just above the waterline. Water splashed through the large hole and the crew had to use a water pump to keep the ship afloat.

Following the shots, the Number 145 hailed the *Shawnee*, saying, "What ship is that?" McLeod answered, "Well, you should know."[2]

The Coast Guard's account was slightly different. Admiral Billard announced in Washington that the Coast Guard cutter fired at the *Shawnee* near Ambrose light vessel because the ship was running without lights and would not stop after the Coast Guard signaled with whistles. The ship was not twenty-six miles out, but sixteen miles out, and the name on the stern was covered with canvas. Billard added that the patrol boat held the vessel in the beam of its searchlight and fired three blank warning shots. Billard went on to explain that:

> "The Coast Guard Boat then fired two shots in the direction of the craft, which then slowed down. There was no name on the stern or hailing port to identify her and the man in charge refused to give the name of the vessel. The vessel was then allowed to proceed and the name Shawnee was made out on her bow. The Coast Guard has no further information on her."[3]

According to statements from Washington, when the Coast Guardsman hailed the *Shawnee* and asked its name, a voice replied, "We know you, and that's enough." The ship then raced away at top speed and the Coast Guardsmen opened fire. The *Shawnee* then pulled up and the Coast Guard boat drew alongside after calling the *Gresham*, another cutter of the division. Although the Coast Guard did not board the rum-ship, the cutters followed it to Nova Scotia to make sure it did not touch American soil.

Coast Guard officials said that they suspected the *Shawnee* of being a rum runner that operated off the North Atlantic Coast from St. Pierre, Miquelon. If the ship was indeed running in ballast from Bermuda to Canada, as McLeod's statement claimed, then it was 400 miles off course.

It turned out that the *Shawnee* was part of a much bigger problem that was to make headlines a month later. At 4:30 PM on October 16, 1929, the US Government made thirty-five simultaneous raids. From Atlantic City, NJ to Sag Harbor, NY, special Treasury agents, deputy US Marshals, and state police all launched their raids on key points in a suspected rum ring. The operations covered an area stretching 200 miles, including landing points, storage stations, warehouses, offices, and salesrooms.

Well before the raids began, six Coast Guard destroyers and ten Customs speedboats left New London and waited off New York. An hour before the raids began, the vessels set out under sealed orders. Their mission was to be on the lookout for ships and speedboats of the syndicate, which might be in the vicinity. They found none. Coasties seized three vessels during the previous two months, which they had identified as property of the syndicate. All three were equipped with radios powerful enough to communicate with the shore.[4]

In the countryside, five miles away from Highlands, NJ, at a far corner of the Lower Bay, agents arrested the syndicate's wireless operator as he was transmitting a code message. A federal man took his place and sent messages to a big boat loaded with liquor off Montauk Point, leading it, unknowingly, to a Coast Guard destroyer. A mile from the wireless station, an even larger group of agents climbed to a hilltop and seized a fortress with gun emplacements, an elaborate armory, telescopes mounted in a cupola observation tower, and underground storage vaults. This turned out to be the principal plant of the syndicate.

The "fortress" turned out to be the former estate of Oscar Hammerstein, the famous songwriter and Broadway producer. The smugglers converted the former mansion into the hilltop armory and observation tower. After Hammerstein no longer used the house, the smugglers had redecorated the place, arming it with sawed-off shotguns, sub-machine guns, tear gas guns, and a variety of large pistols. The radio station occupied a bungalow on a corner of the property remote from the main house. Smugglers used a large cave in the side of the hill for liquor storage.[5]

William J. Calhoun, Prohibition Administrator of New Jersey, was in charge of the raids. He stayed in his office through the night while reports continued to come in and his staff recorded the arrests and seizures. As of midnight, the raiders confiscated liquor at four of the sites. Calhoun and his assistants did not make any official estimates of the syndicate's operations; however, unofficial sources estimated that the syndicate was equipped to smuggle in as much as 10,000 cases of liquor per week, worth $1 million at retail prices.

Forrester F. Redfern, the government's radio operator, maintained contact with the *Shawnee*, which sat off Montauk Point after the raids. However, time is critical in a coordinated raid and by the next day the *Shawnee* broke contact with the Highlands station. The men aboard the ship had become suspicious and turned back. The Coast Guard destroyers continued their search for it during the following day but found nothing.[6]

Planning the Raids

For six months prior to the raids, the government had been building a case and making plans for the day of the raids. The Coast Guard had also been drawing up plans and mapping out the syndicate's operations. The coordinated attack would involve thirty-five deputy marshals, twenty New Jersey State Police, seventy-five special Treasury agents, and, of course, the Coast Guard. The preparations were so complete that on the day of the raids, at the same zero hour of 4:30 PM, every bank which allegedly did business with the syndicate was served with a subpoena to produce all records of the syndicate's accounts. The Bank of America in New York was one of the banks on the list.[7]

Robert Watts, assistant to Calhoun, discussed the case with reporters at New York's Federal Building the next day. In addition to praising Calhoun for organizing and planning the raids, he told the reporters that the Federal Radio Commission played a very big part in discovering the syndicate. It was a Federal Radio inspector who intercepted a strange code message six months earlier. Its source could not be traced and it apparently came from an unlicensed transmitter. The code was baffling, but after weeks of work by government experts under Supervising Radio Inspector Arthur Batcheller, the code was cracked.

After that day, government men intercepted and decoded every message coming out of that hidden station in Highlands. They recorded every order to every ship and small boat of the syndicate. The government claimed it knew every detail of the syndicate's business. Mr. Watts went on to say that the authorities knew about every pint of liquor that the rum ring smuggled in. The government radio operators practiced the code and learned to use it with the same ease as the syndicate's men. During the raids, one of them was ready to step into the place of the arrested wireless man to deceive the ships at sea. Malcolm MacMaster, the arrested radio man, was the first person ever to be indicted under the Federal Radio Act for operating a station without a license.

Like any large business operation, this particular rum syndicate was a complex organization employing a large variety of skilled employees. There were skippers and seamen to man the larger ships, supercargoes to handle the cargo on board, contact men in charge of the speed boat fleet, truck drivers and mechanics, warehouse operators, radio operators, office executives, salesmen and sales managers, and gunmen and racketeers for protection against hijackers. Since the mansion at the top was the hill was the primary cutting plant, it had an unbelievable assortment of machine guns and small arms for protection against competitors and anyone looking to steal the liquor.[8]

There were six vessels working for the syndicate that made regular trips between St. Pierre and Miquelon, and Bermuda. These diesel-powered ships were approximately thirty-five tons, capable of a speed of fifteen knots, and could carry 3,000 cases of liquor. The Coast Guard had recently fired upon one of the six, named the *Shawnee.* These vessels were loaded with liquor at their regular terminal ports and, while passing the New Jersey and Long Island coast, speedboats met them to carry the liquor ashore.

The authorities knew about ten of the rum ring's speedboats but did not know how large the total fleet was. Along the New Jersey and Long Island coasts, smugglers used roadhouses and inns as temporary storage places, the owners of the inns usually being members of the syndicate. From these locations, men loaded the liquor on trucks and drove it to the mansion and the other cutting plants, where the liquor was diluted and re-bottled. From there, the liquor went to warehouses and salesrooms in large cities.

During the coordinated raid, agents stormed the main New York sales office on 43rd Street, where the board of directors met every week and distributed their profits. The New York contingent made three other raids and found liquor in a Bronx garage. Sixteen raids were carried out in New Jersey, including the raid of the mansion where agents arrested fifteen men. In addition, agents raided several spots on Long Island. In total, thirty-two people were arrested on that day, including Mannie Kessler and Morris Sweetwood, who were known bootleg kings five years earlier and had served time in Atlanta's federal prison.[9]

During the next day, the federal court at Trenton, NJ was jammed with lawyers, defendants, and witnesses as arrangements were made to arraign the men before Judge William N. Runyon. Fourteen defendants went before Judge Runyon and bail was set at $1,000 to $30,000. Five men arrested in Manhattan and the Bronx were arraigned in federal court in Manhattan, the highest bail being $15, 000. One man was arraigned in Brooklyn. Mannie Kessler and Morris Sweetwood were released from custody in Trenton. The government supposedly had no information indicating that the two men were involved in the syndicate's operations; they just "happened" to be at one of the smuggling sites when agents raided the place. US Attorney Philip Forman announced that he had no grounds on which to hold them and ordered their release in exchange for their promise to testify.[10]

Malcolm MacMasters, the radio man, was held in $30,000 bail, the highest bail for any of the arrested men. He was indicted not only for conspiracy to violate the Prohibition law, but also for operating an unlicensed wireless transmitting station. He was the first person ever be indicted on the latter charge. Frederic Pearce, MacMaster's attorney, protested vigorously against the bail, arguing that it was excessive. US Attorney Forman, who asked for bail to be set so high, told the court that the government considered the radio violation a very serious charge and the station itself to have been an "extreme hazard," because it was located on the Atlantic Coast, near New York Harbor. MacMasters had to pay a higher bail than the two principal figures arrested in the raids. Harold Lindauer and Andrew Richards, two of the top figures in the syndicate, had their bail set at $25,000 each.

Two Little Black Books

The agents found two little black books in the Highlands mansion, which Calhoun spent most of the following day studying. After leaving his office late on the night of the raids, he came back a few hours later to receive telephone reports from the "front" and sift through the mass of evidence captured during the raids. The black books were 10"x5" account books filled with daily records of the income and expenditures of the syndicate. Calhoun told reporters that the books indicated the syndicate had been expanding, aiming to monopolize the imported liquor market in New York and New Jersey. According to one entry, the syndicate had recently purchased $200,000 worth of liquor in Montreal.[11]

Assistant US Attorney James E. Wilkinson, in charge of the Prohibition Division in Brooklyn, told the press that throughout the black books were bribes. Whether Prohibition agents were on the list in addition to New Jersey local police was unclear. Most of the payments listed as "protection" were recorded with the titles of the officials, but not their names. Some of these bribes ran into the five-figure range.

Wilkinson vehemently denounced the banks and lawyers with whom the syndicate supposedly did business. Of the seven banks in which the syndicate carried accounts, three were in New Jersey. For some mysterious reason, most likely political, he condemned the actions of the New Jersey banks and lawyers but said specifically that the New York banks and lawyers were exempt from the following tirade:

> "When banks lend their palatial offices as a rendezvous for bootleggers and finance bootlegging operations with accounts carried in code to prevent their

identification; and when leading and supposedly respectable lawyers sit in at bootleggers' conferences in their own offices, I consider it is about time for the public to begin to consider a new code of ethics for the business world.

"This is not a question of prohibition enforcement. It is a matter of the financing of all kinds of crime by banks, who are thus misusing their depositors' money. It is no secret that this mob of bootleggers is more or less hooked up with the gang of Scarface Al Capone."[12]

At the time, the notorious Chicago gangster Al Capone was in jail in Philadelphia. Among the documents seized in the raids was a check Capone made out to one of the indicted heads of the syndicate. Wilkinson told reporters that the check was mailed during the previous month, but he had no clue as to how Capone sent it from his cell in Philadelphia.

US Attorney Philip M. Foreman, in Trenton, New Jersey, dismissed Wilkinson's accusations against New Jersey banks, lawyers, and Al Capone. He told reporters that there was no evidence that any of these three factors were connected with the syndicate. Prohibition Administrator William J. Calhoun in Newark, NJ, who built the case against the syndicate and planned the raids, refused to comment. Meanwhile, the Coast Guard continued its search but did not capture any vessels.

Included in the many confiscated documents were complete sets of maps of Long Island's seacoast, worked out to the minutest detail. In addition to the main channels shown on all maritime maps, these maps included small channels running in to the shore, deep enough for speedboats, but free from the traffic of recognized channels.[13]

Another document seized was a list of customers, with addresses. Since the sales were almost exclusively wholesale, the customers listed were mostly speakeasies and other places that sold liquor at retail prices.

Six months later, in April 1930, a federal grand jury in Trenton handed out about fifty indictments based on the evidence seized in the October raids. The accused smugglers made deposits totaling nearly $1 million in different banks, all under false names. Anthony Cassino, identified in the indictment merely as a "driver," deposited $572,678 in a Bank of America account over a six-month period. Another, named Ed Flanagan, deposited a total of $156,439 at a bank in Hampton Bays, NY.

Andrew Richards, another employee of the ring, deposited $241,135 in the New Jersey National Bank and Trust Company of Newark.[14]

An Unhappy Mayor

Mayor George W. Hardy of Highlands, NJ, who was also the station agent in town for the Jersey Central Railroad as well as president of the Board of Education, told reporters that the raids in his town gave it a bad name.

> "Bootleggers can't operate here today because of the change in bootlegging methods. Eight years ago small speedboats, carrying only about a hundred cases were used, and they came up the Shrewsbury from Sandy Hook all the time. Why, I've seen the stuff unloaded and carted away in open trucks in broad daylight. The bootleggers in those days had just started, and most of them never had any money before. So they used to run wild as soon as they made a little money, getting drunk and shooting up the town. This was like a border town in those days, but it's not that way today.
> "They can't use the river today. Now they use big boats which can carry a great many cases. There's no traffic on the river, and if a working boat tried to come up it would be noticed at once. There are three Coast Guard stations right in sight of the town. Two are down by Sandy Hook, where boats would have to pass, and the third is right across the river, in full view of the whole waterfront. The change in method has taken the bootleggers away from here.
> "Why eight years ago it was a common thing to have several gun fights in the streets in one night. I remember one time the bootleggers thought a man here had told on them, and they put two charges of buckshot right through the wall of his house the next night. They were wild fellows then. But the men in it today, why if you met them on the street, you would think they were Sunday school teachers. They aren't taking any chances."[15]

Mayor Hardy told reporters that his election during the previous January had been on a "square deal" issue. He said the bootleggers spent hundreds of dollars to defeat him. He won by five votes in a total poll of more than 1,000. The bootleggers put up money for a recount because they wanted to keep him out of office. After the recount, he won by six votes.

A Coast Guard Leak

Captain Randolph Ridgely, head of the Coast Guard in New York, told reporters that rum syndicates most likely succeeded in getting a few of their men into the Coast Guard. Ridgely declared that it would be surprising if there were no agents of rum-runners or other crooked men among the 10,000 enlisted in the Coast Guard. Assistant Treasury Secretary Lowman announced on October 22, 1929 that the Treasury Department was investigating whether enlisted men were guilty of telling rum-runners where the Coast Guard cutters were during the coordinated raids in New York and New Jersey.[16]

> "We have been suspicious of some of the Coast Guard people, but we have no positive evidence, and our suspicions do not concern officers but rather non-commissioned members of our force. Our suspicions are that these men may have been passing information to rum-runners as to the location of Coast Guard vessels. We do not believe that they have aided in the landing of liquor.
> "We got everything we had expected. We had hopes that we might lure the Shawnee, one of the supply craft of the ring, but it remained outside of the twelve-mile limit and these hopes were dashed."[17]

To be fair, Lowman added that the Coast Guard was "pretty reliable" and its service in capturing rum runners had been excellent.

41

The December Shootings

> "The Coast Guardsmen had no more right to shoot those men than would Boston police officers have to go into hotel dining rooms on New Year's Eve and shoot persons who were drinking at the tables, because the police would know that the people at the tables had violated the law in transporting the liquor there."
>
> — Former Boston Mayor John F. Fitzgerald at Faneuil Hall, January 2, 1930.[1]

On the night of Christmas 1929, Eugene Downey, the 27 year-old son of a Buffalo policeman, and a companion were speeding across the Niagara River in a small boat. Coast Guardsmen on patrol suspected them of rum-running and ordered them to stop. When Downey did not stop, the Coasties opened fire. One round struck him in the thigh and he died less than an hour later in a nearby hospital. His fellow rider ran the craft to shore and escaped. Downey was out on bail after being charged with conspiracy to smuggle. However, the Coast Guardsmen found no liquor or narcotics in his boat.[2]

On the following day, District Attorney Guy B. Moore launched the state's investigation into the fatal shooting by questioning Asa Ennis, Rudolph Thompson, and Orville Lagrant—the crew of the Coast Guard patrol boat who fired the fatal volley of rifle and pistol shots. Martin W. Rassmussen, the Coast Guard district commander, ordered the three men, all boatswain's mates second class, to report to the District Attorney after Attorney General Mitchell in Washington had instructed Federal District Attorney Richard H. Templeton, in Buffalo, to cooperate with Moore in the investigation.[3]

Senator Royal S. Copeland sent a telegram to Admiral Billard the day after the shooting urging that the Coast Guardsmen involved in the shooting be turned over to civil authorities. The letter said, in part:

> "You and I have discussed these Coast Guard outrages and you have expressed the hope they were ended. What can be said now when another apparently needless death is on the shoulders of your Buffalo men?
>
> "My urgent advice in the Hanson case was to submit the officials charged with the crime to the civil authorities. The government cannot afford to take any other action in the Downey matter."[4]

In an effort to control damage to the Coast Guard's image, Assistant Treasury Secretary Lowman made a public statement on the 27th. According to his statement, at 4:40 PM a Coast Guard lookout spotted a rum-runner in Canadian waters proceeding up the Niagara River. The boat sat in Canadian waters for a short time off the Erie Beach dancing pavilion, and then started toward the American shore. The officer in charge of the Buffalo Coast Guard station dispatched boat 2245 to intercept the rum-runner. Darkness set in at 5:20. The Coast Guard boat proceeded to the north breakwater entrance light and tied up to the breakwater.

Ten minutes after the Coasties tied up to the breakwater, the suspected rum-runner was coming from a southerly direction. When the boat was within thirty yards, the Coast Guard used its standard hailing signals and fired six blank warning shots. Lowman continued:

> "The suspected craft kept on its course and the Coast Guard craft fired between twelve and fifteen pistol shots into the rum-runner with the intent of disabling the motor. The shots were aimed low. The rum-runner showed no lights and failed to stop.
>
> "The Coast Guard boat continued the pursuit, but because of the obstruction of floating ice lost track of the rum-runner, and it was fully half an hour before they finally discovered her tied to the pier and it was found that there was a wounded man in the boat, the other man having disappeared.
>
> "The wounded man was removed to the Emergency Hospital with all possible speed. It was found that he had been shot in the leg, and he died a short time after arriving at the hospital. The man shot was Eugene F. Downey, Jr. who was out on $10,000 bail in connection with another smuggling case. No liquor was found in the boat, but this has no significance because there was plenty of time to throw the liquor overboard into the lake…

"The Coast Guards were proceeding under authority of Section 581 of the Tariff Act, which gives them full authority to stop any boat at any time in American waters for inspection."[5]

A highlight in the grand jury hearing was the testimony of three Buffalo policemen, who said that they saw two Coast Guardsmen standing near the dock near where Downey was lying wounded in his boat. Moore asked one of them, Patrolman C.M. Meyers, if the Guardsmen were making any attempt to help. Meyers answered that they were not, as far as he could see. He said policemen called the ambulance to take Downey to the hospital, and that they, the policemen, carried an unconscious Downey up a ladder from the boat.[6]

On December 30, 1929, nearly 1,000 people attended Downey's funeral at Holy Family Church; many of the mourners had to stand outside due to overcrowding. Among them was James G. Higgins, who had recently resigned as Buffalo's police commissioner. A month later, the grand jury returned a no-bill against the three Coast Guardsmen. The refusal of the jury to indict the three men on the charge of second-degree manslaughter came as a surprise to District Attorney Moore and angered many who believed the killing of Downey was unjustified. For those not aware of the difference between a grand jury and trial jury, a grand jury is a panel of citizens assembled by the government to hear evidence against an accused, and determine whether an indictment for a crime should be brought to trial. The men responsible for Downey's death never even went to trial.[7]

The Black Duck

During the same night, Patrol Boat 290, skippered by Boatswain A.C. Cornell, was cruising near Dumpling Light. The dense fog, which hung low over the water, was ideal for rum-running. The patrol boat was moving slowly through the fog when the lookout heard the muffled exhaust of a motorboat. The Coast Guardsmen changed course immediately and pursued the craft at full speed, using the other boat's wake as a guide. As the sound of the motorboat became louder, the patrol boat aimed its searchlight and saw C-5677 on the hull, the number of the *Black Duck*. The patrol boat's siren warned the *Black Duck* to stop, but instead, the boat surged ahead at full speed.[8]

A gunner on the forward deck of the patrol boat loaded a shell in the breech of the one-pounder. After a final blast of the siren failed to stop the *Black Duck*, the gunner fired off a round, which crossed the speedboat's bow and disappeared into the water. Unfazed, the speedboat continued on its course.

The gunner fired another round, but the *Black Duck* ignored it. As the patrol boat gained on the rum-runner, the searchlights revealed the silhouettes of moving figures in the pilot house. The afterdeck was piled with burlap bags, most likely filled with bottles of liquor. Since the warning shots and siren did not work, the Coasties decided to spray the *Black Duck* with machine gun rounds. The speedboat's engine stopped and a man staggered out onto the deck.

The patrol boat quickly caught up and the crew boarded the rum-runner. In the pilot house, three men lay dead on the floor, all victims of the machine gun. The fourth man survived, but his right thumb was shot off and he was shot through his right arm. When the Coasties tried to question him, he refused to answer. The patrol boat towed the speedboat to New London, Connecticut. At first, the surviving member of the crew refused to answer any questions, but when he was finally convinced that his crewmates were dead, he told the interrogators that he was Charles Travers of New Bedford. He also gave the names of the other three men: Jake Weisman of Providence, RI; Dudley Brandt of Boston, MA; and John Goulart of Fair Haven, MA.[9]

The deceased Weisman was 35 years old and was out on bail for a federal charge of conspiracy to violate the Prohibition laws after being arrested at a raid on a liquor plant in Portsmouth. In his pocket were the keys to an expensive car, which police found at a Newport garage. Before his arrest in the Portsmouth case, Weisman had been arrested for transporting Canadian beer. One of the dead men had $127 in his pocket and another had $284, which was enough money to buy a decent used car in the 1920s.

Coast Guardsmen aboard the 290 claimed that the speedboat changed course just as the machine gun opened fire and blamed this for the deaths of the three men. They said that the machine gun fire was directed at the speedboat's stern and intended to disable the rudder. Travers, however, told police, "We never had a chance."[10]

Travers and the bodies of the other three were put ashore at Fort Adams before the *Black Duck* continued on to New London. Colonel Chamberlain, the commanding officer, contacted US District Attorney

Boss at Providence, R.I. The district attorney recommended a coroner and a medical examiner, who examined the bodies. After the autopsy, the medical examiner declared that Weisman and Goulart had died of internal hemorrhages caused by bullet wounds, and Brandt died of a bullet through the brain.

Admiral Billard received first word of the killings from newspaper reporters late the following afternoon. He immediately asked his men at Coast Guard Headquarters for information on the incident. At the DC headquarters, the officers on duty had only skeleton reports from the base at New London. For Billard, the *Black Duck* incident could not have come at a worse time; Congress was in the middle of a fierce debate on Prohibition enforcement and its costs in dollars, prison sentences, and in lives. After learning what happened, Admiral Billard said to reporters:

> "The Coast Guard has the job of stopping liquor smuggling at sea. It is not a job that can be handled with soft words and amiable gestures. The Coast Guard is used to carrying out any duty given it with vigor and determination.
>
> "It means business about this matter and acts strictly within the law. If a smuggler elects to defy the command of a Coast Guard craft to stop, he runs a serious risk of getting hurt through a course of action that the law has specifically authorized for a hundred years."[11]

According to the letter of the law, Admiral Billard was correct. The statute he was referring to is reprinted in the footnote below.[21] Not only did that statute give the Coast Guard the authority to fire into a fleeing craft that did not hail-to after being signaled, it also absolved the commander and crew of liability for doing so. However, many Americans were still outraged over the incident and the wording of some

---

[21] Admiral Billard was referring to US Code Title 14, Part I, Chapter 17, §637 which read: "Whenever any vessel liable to seizure or examination does not bring to when requested to do so, or on being chased by a cutter or boat which has displayed the pennant and ensign prescribed for vessels in the Coast Guard, *the commanding officer of the cutter or boat may fire at or into such vessel* which does not bring to after such pennant or ensign has been hoisted and a gun has been fired by such cutter or boat as a signal, and such *commanding officer and all persons acting by or under his direction shall be indemnified from any penalties or actions for damage for so doing if any person is killed or wounded by such fire,* and if the commanding officer is prosecuted or is arrested therefore he shall be forthwith admitted to bail." As quoted in *The New York Times*, December 31, 1929. Italics added by author.

maritime statute did not, in their minds, justify the killing of three unarmed men and the wounding of another. News of the killings spread to all parts of the nation via newspaper and radio.

One such outraged American was Senator David Walsh of Massachusetts. When he heard the news in Boston, he told reporters that he would demand the disarmament of the Coast Guard and other federal agencies engaged in Prohibition enforcement in order "to safeguard the safety and lives of law-abiding citizens." He went on to tell reporters that, "the enforcement agencies must not be permitted to employ ammunition and guns unless it is known that persons suspected of evading the liquor laws are armed."[12] He described the killing of the three men as one of the most shocking episodes since the adoption of Prohibition. He also sent the following telegram to Treasury Secretary Mellon, which was reprinted in newspapers:

> Much public indignation in Massachusetts as a result of killing three citizens alleged to be violating prohibition law by the Coast Guard off Newport Sunday. Request that you have full investigation made by officers not connected with the Coast Guard and whom the public believe to be disinterested.
>
> Congress and the public should be fully informed as to all facts in this shocking episode, the outcome of a conflict between law violators and government officials.
>
> Your high sense of public duty, I am certain, will lead you to move immediately to determine all the circumstances and punish those who may be found to have exceeded their authority and used their official position to needlessly kill their fellow-citizens, even though violating the law.
>
> I will very willingly cooperate with you in this important service and you may command me in any way.[13]

Senator Walsh added that he did not attempt to justify the breaking of a law which "millions of Americans look upon as a dangerous encroachment of personal liberty," but on the other hand, "it is a murderous act to kill the unarmed whose attempted crime is aided and abetted and encouraged by overwhelming numbers of our citizens, especially in large centers."[14]

Drunken Fistfight

On the day after the *Black Duck* shooting, the Coast Guard and the US District Attorney's office in Providence began investigations. At the same time, the Coast Guard launched another investigation into the disappearance of some of the seized liquor cargo from the *Flor-del-Mar*. While on patrol on the night of December 29th, Coast Guardsmen spotted the *Flor-del-Mar*, a 100-ton vessel of Halifax, Nova Scotia, near Montauk Point, Long Island. The patrol boat *Legare* signaled the former sub-chaser but the *Flor-del-Mar* ignored the signals. Boatswain Otto Bentz, in charge of the patrol boat, changed course at once and headed for the suspicious vessel. As the Coasties approached, they saw flames rising from the ship. As they got closer, they found that the *Flor-del-Mar*'s crew abandoned ship before setting the vessel afire.[15]

As the *Legare* pulled alongside, Coasties rushed to douse the flames with buckets of water and extinguished the fire. When they searched the vessel, the men found 4,000 cases of liquor aboard. The cases were stored in every part of the ship, even in a spare boat, which the escaping crew left behind. While some of the Coast Guardsmen conducted their search, others set out in small boats in search of the *Flor-del-Mar*'s crew. However, after a two hour search of the nearby shoreline, the rum smugglers were nowhere to be found.

When the search party returned, the crew made arrangements to tow the burnt vessel into New London, Connecticut. The fire destroyed most of its superstructure and its deckhouse had completely disappeared, charred into oblivion. The *Flor-del-Mar* was flooded after the fire and in danger of sinking, so the *Legare* took aboard part of the liquor cargo. After the cargo transfer, the two vessels headed to port.

Coast Guardsmen and sailors from the submarine base at New London had a drinking contest, consuming liquor from the *Flor-del-Mar*, and then got into a drunken fistfight. A Coast Guardsman named Jack Easley and a sailor named George Rupert were seriously injured in the brawl. Rupert was taken to the hospital, where doctors told him he might lose sight in one eye. Another sailor named Harry Stone was arrested and charged with assault and battery for attacking both men.[16]

After the brawl, seven Coasties were held in custody while awaiting a court-martial. Several other Coast Guardsmen were reported for being intoxicated. Captain L.T. Chalker, Chief of Staff at the New London Coast Guard Base, ordered a search of all vessels docked at the base for liquor. After the Coast Guard captured the *Flor-del-Mar*, the men stacked the confiscated liquor in a storeroom on a pier, making a pile twelve feet wide, twenty feet long, and eight feet high. Later, many of the burlap bags containing liquor were missing from the pile.

New London police, who were called in during the brawl, reported that the fighting followed a party attended by the Coast Guard basketball team and that they were informed that the liquor was from the *Flor-del-Mar*. The sailor Harry Stone, who attacked the two Coast Guardsmen and was charged with assault, was fined $75 and received a suspended sentence of ten days in jail.[17]

Meanwhile, Coast Guard Commander C.C. Von Paulson was assigned as the investigator who would look into the *Black Duck* shooting. The survivor, Charles Travers, remained in the hospital, recovering from his injuries under close watch by the Coast Guard. Travers' attorney, John H. Backus, attempted to see him but was refused admission. Backus appealed to the Attorney General of Rhode Island, demanding permission for himself and twenty other interested persons to see his client.[18]

Inspector Patrick Furey of the Newport Police was also denied access to Travers. Only two men managed to get past the guards. One of the men was Travers' cousin, and the other was a reverend who was the superintendent of the Seamen's Church Institute at Newport. The chief petty officer on duty at the hospital told reporters that his men were acting under special authority from Washington, transmitted to the Coast Guard Base at New London.

Crew members of Patrol Boat 290 were confined to their vessel on the day following the incident. Although Lt. R.C. Jewell denied that they were being held pending an inquiry, they were not allowed to discuss the case with reporters. And then there was a conflict over jurisdiction.

Federal Attorney Henry M. Boss of Providence, who was also investigating the shootings, said that he saw no reason for presenting the facts to a federal grand jury. However, Assistant Attorney General Benjamin M. McLyman, of Rhode Island, insisted that the case go either before a federal or state grand jury. He announced that if the federal authorities would not take action, then the state would. Mr. Boss held a conference later in the day with Assistant Attorney General Sigmund W. Fischer and both agreed to await the outcome of the Coast Guard inquiry before taking action.[19]

At Providence, R.I. two days after the shooting, Senator Jesse H. Metcalf issued a statement which said that he would ask the Senate to launch an investigation into the shooting if the four or more inquiries underway by other agencies did not get to the heart of the matter. On the same day, Charles Travers was transported from the hospital at Newport to Providence and arraigned before a federal commissioner. He posted $10,000 bail and went to his home in New Bedford.[20]

Fueling the Fire

Congress was already engaged in a heated debate over Prohibition when the *Black Duck* shooting happened. The deaths of the three unarmed men only made matters worse. Assistant Treasury Secretary Lowman defended the shootings, saying:

> "...The loss of life at Newport the other day was unfortunate but unavoidable. The laws of the United States must be maintained. The smugglers defied the government officers and took their punishment. They have no one to blame but themselves."[21]

Secretary Lowman's remarks outraged those who thought the Prohibition law was pointless and had already cost far too many lives. Senator Brookhart of Iowa demanded the removal of the Treasury Department's high command, made up of Secretary Mellon, Under-Secretary Mills, Assistant Secretary Lowman, and Prohibition Commissioner Doran. Brookhart added that he was in agreement with Senator Borah, who charged that the federal Prohibition machine was inefficient from top to bottom and that that first step in the cleaning up process would be the removal of those four Treasury men.[22]

Outrage at Faneuil Hall

On January 2, 1930, angry citizens and politicians met at Faneuil Hall in Boston, where they adopted a resolution calling on President Hoover for a thorough and impartial investigation of the *Black Duck* shooting. The text of the resolution, printed in the footnote below,[22]

---

[22] The resolution read: "Resolved, that we, citizens of the United States, assembled this second day of January 1930, in convention in Faneuil Hall, Boston, are deeply shocked

stated that the attitude of the government "gives the impression that an attempt is being made to suppress the facts and whitewash a criminal act, and all this for the enforcement of an unnecessary and stupid law."[23]

The historic hall, which served as an important meeting place since the American Revolution, was packed to the rafters before noon. Hundreds stood outside the hall, including scores of market-men in white uniforms and straw hats. A band played while the crowd came in. William H. Mitchell, the chairman, opened the meeting by saying:

> "The Boston redcoats had full warrant under the law to order the slaying of Crispus Attucks. Three men were done to death last Sunday morning in Newport Harbor under the guise of authority.
>
> "A Washington paper in the last few days has printed a list of 1,100 done to death throughout the country under similar conditions. When stark wholesale murder stalks abroad under the protection of any law, in God's name repeal that law. Champions of justice were never needed more than now, and some of them are here."[24]

Conrad W. Crooker, general counsel for the Liberal Civic League, added:

---

and indignant at the attitude of Assistant Secretary of the Treasury Lowman who as the responsible head of prohibition enforcement, has justified without examination the killing of three citizens by the Coast Guard in Newport harbor.

"We believe that we have a right to respectfully demand that you, Sir, as President of the United States, order a thorough and searching investigation into the facts surrounding this deplorable incident, by somebody not connected with the Coast Guard or the Treasury Department.

"By the continuance of such governmental practices as the incident above described, we can see nothing by the destruction of the liberties for which our fathers fought, for which free men have bled, from the time of the great charter.

"We are not asserting the guilt of the Coast Guard, but we believe the attitude of the government as at present taken will justly give the impression that attempt is being made to suppress the facts and whitewash a criminal act of the worst kind, and all this for the enforcement of an unpopular, unnecessary and stupid law, which has no proper place in the Constitution of our nation and which all intelligent people know can never be enforced.

"Be it further Resolved, that the original of the above resolution be signed by the chairman of the meeting and duly verified, and that it be sent to the President of the United States and a copy thereof to each member of the Congress, and Secretary of the Treasury Mellon and Assistant Secretary of the Treasury Lowman." As printed in *The New York Times*, January 3, 1930.

"We are meeting here not to glorify rum-runners or bootleggers. These men were known to be rum-runners, but they were human beings, citizens of the United States. If we are going to have law and order we must have law and order on the part of our government."[25]

Mr. Crooker blasted Boatswain Cornell, who skippered the Coast Guard boat, as a "miserable skunk." He denied that Cornell had followed the rules of the sea, saying, "Cornell did not show his pennant in any manner so that the men on the rum-runner could see it. He did not sound his Klaxon [ship horn]."[26]

Joseph Walker, former Speaker of the House of Representatives, said that the killings were "unjustifiable" and "high-handed." Amid applause, he continued:

"I accept the challenge issued by the Governor in his address to the Massachusetts Legislature. If the Legislature does not repeal the baby Volstead act, the people will. Massachusetts will never help enforce a law the repeal of which she has already voted on by an overwhelming majority.

"The Constitution commands our respect, but the Eighteenth Amendment is inconsistent with the Constitution, and deserves no respect whatsoever. I say restore the Constitution. Give us again liberty and self-government."[27]

Representative John J. Douglass also denounced the killings and demanded a change in the Constitution:

"We are not here to defend rum runners. We are here in protest against the action of a Federal department attempting to enforce an unenforceable law. We are here to enforce the command of God, 'Thou shalt not kill.'

"We are here to demand the right of existence from our government. The United States has no more right to kill a man unlawfully than has an individual. Men were slain feloniously Sunday morning by the Coast Guard of the United States. They were murdered."[28]

Former Mayor John F. Fitzgerald criticized the attitude of Governor Allen on the Volstead Act and announced that he, Fitzgerald, would be running for governor the following fall as a Democrat on the platform of repealing Prohibition. He added that:

> "Those three men were bringing in liquor for New Year's Eve celebrations. They knew it would be consumed by governors of states, mayors of cities, selectmen of towns, judges of the Supreme Court, judges of the Superior Court and the municipal court—in fact, by public officials everywhere.
> "The Coast Guard had no more right to shoot those men than would Boston police officers have to go into hotel dining rooms on New Year's Eve and shoot patrons who were drinking at the tables, because the police would know that the people at the tables violated the law in transporting the liquor there."[29]

After the meeting, the crowd poured out of Faneuil Hall and onto the Boston Common, where there was a Coast Guard recruiting station. The petty officer in charge of the recruiting station, greatly outnumbered, stood by helpless as the angry men tore the recruiting posters from their frames and kicked the frames around on the sidewalk. After the demonstration was over, he gathered up the debris and rushed to the local Coast Guard headquarters at the Custom House to report the incident.

The outrage at Faneuil Hall and the petition to Congress did not affect Treasury Secretary Mellon's opinion in the least. On January 3, 1930, Mellon had just returned from a yachting cruise in the Bahamas. Keep in mind that Mellon was in charge of maintaining the financial health of the nation and that this was only a couple of months after the worst stock market crash and the beginning of the Great Depression. While it is true that the Great Depression would have happened whether or not Secretary Mellon took his yachting vacation, it just looked really bad and showed a disconnect with the plight of the average American.

Mellon told reporters that the Coast Guard crew was justified in firing at the *Black Duck* when it failed to halt. He said that the Coast Guard gave the craft warning and that since the *Black Duck* was trying to escape, "the Coast Guard could not do less than it did."[30] Interestingly, as sure as Mellon was on that day that the Coasties did no wrong, he still ordered an investigation conducted by the Collector of Customs at Boston plus two Customs agents. Although the State of Rhode Island intended to prosecute the Coast Guardsmen, the Coasties had the right to request that their trial be moved to a federal court, since they worked as agents of the federal government. However, before the men could exercise that option, they had to be charged in a state court, and as of January 3, no formal charges were brought and the men awaited the results of a grand jury investigation. Once a grand jury found that the state had enough of a case to proceed with a criminal trial, the trial procedure could begin.

Gang Beats Two Coast Guardsmen

During the following night, a gang of men severely beat two Coast Guardsmen at New London, Connecticut. Coxswain George A. Cadorett, who was attached to the destroyer *Erickson*, was the first victim. As he was walking through the freight yard of the Central Vermont Railroad on his way to the base, one of the men asked him:

"Were you on the 290?"

"No," Cadorett answered, "but I am a Coast Guardsman."

"Well, that's good enough for us," replied one of the men, and the gang gave him a severe beating.[31] Soon afterward, another Coast Guardsman, who did not give his name, called the New London police and reported that he had also been beaten in the freight yard, apparently by the same gang.

Police hurried to the scene, and heard several men, who were standing on the opposite side of a parked train, discussing the two beatings. At that moment, one of the officers slipped and fell on the ice, giving away their position, and the gang fled. As a result of the attacks, a double guard was ordered to patrol the State Pier and its perimeter.

Coast Guard Captain L.F. Chalker told reporters that the attacks were a result of the recent bad publicity:

> "The readiness with which many papers have published the statements of liquor smugglers, cheap politicians and wet fanatics has undoubtedly led many ruffians to believe that such action as last night's cowardly attack on two of our men would meet with public approval.
>
> "As was expected, however, the reaction has set in, and the public will soon realize that there has been more falsehood than truth in much that has been published. Many of the ridiculous statements alleged to have come from Charles Travers, survivor of the Black Duck seizure, are being questioned now that the Rhode Island officials have found

that the bullets entered the rear of the Black Duck's pilot house instead of being fired head-on, as stated by Travers.

"Naturally the officers and men of the Coast Guard, with 140 years of humanitarian work to its credit, resent the efforts of an unlawful element to create the impression that the Coast Guard exists merely to chase rum-runners and kill men when it isn't necessary.

"The entire service deeply regrets that these three men were killed, but under the circumstances it could not be avoided if the patrol boat involved was to uphold the law and carry out its specified duty."[32]

On January 4, the general courts-martial of the Coast Guardsmen accused of pilfering the seized liquor from the *Flor-del-Mar* began. Five men, who had been confined since the investigation began, were tried first. Besides them, there were others who would be tried on charges of getting drunk with the seized liquor. On the following day, five bottles from the *Flor-del-Mar* were found on the Coast Guard destroyer *Shaw*.

Meanwhile, US Attorney Boss refused to produce the crew of patrol boat 290 before an inquest for questioning. At the same time, he issued a statement in which he said that the 290 did not fire a warning shot and was not compelled by law to do so. Boss told reporters that he had discovered a new statute, which superseded the old one. Under this new statute, Section 581 of the Tariff Act and Navigation Laws of 1927, any rum-runner may expect to be hailed by a Coast Guard cutter by means of a horn or lights, and if the rum-runner does not immediately heave-to, the pursuing boat could "use all necessary force to compel compliance."[33]

State Attorney General Heltzen, who was at home recovering from a bad cold, was informed of the statute quoted by Boss, but declared it would make no difference to the state's investigation and its presentation of the facts to a special grand jury.

Drunken Guard Runs Amuck

Sixty-four year-old Edward L. Foley of the Boston office of the Internal Revenue Service was the man chosen to guard the *Black Duck* at Providence, Rhode Island. He went on duty at 6 AM on January 5. At 9 AM, when a crowd gathered to look at the boat, the drunken Foley fell on the ground, breaking a bottle of whisky in his inside pocket and saturating his clothes with liquor.

When he stood up, he drew his .45 service pistol and pointed it against the stomach of a man named Gilbert Taylor, then drew another pistol, a .38, which he owned. Taylor grabbed the .45, and later, with the help of another man, somehow convinced the guard to go to a shed nearby. The fact that no one in the crowd was shot by a drunken man brandishing two pistols is nothing short of miraculous.

From the shed, Foley called Boston to ask for reinforcements to help him protect the *Black Duck* from "hijackers," who he said were on their way to attack it. He claimed that he had repelled a similar attack during the night, which was strange, because he was not on duty then. Taylor then made another call to explain the situation from a sober perspective.

Thomas F. Finnegan, of the Boston office of the Customs Service, rushed to Providence. By the time he arrived, there was a large group of officials and police around the boat. He admitted to the press that Foley had been drinking, as did Customs Collector W.W. Lufkin of Boston, who also rushed to the scene. Foley was suspended afterward.

The whole incident inflamed many people, and was yet another black eye for the Coast Guard, Customs, the Treasury Department, the US Government, and Prohibition in general. Conrad Crooker, counsel of the Liberal Civic League, who was denied permission to inspect the vessel earlier, angrily declared that drunken guards were being allowed to watch "this sacred vessel."[34]

On the same day of the drunken-guard incident, Admiral Billard gave a nationwide radio address in which he said:

> "There is no sea-going organization anywhere that has duties more arduous, hazardous and full of hardships, or that requires a higher degree of real seamanship. The Coast Guard is not charged in any way with the enforcement of the national prohibition act. It is charged, and has been since its creation in 1790, with the protection of the custom laws and the prevention of smuggling of contraband from the sea into the United States.
>
> "It has upheld and defended the Constitution since 1790, and it will continue to do so. It enforces at sea the laws of the United States. It does not discuss or question their wisdom or their expediency.

"In one year twenty-six officers and men of the Coast Guard were drowned while on this law-enforcement duty. Picture for yourselves a patrol boat of the Coast Guard on duty at night in the winter time in an endeavor to uphold the Constitution of the United States. Dashing up through the night and without any lights there comes a fast speed boat.

"The Coast Guard patrol turns her searchlight on this boat and immediately recognizes her as a boat engaged in liquor smuggling. There, piled on her decks, are the cases of liquor, and there is not the slightest doubt that the vessel is a rum-runner deliberately violating the laws of the country.

"The rum-runner knows perfectly well that Coast Guard patrol boats are on the lookout for him, hence his dashing through the night at a high speed and without lights, and in a moment he knows that a Coast Guard patrol has discovered him. Trusting in his superior speed, he defies the orders and signals of the patrol to stop, suddenly changes his course and dashes off in the darkness.

"There are just two courses of action open to the Coast Guard patrol boat. One is to do nothing but patiently wait for the time when the smuggler will be kind and gracious enough to accede to the command of the United States to stop, and the other is to take the line of action authorized and indicated by the laws of the United States."[35]

Billard added that during the previous fiscal year the Coast Guard rescued 4,375 persons and assisted vessels in distress whose value, including cargoes, was more than $49 million. These figures beat those of all previous years.

A group of angry men at Shaw's Cove Basin in New London most likely did not listen to Billard's speech, and if they did, they were not impressed. On the morning of January 6, the men were gathered outside the houseboat of Boatswain Alexander Cornell, skipper of patrol boat 290. Mrs. Cornell was alone on the boat at the time; her husband was under arrest pending the outcome of the official investigation into the *Black Duck* shooting. The men threw rocks at the houseboat but were not caught. Late in the afternoon, the Coast Guard towed the houseboat to the State pier, where it was kept under watch.

More Drunken Coast Guardsmen

Admiral Billard surely must have been pulling his hair out at this point. The winter of 1929-1930 was just a really bad time for the Coast Guard, and the nation as a whole. Just when it seemed that the Coast Guard's image could not be tarnished any further, more embarrassing stories appeared in the newspapers.

At 3 AM on January 6, New London Patrolman Dennis Murphy found R.J. Wade and two other Coast Guardsmen drunk in front of a speakeasy on North Bank Street. Wade was in a semi-conscious condition after falling down stairs and severely cutting his scalp. Murphy brought the three men down to the police station, where they admitted having purchased liquor in the speakeasy. Police raided the speakeasy based on the information they gathered from the drunken Coasties.[36]

On the same day, the general court-martial of Coast Guardsmen charged with drunkenness and stealing liquor from the *Flor-del-Mar* reconvened. On that day, ten men from the destroyer *Ericson*'s crew were heard. All of them pleaded guilty to intoxication. Twenty-nine men remained on the docket for trial. Captain H.H. Wolf, commander of the destroyer force, gave an official statement on the investigation which included the following findings: 24 Coast Guardsmen were under the influence of alcohol; 15 men stole or had liquor in their possession; 56 pints of unopened liquor plus four full sacks of liquor bottles were recovered from the patrol boats; and, supposedly, no one above the rank of chief petty officer was involved.[37]

More Fighting In Congress

In early 1930, Rum Row was as big as it ever was. Captain H. Wolf, commander of the Coast Guard destroyer force based in New London, Connecticut, reported that there were at least 150 rum vessels operating off the New England coast. This number only included regular smugglers and not those who only occasionally make trips out to Rum Row. The fleet consisted, as usual, of mother ships, which transported the contraband from foreign ports, and the smaller speedboats and fishing sloops, which took the liquor from the mother ships to shore under the cover of darkness.[38]

Believe it or not, at the beginning of 1930, the US House of Representatives was still overwhelmingly "dry." On January 7, the

House sat in silence as Representative LaGuardia of New York attacked Prohibition, but it burst into applause when Representative Beedy of Maine countered with the defense of the Coast Guard in the killing of the men aboard the *Black Duck*.

LaGuardia began his thirty-minute attack on Prohibition by stating that the law "is not being enforced because it cannot be enforced." He criticized Senator Borah's stand on the enforcement fight and declared that the Idaho Senator's analysis of the causes of the breakdown had failed and that he had "arbitrarily" blamed the Treasury Department.[39]

> "If prohibition is transferred to the Department of Justice, and if the drys want it transferred it will be transferred, the Attorney General of the United States will have the same 100,000,000 people in the United States to deal with as the Secretary of the Treasury now has.
>
> "The transfer will not change public opinion. The transfer will not quench the thirst of the American people.
>
> "Granted that Congress will appropriate hundreds of millions to enforce prohibition, there will still be the same resistance to the law, the same universal desire for drink, the same wholesale importation and manufacture of liquor and the same retail sale in every nook and corner of the United States"[40]

LaGuardia then went on to point out that the Prohibition advocates in Congress were always attacking big cities in the east, especially New York, for lax enforcement. Idaho, which had some of the staunchest drys, had more saloons per capita than Philadelphia and more bootleggers per capita than Chicago. The liquor was of a better quality in Idaho and cheaper than in any of the large cities, LaGuardia argued. He then turned his guns on the Coast Guard, calling the *Black Duck* killings "another paragraph in the shameless annals of Prohibition." He continued:

> "I will not refer to the bloody murder of the three members of her crew lest hardened prohibitionists burst into applause and again stain the pages of the Congressional Record.
>
> "The Treasury Department rushes into print to justify the slaying of these three men. Yet the record is bare of any

facts showing that the Black Duck had refused to or was in actual flight. The Coast Guard officials and the crew of the cutter 220 have been hailed and praised for having well performed their duty. Yes, their duty, as seen in the light of prohibition.

"Part of the liquor seized from the Black Duck was, in turn, sold by members of the Coast Guard. Citizens are prohibited by law to drink alcoholic beverages, and yet on the same day that the Black duck was captured, members of the Coast Guard have been found purloining part of every seizure of liquor made by them."[23]

Representative Beedy's response brought laughter from the "wets" and "drys" alike. He denied the liquor was from the *Black Duck* and gave the following version of what happened:

"That very day there was a ship at sea run down by this Coast Guard patrol, the Flor del Mar. She was laden with liquor. The Coast Guard sent for men in New London to remove the liquor, because the boat was sinking, or about to sink, as she had been set afire. They did rescue the ship and towed her into the harbor, and later sent for a hundred or more men at the base in New London to remove that liquor from the ship.

"I understand the fact is that these men− gobs as we call them− ordinary seamen, yet red-blooded American boys, stood in water for hours on that cold December night unloading this liquor.

"In the explosions which had occurred on board the ship, some of the boxes had been broken open and some of the gobs, to relieve themselves from the cold and suffering, opened a bottle and drank something out of it. [Laughter erupted in the House of Representatives.] You never will get together men in the Coast Guard who under those circumstances will not take a drink of liquor when it is opened before them.

"Two of the men, as I understand it, took a bottle of that liquor and went ashore and got into trouble and boasted that they had stolen the liquor from this seized liquor on the Flor del Mar, and not from the Black Duck."[41]

---

[23] This statement by LaGuardia regarding the law was not true. There was no law against *drinking* alcohol, only transporting, manufacturing, or selling it without a permit.

Mr. Beedy argued that the Coast Guardsmen, who were not particularly interested in Prohibition, still performed their duty in the *Black Duck* incident with the fearlessness and courage which had always characterized the service. Beedy charged that attempts were being made to undermine the morale of the Coast Guard and that rum smugglers were waiting for the day that the Coasties would become "sick of being accused as murderers and suspend vigilance." Then, bringing applause from both Republicans and Democrats, he asked:

"What will you do? Admiral Billard, Commandant of the Coast Guard, says, 'I can send a telegram to those boys tomorrow telling them not to fire on a motor boat under any circumstances.' That is the crux of the enforcement problem. What would you have them do?

"I believe the prohibition officials and the Coast Guard will be permitted to make an honest and conscientious attempt to enforce prohibition. Now we ought not to shoot them down recklessly and regardless of the circumstances, but we have either got to enforce this law or we might as well throw up our hands. The only way to do [it] is to make these people understand that we mean business, and in a law passed since I have been a member of the House, a method was provided for enforcing the provisions of the prohibition law.

"If a rum boat defies the command of a Coast Guard officer to stop and permit a search and starts to escape, then it is time for the officer in charge of that boat to command that they fire on that boat and attempt to disable her, without, if possible, injuring anybody.

"But if she attempts to escape or maneuver herself into such a position— knowing that this is a United States Government boat— that she is within range of their guns, then the members of this House, sworn to uphold the Constitution and to defend it against its enemies, must make these boys know that if they do their duty a majority of the members of Congress and the people of the United States are behind them to a man."[42]

The House again burst into applause, but LaGuardia answered Beedy by saying that there was no difference of opinion as to enforcing the existing law, but, he asked, "How long are we going to continue the use of force to enforce a law which the majority of the people do not want?"

Beedy replied, "I would say that we go far enough to let these flagrant violators of the law and defiers of constitutional provisions and an arm of this government know that we mean business." Once again, the House applauded.[43]

At the same time over in the Senate, Senator Blease, Democrat of South Carolina, gave an hour's speech on the wet-dry issue. He charged that the Prohibition law had been flagrantly violated in the nation's capitol:

> "The newspapers are lying, the grand jury is lying and others are lying when they say there is no crime, that there is no liquor selling in the city of Washington...
>
> "There is prohibition for the poor devil who is not able to buy, but no prohibition to the wealthy man, no prohibition to the commissioners, no prohibition to the embassies, no prohibition to the Cabinet, no prohibition to Mr. Hoover if he wants to have it—he can have it if he wants to—no prohibition to a Senator, no prohibition to a Congressman, no prohibition to any man who wants to buy liquor in Washington.
>
> "Yet a grand jury comes out and says the people who say liquor is sold in Washington, or talk about Washington reeking in crime, do not know what they are talking about. If they do not, these young men in our press galleries ought to report that their papers are publishing most outrageous falsehoods about Washington, the blind tigers, gambling dens, race-horse gamblers and bad women and charge those of us who attempt to help out the situation with falsifying. They must be the falsifiers, because here are their reports.
>
> "Yet Washington is a clean, model city! No young ladies drink in Washington! No young ladies play cards in Washington! No young ladies smoke cigarettes in Washington! Oh, it is the city of all cities!
>
> "We might think it was the New Jerusalem if we had listened to the grand jury and certain newspaper reporters and certain officials who are lying in order to hurt those of us who have endeavored to help clean up this city."[44]

The Grand Jury's Finding

Two weeks after the *Black Duck* shooting, the grand jury announced its findings. The Superior Court Grand Jury, in Providence, Rhode Island, listened to the testimony of twenty-two witnesses, including eight crew members of the patrol boat 290 and Charles Travers, the lone survivor of the *Black Duck*. The foreman of the jury read the following statement after reporting to Judge A.A. Capotosto:

> "In view of the great public interest in the matter under investigation by the grand jury, involving the so-called Black Duck shooting, its members feel that a statement should be made at this time. We believe that the Attorney General's Department has fully and thoroughly presented to us all the evidence available which would assist us in arriving at a decision in the matter. The investigation and consideration has been completely carried out. We accordingly report that we find no true bill."[45]

In other words, the case did not even get to the trial phase and the crew of the patrol boat 290 was completely absolved of any wrongdoing. To add icing to the cake, the Treasury Department's "independent committee," composed completely of Customs men, upheld the Coast Guard's actions.[24]

---

[24] The "independent committee" consisted of Thomas F. Finnegan, Deputy Collector of Customs at Boston; Owen P. McKenna, Customs agent of Washington; and George Murphy, Inspector of Customs in the New England division. "Upholds Coast Guard In Black Duck Killings," *The New York Times,* January 17, 1930.

42
Ten Years of Prohibition

Despite a decade of fighting fiercely against bootleggers and rum-runners, the smugglers kept reappearing on land, at sea, and in the air. The government and its vast army of agents and police officers plus its incredible fleet of Coast Guard and Customs boats were unable to stop millions of people from buying liquor. The 18th Amendment, which banned the manufacture, sale, and transportation of alcohol, had been in effect for ten years in 1930. Yet every day, millions of people were transporting alcohol from one place to another. Millions of people were making their own liquor at home, in city warehouses, and in the hills—as they had done for centuries. Every day millions of customers were purchasing alcohol at speakeasies, and thousands of men—including law enforcement officers, politicians, and other government workers—were making a lot of money.

The Price of Prohibition

In 1929, the Association Against the Prohibition Amendment reported that in the previous year Prohibition had cost the nation $936 million in lost revenue, including federal, state, county, and city revenues. Keep in mind that these figures are in 1929 dollars. Back then, one dollar had as much buying power as $13.83 in 2016. Therefore, one million dollars in 1929 would have been the equivalent of $13.83 million in 2016. Therefore, the lost revenue of $936 million in 1929 would have been close to $13 billion in 2016 dollars. The association's figures read[1]:

```
Federal enforcement
(after subtracting $5,500,000 in fines)..........$36,000,000
Loss in federal revenue..........................850,000,000
Loss in city, state, and county
revenues..........................................50,000,000
Total............................................$936,000,000
```

In 1919, the year before the 18th Amendment became effective, federal revenues from taxes on distilled spirits, wines, and fermented liquors were $483,050,854. The Association Against the Prohibition Amendment estimated that if Prohibition were abandoned, the federal government would have collected $849,918,115 in 1929. Therefore, the association estimated that the dry law was costing the nation hundreds of millions of dollars in lost revenue.

Of course, the federal government's estimates were much different. Dr. Doran, the Prohibition Commissioner, went before a congressional committee in 1929 to give his estimate of how much Prohibition had cost in dollars and how much money would be needed to continue the effort. Dr. Doran said that $300 million would be needed annually to make Prohibition enforcement effective. He gave the following figures of the cost to the Treasury Department during the decade the Eighteenth Amendment had been in force[2]:

EXPENDITURES 1920-1929

Prohibition………………………..$72,622,385
Coast Guard……………………..…..67,556,200
Customs……………………..…….1,000,000
Dept. of Justice………….…………72,000,000
Total………………….………...$213,178,485

COLLECTIONS 1920-1929

Fines and penalties……………..$44,574,832
Taxes on spirits and liquors……..415,927,960
Total………………………….$460,502,792

Looking at Prohibition Commissioner Doran's figures for the decade, one would get the impression that Prohibition was a profitable enterprise. The figures Doran gave imply that the federal government made $247,324,307 in profit while fighting rum runners. Not bad! However, these numbers are misleading. As the Rum War escalated, it became more expensive. Commissioner Doran's expense report for 1928 tells a much different story. These are the figures for *one year* of Prohibition[3]:

EXPENDITURES OF 1928

Prohibition.................................$11,610,669
Customs...450,000
Coast Guard...............................15,426,540
Dept. of Justice............................9,000,000
Total...$36,487,209

COLLECTIONS OF 1928

Fines and penalties......................$6,183,942
Proceeds from seizures and fines..........380,333
Taxes on spirits and liquors............15,307,796
Total...$21,872,071

By its own admission, the federal government had lost $14,615,137 in 1928 in its attempt to fight rum runners and bootleggers. The dry laws were costly in other ways, too. Prohibition put a huge strain on the court system. In 1928 alone, there were 75,298 Prohibition prosecutions in federal courts, with 56,546 convictions. Add to this figure 15,042 Prohibition cases in state and local courts, with 13,605 convictions. The average prison sentence for breaking the liquor laws was 47.3 days. However, that average factors in those defendants who received no jail time. If you average out the sentences of those who actually did receive jail time, the average sentence was 140 days.[4]

Many people lost their lives during that first decade of Prohibition. It is difficult to get an accurate estimate because crime reports from local governments were not collected in a federal database as they are today. The federal government gave the estimate of 263 persons killed, of whom 184 were civilians and seventy-nine federal officers. Senator Tydings of Maryland estimated that the figure was closer to 800 deaths and believed that if one canvassed records throughout the nation, the figure would have been over 1,000.[5] Keep in mind that these figures only cover those who were killed while agents were enforcing Prohibition. These figures do not cover the countless people who were gunned down in gang violence related to booze or those who died of alcohol poisoning.

There was no shortage of proof that Prohibition was a failure; but like any political/moral/religious ideology, it was an idea that died hard and still had a few years yet to live as a federal law. At the very end of 1929, Rum Row, which was supposed to be extinct according to government proclamations, reappeared off the coast near Atlantic City.

People today scoff at the idea that anyone would fight to defend an idea like Prohibition or why anyone would have faith in such an idea after ten years of failure. But Prohibition was in many ways like a war. A nation can fight a war for years and years, costing billions of dollars and thousands of lives, without anything really to show for it. Yet there will always be those who say "stay the course" no matter how costly, no matter how long. People in the future will laugh at our politicians and what is politically popular in our time. They will wonder why we become so inflamed over certain controversial issues because they will have the luxury and safety of hindsight. Americans in the 1920s were in the thick of the fight against alcohol. As in a conventional war, the two sides were entrenched against one another—there were double agents, and there were profiteers who made a fortune both legally and illegally.

There is the old saying that those who don't know history are doomed to repeat it. I wrote this book in the midst of a war and a really bad recession. Was our generation ignorant about war and recession before we got our fair share? No. There are many Americans who know their history. There is no shortage of history enthusiasts, re-enactors, history teachers, professors, and writers of history books. There are thousands of students in colleges and universities all over this nation learning about our past mistakes, yet here we are with the same problems we have created time and again. Perhaps it is a matter of *how many* Americans know their history. If the majority of our population is largely ignorant of even the most basic historical events, then they will easily be led astray again and again.

Prohibition was not a one-time experiment. It was tried several times in different states and in different nations. In a democracy, laws do not come into existence after the general population has done research and comes to a logical conclusion. A bill becomes a law when large numbers of people become *emotional* about an idea and put pressure on their elected officials to enact it.

At the beginning of 1930, there were at least 150 rum vessels off the New England coast. Captain H.H. Wolf, commander of the Coast Guard's destroyer force, told reporters that the figure of 150 only includes those vessels regularly engaged in smuggling and not those who occasionally tried their hand at smuggling. The rum fleet, as usual, consisted of mother ships, which transported the liquor from foreign ports, and the smaller boats, such as fishing sloops and speedboats, which made the dash for land under the cover of darkness. Smuggling activity was greatly affected by the phases of the moon. During a full moon, Coast Guardsmen knew that there was little likelihood of any rum boats trying for land. Instead, they would wait for darker phases of the moon.[6]

The situation off of New England's coast was only part of the larger picture of the rampant rum-running and bootlegging that still existed ten years after the 18th Amendment and the Volstead Act went into effect. In fact, since 1920, smuggling had grown exponentially and had become very well organized while profits continued to increase. Even after ten years of failed enforcement, the politically-correct view was to support Prohibition. To openly support the repeal of Prohibition could be political suicide. "Dry" politicians frequently made character attacks against "wet" politicians as being immoral supporters of vice. Today's reader might scoff at this idea, but there were still millions of supporters of Prohibition in 1930. Many of Prohibition's supporters had great social and political influence and would loudly clamor against anyone who openly defied their views.

It is important to remember that Prohibition originated through grassroots movements in states across the country. From there it went to the respective state assemblies, many of which passed their own state-level dry laws. When the bill went before Congress in 1917, the House and Senate both passed it with an overwhelming majority. Since the bill was for an amendment to the Constitution, it needed to be ratified by a majority of the states. So in turn, each state legislature debated on whether to support the law or not. By January 1919, 36 out of 48 states (Alaska and Hawaii were not states yet) ratified the amendment.

More than a decade later, enforcement of this law was failing miserably and the US Government saw a need to change its battle plan. In May of 1929, President Hoover appointed the former US Attorney General George Wickersham to head the National Commission on Law Observance and Enforcement, commonly known as the Wickersham Commission. Hoover did so pursuant to an act of Congress. The eleven members of the commission were charged with examining problems relating to the enforcement of laws and our judicial system, with particular attention devoted to Prohibition. By January 1930, the commission was ready to present its findings.

On January 13th, the President called upon Congress to make more adequate provisions for enforcing the dry laws. In a message read in the Senate and House, Hoover offered specific recommendations for new legislation and backed them with two extensive reports from the Wickersham Commission, and memoranda from the Treasury Secretary and the Attorney General—17,000 words in total.[7] On the following day, a number of bills were presented in the House of Representatives, approved by the President, intending to carry out the recommendations. Foremost in the recommendations were that the investigating and prosecuting functions of the Prohibition Bureau be transferred from the Treasury to the Department of Justice, and measures to relieve congestion in federal courts due to Prohibition cases. There were also proposals for strengthening the padlocking practice (padlocking the doors of liquor warehouses, etc.); unification of the border patrols under the Coast Guard; requiring all persons entering the US from Canada or Mexico to go through appointed checkpoints; higher salaries for US Attorneys and Marshals; an increase in the number of prosecuting officials; expansion of federal prisons; reorganization of the parole system; and special Prohibition legislation for the District of Columbia.[8]

Neither of the commission's reports proposed any modifications to the Prohibition statutes and stressed that much more time would be needed to investigate the entire problem. Apparently, eight months was not enough. The commission put the problem of Prohibition enforcement into context by describing the historical background of resistance in this country to laws affecting the conduct of people, citing the influence of the pioneers' attitudes toward intrusive laws, the Puritans' objection to administration, and the Whig party's tradition of a "right to revolution." The commission pointed to the arrests of 80,000 people during the previous fiscal year for Prohibition violations to indicate a "staggering number of what might be called focal points of infection."[9] The court congestion arising from so many arrests compelled prosecutors to resort to "bargain days" and "cafeteria courts," i.e. the practice of having days when defendants appear before federal judges, plead guilty to Prohibition violations, and be let off with fines instead of a prison sentences. In one large city, 95% of those arraigned for Prohibition violations did exactly that.[10]

Attorney General Mitchell elaborated on the problem in his memorandum, which was transmitted to Congress via the White House. He described how federal courts were unable to cope with the volume of cases, which resulted in delays, weakening of evidence, and difficulty in obtaining convictions. As stated earlier, courts attempted to clear dockets by wholesale acceptance of guilty pleas with light punishments.[11]

A few days after the Wickersham reports were presented to Congress, Treasury Secretary Mellon appeared before a House committee to voice his approval of transferring Prohibition enforcement from the Treasury Department to the Justice Department. Seated near the head of the committee table, with Seymour Lowman, Assistant Secretary of the Treasury in charge of Prohibition, seated to his right and Commissioner of Prohibition James Doran standing behind his chair, Mellon presented his views in a short statement, which said, in part:

> "...The Treasury, generally speaking, is responsible primarily for managing the finances of the nation, collecting the revenues and protecting the integrity of the revenue laws and of the currency, with all incidental duties relating hereto.
>
> "I know of no reason, therefore, why the Treasury Department should be charged with the duty of enforcing an unrelated penal statute.
>
> "On the other hand, there is a very sound basis for charging the law enforcement department of this government with this task. It is the duty of the Department of Justice, acting through the United States District Attorneys, to prosecute violators of this and other federal statutes, and it seems to me that better results may be obtained if those who are to try the cases are in a position to control and direct investigations of violations of the law and the gathering of evidence necessary for their prosecution..."[12]

He had hardly concluded his statement when the "wets" began firing questions at him. The first was Representative Igoe of Illinois.

Igoe: "Was the Bureau of Prohibition under your direction efficient?"
Mellon: "It doesn't seem to me to be a question of efficiency in any department. It is a question of legislation that is before us."
Igoe: "Do you think your bureau did everything possible to enforce the Prohibition laws?"
Mellon: "I am sure we have made every effort to carry out our responsibility."
Igoe: "Then do you believe the Prohibition law can be enforced?"
Mellon: "It is not a matter of my personal opinion. It is a question of legislation."[13]

Representative Schafer of Wisconsin asked Mellon if it were a fact that when Prohibition agents were involved in law violations, the reports of the charges were sent to the Prohibition Bureau and then covered up. Mellon replied, "I know nothing of anything like that. If such a condition exists, it has never been brought to my attention."[14]

That night, there was a debate broadcast nationwide by the Columbia Broadcasting System (CBS) between Senator Harris of Georgia, a leading dry, and Representative Black of New York. The subject of the debate was "the enforcement of Prohibition and the use of United States commissioners to hear minor cases." Harris argued that Secretary Mellon did not make a serious attempt to enforce the law. When Harris was a member of the Senate Appropriations Committee, he tried to provide additional funds to be used for Prohibition enforcement. Mellon opposed the increased funding, but later agreed to a relatively small increase.[15] Harris continued:

> "It is futile to try to enforce this law with the meager appropriation that has been available in the past when we consider the thousands of miles of Canadian and Mexican borders to be guarded, as well as the Atlantic, Gulf and Pacific Coasts, to say nothing of enforcement in the 2,500 counties and several thousands of cities and towns in the United States."[16]

Representative Black attacked the idea of having commissioners, instead of judges, preside over minor Prohibition cases and said that it would be more constitutional to repeal the 18th Amendment or modify the Volstead Act. He attacked the proposed changes in the judicial system as a breaking down of constitutional safeguards of the American people by denying them a fair trial by jury. He elaborated:

> "Consider how Prohibition has sacrificed the public service by its corrupting influence. Imagine the force of avarice over commissioners clothed with extended powers. Higher qualifications would be required of commissioners, and, of course, higher pay. There is little or no dignity attached to a commissioner's office. Does the majestic United States want justice dispensed in an auction house?"[17]

Senator Harris favored the recommended changes, both in the Prohibition Bureau and in the judiciary. He introduced a bill in Congress to bring those changes about. Harris pointed out that the majorities in both houses of Congress were "dry" and that it was time to act if Prohibition were to succeed:

> "If, with the President and practically two-thirds of both houses of Congress in favor of Prohibition, we fail to do something constructive at this time, the opponents of the law will continue their propaganda so as to make it unpopular. The sentiment of Congress and the country is such that we can give Prohibition a fair trial. It has not been so heretofore. If we fail now it will materially retard the cause. Furthermore, we encourage the enemies of this law to strive for its repeal when we neglect to appropriate the money necessary to secure loyal and efficient employees.
>
> "Most of the Senators and Congressman opposing this law have voted against appropriations to enforce it. When the Coast Guards or other government officials happen to kill violators of the law, even in self-defense, in carrying out their duty, protests and criticisms go up all over the country for those opposed to Prohibition, but no word of protest or sympathy was heard when any one of the 206 government officials was killed by law violators."[18]

In 1930, the "wets" definitely gained ground in Congress. A few years earlier, they were a small minority, subject to being lambasted for opposing Prohibition. If one looks at Congressional debates in that year, it is striking how emboldened the "wets" had become. The pendulum of popular opinion (and politically-correct opinion) had begun to swing in a direction opposing dry laws.

On April 1, Senator Tydings, a Democrat of Maryland, blasted Prohibition for more than two hours before a packed gallery in the Senate. He argued that Prohibition was a failure from practically every standpoint. On that day, he did battle with Senator Brookhart, a Republican of Iowa, and other 'dry' leaders, such as Senators Howell and Norris of Nebraska.[19]

Tydings used the Army-Navy football game of a few years earlier as a case in point. At that game there were 80,000 people in the stands, including the President of the United States, members of his Cabinet, and military service-members. On the following day, the groundskeepers had picked up over 1,000 glass flasks. He pointed out that untold numbers of fans brought their own metal flasks to drink from. Tydings argued that if people did not obey Prohibition laws at a military football game, with the President attending, how could anyone expect that law to be followed anywhere else in the United States?[20]

Senator Brookhart did not like this argument and interrupted Senator Tydings to remind him warningly that Senator Bruce of Maryland lost his re-election after taking a similar "wet" stand. Tydings replied that he would stand up against the "bunk" of Prohibition to the end by saying, "If I can pay that price to render some slight service to my country, at least I will not be running with the crowd just to get re-elected."[21] Listeners in the gallery applauded until the chairman warned that the galleries would be cleared if the applause were repeated.

Tydings pointed out that 872 dry agents had been discharged from the Prohibition Unit for corruption between 1920 and 1927, and 445 had been dismissed for the same reason since then. Tydings also added that 1,365 persons had been killed during Prohibition raids and arrests, almost twice the number of American battle casualties in the Spanish-American war, which was 710. Brookhart interrupted and demanded that Tydings name the man responsible for this Prohibition enforcement mess. Tydings replied that no one man was responsible, but Brookhart insisted that Tydings knew but was afraid to name him. "Who is it?" snapped Senator Tydings.[22]

"His name is Andrew W. Mellon, and the Senator will never name him," Brookhart replied. "He will defend him because he is doing just what the Senator wants done." Tydings replied that Prohibitionists wasted a lot of time trying to find a scapegoat without a shred of evidence to back up their claims.[23]

Senator Tydings was well-prepared that day on the Senate floor. He came armed with nineteen tables or charts to show the failures of Prohibition. One table showed the number of arrests for drunkenness and the annual rate of arrest per 10,000 people in 385 cities. In 1914, before Prohibition, there were 187 arrests per 10,000 for drunkenness. One year after Prohibition became law (1921), arrests had dropped off to 71 per 10,000; but by 1927, that number had increased up to 146 per 10,000.[24]

Another table showed the number of arrests for intoxication in Washington, DC for youths between the ages of 17 and 21. In 1920, there were 73 arrests. In 1927, there were 414 arrests, 390 in 1928, and

368 in 1929. The intoxication arrests of persons under 21 in DC had increased 500% since Prohibition became law. He also argued that deaths from alcoholism had greatly increased since 1920 and that corruption had spiraled out of control due to dry laws.[25]

Senator Tydings gave his speech in front of the Vice President's rostrum, using an easel to display his tables and charts. Brookhart, although frequently interrupting and fighting Tydings at every turn, appeared fascinated by the exhibition. In response to the figures on Prohibition-related deaths, Brookhart remarked that an expert had recently told a Senate committee that there were 9,000 murders a year in the United States. He argued that 1,365 killed in ten years out of a population of 120 million was "a mighty small thing to be hollering about in reference to the enforcement of the greatest reforms in the history of the human race."[26]

Tydings replied that every one of our citizens should have all the protection the federal government can afford. He was greatly disturbed over the applause given in Congress to the report of the killing of a man suspected of carrying half a pint of liquor. "A hundred or so years from now," Tydings exclaimed, "some historian, writing of the decade in which we lived, will say, 'The Senate and House of the United States were in partnership with barbarism to condone the taking of human life on the public highway for no greater crime than transporting a pint, or a quart, or a gallon of liquor.'"[27] Tydings did not have to wait that long because historians were already bashing Prohibition ten years afterward. [However, I am more than happy to fulfill Tydings' prophecy by writing this book.] Tydings continued:

> "The minute we get to the point where we condone the taking of life without a trial for the mere violation of a simple law or any other law, God help the future of the United States. In the first place, I do not believe that drinking is a crime, whether the law decrees it as a crime or not. At any rate, if it is a crime, the criminal so-called or the violator of the law ought to have his day in court.
>
> "When we think there has been a turnover of 330 percent in the Prohibition enforcement personnel in the last seven or eight years, and that some 1,400 or 1,500 men have been dismissed because of discovered corruption, these killings come home to us with a double weight, because a great many of them have no doubt been killed by people who

were subsequently dismissed because they were too corrupt to remain in the Federal service."[28]

On July 1, 1930, Prohibition enforcement was transferred from the Treasury Department to the Department of Justice. The Treasury still retained control over industrial alcohol permits. Amos W. Woodcock, former federal attorney at Baltimore, was sworn in as Director of Prohibition, marking the establishment of the dry unit at the Justice Department. At the Treasury Department, James M. Doran relinquished the post of Prohibition Director to become Commissioner of Industrial Alcohol. Interestingly, the Treasury Department retained control over drug enforcement. Harry J. Anslinger, of the Treasury Department, was made Acting Commissioner of Narcotics under the Porter Act, which set up a separate bureau for drug control.[29]

Although the Prohibition Bureau was transferred to the Justice Department, the Treasury Department still had the task of securing the borders and preventing any contraband from entering the country, including alcohol. The Coast Guard and Customs remained under the Treasury, and the job of those agencies has always been to enforce our laws on the nation's borders, on land or sea. The transfer of the Prohibition Bureau shifted a lot of weight from the Treasury, because the Treasury no longer had to concern itself with chasing bootleggers within America's borders or fighting organized crime in big cities. Treasury agents would no longer have the task of enforcing Prohibition in states that were nowhere near a border, like Kansas, Kentucky, or West Virginia. The Treasury Department no longer had to seek and destroy moonshine distilleries or go on wild car chases in the Appalachian Mountains. Not having to worry about the Appalachians alone was a huge relief. Along the borders and along the coasts, the issue of jurisdiction was more of a grey area, especially in port cities.

Part III: The 1930s

Photo by Dorothea Lange, Farm Security Administration

43
Tiny French Islands

The islands of St. Pierre and Miquelon sit off the southern coast of Newfoundland. The tiny French islands are sparsely populated. In the 1930s, the islands made a perfect port for smuggling after Canada attempted to stop liquor exports to the US. Reporter James C. Young of *The New York Times*, who always seemed to have his finger on the pulse of the rum-running world, paid a visit to St. Pierre. On the steepest and crookedest street in St. Pierre was a tavern called the Café de Paris. Unlike the original in Paris, which was/is a world-famous, glamorous cabaret, this one was a dimly-lit, square, weather-beaten wooden building. Other than the accordion music, one would not have noticed the place passing by. This place was not a speakeasy, because in St. Pierre, there was nothing illegal about serving alcohol.[1]

Inside, the café was lit by old-fashioned oil lamps. There was usually a mademoiselle or two who would sing to entertain the rugged men of the sea. These men from all parts of the globe told tales of icy seas and long watches, pursuit and capture. Champagne was sold there for $1.50 a quart.

Captain Littlejohn, one of the customers, was a big, intimidating man. But on the night James Young came to visit, the captain was in a good, story-telling mood. He told the story of a German rum ship named the *Kaiser Friedrich*:

> "Well, well, poor fellows, they had bad luck. Loaded up here, you know, clear to the water line. Must have had 12,000 cases. Back in Germany they had heard that it was easy to get rich running rum, and over they came, keen for the game. Somebody told her skipper that Providence was the place for a quick trip and quick money, too. So down they went and sent a man ashore. Sure! The Providence crowd would take her cargo. Well, they did, to the last bottle and paid for it in counterfeit money. The skipper didn't know, of

course, until he got back here and tried to break one of his brand new $1,000 bills. Then– it broke his heart, instead. I never saw a man hit so hard. He sat in that chair right over there and cried. Poor fellow! Nobody ever saw him again. Went home, I guess."[2]

Littlejohn's friend, Captain Bill, stoked his pipe and shook his head. Stroking his black beard and frowning, he told Young how rum-running had become a harder game than it once was. A man at another table, called "Shorty," chimed in:

"There's a lot of truth in what you was saying, Bill. First thing you know, we've got to have a union. That's what we need. These owners is getting greedier every day. Here I am, running a speedboat for $400 a month. What's that? Nothing at all. Two trips a month I'm making and these fellows growing rich while I freeze and dodge bullets. Shot at twice this last trip. If I hadn't been for that armor plate on my stern they'd have sunk me, sure. Bullets rattled off'n it like hail. Then they turned a gun on us– but we was gone. For $400 a month! What kind of life is this anyway?"[3]

Captain Littlejohn opined that no union would recognize or protect rum smugglers. The men were all seamen by trade and most of them belonged to seamen's unions, but the unions did not cover that particular kind of work. Littlejohn asked Shorty what kind of union he had in mind. Shorty answered angrily:

"What kind of a union? What kind, Johnnie? A rum-runners' union, says I. Why, we could tie up this whole blooming port and make them pay the price. Here's my crew, getting $100 a month and they don't do nothing but dodge bullets and trim ship. I've got to know, to be watching all the time and worrying about these owners' rum. And me getting only $400 a month. Ain't I worth more'n four times as much as one of them fellows in the fo'castle?"[4]

None of the men answered. Then Captain Bill told a story about a time off the New Jersey shore. Half a dozen ships had been lying there for a week with the Coast Guard's patrol boats swarming around them like mosquitoes. The smugglers were all anxious to be off and the owners were radioing by the hour to do something. The skippers of the other ships came aboard Bill's ship and they had a conference. Captain Bill came up with the idea of setting one of the ships ablaze as a decoy. The other men looked at Bill thinking he had gone crazy. Bill used simple math to justify his plan. The six ships had $100,000 worth of liquor aboard, and the boat they would set on fire was only worth $2,000. The other captains would chip in to compensate the captain of the burned vessel for his loss. The men agreed to go ahead with the plan.[5]

One of the ships radioed an SOS as the old ship burst into flames. All of the Coast Guard vessels made a dash for the burning ship while the rum-runners brought the liquor ashore. Captain Littlejohn disagreed with the strategy:

> "You were smart, Bill. But I don't believe in using SOS. It's not seamanlike. Of course, I probably would have done the same thing in a case of that kind. Because you only had to shoot it once and let them see the fire. But, generally, I am against it. Besides, that has been done so often it is likely to fail anyhow. And some day a ship may be lost because they think ashore that it is only rum-runners radioing. No, I am against it."[6]

That seemed to be the general consensus among the men. Although they were smugglers, they were still seamen, trained in the traditional rules of the sea. The US Government was also not very fond of false distress signals at sea. The Radio Act of 1927, Section 28, states that "no person, firm, company or corporation shall knowingly utter or transmit or cause to be transmitted any false or fraudulent signal of distress or communication." The punishment for such an offense was imprisonment for up to five years and a fine of up to $5,000, or both. However, radio technology in the early 1930s made it easy for operators to get away with their offense.[7]

In one case, nearly twenty ships and boats responded to a false S.O.S. off Barnegat, NJ. There were three cutters and two destroyers from New York, two powered lifeboats from the New Jersey coast and about eleven patrol boats. In addition to these were several commercial ships and a sea plane from Cape May, NJ. Commander Edwin T. Osborn, of the Fifth Coast Guard District at Asbury Park, denounced the hoax as the "most atrocious deed that can be perpetrated."[8] The distress signals seemed suspicious because the sender refused to give the name of his ship. The Munson liner *Pan America*, which was in the general vicinity of the position given by the mysterious radio operator, took a bearing on the radio signal. That bearing was charted along with the bearing obtained by a radio operator at the Manasquan station. When the two bearings were drawn on a chart, they converged in Hoboken, on dry land.[9]

****

Under pressure from the US Government, the Canadian government passed a new law banning liquor exports to the United States. The new law, which went into effect on May 31, 1930, required exporters to post a double-duty bond, which was returned only when exporters satisfied Dominion port officials that the liquor had not been short-circuited to the United States. Basically, the new law made it more expensive to ship alcohol from the Canadian docks, where liquor was, until then, shipped openly. The collector of customs at Windsor shut down ten export docks in border cities near Detroit, refusing clearance to all vessels with liquor cargoes destined for the United States.[10]

Meanwhile, in Buffalo, NY, rum-running across the border had been at a standstill for several days in anticipation of the new Canadian law. Federal officials said that they expected smuggling operations to stop temporarily until smugglers regrouped and figured out how to overcome this new hurdle. The new law targeted larger ships. However, small boats, too small to require clearance papers, were suddenly in great demand.[11]

As usual, the rum syndicates quickly drew up a new battle plan. Two weeks after the new Canadian law went into effect, a Boston newspaper reported that "the most completely organized and equipped armada of rum ships ever reported" was surging down the Atlantic seaboard. As a result of the new law, the center of the rum smuggling shifted from the Canadian border to the Atlantic. St. Pierre and Miquelon, the French islands off the eastern coast of Canada, became a smugglers' oasis. Ships capable of carrying loads of up to 25,000 cases cleared from St. Pierre and transferred their cargoes at points from 50 to 120 miles from the American coast to smaller, faster vessels. Scouting boats helped prevent the rum ships from being seized, along with unlicensed radio stations, and an intricate system of spies.[12]

The rum rings knew that the law would take effect at the end of May, 1930 and planned accordingly. Liquor exports from Canada to St. Pierre and Miquelon and Bermuda skyrocketed during that month. To give a comparison, in May, 1929, Canada exported 16,114 gallons of liquor to St. Pierre. In May, 1930, liquor exporters shipped 98,492 gallons, six times the amount from May of the previous year! Canada exported 222 gallons of whisky to Bermuda in May, 1929; but in May of 1930, that number went up to 14,542 gallons. That is 65 times the amount shipped during the prior May.[13]

The Canadian law banning liquor exports to the United States was a massive failure. Between August 1930 and August 1931, Canada exported 1,815,271 gallons of whisky to St. Pierre and Miquelon, which had a total population of about 4,000. If this amount was consumed by the islanders, each man, woman, and child would have drunk more than 453 gallons over the course of a year—not including imports from France and Scotland. Obviously, the islanders were not consuming that much alcohol and it wound up somewhere on Rum Row. Before the new Canadian law went into effect, the liquor was transported mostly by truck, train, and motorboat across the border. Now the alcohol had to be moved in deep-sea vessels in order to be legal and avoid confiscation. The liquor trade between Canada and St. Pierre and Miquelon was strictly legal because the islands were French colonies. Canadians did wonder why the US Government did not make strong protests to Paris, especially after Washington made such strong protests to Ottawa regarding the exact same issue.[14]

44

The Radio Rum Ring

In New York, Deputy Surveyor John H. McGill was known as the "psychic" Custom House officer because he attributed many of his liquor seizures to dreams and "hunches." However, on July 24, 1930 he directed a big capture that had little to do with psychic ability. McGill used a short-wave radio set, which had been taken from a rum-runner, to intercept radio messages. Although the radio was not working very well, it was still a valuable tool.[1]

Shortly before midnight, when McGill usually received tips on the whereabouts of liquor through "occult" channels, there were no signals from the spirit world. Instead, he twisted the dials on the radio and poked at its tubes impatiently. A message came through the radio in dots and dashes. McGill knew Morse Code from his days in the Navy and recognized two words: "Patria" and "midnight." He also recognized the code for the number 4,000.[2]

Armed with this information, the surveyor called Inspector James Maston and ordered him to take patrol boat 546 to Pier 31 in Brooklyn and search the *Patria*. Maston had a blueprint of the cruise liner *Patria*, which had already been thoroughly searched a few days earlier. He searched the vessel from stem to stern, again. He called McGill to report that he found no liquor. McGill ordered Maston to look in the coal bunkers, acting on a hunch.

Customs men shoveled coal for more than an hour. Finally, they found what they were looking for. Four-thousand bottles of liquor were neatly wrapped in burlap bags. The seizure, which included bottles of Benedictine, yellow and green Chartreuse, Curacao and Cointreau, was valued at $40,000.[3]

****

The use of short-wave radios allowed rum-smugglers to coordinate their operations more easily than before. However, like any communications technology, radio served as a double-edged sword for criminals. Local and federal law enforcement soon learned to monitor radio communications to capture smugglers and really hit pay-dirt via radio in 1930 when they infiltrated a $15 million rum ring. The Justice Department found that this particular rum syndicate came into existence ten years earlier, with the beginning of Prohibition. However, it was not until the late 1920s that the syndicate began using short-wave radios for large-scale operations. Short-wave radios can send a signal very far on very low power. Since the syndicate began using short-wave radios, its operations increased by leaps and bounds, making a profit of $15 million a year by 1930.[4]

The syndicate was backed by American financiers and maintained by agents in Great Britain, France, St. Pierre, and the Bahamas, as well as at numerous locations along the coast from Maine to Delaware. It had built up an impressive logistical system to ship and distribute liquor, establishing a virtual monopoly in that region. That system included the constant operation of twelve rum ships, each capable of carrying a cargo of several thousand cases of liquor. These vessels, loaded at St. Pierre and in the Bahamas, were supplemented by a vast fleet of fast motorboats. The rum ships and the motorboats were equipped with radios, operating on a fixed schedule.

Federal radio inspectors and Justice Department code experts spent months listening to the radio transmissions after they discovered them. They first heard its whining dots and dashes and copied down the unintelligible code, which was at first a seemingly senseless combination of letters and numbers. After a few weeks, the code experts finally succeeded in cracking the code. The messages directed various boats to meet, naming the meeting point, the amount of liquor to be transferred, and the landing point. The points, however, were designated by numerals and only a few of them had been identified by late September 1930. Equipped with a portable radio compass, the federal agents went to various points in New Jersey, Staten Island, and Long Island, taking bearings on the radio signals. The bearings intersected at Coney Island in Brooklyn. After narrowing the search to that neighborhood, the agents brought their instruments there in cars and took numerous additional bearings, sixty in all. The bearings converged on a house at 53 Avenue V. On the outside of the building was a short-wave antenna.[5]

Soon after discovering the location of the building, agents arrived in two automobiles, which they parked two blocks from the house. In one of the cars sat a radio operator wearing headphones. He was awaiting the faint whistling sound that would indicate the illegal radio station was transmitting. Because of defects in the transmitter, no signals were heard until half an hour past the expected time.[6]

The agents closed in on the building and blocked the exits, entering the radio room before the radio men even knew they were there. At his radio, tapping out instructions in code, was Malcolm McMasters, who had been previously arrested in the Atlantic Highlands raid, and released on $30,000 bail pending trial. Nearby was Cecil Molyneaux, the radio operator of the rum ship *I'm Alone*, who was described by federal agents as a "radio genius." He was also wanted by authorities in France and England for violating their radio laws. On that day, Molyneaux was only at the house because McMasters telephoned him to tell him about problems with his radio. The *I'm Alone* was operated by the same syndicate that owned the station in Coney Island and the station raided at Atlantic Highlands a year earlier.

Molyneaux and McMasters attempted at first to escape; but when they saw they stood no chance, they surrendered. The agents confiscated the equipment, which was worth $15,000. It included three complete 75-watt short-wave transmitters and three complete receivers. When arrested, the two were charged with: violating radio laws by operating an unlicensed station, violating the tariff act, violating the Prohibition laws, and conspiring against the United States. However, when they were arraigned before US Commissioner Nicholas M. Pette, they were only charged with the radio violation and the other charges were, for some reason, dropped. The State Department sought to have Molyneaux's bail increased to $50,000 because he was regarded as a valuable aid toward resolving the controversy between the US and Canada as a result of the sinking of the *I'm Alone* a year and a half earlier. However, the commissioner set bail at $7,500 for each man.[7]

The rum syndicate was not about to accept defeat because their radio station in Brooklyn was seized. They immediately set up another station in Long Island. Federal agents used their compasses and antennae and started their search once again. Just as they got near, the syndicate's men moved their radio to New Jersey. They chose the town of Highlands, right next to Atlantic Highlands, where the big radio operation was raided a year earlier. About a month after the Brooklyn raid, two agents appeared in the vicinity of Highlands with new radio-tracing equipment and the usual charts.[8]

The agents traced the signal to the Albion Hotel, a ramshackle building on the waterfront, which the rum-runners had used before. The radio operators somehow learned that they had been discovered and fled before the agents arrived. However, they left the radio equipment behind because it was too large and heavy. In the hotel, the agents found a bar. The 250-watt radio equipment, which could send signals 2,000 miles, was on the second floor. Near the bar was a club room with a card table and numerous packs of cards. One deck was spread out in a half-finished game of solitaire, which one of the radio men abruptly ended. There was also a slot machine in the corner, which was filled with quarters.[9]

In the upstairs room with the radio set, the agents found little heaps of charred paper, most likely the remnants of a code book. In other parts of the room were charts of the Atlantic Ocean, marked with crosses and smudges, most likely to indicate the positions of ships. H.J. Simmons, in charge of the special agents, told reporters that there were plenty more illegal radio stations along the coast.[10]

The Atlantic Highlands Ring on Trial

Simmons was right. Although tracking down the radio operators and stations was frustrating, the government soon had enough evidence to indict 59 defendants, 37 of whom faced their trial in June 1931 at a Newark courthouse. US Attorney Philip Forman said in his opening statement that the syndicate was an enterprise organized on a gigantic scale, with radio-equipped headquarters in Atlantic Highlands and in New York. Forman also stated that the syndicate was headed by a mastermind and had separate departments for shipping, radio, trucking, storage, sales, and distribution.[11]

But there was more. Forman also said that the government would show that a connection between law enforcement officers and the syndicate led to the payment of graft money, and he accused Police Chief Charles A. McGuire of Keansburg and Charles Weiner, former Elizabeth policeman, of receiving bribes.

William S. Fast, a former accountant who became a school teacher, told of having to straighten out certain accounts, or "cook the books," for Alexander Lillien, the alleged mastermind of the operation. Fast said Lillien told him that he was going out of business and wanted to know where he stood. He said that Al Lillien's brother, William, took Fast to the home of Alexander MacMasters, radio operator for the ring.

Lillien dictated the assets and liabilities of the rum ring to Fast, totaling $174,166, for a list of boats, skiffs, and trucks. There were also small items for salaries. Lillein told Fast to divide the remaining balance among eight men, who stood accused of being the principals of the ring at trial.[12]

Fast testified that he went to the Federal Trust Building in Newark, NJ during the previous September to meet some of the defendants in a vault room. He said he gave slips of paper to them stating how much each would receive, and that the men accepted. The list of boats formed the alleged rum fleet of the syndicate and included the *Lucky Strike* and the *Shawnee*.[13]

Not to be outdone, associate defense counsel Louis Halle argued that the evidence obtained in the raid on the Atlantic Highlands headquarters on October 16, 1929 could not be admitted because the government, in its first indictment, charged the conspiracy was completed before that date. Judge J. Lyles Glenn found this argument to be a valid one.[14]

On the following day, Forest F. Redfern took the stand. Redfern was a Department of Commerce assistant radio inspector who had nineteen years of radio experience, which included intercepting radio messages in France during World War I. He told the court that he intercepted and decoded messages from a station giving the call letters 4RD and 3RD, which he traced back to the attic of 33 Shrewsbury Avenue, Atlantic Highlands, NJ, the home of Malcolm McMasters.[15]

Redfern intercepted more than 600 messages to and from the station, beginning March 30, 1929. The prosecution aimed to show that the messages were exchanged with the *Shawnee*, the *Lucky Strike*, and other ships of the rum fleet. Redfern read a number of his interpretations of the messages aloud. They were short and cryptic, but gave enough information to indicate smuggling activity. Here is an excerpt of an evening's messages as given by Redfern, as printed in *The New York Times*:

> "Patrol is with us now."
> "Wire us your highest speed."
> "Ten knots loaded. Patrol boats yet."
> "Say if patrol boat leads you."
> "Oil very low. Think better attempt to stay here till thick fog."
> "How many cases loaded?"
> "Divide load between other two speed boats."

"Give them 400 cases each. They may not want them. But try to fool them."

"Boats left and have returned on account of gale."

"Two boats left. Give them each 100 [here was a word Redford could not translate] and 290 assorted."

"Three, maybe four boats leave. Give them mixed goods if possible."[16]

Frederic M. P. Pearce, defense counsel, objected to the testimony on the grounds that there was no proof that the messages were connected to the defendants. Louis Halle attacked Redfern's system of decoding as guesswork, but Redfern defended its reliability. The court admitted the messages, allowing the jury to decide how reliable the decoding system was.[17] However, the court ruled out testimony as to what Redfern found when he entered the house in the raid on October 16, 1929. The defense's argument that he had no right to enter was upheld.

The prosecution's case took yet another beating on the following day when Redfern admitted on cross-examination that he had assumed certain key words in decoding the messages, or had them supplied by the Coast Guard. The court ordered the words struck out and instructed the jury to disregard them. The words included: "champagne," "Shawnee," "Navesink Light," "Halifax," "Hamilton," "Bermuda," and "Montauk Point."[18]

Thirteen Coast Guardsmen took the stand on that day and told of spotting, following, and picketing British ships off the Atlantic Coast, including the *Shawnee* and the *Lucky Strike*. The ships usually eluded pursuit after two or three days' trailing. The Coast Guard testimony was intended to show that the messages actually came from those ships by matching the content of the messages to what they observed the ships doing. Boatswain Ottar Skothin, who was in charge of the patrol boat *Rush*, said he picked up a ship on June 9, and on June 10 saw burlap bags transferred from the *Lucky Strike* to the *Shawnee*. He caused the people in the courtroom to laugh when he referred to the ships as "rum ships" and the packages as "liquor." The court pointed out that these were his conclusions, not fact, and ordered the words stricken out, adding yet another blow to the prosecution's case.[19]

A few days later, Judge Glenn ruled that the search of the mansion in Atlantic Highlands in October 1929 was not unreasonable; therefore, the evidence gathered there would be admitted. Although the judge could not understand why the officers did not obtain a search warrant, he allowed the search because it was incident to the arrest. The prosecution breathed a sigh of relief as most of their case revolved around evidence from the raid.[20] Among the items seized at the mansion were slips of paper alleged to be orders for whisky shipments. Albert D. Osborn, a handwriting expert of Montclair, NJ, testified that the slips were written by several of the defendants. He compared the writing with that on driver's license application cards and other records filled out by the defendants.[21]

On the following day, Frederick J. Kuegelman, vice president of the New Jersey National Bank and Trust Company of Newark, took the stand. Kuegelman identified credit slips and drafts credited to William B. Moriarty and Frank Flannagan and charged against the account of "A. Silver," who was identified in the court room as Alexander Lillien Jr., alleged master-mind of the ring. Previous testimony was that Flannagan was the assistant sales manager of the Consolidated Distilleries in Montreal, and that Moriarty was the registered agent at Halifax of the *Shawnee* and the *Lucky Strike*.[22]

The trial of the Atlantic Highlands ring concluded on July 10, 1931. Thirty-seven defendants were originally charged, but twenty were absent and not on trial. Charges against 16 of the 37 defendants were dropped the day before when the government admitted it did not have a *prima facie*[25] case against the sixteen. On closing, Special Assistant Attorney General Leslie E. Salter emphasized entries in a little black book seized in the raid on the Atlantic Highlands mansion. He pointed out figures opposite the letters "C.G." and "P.D." which he said were records of protection money paid to members of the Coast Guard and police department. The entry "shake, 1,000," Salter said, meant a $1,000 shakedown.[23]

District Attorney Forman asked the jury to consider the 400 slips of paper found in the mansion raid, which he said were records of liquor shipments, including the name of a truck and a driver. Frederick Pearse, attorney for the defense, argued that the government had not shown that "one drop of liquor" had been transported on the highways of New York or New Jersey. He attacked the government raids as high-handed and illegal.[24]

In his instructions to the jury, Judge Glenn told the jury to disregard eighteen of the thirty-six overt acts named in the indictment as

---

[25] *Prima Facie*: a legal term which in Latin means "at first sight," or "on its face." A *prima facie* case is one that is supported by sufficient evidence.

having no evidentiary support. He instructed them to take the testimony of Forest Redfern, radio expert, with caution. He also told the jury to acquit the defendants if they felt that there was a reasonable doubt of the seizures having been made at the place of arrest.[25]

At 10:30 AM on the following day, Judge Glenn asked the jury if they had reached a verdict. When they told them they had not, he urged them to try further, pointing out that they had sat three weeks listening to the evidence, and that if they failed to agree, another jury would hear the whole case. The jury returned at 12:16. The verdict was "not guilty." The defendants burst into applause and laughter but were quickly silenced by the judge. The verdict was a defeat for the government in one of the biggest prohibition cases ever uncovered. Preparations on the case began in March 1929, and involved the Coast Guard, special Prohibition agents, a Department of Commerce radio expert, and 130 agents who made simultaneous raids on October 16, 1929.[26] The fact that no search warrants were obtained really damaged the government's case. So basically, two years of hard work went down the drain.

For the remainder of the Prohibition era, the government and rum syndicates were in a constant effort to outsmart the other in radio communications. By 1932, there were many government listening posts along the Atlantic seaboard. The federal radio men became so good that they could recognize the "fist" of operators at illegal stations by the way the dots and dashes were formed. It was a difficult task to sort out the professional from the amateur stations, which numbered more than 22,000. However, the federal men managed to detect the smugglers with great accuracy.[27]

Rum Row frequently changed its secret code, but the federal men were quick to crack it. The introduction of new code symbols slowed the investigations, but not for long. After figuring out which short-wave radio stations were transmitting encrypted messages, the next stage involved radio direction finders. Federal agents had a direction finder built in a small suitcase. A tiny loop antenna was part of the equipment. When the length of the suitcase was pointed in the direction of the radio wave, a tiny speaker in the agent's pocket would make noise. In New York, the "traveler" would get in a "taxi" and ride around in ever-decreasing circles. When the agent found the greatest signal strength, the search was narrowed down to a city block. Of course, this particular approach would not work in a small seaside town, because a man riding in a taxi in loops around a small town would raise suspicion. In a smaller town, agents figured out ways to blend in with the locals while tracing the signal. In New York, agents were locating one transmitter per month, on average.[28]

Rum smugglers came up with different ways to hide their equipment. In one case, an agent knew that there was a signal coming from a certain building, but could not find the equipment on his first visit. When he came back the second time with other agents, he decided to inspect the wiring of an innocent looking short wave receiver. As he lifted it away from the wall, a wireless key fell from the niche behind the cabinet. The agent noticed that the wires went through the wall and into the adjacent garage. When he went into the garage, he did not see a transmitter but many old trunks covered with dust. The agents opened fifteen trunks and found nothing inside. Then they opened the last trunk and found a 500-watt short-wave transmitter. A glass bottle filled with a fire extinguishing fluid was fastened near the vacuum tubes, should the trunk on the bottom of the pile catch fire from the tubes. If the equipment did catch fire, heat from the flames would smash the glass, spread the liquid and put out the fire. The aerial antenna was under the rafters.[29]

On another radio hunt, an agent noticed a feint streak of new grass across a 100-foot stretch of carefully mowed lawn. He dug down about a foot and found a cable. He followed the cable in to a building nearby and at the end discovered a transmitter. Wires buried under the grass also led to the operating key hidden in another house.

Some illegal transmitters were found in walls behind paneling or plastered surfaces which showed no traces of tampering. Several were found in steel-barred rooms. The radio locations were visited frequently by handymen and technicians, employed by the rum-runners, to make sure that the equipment remained hidden and running. In one case it took federal investigators and local police a couple of months to track down a radio set, and finally located it in a car. The dials and switches on the dashboard operated the radio, and the transmitter was hidden in the trunk. The radio could send and receive signals over a distance of thirty miles plus. It was not until the operators stayed in one place for a while that agents and police were able to track down the vehicle in a garage in Rockaway, NY.[30]

45

The *Josephine K.*

On January 24, 1931, there was yet another international incident involving the killing of a rum ship captain. William P. Cluett was the captain of a ship called the *Josephine K.*, a two-masted schooner, 100 feet long, equipped with powerful oil-burning auxiliary engines. The ship could travel at a speed of fourteen knots per hour. The ship's home port was Digby, Nova Scotia. After three years as captain of the *Josephine K.*, Cluett was ready to get out of the rum-running business and was making his last planned run. According to officials, the *Josephine K.* was a notorious rum-runner and had been sighted often just outside United States territorial waters. This would probably explain why the Coast Guard had not previously captured Cluett.[1] That all changed on this particular night, when Captain Cluett went inside of the twelve-mile limit.

According to the report from the Stapleton Coast Guard base, located in Staten Island, NY, patrol boat 145 spotted the *Josephine K.* with its searchlight four and a half miles southeast of Ambrose Lightship. Nearby was a tugboat named the *Dauntless No. 6* with a garbage barge named the *Brooklyn* in tow. The *Brooklyn* had just picked up a fresh load of garbage from Newark, New Jersey, and was chartered to go to a point fifteen miles outside of New York Harbor and dump the trash in the ocean. As the patrol boat headed for the schooner the other boats scattered. A launch that was tied up alongside the *Josephine K.* was cast off and sped toward Sandy Hook, thereby escaping.[2]

The Coast Guard boat was too far away to hail the *Josephine K.*, so the men aboard pulled the tarpaulin jacket off of the one-pounder gun. The patrol boat started to chase the schooner, which was making a run for it. Instead of heading out to sea past the 12-mile limit, the schooner headed for Manhattan. The tugboat *Dauntless 6* stayed where it was, most likely because the captain knew he would not have enough speed to escape, especially with a garbage barge in tow.

The first shot fired by the patrol boat was a blank warning shot. The *Josephine K.* sped on and the Coast Guard fired two more blanks. The captain of the schooner pushed his engineers for more and more speed. The commander of the Coast Guard craft then ordered the one-pounder loaded with solid shot. Three solid shots whistled past the *Josephine K.* These were not meant to hit the schooner, but to scare the crew into stopping. The warning shots did not work. The Coasties aimed the next shot at the schooner. The skipper gave the order to fire. The shell struck the pilot house and carried part of it away. The ship hove to, and a few minutes later, the Coast Guardsmen were aboard. They found the 39-year-old Captain Cluett lying unconscious beneath the destroyed pilot house and the wheel he was manning. The round bounced off the heavy timbers and hit the captain in the leg above his knee, shattering his bone.[3]

The C.G. 145 sent a radio message to the Stapleton base asking for immediate medical aid. Within a few minutes, Coast Guard patrol boat 100 cast off from Pier 18 and raced to the scene with a doctor from the Marine Hospital. Cluett was brought onto the C.G. 100 and sped back to Stapleton. Meanwhile, the boarding party ordered the schooner's crew of five into the forecastle and searched the hold for liquor. In the hold, they found 2,500 cases of liquor, mostly Scotch and whisky. During all of the action, the *Dauntless No. 6* and the *Brooklyn* got away. The C.G. 145 sent out another radio message and soon the C.G. 180 was on its way to the scene from Rockaway Inlet. The C.G. 180 escorted the *Josephine K.* and crew to the anchorage at Red Hook Flats, while the C.G. 145 searched for the *Brooklyn* and the *Dauntless No. 6.* Meanwhile, the medical staff at the hospital was making a desperate effort to save Captain Cluett's life. His leg was amputated but he died soon thereafter without regaining consciousness. The medical examiner said the death was caused directly by the gunshot wound.[4]

It must have been comical to watch a tugboat towing a garbage barge while trying to flee a Coast Guard patrol boat. Although the C.G. 145 was diverted for about an hour and a half while dealing with the *Josephine K.*, the patrol boat had no trouble catching up to the tug and barge. They were caught and boarded not far from where the chase had started. The captains and crews of both vessels were arrested and their vessels seized. The Coast Guardsmen found 1,200 cases of liquor aboard the barge, of the same brand carried by the *Josephine K,* there was no liquor aboard the tug. The total value of the liquor seized that night from the two vessels was estimated at $100,000.[5] The vessels were escorted to the anchorage off of Red Hook (a neighborhood in Brooklyn, NY). As the captured vessels sat there anchored, two patrol boats circled them and armed sentries stood on the decks to keep others away.

Of course, the Canadian government was not pleased to hear that the captain of a Canadian vessel was killed by the US Coast Guard and expressed doubts as to whether the ship was within US territorial waters. Representing the crew of the *Josephine K.* at the bail hearing, Louis Halle argued that the vessel was fired on without justification outside of the twelve-mile limit.[6]

The Coast Guard held its own board of inquiry investigating the death of Cluett. The entire crew of the *Josephine K.* testified. At first, the board was only going to allow Coast Guardsmen to testify as witnesses, but the captured crew members were allowed to testify at the request of the British Vice Consul. One of the crew members swore under oath that Carl Schmidt, the Chief Boatswain's Mate commanding the C.G. 145, was drunk when he came aboard. Two others said that while Schmidt seemed sober when he boarded the vessel, he did not remain so for long. They said he spent two hours in the forecastle helping himself to the ship's supply of liquor. Schmidt testified that he was not drunk at any time before, during, or after the ship's seizure. Three crew members of the *Josephine K.* supported his version and said that he did not seem intoxicated, nor did they see him drink in the forecastle.[7] The commander of the Coast Guard tug *Alliance*, which was sent in to tow the captured schooner, testified that he found the *Josephine K.* anchored 11.7 miles offshore. This did not necessarily mean, however, that the incident occurred at that location or that the ship was not moved afterward. This would have put the *Josephine K.* at three-tenths of a mile inside the international limit, which raised doubts from skeptics as to whether the ship actually was within the twelve-mile limit.

Before the board adjourned for the day, the *Josephine K.* was loaded with pig iron equal in weight to the liquor the ship was carrying when seized, in preparation for a test run to determine the ship's real speed. The C.G. 145 was to be put to sea at the same time to take part in a reenactment of the chase, so the board could determine what chance Schmidt would have had of catching the rum-runner without firing the fatal shot. A Coast Guard report on the ship was read into the record, showing that the ship had been pursued 26 times since April 1929, and on each occasion had left the Coast Guard far behind.[8]

After repairs were made to the *Josephine K.*'s steering gear, which had been damaged by the shot that killed Captain Cluett, the two boats were ready for their speed test. The *Josephine K.* was manned by a Coast Guard crew and the C.G. 145 was manned by its regular crew, with Schmidt in command. The three officers of the board of inquiry were aboard the *Josephine K.* Reporters were aboard Coast Guard patrol boat 161, which followed along. The crew on the *Josephine K.* pushed the schooner to full speed and so did the C.G. 145. After the test run, Captain John Bryan, president of the board of inquiry, announced that the *Josephine K.* had run at 9.55 nautical miles, while the C.G. 145 had made 11.15 nautical miles. This shot holes in Schmidt's claim that he had to fire at the *Josephine K.* because it was too fast– no pun intended.[9]

On the following day, the board announced its findings. The board declared that the allegation that Schmidt was intoxicated on the night of the incident was "undoubtedly false" and meant to "discredit the government officer." The board found that the chase and capture of the *Josephine K.* took place within the twelve-mile limit and that Chief Boatswain's Mate Schmidt was simply enforcing the law. The board also came to the conclusion that Schmidt should be commended for seizing the *Josephine K.*, caring for the wounded captain in the manner he did, and afterward seizing the other vessels. The report was submitted to Admiral Billard, forwarded to Seymore Lowman, Assistant Treasury Secretary, and made public at the Treasury Department. The State Department also received a copy and forwarded it to the Canadian legation.[10]

Soon, Captain Cluett's body was back home in Lunenburg, Nova Scotia. On the day of his funeral, there was a fresh blanket of snow on the harbor town, giving it the look of a Christmas card. Cluett was a popular man in Lunenburg. Hundreds of people showed up at St. John's Anglican Church for the funeral service, including Cluett's widow, who was pregnant with their third child. The Orange Lodge, of which Cluett was a member, marched to the church and then to the grave *en masse*. Heads of business firms, legislators, sea captains, and seamen were also present. Reverend Ryder said in his eulogy that the Cluett's was a "fine churchman, thoroughgoing and well-instructed, a good husband and father, a good friend and a master mariner." He added that his death was "nothing more nor less than murder on the high seas" and "one of the inevitable tragedies that follow the hypocrisy of Prohibition."[11] Standing near the spot where William Cluett and June Selig were married six years earlier, he read two prayers the captain wrote for his young wife and himself. After that, he went on to say:

> "This tragedy must not be hushed up. Incidents of this sort are becoming almost a daily occurrence. They are evidence of the futility of trying to make a country dry by Prohibition.
> "Captain Cluett was simply the commander of a supply boat carrying a commodity demanded by the people of the United States. Their laws prohibit its import, yet many in high places who frame these laws are among the creators of that demand. I am confident that British justice will see fair play meted out."[12]

The Canadian government would not let the matter rest and in March sent a 2,000- word letter of protest to the State Department. The letter argued that the *Josephine K.* was more than one-hour's sailing distance from the coast and that the force used was unjustified. In the background of this controversy lingered the case of the *I'm Alone*, which occurred in March 1929. In that incident, the Coast Guard sank the Canadian ship 200 miles off the Louisiana. Two years later, the case of the *I'm Alone* was still in arbitration between the two governments. There were differences, of course. In the *I'm Alone* case, the ship was sunk well outside of the international limit, but no one died.[13]

In April 1931, the US Government filed a libel (the first pleading of the complainant in maritime law) against the *Josephine K.* The libel claimed penalties against the vessel under the Tariff Act, which provides a penalty for a vessel bound for the United States which does not produce a cargo manifest to the Customs or Coast Guard officer upon request. Another count claimed forfeiture of the vessel for transshipment of cargo without a permit within a distance of four leagues (12 nautical miles) of the coast.[14] In July, the *Josephine K.* was still carrying liquor cargoes, and in fact rammed a Coast Guard cutter while making an escape off the New England coast.[15]

In August, months after the shooting, new evidence came to light in the form of a Coast Guardsman's testimony. Wilbur B. Tally was second in command of the C.G. 145 on the night in question. Tally, who had recently resigned from the Coast Guard, told his story to Arthur H. Schwartz, Assistant US Attorney in charge of Prohibition prosecutions. Strangely, the Coast Guard board of investigation had not called upon

Tally to testify at the inquiry. Tally told a much different story than what was previously heard. According to him, the *Josephine K.* was spotted transferring liquor to a barge outside of the twelve-mile limit.[16]

Tally went on to say that after spotting the *Josephine K.* in the act of transferring liquor, Schmidt immediately prepared the one-pounder to fire. The chase only lasted a few minutes and the patrol boat was catching up to the rum ship quickly, never more than 200 feet away. Schmidt, Tally said, fired only one blank, then blasted away with three solid shots directly into the ship, although Coast Guard regulations called for three blank shots, followed by three solid shots across the bow as a warning.[17]

The *Josephine K.* stopped after the third shot pierced it. Tally went aboard as the seizing officer along with Boatswain's Mate John Hoffman. Captain Cluett was lying on the deck with blood pouring from his wound. Tally said that he shouted to Schmidt that he should be taken to a hospital immediately. Schmidt argued with Hoffman for more than ten minutes while Cluett lay there dying. After it was too late, Schmidt decided to have Cluett transported to the hospital, where he died.[18]

Soon, there was a federal grand jury hearing on the actions of Karl Schmidt. At that hearing, Tally retold his story and added that there was intoxication aboard the Coast Guard boat when the fatal shot was fired. He also said that he had not come out with these accusations sooner because he had been coerced into concealing the facts and that he was facing charges for alleged violations of navigation rules.[19] The grand jury did not buy Tally's version of the events and decided not to bring charges against Schmidt.[20]

After several months of negotiations, the US Government reached a settlement with the Liverpool Shipping Company of Nova Scotia, owners of the *Josephine K.* Under the agreement, the ship was released upon receipt of $500 of the $10,000 bond and all of the liquor seized in the raid was forfeited to the government.[21]

Not So Lucky

The *Josephine K.* was definitely not the only ship to have an unfortunate encounter with the Coast Guard in early 1931. A ship ironically named the *Good Luck* was chugging through the Verrazano Narrows with a load of 14,000 pounds of codfish. Coast Guard patrol boat 213 pulled up alongside, and Boatswain O.E. Carlson ordered Captain Bendiksen to stop for his vessel to be searched.[22]

Captain Bendiksen complied, and Coast Guardsmen came aboard, opening up hatches and poking among the fish for an hour. Then, the boatswain ordered Bendiksen to pull into Pier 18, Staten Island, for a more thorough search. Bendiksen replied that he would not and that his only cargo was fish. "If you want to arrest me and take the ship there yourself, go ahead," he said as he stepped away from the wheel.[23]

Farm Security Administration/ Office of War Information

Lower Manhattan at South Ferry. Photo by Dorothea Lange, 1939.

Carlson then tried to use a more friendly approach, "Come on, go to Pier 18." Captain Bendiksen refused again. Carlson then asked him if he would go to the Barge Office and Bendiksen also refused this request. "Oh well, then we will all go to Fulton Market," said the boatswain. And so they went to Fulton Market and when the *Good Luck* was tied up, several Coast Guardsmen came aboard and searched the fishing boat again. Members of the crew were detained on board during the search. They were not allowed to leave the boat until the following night, after yet another search party, this time from Customs, had left.[24]

After the last searchers had left, the ship was a wreck. The bunks were tossed out in the middle of the floor, there were holes punched in the flooring, planks torn up in patches, locker doors were ripped from their hinges, small holes had been drilled in various sections of the craft, and the ship's papers, which were hidden under the Captain's bunk, were missing. They found no liquor. Later on, another Coast Guard boat came alongside, and two men came aboard with tools. While they were patching up some of the holes, a news photographer came aboard. The Coast Guardsmen picked up their tools and hurried off the boat.

Captain Bendiksen told the press that he would file a formal complaint with the Collector of the Port, charging that his vessel had been ransacked and damaged unnecessarily; that his papers were either carelessly lost or taken; that he and his crew were held on his ship for 24 hours without food; that the Coast Guardsmen would not allow his cook to go ashore to purchase food; and that his cargo of fish, valued at $1,000, spoiled during that time.[25]

Bendiksen bought the *Good Luck* two months earlier. Before that, the fishing boat was on the Customs list of suspected rum-runners, which meant it was already a target when Bendiksen took ownership. Although the searchers found no liquor aboard, the *Good Luck* was stuck in port because the ship's papers were missing. The crew was disgruntled, understandably, and threatened to quit.

The Coast Guard repaired the *Good Luck* a few months later, during the summer. But the story does not end there. In December 1931, when the boat was coming out of Jamestown, Rhode Island, a searching crew from the C.G. 231 came aboard. Coasties damaged the *Good Luck*, again, by bringing their craft alongside in a heavy sea, tearing away a section of the aft rail. After that ordeal was over, the *Good Luck* headed for New York, where another Coast Guard vessel came up alongside and searched the boat. No liquor was found in either search.[26] Captain Bendiksen appeared before Coast Guard officials and declared that if the Coast Guard continued searching and damaging his fishing boat, he would change the name of his vessel.

In early August 1932, the Coast Guard cutter *Icarus* was about thirty miles off the Long Island shore when the lookout spotted a British rum runner. The cutter followed the rum runner, but did not attempt to capture it because of its distance from shore. While following the rum runner, the *Icarus* spotted the *Good Luck* with nets over the side. The ship was riding so low in the water that Lieutenant R.L. Raney decided to board it to examine its cargo. Captain Bendiksen was not aboard, but the Coast Guardsmen found 700 cases of liquor aboard, valued at $60,000. The boat was seized 54 miles southeast of Ambrose Lightship, well outside of the twelve-mile limit.

The *Icarus* towed the *Good Luck* into New York Harbor. Bendiksen gave an interview with reporters at his home on 77th Street in Brooklyn and said he was amazed that his ship was seized with liquor aboard. "In all the years I've been at sea I've never run liquor; not only in that boat but any other. My wife just wouldn't believe this when she heard it."[27]

Bendiksen said that he was injured in a fall two months earlier while boarding the *Good Luck* and that since then he had not been able to take the boat to sea regularly. He said that he hired another skipper but was not satisfied with his work and let him go. He then hired a man named Martin, who had master's papers and came well-recommended. He was supposed to have taken the ship out for a cargo of scallops, Bendiksen said, and added, "How this happened is beyond me, and I'm going over to see the Coast Guard tomorrow and see if I can get my ship back."[28]

The attorney who represented the *Good Luck*, Louis Halle, argued that the seizure of the fishing boat was illegal because it happened outside of the twelve-mile limit. Assistant US Attorney George Pfann countered that the twelve-mile limit had nothing to do with the charge that the crew was conspiring to bring liquor into the United States in violation of the Tariff Act.[29]

46

The Tide Turns

In 1931, the Coast Guard continued waging its war on Rum Row on a massive scale. In that year, the Prohibition fleet included 19 destroyers, 39 cutters, and 33 patrol-boats. During the first six months of 1931, the Coasties seized more than 100 vessels and 27,472 cases of liquor and arrested 193 men. However, it would prove difficult to top the job done in 1930. During 1930, the Coast Guard seized 93,288 cases of liquor, 442 kegs, and 8,999 cases of beer and ale. They arrested 476 men and captured 238 vessels in the same year. "There is a constant warfare going on out there on the sea," Admiral Billard told reporters. "We are working harder all the time, keeping up the pressure, but it often rests upon a combination of circumstances whether our seizures are from the big or little fellows."[1]

Treasury Department officials pointed out that despite these constant operations, there had only been two fatal shootings during the first half of 1931. One shooting was that of Captain Cluett aboard the *Josephine K.* The other man shot and killed was a crew member of the motorboat *Diatome*, fired upon ten miles off the California coast. In addition, two more rum smugglers drowned when they jumped overboard, one off the coast of Florida and the other off the Georgia coast.[2]

The New London, Connecticut station alone was extremely busy during the first half of 1931. The Coast Guard patrol along the southern New England coast had seized as much smuggled liquor as it did in all of 1930. The rum fleet in that area took a loss of approximately $2 million, factoring in liquor and boats seized and liquor sunk. Included in that figure were nine ships seized carrying 8,369 bags of liquor, nine others sunk or disabled with an estimated liquor cargo of 10,000 cases, and nine more seized for violating navigation laws. During all of this, two men were shot: one was Harry Barber of Oradell, NJ, whose scalp was creased by a Coast Guard bullet, and Leopold Mousseau of Fall River, Massachusetts, who was shot in the leg during a chase.[3]

Apparently, more than a decade of arrests, seizures, and shootouts had not diminished Rum Row. In June of 1931, there were sixteen "mother ships" anchored in Rum Row and the smaller motorboats that made runs to and from the shore were more numerous than ever. Coast Guard officials told reporters that smugglers were inadvertently helping to defeat themselves. The Coast Guard could not afford to build a fleet of speedboats on par with that of Rum Row. However, despite how fast these boats could move, the Coast Guard still managed to capture a good number of them, and in turn, used the speedboats for patrols. The Coast Guard also copied the rum fleet's system of operations, in a way. They kept their large ships, destroyers, outside of the twelve-mile limit to keep an eye on Rum Row, forming the first line. A second line of large patrol boats operated closer to shore. Supplementing the two lines of defense were small speedboats that sped through coastal waters, maintaining radio contact with the larger vessels.[4]

The government turned up the heat on smuggling operations in the second half of 1931, seizing twice as many vessels as during the first half of the year. The Coast Guard and Customs seized 204 rum-runners, fifteen airplanes, and 1,040 automobiles during those six months. They also seized 58,082 cases of liquor, valued at $1,742,000. As astronomical as those figures sound, it was actually a great decrease compared to previous years. The Treasury Department reported that 755 ships and boats were seized during the 1928-29 fiscal year, 956 vessels the year after that, and 564 during the 1930-31 fiscal year. The Justice Department estimated that about three-fourths of the boats and ships seized were captured off the northeastern coast of the United States. After Canada passed its laws to limit liquor exports to the US, the French Islands of St. Pierre and Miquelon became the headquarters for North Atlantic smugglers. Smuggling provided most of the jobs and revenue on those islands during that period.[5]

One new development in 1931 was the use of poison gas by rum-runners. In July of that year, Coast Guard patrol boat 149 was pursuing the *Cadet of Weymouth* off Nantucket, Mass. The Coasties fired a shot across the fleeing boat's bow when it swung into the wind and released a smoke screen filled with poisonous gas. All eight men aboard the patrol boat were affected and had to be hospitalized. The two worst stricken of the crew were in the hospital for a month afterward.[6] Officials could not identify what type of gas it was, because the Coast Guardsmen did not board the vessel. They did not have the authority to do so, either, because the Canadian boat was more than an hour's sailing distance from the coast. The Coast Guard sent their report to the State Department, which in turn forwarded the report to the American Minister at Ottowa. The complaint pointed out that bootleggers ashore had used smoke screens to escape police, but there had been no previous case where gas had been used by rum-runners at sea.[7]

There was another incident involving poison gas in September. Coast Guard picket boat 2394 was on patrol off Gloucester harbor, Massachusetts, when the crew spotted the *Lassgehn*. The *Lassgehn* was a high-powered, sixty-foot speedboat, whose name in German means "let's go." When the Coast Guardsmen ordered the vessel to stop, the *Lassgehn* ignored the order and sped away. A twenty-minute chase began, and the rum-runner zigzagged back and forth, laying down a poisonous smokescreen. The picket boat fired a few warning shots from a new type of rapid-fire gun, but the *Lassgehn* did not stop. Then, Chief Boatswain's Mate Roy Fitzgerald ordered the machine gun fire directed into its hull. One of the smugglers, Joseph Mello, 30, of New Bedford, Massachusetts, was in the engine room when he was shot and killed. He was the father of five children. Boatswain's Mate First Class William Kelly was overcome by the poisonous gas and was hospitalized in critical condition. The captured craft was brought to Base 7 with its cargo of approximately 400 cases.[8]

The Tide Turns

The early 1930s saw popular opinion turn dramatically against Prohibition. While a good portion of Americans were against Prohibition during the 1920s, it was still not the politically-correct stance to take in public. Today we wonder how on earth such an unpopular law remained in effect for as long as it did. The answer is that there was still a relatively large portion of Americans who supported the ideals of making America dry and eliminating the vices associated with alcoholism. In the early 1920s, to take an official stand against Prohibition as a politician or public official was career suicide. It did not matter how many people were against Prohibition privately if they were afraid to voice their opinions in public. Those few daring individuals who dared to speak up against Prohibition were attacked viciously in newspapers and by organizations like the Women's Christian Temperance Union.

No matter how futile Prohibition enforcement turned out to be, those who supported it argued that Prohibition was not implemented correctly. With a few changes in the way the law was enforced, and with more support from politicians and the average citizen, supporters argued, all would improve within a short time. A dry utopia was always just around the corner, regardless of how many years Prohibition failed. Similar to communist countries, where the answer to problems caused by communism was always "more communism," the dry's answer to Prohibition's problems was "more Prohibition."

The tide of public opinion really began to turn overwhelmingly against Prohibition in 1932. It was an election year, America was two years into the Great Depression, and the federal government needed tax dollars badly. With massive unemployment, homelessness, and hunger on an unprecedented scale, America's priorities changed. Cracking down on alcohol consumption seemed like an absolutely ridiculous waste of time and funds while masses of homeless men, women, and children roamed America's streets.

In early 1932, the *Literary Digest* conducted a poll on Prohibition, in which 4,668,537 votes were cast. The results showed that 73% of those polled wanted to repeal the 18th Amendment, while 27% favored the 18th Amendment. Every state, except Kansas and North Carolina, favored repeal, and those two states who favored the dry law did so by a very slim majority.[9] In November 1932, eleven states held Prohibition referenda. All of them voted to repeal state constitutional dry laws and/or state enforcement acts. Those states were: Louisiana, Colorado, California, Oregon, Washington, New Jersey, Arizona, Michigan, North Dakota, Connecticut, and Wyoming.[10]

The Women's Organization for National Prohibition Reform sent out questionnaires to all Congressional candidates during the fall of 1932. The questionnaire asked candidates for both the Senate and the House if they would vote to repeal the 18th Amendment. In late October, they received replies from 607 candidates; 553 candidates said they would vote to strike down the 18th Amendment and 54 said they would support the 18th Amendment. That is a ratio of 10 to 1 in support of repeal, so regardless who won the presidential election that year, repeal seemed inevitable.[11] To put this political shift into perspective, one should look at the election results of eight years earlier. After the election of 1924, there were 319 members of the House of Representatives who favored Prohibition and 105 who were opposed. In the Senate, there were 72 Senators in favor of Prohibition and 24 opposed—a ratio of approximately 3 to 1 in both houses.[12]

Despite the results of the popular opinion poll and who was running for Congress, the "drys" were still deeply entrenched in Congress in 1932. In May 1932, the House refused to consider, by a vote of 228 to 169, the O'Connor-Hull Bill legalizing beer with 2.75% alcohol. That same month, the Senate shot down an amendment to legalize beer by a vote of 61 to 24. In November, Franklin Delano Roosevelt was elected President, along with a large number of "wets" to Congress. A resolution for the repeal of the 18th Amendment was defeated in the House by a narrow margin in December. However, in the Senate, a resolution for submitting repeal of the 18th Amendment to the states won by a vote of 63 to 23– an almost direct reversal of the vote against beer a few months earlier.[13]

Despite the thousands of ship and boat seizures during the previous few years, there was still a massive fleet of rum ships operating off the US coast in 1932. Admiral Billard testified before the House Appropriations Committee that there were 176 liquor-smuggling vessels operating along our shores in early 1932. Like the head of any large government agency, he wanted more funding for his organization. He told the committee:

> "It is perfectly apparent that if we had a sufficient number of Coast Guard craft to keep all the smuggling vessels under constant surveillance we would have the situation entirely controlled. We really would have to have more than ship for ship, because we, of course, have to find the liquor vessels and then keep the vessels under surveillance and our ships would have to be relieved."[14]

While Admiral Billard was asking for more and more funding for ships, planes, and Coast Guardsmen, public opinion on Prohibition had already turned overwhelmingly against it. The wets in Congress were driving to legalize beer and repeal the 18th Amendment. Because much of the Coast Guard's time was spent chasing rum-runners, House members interested in cutting costs were considering drastic cuts in the Coast Guard's budget. Drys in Congress argued that if Prohibition was modified or repealed, the Coast Guard would still need all of its equipment and manpower to curb smuggling.

Dry members of Congress used the example of Finland, which had recently repealed its own prohibition laws and encountered a large volume of liquor smuggling, most likely in an effort to avoid liquor taxes. Over the years, the US Coast Guard's budget had skyrocketed. In 1924, their budget was about $11.4 million; in 1932, their budget was approximately $28 million. During that same period, the number of commissioned officers rose from 209 to 428, the number of warrant officers rose from 420 to 839, and the number of enlisted men went from 5,260 to 11,250.[15]

One of the biggest money-guzzlers was the Coast Guard's new aviation wing. At the beginning of Prohibition, using planes in the Coast Guard was a novel idea. By 1932, there were eight planes and 32 Coast Guard pilots– a laughable number by today's standards, but enough to make a big difference if they patrolled the skies regularly. The three air bases were located at Gloucester, Massachusetts; Cape May, NJ; and Miami, Florida.[16]

The Coast Guard had a pretty massive fleet of vessels in 1932. It had 36 cruising cutters, 15 destroyers, 34 harbor craft, seven 165-foot patrol boats, thirty-three 125-foot patrol boats, thirteen 100-foot patrol boats, six 78-foot patrol boats, 181 75-foot patrol boats, 34 miscellaneous patrol boats, 88 cabin picket boats, 61 open picket boats, and 17 miscellaneous picket boats– a total of 525 vessels of all shapes and sizes.[17]

Just as Congress was unsure what impact repeal would have on the Coast Guard, anyone connected with the speakeasy business wondered what their futures would hold. In 1932, the Great Depression was in full swing and finding any kind of employment was extremely difficult. At the time, the liquor business was one of America's largest businesses. If it was not *the* largest business, it was certainly the biggest cash business. In New York City alone, there were 32,000 speakeasies in 1929. Many speakeasies had been doing business in the same location for six years or more, keeping the same faithful customers.[18]

The crackdowns on speakeasies were sporadic. Occasionally, a waiter, bartender, or even the owner would go to jail. But overall, the business had been run as a business and the service supplied had been regular and orderly. Raids meant only a temporary break in the routine. Many of the regular speakeasy customers had never even seen a raid after years of visiting the same establishments. The spectacular raids, where agents and police destroyed the bar and smashed furniture got a lot of press coverage, but they were the exception rather than the norm. During the 1920s, speakeasies were highly profitable, but times had changed. In the early 1930s, a good portion of speakeasies were being operated at a loss or just barely scraping by. They were kept running for the same reason as any other businesses during the Depression– to keep their customer base intact for when times improved. The speakeasy owners, however, did not know if their establishments would survive the legalization of liquor and all of the changes it would bring.

Speakeasies sold more than drinks, they also sold food and provided entertainment, so that alone could keep customers returning after repeal. Speakeasy owners were faced with the threat that liquor prices would drop dramatically after legalization. They also wondered how they would be able to maintain their stocks of beverages legally. When speakeasies would become legitimate businesses, there would be an enormous demand and a low supply of alcohol for quite a while. How would the owners survive this shortage? This was a question they grappled with daily as repeal seemed imminent.

A *New York Times* reporter named H.I. Brock interviewed a few men who made their living from a speakeasy. Obviously, he did not reveal their names in the article he wrote, but their comments were insightful. One established speakeasy owner said that he would be glad when Prohibition was over. He looked forward to attracting a higher class of customers and being able to run his business in a way that would save money for everyone involved.[19]

One bootlegger told Brock that the bootleg racket was finished and that the liquor business was ruined, just like everything else in the Depression. People who used to buy twenty cases now hesitated to order two cases. People who used to buy a case occasionally now haggled over the price of a couple of bottles. Collecting the money was slow and painful (literally painful for those who didn't have the money). A boss bootlegger had to pay 25% of his profits for protection and 25% for his men. The remaining 50% was usually tied up in the slow-moving contraband stock. "Myself, I don't have nothing left—never have no money at all," the bootlegger told Brock.[20]

47

Repeal

The year 1933 saw profound political changes—fundamental changes in the role and size of the federal government which endure to this day. The powers of the federal government increase whenever there is a crisis. These crises include wars, civil unrest, natural disasters, economic collapses, crime waves, etc. The pattern is that when a crisis emerges, the federal government passes a new law and/or creates a new agency to deal with the crisis. However, in most cases, after the crisis has passed, the laws and agencies created to deal with the problem remain in existence. This creates a ratchet effect, whereby the federal government becomes more and more powerful, very rarely relinquishing any of its power.

Questions debated hotly during the Great Depression endure to this day. How big and powerful should our federal government be? Where does individual responsibility end and governmental responsibility begin? How much economic regulation should there be and at what point does it become crippling? Is socialism a good or bad thing? If we are going to have social programs, then to what extent? Is government really the answer to all of our economic and social ills? Should government agencies create their own laws without the approval of Congress? Should they even have the power to do so? Should government agencies have the power to spend tax dollars without Congressional oversight? How much power should a President have?

Franklin Delano Roosevelt won the Presidential election of 1932, defeating Herbert Hoover. By popular vote, he won by a vote of 22,821,857 to Hoover's 15,761,845, or 57.4% versus 39.6%. However, in the electoral college, Roosevelt won by a vote of 472 to 59, or 88% versus 12%. This disparity between the electoral college results and the popular vote brings into question why we still keep such a system. Fans of Roosevelt will point to the electoral vote when discussing his presidential victory, but it is worth noting that Hoover received almost 40 percent of the popular vote in 1932.

Roosevelt, or FDR as he is commonly referred to, is still a controversial figure today. He lived his entire life surrounded by wealth and privilege, yet he waged war on wealthy and privileged people on the campaign trail and from the Oval Office. FDR was a political lightning rod, and both his supporters and critics can look at his presidency during the Depression to argue for or against his policies. One thing is certain, regardless of where one stands on FDR, and that is the greatly increased role of the federal government in the everyday lives of Americans after he took office.

FDR's power was greatly enhanced by the congressional election results of 1932. In the House of Representatives, there were 313 Democrats and 117 Republicans. In the Senate, there were now 59 Democrats and 36 Republicans. Roosevelt, a Democrat, now had free reign to implement his policies. During the first 100 days of his administration, fifteen bills went through Congress and became law—an unprecedented number. That averages out to a new federal law every week!

President Roosevelt called for a special session of Congress on March 9, 1933. He began to immediately propose legislation. On March 12, he gave the first of his "fireside chats" to the American people over the radio. His first radio chat was about the banking crisis and how he resolved to fix it, with the support of the American people. At that point, it did not matter whether the American people supported his ideas or not, because the Emergency Banking Act became law three days earlier. Among the other laws passed during the 100 days was the Economy Act, which cut federal costs through the reorganization of government agencies and cuts in salaries and veterans' pensions. The Beer-Wine Revenue Act legalized and taxed wine and beer. The Civilian Conservation Corps Act created millions of jobs for young men between the ages of 19 and 25 through building roads, forestry, and flood control. The Federal Emergency Relief Act established the Federal Emergency Relief Administration, which distributed funds to state and local governments for relief or for wages on public works. The Agricultural Adjustment Act established a new agency to decrease crop surpluses by subsidizing farmers who voluntarily cut back on production, basically paying farmers to produce less. The Thomas Amendment to the Agricultural Adjustment Act allowed the president to inflate currency in different ways. The Tennessee Valley Authority Act provided for the federal government's construction of dams and power plants in the Tennessee Valley, combined with agricultural and industrial planning, in order to generate and sell the power to the area. The Federal Securities Act tightened regulation of the stock market. The grand finale of Roosevelt's first 100 days in office was the National Industrial Recovery Act, which established the National Recovery Administration (NRA) and the Public Works Administration (PWA). The new law regulated the number of hours in a work week, wages, competitive practices, and protected labor unions. The Public Works Administration's purpose was to provide grants or loans to state and local governments in order to fight unemployment, and to use the power of eminent domain to seize land or materials to build transportation infrastructure. This list really only skims the surface of what became known as the New Deal. Each bill that was passed during that period had tentacles reaching far in all directions. It would really take an entire book (or two) to sufficiently discuss all of the details and ramifications of the first New Deal. Congress passed a second set of relief and reform measures in 1935, later known as the Second New Deal.

Against this backdrop was the issue of repeal. No one really knew quite what to expect when Prohibition was repealed. Some guesses were a lot more accurate than others. In 1933, Prohibition was breathing its last breaths. On March 22, 1933, President Roosevelt signed the Cullen-Harrison Act, legalizing beer of 3.2% alcohol and wine. However, the sale of any other type of alcoholic beverage was still illegal and Prohibition was still mainly in effect. In February 1933, Congress proposed the 21st Amendment of the Constitution, which would repeal Prohibition. However, before it could become law, it had to be ratified by a majority of the states. That process took almost ten months. While the gears of repeal turned slowly, the government had the task of figuring out whether repeal would increase or decrease the burden on the Coast Guard. The federal government anticipated that after Prohibition there would be a great deal of rum-running to avoid the high taxes on liquor, and that the profitability of smuggling would become even greater than before. So in September 1933, $14.8 million was allocated to the Coast Guard for equipment. Out of that sum, approximately $1.9 million was allotted for 31 seaplanes. Smugglers increasingly transported liquor by plane to bypass the Coast Guard fleet.[1]

Political cartoon from a 1939 magazine depicting programs and laws created under President Franklin D. Roosevelt.

Other construction authorized for the Coast Guard included six 300-foot cutters, costing $9 million, and two of the 165-foot type, costing $1.1 million. The larger cutters were to be equipped to carry seaplanes and would be the first Coast Guard vessels ever to carry aircraft. The

Coast Guard would have new air stations at Biloxi, Mississippi; Port Angeles, Washington; St. Petersburg, Florida; and Galveston, Texas. The Biloxi station was to be one of the most important air bases, due to the fact that smuggling was rampant along the Gulf Coast near New Orleans. In addition to the seaplanes and new cutters would be nine new patrol boats, costing $2,250,000. These patrol boats would replace the obsolete destroyers being used by the Coast Guard and were projected to save about $1.2 million in annual operating expenses.[2]

Three of the six new 300-foot cutters would replace the *Seneca, Snohomish,* and the *Yamacraw,* each of which was more than 24 years old. The other three cutters would be stationed at San Pedro, California; the Panama Canal; and Alaska. The coasts in the vicinity of San Pedro and Alaska were dangerous for shipping and the need for extra cutters in the Panama Canal had been on the priority list for several years.

Despite these new ships and planes, the Coast Guard still felt the pinch of the Great Depression. As FDR came into office as President, he sought to slash government spending in some areas and increase it in other areas. Under the Economy Act, 150 warrant officers and 1,500 enlisted men were cut from the Coast Guard. In addition, 150 inshore patrol vessels and some of its destroyers were decommissioned.[3]

As the Coast Guard fleet was shrinking, the rum fleet was growing. All along the US coast, the number of liquor smuggling vessels was increasing. At the end of October 1933, when repeal was imminent, the number of liquor smuggling vessels off the northeastern coast almost doubled from its normal size. In the waters between Cape May, NJ and Nantucket Island, Mass., there were about fifty rum boats of all sizes, the largest number since 1925. Three months prior, there were only thirty. In some ways, it would be easier for smugglers to get liquor ashore after Prohibition was repealed. Ships filled with liquor could legally clear for American ports and, once inside the twelve-mile limit, make a detour to drop off the cargo at another point, thereby avoiding liquor taxes. One official calculated that if the illegal rum fleet were allowed to operate after Prohibition, it would cost the government $50 million annually in lost duties.[4]

The Big Day Arrives

On December 5, 1933, Pennsylvania, Ohio, and Utah ratified the 21st Amendment. Three-fourths of the states must ratify an amendment before it can be added to the Constitution. When Utah ratified the amendment at 5:32 P.M., it brought the count up to 36 states, providing the three-fourths majority, thereby repealing the 18th Amendment. At 6:55 P.M., President Roosevelt signed an official proclamation which announced the end of federal Prohibition. He asked all citizens to cooperate with the government in its effort to restore a greater respect for law and order, especially by purchasing liquor only from licensed businesses. This practice, he said, would bring about the "break-up and eventual destruction of the notoriously evil illicit liquor traffic" and provide the government with tax dollars. Roosevelt also said, "I ask especially, that no state shall, by law or otherwise, authorize the return of the saloon, either in its old form or in some modern guise."[5] What Roosevelt meant by this was that drinks should only be served to people sitting at tables, and the traditional bar complete with brass rail and stools should be banned. This was not a provision included in the 21st Amendment, but something Roosevelt pushed for at the last minute.

Roosevelt promoted drinking in moderation and proposed education as a way to bring about greater temperance throughout the nation. Along with repeal came the new Federal Alcohol Control Administration (FACA), ready to regulate the nation's liquor supply and trade. FACA officials told the public that they were confident that the country would have an adequate supply of good liquor within the next few days. Their chief concern was that profiteers should not reap the rewards of the immediate post-repeal demand, or that customers should buy from bootleggers who were trying to sell tax-free liquor.

Since many states still had their own Prohibition laws and the federal government wanted its tax dollars, the force of 1,300 former Prohibition agents kept their jobs at the Department of Justice. The only real difference was that their division was renamed the Alcoholic Beverages Unit, as opposed to the Prohibition Division. Lawyers who worked for the Industrial Alcohol Bureau during Prohibition now worked for the Bureau of Internal Revenue (today's IRS).[6]

On the night of repeal, big crowds of New Yorkers flowed into Times Square and the thousands of restaurants, hotels, and clubs fortunate enough to already have liquor licenses were overwhelmed. The NYPD did not receive the official word about repeal until 9:20 PM, four hours after Utah ratified the amendment. Although the city's entire police force of 19,000 was mobilized that night, arrests did not exceed the normal number.[7]

Because Utah made repeal so late in the day, retail liquor stores were unable to obtain inventory from the warehouses in time for the glut of customers that night. The supply of legal liquor in the licensed businesses was really short. Only 54 truckloads of bonded liquor were released from the warehouses before they closed that night; the two largest warehouses shut their doors before repeal took effect. With 3,000 places licensed to sell liquor in the city, plus another 2,000 in upstate New York, only about one in one-hundred was able to move in a stock in the few hours available. Some of the others had the very smart idea of increasing their supplies using medicinal permits while Prohibition was breathing its last breaths. The few trucks that got under way from bonded warehouses and distilleries that night had armed guards. The trucks bound for Connecticut were armed with machine guns to guard against hijackers.[8]

Bootleggers and speakeasies took advantage of the alcohol shortage, despite a stern warning against such activity from the police commissioner. Others were not so bold and took heed to the commissioner's warning. Hundreds of cordial shops closed their doors that night and others dealt only with long-known and trusted customers. Most of those that closed their doors that night removed their inventory and left their shelves empty. The wave of cordial shop closures began in the Bronx, NY. There, a syndicate that operated 250 shops had cars and trucks in front of its largest stores right as the news came from Utah. Only a few cordial shops, mostly in downtown Manhattan, carried on business as usual. Some of them posted signs promising to open as licensed liquor stores in a few days.[9]

The *White Star* arrived from France late in the afternoon with a cargo of 6,200 cases of assorted wines and spirits. However, the ship was delayed five hours by bad weather and did not dock until after Customs had closed, delaying the unloading until the next morning.

In New York, the first legal sale of wine and liquor under repeal was made at Bloomingdale's. The department store, located at 60th Street and Lexington Avenue in Manhattan, had a liquor and wine shop inside. Bloomingdale's obtained its stock in advance under a medicinal permit. Other department stores, such as Macy's, Gimbel's, and Abraham & Straus did not attempt to open their wine and liquor shops until the next day. During the hour before repeal became official, a huge crowd stood outside Bloomingdale's with their noses pressed to the window, watching the clerks load the shelves with medicinal liquor. In the main part of the store, employees listened intently to radio coverage of the proceedings in Utah. The employees formed a relay line to pass the messages on to the liquor department.

Then came the big moment. "Open the door!" the store's officers shouted, practically in sync. The security guards admitted twenty people at 5:21 PM. As they waited at the counter, most of them rested their elbows on the counter as if it were a bar and looked eagerly at the shelves, where there were about 300 bottles of various liquors. The store employees brought case after case from an upstairs storeroom and loaded it on the shelves. Out of habit, quite a few of the customers raised a foot up below the counter, expecting a brass rail to be there. Of course, there was none because this was Bloomingdale's and not a speakeasy.[10]

The first customer, Aubrey Hollingsworth, was a tile-maker from Queens who was still in his work clothes. He wanted a bottle of port and a pint of rye. Bloomingdale's had both, and at reasonable prices compared to those of Prohibition. Because of a miscommunication between the employee monitoring the radio news and those working in the liquor department, the first patrons came in a few minutes before repeal became official. Fortunately for everyone involved, Mr. Hollingsworth purchased the liquor at 5:33 PM, one minute after repeal went into effect. Camera bulbs flashed away, recording the event.[11]

On the following day, hotels and restaurants were packed full. Long lines of people waited in the rain outside of department store wine and liquor shops. Approximately 100,000 homes had legal liquor on the first night after repeal. However, the supply simply could not keep up with the demand. Government restrictions caused long delays at warehouses. Exhausted truck drivers, who had worked all night, also slowed deliveries. Many of the smaller shops were unable to get any liquor. Compounding this problem was the relatively small number of places that were licensed right after repeal. For example, in New York, 120 stores on Broadway applied for liquor licenses, but only nineteen had licenses on the day after repeal. The few inspectors of the State Alcoholic Beverage Control Board could not keep up with the flood of applications. In addition, Police Commissioner Bolan made good on his threats and had 52 places raided in one night for selling unlicensed liquor.[12]

The higher-class speakeasies, some of which had obtained licenses, were packed with happy crowds that toasted the occasion with legal beverages. The prices were cheaper than a few days earlier by

40%. High-end hotels began selling drinks briskly in the early afternoon. Some of them ran out of stock by the cocktail hour, but most of them managed to keep up with the demand.[13]

The Assistant Collector of Customs of New York, H.C. Stuart, estimated that about 50,000 cases of liquor had been removed from more than seventy bonded warehouses during the first day after repeal. Customs collected duties totaling $385,000 on foreign wines and liquor. Of this figure, about 90% was collected on goods withdrawn from warehouses, the rest was collected at the piers.[14]

The real celebration of repeal came on New Year's Eve. In New York, the turn-out was the biggest it had been in fifteen years. In Times Square alone, about 300,000 showed up to celebrate. Police estimated the entire midtown crowd at 750,000.[15] People were celebrating their new freedom, now that the shackles of Prohibition had fallen off. For the first time in years, millions would be able to toast the New Year with champagne legally. They were able to have their New Year's parties without fear that police or federal agents would come busting through the doors. Massive crowds celebrated in the streets, hotels and restaurants were filled to capacity, and millions of Americans celebrated in their homes with bottles of legal alcoholic beverages. They were not only celebrating the end of Prohibition, they were also celebrating the New Deal, and the optimism that came with the belief that things were about to change for the better. In reality, the Great Depression would drag on for the rest of the 1930s, followed by World War II– arguably the darkest period in human history. But on the eve of 1934, as with any other year, no one knew how events would unfold. What they did know was that they had a new president, who was very popular and willing to try new, radical ideas to solve the nation's problems. Along with the new administration came new jobs, government assistance, and massive new infrastructure projects under the New Deal. To top it all off, Prohibition was dead. Those things alone were worth celebrating.

****

Like any other major changes in federal law, repeal brought a lot of uncertainty– not only for those in the alcoholic beverage business, but also for those who were in trouble with the law. Not long after repeal took effect, the US Supreme Court scheduled a test case to determine whether federal Prohibition charges should be prosecuted or dismissed.

There were still thousands of Prohibition cases waiting to be heard in federal district courts throughout the country. Solicitor General James C. Biggs told the Court that the Justice Department was without precedent to guide its action in such cases and requested a ruling as soon as possible.[16]

The case to be heard was against Byrum Gibson and Claude Chambers, charged with conspiracy to violate the federal Prohibition law in Rockingham County, North Carolina. The federal district court dismissed the indictments on the ground that repeal had nullified the Volstead Act. The Ninth Circuit Court of Appeals at San Francisco went a step further by holding that sentences imposed by trial courts in liquor cases must be set aside because of Prohibition repeal. The Supreme Court case was scheduled for the following month, which is lightning speed as far as the Supreme Court is concerned. Normally a case will take months or years to be heard, if it ever makes it to the Court at all. This was a special case in which the lives of thousands of Americans were held in limbo, not to mention the time and resources of federal courts across the nation, so time was of the essence. Until then, however, thousands who violated the Prohibition law languished in jail awaiting trial.[17] After repeal, the Justice Department still wanted to prosecute all those who were charged with violating Prohibition before repeal. Solicitor General James Biggs filed a brief with the Supreme Court urging the Court not to release those who had violated the now-defunct federal Prohibition law.[18]

On February 5, 1934, the Supreme Court gave its ruling. The Court decided that pre-repeal Prohibition cases were to be stricken from the dockets of federal courts throughout the nation. The decision affected not only cases where indictments had been returned, but where convictions had been obtained and appealed. In all, about 9,000 Prohibition cases pending in federal courts were dismissed.[19]

48

Hangover

Most accounts of Prohibition stop at repeal in 1933. Whether the story is told through a documentary or in writing, it almost invariably goes something like this: Franklin D. Roosevelt was elected President, the Beer Bill was passed, Prohibition was repealed, the end. Documentaries usually show old footage of people popping wine corks and dancing in celebration at speakeasies, or long lines of people waiting to buy beer and wine legally for the first time in thirteen years. These accounts would have us believe that everything went back to normal overnight and that rum-running and bootlegging stopped dead in its tracks, with the exception of a few moonshiners in the mountains. That was definitely not the case. What makes this story more interesting is finding out what happened in the aftermath.

With the repeal of the federal Prohibition law, liquor control became a confusing mess. There were still many states that had Prohibition written into their state constitutions, states with their own Prohibition statutes, and states that had no Prohibition laws whatsoever. Since the federal government controls interstate commerce, this would become a very messy issue. At least under federal Prohibition, the 18th Amendment and the Volstead Act applied regardless of where you went in the United States. Now, the liquor laws were a confusing patchwork.

The magnitude of this confusing legal mess was apparent in all parts of the nation. In the western states, such as Colorado, Utah, Nevada, Wyoming, Montana, and Nebraska, the illegal distilling of corn whisky had developed into a major industry. Shortly after repeal, the illicit whisky stock was estimated at one million gallons in the mountain states. Single distilleries in Wyoming and Nevada had as much as 5,000 gallons on hand. Bootleggers could easily undersell legal liquor prices and were willing to deliver anything from a pint to ten gallons, anywhere, anytime, at low prices.[1]

Rum Row did not vanish overnight; it took several years for that to happen. However, there were some immediate signs that the days of large-scale liquor smuggling by sea were numbered. A month after repeal, word reached Rum Row that the Coast Guard planned a strict illegal-liquor blockade, but there was a legal loophole. Under new government regulations, if the rum ships brought their stocks to Honduras, or islands such as the Bahamas and Bermuda, shipments of unlimited quantities could be made legally. As a result, rum ships brought two million gallons of whisky to foreign ports for legal reshipment to the US.[2]

In April 1934, the federal government began yet another campaign against eliminating bootleggers and illicit distilleries. Treasury Secretary Henry Morgenthau told the press that the illegal distilleries formed a "husky industry" and showed no signs of slowing down after repeal. "We hope to hit and hit hard this illicit industry," he added. "So far as big stills are concerned there appear to be as many in operation as before Prohibition repeal." In order to fight illicit distilling, a special unit made up of more than 600 men was established in the Bureau of Industrial Alcohol. In yet another bureaucratic change, the Justice Department's Alcoholic Beverage Unit was transferred to the Treasury Department. Most of the 1,000 agents became a part of the Internal Revenue Bureau. The job of combating illicit distilleries was given to the Treasury because those distilleries were costing the federal government a lot of lost revenue. During one week in April, Treasury agents seized 73 stills, which had an average output of 239 gallons a day. In that same week, they captured a large quantity of distilled spirits and mash and property valued at $17,600.[3]

Included in the New Deal's program of tight government controls were the Federal Alcohol Control Administration (FACA) and the Distiller's Code. When the code took effect on November 7, 1933, the federal government believed that the alcohol production of licensed distilleries would exceed the demand, so the government set limits. As of February 1934, the government estimated that the legal distilleries would have a yearly output of about 240 million gallons of liquor. This figure did not include industrial alcohol. After making further studies on the demand for alcohol, FACA authorized the production of another 40 million gallons annually. However, as astronomical as 280 million gallons sounds, illicit distilleries were still out-producing legal ones.[4]

Up against this massive illegal liquor problem was a diminished force of agents. During June 1933, the government made a large cut in enforcement personnel, followed by a 50% cut in August. As a result, the number of illicit distillery seizures dropped by two-thirds, averaging a little under 500 per month during the last quarter of the year. In 1934, those agents who still had jobs were picking up the pace. In January there were 732 distillery seizures, followed by 582 in February, and 674 in March. These were not backyard stills made from tea kettles and other household items, these were active distilleries. Many of them were large plants with modern equipment and stills three or four stories high. FACA estimated that the distilleries seized during those three months had an annual capacity of approximately 68 million gallons. The government estimated that there were still at least 7,952 illicit plants in operation, capable of producing roughly 272 million gallons annually. The government had been seizing thousands of illicit distilleries per year since Prohibition began and new ones would pop up as fast as other ones were seized.[5] One estimate of federal taxes lost in 1934 through bootlegging and smuggling was $400 million.[6]

These figures show that the demand for alcoholic beverages of all types had skyrocketed since Prohibition took effect. To make a comparison, from 1912 to 1916, the tax-paid withdrawals of alcoholic beverages averaged about 130 million gallons per year. Illegal production existed during those years, but was on a very small scale. In 1934, legal and illegal production combined was well over 500 million gallons annually.[7] So the irony is that Americans drank more after thirteen years of Prohibition than before. During the 1920s, the thrill of doing something taboo attracted many Americans to speakeasies. In the 1930s, millions of Americans used alcohol to drown the sorrows that came from living through the Great Depression.

FACA was not very popular with distillers, brewers, distributors, or anyone else in the alcoholic beverage trade. In a written formal protest to President Roosevelt bearing the signatures of twelve Congressmen, Representative Celler of New York complained of the "intense bureaucratic control of the industry," which he said had put it in a straightjacket. Celler characterized the Federal Alcohol Control Administration as "foolish, piddling and annoying," and argued that it had increased the cost of doing business for small merchants and increased prices for consumers. The letter said, in part:

"...These rigid regulations give aid and comfort to the bootlegger, who can easily avoid the regulations due to inability and failure of enforcement, whereas the legitimate trader must live up to them. The FACA cannot enforce its regulations.

"We thought we had destroyed the rum rows along our seacoasts. It is noted now Rum Row lives again. St. Pierre et Miquelon has again become a haven of rum runners and smugglers. It is reported that large supplies of liquor destined for United States bootleggers are warehoused there.

"Smuggling, particularly as a result of rigid quota regulations, has increased tremendously. Only due to vehement protests were quotas for the third period lifted. They must be abolished entirely. They served no good purpose. They encouraged smuggling..."[8]

The Coast Guard faced the challenges of 1934 with a greatly-reduced force. The fleet had been reduced by more than 30% between July 1933 and July 1934. Among the craft removed by government spending cuts were a score of destroyers and between 150 and 200 patrol boats, picket boats, and other smaller vessels. In addition to that, the Navy was planning to take control of several key Coast Guard radio posts at New London, Connecticut; Rockaway, NY; and Wintrop, Mass., making the surveillance of rum ships far more difficult for the Coasties.[9]

In July 1934, the Coast Guard was aware of about twenty large rum ships cruising up and down the East Coast, most of them off New England and the Mid-Atlantic states. The rum fleet was growing larger as tight government regulation and high liquor taxes and duties ($7 a gallon in 1934 dollars) made illegal liquor a more appealing option. At Red Bank, NJ, Coast Guard officials reported at least twenty-two known rum-runners standing by offshore, waiting for their chance to unload their illicit cargoes. With its fleet depleted, the Coast Guard was powerless to do anything except trail a few rum ships offshore. Smugglers could land their land their cargoes at just about any point on the East Coast with little opposition.[10]

During that same month, bootleggers and liquor law violators were going to federal prison at a faster rate than in the fifteen months prior to repeal. Oh, the irony! The federal government was cracking down on anyone who violated the new FACA regulations and evaded liquor taxes. Treasury Secretary Morgenthau proudly told reporters that the federal government was increasing the pace of arrests for liquor violations. In the previous three months, an average of 313 persons per month wound up in federal prison for breaking liquor laws. Compare that to an average of 178 monthly for the previous fiscal year and 278 per month for the fiscal year from July 1, 1932 to June 30, 1933. Repeal was supposed to ease the burden on federal courts, but instead, hundreds of cases were piling up in federal courts.[11]

In early 1935, the cuts to the Coast Guard became painfully obvious. The Coast Guard was reduced to 10,000 personnel. That averaged out to one man to guard each mile of the 10,000-mile American coast. The Coast Guard's budget shrank from $25,772,950 in 1934 to about $18 million in 1935.[12] Rum-runners had regrouped and slightly changed their strategies to adapt to the changing times. Facing this resurgence in rum-running was a greatly depleted Coast Guard. The bases at Boston, Woods Hole, and Gloucester, Massachusetts were shut down. The force of 49 boats that once patrolled the area was reduced to one boat. At the Staten Island, NY base, there were once thirty craft and now there were only two. The fifteen destroyers that once patrolled the New York/ New Jersey area were sent to other places. At Cape May, NJ, only six of twenty-two inshore patrol boats remained. The results of the cuts showed in the number of seizures. Between July 1 and November 30, 1934, the Coast Guard and Customs combined seized only twenty boats, one plane, 122 automobiles, 10,921 gallons of spirits and wine, 172 gallons of beer, and 31,422 gallons of alcohol. These seizures were only a fraction of what they once were. Meanwhile, rum-runners were still as active as ever.[13]

After repeal, not only was it easier for smugglers to get their illegal shipments past a diminished Coast Guard, it was also easier to disguise illicit liquor as legitimate. Now that alcohol manufacture was legal, the bootleg alcohol was of a higher quality than during Prohibition. The days of making drinks with industrial alcohol were over. Now, a more refined, safer product flooded the illicit market. Distillers began producing knock-offs of imported and domestic liquors that were hard to distinguish from the real thing. A cargo of legally-imported alcohol could be increased fourfold, meaning that one gallon of alcohol could be made into four gallons of illicit spirits in a single operation. These beverages were put into bottles with well-known names blown into the glass and convincing labels affixed, with false revenue stamps to add the finishing touch.[14]

As usual, every time the federal government came up with a new obstacle to the illegal liquor trade, smugglers and bootleggers figured out a way to overcome it. On January 1, 1935, it became a jailable offense to use bottles for domestic liquor without a permit number blown into the glass, plus other markings and the words, "The Federal law prohibits the sale or re-use of this bottle." Soon after the law went into effect, federal agents raided a number of warehouses in New York in search of "illegal" bottles. The government estimated that some 90 million bottles would have to be destroyed. However, this new law did not apply to foreign bottles, creating yet another loophole for smugglers and bootleggers to exploit.[15]

In March 1935, Treasury Secretary Morgenthau appeared before the House Ways and Means Committee to ask for more funding for the Coast Guard. He told the committee that during the previous year liquor smugglers cost the government more than $30 million dollars in lost taxes and customs duties. At the time, there were 39 vessels known to be carrying contraband alcohol and Scotch malt, waiting beyond the 12-mile limit for their chance to make dash for shore. Morgenthau estimated that illicit alcohol was entering the country at a rate of more than 2,225,000 gallons per year and being sold at prices far below legitimate market rates. The tax on legally-imported alcohol was $3.80 per gallon and the customs duty was $9.50 per gallon. Smugglers were buying alcohol in Belgium, Holland, Guatemala, British Honduras, Mexico, the Bahamas, and other places at prices of 20 to 50 cents a gallon and delivering it to American shores for $3.50 a gallon—a very handsome profit. Most of the liquor was entering northeastern ports or coming in on the Gulf Coast. Despite the fact that the rum ships were known to contain contraband, the Coast Guard could not touch them outside of the international limit. They could, however, follow them. Because the rum ships were loaded to the gunwales with their liquid cargo, they were unable to carry much fuel. In some cases, Coast Guard craft trailed rum ships more than 700 miles until the smugglers ran out of fuel and were forced into neutral ports.[16]

****

Although it seemed like Rum Row would never disappear, it did…gradually. During 1936 and 1937, the supply of legal liquor caught up with the demand. Taxes on domestic brands and duties on liquor imports dropped, making legally-purchased liquor more affordable. The figures speak for themselves. In 1937, the federal government collected more than a billion dollars in taxes on legal liquor.[17] The number of rum boat seizures dropped dramatically during those years. In the fiscal year ending June 30, 1937, the Coast Guard seized only eleven vessels, compared to 34 seizures during the previous year. Liquor seizures dropped from $176,890 in 1936 to $2,176 in 1937. The Coast Guard's arrests of alcohol smugglers dropped from 48 in 1936 to half a dozen in 1937.[18]

By 1938, rum-running was scarcely mentioned in newspapers because it had been reduced to such a small scale. The making of moonshine in places such as the Appalachians and the Ozark Mountains continued to thrive after Prohibition and lives on to this day. Hitler's invasion of Poland in the fall of 1939 marked the beginning of World War II. During those years, shipping across the Atlantic and Pacific became extremely dangerous as the seas were infested with German and Japanese submarines and mines. Rum runners had very little incentive to risk their lives as enemy subs were on a ship-sinking frenzy. America's focus rapidly shifted from the Great Depression and the remnants of Prohibition to fighting the biggest war in the history of mankind. The popular version of Prohibition came to focus on gangsters, bootleggers, moonshine, flappers, and speakeasies, ignoring the fact that most of the liquor arrived by sea. The once famous rum smugglers were forgotten. The Coast Guardsmen who risked their lives, or gave their lives, chasing them were forgotten. Within a few decades, Rum Row became a footnote in history, eventually known only to a few history buffs.

Appendix A

Excerpts from the Volstead Act of 1920, also known as the War Prohibition Act and the National Prohibition Act.
41 Stat. 305–323, ch. 83

TITLE I.
TO PROVIDE FOR THE ENFORCEMENT OF WAR PROHIBITION.

The term "War Prohibition Act" used in this Act shall mean the provisions of any Act or Acts prohibiting the sale and manufacture of intoxicating liquors until the conclusion of the present war and thereafter until the termination of demobilization, the date of which shall be determined and proclaimed by the President of the United States. The words "beer, wine, or other intoxicating malt or vinous liquors" in the War Prohibition Act shall be hereafter construed to mean any such beverages which contain one-half of 1 per centum or more of alcohol by volume: . . .

SEC. 2. The Commissioner of Internal Revenue, his assistants, agents, and inspectors, shall investigate and report violations of the War Prohibition Act to the United States attorney for the district in which committed, who shall be charged with the duty of prosecuting, subject to the direction of the Attorney General, the offenders as in the case of other offenses against laws of the United States; and such Commissioner of Internal Revenue, his assistants, agents, and inspectors may swear out warrants before United States commissioners or other officers or courts authorized to issue the same for the apprehension of such offenders and may, subject to the control of the said United States attorney, conduct the prosecution at the committing trial for the purpose of having the offenders held for the action of a grand jury...

TITLE II.
PROHIBITION OF INTOXICATING BEVERAGES.

SEC. 3. No person shall on or after the date when the eighteenth amendment to the Constitution of the United States goes into effect, manufacture, sell, barter, transport import, export, deliver, furnish or possess any intoxicating liquor except as authorized in this Act, and all the provisions of this Act shall be liberally construed to the end that the use of intoxicating liquor as a beverage may be prevented.

Liquor for non beverage purposes and wine or sacramental purposes may be manufactured, purchased, sold, bartered transported, imported, exported, delivered, furnished and possessed, but only as herein provided, and he commissioner may, upon application, issue permits therefor: Provided, That nothing| in this Act shall prohibit the purchase and sale of warehouse receipts covering distilled spirits on deposit in Government bonded warehouses, and no special tax liability shall attach to the business of purchasing and selling such warehouse receipts....

SEC. 6. No one shall manufacture, sell, purchase, transport, or prescribe any liquor without first obtaining a permit from the commissioner so to do, except that a person may, without a permit, purchase and use liquor for medicinal purposes when prescribed by a physician as herein provided, and except that any person who in the opinion of the commissioner is conducting a bona fide hospital or sanitarium engaged in the treatment of persons suffering from alcoholism, may, under such rules, regulations, and conditions as the commissioner shall prescribe, purchase and use, in accordance with the methods in use in such institution liquor, to be administered to the patients of such institution under the direction of a duly qualified physician employed by such institution.

All permits to manufacture, prescribe, sell, or transport liquor, may be issued for one year, and shall expire on the 31st day of December next succeeding the issuance thereof: . . . Permits to purchase liquor shall specify the quantity and kind to be purchased and the purpose for which it is to |be used. No permit shall be issued to any person who within one year prior to the application therefor or issuance thereof shall have violated the terms of any permit issued under this Title or any law of the United states or of any State regulating traffic in liquor. No permit shall be issued to anyone to sell liquor at retail, unless the sale is to be made through a pharmacist designated in the permit and duly licensed under the laws of his State to compound and dismedicine prescribed by a duly licensed physician. No one shall be given a permit describe liquor unless he is a physician licensed to practice medicine and actively engaged in the practice of such profession. . .

Nothing in this title shall be held to apply to the manufacture, sale, transportation, importation , possession, or distribution of wine for sacramental purposes, or like religious rites, except section 6 (save as the same requires a permit to purchase) and section 10 hereof, and the provisions of this Act prescribing penalties for the violation of either of said sections. No person to whom a permit may be issued to manufacture, transport, import, or sell wines for sacramental purposes or like religious rites shall sell, barter, exchange, or furnish any such to any person not a rabbi, minister of the gospel, priest, or an officer duly authorized for the purpose by any church or congregation, nor to any such except upon an application duly subscribed by him, which application, authenticated as regulations may prescribe, shall be filed and preserved by the seller. The head of any conference or diocese or other ecclesiastical jurisdiction may designate any rabbi, minister, or priest to supervise the manufacture of wine to be used for the purposes and rites in this section mentioned, and the person so designated may, in the discretion of the commissioner, be granted a permit to supervise such manufacture.

SEC. 7. No one but a physician holding a permit to prescribe liquor shall issue any prescription for liquor. And no physician shall prescribe liquor unless after careful physical examination of the person for whose use such prescription is sought, or if such examination is found impracticable, then upon the best information obtainable, he in good faith believes that the use of such liquor as a medicine by such person is necessary and will afford relief to him from some known ailment. Not more than a pint of spiritous liquor to be taken internally shad be prescribed for use by the same person within any period of ten days and no prescription shall he filled more than once. Any pharmacist filling a prescription shall at the time endorse upon it over his own signature the word "canceled," together with the date when the liquor was delivered, and then make the same a part of the record that he is required to keep as herein provided....

SEC. 18. It shall be unlawful to advertise, manufacture, sell, or possess for sale any utensil, contrivance, machine, preparation, compound, tablet, substance, formula direction, recipe advertised, designed, or intended for use in the unlawful manufacture of intoxicating liquor....

SEC. 21. Any room, house, building, boat, vehicle, structure, or place where intoxicating liquor is manufactured, sold, kept, or bartered in violation of this title, and all intoxicating liquor and property kept and used in maintaining the same, is hereby declared to be a common nuisance, and any person who maintains such a common nuisance shall be guilty of a misdemeanor and upon conviction thereof shall be fined not more than $1,000 or be imprisoned for not more than one year, or both....

SEC. 25. It shall be unlawful to have or possess any liquor or property designed for the manufacture of liquor intended for use in violating this title or which has been so used, and no property rights shall exist in any such liquor or property.... No search warrant shall issue to search any private dwelling occupied as such unless it is being used for the unlawful sale of intoxicating liquor, or unless it is in part used for some business purposes such as a store, shop, saloon, restaurant, hotel, or boarding house....

SEC. 29. Any person who manufactures or sells liquor in violation of this title shall for a first offense be fined not more than $1,000, or imprisoned not exceeding six months, and for a second or subsequent offense shall be fined not less than $200 nor more than $2,000 and be imprisoned not less than one month nor more than five years.

Any person violating the provisions of any permit, or who makes any false record, report, or affidavit required by this title, or violates any of the provisions of this title, for which offense a special penalty is not prescribed, shall be fined for a first offense not more than $500; for a second offense not less than $100 nor more than $1,000, or be imprisoned not more than ninety days; for any subsequent offense he shall be fined not less than $500 and be imprisoned not less than three months nor more than two years....

SEC. S3. After February 1, 1920, the possession of liquors by any person not legally permitted under this title to possess liquor shall be prima facie evidence that such liquor is kept for the purpose of being sold, bartered, exchanged, given away, furnished, or otherwise disposed of in violation of the Provisions of this title.... But it shall not be unlawful to possess liquors in one's private dwelling while the same is occupied and used by him as his dwelling only and such liquor need not be reported, provided such liquors are for use only for the personal consumption of the owner thereof and his family residing in such dwelling and of his bona fide guests when entertained by him therein; and the burden of proof shall be upon the possessor in any action concerning She same to prove that such liquor was lawfully acquired, possessed, and used....

SOURCES

Published Books

Behr, Edward. *Prohibition: Thirteen Years That Changed America.* NY: Arcade Publishing, 1996.
Canadeo, Anne. *Warren G. Harding: 29th President Of The United States.* Ada, Oklahoma: Garrett Educational Corporation, 1990.
Cannadine, David. *Mellon: An American Life.* NY: Alfred A. Knopf, 2006.
Coolidge, Calvin. *The Autobiography Of Calvin Coolidge.* NY: Cosmopolitan Book Corporation, 1929.
Dean, John W. *Warren G. Harding.* NY: Times Books, 2004.
Haynes, Roy A. *Prohibition Inside Out.* NY: Doubleday, Page & Co., 1923.
Hevenor, Darrell Smith and Powell, Fred Wilbur. *The Coast Guard: Its History, Activities and Organization.* Washington, DC: The Brookings Institution, 1929.
Hoover, Herbert. *The Memoirs Of Herbert Hoover: The Cabinet And The Presidency, 1920-1933.* NY: The Macmillan Company, 1952.
Hoover, Herbert. *The Ordeal Of Woodrow Wilson.* NY: McGraw-Hill Book Company Inc., 1958.
Hoover, Irwin Hood. *Forty-Two Years In The White House.* NY: Houghton Mifflin Co., 1934.
Kyvig, David E., *Daily Life In The United States, 1920-1940.* Chicago: Ivan R. Dee, 2002.
Leinwand, Gerald. *1927: High Tide of the 1920's.* New York: Four Walls Eight Windows, 2001.
Levin, Phyllis Lee. *Edith And Woodrow: The Wilson White House.* NY: Scribner, 2001.
Potter, Claire Bond. *War On Crime: Bandits, G-Men, And The Politics of Mass Culture.* New Brunswick, NJ: Rutgers Univ. Press, 1998.
Rogers, James T. *Woodrow Wilson: Visionary For Peace.* NY: Facts On File Inc., 1997.
Smith, Gene. *When The Cheering Stopped: The Last Years Of Woodrow Wilson.* NY: William Morrow And Company, 1964.
Tumulty, Joseph P. *Woodrow Wilson As I Know Him.* Garden City, NY: Doubleday, Page & Company, 1921.

Government Documents

Note: All of the following documents are located at US Coast Guard Headquarters unless otherwise noted.

Appleby, John D. Attorney at Law. Letter to Federal Prohibition Commissioner Roy A. Haynes. New York, 28 April 1923. Forwarded to Secretary of the Treasury Andrew Mellon. 1 May, 1923.
Billard, F.C. Commandant of the Coast Guard. Letter to Wayne B. Wheeler. General Counsel of the Anti-Saloon League of America. Washington, DC 25 July 1924.
Camp, E.W. Office of the Secretary of the Treasury/ Division of Customs. Memorandum

for Assistant Treasury Secretary Clifford. Washington, DC, 18 January 1923.
Clifford, Edward. Assistant Treasury Secretary. Memorandum for the Secretary of the Treasury. Washington, DC 25 January 1923.
Gordon, James L. Special Agent In Charge. Letter to the Secretary of the Treasury. Buffalo, NY 11 July 1923.
Haynes, R.A. Federal Prohibition Commissioner. Memorandum for Mr. Blair. Washington, DC 3 February 1923.
Reynolds, W.E. Commandant of the Coast Guard. Memorandum for General Lord, Director of the Budget. Washington, DC 3 May 1923. Forwarded to Treasury Secretary Mellon. 3 May 1923.
R.G. 26. Records of the US Coast Guard. Logbooks of Revenue Cutters and Coast Guard Vessels, 1819-1941. National Archives.
Scott, Philip H. Captain, US Coast Guard. Letter to Captain Byron L. Reed. Commander of the New York Division. Sandy Hook, NJ 5 March 1924. Forwarded to the US Attorney General. 17 March 1924.
Stuart, H.C. Collector of Customs. Letter to Assistant Treasury Secretary Edward Clifford. New York, 24 January 1923.
US Congress. House. Committee On Interstate And Foreign Commerce. *United States Coast Guard Law Enforcement Hearing.* H.R. 6815, 68th Congress, 1st sess., 1924.
Van Doren, Nathaniel. Director of the Special Agency Service, US Customs. Memorandum for Assistant Treasury Secretary Clifford. Washington, DC 19 January 1923.
Van Doren, Nathaniel. Director of the Special Agency Service, US Customs. Memorandum for Assistant Treasury Secretary Moss. Washington, DC 29 July 1924.
Willebrandt, Mabel Walker. Assistant US Attorney General. Letter to the Secretary of the Treasury. Washington, DC, 13 December 1923.
Willebrandt, Mabel Walker. Assistant US Attorney General. Letter to Assistant Treasury Secretary Clifford. Washington, DC, 7 February 1923.
Yellowley, E.C. Federal Prohibition Director. Letter to Acting Collector of Customs H.C. Stuart. New York, 24 January 1923.

Government Publications

Clark, Edward F. "US Coast Guard Commandants, 1889 to 1933." *The US Coast Guard: The National Publication of the United States Coast Guard,* April 1933.
Willoughby, Malcolm F. *Rum War At Sea.* Washington, DC: US Government Printing Office, 1964.

Newspapers

The Atlanta Constitution. 1920-1924.
The Chigago Tribune. 1920-1924.
The London *Times.* 1920-1921.
The New York Times. 1920-1938.
The New York Tribune. 1920-1924.
The Washington Post. 1920-1924.

Statistical Abstracts

"Table Dg34-45- Telephone Industry- telephones, access lines, wire, employees, and plant: 1876-2000." Cambridge University Press, 2007.

ENDNOTES

CHAPTER 1

[1] David E. Kyvig, *Daily Life In The United States, 1920-1940.* (Chicago: Ivan R. Dee, 2002.) pp.66-67
[2] "Table Dg34-45- Telephone Industry- telephones, access lines, wire, employees, and plant: 1876-2000." (Cambridge University Press, 2007.)
[3] Kyvig, pp.75-76.
[4] Ibid., p.49.

CHAPTER 2

[1] Gene Smith, *When The Cheering Stopped: The Last Years Of Woodrow Wilson,* (NY: William Morrow And Company, 1964) p. 72.
[2] Ibid., p.82.
[3] Ibid., p.83.
[4] Ibid., pp. 84-85.
[5] Irwin Hood Hoover, *Forty-Two Years In The White House,* (NY: Houghton Mifflin Co., 1934.) p. 100.
[6] Smith, p.122.
[7] Ibid., p.121.
[8] Ibid., p.125-126.
[9] "Biggest Liquor Haul," *The Washington Post,* January 15, 1920.
[10] Edward Behr, *Prohibition: Thirteen Years That Changed America.* (NY: Arcade Publishing, 1996) p.81.
[11] "Heavy Exports Of Liquor," *The New York Times,* March 5, 1920.
[12] Behr, pp. 82-83.
[13] "Lid On, Palmer Says," *The Washington Post,* January 16, 1920.
[14] Smith, pp.83-84.
[15] Smith, p.127.
[16] "Asks For $2,000,000 To Keep Out Liquor," *The New York Times,* Feb. 4, 1920.
[17] RG 26 Records of the US Coast Guard. Logbooks of Revenue Cutters and Coast Guard Vessels, 1819-1941. NARA.
[18] Edward F. Clark, "US Coast Guard Commandants, 1889 to 1933," *The US Coast Guard: The National Publication Of the United States Coast Guard,* April 1933, p. 2.
[19] Smith., p.143.
[20] Ibid., p.140.
[21] Hoover pp.276-277; Smith pp.154-155.
[22] "Seamen's Objections To 'Dry' US Ports," The London *Times,* January 28, 1920.
[23] Ibid.
[24] "Puts 'Dry' Guard Aboard Whisky Ship," *The New York Times,* January 30, 1920.
[25] "5,000,000 Liquor Cargo Is Seized," *The New York Times,* February 4, 1920.
[26] Ibid.
[27] Ibid.
[28] Ibid.
[29] "Yarmouth To Sail With Liquor Cargo," *The New York Times,* February 5, 1920.
[30] "The Yarmouth Off With Whisky Cargo," *The New York Times,* February 3, 1920.

[31] "Bootleggers Seize Agent As Hijacker," *The New York Times*, August 9, 1924.
[32] Ibid.
[33] Ibid.
[34] Ibid.
[35] Ibid.
[36] "McCarthy Upbraids Prohibition Agents," *The New York Times*, March 4, 1920.
[37] "Liquor Is Seized On Italian Liner," *The New York Times*, October 15, 1920.
[38] "Crew Resents Raid On Ship For Liquor," *The New York Times*, November 2, 1920.
[39] Ibid.
[40] Ibid.
[41] "Liquor Smuggling Scare," The London *Times*, April 30, 1920.
[42] "Chaser Fires On Submarine, Thinking Her Liquor Smuggler," *The New York Times*, April 29, 1920.
[43] "Report Torpedoes Used To Shoot Whisky Into Detroit," *The New York Times*, May 8, 1920.
[44] Smith, p. 296-297.
[45] Ibid., p.166.
[46] "Service Inadequate To Curb Smuggling," *The New York Times*, Aug. 10, 1920.
[47] "Free Rum-Running On Canadian Border," *The New York Times*, September 19, 1920.
[48] Ibid.
[49] "Big Seizure of Liquor," The London *Times*, March 2, 1921.
[50] "Threat To Seize Alien 'Rum' Ships," *The New York Times*, Oct. 12, 1920.
[51] "Newton Denies Plan To Seize Liquor Ships," *The New York Times*, Oct. 14, 1920.
[52] "Imperial and Foreign News Items," The London *Times*, December 9, 1920.
[53] Smith, p.167-168.
[54] Ibid., p.168-169.

CHAPTER 3

[1] Herbert Hoover, *The Ordeal Of Woodrow Wilson* (NY: McGraw-Hill Book Company Inc., 1958) pp.297-298.
[2] Ibid., p.298.
[3] Canadeo, p.73-74.
[4] Ibid.
[5] Ibid., pp.87-88.
[6] David Cannadine, *Mellon: An American Life* (NY: Alfred A. Knopf, 2006.) p.271.
[7] Ibid., p.272.
[8] Ibid., pp.272-273.
[9] Ibid., p.278.
[10] Ibid.
[11] Ibid., p.291.
[12] Dawes as quoted in Dean, pp.105-106.
[13] Dean, pp.105-106.
[14] "Hunt Custom Graft In Smuggled Goods," *The New York Times*, February 4, 1921.
[15] Ibid.
[16] "US Ban On Ships With Bars," The London *Times*, February 10, 1921.
[17] "Bimini's Behavior; Mr. Bryan Shocked," The London *Times*, April 26, 1921.
[18] "The 'Booze Fleet;' Running the Dry Blockade," The London *Times*, May 23, 1921.
[19] "Sees Smuggling Clue In $75,000 Rum Seizure," *The New York Times*, May 12, 1921.
[20] "$500,000 Contraband Rum Fleet Hovers Outside 3-Mile Limit, Off Atlantic City," *The New York Times*, May 20, 1921.
[21] Ibid.
[22] "Rumors Of A Rum Ship," *The New York Times*, July 10, 1921.
[23] "Rum-runners Busy Again," *The New York Times*, July 14, 1921.
[24] "Foreign Ships Plan Test Of Volstead Curb," *The New York Times*, July 14, 1921.

ALCOHOL, BOAT CHASES, AND SHOOTOUTS!

[25] "Planes Hunt Wet Smuggler," *The New York Times*, July 15, 1921.
[26] "Unite In Coast Rum Hunt," *The New York Times*, July 18, 1921.
[27] "Ship At Atlantic City May Be Rum-runner," *The New York Times*, July 21, 1921.
[28] "Millions Behind Rum Plot, He Says," *The Washington Post*, July 25, 1921.
[29] "Unite To Run Down Coast Rum Ships," *The New York Times*, July 22, 1921.
[30] "Liquor Smugglers Captured," The London *Times*, July 25, 1921.
[31] "Seize British Ship But Find No Liquor," *The New York Times*, July 24, 1921.
[32] Ibid.
[33] Ibid.
[34] "Wireless to Warn Rum Ship Inbound," *The New York Times*, July 25, 1921.
[35] Ibid.
[36] Ibid.
[37] Ibid.
[38] Ibid.
[39] Ibid.
[40] "Seek All Who Met $100,000 Rum Ship," *The New York Times*, July 25, 1921.
[41] "New Raid In New Haven," *The New York Times*, July 26, 1921.
[42] "Rum-runner Accuses Police," *The New York Times*, July 26, 1921.
[43] Ibid.
[44] "Hunt For Pocomoke's Cargo," *New York Times*, July 26, 1921.
[45] "Rum Hunters Baffled," *The New York Times*, July 27, 1921.
[46] "Holds Dry Sleuth Ships Impractical," *The Washington Post*, July 27, 1921.
[47] "Ex-Revenue Men Accused," *The New York Times*, July 26, 1921.
[48] "Charges Insanity To Bootleg Rum," *The New York Times*, July 26, 1921.
[49] "Ship Mystery Solved?" The London *Times*, July 30, 1921.
[50] "Rum Ship Seized Under Act Of 1790," *The New York Times*, August 14, 1921.
[51] "3-Mile Limit Won't Shield Smugglers," *The New York Times*, August 7, 1921.
[52] "Boatmen Arrested As Rum Carriers," *The New York Times*, August 10, 1921.
[53] "Britain Bars Seizure Of Rum Ship At Sea," *The New York Times*, August 19, 1921.
[54] "Hudson Maxim Assails Dry-Law 'Parasites,' " *The New York Times*, August 13, 1921.
[55] Ibid.
[56] Ibid.
[57] "Canada Won't Help To Stop Rum Smuggling," *The New York Times*, August 13, 1921.
[58] "Right To Make Wine Reported," *The New York Times*, August 14, 1921.
[59] "Reporter Finds British Craft Supplying Boat Customers Off New Bedford," *The New York Times*, August 13, 1921.
[60] Ibid.
[61] "Liquor Runners: Lorry Loads From Canada," The London *Times*, August 15, 1921.
[62] "Imperial And Foreign News," The London *Times*, August 19, 1921.
[63] "Canadians Speed Up Flood Of Liquor," *The New York Times*, August 14, 1921.
[64] "Liquor Shipments Via US Ports," The London *Times*, October 24, 1921.
[65] "Right Of Search For Liquor," The London *Times*, August 20, 1921.
[66] Ibid.
[67] Ibid.
[68] Ibid.
[69] "Thriving On Liquor," The London *Times*, August 23, 1921.
[70] Ibid.
[71] Ibid.
[72] "US Whisky Imports: Large Increase Under Prohibition," The London *Times*, September 7, 1921.
[73] "Bootlegger Heirs Of The Buccaneers Of Baratia," *The New York Times*, October 23, 1921.
[74] Ibid.
[75] Ibid.
[76] Ibid.
[77] Ibid.

CHAPTER 4

[1] "R.A. Day Resigns As Dry Chief Here," *The New York Times*, October 5, 1921
[2] "Rum Running Vessels Listed By Government," *The New York Times*, January 12, 1922.
[3] Ibid.
[4] "Former Canadian Submarine Sought As A Whisky Runner," *The New York Times*, January 12, 1922.
[5] "How Prohibition Flotilla Will Make War On Rum-Runners—Armed With 3-Inch Guns," *The New York Times*, April 9, 1922.
[6] Ibid.
[7] "Two Rich Years For Rum-runners," *The New York Times*, January 15, 1922.
[8] Ibid.
[9] "To Stop Smuggling Of Liquor Here," *The New York Times*, February 18, 1922.
[10] "Seek To Dam Flood Of Rum Into South," *The New York Times*, March 5, 1922.
[11] Ibid.
[12] Ibid.
[13] "Dry Navy's Drag Net," *New York Times*, April 9, 1922.
[14] Ibid.
[15] Ibid.
[16] "Seek To Dam Flood Of Rum Into South," *The New York Times*, March 5, 1922.
[17] "Prohibition 'Navy' To Hunt Liquor Runners; Nine Sub. Chasers to Operate in the Atlantic," *The New York Times*, March 6, 1922.
[18] "How Prohibition Flotilla Will Make War On Rum-runners—Armed With 3-Inch Guns," *The New York Times*, April 9, 1922.
[19] Ibid.
[20] Ibid.
[21] Ibid.
[22] Ibid.
[23] Ibid.
[24] Ibid.
[25] "Calls On Veterans To Man 'Dry' Guns," *The New York Times*, April 11, 1922.
[26] "Revenue Boat Nabs Floating Winery At Sea," *Lima News*, May 13, 1922.
[27] Ibid.
[28] "Seize Mystery Ship With $1,500,000 Rum," *The New York Times*, May 12, 1926.
[29] Ibid.
[30] Ibid.
[31] Ibid.
[32] "Bail For Tipsy Crew Of Prize Rum Ship," *The New York Times*, May 13, 1926.
[33] Ibid.
[34] Ibid.
[35] "Rum Ship An Outcast; Alcohol Blast Feared," *The New York Times*, May 14, 1926.
[36] "Donnetta Finds A Pier," *The New York Times*, May 16, 1926.
[37] "Bootleggers Fire On 20 Dry Raiders," *The New York Times*, April 2, 1927.
[38] "Hughes Opposes Drastic Navy Cut," *The New York Times*. April 12, 1922.
[39] Ibid.
[40] "$250,000 In Liquors Seized With 3 Ships," *The New York Times*. July 28, 1922.
[41] Ibid.
[42] Ibid.
[43] Ibid.
[44] Ibid.
[45] Ibid.

[46] "Respected Citizen Of Patchogue," *The New York Times*,. July 29, 1922.

CHAPTER 5
[1] "Begin Rum Blockade Here," *The New York Times*. August 1, 1922.
[2] Ibid.
[3] "65 Cases Of Rum Seized By Police, Are Sought In Vain," *The New York Times*. August 5, 1922.
[4] Ibid.
[5] Ibid.
[6] Ibid.
[7] Ibid.
[8] "Rum Seized In Bay Is Still Missing," *The New York Times*. August 6, 1922.
[9] Ibid.
[10] Ibid.
[11] Ibid.
[12] Ibid.
[13] Ibid.
[14] "Order Liquor Ship Seized On High Sea," *The New York Times*, August 7, 1922.
[15] Ibid.
[16] Ibid.
[17] "Policeman and Waiter Victim Reported Dying," *The New York Tribune*, August 8, 1922.
[18] "Policeman, Rum Crazed, Shoots Two And Is Shot," *The New York Tribune*, August 7, 1922.
[19] "Drunken Policeman On A Rampage, Shot After Wounding 2," *The New York Times*. August 7, 1922.
[20] "Policeman, Rum Crazed, Shoots Two And Is Shot," *The New York Tribune*, August 7, 1922.
[21] "Drunken Policeman On A Rampage, Shot After Wounding 2," *The New York Times*. August 7, 1922.
[22] Ibid.
[23] Ibid.
[24] Ibid.
[25] Ibid.
[26] Ibid.
[27] "Awaits Seizure Of Ship," *The New York Times*. August 10, 1922.
[28] "Scrapping Five Warships," *The New York Times*. August 8, 1922.
[29] "Enright Asks For $77,500 For Fast Boats To Cope With Flying Rum Squadrons," *The New York Times*. September 23, 1922.
[30] "Gunmen On Rum Ship Force Crew To Obey Radio-Sent Orders," *The New York Times*. September 22, 1922.
[31] Ibid.
[32] Ibid.
[33] Ibid.
[34] Ibid.
[35] Ibid.
[36] "Says US Rum Ban Ends On High Seas," *The New York Times*, September 23, 1922.
[37] Ibid.
[38] "Coast Guard's Life Has Thrills A-Plenty Today," *The New York Times*, August 30, 1925.
[39] "Rum Ship's Master Is Held In $50,000," *The New York Times*, February 10, 1925.
[40] "Coast Guard's Life Has Thrills A-Plenty Today," *The New York Times*, August 30, 1925.
[41] Ibid.
[42] Ibid.
[43] Ibid.
[44] Ibid.

45 Ibid.
46 Ibid.
47 Ibid.
48 Ibid.
49 Ibid.
50 "Seize British Ship Under Dry Treaty," *The New York Times*, February 8, 1925.
51 "Rum Ship's Master Is Held In $50,000," *The New York Times*, February 10, 1925.
52 Ibid.
53 Ibid.
54 "US Releases Rum; May Be Baronet's," *The New York Times*, May 6, 1925.

CHAPTER 6

1 "R.A. Day Resigns As Dry Chief Here," *The The New York Times*, October 5, 1922.
2 Ibid.
3 "R.A. Day Resigns As Dry Chief During Probe," *The New York Tribune*, October 5, 1922.
4 "Day Says He Quits As Dry Official To Run Own Business," *The New York Tribune*, October 6, 1922.
5 "Charges Day Got Bootlegger Loan," *The New York Times*, October 9, 1922.
6 "Dry Director Day Is Haled Into Court," *The New York Times*, October 28, 1922.
7 "Day Denies He Had Any Part In Rum Theft," *The New York Tribune,*, October 29, 1922.
8 Ibid.
9 "Day Not In Contempt In Rum Jury Inquiry," *The New York Times*, November 2, 1922.
10 "Books of Day's Firm Go Before US Jury Today," *The New York Tribune*, November 2, 1922.
11 "Trap-Bottom Planes" *The New York Times*, October 5, 1922.
12 "Court Confiscates British Rum Ship," *The New York Times*, October 17, 1922.
13 "British Complain Of Rum Ship Seizure," *The New York Times*, October 19, 1922.
14 Ibid.
15 "Hughes Releases Schooner Emerald," *The New York Times*, October 28, 1922.
16 Ibid.
17 "*Marina* Sails With Liquor," *The New York Times*, November 4, 1922.
18 "Land Liquor In Providence," *The New York Times*, November 7, 1922.
19 "Liquor Fleet Near; Dry Navy On Guard," *The New York Times*, November 4, 1922.
20 "Frees Ships Seized Beyond 3-Mile Line," *The New York Times*, November 11, 1922.
21 "Dry Law Rules Modified," *The New York Times*, November 23, 1922.
22 "Rum Running By Sea Ended, Says Dry Chief," *The New York Times*, December 21, 1922.
23 "Jail Or Drowning Is Choice As Rum Craft Intrude On Montauk," *The New York Tribune*, December 29, 1922.
24 "2 Rum Ships Ground, Pirates Loot Third," *The New York Times*, December 29, 1922.
25 Ibid.
26 "Jail Or Drowning Is Choice As Rum Craft Intrude On Montauk," *The New York Tribune*, December 29, 1922.
27 Ibid.
28 "Dry Navy Laid Up, Liquor Rushed In; Murder Follows," *The New York Times*, December 31, 1922.
29 "Dry Navy Flagship Inert; Rum-runners Steal In," *The New York Tribune*, December 31, 1922.
30 Dry Navy Laid Up, Liquor Rushed In; Murder Follows," *The New York Times*, December 31, 1922.
31 Ibid.
32 "Dry Navy Flagship Inert; Rum-runners Steal In," *The New York Tribune*, December 31, 1922.
33 "Get 4 Rum Boats; Miss 35,000 Cases," *The New York Times*, January 12, 1923.
34 Ibid.
35 Ibid.
36 "Scoff At Rum Tale, But Fear Its True," *The New York Times*, January 13, 1923.

ALCOHOL, BOAT CHASES, AND SHOOTOUTS!

[37] Ibid.
[38] Ibid.
[39] "Wants An Inquiry Into Whisky Fleet," *The New York Times*, January 14, 1923.
[40] Letter to Acting Collector of Customs H.C. Stuart, from E.C. Yellowley, Acting Federal Prohibition Director. New York, 18 January 1923.
[41] Ibid.
[42] Ibid.
[43] Memorandum for Assistant Secretary Clifford, from E.W. Camp, Division of Customs. Washington, DC, 18 January 1923.
[44] Letter to Assistant Treasury Secretary Clifford, from Mabel Walker Willebrandt, Assistant Attorney General. Washington, DC, 7 February 1923.
[45] Memorandum for Mr. Blair, from R.A. Haynes, Federal Prohibition Commissioner. Washington, DC, 3 February 1923.
[46] Memorandum for Assistant Secretary Clifford, from E.W. Camp, Division of Customs. Washington, DC, 18 January 1923.

CHAPTER 7

[1] "Vast Rum Running Baffles Officials," *The New York Times*, January 20, 1923.
[2] Ibid.
[3] "Finds 17 Vessels In Liquor Fleet," *The New York Times*, January 21, 1923. Also see Letter from Customs Collector H.C. Stuart to Assistant Treasury Secretary Edward Clifford, January 24, 1924.
[4] "4,000 Business Men Join Dry Law Fight," *The New York Times*, January 24, 1923.
[5] Memorandum for Assistant Secretary of the Treasury Clifford, from Nathaniel Van Doren, Division of Customs. Washington, DC, 19 January 1923.
[6] Memorandum for the Secretary of the Treasury, from Edward Clifford, Assistant Secretary, Washington, DC 25 January 1923.
[7] "Ship's Liquor Gone; Say Pirates Got It," *The New York Times*, February 8, 1923.
[8] Ibid.
[9] Ibid.
[10] "Mobile Dry Squad For 3 Wet Centres," *The New York Times*, February 13, 1923.
[11] Ibid.
[12] Roy A. Haynes, *Prohibition Inside Out* (NY: Doubleday, Page & Co., 1923) p.85.
[13] Ibid., pp.84-85
[14] Ibid., p.15.
[15] "Pirates Board Ship, Get $400,000 In Rum," *The New York Times*, February 15, 1923.
[16] Ibid.
[17] Ibid.
[18] "Deserted Rum Ship Found Adrift With Dinner On Table," *The New York Times*, March 4, 1923.
[19] Ibid.
[20] "Refuses To Quash Hart Indictments," *The New York Times*, March 17, 1923.
[21] Ibid.
[22] "Think Edge Seeks To Oust Appleby," *The New York Times*, February 22, 1923.
[23] "Appleby Gives Up Prohibition Post," *The New York Times*, March 13, 1923.
[24] Letter to Federal Prohibition Commissioner Roy A. Haynes, from John D. Appleby, Attorney At Law. New York, 28 April 1923. Forwarded to Secretary of the Treasury Andrew Mellon. 1 May 1923.
[25] "Savannah Is Called Rum-runners Paradise," *The New York Times*, March 11, 1923.
[26] "Army Of Baymen Now Rum-runners," *The New York Times*, March 11, 1923.
[27] "Rum Pirates Loot Steamer At Pier," *The New York Times*, March 10, 1923.
[28] "Dry Ships Ruinous, American Line Says," *The New York Times*, December 23, 1922.
[29] "Battle With Police To Save Liquor," *The New York Times*, March 12, 1923.
[30] "Crew Say Pirates Got Liquor Cargo," *The New York Times*, March 12, 1923.

[31] Ibid.
[32] "Hears Rich Man Backs Rum Fleet," *The New York Times*, March 13, 1923.
[33] "Bootlegger's List Startles Capital," *The New York Times*, March 13, 1923.
[34] Ibid.
[35] Ibid.
[36] Ibid.
[37] Ibid.
[38] "Beacons Blaze Out On Coast Rum Fleet," *The New York Times*, March 16, 1923.
[39] "Rum Smugglers Stir Many Towns," *The New York Times*, March 17, 1923.
[40] Ibid.
[41] Ibid.
[42] "Bullets Fly In War With Rum Pirates," *The New York Times*, March 23, 1923.
[43] Ibid.
[44] Ibid.
[45] Ibid.
[46] Ibid.
[47] "Seize 2 Rum Boats, But Many Escape," *The New York Times*, March 24, 1923.
[48] Ibid.
[49] Ibid.
[50] "Ask Harding To Act Against Rum Fleet," *The New York Times*, April 6, 1923.
[51] "Haynes To Ask Navy To Fight Rum Fleet," *The New York Times*, April 11, 1923.
[52] Ibid.
[53] Cannadine p.310.

CHAPTER 8
[1] Ibid.
[2] "Think 8 on Rum Ship Were Slain In Fight," *The New York Times*, April 9, 1923.
[3] "Ship Sinks In Fog, Crew Are Missing," *The New York Times*, April 7, 1923.
[4] "Find 8 Dead In Sea And Barrels Of Ale," *The New York Times*, April 8, 1923.
[5] Ibid.
[6] "Think 8 On Rum Ship Were Slain In Fight," *The New York Times*, April 9, 1923.
[7] Ibid.
[8] "Rum Ship Victim Secretly Buried," *The New York Times*, June 1, 1923.
[9] Ibid.
[10] Ibid.
[11] "Naval Divers Used In Dwight Mystery," *The New York Times*, June 27, 1923.
[12] Ibid.
[13] "Blow Up Wreck Of Dwight," *The New York Times*, July 1, 1923.
[14] "Think Pirates Slew Crew Of Liquor Ship Abandoned At Sea," *The New York Times*, April 16, 1923.
[15] Ibid.
[16] Ibid.
[17] Ibid.
[18] Ibid.

CHAPTER 9
[1] "Tells Woes Of Life On Liquor Armada," *The New York Times*, April 14, 1923.
[2] "Prohibition Chief To Visit Rum Fleet," *The New York Times*, April 17, 1923.
[3] Ibid.
[4] "Dry Chief Visits Bootlegging Fleet Off Ambrose Light," *The New York Times*, April 10, 1923.
[5] Ibid.
[6] Ibid.

[7] Ibid.
[8] Ibid.
[9] Ibid.
[10] Ibid.
[11] Ibid.
[12] Ibid.
[13] "Rum Fleet Problem Before The Cabinet," *The New York Times*, April 21, 1923.
[14] Ibid.
[15] "Dry War Hampered By Lack Of Funds," *The New York Times*, April 24, 1923.
[16] "Dry Chief Wants Planes, Cars, Ships," *The New York Times*, April 24, 1923.
[17] "Treasury Men Visit Liquor Smugglers," *The New York Times*, April 26, 1923.
[18] "President Decides To Use Navy To War On Rum Smugglers," *The New York Times*, April 28, 1923.
[19] Ibid.
[20] Memorandum for General Lord, Director of the Budget, from W.E. Reynolds, Rear Admiral, US Coast Guard. Washington, DC 3 May 1923. Forwarded to Treasury Secretary Mellon. 3 May 1923.
[21] Ibid.
[22] "Teapot Dome," *The New Encyclopedia Britannica*, Vol.1, (London: Encyclopedia Britannica Inc., 1997) p.599.

CHAPTER 10

[1] "President Decides To Use Navy To War On Rum Smugglers," *The New York Times*, April 28, 1923.
[2] "Foreign Conference Proposed On Liquor," *The New York Times*, May 3, 1923.
[3] "Big Liquor Armada Is Leaving Coast," *The New York Times*, May 3, 1923.
[4] "Baldwin Scouts Talk Of Clash On Liquor," *The New York Times*, May 3, 1923.
[5] "Trip By Air Shows Few Liquor Ships," *The New York Times*, May 4, 1923.
[6] Ibid.
[7] "Liquor Fleet Has Airplane Adjunct," *The New York Times*, May 5, 1923.
[8] "Liquor Fleet Edges Back To Old Stand," *The New York Times*, May 9, 1923.
[9] "Dry Officers Admit Big Rush Of Liquor," *The New York Times*, May 12, 1923.
[10] "Seized Ship Center Of Big Bootleg Plot," *The New York Times*, May 16, 1923.
[11] "Bootlegging Yacht Surrenders Here," *The New York Times*, May 15, 1923.
[12] Ibid.
[13] "Seized Ship Center Of Big Bootleg Plot," *The New York Times*, May 16, 1923.
[14] Ibid.
[15] "Get 3 of 8 Wanted As Liquor Plotters," *The New York Times*, May 18, 1923.
[16] "Officials In A Fog On Ship Liquor Ban," *The New York Times*, May 24, 1923.
[17] "Dry Rule Confusion As 5 Nations Plead," *The New York Times*, May 27, 1923.
[18] "Japan Joins Protest On Ship Liquor Rules," *The New York Times*, June 1, 1923.
[19] "Rum-runners Plan To Flood State With Canadian Liquor," *The New York Times*, June 5, 1923.
[20] "Great Beer Fleet Keeps Detroit Wet," *The New York Times*, June 10, 1923.
[21] "Ford Urges Army Keep Country Dry," *The New York Times*, June 10, 1923.
[22] Ibid.
[23] "Detroit Dry Navy Told To Use Guns," *The New York Times*, June 13, 1923.
[24] "Arrests Disclose Huge Liquor Ring," *The New York Times*, May 27, 1923.
[25] Ibid.
[26] "Report Big Britishers With The Liquor Fleet," *The New York Times*, May 28, 1923.
[27] "Country 'Dried Up' Haynes Maintains," *The New York Times*, May 29, 1923.
[28] Ibid.
[29] Ibid.
[30] Ibid.

[31] "Two Rum Ships Hit By Solid Shot From Dry Navy's Guns," *The New York Times*, June 10, 1923.
[32] Ibid.
[33] "Bootleg Crew Drive Bathers From Beach So They Can Land Liquor At Riverhead," *The New York Times*, June 22, 1923.
[34] Ibid.
[35] Letter to the Secretary of the Treasury, from James L. Gordon, Special Agent in Charge, Buffalo, NY 11 July 1923.
[36] Ibid.
[37] "Drys Seize Fleet In Detroit River," *The New York Times*, July 15, 1923.
[38] Ibid.
[39] Ibid.
[40] "Sight New Liquor Fleet," *The New York Times*, July 20, 1923.
[41] "Coast Guard Spurns $70,000 liquor bribe," *The New York Times*, July 25, 1923.
[42] Ibid.
[43] Ibid.
[44] "Hold Dry Law War By Army Illegal," *The New York Times*, July 28, 1923.
[45] Ibid.
[46] Ibid.
[47] "Britain Answers On 12-Mile Limit," *The New York Times*, August 1, 1923.
[48] "Britisher Advertises Liquor Running Plan," *The New York Times*, August 1, 1923.

CHAPTER 11

[1] Francis Russell, *The Shadow Of Blooming Grove*, (NY: McGraw Hill Book Company, 1968.) p. 574.
[2] "Harding Pledges Dry Enforcement; Hits Smith's Stand," *The New York Times*, June 26, 1923.
[3] "Dry Leaders Gather For 'War Council,'" *The New York Times*, June 26, 1923.
[4] "Harding Pledges Dry Enforcement; Hits Smith's Stand," *The New York Times*, June 26, 1923.
[5] Herbert Hoover as quoted in Russell, p.582.
[6] Russell, p.586.
[7] Hoover as quoted by Russell, p.582.
[8] Russell, p.450.
[9] Charles L. Mee, Jr., *The Ohio Gang: The World of Warren G. Harding*, (NY: M. Evans And Company, Inc., 1981) pp. 29-31.
[10] Russell, p.588.
[11] Ibid., p.592.
[12] Ibid., p.605.
[13] Robert Sobel, *Coolidge: An American Enigma*, (Washington: Regnery Publishing Inc, 1998.) p.231.
[14] Ibid., p.232.
[15] Ibid.
[16] Ibid.
[17] Ibid., p.235.
[18] Cannadine, p.317.

CHAPTER 12

[1] "Pirates Surprise Crew," *The New York Times*, August 23, 1923.
[2] "Pirates Took $20,000 In Rum-runner Raid," *The New York Times*, August 22, 1923.
[3] "Police Trace Band Of Liquor Pirates," *The New York Times*, August 28, 1923.
[4] "Pirates Surprise Crew," *The New York Times*, August 23, 1923.
[5] Ibid.
[6] "Police Trace Band Of Liquor Pirates," *The New York Times*, August 28, 1923.

[7] "Pirates Took $20,000 In Rum-runner Raid," *The New York Times*, August 22, 1923.
[8] Ibid.
[9] "Police Trace Band Of Liquor Pirates," *The New York Times*, August 28, 1923.
[10] "200 Cases Of Whisky Drift Ashore, Vanish," *The New York Times*, August 30, 1923.
[11] "British Liquor Runner Derides 'Dry' Forces," *The New York Times*, August 30, 1923.
[12] Ibid.
[13] "Dry Chief To Fight Bootlegger Knight," *The New York Times*, September 8, 1923.
[14] Ibid.
[15] "Rum-Running Baronet Loses A Liquor Cargo," *The New York Times*, April 20, 1925.
[16] "Rum Fleet Beaten, Treasury Asserts," *The New York Times*, April 21, 1925.
[17] "Shrinkage In British Exports," *The New York Times*, April 21, 1925.
[18] " 'Rum-Running Baronet' Fears He Is Stranded," *The New York Times*, April 28, 1925.
[19] "Rum Baronet Lost $1,250,000 on Final Cargo; British Creditors Find Assets Are Worthless," *The New York Times*, December 31, 1925.
[20] "Cannot Use Navy In Dry Enforcement," *The New York Times*, September 14, 1923.
[21] "Big World Balance Against America," *The New York Times*, September 17, 1923.
[22] "Coolidge Upholds Dry Chief's Work," *The New York Times*, September 15, 1923.
[23] "Rum-runners' Rifles Cause 40 Coast Guardsmen To Quit," *The New York Times*, October 18, 1923.
[24] "Favors $28,500,000 For Big Dry Navy," *The New York Times*, November 18, 1923.

CHAPTER 13
[1] "Cutter's Guns Halt British Liquor Ship Beyond 3-Mile Line," *The New York Times*, November 26, 1923.
[2] Ibid.
[3] "Sea Rumrunner Held On 2 Liquor Charges," *The New York Times*, November 27, 1923.
[4] "Cutter's Guns Halt British Liquor Ship Beyond 3-Mile Line," *The New York Times*, November 26, 1923.
[5] Ibid.
[6] "Await Seizure Report," *The New York Times*, November 26, 1923.
[7] "Sea Rumrunner Held On 2 Liquor Charges," *The New York Times*, November 27, 1923.
[8] Ibid.
[9] "Capital Confident In Tomaka Seizure," *The New York Times*, November 29, 1923.
[10] "Tomaka Seizure Stirs Rum Row," *The New York Times*, November 29, 1923.
[11] "British Ship's Crew Freed," *The New York Times*, January 17, 1924.
[12] "Holiday Develops A Volstead Record," *The New York Times*, February 24, 1924.

CHAPTER 14
[1] "Shows Liquor Cases Are Filling Courts," *The New York Times*, December 5, 1923.
[2] Ibid.
[3] "The Far-Flung Prohibition Battle Line," *The New York Times*, December 16, 1923.
[4] Ibid.
[5] "Scout Airplane Aids Liquor Fleet," *The New York Times*, December 11, 1923.
[6] Letter to the Secretary of the Treasury, from Mabel Walker Willebrandt, Assistant Attorney General, Washington, DC 13 December 1923.
[7] Ibid.
[8] Ibid.
[9] Ibid.
[10] "Bootleggers Begin Price-Cutting War," *The New York Times*, December 12, 1923.
[11] "Gale Aids The Drys; Sends Ships To Sea," *The New York Times*, December 15, 1923.
[12] "Liquor Smugglers Have A Good Day," *The New York Times*, December 16, 1923.
[13] Ibid.

[14] "Aboard The Christmas Rum Flotilla," *The New York Times*, December 16, 1923.
[15] Ibid.
[16] Ibid.
[17] Ibid.
[18] Ibid.
[19] Ibid.
[20] Ibid.
[21] Ibid.
[22] Ibid.
[23] Ibid.
[24] Ibid.
[25] Ibid.
[26] "Speed Boats Bring Liquor," *The New York Times*, December 24, 1923.
[27] Ibid.
[28] "Arrest Six At Sea With $46, 356 In Cash; Scent Liquor Plot," *The New York Times*, December 25, 1923.
[29] Ibid.
[30] "Fothergill To Fight It Out," *The New York Times*, December 27, 1923.

CHAPTER 15

[1] "Huges And Geddes Sign Liquor Treaty," *The New York Times*, January 24, 1924.
[2] "Sees A Curb On Smuggling," *The New York Times*, January 24, 1924.
[3] "Agreement Pleases London," *The New York Times*, January 24, 1924.
[4] "Fourth Bootleg Cruise By A Knight," *The New York Times*, February 1, 1924.
[5] "Whisky Imports Active," *The New York Times*, January 17, 1924.
[6] Ibid.
[7] "House of Commons Debate: Liquor Smuggling," The London *Times*, May 29, 1924.
[8] "Whisky Imports Active," *The New York Times*, January 17, 1924.
[9] "Synthetic Liquor: The 'Rum Fleet's' Imitations," The London *Times*, January 18, 1924.
[10] Ibid.
[11] "Rum-Runners Of The Air," *The New York Times*, January 20, 1924.
[12] Ibid.
[13] Ibid.
[14] Ibid.
[15] Ibid.
[16] Ibid.
[17] Ibid.
[18] Ibid.
[19] Edward F. Clark, "US Coast Guard Commandants, 1889 to 1933," *The US Coast Guard: The National Publication of the United States Coast Guard*, April 1933.
[20] US, Congress, House, Committee On Interstate And Foreign Commerce, *United States Coast Guard Law Enforcement Hearing*, H.R.6815, 68th Congress, 1st Sess., 1924. p.13.
[21] Ibid., p.14.
[22] Ibid., pp.14-15.
[23] "115,000 'Dry' Cases Tried In Four Years," *The New York Times*, February 18, 1924.
[24] Ibid.
[25] "Reports Increase In Liquor Running," *The New York Times*, February 22, 1924.
[26] Letter to Commander, New York Division, from Captain Philip H. Scott, US Coast Guard. Sandy Hook, NJ 5 March 1924.
[27] Ibid.
[28] "Reports Increase In Liquor Running," *The New York Times*, February 22, 1924.
[29] "Recommended $13,850,622 For Rum Fleet Chasers," *The New York Times*, March 2, 1924.
[30] Darrell Hevenor Smith and Fred Wilbur Powell, *The Coast Guard: Its History, Activities and*

Organization (Washington, DC: The Brookings Institution, 1929) p.231.
[31] "Violent Storm In The United States," The London *Times*, March 13, 1924.
[32] Ibid.
[33] Ibid.
[34] "Royal Mail Liner Seized As Wet Ship," *The New York Times*, March 13, 1924.
[35] Ibid.
[36] Ibid.
[37] " Col. Hayward Files A Libel On Orduna," *The New York Times*, March 14, 1924.
[38] Ibid.
[39] Ibid.
[40] "Orduna's Men Tell Of Selling Liquor," *The New York Times*, March 15, 1924.
[41] Ibid.
[42] Ibid.
[43] "S.S. Orduna's Owner's Are Cleared," *The New York Times*, March 15, 1924.
[44] "Men Of The Orduna Get Off With Fines," *The New York Times*, March 20, 1924.
[45] "Orduna Is Cleared Of Liquor Charges," *The New York Times*, October 17, 1924.
[46] "Shots Halt Rum Ship After 50-Mile Chase," *The New York Times*, March 16, 1924.
[47] Ibid.
[48] Ibid.
[49] Ibid.
[50] "Liquor Fleet Drive By 5 Navy Ships," *The New York Times*, March 27, 1924.
[51] Ibid.
[52] Ibid.
[53] "Prohibition 'Navy' Prepares For Sea," *The New York Times*, April 6, 1924.
[54] John C. Young, "A Week On The Rum Patrol," *The New York Times*, May 11, 1924.
[55] Ibid.
[56] Ibid.
[57] Ibid.
[58] Ibid.
[59] Ibid.
[60] Ibid.
[61] Ibid.
[62] Ibid.
[63] Ibid.
[64] Ibid.
[65] Ibid.
[66] Ibid.
[67] Ibid.
[68] Ibid.
[69] Ibid.
[70] Ibid.
[71] Ibid.
[72] Ibid.
[73] Ibid.
[74] Ibid.
[75] "Liquor Treaty With US," The London *Times*, May 7, 1924.
[76] Howard Mingos, "Rum-runners Laugh At New 12-Mile Treaty," *The New York Times*, May 11, 1924.
[77] Ibid.
[78] Ibid.
[79] Ibid.
[80] Ibid.
[81] Ibid.
[82] Ibid.

[83] Ibid.
[84] Ibid.
[85] Ibid.
[86] Claire Bond Potter, *War On Crime: Bandits, G-Men, And The Politics of Mass Culture*, (New Brunswick, NJ: Rutgers Univ. Press, 1998.)p. 10.
[87] Ibid., p.34.
[88] Ibid.p.12.
[89] Ibid.p.13.
[90] Ibid. p.36.

CHAPTER 16
[1] "Capture Liquor Ship In Battle On River," *The New York Times*, January 21, 1924.
[2] Ibid.
[3] Ibid.
[4] Ibid.
[5] "Patrolmen In Command," *The New York Times*, February 17, 1924.
[6] Ibid.
[7] "Liquor Yacht Runs Gauntlet Of Shots," *The New York Times*, March 3, 1924.
[8] Ibid.
[9] Ibid.
[10] "Fastest Rum Boat Wrecked In Chase By Police Boat," *The New York Times*, May 12, 1924.
[11] Ibid.
[12] Ibid.
[13] Ibid.
[14] Ibid.
[15] Ibid.
[16] Ibid.
[17] Ibid.
[18] Ibid.
[19] Ibid.
[20] Ibid.
[21] Ibid.
[22] "Rum-Runner In Bay Rams Police Boat," *The New York Times*, November 13, 1924.
[23] Ibid.
[24] Ibid.
[25] Ibid.
[26] "Liquor Boat Chase Ends In Captures," *The New York Times*, November 14, 1924.
[27] Ibid.
[28] Ibid.
[29] "Shot On Police Boat By Dry Navy In Dark," *The New York Times*, July 13, 1924.
[30] Ibid.
[31] Ibid.
[32] Ibid.
[33] Ibid.
[34] Ibid.

CHAPTER 17
[1] "Says Mellon Owned Whisky Last March," *The New York Times*, May 12, 1924.
[2] "Mellon Is Accused By Means In Tale Of Whisky Frauds," *The New York Times*, May 30, 1924.
[3] Ibid.
[4] Ibid.
[5] Ibid.
[6] "Mellon Answers Charges By Means," *The New York Times*, June 7, 1924.

[7] "Mellon To Testify At Trial Of Means," *The New York Times*, June 21, 1924.
[8] Ibid.
[9] "Mellon Testifies No Liquor Permits Were In His Bank," *The New York Times*, June 27, 1924.
[10] Ibid.
[11] "Contradicts Mellon," *The New York Times*, June 27, 1924.

CHAPTER 18

[1] "Swift Pirate Craft Terrorize Rum Row," *The New York Times*, July 15, 1924.
[2] Ibid.
[3] "Pirates Of Rum Row Play For High Stakes," *The New York Times*, July 27, 1924.
[4] Ibid.
[5] Ibid.
[6] "Pirates Seize Liquor Valued At $500,000," *The New York Times*, July 11, 1924.
[7] "Promise A Sequel To Mulhouse Piracy," *The New York Times*, August 28, 1924.
[8] "German-American Held as Rum Fleet Pirate; Accused in Paris of Attack on French Ship," *The New York Times*, September 18, 1924.
[9] Ibid.
[10] "Pfaff In Brest Jail For Piracy Trial," *The New York Times*, September 25, 1924.
[11] Ibid.
[12] Ibid.
[13] Ibid.
[14] "Tells How Smugglers Handle Liquor Trade," *The New York Times*, September 28, 1924.
[15] "Pfaff To Be Tried On Piracy Charge," *The New York Times*, October 1, 1924.
[16] Ibid.
[17] Ibid.
[18] Ibid.
[19] "Pfaff Case Starts Pirate Hunt Here," *The New York Times*, October 2, 1924.
[20] Ibid.
[21] Ibid.
[22] Ibid.
[23] Ibid.
[24] "French Magistrate Names Bootleg King," *The New York Times*, October 3, 1924.
[25] "Pfaff Case Starts Pirate Hunt Here," *The New York Times*, October 2, 1924.
[26] Ibid.
[27] Ibid.
[28] "Report Rum Pirate Chief Is Montreal Tailor; Fast Cars Stop All Day at Adelman's Shop," *The New York Times*, October 4, 1924.
[29] "Pfaff Case Starts Pirate Hunt Here," *The New York Times*, October 2, 1924.
[30] "Report Rum Pirate Chief Is Montreal Tailor; Fast Cars Stop All Day at Adelman's Shop," *The New York Times*, October 4, 1924.
[31] Ibid.
[32] Ibid.
[33] Ibid.
[34] "French Magistrate Names Bootleg King," *The New York Times*, October 3, 1924.
[35] Ibid.
[36] Ibid.
[37] "Smuggler Reveals Rum Row 'Secrets,'" *The New York Times*, October 9, 1924.
[38] "Phaff Is Exonerated By Mulhouse Men," *The New York Times*, October 26, 1924.
[39] "Two Jailed For Transporting Liquor," *The New York Times*, November 4, 1924.
[40] "Schooner Raided by Hijacker Pirates, Adrift Six Weeks, Located in Midocean," *The New York Times*, November 21, 1924.
[41] Ibid.
[42] "Pirates Held Ship Three Weeks At Sea," *The New York Times*, November 22, 1924.

[43] Ibid.
[44] "Max J. Phaff Here After French Trial," *The New York Times,* November 22, 1924.
[45] "Rum-runner Tells Of Pirates' Work," *The New York Times,* February 15, 1925.
[46] Ibid.

CHAPTER 19

[1] "Liquor Boat Doctor Brings Dying Man In," *The New York Times,* July 18, 1924.
[2] Ibid.
[3] Ibid.
[4] "Aliens And Drugs Come From Rum Row," *The New York Times,* July 25, 1924.
[5] Ibid.
[6] Memorandum for Assistant Treasury Secretary Moss, from Nathaniel Van Doren, Director of the Special Agency Service, US Customs. Washington, DC 29 July 1924.
[7] "Beach Mobs Grab Lost Liquor Cargo," *The New York Times,* July 25, 1924.
[8] Ibid.
[9] "600 Bullets Fired Into A Rum-Runner," *The New York Times,* July 29, 1924.
[10] Ibid.
[11] Ibid.
[12] Ibid.
[13] "War Craft Coming To Join Dry Fleet," *The New York Times,* August 13, 1924.
[14] Ibid.
[15] Ibid.
[16] "One-Man War Boat Ends As Rum Craft," *The New York Times,* August 17, 1924.
[17] Ibid.
[18] Ibid.
[19] Ibid.
[20] Ibid.
[21] Ibid.
[22] "Rum-runners Use German Submarine," *The New York Times,* August 3, 1924.
[23] Ibid.
[24] "Shenandoah Shows Power As A Rum Chaser; Searchlight Puts 3 Bootleg Craft To Flight," *The New York Times,* August 11, 1924.
[25] Ibid.

CHAPTER 20

[1] "Officers For Liquor Fleet," *The New York Times,* August 13, 1924.
[2] "Liquor War At Sea Opens In September," *The New York Times,* August 14, 1924.
[3] Ibid.
[4] Ibid.
[5] "Man Shot In Chase By New Dry Cruiser," *The New York Times,* August 15, 1924.
[6] Letter to Wayne B. Wheeler, General Counsel of the Anti-Saloon League of America, from Rear Admiral Billard, Commandant of the Coast Guard. Washington, DC, 25 July 1924.
[7] "Coast Guard Acts To Close Cabaret 15 Miles Out To Sea," *The New York Times,* August 17, 1924.
[8] Ibid.
[9] Ibid.
[10] Ibid.
[11] Ibid.
[12] Ibid.
[13] Ibid.
[14] "Beach Whisky Boat To Escape Shots," *The New York Times,* August 18, 1924.
[15] "Want Dry Ban Off 2 Broadway Cafes," *The New York Times,* August 19, 1924.
[16] "Movie Covets Café Ship," *The New York Times,* August 21, 1924.

[17] Ibid.
[18] "Floating Cabaret A Reporter's Myth," *The New York Times*, August 23, 1924.
[19] Ibid.

CHAPTER 21

[1] "300 Rum-Runners Caught by Patrol," *The New York Times*, August 24, 1924.
[2] Ibid.
[3] Ibid.
[4] Ibid.
[5] Ibid.
[6] "Two Destroyers Here Dry Fleet's Vanguard," *The New York Times*, August 30, 1924.
[7] "New Dry Navy Ordered To Work In Secret; Four More Destroyers On Their Way Here," *The New York Times*, September 8, 1924.
[8] "Whisky Chaser Launched," *The New York Times*, September 14, 1924.
[9] "Strikes Hard Blow At Liquor Fleet," *The New York Times*, October 27, 1924.
[10] Ibid.
[11] Ibid.
[12] Ibid.
[13] "Seized Liquor Ship Will Charge Piracy," *The New York Times*, October 29, 1924.
[14] Ibid.
[15] "British Boat Seized In $1,000,000 Plot To Smuggle Liquor," *The New York Times*, October 5, 1924.
[16] Ibid.
[17] Ibid.
[18] Ibid.
[19] Ibid.
[20] Ibid.
[21] Ibid.
[22] Ibid.
[23] "Liquor Ship's Crew Weak On Memory," *The New York Times*, October 11, 1924.
[24] Ibid.
[25] "Guard 2 Seized Vessels," *The New York Times*, October 14, 1924.
[26] Donald Lawder, "Rum Row's Baronet Speaks Out," *The New York Times*, November 9, 1924.
[27] Ibid.
[28] Ibid.
[29] Ibid.
[30] Ibid.
[31] Ibid.
[32] "Long Island Liquor Blockade Pierced," *The New York Times*, November 23, 1924.
[33] "Big Shake-Up In State Dry Force," *The New York Times*, December 9, 1924.
[34] "Wide Bootleg Hunt Is Now Demanded," *The New York Times*, December 15, 1924.
[35] Ibid.

CHAPTER 22

[1] John C. Young, "Christmas Rum Meets Stiffer Blockade," *The New York Times*, December 14, 1924.
[2] Ibid.
[3] Ibid.
[4] Ibid.
[5] Ibid.
[6] Ibid.
[7] Ibid.
[8] Ibid.

⁹ Ibid.
¹⁰ "332 Foreign Ships Found In Rum Trade," *The New York Times*, February 3, 1925.
¹¹ Ibid.
¹² Ibid.
¹³ "Smuggling Up In Cabinet," *The New York Times*, February 4, 1925.

CHAPTER 23

¹ "South Street Whispers Of Shanghaing," *The New York Times*, March 1, 1925.
² Ibid.
³ Ibid.
⁴ "Rum Runner Tells of Pirates' Work," *The New York Times*, February 15, 1925.
⁵ Ibid.
⁶ Gerald Leinwald, *1927: High Tide Of The 1920s* (New York: Four Walls Eight Windows, 2001.) p.9 & 37.
⁷ Ibid., p.36
⁸ Ibid., p.9
⁹ Ibid., p.10
¹⁰ Ibid., p.11
¹¹ Ibid., p.14
¹² Ibid.
¹³ Ibid., p.56-7
¹⁴ Ibid., p.57
¹⁵ Ibid., p.58
¹⁶ "Dry Fleet Picks Up Big Liquor Armada," *The New York Times*, February 7, 1925.
¹⁷ Ibid.
¹⁸ Ibid.
¹⁹ "Chase Proves Fatal To Rum-Runners' Foe," *The New York Times*, February 4, 1925.
²⁰ Ibid.
²¹ "Liquor Boat Caught After A Gun Chase," *The New York Times*, February 23, 1925.
²² Ibid.
²³ Ibid.
²⁴ "Question Release Of Liquor Prisoners," *The New York Times*, February 26, 1925.
²⁵ "Liquor Cases Returned," *The New York Times*, February 26, 1925.
²⁶ "Dry Boats Ordered To 'Shoot First,'" *The New York Times*, April 2, 1925.
²⁷ Ibid.
²⁸ "Plane Stops Rum Landing," *The New York Times*, April 25, 1925.
²⁹ Ibid.

CHAPTER 24

¹ "New Dry and Wet Fleets Mobilize for War," *The New York Times*, March 29, 1925.
² "New Dry Fleet Is Equipped With Latest Radio Equipment," *The New York Times*, April 19, 1925.
³ "New Dry and Wet Fleets Mobilize for War," *The New York Times*, March 29, 1925.
⁴ Ibid.
⁵ Ibid.
⁶ Ibid.
⁷ Ibid.
⁸ "New Dry Fleet Is Equipped With Latest Radio Equipment," *The New York Times*, April 19, 1925.
⁹ "New Dry and Wet Fleets Mobilize for War," *The New York Times*, March 29, 1925.
¹⁰ Ibid.
¹¹ Robert T. Small, "Chief of Offensive Is Sea-Going General," *Oakland Tribune*, May 5, 1925.

[12] "Mobilize Dry Fleet For Big Liquor Drive," *The New York Times*, May 5, 1925.
[13] Ibid.
[14] Ibid.
[15] "35 Ships Put To Sea To Smash Rum Row," *The New York Times*, May 6, 1925.
[16] Ibid.
[17] "Rum-Runners Take Reprisals On Fleet; Real War Declared," *The New York Times*, May 9, 1925.
[18] Ibid.
[19] Ibid.
[20] Ibid.
[21] Ibid.
[22] "Coast Guardsmen Kin Threatened," *Bridgeport Telegram*, May 9, 1925.
[23] "Liquor Ships Retire Southward, Dogged By the Dry Fleet," *The New York Times*, May 12, 1925.
[24] Ibid.
[25] Ibid.
[26] Ibid.
[27] Ibid.
[28] "Dry Navy Chief Says War Is Yet To Begin," *The New York Times*, May 13, 1925.
[29] "Extend Rum War To Border Sectors And Western Coast," *The New York Times*, May 14, 1925.
[30] Ibid.
[31] "Rum Row Vanished Says Dry War Chief," *The New York Times*, May 17, 1925.
[32] "Senators Charge Dry Law Collapse," *The New York Times*, May 19, 1925.
[33] "Rum Row Cleaned Up," *The New York Times*, May 20, 1925.
[34] "Reports Nine Ships Now In Rum Fleet," *The New York Times*, May 21, 1925.
[35] "Country Spends Millions To Enforce Dry Law," *The New York Times*, June 14, 1925.
[36] Ibid.
[37] "Seaplanes Used By Rum Runners," *The New York Times*, May 29, 1925.
[38] "Rum Chaser Fires On Harvard Craft," *The New York Times*, May 30, 1925.
[39] Ibid.
[40] "Scores Dry Navy Shooting," *The New York Times*, May 30, 1925.
[41] "Dry Chief Rebuffs Plea Made By Edge," *The New York Times*, June 6, 1925.
[42] Ibid.
[43] "Dry Agents Fire on Auto Body Maker's Boat," *San Antonio Express*, June 13, 1925.
[44] "Couzens Protests Firing On Boats," *The New York Times*, June 21, 1925.
[45] Ibid.
[46] "Coast Guard Eases Search For Liquor," *The New York Times*, June 18, 1925.
[47] Ibid.
[48] "Coolidge Approves New Liquor Drive On Coast Resorts," *The New York Times*, June 21, 1925.
[49] Ibid.
[50] "Add To Coast Guard Near Swampscott," *The New York Times*, June 22, 1925.
[51] Ibid.
[52] "Coolidge Asks War On Boston Rum Row," *The New York Times*, July 7, 1925.
[53] Ibid.
[54] Ibid.
[55] "Three Liquor Ships Back," *The New York Times*, July 18, 1925.
[56] "Liquor Ships Quit Cape Ann Rum Row," *The New York Times*, July 19, 1925.

CHAPTER 25

[1] "6 In Dry Navy Guilty of Smuggling Rum," *The New York Times*, May 18, 1925.
[2] "Dry Petty Officer Held," May 22, 1925.
[3] "6 In Dry Navy Guilty of Smuggling Rum," *The New York Times*, May 18, 1925.
[4] Ibid.
[5] Ibid.

[6] "Four Coast Guards Saw Bars, Flee Jail," *The New York Times,* May 18, 1925.
[7] "Coast Guardsmen Quit The Dry Fleet," *The New York Times,* June 2, 1925.
[8] "5 Coast Guardsmen Quit The Dry Fleet," *The New York Times,* June 3, 1925.
[9] Ibid.
[10] Ibid.
[11] "Liquor Is Seized On Navy Transport," *The New York Times,* February 26, 1925.
[12] "Liquor On Beaufort Brings Navy Trials," *The New York Times,* March 28, 1925.
[13] "Court-Martial for Six Officers of Beaufort Because Liquor Was Found on the Transport," *The New York Times,* April 12, 1925.
[14] "Upholds Penalties In Navy Liquor Case," *The New York Times,* August 21, 1925.

CHAPTER 26

[1] "Wrecked Plane Found By Freighter In Fog," *The New York Times,* January 7, 1926.
[2] "Identifies Wreckage As Husband's Plane," *The New York Times,* January 9, 1926.
[3] Ibid.
[4] "Wrecked Airmen Picked Up At Sea," *The New York Times,* January 11, 1926.
[5] "Can't Dry Up Nation, Andrews Admits," *The New York Times,* January 26, 1926.
[6] Ibid.
[7] "8 In Dry Navy Force Get Year In Prison," *The New York Times,* January 31, 1926.
[8] Ibid.
[9] "Rum Bribery Laid To 24 Coast Guards," *The New York Times,* July 22, 1926.
[10] Ibid.
[11] "Coast Guards Sent To New Stations," *The New York Times,* July 25, 1926.
[12] "$30,000 Bribe Is Laid to a Coast Guardsman; Commander Is Said to Admit Rum Running," *The New York Times,* August 18, 1926.
[13] "Coast Guard Bribery Suspected For Year," *The New York Times,* August 19, 1926.
[14] "$30,000 Bribe Is Laid to a Coast Guardsman; Commander Is Said to Admit Rum Running," *The New York Times,* August 18, 1926.
[15] "End Liquor Trial Of Coast Guards," *The New York Times,* August 24, 1926.
[16] "Congress Wets Ask For National Vote On Modifying Law," *The New York Times,* March 27, 1926.
[17] Ibid.
[18] Ibid.
[19] "Urge Andrews To Stay For A Year," *The New York Times,* July 4, 1926.
[20] "Andrews's Decision Helps Republicans," *The New York Times,* July 8, 1926.
[21] Ibid.
[22] "Boston's Rum Row Has Seven Visitors," *The New York Times,* July 8, 1926.
[23] A. H. Ulm, "Dry Navy And Army Are Stripped For Action," *The New York Times,* July 18, 1926.
[24] Ibid.
[25] "Radio Direction Finders To Locate Rum-Runners," *The New York Times,* July 14, 1926.
[26] "Forty Customs Men Put On Patrol Here To Dry Waterfront," *The New York Times,* August 22, 1926.
[27] Ibid.
[28] "Patrol Ferried Rum Coast Guard Says," *The New York Times,* November 4, 1926.
[29] Ibid.
[30] Ibid.
[31] "Andrews Lauds The Guard," *The New York Times,* November 6, 1926.
[32] "Lowman Gets Post As Andrews Quits In Big Dry Shift," *The New York Times,* May 20, 1927.
[33] Ibid.
[34] A.H. Ulm, "New Prohibition Chief Seeks an Honest Staff," *The New York Times,* August 7, 1927.
[35] Ibid.

CHAPTER 27

[1] Department of Commerce, *Statistical Abstracts of the United States: 1926* (Washington, DC: US Government Printing Office, 1927). p. 8, figure 11.
[2] Department of Commerce, *Statistical Abstracts of the United States: 1930* (Washington, DC: US Government Printing Office, 1930) p.4, figure 7.
[3] "Rum Row Off West Coast," *The New York Times*, May 14, 1925.
[4] "$3,000,000 Rum Fleet Plies Coast," *Oakland Tribune*, May 12, 1925.
[5] Ibid.
[6] Ibid.
[7] "L.A. Flooded With Stream of Booze From Rum Fleet," *Oakland Tribune*, May 15, 1925.
[8] "Water Routes Open To Smuggling Crews," *Oakland Tribune*, May 17, 1925.
[9] Ibid.
[10] "NY Crusher Of Rum Row Sent To S.F.," *Oakland Tribune*, August 20, 1925.
[11] "Pacific Coast, Too, Has Its 'Rum Rows'; No Dryer Than East," *The New York Times*, March 22, 1926.
[12] Ibid.
[13] "Banks Aided In Financing Bootleggers, Solons Told," *Modesto News-Herald*, June 17, 1926.
[14] Ibid.
[15] "Congressional Liquor Witness Sought In Fraud," *Oakland Tribune*, June 18, 1926.
[16] "16 Rum Runners Seeking To Land Cargoes On Coast," *Fresno Bee*, June 30, 1926.
[17] Ibid.
[18] Ibid.
[19] "Dry Chief Under Inquiry," *The New York Times*, July 23, 1926.
[20] "Dry Chief Under Suspension," *The New York Times*, July 25, 1926.
[21] Ibid.
[22] Ibid.
[23] Ibid.
[24] Ibid.
[25] "Col. Green Indicted By Federal Jury," *The New York Times*, July 27, 1926.
[26] "Col. Green Reinstated In Federal Dry Post," *The New York Times*, December 23, 1926.
[27] Ibid.
[28] "Rum Ship Off S.F. Watched," *Orangeburg Times*, March 1, 1927.
[29] "Question Legality Of Rum-Ship Seizure," *The New York Times*, March 20, 1927.
[30] "61 Are Indicted As Rum-Runners," *The New York Times*, March 6, 1927.
[31] "Question Legality Of Rum-Ship Seizure," *The New York Times*, March 20, 1927.
[32] Ibid.
[33] "Rum Boat With Rich Cargo Towed To San Francisco," *Fresno Bee*, March 3, 1927.
[34] "Question Legality Of Rum-Ship Seizure," *The New York Times*, March 20, 1927.
[35] "Fifty Shots Take Coast Booze Ship," *Oakland Tribune*, March 3, 1927.
[36] "Question Legality Of Rum-Ship Seizure," *The New York Times*, March 20, 1927.
[37] Ibid.
[38] Ibid.
[39] "Panama After Rum Ship," *The New York Times*, April 3, 1927.
[40] "Court Upsets Seizure Of Canadian Rum Ship," *The New York Times*, April 21, 1927.
[41] "Orders Release Of Federalship," *The New York Times*, May 1, 1927.
[42] "Gen. Andrews Orders Federalship Held Up," *The New York Times*, May 3, 1927.
[43] "Orders Federalship Freed," *The New York Times*, May 4, 1927.
[44] "Panama Opens Inquiry On The Federalship," *The New York Times*, May 5, 1927.
[45] "Rum Runner Is Reported Lying Off Coast Again," *Modesto News-Herald*, April 7, 1928.

CHAPTER 28

[1] "Seize Tug and Rum Worth $1,000,000," *The New York Times*, January 22, 1926.
[2] Ibid.
[3] "Seeks To Extradite Dwyer Defendants," *The New York Times*, March 23, 1926.
[4] "Swears Police Saw Dwyer Boats Land," *The New York Times*, July 13, 1926.
[5] Ibid.
[6] Ibid.
[7] Ibid.
[8] Ibid.
[9] Ibid.
[10] "Testify To $75,000 Liquor Bribe Offer," *The New York Times*, July 15, 1926.
[11] Ibid.
[12] Ibid.
[13] "'Fugitive' Appears And Turns on Dwyer," *The New York Times*, July 16, 1926.
[14] Ibid.
[15] Ibid.
[16] Ibid.
[17] Ibid.
[18] "Dwyer's Counsel Faced By Bielaski, Won't Question Him," *The New York Times*, July 20, 1926.
[19] "'Fugitive' Appears And Turns on Dwyer," *The New York Times*, July 16, 1926.
[20] Ibid.
[21] Ibid.
[22] "Testifies Dwyer Said He Had 'Pull,'" *The New York Times*, July 17, 1926.
[23] Ibid.
[24] Ibid.
[25] Ibid.
[26] Ibid.
[27] Ibid.
[28] "Bielaski Revealed As Chief 'Dry' Aid At Dwyer's Trial," *The New York Times*, July 21, 1926.
[29] Ibid.
[30] Ibid.
[31] "Catch Chief Witness Who Quit Rum Trial," *The New York Times*, July 23, 1926.
[32] Ibid.
[33] Ibid.
[34] "Rum Trial Witness Held For Perjury," *The New York Times*, July 24, 1926.
[35] Ibid.
[36] Ibid.
[37] "Dwyer Found Guilty Of Rum Conspiracy; Gets 2 Years In Jail," *The New York Times*, July 27, 1926.
[38] "Admits Perjury In Trial Of Dwyer," *The New York Times*, August 6, 1926.
[39] "Laguardia Assails Bielaski's Status," *The New York Times*, August 3, 1926.
[40] "Dwyer Finds Living In Tombs Good, Cheaper Than Outside," *The New York Times*, July 29, 1926.
[41] "Dwyer Out of Tombs Three Times a Week," *The New York Times*, July 31, 1926.
[42] Ibid.
[43] "Dwyer and Cohron Released On Bail," *The New York Times*, August 21, 1926.
[44] "Seized After Fight As Ally of Dwyer," *The New York Times*, August 25, 1926.
[45] Ibid.
[46] Ibid.

CHAPTER 29

[1] "18 Go On Trial As Rum Ring," *The New York Times*, January 4, 1927.
[2] "Used Plane To Hunt Lost Liquor Ship," *The New York Times*, January 5, 1927.
[3] Ibid.
[4] "Once Rum-Runner, Now With Bielaski," *The New York Times*, January 6, 1927.
[5] "Says Patrol Boats Guided Rum Ships," *The New York Times*, January 7, 1927.
[6] "Admits Rum Trade Of Coast Guard," *The New York Times*, January 7, 1927.
[7] "Says Patrol Boats Guided Rum Ships," *The New York Times*, January 7, 1927.
[8] "Admits Rum Trade Of Coast Guard," *The New York Times*, January 8, 1927.
[9] Ibid.
[10] Ibid.
[11] Ibid.
[12] "Andrews Is Named In Rum Graft Trial," *The New York Times*, January 13, 1927.
[13] Ibid.
[14] "Tells of Distrust In the Coast Guard," *The New York Times*, January 14, 1927.
[15] "Liquor Ring Case In Hands Of Jury," *The New York Times*, January 20, 1927.
[16] Ibid.
[17] Ibid.
[18] "Costello Jurors Clear 8, Split on 6 in Liquor Ring Trial," *The New York Times*, January 21, 1927.
[19] "Costello Case Seen As Blow To Dry Force," *The New York Times*, January 22, 1927.
[20] Ibid.

CHAPTER 30

[1] "Abducted In Rum Battle," *The New York Times*, May 13, 1926.
[2] Ibid.
[3] "$20,000 Bribes Paid By Alcohol Ship," *The New York Times*, May 1, 1926.
[4] Ibid.
[5] "$9,500 Left On Desk Of A Police Captain," *The New York Times*, May 4, 1926.
[6] Ibid.
[7] Ibid.
[8] "$9,500 Liquor Bribe Mystery Deepens," *The New York Times*, May 7, 1926.
[9] Ibid.
[10] "McLaughlin Orders Changes In Rank," *The New York Times*, January 11, 1927.
[11] "Rum Boat's Captain Held," *The New York Times*, June 6, 1926.
[12] "Kidnapped, He Tells Of Rum Ship's Trip," *The New York Times*, June 12, 1926.
[13] "Britain Asks Return Of Rum Ship's Crew," *The New York Times*, June 13, 1926.
[14] Ibid.
[15] "Rum Runner's Crew Held For Extradition," *The New York Times*, June 19, 1926.
[16] "Ship Captain Extradited," *The New York Times*, July 30, 1926.
[17] "Indict Jersey Mayor And 32 In Rum Plot," *The New York Times*, December 15, 1926.
[18] "Seek Arrest In Rum Case," *The New York Times*, December 17, 1926.
[19] "Ignore Eker Indictments," *The New York Times*, December 24, 1926.
[20] "Wissel and Dinan Give Up," *The New York Times*, December 25, 1926.
[21] "Said Jersey Mayor Took $50,000 Bribe," *The New York Times*, November 11, 1926.
[22] Ibid.
[23] "Three Admit Guilt In Ecker Rum Case," *The New York Times*, February 1, 1927.
[24] Ibid.
[25] Ibid.
[26] "Testified He Bribed Edgewater Mayor," *The New York Times*, February 3, 1927.
[27] Ibid.
[28] Ibid.
[29] Ibid.

[30] "Edgewater Mayor, Chief and 12 Guilty In Eker Liquor Case," *The New York Times*, February 5, 1927.
[31] Ibid.
[32] "Weep As Ex-Mayor Is Sent To Prison," *The New York Times*, February 10, 1927.
[33] Ibid.
[34] "Wissel Conviction Is Upset On Appeal," *The New York Times*, November 15, 1927.
[35] Ibid.

CHAPTER 31

[1] "Rum Treaty Fails In $350,000 Seizure 14 Miles Off Shore," *The New York Times*, October 30, 1926.
[2] Ibid.
[3] Ibid.
[4] "Holidays to Be Dry, Says Coast Guard Head; Denies Big Liquor Fleet Lies Off New Jersey," *The New York Times*, November 22, 1926.
[5] "Rum Row Picture Declared A Fake," *The New York Times*, December 28, 1926.
[6] "$20,000,000 Liquors From Canada In 1926," *The New York Times*, January 13, 1927.
[7] Ibid.
[8] "Blanton Attacks Mellon As A Wet," *The New York Times*, February 1, 1927.
[9] Ibid.
[10] A.H. Ulm, "Next Big Dry Problem Is To Stop Distilling," *The New York Times*, March 6, 1927.
[11] "Andrews Summons Liquor Distillers," *The New York Times*, March 15, 1927.
[12] Ibid.
[13] "New Rum Chasers To Go Into Service," *The New York Times*, March 21, 1927.
[14] William Atherton DuPuy, "Drys Win Office In Contests With Wets," *The New York Times*, May 15, 1927.
[15] Ibid.
[16] "Our Buying Abroad In 1926 Above Sales," *The New York Times*, August 26, 1927.

CHAPTER 32

[1] "Shooting Of Skipper Linked In Rum Plot," *The New York Times*, March 7, 1927.
[2] Ibid.
[3] Ibid.
[4] Ibid.
[5] "Faces Two Charges As Rum Smuggler," *The New York Times*, July 17, 1927.
[6] "Whaleback Turns Pirate," *The New York Times*, July 17, 1927.
[7] "'Pirate Ship' Seized With $1,000,000 Rum," *The New York Times*, June 22, 1927.
[8] "26 of Rum Ship Crew Free," *The New York Times*, July 2, 1927.
[9] "Jurors In Uproar Over Lock-Up Order," *The New York Times*, January 26, 1928.
[10] "Liquor Ship Captain Reveals Ventures," *The New York Times*, January 28, 1928.
[11] Ibid.
[12] Ibid.
[13] "Capt. Willis Guilty Of Liquor Running," *The New York Times*, January 29, 1928.

CHAPTER 33

[1] "Ontario Goes Wet And The Border Seethes," *The New York Times*, May 15, 1927.
[2] Ibid.
[3] Ibid.
[4] Ibid.
[5] Ibid.

[6] "Curb Tightened On Canadian Liquor," *The New York Times*, June 4, 1927.
[7] "Exports Of Liquor By Britain Decline," *The New York Times*, July 25, 1927.
[8] "Lowman To Double Border Dry Patrol," *The New York Times*, August 31, 1927.
[9] "Lowman Plans 'Plug' For Canadian Rum," *The New York Times*, August 19, 1927.
[10] Ibid.
[11] "Lowman To Double Dry Patrol," *The New York Times*, August 31, 1927.
[12] "Smuggling That Goes On Across American Borders," *The New York Times*, March 30, 1930.
[13] Ibid.
[14] "Rum Runner Slain By Coast Guard," *The New York Times*, October 13, 1927.
[15] Ibid.

CHAPTER 34

[1] "Big Seas Lash Coast, Damage In Millions; Shore Resorts Flooded, Tides Hit City; Thousands Flee; Ships Driven Ashore," *The New York Times*, February 27, 1927.
[2] "Rum Ship Wrecked, Townsfolk Save Crew, Then Brave Raging Sea To Share In Liquor," *The New York Times*, February 21, 1927.
[3] "Wrecked Schooner Yields More Liquor," *The New York Times*, February 27, 1927.
[4] "Coast Guard Boat Lost With 8 Men," *The New York Times*, February 27, 1927.
[5] Ibid.
[6] "Lone Ensign Takes $500,000 Rum Craft, Subdues 22 In Crew," *The New York Times*, July 5, 1927.
[7] Ibid.
[8] Ibid.
[9] Ibid.
[10] Ibid.
[11] Ibid.
[12] Ibid.
[13] "Lone Guard Seizes 36 On Liquor Ship," *The New York Times*, August 13, 1927.
[14] Ibid.
[15] "Gun Battle On Ship Marks Liquor Raid," *The New York Times*, November 18, 1927.
[16] Ibid.
[17] Ibid.
[18] Ibid.

CHAPTER 35

[1] "LaGuardia Renews Liquor Plot Charge," *The New York Times*, January 8, 1928.
[2] Ibid.
[3] "Customs Men Seize Liquor On 2 Ships," *The New York Times*, January 10, 1928.
[4] Ibid.
[5] "Lowman Will Sift LaGuardia Charges," *The New York Times*, January 15, 1928.
[6] Ibid.
[7] "Lowman Discovers Vast Smuggling Here," *The New York Times*, January 17, 1928.
[8] Ibid.
[9] "Rum Row Smashed, Dr. Doran Asserts," *The New York Times*, July 18, 1928.
[10] "Night Club Truce Remains Unbroken," *The New York Times*, August 26, 1928.
[11] "Reveals Seizure At The Ile De France," *The New York Times*, September 2, 1928.
[12] Ibid.

CHAPTER 36

[1] "Move To Stop Flow Of Canadian Liquor," *The New York Times*, April 1, 1928.
[2] Ibid.

[3] "Armored Rum Craft Told of In Ontario," *The Toronto Globe*, April 9, 1928.
[4] Ibid.
[5] "Armed Liquor Craft Gather On Lake Erie," *The New York Times*, May 8, 1928.
[6] "Lake Liquor War To Open," *The New York Times*, May 21, 1928.
[7] Ibid.
[8] "Report Rum-Runners Row In From Canada," *The New York Times*, July 9, 1928.
[9] "Defends Firing At Yacht," *The New York Times*, July 11, 1928.
[10] Ibid.
[11] "Coast Guard Kills Man In Lake Chase," *The New York Times*, November 30, 1928.
[12] Ibid.

CHAPTER 37

[1] "Randell Has War Medals," *The New York Times*, March 26, 1929.
[2] "Rum Boat Skipper Tells of Sinking Under Fire In Gale," *The New York Times*, March 25, 1929.
[3] Ibid.
[4] Ibid.
[5] Ibid.
[6] Ibid.
[7] "'Worse Than War,' Chief Says," *The New York Times*, April 16, 1929.
[8] Ibid.
[9] "Rum Boat Skipper Tells of Sinking Under Fire In Gale," *The New York Times*, March 25, 1929.
[10] Ibid.
[11] "British See Test of Treaty Involved," *The New York Times*, March 26, 1929.
[12] "British Envoy Acts On Rum Ship Sinking By The Coast Guard," *The New York Times*, March 24, 1929.
[13] "Bases Case On Old Offense," *The New York Times*, March 26, 1929.
[14] "Mellon Holds Law Justifies Sinking of Rum Runner," *The New York Times*, March 26, 1929.
[15] "British Envoy Acts On Rum Ship Sinking By The Coast Guard," *The New York Times*, March 24, 1929.
[16] "Bases Case On Old Offense," *The New York Times*, March 26, 1929.
[17] "Ship's Crew Freed; Canada Files Note Protesting Sinking," *The New York Times*, April 10, 1929.
[18] Ibid.

CHAPTER 38

[1] "Picturesque King Of Rum Runners Killed In Action," *The Fresno Bee*, March 5, 1926.
[2] Ibid.
[3] Ibid.
[4] Ibid.
[5] Ibid.
[6] "Coast Guard Tells Of A Sea Battle," *The New York Times*, August 28, 1927.
[7] Ibid.
[8] Ibid.
[9] Ibid.
[10] Ibid.
[11] Ibid.
[12] James C. Young, "Where Rum Ships Play Hide and Seek," *The New York Times*, April 21, 1929.
[13] Ibid.
[14] Ibid.
[15] Ibid.
[16] Ibid.

ALCOHOL, BOAT CHASES, AND SHOOTOUTS!

CHAPTER 39
[1] Charles A. Selden, "Our 'Rum Capital': An Amazing Picture," *The New York Times*, May 27, 1928.
[2] Ibid.
[3] Ibid.
[4] Ibid.
[5] Ibid.
[6] Ibid.
[7] Ibid.
[8] Ibid.
[9] Ibid.
[10] "Detroit River Fleet Vanishes With Liquor," *The New York Times*, August 19, 1928.
[11] Ibid.
[12] "Inspectors Arrested. Docks Closed," *The New York Times*, December 1, 1928.
[13] Ibid.
[14] "Start Using Machine Guns," *The New York Times*, June 2, 1929.
[15] Ibid.
[16] "Dry Chiefs Order Drive in Detroit," *The New York Times*, June 11, 1929.
[17] Ibid.
[18] "Rum War Forces Mass On The Detroit Front," *The New York Times*, June 23, 1929.
[19] Ibid.
[20] Ibid.
[21] "90 Per Cent of Canadian Liquor Sent Here, Says Anti-Drys, Putting Value at $30,000,000," *The New York Times*, July 1, 1929.
[22] Ibid.
[23] "Rum War Forces Mass On The Detroit Front," *The New York Times*, June 23, 1929.
[24] Ibid.
[25] Ibid.
[26] "Rum Runners Kidnap Man," *The New York Times*, June 19, 1929.
[27] "Rum War Forces Mass On The Detroit Front," *The New York Times*, June 23, 1929.
[28] "Lake Liquor Runners Combine For New War," *The New York Times*, June 13, 1929.
[29] Ibid.
[30] "Land Liquor Cargoes In Heart of Detroit," *The New York Times*, August 15, 1929.
[31] "Canada Steers Clear Of Rum-Running Row," *The New York Times*, July 3, 1929.
[32] "Border Liquor Curb Is Asked In Canada," *The New York Times*, July 12, 1929.
[33] "Liquor Boats Shift Route," *The New York Times*, July 8, 1929.
[34] James C. Young, "In the 'Rum Capital' of Dry America," *The New York Times*, July 14, 1929.
[35] Ibid.
[36] "Big Craft Join War On Lake Rum Fleet," *The New York Times*, August 17, 1929.
[37] "Small Rum-Chasers To Lose Big Guns," *The New York Times*, August 18, 1929.
[38] Ibid.
[39] "More Liquor Crossing The Detroit River," *The New York Times*, September 23, 1929.

CHAPTER 40
[1] "Rum Chaser's Shots Hit Canadian Craft," *The New York Times*, September 20, 1929.
[2] Ibid.
[3] Ibid.
[4] "Rum Ring Paid Big Bribes, Seized Records Reveal; 6 Months' Profit $2,000,000," *The New York*

Times, October 18, 1929.
[5] "130 Dry Raiders Sweep Along Coast; Get Arsenal And Rum Ring's Wireless," *The New York Times*, October 17, 1929.
[6] "Rum Ring Paid Big Bribes, Seized Records Reveal; 6 Months' Profit $2,000,000," *The New York Times*, October 18, 1929.
[7] "130 Dry Raiders Sweep Along Coast; Get Arsenal And Rum Ring's Wireless," *The New York Times*, October 17, 1929.
[8] Ibid.
[9] Ibid.
[10] "Rum Ring Paid Big Bribes, Seized Records Reveal; 6 Months' Profit $2,000,000," *The New York Times*, October 18, 1929.
[11] Ibid.
[12] Ibid.
[13] "Agents On New Trail In Liquor Case," *The New York Times*, October 19, 1929.
[14] "Say Liquor Ring Put $1,000,000 in Banks," *The New York Times*, April 16, 1930.
[15] "Rum Ring Got Hint Of Raids In Advance," *The New York Times*, October 21, 1929.
[16] "Seek Coast Guard Leak," *The New York Times*, October 23, 1929.
[17] Ibid.

CHAPTER 41

[1] "Bostonians Tear Up Coast Guard Bills," *The New York Times*, January 3, 1930.
[2] "Coast Guards Kill Boatman, Buffalo Police Officer's Son," *The New York Times*, December 26, 1929.
[3] "3 Guardsmen Held In Booze Killing," *The New York Times*, December 27, 1929.
[4] Ibid.
[5] "Lowman Upholds Buffalo Killing," *The New York Times*, December 28, 1929.
[6] Ibid.
[7] "Clears Coast Guardsmen," *The New York Times*, February 1, 1930.
[8] Ibid.
[9] Ibid.
[10] Ibid.
[11] "Stop Or Get Hurt, Billard Warns," *The New York Times*, December 30, 1929.
[12] "Would Disarm Coast Guard," *The New York Times*, December 31, 1929.
[13] Ibid.
[14] Ibid.
[15] "Three On Rum Boat Slain By Coast Guard In Chase; Three Vessels Captured," *The New York Times*, December 30, 1929.
[16] "Coast Guard Held For Liquor Brawl," *The New York Times*, December 31, 1929.
[17] "Bars Federal Men In Rum Ship Inquest," *The New York Times*, January 3, 1930.
[18] "Coast Guard Held For Liquor Brawl," *The New York Times*, December 31, 1929.
[19] Ibid.
[20] "Threatens Inquiry On Liquor Killings," *The New York Times*, January 1, 1930.
[21] "Lowman Defends Shootings," *The New York Times*, January 1, 1930.
[22] "Brookhart As A Dry Calls For Removal Of Treasury Heads," January 1, 1930.
[23] "Bostonians Tear Up Coast Guard Bills," *The New York Times*, January 3, 1930.
[24] Ibid.
[25] Ibid.
[26] Ibid.
[27] Ibid.
[28] Ibid.
[29] Ibid.

[30] "Rum Row Killings Upheld By Mellon," *The New York Times*, January 4, 1930.
[31] "Gang of Men Beats 2 Coast Guardsmen," *The New York Times*,
[32] Ibid.
[33] Ibid.
[34] "More Liquor Found On Patrol Boats," *The New York Times*, January 6, 1930.
[35] "Billard Says Duty Rules Coast Guard," *The New York Times*, January 6, 1930.
[36] "Crowd Terrifies Coast Guard's Wife," *The New York Times*, January 7, 1930.
[37] Ibid.
[38] "Reports 150 Ships In Rum Row Fleet," *The New York Times*, January 8, 1930.
[39] "House Cheers Dry Demanding Support For Coast Guard," *The New York Times*, January 8, 1930.
[40] Ibid.
[41] Ibid.
[42] Ibid.
[43] Ibid.
[44] Ibid.
[45] "Jury On Rum Killing Absolves Coast Guard," *The New York Times*, January 15, 1930.

CHAPTER 42

[1] "Dry Conflict Acute After 10-Year Test," *The New York Times*, January 1, 1930.
[2] Ibid.
[3] Ibid.
[4] Ibid.
[5] Ibid.
[6] "Reports 150 Ships In Rum Row Fleet," *The New York Times*, January 8, 1930.
[7] "Many Weaknesses Found: President Cites Growing Problem Involved In Scores of New Laws," *The New York Times*, January 14, 1930.
[8] Ibid.
[9] Ibid.
[10] Ibid.
[11] Ibid.
[12] "Mellon On Stand Presses Transfer Of Prohibition Unit," *The New York Times*, January 23, 1930.
[13] Ibid.
[14] Ibid.
[15] "Harris, Dry, Calls Mellon Lax On Laws," *The New York Times*, January 24, 1930.
[16] Ibid.
[17] Ibid.
[18] Ibid.
[19] "Tydings In Attack On Prohibition Rule Stings Senate Drys," *The New York Times*, April 2, 1930.
[20] Ibid.
[21] Ibid.
[22] Ibid.
[23] Ibid.
[24] Ibid.
[25] Ibid.
[26] Ibid.
[27] Ibid.
[28] Ibid.
[29] "Sees Cooperation In Dry Law Tasks," *The New York Times*, July 2, 1930.

CHAPTER 43

[1] James C. Young, "When Rum-Runners Spin Their Yarns," *The New York Times,* August 10, 1930.
[2] Ibid.
[3] Ibid.
[4] Ibid.
[5] Ibid.
[6] Ibid.
[7] "SOS Viewed As Hoax Or Rum-Runner Ruse," *The New York Times,* March 29, 1931.
[8] Ibid.
[9] Ibid.
[10] "Canadians Put Ban On Rum Shipments," *The New York Times,* June 1, 1930.
[11] Ibid.
[12] "Reports Rum Fleet Is Plying Coast," *The New York Times,* June 18, 1930.
[13] Ibid.
[14] "French Islands Got $8,856,320 Whisky," *The New York Times,* October 22, 1931.

CHAPTER 44

[1] "Wireless Tip Leads To Liquor On Liner," *The New York Times,* July 25, 1930.
[2] Ibid.
[3] Ibid.
[4] "$15,000,000 Rum Ring Bared By Radio Raid," *The New York Times,* September 28, 1930.
[5] Ibid.
[6] Ibid.
[7] Ibid.
[8] "Fourth Radio Plant Of Rum Ring Seized," *The New York Times,* October 8, 1930.
[9] Ibid.
[10] Ibid.
[11] "Rum Trial On; Police Implicated," *The New York Times,* June 23, 1931.
[12] Ibid.
[13] Ibid.
[14] Ibid.
[15] "Radio Expert Bares Rum Ring Messages," *The New York Times,* June 24, 1931.
[16] Ibid.
[17] Ibid.
[18] "Coast Guard Tells of Rum Chases," *The New York Times,* June 26, 1931.
[19] Ibid.
[20] "Upholds Rum Search In Atlantic Highlands," *The New York Times,* June 29, 1931.
[21] "Testify To Whisky Orders," *The New York Times,* July 7, 1931.
[22] "Links Drafts To Rum Ring," *The New York Times,* July 8, 1931.
[23] "'Rum Ring' Charges Go To Newark Jury," *The New York Times,* July 10, 1931.
[24] Ibid.
[25] Ibid.
[26] "Jury Acquits 17 In 'Rum Ring' Trial," *The New York Times,* July 12, 1931.
[27] "A Drama Listeners Miss," *The New York Times,* February 7, 1932.
[28] Ibid.
[29] Ibid.
[30] "Liquor Gang's Radio Is Found In An Auto," *The New York Times,* March 26, 1932.

CHAPTER 45

[1] "Canadian Is Killed By Coast Guard Shot In Harbor Rum Chase," *The New York Times,* January 26, 1931.

ALCOHOL, BOAT CHASES, AND SHOOTOUTS!

[2] Ibid.
[3] Ibid.
[4] Ibid.
[5] Ibid.
[6] "Canada Asks Facts On Cluett Killing," *The New York Times*, January 27, 1931.
[7] "Captor Was Drunk, Rum-Runner Says," *The New York Times*, January 29, 1931.
[8] Ibid.
[9] "Coast Guard Seizes Sixth Rum Vessel," *The New York Times*, January 30, 1931.
[10] "Coast Guard Upheld In Rum Boat Killing," *The New York Times*, January 31, 1931.
[11] "Lunenburg Buries Captain Cluett," *The New York Times*, February 1, 1931.
[12] Ibid.
[13] "Canada Protests On The Josephine K." *The New York Times*, March 18, 1931.
[14] "Government Libels The Josephine K." *The New York Times*, April 14, 1931.
[15] "Josephine K. Damaged On New England Coast," *The New York Times*, July 23, 1931.
[16] "Cluett Case Action By Grand Jury Seen," *The New York Times*, August 23, 1931.
[17] Ibid.
[18] Ibid.
[19] "Rum-Runner Seized With $50,000 Cargo," *The New York Times*, August 27, 1931.
[20] "No Indictment Found In Josephine K Case," *The New York Times*, September 5, 1931.
[21] "Canadian Owners Agree To The Forfeiture Of Liquor Taken Here And Ship Is Released," *The New York Times*, May 15, 1932.
[22] "Says Dry Raiders 'Wrecked' His Ship," *The New York Times*, January 29, 1931.
[23] Ibid.
[24] Ibid.
[25] Ibid.
[26] "The Good Luck Not Lucky," *The New York Times*, December 24, 1931.
[27] "Ship Yields Liquor After Third Raid," *The New York Times*, August 9, 1932.
[28] Ibid.
[29] Ibid.

CHAPTER 46

[1] "Coast Guard Gains In War On Rum Row," *The New York Times*, June 28, 1931.
[2] Ibid.
[3] Ibid.
[4] Ibid.
[5] "600 Rum-Runners Seized Every Year," *The New York Times*, January 24, 1931.
[6] "Coast Guard Crew Gassed By Escaping Rum-Runner," *The New York Times*, July 20, 1931.
[7] "Protest Sent to Canada on Gas Attack by Rum Ship on Coast Guard Patrol Boat," *The New York Times*, July 20, 1931.
[8] "Rum-Runner Killed By Guard Boat Fire," *The New York Times*, September 5, 1931.
[9] "73% Favor Repeal In Prohibition Poll," *The New York Times*, April 29, 1932.
[10] "Prohibition Breaking Up," *The New York Times*, November 11, 1932.
[11] "Congress Nominees Found Wet By 10 to 1," *The New York Times*, October 24, 1932.
[12] "House 'Drys' 319, Wheeler Estimates," *The New York Times*, November 7, 1924.
[13] Frank S. Adams, "Swing To Prohibition Repeal Came Suddenly After Long Fight," *The New York Times*, February 21, 1933.
[14] Untitled article. *The New York Times*, February 25, 1932.
[15] "House Wets To Ask Cut In Coast Guard," *The New York Times*, November 26, 1932.
[16] Ibid.
[17] Ibid.
[18] H.L. Brock. "Our Speakeasies Consider Their Future," *The New York Times*, September 11, 1932.
[19] Ibid.

[20] Ibid.

CHAPTER 47
[1] "Allots $14,800,000 In Smuggling Fight," *The New York Times*, September 22, 1933.
[2] Ibid.
[3] Oliver McKee Jr., "After-Repeal Task Of The Coast Guard," *The New York Times*, October 22, 1933.
[4] "Rum Fleet Grows As Repeal Nears," *The New York Times*, October 31, 1933.
[5] "Final Action At Capital," *The New York Times*, December 5, 1933.
[6] Ibid.
[7] "City Toasts New Era," *The New York Times*, December 6, 1933.
[8] Ibid.
[9] "Police Raids Start Clean-Up of Speakeasies and Cordial Shops," *The New York Times*, December 6, 1933.
[10] "Liquor Stores Dry As Deliveries Fail," *The New York Times*, December 6, 1933.
[11] Ibid.
[12] "Crowds Besiege Stores," *The New York Times*, December 7, 1933.
[13] Ibid.
[14] "Liquor For Homes Is Scarce In City," *The New York Times*, December 7, 1933.
[15] "First New Year's Revel Since Repeal Is Orderly; The Gayest In 14 Years," *The New York Times*, January 1, 1934.
[16] "High Court To Rule On Dry Law Status," *The New York Times*, December 19, 1933.
[17] Ibid.
[18] "Government Acts To Push Dry Cases," *The New York Times*, January 4, 1934.
[19] "Court Edict Ends 9,000 Liquor Cases," *The New York Times*, February 6, 1934.

CHAPTER 48
[1] "Repeal In West Changes Nothing," *The New York Times*, December 6, 1933.
[2] "Rum Ships Quit Coast To Legalize Cargoes," *The New York Times*, January 17, 1934.
[3] "Washington Opens Wide Bootleg War," *The New York Times*, April 20, 1934.
[4] Joseph M. Choate, Jr., "Choate Finds Bootlegging Is Active Despite Repeal; Illicit Output Colossal," *The New York Times*, April 29, 1934.
[5] Ibid.
[6] "Loss In Liquor Taxes Put At $400,000,000," *The New York Times*, April 30, 1934.
[7] Joseph M. Choate, Jr., "Choate Finds Bootlegging Is Active Despite Repeal; Illicit Output Colossal," *The New York Times*, April 29, 1934.
[8] "Choate Assailed For Liquor Policy," *The New York Times*, May 1, 1934.
[9] "New Rum Row Era Is Held Imminent," *The New York Times*, July 25, 1934.
[10] Ibid.
[11] "Traps Many Bootleggers," *The New York Times*, July 31, 1934.
[12] Frank L. Kluckhohn, "Alcohol-Running A Vast Business," *The New York Times*, March 17, 1935.
[13] James C. Young, "Rum-Runners Again Challenge The Law," *The New York Times*, January 13, 1935.
[14] Ibid.
[15] Ibid.
[16] Frank L. Kluckhohn, "Alcohol-Running A Vast Business," *The New York Times*, March 17, 1935.
[17] Mrs. John S. Sheppard, "After Five Years, What Has Repeal Achieved?" *The New York Times*, December 4, 1938.
[18] "Bad Money Is Cut One-Third In Year," *The New York Times*, August 8, 1937.

Index

A

Adelman, Alexander, 229, 230
Airplanes, 2, 35, 36, 74, 83, 89, 101, 108, 123, 131, 132, 147, 172, 177-179, 199-203, 212, 231, 238, 242, 243, 265, 280, 282, 291, 293, 296, 304, 305, 311, 320, 345, 346, 365, 379, 394, 414, 415, 483, 505, 508, 509, 513-15, 525
Alaska, 129, 146-148, 470, 515
Anchor Line, 46, 248
Andrews, Lincoln C., 283, 285, 287, 292, 294-297, 305, 309-314, 320, 322, 323, 327, 328, 336, 341, 346, 349-351, 367, 368, 378, 409, 410
Anti-Beer Bill, 47
Anti-Saloon League, 1, 47, 117, 247, 259, 267, 288, 314
See also Wheeler, Wayne
Appleby, John D., 64, 67, 70, 81, 85-91, 100, 101
Appliances, household, 3, 4, 5, 274, 276
Arctic Steamer *Jeannette*, 17, 63
Armaments,
See Naval Guns
Armistice, 33, 125, 181, 283
Army, US, 33, 63, 85, 105, 124, 136, 142, 143, 146, 155, 157, 158, 166, 177, 180, 241, 242, 256, 265, 283, 299, 310, 329, 382, 386, 433, 466, 474
Atlantic City, NJ, 35-41, 43, 60-63, 97, 100-102, 162, 165, 172, 279, 280, 284-286, 293, 299, 302, 304, 306, 307, 365, 381, 394, 410, 415, 436, 469
Atlantic Highlands, NJ, 106-108, 179, 201, 230, 231, 250, 488-492
Attorneys General,
See
Daugherty, Harry
Palmer, A. Mitchell
Attorneys, US,
Caffey, Francis G., 21
Clark, John Holley, 54, 69, 71, 81-83, 116, 163, 189, 191, 255, 364

Attorneys, US (*continued*),
Cohen, Sanford H., 117
Hayward, William, 43, 44, 82, 177, 188-190, 229
Harris, Robert O., 243
Mattuck, Maxwell S., 100
McGurk, Francis S., 80, 255
Ross, Leroy W., 38
Stichman, Herman T., 60-62, 358, 360, 361, 373
Automobiles, 6, 7, 67, 102, 108, 109, 133, 151, 166, 218, 239, 275, 276, 394, 397, 420, 424, 430, 487, 505, 525

B

Bahamas, 37, 39, 42, 44, 48, 59, 85, 101, 103, 138, 164, 171, 197, 199, 354, 357, 359, 410, 455, 487, 522, 526
Bermuda, 42, 46, 65, 75-77, 137, 199, 231, 263, 273, 401, 436, 438, 485, 491, 522
Bielaski, A. Bruce, 333-337, 339-343, 346, 348, 351-353
Billard, Frederick, 180-184, 201, 244, 245, 247, 251, 280, 283-288, 292, 295, 296, 299, 366, 378, 407, 435, 436, 444, 448, 458, 459, 462, 463, 498, 504, 508
Bimini, 35, 36, 39, 263, 411, 415-417
Black Star Line, 20, 21
Blimps, 243
Bonded warehouses, 2, 14, 20, 97, 102, 177, 218, 221, 367, 517, 519, 529
Border Patrol, US, 309, 423, 426, 430, 434, 471
Borders, U.S.,
See
Canada
Mexico
Boston, 23, 25, 42, 44-46, 59, 101, 128, 133, 153, 242, 289, 296, 297, 310, 312, 346, 348, 371, 372, 383, 415, 444, 447, 449, 452, 453, 455, 457, 458, 465, 484, 525

567

Index

Boston Herald, 147
Bribery, 28, 126, 147, 186, 233, 259, 285, 293, 306, 307, 331, 336, 337, 339, 340, 345, 348, 349, 351, 354, 357-359, 361, 378, 423, 426, 427, 434, 440, 489
British Columbia, 52, 53, 263, 321, 324
British Consul, 43,121, 162, 256
British Government, 35, 44, 74, 130, 143, 144, 155, 162, 190, 358, 368, 408
   See also Parliament
British smuggling,
   See
   England
   Ireland
   Scotland
Bronx, NY, 333, 371, 439, 517
Brooklyn, NY, 38, 63, 85, 113, 186, 209, 211, 212, 215, 271, 304, 329, 340, 372, 382, 391, 439, 440, 486-488, 497, 503
Bryan, John, 286, 291, 498
Bryan, William Jennings, 35
Buffalo, NY, 140, 379, 394-399, 426, 429, 430, 444-446, 484
Bureau of the Budget, 33, 124, 184
Bureau of Investigation, 15, 147, 148, 204, 205, 265

C

California, 51, 52, 126, 249, 316-328, 504, 507, 515
Camp, E.W., 91, 92, 426
Canada, 1, 26-28, 46, 60, 64, 86, 90, 130, 135, 138, 164, 185, 197, 225, 227-231, 252, 320, 333, 345, 346, 364, 366, 375-380, 392, 408, 419, 420, 423-434, 436, 471, 481, 484, 485, 488, 505
   Canadian Border, 27, 51, 60, 97, 379, 391, 484
   Montreal, 83, 112, 227, 230, 232, 333, 440, 492
   Ontario, 45, 46, 140, 263, 376, 377, 379, 394, 396, 398, 422, 423, 427, 430, 433, 434

Canada (*continued*),
   Ontario Temperance Act, 45, 46
   Quebec, 37, 377
   Vancouver, 27, 53, 131, 263, 320, 324, 325, 379
   Windsor, 28, 45, 46, 263, 376, 420, 422, 427, 428, 430, 484
Canfield, Palmer, 117-123, 131
Camden, Bernard H., 224, 248
Campbell-Willis Bill, 47
Cannadine, David, 32
Cape May, NJ, 36, 37, 128, 142, 158, 172, 248, 259, 299, 305, 307, 335, 365, 483, 509, 515, 525
Capone, Al, 441
Captain of the Port of NY,
   See Reed, Byron L.
Captain Roy, 38, 41
Caribbean, 51, 230, 302, 317, 378, 392
   See also
   Cuba
   Nassau
   Bahamas
   Bermuda
   Bimini
Chalker, L.T., 450, 456
Chesapeake Bay, VA, 138, 164
Chiswell, R.M., 433
Chicago, 6, 14, 164, 185, 359, 360, 410, 411, 441, 461
Clifford, Edward, 91, 94, 95
Coast Guard Captains,
   See
   Bryan, John
   Camden, Bernard H.
   Chalker, L.T.
   Chiswell, R.M.
   Dizer, George
   Ford, F.T.
   Holdzkom, John
   Jacobs, William V.E.
   Moran, G.
   Newman, Quinton R.
   Rasmussen, M.W.
   Reed, Byron L.
   Ridgely, Randolph
   Scott, Philip

Index

Coast Guard Captains (*cont.*),
  See
  Tawes, George W.
  Weightman, R.C.
  Wolf, H.H.
Coast Guard Cutters
  Algonquin, 129, 325
  Cahokia, 129, 325, 326
  Calumet, 62, 90, 386
  Chase, 182
  Corwin, 17, 182
  Gresham, 17, 128, 138, 191-193, 284, 384, 436
  Guide, 128, 134
  Hahn, 17, 57, 70, 71, 84, 85
  Hansen, 57, 64, 65, 70, 71, 86-89, 93
  Hudson, 99, 128, 193
  Johansson, 57
  Kickapoo, 128, 141, 229, 305
  Larsen, 57, 70, 71
  Lexington, 89, 93, 105, 116, 128, 159
  Manhattan, 17, 90, 95, 114, 115, 117-123, 128, 138, 193, 229, 255, 284, 382
  Mehalatos, 60
  Newbury, 57
  Ossipee, 114, 298
  Porpoise, 105
  Seminole, 79, 129, 138, 142, 173, 174, 186, 194-199, 284, 433
  Seneca, 17, 43, 60-62, 128, 132, 138, 139, 159, 160, 193, 247-249, 266, 284, 301, 302, 348, 515
  Surveyor, 89-91, 93, 214
  Tamaroa, 129, 317, 318
  Tampa, 59, 128, 153, 252
  Taylor, 57, 70, 71
  Vaughn, 317, 318
  Vidette, 56, 129
Coast Guard Destroyers,
  Conyngham, 246
  Ericson, 460
  Jouett, (Jewett), 78, 246, 252, 284, 384
  Porter, 246, 299

Coast Guard Headquarters, DC, 57, 58, 59, 285, 286, 448
Coast Guard patrol boats, 39, 45, 60, 78, 92, 103, 136, 184, 209, 281, 282, 286, 287, 289, 291, 293, 294, 295, 297-300, 310, 311, 313, 318, 332, 347, 349, 365, 379, 383, 384, 386, 396, 406, 407, 409, 414, 420, 424, 429, 430, 433, 436, 444, 446, 447, 450, 451, 457, 459, 460, 465, 482, 483, 486, 490, 491, 495-498, 500, 501, 505, 509, 515, 524, 525
Cocaine, 34, 238
Commandants of the Coast Guard,
  See
  Billard, Frederick
  Reynolds, William
Connecticut, 40, 47, 77, 134, 145, 198, 228, 240, 248, 250, 251, 286, 289, 330, 345, 345, 348, 349, 369, 370, 447, 450, 456, 460, 504, 507, 517, 524
  New Haven, 40, 42, 134
  New London, 77, 78, 198, 240, 248, 251, 286, 289, 293, 330, 348-351, 436, 447, 448, 450, 451, 456, 459, 460, 462, 504, 524
Congress, US, 6, 8, 9, 11, 12, 15-18, 27, 47, 63, 64, 91, 92, 103, 123-126, 132, 143, 145, 148, 157, 158, 164, 180-183, 187, 193, 194, 201, 206, 221, 245, 250, 267, 281, 282, 288, 291, 293, 295, 300, 308, 309, 310, 314, 342, 343, 353, 367-370, 378, 390, 448, 449, 452, 455, 460, 461, 463, 464, 467, 470-472, 474, 476, 507, 508, 509, 511, 512, 513, 523
  House of Representatives, 63, 181, 184, 187, 193, 308, 320, 367, 454, 460, 462-464, 470, 471, 472, 476, 507, 508, 512, 526
  Senate, 13, 30, 31, 47, 126, 148, 183, 193, 218, 219, 291, 292, 308, 452, 464, 470, 471, 473, 474, 475, 476, 507, 508, 512

Index

Senate (*continued*),
  See also
  Representatives, US
  Senators, US
Constitution, US, 13, 47, 143, 186,
  216, 217, 259, 264, 315, 369,
  392, 454, 458, 463, 470, 473,
  507, 513, 516, 528
Coolidge, Calvin, 5, 26, 150, 151,
  158, 180, 181, 184, 204, 244,
  264, 287, 295-298
Courts-martial, 299, 300, 303,
  306-308, 336, 338, 395, 450,
  457, 460
Cox, George, 64, 65
Cox, James M., 26, 29
Cuba, 20, 21, 23, 80, 131, 133,
  134, 165, 263, 368, 414
Customs, US, 1, 2, 7, 8, 14, 16,
  17, 19, 23-25, 27-29, 34-46, 56,
  59, 63-71, 73-75, 77, 78, 80, 81,
  84-95, 97-99, 102, 104, 105,
  108, 109, 115, 116, 123, 131,
  134, 141, 153, 156, 159-162,
  168, 173, 177, 181, 182, 189,
  190, 192, 208, 213, 214, 224,
  232, 238-243, 250-255, 264,
  265, 283, 287, 292, 302, 309,
  311, 312, 313, 315, 328, 331,
  332, 352, 354, 355, 358, 359-
  362, 370, 373, 379, 384, 388-
  394, 397, 406, 419-426, 428,
  430, 431, 433, 434, 436, 455,
  458, 465-468, 477, 484, 486,
  499, 502, 505, 517, 519, 525

D

Daugherty, Harry, 43, 84, 142,
  147-150, 157, 158, 164, 184,
  185, 204, 217
Dawes, Charles, 33
Day, Ralph A., 51, 55, 60, 81-83
Democrats, 16, 26, 63, 199, 201,
  308, 455, 463, 464, 474, 512
Denby, Edwin, 126, 143, 217, 242
Department of Commerce, 48,
  157, 366, 490, 493

Department of Justice, 15, 33, 34,
  80, 90, 124, 143, 147, 151, 157,
  162, 164, 204, 205, 218, 220,
  221, 229, 259, 260, 263, 264,
  283, 291, 292, 308, 313, 327,
  328, 342, 372, 461, 471, 472,
  477, 487, 505, 516, 520, 522
Detroit, 25-28, 46, 47, 125, 129,
  135, 136, 141, 185, 295, 312,
  376-379, 418-434, 484
Distilleries, 2, 14, 32, 86, 140,
  218-221, 256, 257, 287, 367,
  369, 395, 419, 426, 427, 477,
  492, 517, 521, 522, 523, 525
  Also see Overholt Distillery
Dizer, George, 64, 88, 89
Doran, James M., 313, 314, 378,
  391, 425, 428, 452, 467, 472,
  477
Drugs,
  See
  Cocaine
  Heroin
  Morphine
  Narcotics
  Opium
Duke, Charles L., 384-387
Dwyer, William V., 329-343

E

Eagle Boats, 2, 124, 125
Economy, U.S., 4, 6, 32, 110, 124,
  146, 276, 277, 415, 512, 515
Edgewater, NJ, 330, 357-362
Eighteenth Amendment, 11, 12,
  15, 103, 143, 145, 216, 217,
  259, 264, 315, 369, 454, 466,
  467, 470, 473, 507, 508, 516,
  521, 528-531
Election, Presidential, 29, 147,
  507, 511
England, 138, 155, 156, 171, 174,
  176, 197, 199, 200, 203, 227,
  232, 237, 256, 257, 262, 274,
  338, 359, 400, 407, 416, 488

Index

Expenses, Rum War, 16, 17, 21, 33, 124, 125, 158, 184, 187, 193, 265, 281, 292, 293, 300, 308, 310, 350, 391, 466-468, 508, 509, 513-515, 525
Exports, US liquor, 14, 86, 528, 529

F

FBI, see Bureau of Investigation
Films, 2, 6, 90
Florida, 25, 35, 44, 48, 55, 56, 57, 70, 159, 162, 165, 185, 296, 304, 318, 354, 378, 409-417, 504, 509, 515
    Daytona, 44, 161, 162
    Miami, 25, 55, 56, 129, 133, 354, 409-411, 416, 509
Ford, Henry, 6, 125, 137, 146, 154, 220, 275, 303, 357
France, 20, 26, 51, 87, 135, 138, 142, 199, 222-229, 233-235, 243, 263, 264, 289, 309, 335, 379, 392, 406, 408, 426, 481-485, 487, 488, 490, 505, 517

G

Gaskill, Burton L., 43, 44
Geddes, Auckland, Sir, 175
Germany, 10, 26, 34, 181, 203, 226, 241, 243, 244, 248, 263, 292, 299, 309, 314, 335, 384, 400, 481, 506, 527
Globe Line, 64, 66, 74-77
Grayson, Cary, Dr., 10, 11, 19
Great Lakes, 27, 46, 64, 129, 140, 164, 281, 287, 367, 372, 379, 380, 395-398, 429, 430, 433, 434
    Lake Erie, 140, 367, 380, 395, 397, 424, 429, 430
    Lake Huron, 379, 429
    Lake Michigan, 46
    Lake Ontario, 140, 367, 398
Great War, 1, 2, 6, 12, 18, 32, 33, 42, 44, 89, 111, 145, 165, 244, 246, 256, 276, 281, 384, 400, 416, 490

Grill, Saul, 55, 253, 364
Gulf Coast, 128, 165, 257, 316, 384, 407, 515, 526

H

Harding, Warren G., 16, 26, 29, 30-33, 96, 109, 123, 124, 142, 145-150, 152, 157, 180, 204, 221
Harris, William Julius, 473, 474
Hart, Harold L., 99, 100
Harvard University, 293-295
Hartwell, Broderick, Sir, 80, 144, 155-157, 176, 177, 256, 283
Haynes, Roy A., 33, 41, 45, 55, 57, 64, 81, 82, 86, 91, 92, 96, 97, 100, 101, 105, 109, 123, 135, 138, 151, 161, 313, 314
Heroin, 238, 410
Highlands, NJ, 89, 90, 96, 104-108, 196, 250, 437, 438, 440, 442, 488
Holdzkom, John, 43
Holland, 135, 526
Hoover, Herbert, 146-148, 425, 452, 464, 470, 471, 511, 512
Hoover, John Edgar, 205, 206

I

Imports, 1, 48, 84, 97, 138, 159, 177, 258, 319, 345, 366, 373, 427, 440, 461, 499, 526, 528, 529
Income Tax, 32, 217
Internal Revenue Bureau, 16, 22, 29, 42, 81, 119, 134, 162, 221, 232, 259, 314, 322, 457, 516, 528
Ireland, 176
Italy, 135, 138, 199, 256, 264

J

Jack, Raymond L., Lt., 58
Jacobs, William V.E., 80, 193, 247, 248, 292, 318, 319
Japan, 1, 52, 135, 326, 374, 375, 527
Jarrell, Sanford, 247, 249

571

Index

Judges,
  Bourquin, George M., 327
  Capotosto, A.A., 465
  Foster, Rufus A., 82
  Garvin, Edwin L., 190, 191
  Glenn, J. Lyles, 490-493
  Guthrie, 22
  Hand, Augustus N., 80, 190, 191, 363
  Hand, Learned, 103, 363
  Hazel, John R., 83
  Kerrigan, Frank H., 323, 328
  Knox, John C., 83, 132, 359
  Mack, Julian W., 330, 334, 336-342
  Manton, 363
  Mayer, 46
  Meekins, Isaac, 361, 362
  Morris, 373
  Morton, 253
  Payne, John Barton, 19
  Runyon, William N., 439
  Stone, Harlan Fiske, 204, 205, 263, 264
  Winslow, Francis A., 100, 345, 349, 351-353, 365
  Wolverton, 220

K
Kremer, John F., 21

L
LaGuardia, Fiorello H., 320, 341, 343, 390, 391, 461, 463
League of Nations, 9, 10, 12, 26, 29, 145
Liberty engines, 2, 203, 278
Limits of US sea jurisdiction,
  3-mile limit, 27, 29, 34-37, 39-41, 43-45, 75, 77, 84-85, 89, 90, 99, 103, 106, 107, 109, 117, 121, 124, 131, 135, 159, 161-163, 182, 189, 199, 202, 262, 407
  12-mile limit, 43, 61, 63, 67, 70, 71, 78, 85, 85, 132, 141-143, 162, 173, 175, 182, 183, 193, 197, 199, 201, 203, 238, 247,

12-mile limit (*continued*), 326, 327, 365, 407, 408, 443, 495, 497, 498, 500, 503, 505, 515, 526
  Hovering Act of 1736, 43
  Long Island, NY, 20, 37-39, 65, 91, 95, 106, 114, 116, 133, 139, 140, 153, 154, 159, 164, 179, 186, 188, 194-196, 198, 202, 222, 230, 235, 236, 240, 241, 247-251, 259, 263, 264, 271, 273, 284, 289, 290, 292, 335, 345, 349, 373, 381, 437, 439, 441, 450, 487, 488, 491, 503
  Lowman, Seymore, 313-315, 378, 379, 390-393, 397, 424, 425, 433, 443, 445, 452, 472, 498

M
Maine, 1, 27, 35, 101, 128, 159, 185, 228, 246, 296, 369, 379, 461, 487
Maritime Act of 1790, 43
Martha's Vineyard, 111, 335
Marshals, US, 41, 134, 158, 243, 292, 339, 359, 372, 373, 436, 438, 471
Massachusetts, 1, 5, 45, 59, 63, 111-113, 145, 152, 185, 228, 243, 286, 288, 293, 296, 297, 312, 346, 383, 449, 454, 505, 506, 509, 525
  See also
  Boston
  Martha's Vineyard
  New Bedford
  Provincetown
  Salem
Maxim, Hudson, 44
McCoy, William F., 44, 159-163, 229, 233
Means, Gaston, 147, 148, 218-220
Mellon, Andrew, 31-33, 46, 85, 86, 109, 110, 123, 134, 151, 165, 216-221, 267, 283, 287, 294, 297, 309, 313, 367, 368, 390, 407, 449, 452, 455, 472, 473, 475

572

Index

Merrick, Romaine Q., 22, 101, 104, 154, 155, 201, 230, 249, 259
Mexico, 1, 135, 158, 164, 165, 263, 293, 317-319, 375, 392, 415, 471, 526
Miami, FL, 25, 55, 56, 129, 133, 354, 409-411, 416, 509
Moonshine, 1, 56, 97, 98, 165, 319, 477, 521, 527
Morphine, 25, 188, 238
Moyle, James Henry, 25
Mullan-Gage Act, 132, 135, 315

N

Narcotics, 23, 34, 187-190, 197, 237, 244, 318, 393, 416, 444
    Also see "Drugs"
Narcotics Bureau/ Division, 86, 188, 265, 477
Nassau, 35-38, 44, 48, 56, 64, 65, 85, 87, 99, 115, 120, 133, 152, 154, 160, 161, 164, 165, 173, 263, 354, 357, 358, 360, 401
Naval Disarmament Treaty, 63, 74, 265
Naval guns, 10, 57, 59, 67, 78, 89, 92, 107, 137-139, 159, 181, 182, 193, 195, 196, 201, 242, 244, 245, 267, 281, 282, 284, 300, 347, 369, 397, 398, 402, 405, 433-435, 447, 495
Navy, US, 2, 9, 25, 33, 57, 58, 63, 64, 74, 91, 104, 105, 109, 111, 113, 114, 123-126, 136, 142, 143, 145-147, 157, 158, 177, 178, 181, 187, 193, 194, 240-242, 245, 246, 265, 300-303, 308, 311, 336-338, 384, 433, 474, 486, 524
    Assistant Navy Secretary,
        See Roosevelt, Franklin D.
    Boats,
        Sea Hornet II, 241, 242
    Secretary of the Navy,
        See Denby, Edwin

Navy Ships,
    Aphrodite, 181
    Beaufort, 302, 303
    Falcon, 113
    Henderson, 146-148
    Pickering, 306
New Bedford, Mass., 45, 85, 447, 452, 506
New Deal, 513, 519, 522
New Jersey, 22, 36, 37, 41, 42, 45, 51, 67, 84-91, 93, 95, 96, 99, 101-108, 112, 117, 128, 130, 131, 137-139, 141, 142, 145, 159, 163-167, 179, 185, 188, 191, 192, 196, 202, 203, 209, 213, 222, 231, 243, 245, 249, 250, 253, 254, 259, 260, 262, 263, 277, 278, 280, 284, 288, 292, 294, 304-306, 308, 330, 345, 358-365, 373, 381, 382, 383, 385, 410, 436-443, 482, 483, 487, 488, 490, 492, 495, 504, 507, 509, 515, 524, 525
    See also,
    Atlantic City
    Atlantic Highlands
    Cape May
    Edgewater
    Highlands
    Newark
    Trenton
New Orleans, 49, 55, 129, 135, 403, 405, 406, 515
New York City, 5-7, 14, 17, 20, 21, 23, 34-36, 38, 39, 42, 43, 46, 48, 54-57, 64, 65, 67, 69, 70, 74-77, 78, 79, 81-91, 93, 94, 96, 97, 99, 101, 102, 112-114, 116, 117, 128, 129, 132, 134, 135, 137, 140, 142, 154, 159, 161, 170, 173, 178, 187-190, 198-201, 204, 207-215, 224, 226, 228, 230-234, 240, 243, 248, 249, 251, 253-256, 258, 262, 271-273, 278-279, 286, 287, 289-291, 299, 300, 301, 305, 311, 312, 317, 329-333, 335, 337, 341, 342, 345, 346,

Index

New York City (*continued*), 348, 351-354, 357-360, 361, 366, 371-375, 384, 385, 387, 389-391, 393, 397, 415, 418, 435, 436, 438-440, 443, 461, 473, 483, 486, 489, 493-495, 501-503, 509, 516-519, 526
   See also
   Bronx
   Brooklyn
   Queens
   Staten Island
New York Herald-Tribune, 249
New York Police Dept., 65, 67, 69, 71-74, 88, 208-215, 255, 278, 279, 286, 329, 357, 358, 360, 361, 387, 516
   Marine Division, 71, 73, 208, 213, 278, 329, 355, 356, 358, 361
   Police boats, 65, 67-69, 74, 116, 202, 207-215, 278, 279, 286, 330, 361, 387, 388
      Blue Boy, 67-69, 74, 116
      Gypsy, 210-213, 278, 279, 330, 387
      Manhattan, 65-67, 207-209, 213
   Shooting spree,
      See Owens, David A.
New York State, 51, 97, 101, 132, 135, 145, 227, 259, 264, 314, 376
   See also
   Buffalo
   Long Island
   New York City
New York Times, 45, 58, 59, 68, 72, 74, 77, 84-86, 93, 107, 116, 117, 156, 158, 161, 198, 201, 220, 224, 227, 237, 242, 245, 257, 261, 312, 319, 368, 372, 398, 414, 418, 422, 481, 490, 510
   See also Young, James C.
New York World, 32

Newark, NJ, 22, 23, 90, 166, 278, 441, 442, 489, 490, 492, 495
Newman, Quinton R., 282
Nineteenth Amendment, 27
No Man's Land, 45, 289
Norway, 1, 142, 192, 197, 262-264, 400
Nova Scotia, 51, 70, 103, 104, 115, 119, 154, 225, 234, 263, 286, 298, 321, 345, 373, 400, 435, 436, 450, 495, 498, 500

O

Opium, 238
Oregon, 52, 317, 318, 320, 507
Overholt Distillery, 32, 217-221
Owens, David A., 71-74

P

Pacific Coast, 6, 51, 52, 54, 129, 165, 264, 316-328, 317, 473
   See also
   California
   Oregon
   Washington State
Palmer, Alexander Mitchell, 4, 14, 19, 205
Parliament, British, 137, 176
   House of Lords, 143
   House of Commons, 155, 176, 407
"The Pelican," 70
Peru, 74, 75
Pfaff, Max Jerome, 226-235
Philadelphia, 38, 40, 42, 44, 45, 97, 99, 128, 131, 188, 193, 194, 200, 244-246, 307, 349, 441, 461
Philadelphia Public Ledger, 42
Pinchot, Gifford, Gov., 216, 218
Pirates, 37, 70, 93, 95, 98, 99, 102-104, 106, 107, 114, 115, 118, 152, 153, 199, 222-236, 273, 274, 278, 351, 371-373, 415
Pittsburgh, PA, 31, 33, 217, 218, 220

Index

Prohibition,
  Agents, 16, 20-23, 33-42, 44, 45, 47, 49-51, 55, 57, 60, 64, 65, 67, 70, 71, 74, 76, 81, 83-85, 89, 93, 96-99, 101, 102, 104, 105, 107, 132, 134, 137, 138, 140, 141, 151, 153, 156, 159-161, 164, 173, 188, 201, 203, 220, 222, 229, 230, 238, 249, 253-255, 259, 283, 300, 305, 309, 311, 319, 322, 343, 346, 350, 351, 357, 364, 371, 382, 411, 412, 432, 436-440, 466, 468, 473, 475, 477, 487-489, 493, 494, 510, 516, 519, 522, 523, 526, 528
  Bureau, 16, 19, 57, 74, 83, 93, 102, 205, 206, 265, 287, 314, 315, 379, 425, 471, 473, 474, 477
  Commissioners,
    See
    Doran, James M.
    Haynes, Roy A.
    Kremer, John F.
    Lowman, Seymore
  History, pre-1920s, 1, 2
  Laws,
    See
    Eighteenth Amendment
    Volstead Act
  Polls, 507, 508
  Prohibition "navy," 2, 37, 51, 57, 58, 60, 64, 67, 71, 88, 89, 101, 123, 124, 139, 165, 193, 244-246, 251, 252, 265, 267, 277, 281-286, 292, 293, 296, 298, 299, 308, 311, 312, 319, 321, 394, 397, 414, 433, 466, 504, 505, 509, 513, 515, 524
Provincetown, MA, 383

Q
Queens, NY, 518

R
Railroads, 6, 10, 11, 19, 102, 135, 145, 146, 149, 188, 207, 267,

Railroads (*continued*), 309, 316, 330, 333, 381, 395, 428, 442, 456, 485
Randell, John T., 400-408
Rasmussen, M.W., 245, 277, 307, 308, 394, 397
Reed, Byron L., 38, 65, 93, 94, 117, 118, 121, 142, 175, 186
Representatives, US,
  Beedy, Carroll L., 461-464
  Celler, Emanuel, 117, 392, 393, 523
  Cooper, John G., 183
  Denison, Edward E., 181-183
  Fess, Simeon D., 110
  Gallivan, J. Ambrose, 63, 64
  Igoe, James T., 472
  LaGuardia, Fiorello H., 320, 341, 343, 390, 391, 461, 463
  Schafer, John C., 473
  Shallenberger, Ashton C., 185
Republicans, 12, 16, 26, 29, 146, 204, 217-220, 288, 295, 308, 310, 314, 393, 463, 474, 512
Remus, George, 147, 148, 157
Revenue Cutter Service, 17, 18, 75, 77, 89, 181, 235, 273, 300
Revenue Cutters
  Corwin, 17, 181
  McClane, 18
  Surveyor, 89, 90, 93
Reynolds, William Edward, 17, 18, 58, 124, 125, 179-181
Rhode Island, 85, 91, 145, 243, 286, 312, 360, 369, 451, 455-457, 465, 502
Ridgely, Randolph, 304, 443
Ritz-Carlton Hotel, 43
Roosevelt, Franklin D., 26, 105, 508, 511-514, 516, 521, 523
Royal Mail Line, 102, 188, 190
Rum Row, 35, 36, 87, 94, 97, 98, 119, 130, 133, 142, 156, 162, 165-167, 173, 197, 199, 202, 203, 224, 233, 239, 243, 245, 248, 257, 258, 261-263, 271, 272, 283, 285-292, 297, 298, 305, 306, 312, 313, 318, 319,

Index

Rum Row (*continued*), 330, 332, 334, 345-347, 351, 365, 366-369, 390, 391, 460, 469, 485, 493, 504, 505, 522, 524, 526, 527
Rum-runners,
  Aubrie, Tessie, 233
  Bell, Jennie, 86, 88
  Bradner, Mary, 233
  Capitol No. 1, 207, 208
  Cigarette, 212, 212
  Com-an-Go, 240, 241
  Elsie B., 237, 238
  Fox, 87
  Genevieve, 233
  Gorcum, 233
  Linwood, 184
  Man of War, 213, 331
  Marie, Rose, 213
  Marie, Catherine, 233
  Milk Maid, 53
  Monon, 209
  Pandora, 85
  Petara, 233
  Peerless, 116
  Plymouth, 231
  Quacco Queen, 233
  Shark, 239, 240
  Smith, Bessie, 167-172
  Williams 18, 240
Russia, 1, 4, 33, 274

S

Salem, Mass., 59
Savannah, Georgia, 101, 102, 104, 129
Saunders, William R., 69, 71
Scotland, 116, 138, 164, 168, 176, 185, 238, 485
Scott, Philip, 173, 186, 194-199
Seattle, WA, 9, 27, 52, 54, 135, 148, 320, 379
Secretary of the Navy, 9, 126, 242, 303
Secret Service, 15, 56, 77, 145, 297, 411

Senators, US,
  Ashurst, Henry, 47
  Blease, Coleman L., 464
  Brandega, 47
  Brookhart, Smith, 218, 220, 452, 474-476
  Dial, Nathaniel, 109
  Edge, Walter, 100, 294, 295, 308
  Harris, William Julius, 473, 474
  Knox, Philander, 32
  Reed, David, 47
  Tydings, Millard E., 468, 474-476
  Volstead, Andrew, 47
  Wheeler, Burton, 218
  Sheldon, Rex, 218, 219
Shipping Board, US, 16, 19, 41, 44, 55, 77, 109, 248
Ships,
  Acadia, 86
  Albatross, 191, 192
  Andora, 197, 331
  Antilla, 103
  Arakaka, 249
  Arethusa, 45
  Atalanta, 60
  Bachman, Marjorie, 252
  Beatrice, Mary, 137, 310
  Beman, Patricia M., 114, 115
  Cartona, 137
  Catherine and Mary, 197, 198
  Competitor, 111
  Cretic, 23, 25
  Donnetta, 60-63
  Dante d'Alighieri, 23
  Dwight, John, 111-114
  Economy, 384-387
  Eker, 354-361
  Emerald, 84, 85
  Federalship, 321, 324-328
  Flor-del-Mar, 450, 451, 457, 460
  France, 392
  Frederick B., 253-255, 364, 365
  Gardner, M.M., 86, 121, 122
  Glasgow, 199
  Good Luck, 500-503

576

Index

Ships (*continued*),
  Hankerson, J. Scott, 152, 153
  Harding, President, 233-235
  Hill, Strand, 137
  Himmelman, 302, 310
  I'm Alone, 310, 313, 400-408, 488, 499
  Istar, S.V., 116, 121, 131, 132, 137
  James, Eddie, 103, 104
  Jenny T., 40
  Josephine K., 495-500, 504
  J.H.B., 64, 65
  Kaiser Friedrich, 481
  Katherine M., 119, 120
  Korona, 74-76
  Lutzen, 227, 230-232
  Lyon, 231
  Madonna V., 86
  Margaret B., 89
  Marina, 85
  Marshall, Henry L., 43, 44, 54, 83, 84, 162
  Mary, Catherine (a.k.a. Catherine and Mary), 120, 197, 198, 331
  McLaughlin, 100, 101
  Mosher, Marion, 64, 65, 86, 90, 93, 95, 96, 99
  Mulhouse, 142, 222, 225-229, 232-234
  O'Conner, Mary, 120
  Orbita, 102, 103
  Orduna, 188-191
  Pocomoke, 37, 38, 40, 41, 54
  Rask, 197, 237, 238
  Sea Witch, 170
  Shawnee, 129, 328, 435-437, 439, 443, 490-492
  Smith, Bessie, 167-172
  Strudsholm, 192
  Tilley, 329
  Tomaka, 159-162
  Turner, 372-374
  Veronica, 233-235, 273, 274
  Victor, 99
  Wallace, Minnie, 68, 70, 71, 74
  Warszawa, 120, 121, 131, 132

Ships (*continued*),
  Washington, Martha, 77
  White, 302, 345-348
  Waldic, 304
  Wilson, Presidente, 23
  Witch, 56
  Wrack, 173, 174
  Yankton, 133, 134
  Yarmouth, 20-22
Shootings, 71-73, 103, 137, 152, 153, 159, 214, 278, 280, 329, 371, 374, 380, 398, 402-413, 442, 444-447, 496, 500, 504-506
Shouse, Jouette, 27
Smith, Al, 314
Smith, Jess, 147, 148, 218
Southern U.S., 55, 56, 101, 110, 165, 287, 407
  See also
  Florida
  Gulf Coast
  Savannah, GA
Spain, 74-77, 135, 138, 199
Speedboats, 2, 57, 68, 101, 103, 108, 136, 138, 139, 153, 166-168, 172, 175, 199, 208-213, 225, 231, 237, 239, 244, 251, 252, 254, 261, 277, 278, 282, 312, 313, 318, 330, 378, 379, 386, 396, 409, 415, 418, 419, 424, 429, 430, 436, 439, 442, 447, 460, 470, 482, 505, 506
Spies, 148, 245, 253, 285, 305, 346, 484
State Department, 15, 36, 84, 85, 90, 104, 105, 109, 121, 135, 155, 161, 175, 222, 238, 265, 266, 392, 406, 408, 488, 498, 499, 506
Staten Island, NY, 131, 209, 210, 212-215, 237, 278, 283, 285, 286, 299-302, 372, 381, 385-388, 487, 495, 501, 525
Stone, Harlan Fiske, 204, 205, 263, 264
Submarine-chasers, 2, 124, 128, 262

Index

Submarines, 2, 25, 52, 57, 241, 243, 244, 293, 450, 527
Supreme Court, US, 47, 103, 130-135, 137, 145, 147, 455, 519, 520
Surplus military equip., 2, 33, 178

T
Tawes, George W., 70
Teapot Dome Scandal, 126, 127, 148
Tombs Jail, 42, 66, 190, 342, 358
Torpedoes, 2, 25, 26, 57, 242, 281, 286
Treasury Department, 15, 16, 20, 32, 34, 84, 85, 93, 121, 123, 124, 135, 151, 156, 158, 159, 161, 189, 204, 216, 221-223, 225, 259, 283, 287, 291, 294, 295 308, 309, 314, 324, 330, 337, 342, 379, 407, 410, 426, 443, 452, 458, 461, 465, 467, 472, 477, 498, 504, 505, 522
   Assistant Secretaries,
      See
      Andrews, Lincoln C.
      Clifford, Edward
      Moyle, James Henry
      Shouse, Jouett
   Secretaries,
      See
      Houston, David
      Mellon, Andrew
Treaty of Versailles, 12, 26
Trenton, NJ, 41, 44, 141, 166, 220, 439, 441
Tumulty, Joseph, 10-12

V
Vermont, 27, 28, 150, 456
Virginia, 14, 21, 26, 42, 137, 138, 165, 188, 242, 302, 357, 369, 372
Volstead Act, 15, 22, 29, 31, 36, 40, 47, 96, 98, 99, 136, 173, 219, 247, 253, 259, 287, 297, 309, 326, 339, 360, 454, 470, 473, 520, 521, 528-531

W
Waldorf-Astoria Hotel, 55, 173
War Department, 104, 242
Warner, Joseph E., 113
Wartime Prohibition Act, 2
Washington, DC, 11, 15, 17, 20, 21, 26, 29, 30, 32, 43, 44, 51, 55, 58, 77, 78, 81, 84, 93, 96, 104, 105, 117, 123, 137, 138, 145, 147, 164, 181, 187, 189, 190, 205, 221, 242, 250, 251, 285, 286, 305, 307, 312, 320, 337, 338, 378, 391, 435, 453, 464, 475
Washington Post, 104, 165
Washington State, 53, 317, 319, 379, 507, 515
Weightman, R.C., 141
West Coast,
   See
   California
   Oregon
   Pacific Coast
   Pacific Ocean
   Washington State
Wheeler, Wayne, 47, 48, 64, 218, 247
White House, 11-13, 30, 31, 123, 124, 147, 151, 158, 264, 471
Wickersham Commission, 470-472
Willebrandt, Mabel Walker, 91, 142, 164, 165, 251, 259, 393
Willis, Browne, 371-375
Wilson, Edith, 9, 10, 12, 13
Wilson, Woodrow, 9-13, 16, 19, 26-31
Wolf, H.H., 460, 469
World War I,
   See Great War

Y
Yarmouth, Nova Scotia, 152, 263
Yellowley, E.C., 51, 55, 88, 93, 101, 108
Young, James C., 167-172, 194-199, 261-263, 272, 414-417, 481, 482

www.ingramcontent.com/pod-product-compliance
Lightning Source LLC
Chambersburg PA
CBHW071956150426
43194CB00008B/896